The Computer Challenge

The Computer Challenge

Technology, Applications, and Social Implications

Donna S. Hussain
Khateeb M. Hussain

Burgess Communications
A Division of Burgess International Group, Inc.

Publisher: Brete C. Harrison

Editor: Philip Alan Cecchettini

Production Manager: Larry Lazopoulos

Production Coordinator: Lynn R. Hurst

Assistant Editor: Barbara Pickard

Cover and Interior Design: Detta Penna

Art Direction: Detta Penna

Production Management: Liz Powers and Bettina Borer

Art Editor: Cathy Aydelott

Photo Research: Jenny Forbes, Joyce M. Konigsberg

Composition: Jonathan Peck Typographers, Ltd.

Printing and Binding: Arcata Graphics/Kingsport Press

Credits for photographs appearing in the color section, and in the individual chapters, are listed immediately following the index.

Library of Congress Cataloging in Publication Data

Hussain, Donna.
The computer challenge.
Includes bibliographies and index.
1. Computers. I. Hussain, Khateeb M., 1924–
II. Title.
QA76.H87 1986 004 86-997
ISBN 0-8087-6428-4

Printed in the United States of America

J I H G F E D C B

Address orders to:
The Burgess International Group, Inc.
7110 Ohms Lane
Edina, Minnesota 55435

Address editorial questions to:
Burgess Communications
900 College Avenue
Santa Rosa, California 95404

Burgess Communications
A Division of The Burgess International Group, Inc.

Brief Contents

Table of Contents

PART TWO: COMPUTER APPLICATIONS 121

PART THREE: THE SOCIAL IMPLICATIONS OF COMPUTERS 281

Supplements

Chapter 9

Chapter 10

Chapter 11

Chapter 12

Chapter 13

Chapter 14

Chapter 15

Chapter 16

Chapter 17

Chapter 18

Chapter 19

Chapter 20

Preface

The 1980s have been dominated by the computer revolution, and few fields of endeavor remain untouched by the computer's influence. In summarizing the year's top 100 scientific innovations, the December 1985 issue of *Science Digest* lists 31 directly related to computers; the balance would likely not have been possible without computers. The January 1986 issue arrives and chronicles "The Stories, The Breakthroughs, The People" of the past year. With the race of time, the magazine includes more computer innovations, technological breakthroughs, company mergers, internal corporate wars, computer-assisted crimes, developments in the Third World, and more. The pace of innovation is staggering!

This pace has influenced the way we have taught computers over the last half-decade. Textbooks, lecture notes, programming assignments, and class projects from only a few terms ago quickly become antiques. We chuckle at the lack of coverage of microcomputers, the almost nonexistent sections on applications, and the blasé and/or doomsday concern about the impact of computers on our lives and values. Our computer literacy courses coexist with new courses like Business Information Systems, Information Processing, and Microcomputer Applications.

The fact that modern society is quickly becoming computerized places a new burden on us all. Effective human-to-computer interaction requires knowledge of basic computer technology, and a lifelong learning style for absorbing the "input." Computer literacy is a *process* and not a state in life, or a single required course! An understanding of computer uses and limitations is necessary to gain the full benefits of living in the information age. Furthermore, social concerns such as data privacy, job displacement, and the changing nature of work must be understood by students as they embark on careers.

The Computer Challenge addresses each of these areas, and reflects a structure we've found valuable teaching a variety of computer courses.

Part One examines computer development and provides students with a framework for understanding technical concepts and the capabilities and limitations of computers. This section gives students an introduction to history, basic concepts of hardware and software, processing techniques, and programming languages.

Part Two explores contemporary applications such as office administration, smart products, education, health and medicine, the arts, government, science, and daily life. Students are exposed to the latest applications known by the authors at press time.

Part Three confronts the social implications of computers and deals with such issues as privacy, artificial intelligence, employment, the "cashless" society, and the "telematic world." As teachers, we've found these topics among the most difficult to teach, and this section carefully relates issues to current events likely to impact students today.

All chapters contain numerous Supplements that explore fascinating aspects of computers as they are introduced, and provide students with a magazine-like "sidebar" to amplify the main text. Supplements include many of the latest applications of computers such as computer-enhanced imaging of the Giaccobini–Zinner comet fly-through, the Cauzin Softstrip low-cost method of printing software into books and magazines, the computer-aided manufacture of "designer bones," and the role of computers in the search for missing children. A list of Supplements appears on page xiii.

Despite the changes in the computer field and computer courses, this balance of concepts, applications, and social issues has served instructors well in the introductory course. What varies among instructors is the amount of exposure in the first course to a programming language and/or hands-on experience with productivity software. To provide instructors with maximum flexibility, *The Computer Challenge* is language free and is easily reinforced with Burgess Communications texts on BASIC and Pascal programming.

In addition, *The Computer Challenge* can be used effectively with Intro-Software and the accompanying study guide/workbook, *Using Computer Applications,* available in IBM PC/compatibles and Apple versions. Intro-Software offers free, unrestricted, copyable software to teachers. Intro-Software offers students a hands-on experience with the concepts and operation of a spreadsheet (Intro-Calc), a database management system (Intro-File), and word processing (Intro-Word). They learn basic operations and applications through self-paced and carefully guided assignments that reinforce concepts learned in *The Computer Challenge.* Each program contains an easy-to-use menu and operating instructions.

Intro-Software was created by Fred Beisse of the University of Oregon. He wrote the programs and the study guide/workbook which accompany the text. As an instructor, Fred is aware of the pressures on instructors to provide a balanced presentation in one term. In order to be of maximum value to the student and instructor, Intro-Software is designed with a few simple commands that demonstrate typical capabilities and features contained in major commercial programs. As teachers, the concepts of generic applications software fit well with our approach—the goal is to educate students about concepts rather than to train them in the use of a particular approach.

The text contains many learning aids that we've found valuable in the textbooks we've written and taught over the years.

- A key words list begins each chapter, and key words appear in boldface on first use.
- Introductions focus student attention on the material that follows.
- Annotated bibliographies conclude each chapter and give students important clues to sort through the vast array of computer literature.
- Summing Up sections at the end of each chapter review and capsulize topics, concepts, and terms already presented.
- Three types of study questions are included in each chapter: Review Questions for mastery of chapter test material; Discussion Questions for research papers or classroom oral reports, panel discussions, and debates; and Exercises requiring additional exploration outside the classroom.

The ancillary package designed to accompany the text includes an Instructor's Manual, a Student Study Guide, Transparency Masters, a printed Test Bank with over 1000 questions, and a computerized version, TEST ONE, for the IBM PC/compatibles and Apple IIe.

ACKNOWLEDGMENTS

We wish to express our appreciation to friends and colleagues who made helpful suggestions as we wrote this book or who read chapters in their fields of expertise. Our thanks go to J. Mack Adams,

Kathleen Brook, Herbert Hamilton, Warner Hutchison, Kim Knauf, James Mensching, Conrad Milne, Derek Partridge, Emery Peterson, Timothy Pettibone, Debbie Treat, and Barbara Weber. The administrative and secretarial support of Karen Cavert and Stella Rodrigues is also gratefully acknowledged.

The manuscript was reviewed by a number of teachers at two- and four-year colleges and universities, and we thank them for their careful technical and pedagogical scrutiny. They are:

Robert Aiken, Temple University

William Atchison, University of Maryland

Carole Bergen, Mercy College

Grady Early, Southwest Texas State University

David Feinstein, University of Alabama

Patrick Graham, Austin Community College

Bart Green, St. Louis Community College

Carla Hall, St. Louis Community College

Lee T. Hill, Southern Oregon State College

James Jones, Graceland College

William Kelly, University of Arizona

Ronald Lancaster, Bowling Green State University

Donald McClain, University of Iowa

Alex T. Prengel, Brandeis University

Ann Sobell, Ohio State University

Finally, we wish to thank the entire staff of Burgess Communications for their editorial responsiveness to our manuscript, their fine job of book building, and their sales and marketing energy. Thank you.

Donna S. Hussain
Khateeb M. Hussain
Las Cruces, New Mexico
January 1986

Computer Technology

What is a computer? How does it work? What types of operations can it perform? Are processing results always accurate?

The purpose of Part I is to answer these questions. The basic components of computer systems—hardware, software, and data—are discussed. Instead of technical detail, the chapters present an overview of basic computing concepts and introduce computer terminology. The material in these chapters will provide you with the background you need to understand Parts II and III of this book, which focus on how computers are used and on the impact of computers on society.

Chapter 1 opens by explaining how the need for improved methods of data handling led to the invention of electromechanical data processing machines and then to the invention of computers. This chapter also describes the technological advances that have given rise to different computer generations.

Chapter 2 introduces the basic resources needed for processing. The chapter gives an overview of the role of the central processor and describes modes of processing and types of computers.

Peripherals, including input, storage, and output devices, are the subject of Chapter 3. Telecommunications and networks are also described.

Chapter 4 explains how to communicate with a computer. Programming languages and system software are introduced.

The collection, preparation, organization, and administration of data are surveyed in Chapter 5.

The final chapter in this part, Chapter 6, deals with human mistakes, hardware malfunction and breakdown, and criminal activity that lead to computer error. Common control measures to prevent errors are outlined.

PART ONE

Enter Computers

We are reaching the stage where problems that we must solve are going to become insoluble without computers. I do not fear computers; I fear the lack of them.

ISAAC ASIMOV

CHAPTER ONE

Key Words

ABC	first generation computers	minicomputer (mini)
Atanasoff, John	fourth generation computers	nanosecond
chip	hardware	network
computers	Hollerith, Herman	second generation computer
data	information	semiconductor
data processing	integrated circuits (IC)	supercomputer
Eckert, J. Presper	large-scale integration (LSI)	third generation computers
electromechanical device	mainframe	time sharing
electronic data processing (EDP)	manual data processing	transistor
electronics	Mauchly, John	UNIVAC
ENIAC	microminiaturization	vacuum tube
fifth generation computers	microprocessor	very large scale integration (VLSI)

It is here. The age of computers has arrived. The fantasies of childhood are no longer the raw material for science fiction: they are blueprints for computer engineering. We have robots to assist the Sorcerer's apprentice, terminals that talk like Hal in the films *2001: A Space Odyssey* and *2010*, and microcomputers the size of a dental filling for Buck Rogers. Computers have become so commonplace that we have even ceased to marvel at their technology. We take computers for granted instead.

American society today is becoming a computer-based society. Electronic record-keeping systems for payrolls, sales, inventories, and banking are the norm. Transmission of power and communications is monitored and managed by computer. Computers process text and numerical data in the office. They provide information for decision makers; they control manufacturing processes; and they analyze scientific measurements in research. Many household appliances, such as microwave ovens and thermostats, have electronic controls. Terminals are even used by musicians and artists for creative expression; they are used by the military to organize this country's defense.

Imagine the chaos if all computers suddenly stopped working. Utilities would be interrupted, assembly lines would stop moving, planes would be grounded, and banks would have to close their doors. All organizations that today rely on computers, such as hospitals, law enforcement agencies, warehouses, shops, government bureaus, factories, corporations, and universities, would be thrown into disarray. We have become dependent on computers for the delivery of modern goods and services. Without computers, society could no longer function.

WHAT *IS* A COMPUTER?

Computers are electronic machines that perform a specified sequence of operations on a set of **data**

(observations, facts, and concepts) in order to generate **information** (processed data), which in turn assists computer users in decision making. The manipulation of data is called **data processing**. The football coach who records the yardage gained per completed pass and calculates the average number of yards gained per successful pass is in a sense doing what a computer does. In this case, the record of yardage gained is the data and the calculation of yards per pass is data processing. And the result of the calculation is a statistic that helps the coach to evaluate passing effort and thus to make a decision on team performance.

Most work requires records and data manipulation. The wholesaler who keeps inventory lists and sends bills to customers is processing data. So is the farmer who keeps data on breeding stock and the doctor who evaluates patient symptoms, makes a diagnosis, and writes a prescription. Every citizen who fills out an annual tax return is processing data.

Manual data processing—that is, processing data by hand without aid of a machine—is satisfactory when the amount of data to be processed is small. But manual processing is slow, often monotonous, and subject to human error. It is also impractical to hand process large amounts of data, particularly when complex operations must be performed on that data.

As one might expect, machines have been developed to improve the speed, accuracy, and facility of data handling. Adding machines, typewriters, cash registers, and calculators are all examples. As technology has advanced, machines have also begun doing tasks that would be impractical, if not actually impossible, to do by hand. For example, a modern computer is needed to take the space shuttle out of orbit. The complex time sequence of rocket firings needed to bring the craft back to earth cannot be done manually by an astronaut.

COMPUTER HISTORY BEGINS

The data processing machine that has had the greatest impact on society is the computer. The origin of computers in fact dates back to the first occasion when prehistoric man picked up a few stones to use as a counting aid. The realization that a number or quantity could be represented by a physical unit led to other ways of expressing numbers—to beads and marks on paper and to the representation of numbers by means of mechanical gear wheels, electrical relays, and vacuum tubes. Modern computers represent numbers as submicroscopic areas of magnetized material.

The concept that numbers can be expressed in physical units resulted, in time, to the construction of machines able to perform calculations by manipulating the units. Supplement 1.1 describes some of the historical landmarks in the evolution of computing machines. By the end of the nineteenth century, a number of **electromechanical devices** (mechanical devices driven by electricity) for data processing had been developed. Because these devices were used primarily for accounting functions, they were called electrical accounting machines or EAM equipment.

HOLLERITH AND THE CENSUS

Among the leading nineteenth century pioneers in data processing was **Herman Hollerith**, who developed electromechanical punched-card equipment to process the 1890 census data. Hollerith drew inspiration from Joseph Jacquard, a French inventor. Jacquard had automated a weaving machine by punching a pattern of holes into cards to represent weaving instructions. The basic theory of Hollerith's machine was similar. Hollerith represented answers to census questions by means of holes punched in cards. Each possible census answer was assigned a specific location on the card.

How did Hollerith's machine work? In order to read the answers, Hollerith placed punched data cards into a circuit-closing press. The press contained rows of telescoping electrical pins (one for each possible hole location) that dropped onto the surface of the card. Wherever there was a hole, the pins passed through the card to complete an electrical circuit. Each completed circuit caused an electromagnet to advance a counting dial one or more spaces, depending on the information on the

Supplement 1.1 Landmarks in the Evolution of Computers

Antiquity The abacus, an apparatus of pebbles or other moving counters, was known to ancient Egyptians, Greeks, Romans, and Chinese. It is a simple calculating device.

1617 John Napier, a Scot, invented a device called Napier's Bones. It is a mechanical arrangement of bone strips on which numbers are stamped out that can be used to perform direct multiplication.

1640s Blaise Pascal, a French mathematician, invented a numerical wheel calculator. It is a mechanical device consisting of small wheels connected by gears, each wheel having a dial marked with the numbers 0 through 9. After one complete revolution of a wheel, action of the gears made the next wheel move ahead one-tenth of a revolution. In this manner, addition could be performed. Subtraction was done by reverse revolutions.

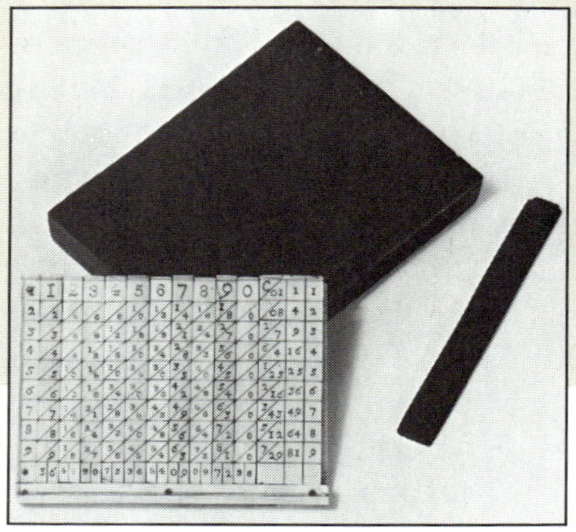

Napier's Bones (also called Napier's Rods), a device for direct multiplication. (International Business Machines Corporation)

1694 Gottfried Leibniz, a German philosopher and mathematician, built a general-purpose calculating device that could multiply and divide as well as add and subtract. Multiplication was rapidly repeated addition, while division was repeated subtraction. The device ran on gears and levers like Pascal's machine.

1801 Joseph Marie Jacquard, a French weaver, invented a textile loom attachment consisting of a belt of stiff punched cards. In weaving, a series of rods carried threads into the loom. The punched cards blocked some of the rods and allowed others to slip through to complete the weave. At each throw of the shuttle, a new card with a particular pattern of holes appeared in the path of the rods, determining which rods were engaged. In this way, the cards controlled the pattern of the weave. Jacquard cards were predecessors of the Hollerith card used in the 1890 census.

1830 Charles Babbage, an English mathematician, began construction on a "difference engine" with steam-driven rods, ratchets, and gears to perform arithmetic operations. It was the first mechanical calculator. Babbage hoped to be accurate to twenty digits and to produce and print mathematical tables such as logarithms. The underlying logic of the machine contributed to later work in the evolution of computers.

Babbage subsequently envisioned another machine, an "analytical engine," that would solve more general problems. This machine was never actually constructed by him but his design foreshadowed modern general-

card. Hollerith's machine had forty dials, with the result that forty questions could be tabulated simultaneously. At the end of each day, the total on each dial was recorded by operators and the dials were reset to zero. Using Hollerith's machine, the 1890 census data was processed in under two months, compared to the seven and a half years required for manual tabulation of the 1880 census. The census count was more accurate as well.

The value of Hollerith machines was quickly recognized. Austria and Canada used them for their own census. Hollerith entered the commercial market in 1896, founding the Tabulating Machine Company to market his inventions. The railroads purchased punched-card machines to audit freight statistics. Telephone companies purchased them for billing, and insurance companies purchased them to correlate actuarial statistics and make mortality predictions.

purpose digital computers. Augusta Ada, Countess of Lovelace, the daughter of the poet Byron and a skilled mathematician, assisted Babbage. She mastered Babbage's plans and used her influence to get others interested in his ideas. She also developed the essential ideas of programming. The programming language Ada is named in tribute to her contributions to the field of computing.

1854 George Boole, English mathematician and logician, published his principles of Boolean logic. This logic is used in computing.

1890s Herman Hollerith, American inventor, developed punched-card equipment for use in processing the 1890 U.S. census.

1937 Howard Aiken, an American computer pioneer at Harvard University, proposed a new kind of calculating machine with mechanical relays, wired control boards, and instructions fed in on paper tape. IBM backed the project. The machine, called the Mark 1, was completed in 1943. Addition and subtraction of two numbers took three-tenths of a second.

1939 John Atanasoff, faculty member at Iowa State University, began work on a machine to solve linear algebraic equations. The machine, known as the ABC (Atanasoff-Berry Computer), has come to be regarded as the first true electronic, digital computer.

1943 John Eckert and John Mauchly, two Americans, began work on ENIAC (Electronic Numerical Integrator and Calculator), designed to calculate trajectories of bombs and shells. It used more than 17,000 vacuum tubes, weighed 60,000 pounds, and was 1000 times faster than the Mark 1. ENIAC, a very useful machine, was kept secret until 1955.

1940s John Von Neumann, the Hungarian-born mathematician who worked on the ENIAC project, proposed both computer memories to store programs and the introduction of conditional transfer. He also contributed to adapting binary arithmetic to represent decimal numbers so that computations could be reduced to a simple on-off switch.

1951 UNIVAC (Universal Automatic Computer), brainchild of Eckert and Mauchly and the first commercial computer, was installed by Remington Rand in the U.S. Census Bureau. Within two years, thirteen companies were manufacturing computers for the commercial market.

The Leibniz Calculator, a general-purpose calculating device. (International Business Machines Corporation)

IMPROVED TABULATION EQUIPMENT

By the 1920s, card tabulating equipment had become quite common throughout the United States. The equipment had been enhanced since the early Hollerith machines. For example, machines gained the ability to interpret alphabetic data by representing the data as machine-readable code. James Powers, Hollerith's successor at the census bureau, patented a number of other improvements and marketed them through his own company, the Powers Accounting Company, which later became part of Remington Rand.

Hollerith's company had expanded through a number of acquisitions and mergers. Its president, Thomas J. Watson, was a personal force in the invention and popularization of information handling machines. When the company reorganized in 1924, it changed its name to International Business Machines Corporation (IBM). IBM is a company

Figure 1.1 A typical accounting department in the 1920s. Compare the atmosphere here with the more comfortable feel of today's electronic office. (International Business Machines Corporation)

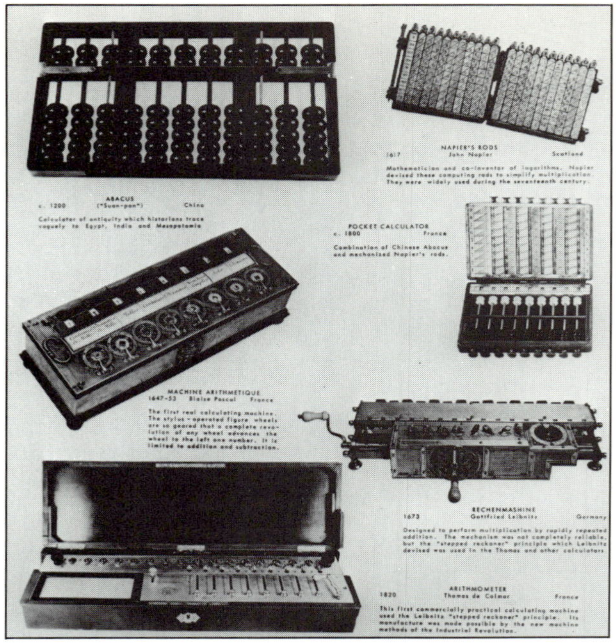

Figure 1.2 A photographic overview of significant steps in the history of the calculator. Each invention made possible a significant increase in the efficiency and speed of counting. (International Business Machines Corporation)

that continues to dominate the information processing industry today.

The demand for faster and more reliable calculators, primarily for scientific use, led to continued research in data processing. In the 1930s, many contributions were made to improve electromechanical devices. Vannevar Bush built a differential analyzer, the first general equation solver. Konrad Zuse pioneered some basic ideas of automatic computing, including binary arithmetic, the floating decimal point, and program control by punched tape. Claude Shannon described a way of using symbolic logic to improve electrical switching circuits. Howard Aiken started work on an electromechanical computer to solve complex equations, a machine called the Mark 1, that was built with financial and technical support from IBM. These are just a few of the many mathematicians, engineers, and scientists whose work laid the foundation for subsequent advances in data processing. (Concepts such as binary arithmetic will be discussed in the next chapter.)

Two major problems exist with electromechanical data processing machines: namely, speed is limited by the time taken to align moving parts, and repeated movement causes parts to wear, leading to machine failure. These problems led designers in the 1930s to turn to **electronics**. With electronics, faster speeds and improved reliability could be achieved since electronic devices have no moving mechanical parts.

FROM RELAYS TO TUBES

John Atanasoff was the first person to design an electronic computing machine. His device, built in 1939 with the help of a graduate student, Clifford Berry, used vacuum tubes and performed arith-

Supplement 1.2 Ways of Representing the Number 2

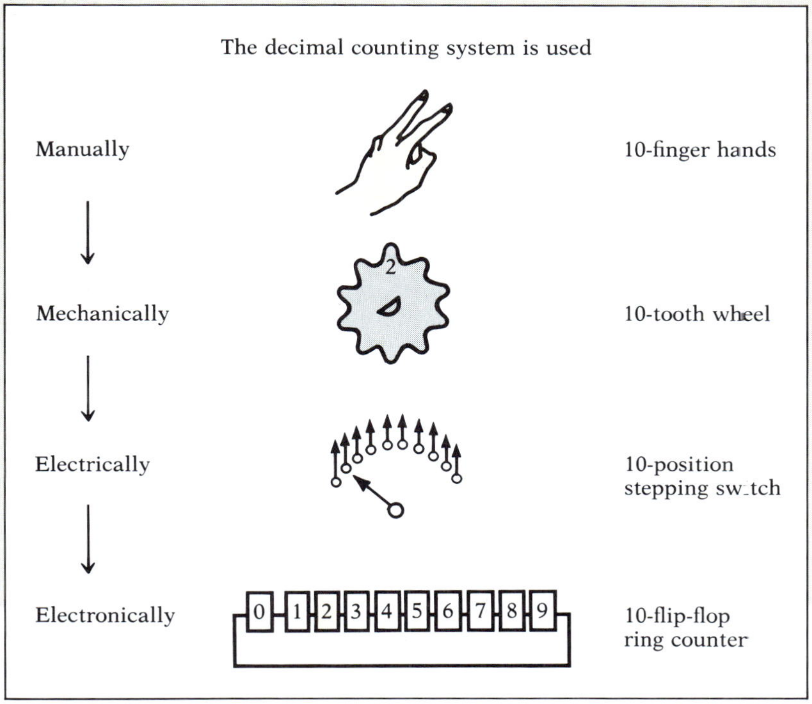

Manual Count two fingers.

Mechanical Turn a ten-tooth wheel until tooth representing the number 2 is in line with a viewing window.

Electrical Two electrical pulses will register as 2 on a ten-position, high-speed stepping switch.

Electronic A ten flip-flop ring counter is advanced electronically by two incoming pulses that reset the flip-flops to 2. This system was used by ENIAC. Modern computers do not require the ten flip-flop counter since they compute in binary.

metic and logical tasks by manipulating numbers. The ultimate goal of the machine, called the **ABC** (Atanasoff-Berry Computer), was to solve twenty-nine simultaneous algebraic linear equations with twenty-nine unknowns. The machine never achieved its objective.

World War II spurred the development of **electronic data processing (EDP) machines** to replace electromechanical models. The British government worked on a special electronic computer called Colossus to crack German war codes. The American government focused efforts on an electronic computer to calculate firing and ballistic tables for gunners, and trajectories for new weapons. A contract to **John Mauchly** and **J. Presper Eckert** resulted in construction of the **ENIAC** (Electronic Numerical Integrator and Calculator), usually considered the world's first large-scale digital computer, completed in 1946. (A digital computer processes data represented in the form of digits. Chapter 2 will explain digital processing in more detail.) However, ENIAC lacked the ability to process a conditional instruction. A conditional instruction is one that is executed only when a specified condition or set of conditions is satisfied. Today we regard this feature the essential feature distinguishing a digital computer from a calculator.

With the transition from electromechanical devices to electronic machines, the computer revolution began.

COMPUTER GENERATIONS

In 1951, **UNIVAC** (Universal Automatic Computer) became the first commercial electronic computer to reach the market. Unlike earlier computers which were one of a kind machines dedicated to particular scientific or engineering problems,

Supplement 1.3 How Modern Computers Work

Modern computers use an internal representation based on the binary number system (zeros and ones, not the ten digits of the decimal number system that people use). George Boole, a nineteenth century mathematician, codified a system of algebra based on the binary number system that could be used to deal with the truth or falsity of algebraic expressions. More recently, other mathematicians, notably Alan Turing in the 1930s, showed that three simple functions, that of AND, OR, and NOT, could be designed into electronic circuitry.

One of the simplest circuits in modern computers is called a half-adder. By linking many of these half-adders together, it is possible to construct circuits that add large numbers expressed as a sequence of zeros and ones. Such circuits, plus the judicial use of other AND, OR, and NOT circuits (or more elementary yet, only AND and NOT-OR circuits) take care of all of the mathematical and logical functions of the modern computer.

UNIVAC was a general-purpose computer designed for business data processing applications. Who was UNIVAC's first client? The U.S. Bureau of Census.

The key component of UNIVAC and other **first generation computers** was electronic tubes, called **vacuum tubes**, which served to control internal machine operations. The tubes acted as electronic on-off switches, replacing earlier electromechanical relays. The thousands of tubes made UNIVAC enormous in size; the computer in fact filled a very large room. The tubes generated considerable heat so that special air conditioning was needed, and frequent failure of tubes meant machine reliability was poor.

First generation computers—that is, computers developed between 1951 and 1958—were slow by today's standards. Early computers executed approximately 1000 instructions per second. Their high-speed memories could hold only 10,000 to 20,000 characters (including both instructions and data). Programming (the preparation of instructions telling the computer what to do) was time-consuming as well since convenient computer languages had not been developed. Programming and computer languages will be discussed in detail in Chapter 4.

Because of these drawbacks, it was assumed that the market for electronic computers would be limited. IBM planned to build only eighteen when it launched the IBM 701 series, expecting that number would saturate the market. Demand proved much greater than originally predicted however. By 1956, IBM, UNIVAC, Monroe, National Cash Register, Burroughs, Radio Corporation of America, and Underwood were all producing computers for the marketplace.

THE SECOND GENERATION

Computer technology advanced at a fast pace in the 1950s. By 1959, solid-state **transistors** replaced vacuum tubes in computer circuits. Because transistors represented such a dramatic change in technology, the new machines were classified as **second generation computers**. (The second generation extended from 1959 to 1964. See Table 1.1 for a time line of computer generations.)

Why were transistors such an improvement? They were very small in size compared to vacuum tubes, required less power to operate, generated less heat, and were more reliable. In addition, circuits using transitors could be designed to operate at much higher speeds. One reason is that an electrical impulse in a transistor has less distance to travel than in a vacuum tube. Instructions could also be executed significantly faster by second generation machines because of improved circuitry.

Supplement 1.4 ENIAC

Weighed: Thirty tons

Stood: Two stories high

Occupied: 15,000 square feet floor space

Cost: $486,840.22 (in 1946 dollars)

Required: 1500 relays
70,000 resistors
10,000 capacitors
More than 17,000 vacuum tubes
174 KW consumption

Speed: Addition and subtraction twenty times slower than the time required for a $2000 kneetop portable today.

Computing power: Equivalent to the average digital watch projected for 1990.

Work begun: May 31, 1943

Completed: June 1, 1946

In service: Until October 2, 1955, when it was disassembled and parts sent to the Smithsonian Institution, Washington, D.C.

ENIAC, generally considered the first large-scale digital computer. This 1946 thirty-ton installation is a far cry from today's compact fourth-generation computers. (Sperry Corporation)

Furthermore, second generation computers incorporated improved methods of data storage.

Another advantage was that programming was simplified. FORTRAN, COBOL, and other high-level programming languages were now on the market, and they facilitated communication between computers and users.

The cost of computing dropped with second generation computers. The technology that improved performance also lowered the price of equipment and reduced operating expenditures. With second generation computers, demand surged. Computers were now within the budget of many large corporations, universities, and governmental agencies. What is more, the range of computer programs broadened as the number of users grew. In 1960, Bethlehem Steel became the first company to handle orders, inventory, and production control by computer. The Bank of America installed automatic check-processing equipment. In 1963, the Oklahoma City Times began to typeset by computer, and American Airlines inaugurated the first computerized system for seat reservations. By 1965, the value of installed computers had risen to an estimated three to four billion dollars.

THE THIRD GENERATION

It was not, however, until the **third generation** of computers (1965 to 1970), characterized by miniaturized **integrated circuits (IC)**, that computers were produced in the price range of most organizations. Integrated circuits, an advance of the mid-1960s, made it possible to print and etch thousands of small circuits onto a small **chip** of silicon less than one-eighth inch square. Silicon, one of the most plentiful elements on earth, is a **semiconductor**, which means that it is able to conduct electric current when "doped" with chemical impurities. (Silicon chips have greater electrical conductivity than an insulator, but less than a good conductor: hence the term "semiconductor.") The size of computers became smaller as a result of these tiny components. Because electrical signals had shorter distances to travel on chips, computing speed increased. Techniques of mass producing chips contributed to lower component costs.

Other improvements of third generation computers included:

- Further expansion of storage capacity.
- The use of telephone wires, cable and other communication channels to connect user terminals with distant computers.
- The development of **time sharing**, whereby several users simultaneously share the resources of a single, large, centralized computer. (Time sharing is explained in Chapter 2.)
- The development of new high-level languages such as BASIC.
- The development of more powerful programs to automate many computing tasks previously done by human operators. (See Chapter 4 for a discussion on operating systems.)

In the third generation, a smaller computer, called a **minicomputer** or **mini**, was also introduced by Digital Equipment Corporation (DEC) to compete with **mainframes**, the larger computers of the day. Although less powerful than mainframes, DEC's minis were less expensive and other companies soon started to manufacture minis as well. At first, minis were designed for scientific and engineering uses. By the early 1970s, however, minis were also being packaged for the small business market.

COMPUTERS TODAY

A primary characteristic of **fourth generation computers**, the computers of today, is **microminiaturization** and the use of **large-scale integration (LSI)** and **very large-scale integration (VLSI)** of circuits. With this technology, the integrated circuitry of a complete processor can be etched on a single chip. Such chips, called **microprocessors**, are today embedded as control devices in industrial equipment and household appliances. Microprocessors have also made possible the advent of **microcomputers**. Microcomputers are low-cost, desk top computer models appropriate for small organizations and personal use. An entire chapter in this book, Chapter 14, is devoted to the subject of microcomputers. Finally, in addition to leading to microcomputers, microminiaturization has led to **supercomputers**, very fast and very powerful computers like the Cray 2. Supercomputers are designed for engineering or scientific research rather than for business environments. (Supercomputers are discussed in detail in Chapter 13.)

Some fourth generation machines operate at **nanosecond** speeds. A nanosecond is one billionth of a second. Supplement 1.5 compares the operations that can be performed by computers operating at nanosecond speeds with the half second it takes for spilled coffee to reach the floor.

Figure 1.3 A wealth of hardware options. One hallmark of the optimum modern office system is the choice of computers—minicomputers, mainframes, and even portables—all linked into the same system. (Hewlett-Packard Company)

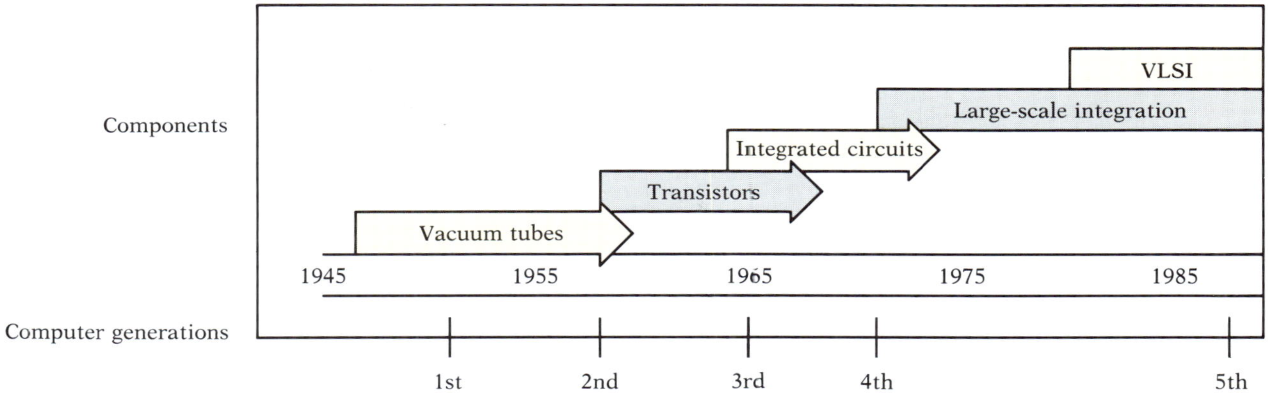

Figure 1.4 The relationship of component development and computer generations in time. Advances in component technology are largely responsible for the first four computer generations. Although fifth-generation computers will harness thousands of microprocessors in parallel (very large-scale integration), advances in the technology of components will have less bearing on improved performance than programs that incorporate artificial intelligence.

Other characteristics of fourth generation computers include their greater reliability, lower cost, and larger storage facilities than previous computers, all of which is the result of microtechnology. As for applications, a distinguishing feature of this period in the evolution of computers is the development of database management systems, often referred to as DBMS. The function of database management systems, which are explained in Chapter 5, is to store an integrated collection of data and provide easy access to the stored data.

We can expect **fifth generation computers** in the near future. These computers will have "intelligent" processors—that is, processors that can make inferences. Users will also be able to communicate with these computers in natural languages, such as English and Japanese. (Natural language research has high priority in Japan.) Chapter 20 discusses fifth generation computers in detail. Table 1.1 is a comparison of computer generations. Table 1.2 shows relative changes in computer **hardware** (physical equipment) over time.

Later chapters of this text will explain the meaning of the many new terms introduced in this section in greater detail and will introduce readers to applications for microminiature technology. In addition, brief definitions of terms used in this chapter can be found in the Glossary.

THE COMPUTER REVOLUTION

Each new generation of computers has been characterized by improvements in speed, reliability, and productivity. For example, processing that cost $1 in 1952 cost only $.0076 in 1985. A frequently quoted statistic summarizes the improvement in computers this way: had the pace of advance in the computer industry been matched in the automobile industry, a Rolls Royce today would cost only $2.50 and get two million miles per gallon. (Readers, note that the figures in this paragraph measure different aspects of improved performance. Incidentally, the Rolls in this performance statistic would be miniaturized, hardly suitable for carrying unminiaturized people!)

The number of users has grown as each new computer generation has reached the market and the number of available programs has also expanded. At the present time we are experiencing explosive growth in the sale of microcomputers for business and home use. The number of jobs in data processing is on the rise, and the number of users is

Table 1.1: Comparison of Computer Generations

Major Characteristics	First Generation	Second Generation	Third and Fourth Generation	Fifth Generation
Introduced	1951–58	1959–64	1965–80s	1990s
Electronic circuitry	Vacuum tubes	Transistors	Integrated circuits (IC, LSI, VLSI)	Very, very large scale integration (VVLSI)
Size	Room size	Closet size	Desk-top to chip	Not known
Speed	Millisecond	Microsecond	Nanosecond	Picosecond
Most common languages used	Symbolic, machine language	Assembler, high level, e.g., FORTRAN, COBOL	High and higher levels, e.g., query languages	Artificial intelligence-oriented language
Main memory	Williams storage tubes	Magnetic	Solid state	Solid state
Reliability:				
• Relative reliability	1	1,000	100,000	Infinity
• Failure rate	1 every few hours	1 every 100–1,000 hours	1 every million hours	Approaching 0
Applications	Scientific and engineering	Business	Integrated	Artificial-intelligence-oriented
Early examples	ENIAC IBM 650	IBM 1401 Honeywell 200	IBM 360 IBM 370 NCR 395 Minis Microcomputers	Super super-computer

Supplement 1.5 Nanosecond.

In the computer, the basic operations can be done within the order of a

NANOSECOND

(one thousandth of a millionth of a second.)

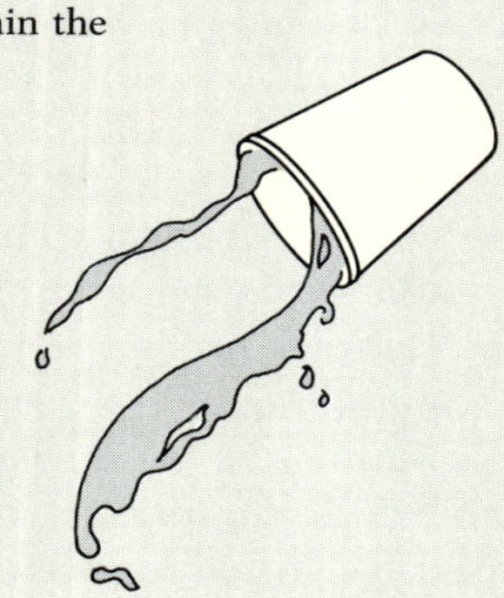

Within the half second it takes this spilled coffee to reach the floor, a fairly large computer could—(given the information in magnetic form)

Debit 2000 checks to 30 different bank accounts.

and examine the electrocardiograms of 100 patients and alert a physician to possible trouble,

and score 150,000 answers on 3000 examinations and evaluate the effectiveness of the questions,

and figure the payroll for a company with a thousand employees.

and a few other chores.

Courtesy International Business Machines Corporation

Computer processing speeds have increased since IBM first published this definition of a nanosecond, one thousandth of a millionth of a second (a billionth of a second). Many more chores can today be performed in a millionth of a second than listed here.

Table 1.2: Relative Changes in Hardware Characteristics

	1950s	1960s	1970s	1980s	1990s*
Size (of circuit per cubic foot)	1,000	100,000	10 million	1 billion	Many billion
Speed (time to execute an instruction in CPU)	300 ms	5 ms	80–10 ns	25–5 ns	5 ns
Reliability (mean average in between failures in CPU)	Hours	Tens of hours	Hundreds of hours	Thousands of hours	Tens of thousands of hours
Cost (for 1 million basic instructions)	28	1	0.02	0.001	less than 0.001
Cost (of storage)	2.61	0.85	0.05	0.001	less than 0.001

ms = microsecond (millionth of a second)
ns = nanosecond (billionth of a second)
*Estimated

doubling every two years. It is estimated that six out of ten persons in the U.S. labor force will have direct involvement with data processing by 1990.

The amount of money spent on data processing is also rising: up from 2.1 percent of the gross national product in 1970 to a projected 13 percent in 1990, or in other words, from $101 per capita in 1970 to an estimated $1253 in 1990. Indeed, expenditures on data processing double approximately every five years. What is more, this increase is occurring in spite of the fact that actual equipment costs are dropping. The increase can be attributed to increased volume of computer sales and greater expenditures in the development of computer applications overall. In 1984, annual American revenues for the computer industry exceeded $110 billion. Growth statistics can be cited in almost every aspect of computing.

In addition to this phenomenal growth, new generations have added new dimensions to computing. Today computers process text, images, and voice as well as numbers. Although computers are still used primarily to process business transactions and compute scientific formulas, people use computers for all types of endeavors. With a computer, decision makers can plan for the future (for example, by answering "What if?" questions), maintain control (for example, by verifying whether products and performance meet design specifications), and manage day-to-day operations (for example, scheduling work assignments of employees.) Writers, artists, musicians, anthropologists, politicians, librarians, law enforcement officers, doctors, and athletes all apply computer technology to their specialities. Increasingly, young children are using computer terminals in the classroom and personal computers are being used in the home. No longer is computing the prerogative of the corporate elite or scientific researcher.

COMPUTING IN THE 1980s

The 1980s is a crucial decade in the evolution of computers. The computer industry is standing at a threshold, ready to capitalize on technological advances of recent years. Low-cost, miniaturized computers for an enlarged range of applications have reached the market, as have computers that are able to tackle previously unsolvable problems.

Figure 1.5 Demonstrating a portable computer. This compact, convenient, "lap" machine goes anywhere, communicating by telephone and modem to the home- or office-based system. (Hewlett-Packard Company)

(Supplement 1.6 lists some sample applications that may become commonplace.) At the same time, research and development in computing have reached an all-time high, constituting more than one-fifth of all industrial research and development in the United States. We can expect even faster processing speeds, greater reliability, lower costs, and smaller computers in the future.

Public acceptance of computers is also on the rise. Although people still resist the introduction of computers at work if their jobs are threatened by the technology, they expect to deal with computers when transacting business, paying bills, banking, and shopping. Indeed, computers have become so commonplace that they are usually blamed when things go wrong, even though the blame is rarely justified.

Another reason why the 1980s will be a crucial decade is that the American government is redefining its relationship with the computer industry. One example of changed policy is the government's 1982 settlement of its antitrust suit against American Telephone and Telegraph (AT&T). This settlement allows for the merger of computer manufacture and communications by AT&T, a merger formerly prevented by the Federal Communications Commission. (In effect, the settlement frees computer firms to challenge AT&T in communications as well. That they will begin to do so is shown by IBM's 1984 acquisition of Rolm.) The merger of computers and communications will not only help promote competition in the computer industry, but will also facilitate the development of computer **networks**, which are simply interconnected computing facilities. Computer networks are the key to the realization of many applications that are merely dreams today, such as widespread use of home banking and electronic mail.

Another antitrust case, the government's thirteen-year-old suit against IBM that was dismissed in 1982, will also have far-reaching repercussions. IBM is already a domineering presence in the computer industry. Now that legal and political shackles have been removed by dismissal of the suit, the company is expected to search for new markets and move relentlessly against competitors. The computer industry and consumers will both be affected.

In short, advances in technology, new computer applications, a receptive public, and fewer restrictions on industry growth will all contribute to make the 1980s a period of accelerated change.

Figure 1.6 A wristwatch terminal, a new twist on portability. Using a controlling device, the user loads up to 2000 characters of information—phone numbers, addresses, schedules—from a base computer and reads it out through any other computer at the touch of a button. (Hattori Corporation of America)

Supplement 1.6 Computer Applications That Might Become Commonplace

Agriculture: A computer with access to information on market conditions will advise farmers what to sow and when to sell.

Education: A student's pronunciation in a foreign language will be drilled and corrected by a computer that can listen and respond.

Law: Lawyers will use computers to search law databases for relevant precedents in a given case, saving hours of library search.

Publishing: Manuscripts will be stored on magnetic tape, with books printed by publishers on demand. An alternative to such "instant publishing" will be to send material through communications channels for display on computer terminals or for local printing.

Management: Given figures on market demand, plant capacity, and the price of raw materials, computers will suggest the optimal mix of products to be manufactured.

Medicine: A computer will identify diseases that fit a patient's symptoms and recommend treatment.

Shopping: Information on a store's inventory (such as one might find printed in a store catalog) will be available to consumers, who will be able to compare offerings from several stores, place an order, specify home delivery, and authorize payment through electronic transfer of funds—all without leaving home.

Transportation: Automobiles will have autopilots controlled by computer. In airplanes, the instrument panel will be replaced by dial displays projected in space when requested by the pilot, and audible status reports will supplement the displays.

ISSUES TO BE RESOLVED

While an expanded role for computers in society will have beneficial effects, there are many social and ethical problems which arise from this expanded role that will need to be resolved. For example, will there be jobs for workers displaced by computers? If not, how will we redistribute income to provide for the families of the unemployed? Nations that depend on their cheap labor to accumulate capital may find that robots are undermining their economies. Will computers disrupt a fragile world order?

Security of computerized information is also an issue. Are secrets, such as chemical formulas for products or strategies for national defense, safe when stored in a computer? Do we have adequate safeguards to thwart embezzlement in electronic banking? How will a cashless society change our lifestyle?

Personal privacy, like data security, is jeopardized by computer technology. Our bank statements, medical files, credit ratings, school records, and job vitae may become part of vast integrated data banks. Will we lose control over the distribution and use of such information? Will government become the Big Brother of George Orwell's *1984*? Will computer specialists become the new elite?

Many observers are concerned lest we rely on computers for all problem solving in the future even though not all types of problems can be solved by computer. Many people may cease to be creative thinkers and limit their vision to machine solutions, ignoring the nuances of interpersonal relationships because such relationships are hard to quantify. Will a time come when human attributes such as courage, sympathy, integrity, and love become less important than machine efficiency? Will we so rely on computers to do our thinking that we stop thinking altogether? With computers to calculate, plan, manage, and design, why bother to learn multiplication tables and how to spell? Will the value of human life be diminished if computers become smarter than we are?

In the past, people have had pride in work and earned the esteem of others through the contributions they made in their work. What will replace the work ethic in American society when computers displace humans in many jobs? Will displaced workers find employment in higher pursuits? Do people have the inner resources to cope with increased leisure? Do we have social structures to facilitate change in society—change that it fostered by computerization?

WHAT LIES AHEAD?

These are some of the questions that arise because of our increased dependence on computers. Without doubt, social adjustments will have to be made as our society becomes more and more dependent on computers. We must begin planning now if we want to assimilate computer technology without social turmoil. It may be necessary to reshape the legal framework of corporate activity to protect individual privacy and data security in a computerized society. We may need to redefine the role of government and the rights of citizens. Perhaps we will have to revise our educational system so that all students learn computer skills and can frame problems for computer solution.

The authors hope that this book will help prepare readers for the years ahead. In this text, basic computer technology is explained, applications of this technology are described, and the impact of computer technology on society is discussed. Both the potential and limitations of computers are examined. Computers are going to play an increasingly important role in coming years. This book should provide readers in all disciplines with the background they need to realize the full benefits of computer technology in their jobs, in their communities, and in their homes.

REVIEW QUESTIONS

1. What are the advantages of machine data processing over manual data processing?
2. Discuss early contributions to machine data processing, including those of Pascal, Jacquard, and Babbage.
3. Why is Herman Hollerith considered a leading pioneer in data processing equipment? What contributions did he make?
4. What are the limitations of electromechanical machines?
5. Discuss work that was done in the 1930s and 1940s that led to the first electronic computer.
6. Why is computer history divided into generations? What were the characteristics of the first generation of computers?
7. Discuss briefly major technological advances of the second, third, and fourth generations of computers.
8. Why will the 1980s be a decade of accelerated change?
9. Does the growing dependence of society on computers pose ethical problems? What problems?

DISCUSSION QUESTIONS

1. What has been the greatest contribution of computers to data processing? Speed? Accuracy? Ability to process complex problems and handle large amounts of data?
2. Comment on the following statement: We are now in the stage of the computer revolution comparable to the Model T in the automobile revolution.
3. What three computer applications of the 1980s do you think will have the greatest impact on society? Why?
4. What do you think Asimov means by saying, "I do not fear computers; I fear the lack of them"?
5. To what extent do you think that the United States is becoming a computerized society? Do you consider computerization a challenge and opportunity, or do you look upon computerization with apprehension?

6. Comment on the following statement: Soon computers in the home will be as common as the telephone.
7. Do you agree with the opinion that computers are essential for business and industry if America is to remain competitive in the world of the 1990s? Give reasons to support your answer.
8. Do you believe that knowledge of computers is essential for all university students irrespective of their discipline? Explain your position.

EXERCISES

1. List the ways in which computers are used in your daily life:
   a. As a student.
   b. At home.
   c. In your community.
2. List all the ways you have personally used computers (or information processed by computer) in the past week.
3. Make a list of social implications of computers. Keep the list so that you can compare it with your views after you have finished reading this book.
4. Write a report on one of the early pioneers in data processing. Did the environment in which the individual worked play a role in the contribution?
5. Draw a time chart for important events in the history of computing. Use arrows to show how one invention led to another if you feel that there is a strong relationship between inventions.
6. Write a scenario of the year 1995 as you envision it, describing how computers will affect your life.
7. Write an outline of the new concepts that you learned in this chapter.
8. Write several paragraphs describing what you expect to learn from this book.

Selected Annotated Bibliography

Austrian, Geoffrey D. *Herman Hollerith.* New York: Columbia University Press, 1982. This biography of Hollerith describes the punches, tabulators, and sorters Hollerith invented and Hollerith's role as a pioneer in data processing.

Corvey, H. Dominic and McAlister, Neil H. *Computer Consciousness.* Reading, Mass.: Addison-Wesley, 1982. This book has a good discussion of computer hardware and software for persons new to the computing field. It also describes what advances to expect in coming years.

Crichton, Michael. *Electronic Life: How to Think About Computers.* New York: Alfred A. Knopf, 1983. Crichton introduces the computer scene to novices with chapters such as "Afraid of Computers" and "Following Zenith: The Final Days of Man Before the Machines Take Over?"

Eames, Charles and Ray. *A Computer Perspective.* Cambridge, Mass.: Harvard University Press, 1973. This is an illustrated essay on the origins and first lines of development of the computer. The book is based on an exhibition assembled for IBM.

Evans, Christopher. *The Making of the Micro.* New York: Van Nostrand Reinhold, 1981. Numerous photos and drawings are used in this brief history of computers. This is an excellent source.

———, *The Mighty Micro.* London: Victor Gallancz, 1979. The author, a psychologist turned computer scientist, was an acknowledged expert on microcomputers. Although Evans focuses on British contributions to the microcomputer revolution in this book, he does present a world view when discussing the future of computing.

Kidder, Tracy. *The Soul of a New Machine.* New York: Avon, 1982. The author, a Pulitzer Prize winner, describes how a computer works and how both designers and users view "la machine." The use of computers as a whole is also discussed.

Lafferty, Peter. *An Introduction to Computing.* New York: Simon and Schuster, 1983. The topics discussed are how to select a computer, how computers work, how to use a computer, and how to extend a simple system.

Laurie, Peter. *The Joy of Computers.* Boston: Little, Brown and Company, 1983. This book describes computers in nontechnical language. The text is well supported by colorful diagrams.

Martin, James. *The Telematic Society.* Englewood Cliffs, N.J.: Prentice-Hall, 1981. This book is an update of *The Wired Society* by the same author. Martin discusses the technology of wired communities and the social impact of teleshopping, telenews, telebanking, and teleschools. The book can be read either before or after one is introduced to computers. The author has written more than twenty books on computing. This is perhaps his most thought-provoking volume.

Pagels, Heinz R., (ed.) *Computer Culture: The Scientific, Intellectual, and Social Impact of the Computer.* New York: National Academy of Sciences, 1984. The computer revolution is causing important changes in our world view. This book is a product of a symposium on these changes sponsored by The New York Academy of Sciences. The 29 contributors to the book include well-known names in the computer field such as John McCarthy, Seymour Papert, Edward Feigenbaum, Alphonse Chapanis, and Michael Dertouzos.

Sommerfeld, Amy. "A Walk Through The Computer Museum with Gordon Bell," *Computerworld,* vol. 19, no. 41 (October 14, 1985), ID/10-22. The Computer Museum, located in Boston in a converted warehouse, houses the world's largest collection of computer industry artifacts. Bell, a trustee of the museum, gives his comments on the exhibits to the author as they tour the facility.

Willis, Jerry and Miller, Merl. *Computers for Everybody.* Beaverton, Oregon: Dilithium Press, 1981. This book tries to remove the misconception that computers are magical machines to be feared. Basic computing concepts are discussed, home computers and teaching computers are described, peripherals are introduced, and use of computers is examined.

A Closer Look at Processing

The extension of man's intellect by machine, and the partnership of man and machine in handling information may well be the technological advance dominating this century.

SIMON RAMO

CHAPTER TWO

Key Words

- analog computer
- application program
- arithmetic and logic unit (ALU)
- batch processing
- binary digits
- bits
- bubble memory
- byte
- central processing unit (CPU)
- chip
- computer
- control unit
- CPU-on-a-chip
- data
- data processing
- digital computer
- downtime
- electronic data processing (EDP)
- execution cycle
- hardware
- hybrid computer
- information processing
- input equipment
- instruction cycle
- instruction register
- interactive processing
- interface
- internal memory
- internal storage
- K
- mainframe
- microcomputer (micro)
- microprocessor
- minicomputer (mini)
- online processing
- online real time (OLRT)
- operating system programs
- output equipment
- peripheral equipment
- picosecond
- primary storage
- programmable read-only memory (PROM)
- programming language
- programs
- random-access memory (RAM)
- read-only memory (ROM)
- real-time processing
- remote processing
- software
- software packages
- storage registers
- supercomputer
- telecommunications
- time sharing
- vendor

Do you stand in front of your closet mornings, half-awake, trying to decide what to wear? You check the weather, consider the activities you have planned for the day, and look to see what is clean. In making a clothing choice, your brain acts as a data processor.

Machines can also be used to process data. In fact, machines are far more efficient and effective than brain power when:

- A large volume of data must be processed.
- Fast processing is crucial.
- Processing must be done frequently.
- Complex operations on data are required.
- A high degree of accuracy is essential.

Indeed, the term **data processing** has become synonomous with machine data processing.

Chapter 1 described the development of computers. Processing by computer is commonly called **EDP (electronic data processing)**. Unfortunately, many people associate the term "data" with numbers; that is, they interpret the acronym

EDP as restricted to numerical data processing. Computers also process nonnumeric data, however, including text, voice, and images. The ability of computers to process this broad range of data is better expressed by the term **information processing**.

This chapter will explain how computer systems for information processing are organized. We will begin with a discussion of how computers operate, illustrating computer processing with a sample application: the calculation of a grade point average. Modes of processing will be introduced next. Finally, we will outline the differences between microprocessors, microcomputers, minicomputers, mainframes, and supercomputers.

WHAT DOES A COMPUTER DO?

A **computer** is a machine designed to receive data and perform operations on this data according to a given set of instructions. It can perform two basic functions:

- Arithmetic operations: addition, subtraction, multiplication, division.
- Comparisons: determining whether one value is smaller than, equal to, or larger than another.

Computers are classified in terms of the type of information processed. When data is discrete—that is, when the items to be counted are separate and distinct parts, like the units coming off an assembly line—a **digital computer** is used. When data is processed continuously—for example, when the temperature, pressure, or flow of liquids in manufacturing are monitored—an **analog computer** is used. A **hybrid computer** handles both discrete and continuous data.

In the past, a distinction was also made between computers dedicated to business problems and those used for scientific purposes. Formerly, business programs involved relatively simple and repetitive computations with large amounts of input and output: for example, multiplying hours worked times wages for each employee in order to calculate a payroll. Scientific programs, on the other hand, required solving complex formulas with little input and output. A computer designed for business use was not appropriate for scientific use, and vice versa. We now have general-purpose computers designed to solve problems in both domains. Furthermore, the distinction between business and scientific processing is no longer so clear-cut since many of today's business problems are as complex as those in scientific fields.

BASIC RESOURCES REQUIRED FOR PROCESSING

In order to process information, a computer system requires three basic resources: hardware, software, and data.

Computer Hardware

The physical equipment of computer systems is called **hardware**. Hardware components are needed to introduce data into the computer (input equipment), to process and store data and programs (processing units), and to deliver processed results to the user (output equipment).

Input equipment collects data, converts it into machine-readable form, and conveys it to the processing unit of the computer. There are many types of input devices. The **input equipment** used in a given application will depend on the type of input to be collected. For example, in an office, sales data may be typed on a terminal keyboard (see Figure 2.1). Badge readers are used to input data on the movement of personnel at security checkpoints in factories. Other machines have been developed to read data recorded on punched cards, tape, cassettes, and disks.

Central Processing Unit and Internal Memory

The **central processing unit (CPU)**, often thought of as the heart or brain of the computer, has the following parts:

Figure 2.1 A portable teleprinter. This lightweight data terminal links to a host computer via the telephone system and prints out the information it receives. (Texas Instruments Incorporated)

1. The **arithmetic and logic unit (ALU)**. Contains circuits that perform both arithmetic and logical operations.
2. The **control unit**. Coordinates the sequence of instructions and the flow of data within the CPU.
3. **Storage registers**. Temporarily stores instructions and intermediate results.

Internal memory, also called **internal storage** or **primary storage**, is often housed within the same physical unit as the CPU. (Some authors consider internal memory an integral part of the CPU. In spite of the fact that the term CPU is more than twenty years old, there is still no clear consensus regarding its definition.) The purpose of internal memory is to store data until it is ready to be processed. It also stores instructions concerning computations to be performed. Most current internal storage hardware consists of semiconductors that have memory circuitry etched on silicon chips. Bubble memory is another storage technology of promise. It consists of magnetized spots, which resemble magnetic bubbles when seen under a microscope, resting on a thin film of a semiconductor material such as garnet.

Many of the complex functions performed by computers, like taking square roots and evaluating exponents, are performed by programs that are placed in **read-only memory (ROM)**, a nonerasable, permanently programmed memory that is burned in memory chips. Sometimes all of the instructions a computer can execute are placed in ROM. This is true, for example, of a child's computer that plays only a single game.

Output equipment is used to deliver processed results. Results may appear on a computer terminal screen, be printed in a hard-copy report, or stored on tape or disk for later use. Sometimes voice output is used; sometimes a plotter produces graphs or drawings of the output. Output might also control the movements of a robot. The exact **output equipment** included in the configuration of a given computer system will depend on the needs of users and on their financial resources.

The term **peripheral equipment** is used to describe all hardware distinct from the central processor and internal storage. Peripherals include input/output devices, secondary storage devices to supplement internal memory, and communication equipment used to link the processor unit with these devices. Chapter 3 discusses peripherals at length.

Supplement 2.1 gives a list of the components of a computer. Parts of the CPU and the relationship of the CPU to internal and secondary storage are illustrated in Part A. The arrows represent the flow of data within the CPU and between the CPU and memory units during processing. Part B illus-

Supplement 2.1: Computer Components

Part A. Relationship of CPU to Memory.

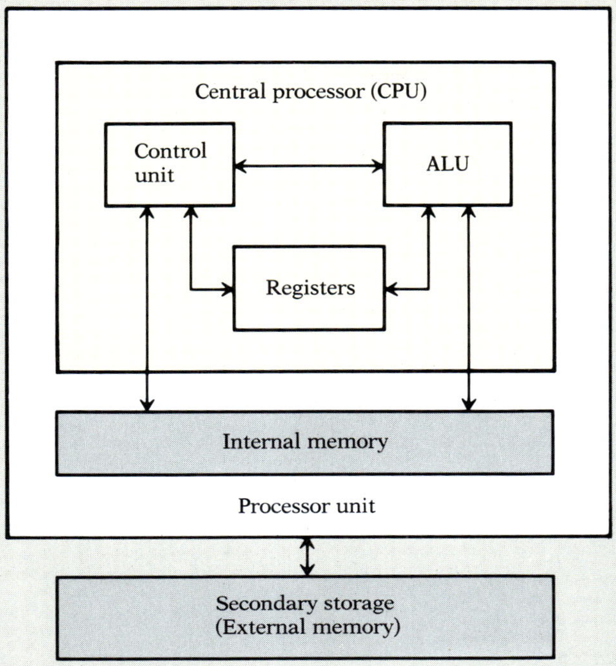

- *Central Processing Unit.* Performs instructions specified in programs
- *Memory.* Stores programs and data
- *Clock(s).* Determines order in which computer operations are performed
- *Bus.* A circuit used for transmitting data or power

Part B. Relationship of CPU to Peripherals.

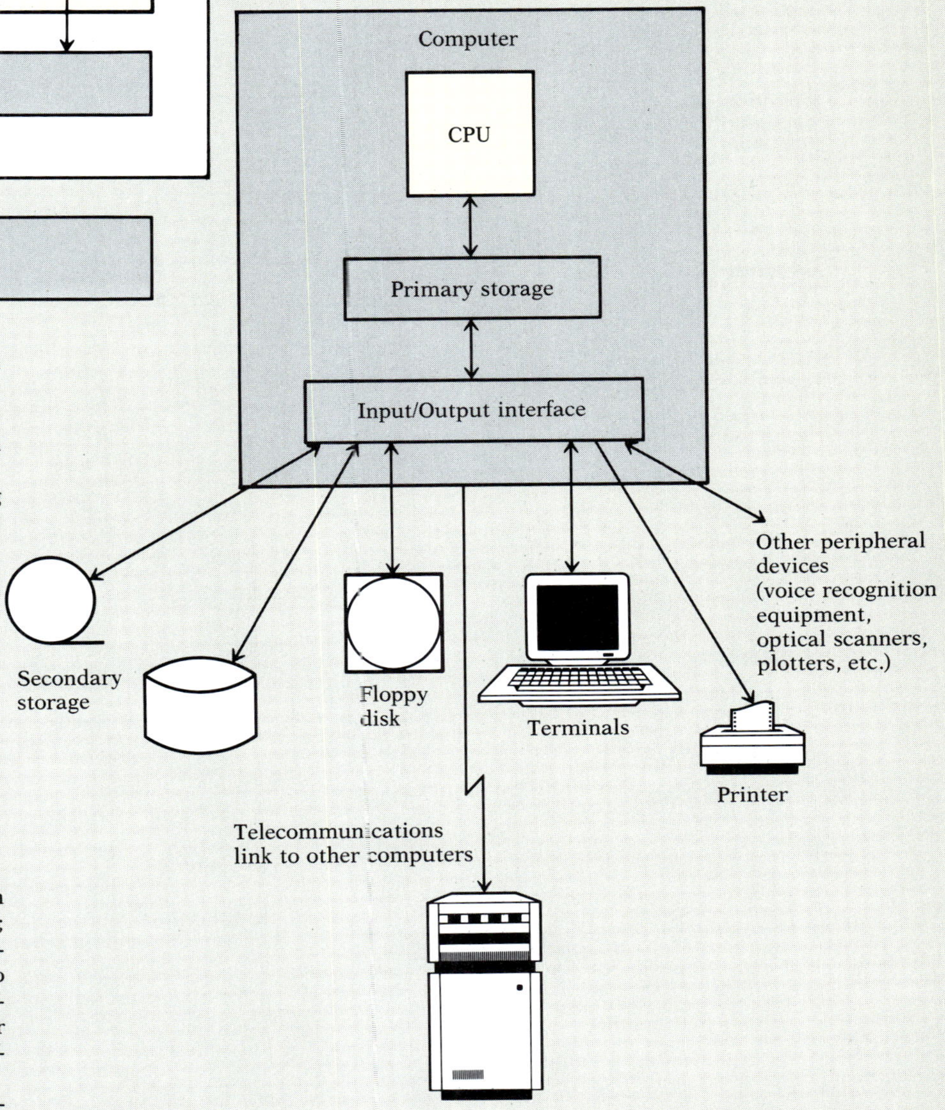

- *Interfaces.* Connect computer with other devices to extend its capabilities; e.g., terminal interface allows the computer to communicate with a video screen and keyboard. Telephone interface, called a modem, allows a computer to interact with other computers or peripherals through a telephone system.
- *Power supply.* Provides electrical current to run the computer.

(Part C on next page)

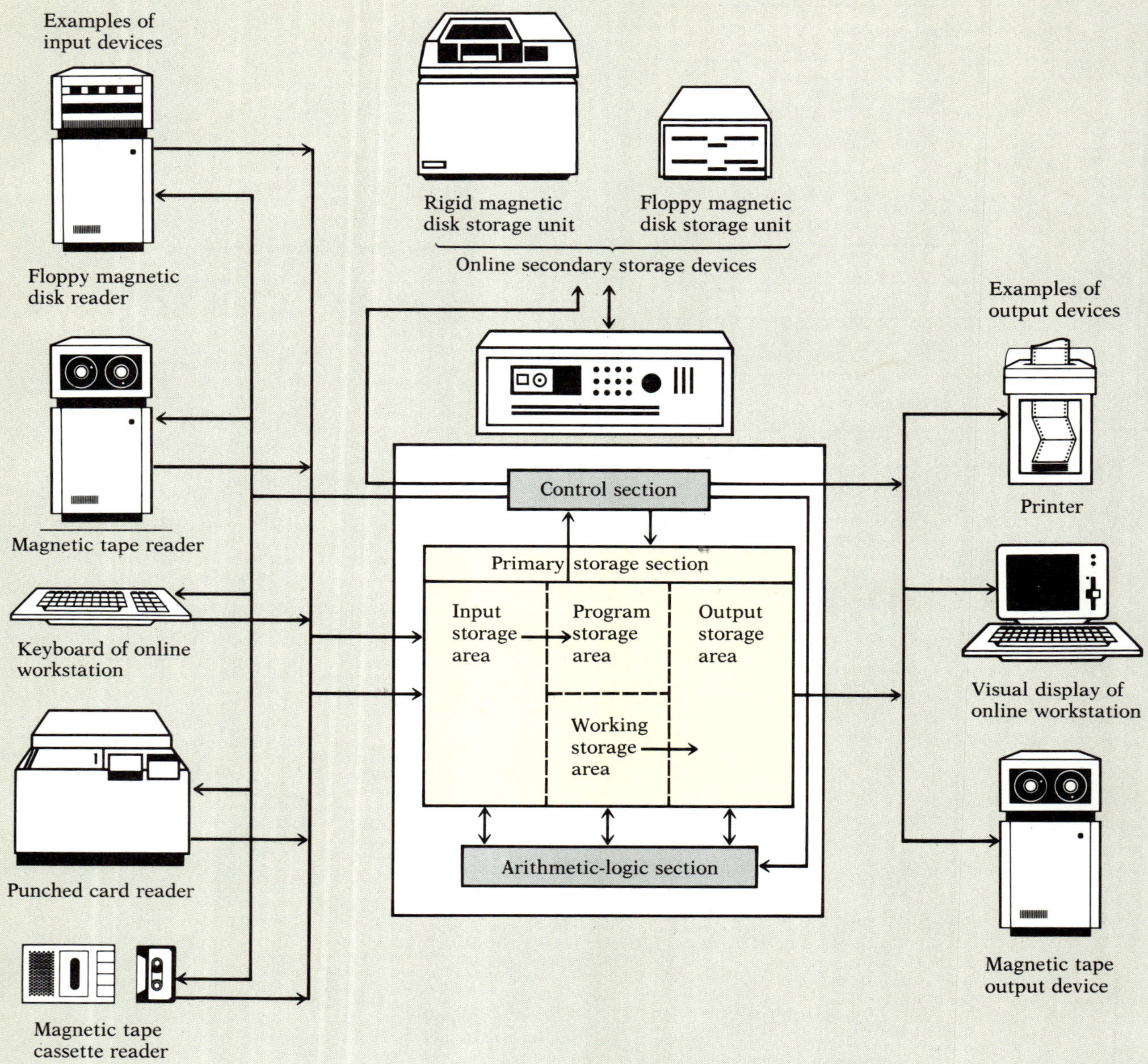

Part C. A Typical Computer System.

trates the relationship of the CPU with peripherals. Here again, the arrows represent data flow. Input peripherals send data to the CPU; output devices receive data from the CPU. Note that some peripherals (for example, terminals) serve both input and output functions. The hardware component that links the processor with external devices is called an **interface**. Finally, Part C shows the hardware components of a typical computer system. You will become more familiar with the peripherals shown in this figure when you read the next chapter.

Software

The term **software** is used to describe program sets needed to operate an information processing system. These **programs** give life to the circuitry and metal of computer hardware. They consist of a sequence of instructions and decision rules that direct the computer in executing a given task. The CPU must be told what data to process, what computations are to be performed on the data, the exact order of computation, and how output is to appear. The programs that tell the computer all this must be written in a form that the computer can understand; that is, the programs must be written in a **programming language**. Chapter 4 will describe how programming languages differ and how they work.

Two types of software are required in computing: operating system programs and application programs.

Operating system programs, usually supplied by the computer manufacturer, control the overall operations of a computer. Operating systems perform a variety of tasks. They translate the languages in which application programs are written into a language the CPU can understand. They also retrieve data from storage, schedule the jobs the computer is to perform, and maintain logs. In addition, they coordinate the operation of computer circuitry and of input and output. Operating system programs might be compared to a traffic officer who directs the flow of traffic. The traffic, in this case, consists of requests from users for information processing—requests that require use of many different types of peripherals and of different application programs.

Application programs enable the computer to solve a particular type of problem or do useful work—that is, to do "applications." Application programs can be used, for example, to write music, calculate payrolls, draw blueprints, edit reports, monitor a manufacturing process, display information in color graphs and charts, or perform analysis of hospital laboratory tests. Computer applications is the subject of Part II of this book.

Standard application programs may be purchased from software **vendors** (sellers of software). These predeveloped **software packages** may require modification to fit the needs of a given user, but generally they are ready for immediate use. When specialized custom software is preferred, users must write their own application programs or hire programmers to do so.

Data

Data consists of facts, observations, or concepts. These are the basic ingredients of processing. Since digital computers can process only **binary digits** (the characters 0 or 1), all input data must be converted into binary notation. When input data is decimal numbers, decimal to binary conversion is a preliminary step to CPU processing. To understand how this is done, one must first understand the difference between decimal numbers, which are the numbers people use in daily life, and the binary number system.

Binary Numbers Young children learning to count are given objects to handle, such as sticks. A teacher will bundle ten sticks together and tie them with a string, and then write 10 on the blackboard. The child will be taught that the 1 in the 10 represents the number of bundles. The 0 means no sticks are left over. Eleven sticks (11) means one bundle plus one stick.

If children were taught the binary number system, the bundling would occur whenever two sticks were gathered, not ten. For example, three in binary would be expressed as 11 (one bundle of two sticks, one stick left over).

Another way of explaining decimal and binary numbers is to speak of the position of digits. Each digit in the decimal system represents a power of 10 when starting from right to left. The first position represents 10^0, the second 10^1, the third 10^2, and so forth. In binary, the positional value is not the power of 10, but the power of 2: 2^0, 2^1, 2^2, and so on.

The number eleven can be represented in exponents of 2 as follows:

$$8(\text{or } 2^3) + 2(\text{or } 2^1) + 1(\text{or } 2^0)$$

Each of these positional values must be represented by a 1. There is no 2^2 in the equation, but its position must be held by a 0. Therefore, the binary number eleven equals 1011, as shown here:

1	0	1	1

$$(1 \times 2^3) + (0 \times 2^2) + (1 \times 2^1) + (1 \times 2^0)$$

$$8 \quad + \quad 0 \quad + \quad 2 \quad + \quad 1$$

Not all data processed by computer is numeric data. Alphabetic characters of data are common. Symbols, images, and speech are also used as data input. All such data must be coded into **bits** (a shortened form of the term *b*inary dig*its*) before it can be processed by a digital computer.

Bits and Bytes Because bits are very small units of data, they are usually combined into larger units. A sequence of consecutive binary digits is called a **byte**. An 8-bit byte is common. A microcomputer with 64**K** (K = 2^{10} or 1024) of memory can store approximately 64,000 bytes, roughly equivalent to forty double-spaced typewritten pages. (This is in addition to storage required for the operating system of the computer and the instructions accompanying the data to be processed.)

Supplement 2.2 Decimal Numbers Expressed in Binary

0 =	0000	15 =	1111
1 =	0001	25 =	11001
2 =	0010	35 =	100011
3 =	0011	45 =	101101
4 =	0100	150 =	10010110
5 =	0101	500 =	111110100

In the early days of computing, users had to punch coded patterns of holes on cards using a machine called a keypunch to represent their data and prepare it for processing. Today, a variety of input peripherals can be used to prepare data in machine-readable form. These peripherals are described in Chapter 4. Data is the subject of Chapter 5.

SAMPLE PROBLEM: HOW THE CPU CALCULATES GPA

To illustrate how a computer works, let us examine how the grade point average (GPA) of a student would be calculated by computer. We will start with the assumption that the computer is already provided with operating system programs and a GPA application program that instructs the computer in the steps required to calculate a GPA. We will also assume that the GPA program is written in a language that the computer can interpret.

The first step is to enter the GPA program into the computer's CPU through an appropriate input device and enter the current student grades. (When GPA is based on previous grades, a disk containing data on past grades is placed in a disk drive, or a tape with the grades in a tape drive.)

In a typical computer system, the control unit "fetches" one instruction of the program at a time from internal memory and places it in temporary storage, called the **instruction register**, in the central processor. The control unit of the CPU then decodes the instruction so that the central processor will know what action to take. These steps are called the **instruction cycle**.

Supplement 2.3 The Decimal Number 324 and Binary Equivalent

Decimal representation: 324

Positional values	10^2 = 100	10^1 = 10	10^0 = 1
Decimal number	3	2	4

$4 \times 1 = 4$
$2 \times 10 = 20$
$3 \times 100 = \underline{300}$

Total = $(300 \times 100) + (2 \times 10) + (4 \times 1) = 324$

Binary representation of decimal number 324 = 101000100

Positional values	2^8 = 256	2^7 = 128	2^6 = 64	2^5 = 32	2^4 = 16	2^3 = 8	2^2 = 4	2^1 = 2	2^0 = 1
Binary number	1	0	1	0	0	0	1	0	0

$0 \times 1 = 0$
$0 \times 2 = 0$
$1 \times 4 = 4$
$0 \times 8 = 0$
$0 \times 16 = 0$
$0 \times 32 = 0$
$1 \times 64 = 64$
$0 \times 128 = 0$
$1 \times 256 = \underline{256}$

Total = $(1 \times 256) + (0 \times 128) + (1 \times 64) + (0 \times 32) + (0 \times 16) + (0 \times 8) + (1 \times 4) + (0 \times 2) + (0 \times 1) = 324$

After the instruction cycle is completed, the control unit "fetches" stored data (when it is needed) to execute the instruction. The exact location of the stored data is specified or implied in the program instruction. Next, the control unit places the data in registers available to the arithmetic/logic unit in the CPU. Then the specified action is performed by the arithmetic/logic unit using relevant circuitry. The result is stored by the control unit in primary memory. This is called the **execution cycle**.

This basic process—fetch instruction, decode instruction, fetch data, execute instruction, and store the results—continues until each instruction in the program has been executed.

Final results constitute output. How this output is produced for the user is specified in the program. Results might be displayed on a terminal screen, printed in a report, or added to the student's permanent academic record. Control of equipment used for processing output is another role of the control unit of the CPU.

Now look at Figure 2.2, which shows in detail how the CPU executes the GPA program. The twelve program instructions in the GPA program (expressed in this figure in English rather than in a programming language) are listed. The yellow arrow traces the flow of control; the black arrows trace the data flow and the instruction flow.

The preceding paragraphs explain what a computer does but not how it does it. Even though computers are based on principles that are funda-

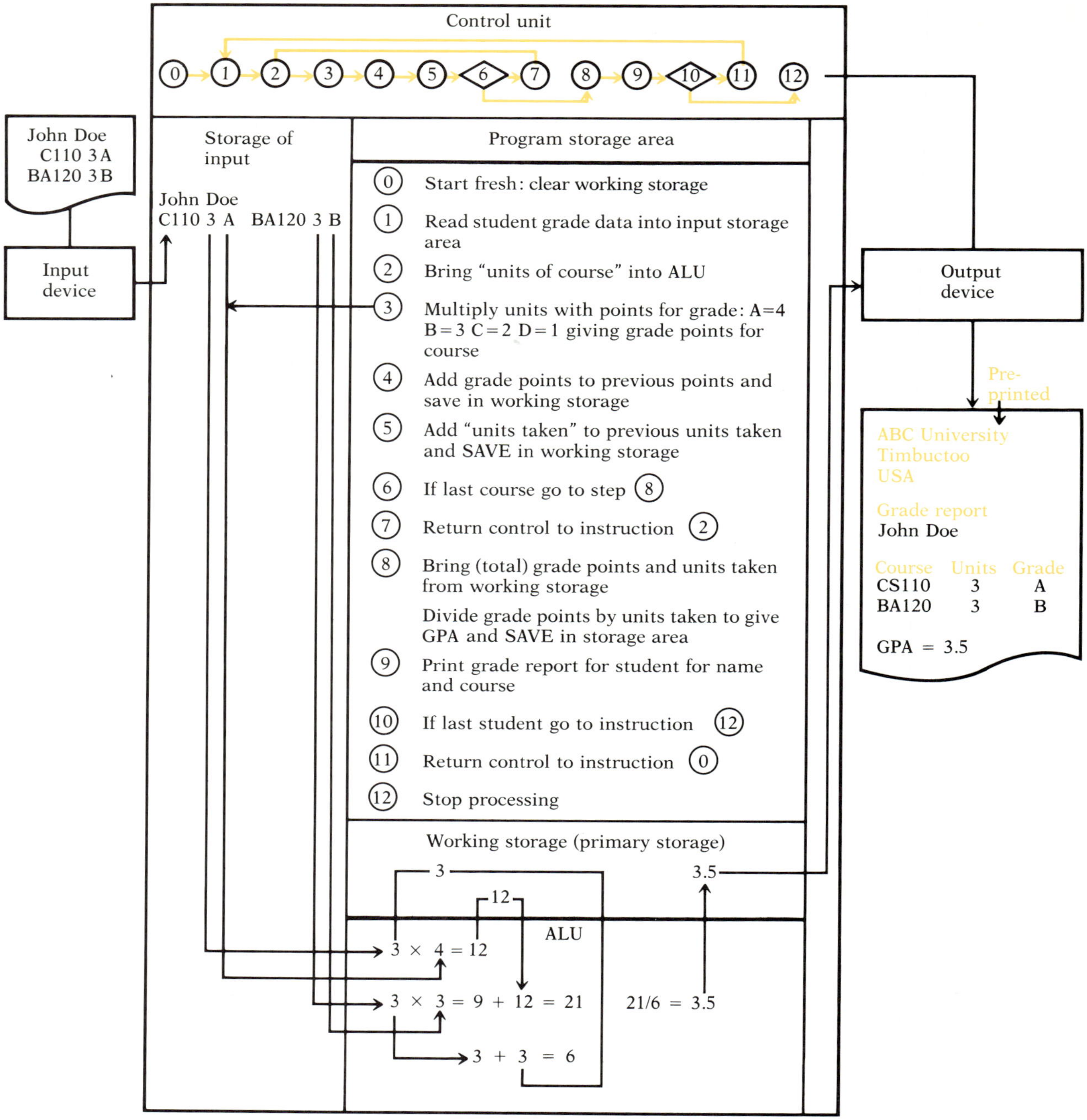

Figure 2.2 Execution of a Program to Calculate GPA. This figure illustrates the principles of computer computation. This grade point average example has been simplified for the reader. John Doe has no previous grade point average, and has taken only two courses. (In the real world, students take many courses per semester and their GPA is based on past as well as present performance.) The example also shows an incomplete output. A real GPA report would include name and address of the university as well as the student's address, student number, and other personal data. These have been deleted for the sake of simplicity.

Supplement 2.4 Computer Codes

Most computers use a coded version of binary to represent numbers, letters, and special symbols. Here are selected characters in two coding schemes that are popular: **EBCDIC** (**E**xtended **B**inary **C**oded **D**ecimal **I**nterchange **C**ode) and **ASCII** (**A**merican **S**tandard **C**ode of **I**nformation **I**nterchange). EBCDIC, developed by IBM, is a code used in IBM 360/370 model computers. ASCII representation is found in a variety of computers, particularly minicomputers and microcomputers.

Character	EBCDIC	ASCII
0	11110000	01010000
1	11110001	01010001
2	11110010	01010010
3	11110011	01010011
4	11110100	01010100
5	11110101	01010101
6	11110110	01010110
7	11110111	01010111
A	11000001	10100001
B	11000010	10100010
C	11000011	10100011
D	11000100	10100100
E	11000101	10100101

mentally simple, such as binary arithmetic and on-off switches, the engineering of computers is complex. You are not expected to understand the electronics of computing, but you should understand the manner in which computers work. The computer user, in effect, might be compared to the driver of a car. Although few drivers understand how an internal combustion engine works, they must know the consequence of pressing the accelerator and of pressing the brake. Likewise, a computer user need not understand the internal circuitry of computers but should be aware of what happens to data and program input.

PROCESSING CAPABILITIES

What makes computers such powerful machines?

One reason is their speed. Many small computers can do more than a million additions in one second; large computers can execute an instruction in nanoseconds. **Picosecond** (one trillionth of a second) speeds may soon become commonplace.

Another reason for the power of computers is their accuracy. Computers can process large amounts of data and data with large values virtually error-free. Unlike humans, computers neither tire nor suffer from memory lapses. Mistakes attributed to computers are generally human errors, such as faulty programming logic (the responsibility of the person who wrote the program), incorrect data entry (a clerical error), or use of a wrong tape or disk (an error made by the employee responsible for operations).

Central processors are also extremely reliable. **Downtime** (time a computer is inoperative because of malfunction) that is attributed to hardware failure is usually caused by peripheral breakdown, not by failure of the CPU.

Still another reason for the power of computers is their ability to store large amounts of data and to retrieve that data at incredible speeds when it is needed in processing.

Finally, computers do many useful tasks. They can manipulate data by performing basic arithmetic calculations, and they can match or compare data. They can also rearrange, sort and merge data. Furthermore, computers can be used to classify and summarize data, and to make inquiries regarding stored data.

Supplement 2.7 presents some examples of computer applications to illustrate these basic operations. Additional examples of computer appli-

Supplement 2.5 What Does 2 Bits Mean?

Characters of data are converted to binary digits (bits) when they are introduced into a digital computer. Binary code uses the digits 0 and 1. These single digits can be represented by a single circuit. No current (or electrons) flowing in the circuit represents 0; current flowing in the circuit represents 1. If the code for male is 0 and the code for female is 1, a single circuit can be used to store the answer to the question, "What is your sex?" (If the respondent answers "male," no current is turned on. If the answer is "female," the circuit is turned on.) In other words, a single bit (a binary number written with a single digit) can represent two answers.

But suppose a question is asked that has more than two possible answers, such as "What is your favorite color?" A computer can represent four alternatives with two circuits:

- No current in either circuit = 00
- Current in the first, no current in the second = 01 (Right to left)
- No current in the first, current in the second = 10
- Current in both circuits = 11

Therefore, four choices can be represented using binary code of two digits (for example, four colors when the following codes are used: Red = 00, Orange = 01, Yellow = 10, Blue = 11).

Sometimes the choices are codes for instructions, such as add and multiply.

The number of choices determines the power of the computer. Three-bit codes give eight possible alternatives. This is represented mathematically as 2^3. Four-bit codes allow sixteen possible alternatives (2^4). Eight-bit codes allow 256 (2^8), and so on.

Computer models vary in their design. Although a 4-bit computer is adequate for some applications, modern computers are being designed for greater capability. Most microcomputers today are 8-bit and 16-bit machines. Supercomputers of tomorrow may well be 256-bit computers.

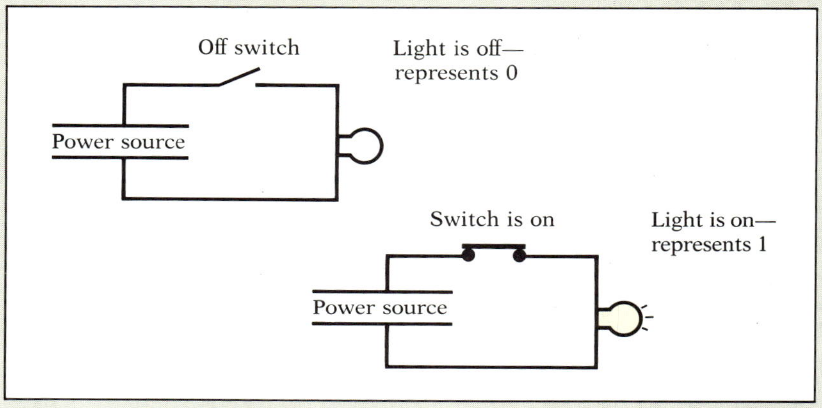

cations that require these operations appear in Part II of this book.

All of these processing capabilities can be performed at low cost. The performance/cost ratio in 1975 was 10,000 times that of 1955. By the end of the 1980s, it is estimated that this ratio will increase one million times the 1955 value.

Another advantage of computers is their ability to function in hostile environments, such as in outer space or in the presence of radioactive material. Furthermore, computers never get sick, complain, or go on strike.

Without computers, society as we know it would not exist since most modern services and goods are the product of our partnership with computers. We simply do not have the time or manpower to manually process the deluge of information that is used in decision making today.

MODES OF PROCESSING

In the early days of computing, only batch processing was available. Users today have many processing options.

Batch Processing

In **batch processing**, jobs are collected into groups,

Supplement 2.6 The Difference Between Computers and Other Machines

Many machines perform a number of operations. Consider a car, for example. It will accelerate, brake, turn, honk, signal lane changes, light the road ahead, clear windows of rain, and heat (or cool) the interior space. A driver controls the sequence of these operations when the car is in use.

A computer can also perform a number of operations. These operations include adding two numbers, comparing two numbers to decide which is larger, recording information entered on a keyboard, sorting data, and so forth. Just as a compact car differs from a eighteen-wheel semitrailer truck, computers vary somewhat from one make and model to the next. But in general, all computers perform similar information processing tasks.

What makes a computer a unique machine is that an operator does not need to control the sequence of operations when the computer is in use. Instead, the sequence is determined in advance. A program is prepared by a programmer listing the order of operations to be performed, and this program can be stored within the computer itself. Furthermore, a conditional instruction can be part of the program. That is, the instruction may be IF X, THEN do Y. No other kind of machine possesses this capability.

Supplement 2.7 The Kinds of Operations Computers Perform

- *Calculate.* Design new products. Prepare monthly payrolls. Determine optimal altitude for minimum fuel consumption in an airplane. Determine the trajectory of a rocket.
- *Rearrange.* Delete a paragraph from newspaper copy being edited for publication. Restructure a data column or row in a table.
- *Match/compare.* Check whether manufactured products are within allowable tolerance ranges (for example, size and weight).
- *Sort.* List alphabetically students in a university class. Arrange library records by author, call number, or title.
- *Merge.* Update bank records of customer accounts when money is withdrawn.
- *Classify.* List all insecticides that could be used to eradicate cutworms.
- *Summarize.* List outstanding accounts receivable.
- *Inquire.* Check medical records to determine when a patient was last hospitalized.

or batches, until a number have been accumulated. Then processing is initiated.

Many persons use batch processing in paying their monthly bills. They do not write and mail a check each time a bill is received; instead they collect bills until payday. Then all checks are written at one sitting.

In computer batch processing, either the computer operator or the system itself collects jobs in batches. A decision rule will determine when processing begins. For example, some computer systems are programmed to start processing when a given number of transactions have been received. Others may be programmed to start batch processing at a certain hour of the day regardless of the number of jobs waiting to be processed.

Batch processing is efficient when a large volume of nonurgent data that could tie up the computer for long periods of time must be processed. Since many repetitive operations need to be done only once for all jobs in the batch, overhead costs are minimized. One disadvantage of batch processing is that a processing delay of hours or days may result.

It should be noted that input/output devices need not be in the same location as the CPU for batch or other types of processing. Processing when input/output is physically distant from the central processor is called **remote processing**. Data stored on tape or disk might be mailed to the location of the CPU for processing. More commonly, remote input/output devices are connected to the central processor by cable, telephone wire, microwave, satellite, or some other communication link. (The transfer of data from one place to another over communication lines is called **telecommunications**.) For example, many firms have input terminals in regional offices connected by telecommunications to the CPU at company headquarters.

Real-Time Processing

An alternative to batch processing is **real-time processing**. Real time is used for instantaneous processing and continuous updating of data. For example, a real-time system is required for up-to-the-minute information on airline ticket sales. In manufacturing, real-time processing might be used to monitor data (for example, to check whether predetermined standards are being met) and provide feedback for control. A computer might monitor pressure in a refinery and issue instructions to shut off valves when pressure is too high.

Real time is also desirable for **interactive processing**. This kind of processing involves an exchange or dialogue between computer and user, such as a query to a reservation system regarding the availability of no-smoking seating for a given flight.

Real time requires **online** input and output. In other words, both input and output devices are under the control of the central processing unit: they are either plugged into the CPU or connected by a communication channel. The term **online real time (OLRT)** is therefore used to describe processing in the real-time mode.

TIME SHARING

Time sharing is a method of operation allowing several users to share a block of computer time. Figure 2.3 illustrates this concept. The computer

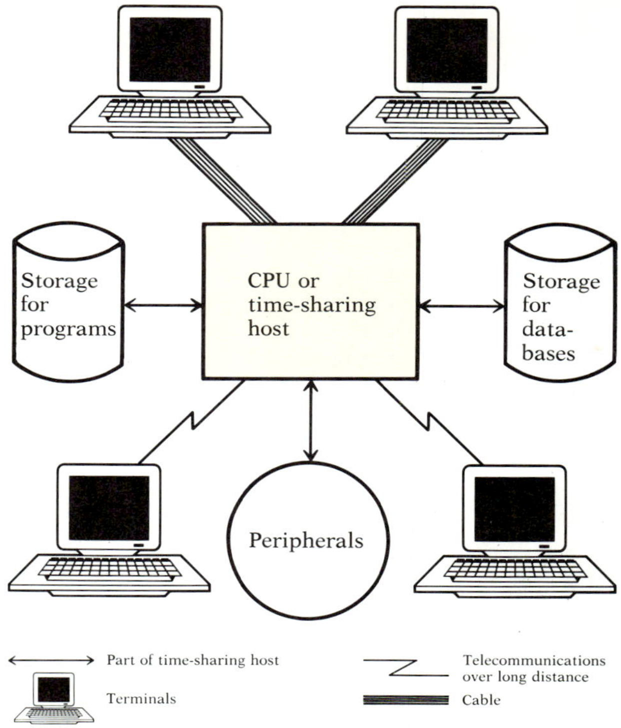

Figure 2.3 Time Sharing. A CPU can be shared by local terminals connected by cable, or by distant terminals connected by telecommunications.

actually processes each user's data in sequence, but the response time of the computer is so fast that it seems as if all processing is being handled simultaneously. Users are under the illusion that the computer is dedicated to their sole use.

Time sharing is of particular value to small businesses unable to afford their own large computer systems. Some organizations supplement in-house computing with time sharing in order to take advantage of specialized peripherals, computer software, data, or programming languages offered by the time-sharing host.

Another advantage of time sharing is that it allows users to economize by sharing computer costs. A disadvantage is that response time will drop when many users want service, or when a single user has a complex problem to solve that requires a great deal of processing time. To be fair to users, most time-sharing installations have had to formulate fair-use rules for the assignment of processing priorities. Some operate on a first-come, first-served basis. Others provide round-robin service, giving each user a small slice of computing time in turn. Sometimes priority depends on the status of the user or the urgency of the job. Priority rules will vary from one time-sharing installation to another. They determine the order of access to the CPU when more jobs need processing than the computer can service at one time.

TYPES OF COMPUTERS

Computers differ in their processing speeds and storage capacity. They also vary in their size and cost. A desktop microcomputer may be all that is needed to handle the finances of an art gallery, while a mainframe computer occupying a large room may be required to monitor and control a nuclear power station. Some hardware is capable of solving only a few selected types of numerical or logical problems. Microprocessors incorporated in microwave ovens, cameras, and other consumer products are examples of this. Some computers are dedicated to a specific purpose, such as controlling the manufacture of products in a factory. Other computers are designed to solve a wide class of problems. This section will first introduce microprocessors, and then describe microcomputers, minicomputers, mainframes, and supercomputers.

Microprocessors

A **microprocessor** processes data but has no input or output capabilities. It can serve as a component for the central processing unit of a large computer or be used for specialized computing tasks; for example, it can control the mixture of gasoline and air in the engine of a car to maximize mileage per gallon. Recent advances in microtechnology now make it possible to fit a microprocessor on a single **chip** the size of a child's fingernail. This is sometimes called a **CPU-on-a-chip**. Already it is clear that such miniaturization may have more impact on consumers and industry than any other type of computing.

Microprocessors are found in a wide range of industrial and consumer products. They are used in video games, checkout registers in stores, microwave ovens, gas station pumps, pacemakers, taxi meters, and burglar alarms, to name just a few applications. Other examples appear in Figure 2.4 and Supplement 2.8.

Whether a microprocessor should be classified as a computer or not is in dispute. The problem is that the word "computer" has many definitions. Unfortunately, there is no consensus among computer scientists regarding the meaning of many computer terms. This is because the field of computer science is new and technology in the field is moving at such a fast pace. It takes time to reach agreement on meaning of terms. Lack of a standardized computer vocabulary hampers communication among researchers, computer manufacturers, vendors, and users.

The term "microprocessor" is an example of a word with many definitions. Some glossaries define a microprocessor as a small, simple computer. Most computer professionals disagree. They argue that since additional facilities must be added to a microprocessor to make it suitable for general processing purposes, a microprocessor cannot be classified as a computer; it is merely a computer component.

Microcomputers

A **microcomputer** (or **micro**) is a low-cost, small but complete computer system built around microprocessors. Personal computers (for example, the desktop computer) or the models used in many offices for accounting and inventory control, are examples. Chapter 14 is devoted to the subject of microcomputers.

A common feature of microcomputers is **random-access memory (RAM)** used for primary storage. This type of memory is nonpermanent: everything is erased when the power is turned off. Systems programs stored in internal memory have to be reloaded into RAM each time the computer is turned on. In contrast to read-only memory discussed earlier in this chapter, users can not only read from but also add to RAM. Microcomputers are commonly designed so that the installation of additional RAM chips increases memory capacity. In some models, the user can install these extra chips simply by plugging them into the circuit board.

Sample Uses of Microprocessors

Industrial products	Consumer products
Aircraft subsystems	Automobile subsystems
Blood analyzers	Blenders
Cash registery	Burglar alarms
Communication devices	Calculators
Copying machines	Cameras
Dictating machines	Clocks
Gasoline pumps	Clothes dryers
Lab equipment control	Dishwashers
Machine control	Electric slicing knives
Measuring instruments	Fire alarms
Medical diagnostics	Hair dryers
Pacemakers	Heating systems
Robots	Microwave ovens
Scales	Monitoring of
Scanners	home utilities
Taxi meters	Fuel/heat/water/ light
Telephone switching	Ovens
Testing instruments	Pinball machines
Toasters	Radios
Traffic lights	Refrigerators
TV camera	Slow cookers
Vending machines	Stereo systems
etc.	Telephones
	Television sets
	Washing machines
	Watches
	etc.

Figure 2.4

Programmable read-only memory (PROM) is yet another variety of storage used in microcomputers. PROM is internal memory that is programmed, not hard-wired. Once programmed, however, memory contents cannot be altered. The programming can be done by the manufacturer or blank memory chips can be shipped to the user to program.

Minicomputers

Minicomputers (also called **minis**) have been on the market since the late 1960s. When first introduced, minicomputers were smaller in speed, size, and capacity than other computers on the market, and the name "mini" was descriptive of the size and character of the computer (see Figure 2.5). Since then, microcomputers and microprocessors have been developed, taking over the slot formerly occupied by minis, while many minis themselves have grown in physical size. In addition, technological advances have made minis very fast in computation. Indeed, modern minis are more powerful than the large computers (mainframes) manufactured ten years ago. Today, the term mini is thus somewhat of a misnomer.

Another problem with the category of the minicomputer is that some microcomputers perform at the level of minis. In general, however, minis have a higher performance level than micros, and they have more powerful instruction sets and a wider selection of available programming languages and operating systems. One can place minis between microcomputers and mainframes in processing capability. Figure 2.6 lists sample uses of minis and micros.

It is likely that the minicomputer category will disappear in time. The line of division between micros and minis is continually becoming less distinct, just as the line between minis and mainframes is no longer as clear-cut as it was.

Mainframes

Mainframes are large-scale computers that range in cost from a few hundred thousand to several million dollars; they are the type of computer used in corporate headquarters, in research organizations, in governmental agencies, and in universities. Mainframes are usually general-purpose computers capable of performing most of the information processing needs of the organization they serve. The management, operation, and maintenance of such computers requires a professional staff. Obviously, such computers are appropriate for large organizations rather than individuals.

Supercomputers

The **supercomputer** category is reserved for the largest, fastest, and most expensive computers.

Figure 2.5 Electronic publishing. With this electronic printing system, complete black and white publications can be published electronically in a matter of hours. While text is being created on word processing systems, an operator communicates with the minicomputer using a keyboard display console. (Xerox Corporation)

Sample Uses of Minis and Micros

Minis	Micros
Bank terminals	Badge and credit-card checking
Blood analyzer	Bartenders
CAI (computer-assisted instruction)	Elevator control
Cash register	Gas pump control
Communication	Medical diagnosis
Storing and forwarding messages	Online calculations in hotel
Monitoring telephone lines	Hotel bill
Education	Restaurant
Input validation on terminals	Tip
Instrumentation	Passenger movement control
Mixers (e.g., paint and other substances)	Physician control of information on patients
Numerical control	Plant schedule control
Personal computer	Process control
Printing	Security and access control
Editing	Shopping scales
Typesetting	Simulation
Page layout	Stock and commodity applications
Process control	Typewriters
Stand-alone computer for small businesses	Vending machines
Text editing	

Figure 2.6

The cost of a supercomputer begins at about ten million dollars. Supercomputers compute four to five times faster than conventional mainframes. They are used to solve complex problems that require a massive amount of computation, such as weather forecasting, weapons research and development, sending rockets to Jupiter, and energy and power modeling. They process numbers in such large quantities that they are colloquially referred to as "number crunchers." Supercomputers are discussed in Chapter 13.

SUMMING UP

Computers are machines that accept data, perform prescribed operations (mathematical and logical) electronically on that data, and supply the results of the operations. The hardware (equipment) necessary includes a central processor and peripherals (input/output equipment). Programs (software) are also needed to tell the CPU exactly what operations must be performed as well as the order of those operations.

The operations themselves are very basic. The computer can add, subtract, multiply, divide, and perform logical operations. The power of computers comes from the fact that they can store large amounts of data and process that data at incredible speed, with astounding accuracy, and all at low cost.

Not all computers utilize the same processing mode. Some perform batch processing; others do real-time processing. Remote processing and time sharing are two common methods of operation.

Since computers are used for many different types of problem solving, it is not surprising that a

Supplement 2.8 Use of Computers in Boeing's Two-crewmember Airliner Flight Deck

Modern jet aircraft depend on a variety of sophisticated subsystems for navigation, communication, music, passenger comfort and safety, engine control, and the control of aerodynamic surfaces. The sensors that monitor these various systems transmit their data to related central computers.

The flight deck of the new-generation Boeing 757 and 767 twin-jets features digital electronics including an engine indicator and crew alerting system. Graphically and by alphanumerics displayed on the center instrument panel, on two color cathode-ray tubes, the crew alerting system provides:

- engine operating parameters.
- caution and warning alerts.
- airplane systems status before takeoff.
- for ground personnel, a readout of electronic systems discrepancies to indicate maintenance requirements.

Developed by Rockwell International's Collins Air Transport Division, this system centralizes all engine displays for two-crew operation. It replaces electromechanical instruments with high-technology digital electronic equipment and provides automatic monitoring of engine operation.

The flight decks employ the latest state-of-the-art digital electronic instruments, which reduce crew workload, and lower fuel consumption. Use of the latest digital electronics also makes it possible to upgrade navigation capability as air traffic control systems change.

The flight deck also includes a flight management computer system that integrates navigation, guidance, and performance data functions. When coupled with the

The flight deck panel on a commercial airliner. Electronic indicators and data terminals help crew members fly the airplane as to the best configuration, speeds, and altitudes for optimum fuel economy. (Boeing Commercial Airplane Company)

range of computers have been developed to meet user needs. Computers vary in size, speed, and storage capability. The most limited processing unit is the microprocessor, which is embedded in many household appliances and consumer goods. General-purpose computers range from microcomputers, usually small desktop models, to supercomputers. Supercomputers are needed when problems require the processing of massive amounts of data, as in airplane design, weather forecasting, and cryptography.

Price is another way to distinguish the difference between computers. Microcomputers are generally in the one thousand to ten thousand dollar range; minis range from ten thousand to one automatic flight control system ("automatic pilot"), the flight management system provides accurate engine thrust settings and flight path guidance during all phases of flight, from immediately after take-off to final approach and landing. The system can predict the speed and altitude which will result in the best fuel economy, and command the airplane to follow the most fuel-efficient (or the "least time") flight paths. Flight planning, terminal area procedures, and airliner route information can be stored for use as required.

Innovations in this new generation flight deck are not limited to computer-based systems. The flight decks also include independent zone ventilation that provides fresh air to each side of the flight deck. For full-time windshield defogging, the air is directed downward to prevent eye irritation. Instrument panel cooling is separate from flight-deck ventilation. Design of the nose section and location of air-conditioning outlets means lower cockpit noise levels.

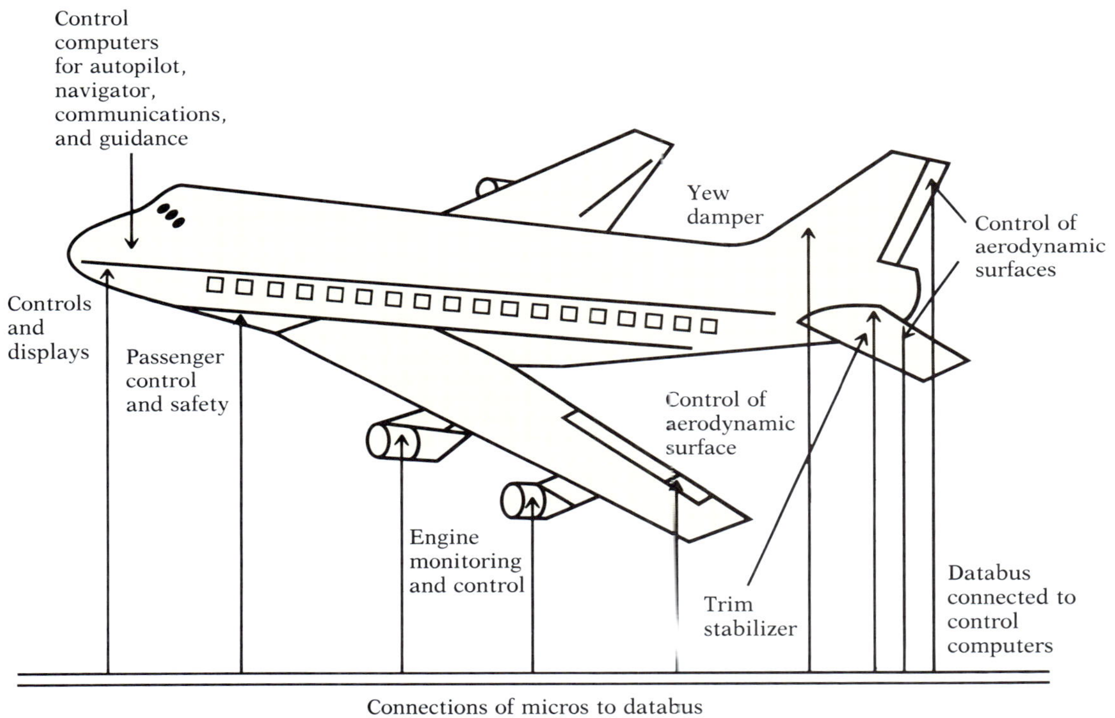

hundred thousand dollars, and mainframes from one hundred thousand to one million dollars. Supercomputers usually cost over one million dollars.

REVIEW QUESTIONS

1. List the main advantages of computer processing over manual processing. In what circumstances would each be used?

2. What are the principal parts of a computer system? What function does each part perform?

3. What basic operations can a computer do?
4. What is computer hardware? How does it differ from software? Give three examples of each.
5. What is the difference between batch processing and real-time processing? Give an example of each for:
   a. government
   b. industry
   c. an office
   d. a university
   e. a medical clinic
   f. publishing
   g. a museum
6. What are the differences among a microprocessor, microcomputer, and minicomputer? Are these three terms appropriate today?
7. How do system programs and application programs differ? Identify two functions that each can perform.
8. Why would one want remote processing?
9. Why do we need so many types of computers?
10. What are the differences among digital, analog and hybrid computers?
11. Describe the instruction and execution cycles in a CPU and draw a diagram showing the sequence of events.

DISCUSSION QUESTIONS

1. Comment on the following: Computers are neutral and unbiased; they only do what they are instructed to do.
2. Hardware is the body of a computer and software is its brain. Comment.
3. Compare the human brain and computers. Where does each have a comparative advantage? For what work and under what conditions would each be appropriate, efficient, and effective?
4. What do you think are the primary functions and advantages of computers for the following users:
   a. small organizations?
   b. large organizations?
   c. families?
   d. students?
   e. doctors?
5. How do microprocessors affect your daily life?
6. Give three examples of organizations you know that could and should use computers for data processing but do not. Explain the reasons why a switch to computers has not been made.
7. Comment on the following statement: A brain takes nine months to develop organically and many more months in educational development before it is capable of computational and intellectual activity. A computer is cheaper to produce and can be put in service far faster.
8. Which is more important, the CPU or peripherals? Which constrains modern data processing? Why?
9. How has microminiaturization affected:
   a. business?
   b. office?
   c. home?
   d. the arts?
   e. sports?
   f. handicapped persons?

EXERCISES

1. In the table on the next page, fill in the appropriate space with the best mode of processing for each application listed. Choose *Batch*, *Time Sharing*, *Online*, or *OLRT* processing.

Application	Mode of Processing
Airline reservations	....
Hotel nationwide reservations	....
An auto dealer	
Accounting	....
Contract calculations with buyer	....
Instructor keeping grades	....
University keeping grades	....
University admissions	....
University registration	....
University computing for class	....
University alumni records	....
Retailer point-of-sales credit checking	....
Bank account status monthly ledger	....
Wholesale inventory	
For perishables	....
For nonperishables and stable demand	....
Large database computing and computing for sale	....
Hospital admissions	....
Textbook manuscript copy editing	....
Library search for a book	....
Keeping welfare records	....

2. What type of computer will you recommend for each of the following applications? Choose *microprocessor*, *microcomputer*, *minicomputer*, *mainframe*, or *supercomputer*.

   Home/personal use
   Vacuum cleaner
   Racing automobile
   NASA space flights
   Automobile agency
   Large manufacturer
   Auto rental reservation
   Retail store
   Lawyer's office
   Hotel reservation
   Pharmacy
   U.S. air defense system
   Small college
   Large university
   Studying at home
   Large warehouse
   Hospital patient care

3. Interview someone who uses a computer on the job. Draw up a list of the advantages the individual derives from computer use and problems associated with computer use.

Selected Annotated Bibliography

Boraiko, Allen A. "The Chip," *National Geographic*, vol. 162, no. 4 (October 1982), pp. 421–76. A superb article on computers and how they work with many colorful and well-explained photographs on the production of computers.

Forester, Tom. *The Microelectronics Revolution*. Cambridge, Mass.: MIT Press, 1980. This is an excellent selection of some forty articles organized into eight chapters, each chapter ending with a guide to further reading. The selections are well balanced between optimists, such as Herbert Simon, and critics, like Joe Weizenbaum. Microelectronics is such a fast moving field that everything written soon becomes obsolete. This book, however, is worth having as a reference volume.

Healey, Martin. "Junking the Mainframe," *Datamation*, vol. 29, no. 3 (August 1983), pp. 120–32. The author argues that the mainframe will not die but will fade away in the next ten years as the micro takes over. Teleprocessing networks, specifically local area networks (LANs), will be largely responsible.

Immel, A. Richard. "Small Business Computing: The Micro-Mainframe War," *Popular Computing*, vol. 2, no. 8 (June 1983), pp. 46–60. The author describes the encroachment of micros on mainframe turf in corporate America. The conversion from mainframes to micros is also discussed.

"The Battle of the Supercomputers: Japan's All-Out Challenge to the U.S.," *Business Week*, (October 17, 1983), pp. 156–66. A good discussion of supercomputer number crunchers under development in both the U.S. and Japan.

Verity, John W. "Alas, Poor Mini," *Datamation*, vol. 28, no. 10 (September 1982), pp. 223–28. The author asks the question: Is the mini doomed to extinction? He concludes that the mini may live on in spirit, having helped create a marketplace for small processors.

Hardware to Support the CPU: Peripherals and Telecommunications Equipment

If computers are so fast, why do we spend so much time waiting around the computer center?

COMPUTER GRAFFITI

CHAPTER THREE

Key Words

analog signal
baud
buffer
cartridge
cathode-ray tube (CRT) monitor
CRT terminal
computer output on microfilm (COM)
concentrator
conversion equipment
cursor
daisy wheel printer
demodulation
digital signal
direct access
direct-access storage
disk drive
disk pack
dot matrix printer
electrostatic printer
electrothermal printer
external memory
external storage
final output
floppy disk
front-end processor
graphics capability
graphics display
hard copy
hard disks
impact printer
ink jet printer
input peripheral
input terminal
intelligent terminal
interconnected network
intermediate output
joystick
key terminal
laser printer
laser/optical disk technology
light pen
local area network (LAN)
machine-readable
magnetic drum
mass storage devices
microfiche
modem
modulation
mouse
multiplexer
network
nonimpact printer
offline
offline peripheral
online
optical character recognition (OCR) devices
output
peripheral-bound
peripheral equipment
plotter
point-of-sale terminal
printer
random access
read/write head
ring network
secondary storage
sequential access
sequential processing
soft output
star network
storage
tape drive
telecommunications
telecommunications equipment
teleprocessing
terminal
voice output
voice recognition equipment
wand
xerographic printer

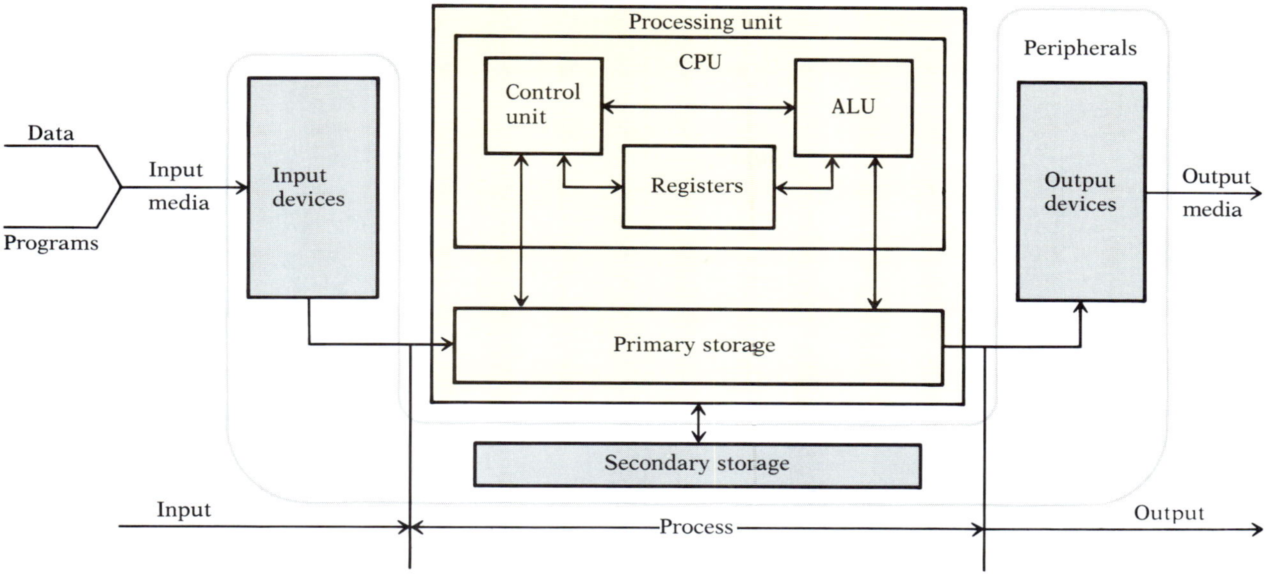

Figure 3.1 Relationship of peripherals to processing.

Peripheral equipment is used to get data into and out of the central processing unit. External storage for data to supplement the internal memory of the CPU is also provided by peripheral devices. The relationship of peripherals to processing is illustrated in Figure 3.1. In many systems, peripheral equipment represents a major share of hardware costs—as high as 90 percent in some operations.

This chapter will examine the characteristics of input, storage, and output peripherals. In addition, it will also describe **telecommunications equipment** needed to connect peripherals to computers when the former are remote from the CPU. Telecommunications equipment is also used to connect one computer to another in a computer network.

INPUT EQUIPMENT

Input equipment has two functions. It is used to represent data in a form that is **machine-readable** (translated into a code recognized by the computer and stored on a medium acceptable to the computer), and it is also used to channel machine-readable code into the CPU for processing. A machine that performs one (or both) of these functions is called an **input peripheral**.

Some input peripherals are offline; others are online. **Offline** means that the peripheral is not under the direct control of the CPU. **Online** equipment must be either plugged into the computer or connected to the CPU by telecommunications equipment—that is, equipment that transfers data from one place to another over a communications line, such as a telephone line or a satellite.

Offline Conversion Equipment

A keypunch, which is used to punch holes in cards to represent data, is an example of an **offline peripheral** used to prepare data for input. Other examples of offline equipment associated with input include devices for keying data onto paper tape (paper tape converters), onto magnetic tape (magnetic tape converters), or onto magnetic disk (disk converters). Such machines are categorized as **conversion equipment** because they convert (change) the form of data representation from characters of data that humans use into code that a computer can process. Two codes commonly used in data conversion are EBCDIC and ASCII. These standard codes represent each character of data as a unique

Supplement 3.1 Human Factors

Physiological, psychological, and training factors are considered when computer hardware (and software) is being designed. The purpose is to ensure that humans interface efficiently and effectively with computer systems. The field of effort concerned with ways to improve human-machine interaction is called "human factors." (The Europeans use the word "ergonomics" instead. Historically they have placed an emphasis on physiological rather than psychological considerations.)

For example, eye fatigue when using computer terminals is a human factors problem. Eye fatigue may be caused by the angle at which light hits the computer screen. Sometimes eye fatigue is caused by the screen image itself. Many experiments have been done with colors, fonts, size of image, blinking, and flickering in order to determine what factors produce eye strain. The results have influenced screen design. To accommodate differences between users, some manufacturers provide a choice in screen color combinations and screen size.

One early microcomputer had small keys placed close together. Users made many errors on this keyboard, striking the wrong keys because finger position was unnatural and uncomfortable. It is this type of problem that can be avoided when attention is paid to human factors. Noise levels can affect user concentration, operational procedures can affect user patience, and emissions from the machine may affect user health. (Whether the latter is true or not is a highly debated issue.) Vague or ambiguous error messages can hamper effective system use. Some systems seem to scold the user for errors instead of providing solution-oriented messages that are less frustrating and easier to use.

Standards for computer design and use are beginning to be developed based on human factors research. In 1984, eleven states were considering laws on machine design and required rest periods for computer workers. Industrial de facto standards are in existence, such as a 12° slope of the keyboard and a 15° tilt for a twelve-inch monitor.

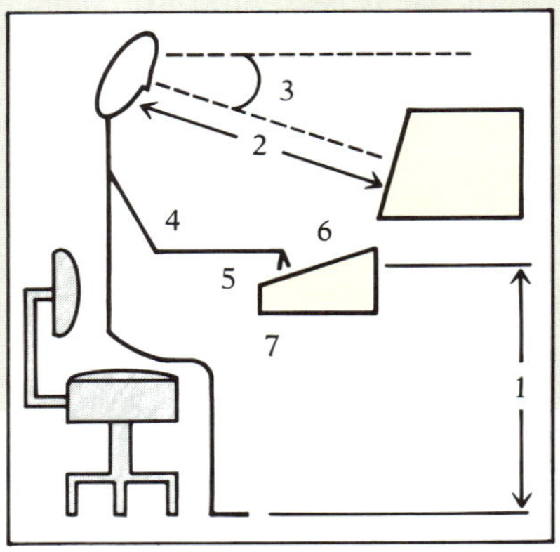

In 1984, over 800 human factors specialists and ergonomists were working for computer hardware manufacturers.

1. The European recommendation for the height of the home row keys is 28¼ to 29½ inches. The U.S. military standard is 29¼ to 31 inches.

2. The viewing distance should be between 17¼ and 19¾ inches, with a maximum of 27½ inches.

3. Generally, the center of the screen should be at a position between 10 and 20 degrees below the horizontal plane the the operator's eye height. One researcher recommends that the top of the screen be below eye height, another that the top line of the display be 10–15 degrees below the horizontal, with no portion of the screen at an angle greater than 40 degrees below the horizontal.

4. One researcher recommends that the angle between the upper and lower arms be between 80 and 120 degrees

5. The angle of the wrist should be no greater than 10 degrees.

6. The keyboard should be at or below elbow height.

7. Don't forget enough room for your legs.

—Taken from *Potential Health Hazards of Video Display Terminals*

set of bits. For example, an A in EBCDIC is represented as 11000001 (see Chapter 2, Supplement 2.4).

Offline conversion equipment also functions to place the coded data onto a storage medium acceptable to the computer. (A description of storage media appears later in this chapter.)

Once data is machine-readable, it can be entered into the computer by one of the online input devices described next.

Online Data Input Equipment

Online card readers, cassette readers, disk drives, or paper tape readers are examples of peripherals

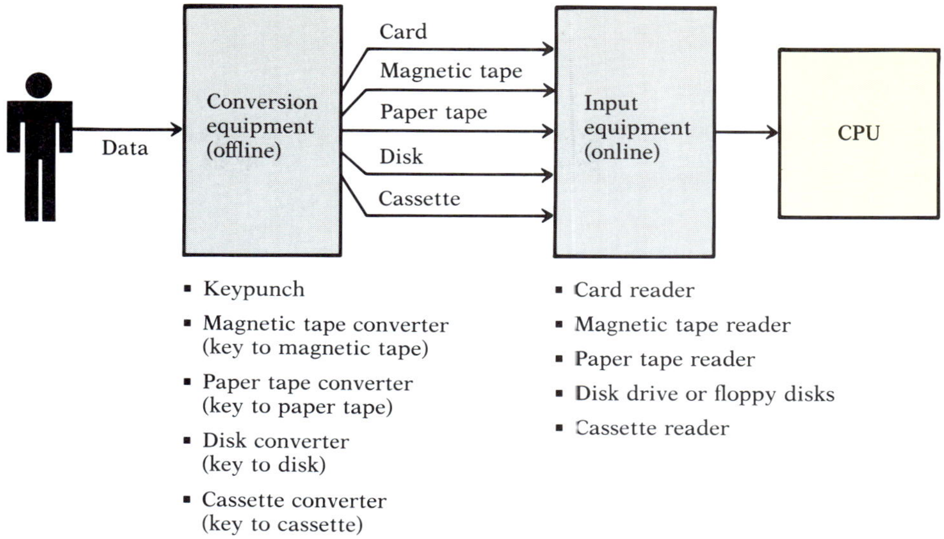

Figure 3.2 Conversion and input equipment. Data that is collected by humans may be converted into machine-readable form by conversion equipment and stored on a media such as magnetic tape. This stored data is subsequently read by input equipment and conveyed to the CPU for processing. Sometimes source data is already in machine-readable form—for example, UCP labels (universal product code) on grocery items.

that read data stored on a machine-readable medium and convey it to the CPU for processing. The relationship of this input equipment to conversion equipment is illustrated in Figure 3.2.

Some online **input terminals** (a peripheral used to enter data into a computer system) convert and input data in one step, thereby reducing handling of input. As a result, there is less likelihood that the input will be flawed by human error. An online terminal with a keyboard on which input is typed is an example. In addition, many online input terminals are **intelligent terminals**. This means that the terminal has a small, built-in computer or a microprocessor that can perform intelligent functions, such as editing and validating data at the point of entry. Input validation is particularly useful in banking, reservations, insurance, and accounting, where the accuracy of large-volume data entry is crucial.

Recent technological advances have reduced the cost of online equipment used for one-step data conversion and input. As a result, such equipment is becoming increasingly competitive with offline peripherals in price. Sections that follow will describe three examples of such online equipment: key terminals and CRT terminals, optical character recognition devices, and voice recognition equipment.

Input terminals **Key terminals** may have a keyboard like that of a typewriter or push-buttons like a calculator. Many department stores and grocery checkout counters have **point-of-sale terminals** that fit this description. These terminals act like a cash register to generate a sales slip. They also convey data on sales to the store's computer, which in turn compiles the data with input from other terminals in the store to process inventory records and financial reports.

Many key terminals include a screen resembling that of a TV where input is displayed as it is entered. This screen, a **cathode-ray tube (CRT) monitor**, allows users to interact with the computer and visually check input before processing begins. (Some home computer systems do not include a CRT monitor but connect to the family TV for screen display.) When an input error is sighted, a correction can be made. For example, a key (or keys) may be pressed to move a **cursor** (a symbol

Supplement 3.2 Online Terminals to Key Oriental Symbols at Library of Congress

A Chinese-Japanese-Korean system is operating at the Library of Congress to catalog Each Asian books by computer in actual Oriental characters. The system, which includes a microprocessor and four terminals, was developed by the Research Libraries Group (RLG), with headquarters located at Stanford University. It enables American East Asian libraries to create and retrieve bibliographic information in Chinese, Japanese, and Korean vernacular scripts, as well as Roman alphabet languages.

According to Russell Fischer, Director of the San Jose City College Library, "American libraries have long used the Roman alphabet to Romanize East Asian scripts for the purpose of bibliographic description and filing. Even though Romanization provides a useful function in libraries, it does have a serious drawback because of the homophonic nature of the Chinese language; that is, many characters which are written differently and have different meanings can have the same sound. Consequently, when such characters appear in their Romanized form, it can be difficult to determine the correct meaning. The use of East Asian vernacular scripts solves this problem

such as a dash) to a position on the screen where the mistake is found. A change (either the addition, replacement, or deletion of a character) can then be made where the cursor is positioned. In some systems, the pointer used to identify positions on the screen is controlled by a lever, called a **joystick**, or a device called a **mouse**. Many users find these latter devices faster and easier to use than a cursor that is controlled from the keyboard.

CRT terminals (that is, terminals that include both a keyboard and a CRT monitor) are general-purpose tools. They are used to input data on accounts payable and receivable, and to update payroll, inventory, personnel, and customer records. Secretaries use them to write letters; advertisers, to prepare copy and layouts; salesmen, to record sales; nurses, to input patient symptoms; and patrol officers, to record arrests. A comprehensive list of how CRT terminals are commonly used would be lengthy indeed. And new functions are continually being introduced. (It should be noted at this point that CRT terminals perform output functions as well as input functions. They are really input and output devices all in one.)

Some CRT terminals have **graphics capabilities**; that is, keyed data can be displayed as lines and curves on the tube instead of as characters of data. Graphics CRTs differ from one another in cost and sophistication. Some include a data tablet for input that digitizes the coordinates of points on a hand-drawn sketch. Others have touch-sensitive screens that allow the user to input commands by touching specific locations on the screen. Still others have both a keyboard and a hand-held, pencil-like device, called a **light pen**, that can generate input when it is used to draw on the screen. Software that permits zooming and scaling (enlargement or reduction) of material on the screen or color choices is also available.

One of the most common uses of graphics CRTs is to display keyed input as graphs and charts. CRT terminals that can display graphics enable designers, for example, to visualize products or schemas from keyed design specifications. With appropriate hardware and software, graphics CRTs will even input data from maps or pictures.

Optical character recognition (OCR) devices are online input terminals that scan documents, such as inventory tags, plastic credit cards, or badges.

of ambiguity."

The CJK terminal looks much the same as any other computer terminal except for the keyboard which holds 179 keys—three times as many keys as a typical one. Operators enter individual components or word roots of the Oriental characters. (Characters look like complex stick figures; the Chinese language has more than 4800 frequently-used characters.) The computer combines the components to form the actual character. Some characters require only one keystroke; others require a number of keystrokes to compose a character. Characters are composed on the screen's "scratch pad," checked for accuracy, and then entered into the actual data stream of the bibliographic reference. It has been demonstrated that it takes only five or six months for regular library staff to learn the system and outpace manual cataloging methods for East Asian books.

An RLIN Chinese Record

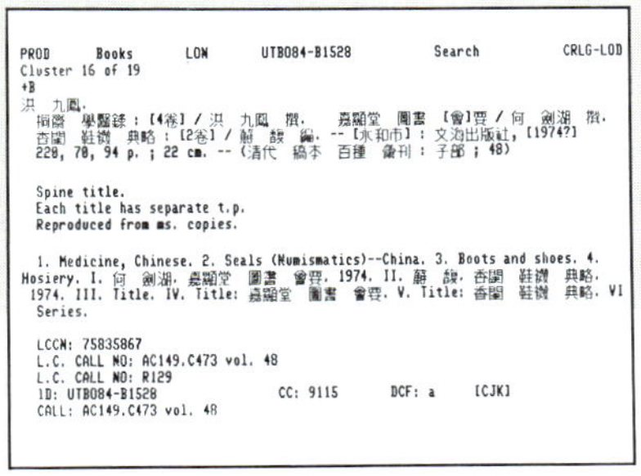
PROD Books LON UTB084-B1528 Search CRLG-LOD
Cluster 16 of 19
+B
洪 九鳳.
搁齋 學醫錄 : [4卷] / 洪 九鳳 撰. 嘉顯堂 圖書 [會]要 / 何 劍湖 撰. 香閨 鞋襪 典略 : [2卷] / 解 韻 編. -- [永和市] : 文海出版社, [1974?]
228, 70, 94 p. ; 22 cm. -- (清代 稿本 百種 彙刊 : 子部 ; 48)

Spine title.
Each title has separate t.p.
Reproduced from ms. copies.

1. Medicine, Chinese. 2. Seals (Numismatics)--China. 3. Boots and shoes. 4. Hosiery. I. 何 劍湖. 嘉顯堂 圖書 會要. 1974. II. 解 韻. 香閨 鞋襪 典略. 1974. III. Title. IV. Title: 嘉顯堂 圖書 會要. V. Title: 香閨 鞋襪 典略. VI Series.

LCCN: 75835867
L.C. CALL NO: AC149.C473 vol. 48
L.C. CALL NO: R129
ID: UTB084-B1528 CC: 9115 DCF: a [CJK]
CALL: AC149.C473 vol. 48

An RLIN Japanese Record

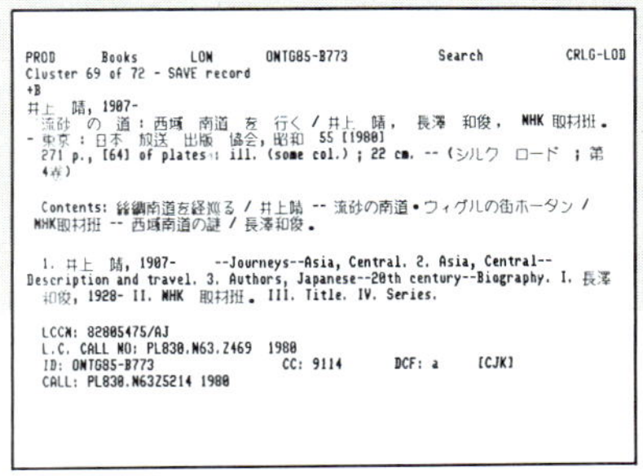
PROD Books LON ONTG85-B773 Search CRLG-LOD
Cluster 69 of 72 - SAVE record
+B
井上 靖, 1907-
流砂 の 道 : 西域 南道 を 行く / 井上 靖, 長澤 和俊, NHK 取材班. - 東京 : 日本 放送 出版 協会, 昭和 55 [1980]
271 p., [64] of plates : ill. (some col.) ; 22 cm. -- (シルク ロード ; 第4巻)

Contents: 絲綢南道を経巡る / 井上靖 -- 流砂の南道・ウィグルの街ホータン / NHK取材班 -- 西域南道の謎 / 長澤和俊.

1. 井上 靖, 1907- --Journeys--Asia, Central. 2. Asia, Central--Description and travel. 3. Authors, Japanese--20th century--Biography. I. 長澤 和俊, 1928- II. NHK 取材班. III. Title. IV. Series.

LCCN: 82805475/AJ
L.C. CALL NO: PL830.N63.Z469 1980
ID: ONTG85-B773 CC: 9114 DCF: a [CJK]
CALL: PL830.N63Z5214 1980

They then convert data encoded on these documents (prerecorded as special marks, bars, or characters) into a form the CPU can process. Such scanning terminals reduce the time required for data entry (though time was initially spent preparing the codes). They also minimize human handling of data at the time of input. A problem with such terminals, is that documents in poor condition (because of smudges, creases, tears, or dirt) may be misread. Human operators who exercise judgment in data entry may be more accurate than optical scanning devices in some circumstances.

One OCR device commonly found in retail stores for use in taking inventory is a portable **wand** that resembles a toy pistol. The wand, connected by cable to the data collection terminal, captures price and product identification data through a sensor at its tip when waved past encoded labels.

Most students are familiar with another use of optical scanning: mark-sense test answer sheets. These answer sheets can be scanned by an online device that reads the marks and sends answer data to a computer for grading. Offline mark-sense readers are also available.

Voice recognition equipment converts speech, which is an airborne signal, into digital data (which, as we have learned, is data represented by the binary digits 0 and 1) for computer processing. This process is far more complex than reading a pattern of marks or bars because there are so many variables in speech. Voices differ in sound, pitch, tone, and loudness. Pronunciation also varies from individual to individual, and even the voice patterns of a single speaker will not always be alike since mood, circumstance, and health can affect speech characteristics. The equipment, furthermore, must be able to distinguish a voice from background noise.

One method of overcoming some of these problems is to create user voice profiles. Words are flashed on a screen (words that would be used to input data). These words are repeated by the individual who will be inputting data, and the sound patterns created are digitized and stored. When input data is subsequently spoken, the computer is able to interpret meaning by matching the sound patterns of the speaker with the stored voice profile.

Figure 3.3 Inventory control by voice. The worker speaks into the computer via a headset, leaving his hands free to do other work. (Interstate Electronics Corporation)

When more than one user will be inputting data, several voice profiles can be stored for a limited vocabulary, a vocabulary chosen according to use of the input equipment. For example, a robot used to move items on an assembly line might be programmed to recognize commands such as "Go left" or "Lift two inches."

At the present time, use of voice recognition equipment is limited. The storage capacity required and the computer time needed to process voiced input is too expensive for widespread use. The most common application is in factories where a worker using both hands for a task needs to input data. For example, when examining products being assembled, an inspector may be required to handle items and move from one location to another. In this instance it is more practical to input inspection data by voice through a headset than it is to key the input on a stationary terminal (see Figure 3.3). The spoken input would identify the type and cause of assembly errors detected during inspection.

Improved technology and lower computing costs will undoubtedly make voice recognition equipment cost-effective for many other applications in the future. For example, voice recognition devices may be used to control access to restricted areas in factories or for customer identification in banking and cash dispensing. Phone-in orders to stores in which the customer talks to a computer may become commonplace. Voice-directed equipment may soon assist bedridden and handicapped persons in a variety of tasks. Machines are being developed to dispense medicine, turn on and tune a TV, type letters, and control the movement of an electric wheelchair at a patient's spoken command.

STORAGE

When offline peripherals are used to key data onto cards, tape, or disks, the keyed data is stored until the time of processing. The cards, tape, or disks act as **storage** media. (It should be mentioned that storage may also be needed for online input to compensate for the difference in rate of flow of data from the input device and the processing speed of the CPU. However, this is not a responsibility of peripherals. A temporary storage area of relatively small capacity within the computer, called a **buffer**, performs this function.)

The need for storage may occur after data has been processed as well. This happens when processed data will be used at a later time for additional processing. For example, when a bank client withdraws funds, online processing will update the customer's balance. The new balance will be stored until it needs to be updated once again as a result of subsequent deposits or withdrawals.

Although the CPU has internal memory, this memory cannot store both an application program and data indefinitely. The storage space must be yielded to the next CPU user. After a processing run, the program and data are stored in **external storage** (also called **external memory** or **secondary storage**). Such storage may be either online or offline. An additional use of online external storage is to provide auxiliary storage for the CPU when the amount of data required by a program exceeds the capacity of internal memory.

The most common media for external storage are magnetic tapes and magnetic disks. Magnetic drums and mass storage devices are also possibilities.

Magnetic Tape

Magnetic tape has an iron oxide coating that can be magnetized. Data is stored in the form of magnetized spots on this tape by a peripheral device called a **tape drive**. Tape drives have a **read/write head** (an electromagnet) that detects magnetized areas and converts them into pulses for CPU processing (read). The head also creates magnetized spots (write) when data is received from the CPU for storage.

Magnetic tape is used when a large amount of data must be stored and processed sequentially, as in payroll processing. It is commonly used for backup storage of data and software and also when data and software must be transported from one location to another.

Figure 3.4 A Winchester hard disk assembly. The disks will be sealed off together with the access mechanisms and the heads to prevent contamination. (Cogito Systems)

Magnetic Disk

Floppy disks are commonly used as the media for external storage by minicomputer and microcomputer systems. They are low-cost, flexible disks resembling a 45 RPM record and are made of oxide-coated plastic. As with tape, the oxide-coated surface of disks can be magnetized. Unlike tape, however, the surface of disks is made up of concentric tracks, with data recorded on the tracks as magnetized spots. Whenever data sets must be accessed individually (for example, police department storage of criminal records), data storage on disks is appropriate.

Floppies are lightweight (less than two ounces), inexpensive, and reusable. They can also be handled and even transported in a briefcase or through the mail without being damaged. A **disk drive** is the peripheral that records and reads data on floppy disks.

Large systems frequently use magnetic disks that are metal platters coated with ferrous oxide, many of which are fourteen inches in diameter although there is no universal standard. These disks are called **hard disks** and are assembled in a **disk pack**, a storage device containing a set of disks (see Figure 3.4). A disk drive also records and reads data on hard disks. One example is a Winchester disk drive, which encloses the disks, the access mechanism, and the read/write heads in a sealed cartridge to prevent dust and airborne contaminants from damaging the disk surface. As a result, a high degree of reliability is achieved.

Magnetic Drum

A **magnetic drum** is a peripheral storage device consisting of a cylinder with a surface that can be magnetized. Multiple read/write heads placed around the spinning drum read and record data as magnetized spots on tracks on the drum.

Mass Storage

Mass storage devices have been developed to handle enormous volumes of data. While retrieval

Table 3.1 Average Access for Storage Technologies

Type	1982	1987*	1992*	1997*
Random access				
Fast semiconductor (RAM)	12 ns	8 ns	5 ns	4 ns
Medium-speed semiconductor (RAM)	60 ns	40 ns	25 ns	15 ns
Slow semiconductor (RAM)	250 ns	150 ns	80 ns	60 ns
Fixed, nonvolatile semiconductor (ROM)	350 ns	150 ns	80 ns	60 ns
Fuze, nonvolatile semiconductor (PROM)	70 ns	50 ns	30 ns	20 ns
Rewritable, nonvolatile semiconductor (EEPROM)	250 ns	150 ns	80 ns	60 ns
Serial access (latency)				
Serial semiconductor	0.4 ms	0.25 ms	0.15 ms	0.1 ms
Bubble	2 ms	1 ms	0.7 ms	0.5 ms
Magnetic	25 ms	20 ms	15 ms	10 ms
Video disc		0.1–3 sec	0.05–3 sec	0.02–2 sec

*Estimated
ms = microsecond
ns = nanosecond

Source: "A Five-Year Plan: Meeting the Automatic Data Processing and Telecommunications Needs of the Federal Government." Washington, D.C.: Government Printing Office, April 1983, p. 38.

of data is slow, these devices store data at low cost. They are appropriate for large files, backup files, or files that are used infrequently. (In computer jargon, a "file" is a collection of related information. Files will be discussed in the chapter on data and its organization, Chapter 5.)

The storage media are usually **cartridges** of high-density magnetic tape stored in a cartridge container that is not directly connected to the CPU. When data is needed, a mechanical arm places the cartridge in a device that transfers the data onto a magnetic disk from which the data is retrieved by the CPU.

Laser/optical disk technology, which is the use of a beam of laser light to burn tiny spots into the disk coating, has potential for mass data storage. The problem is that this type of data recording does not allow data to be erased when it is no longer needed so that the space can be reused. As a result, optical disk systems are useful only for permanent archival storage. The advantages over magnetic tape and magnetic disk systems include greater data density (millions of bits per inch instead of 1600 to 6250 bits per inch for magnetic tape and disks), lower cost (one-tenth that of magnetic tape, one-hundredth that of magnetic disk), and faster access time.

Differences Between Storage Media

Speed of access to data in storage, the cost of storage, and storage capacity differ according to the storage media used (see Tables 3.1 and 3.2). Type of access also differs according to the storage medium employed. Magnetic tape provides **sequential access**; that is, the tape must be read from the beginning until it comes to the desired data. Storage on tape is appropriate when all records on the tape need processing. This type of processing is called **sequential processing**. But tape is inappropriate for processing individual records of data located on particular segments of the tape. An analogy can be made to taped music. For listening to a series of songs, tapes are excellent. But when a listener wants to hear a specific song over and over or wants to change the listening order of songs, then a tape is inappropriate (unless, of course, segments are rerecorded).

Magnetic disks and drums allow data to be

Table 3.2 Cost Comparisons of Storage Technologies (User cost in millicents per bit)

Type	1982	1987*	1992*	1997*
Random access				
Fast semiconductor (RAM)	300	70–100	20–40	5–10
Medium-speed semiconductor (RAM)	100	20–30	7–12	1.5–3
Slow semiconductor (RAM)	25	7–10	2–4	0.5–1
Fixed, nonvolatile semiconductor (ROM)	20	5–7	1.5–3	0.5–1
Fuze, nonvolatile semiconductor (PROM)	300	50–100	10–30	2–5
Rewritable, nonvolatile semiconductor (EEPROM)	300	50–70	10–20	3–5
Serial access				
Serial semiconductor	75	10–15	2–4	0.3–0.5
Bubble	100	20–30	5–10	3–5
Magnetic disk	0.4	0.12	0.03–0.06	0.01–0.03
Video disc		0.05–0.1	0.01–0.02	0.001–0.003

*Estimated

Source: "A Five-Year Plan: Meeting the Automatic Data Processing and Telecommunications Needs of the Federal Government." Washington, D.C.: Government Printing Office, April 1983, p. 37.

accessed by positioning the read mechanism (or the disk or drum itself) directly at the data required, a process called **direct access**. (Direct access is also called **random access**.) The term **direct-access storage** is used in relation to disk and drum storage. Disks and drums are appropriate when a single record, or group of records, needs frequent processing.

OUTPUT PERIPHERALS

Output is simply information that has been processed by a computer. As Figure 3.5 shows, this processed information may be either **intermediate output** (output that is stored and used as input for later processing), or **final output** delivered to users. Output peripherals are pieces of equipment that provide for this storage or delivery. These devices may be online or offline, depending on whether they are under the control of the CPU or not. The sections that follow describe common output devices.

Printers

A **printer** produces output in a visually readable form on paper. There are two categories of printers: impact and nonimpact printers.

Impact printers produce **hard-copy** output by pressing print elements against paper when the printer is activated by signals from the CPU. Impact printing may use either formed or dot matrix characters. Some of the printers with formed characters resemble a typewriter. A **daisy wheel printer** also has formed characters, but these characters are on the tips of spokes of a wheel—a wheel that spins the characters into position for impact with the paper (Figure 3.6). Other kinds of impact printers place character sets on a revolving chain or in rows on a metal drum. The average speed of letter-quality, formed-character printers is between eighteen and eighty characters per second.

A **dot matrix printer**, which is also in the impact printer category, selects specific pins within a matrix (a rectangle of pins, usually seven pins high and five pins wide), and then presses the pins against a ribbon (Figure 3.7). Since such printers can arrange dots in unlimited patterns, they can produce graphics as well as text and numbers.

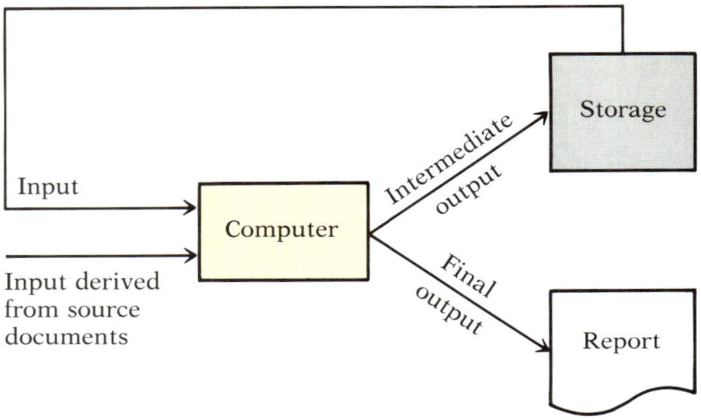

Figure 3.5 Intermediate and final output. Final output is delivered to the user whereas intermediate output is stored. A monthly report of sales processed by computer and delivered to management is an example of final output. The result of processing inventory records to incorporate recent sales data is an example of intermediate output since these records must be placed in storage for subsequent updating. Tape or disk can be used for both intermediate and final output.

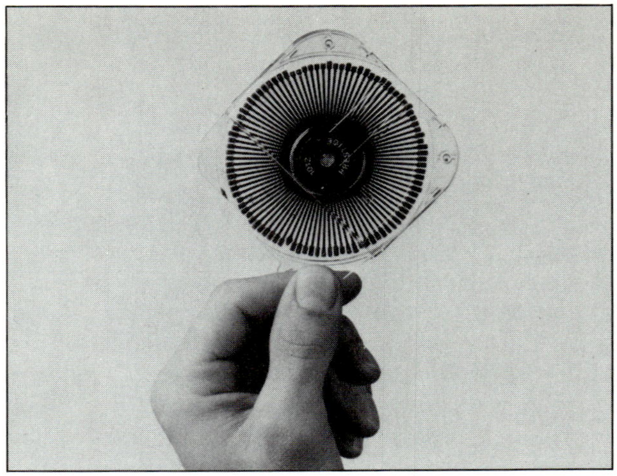

Figure 3.6 A print wheel for a daisy wheel printer. Each wheel contains a full array of characters in a particular font, and the wheels are interchangeable, making it a simple matter to change type styles. (Datasouth Computer Corporation)

Many dots printed close together form dark lines and shaded areas when a graphics image is printed, whereas dots more widely spaced are used in the lighter areas of the image. Dot matrix printers are faster than formed-character printers, with speeds up to 400 characters per second, and less expensive as well.

Electrothermal printers heat dot pins and press them against heat sensitive paper. Their biggest drawback is that the specially coated paper is expensive.

Nonimpact printers use a variety of techniques to print hard copy. But all nonimpact printers have one characteristic in common: the print elements never touch the paper. **Electrostatic printers**, for example, use a dot matrix in which the pins do not strike the paper; instead, an electrical charge is sent through the pins. The paper is then passed through a toner containing ink particles with the opposite charge. These stick to the paper in the charged areas to create the desired image.

Xerographic printers use processes similar to photocopying. **Ink jet printers** produce hard copy by controlling ink drops with an electric charge or by shooting ink from nozzles contained in the print head. These printers print up to 270 characters per second. **Laser printers** use a laser beam to trace characters or images onto a light-sensitive drum, which attracts a toner that sticks to the paper in the form outlined by the laser. The speed, 300 characters per second, is similar to a fast dot matrix unit, but the print quality is far better. Because laser printers are expensive machines (costing between $17,000 and $20,000 in 1984), they are only suited to businesses that generate large volumes of printed matter.

Plotters

A **plotter** is a device that makes pen and ink drawings of lines, curves, and complex shapes. It is used to produce graphs, charts, engineering drawings, maps, and pictures. The paper used by a plotter is put in either a flat bed or on a drum. A carriage holding one or more pens moves across the paper to draw lines according to output signals from a computer. An ink jet plotter substitutes ink jets for pens on the moving carriage.

Plotters produce a colored product when many colored pens are used. In this case, a program will control which pens color which portions of the picture.

CRT Terminals

CRT terminals, described earlier in this chapter as input devices, can also be used to deliver output. In this case, processed results are displayed on the CRT screen for temporary viewing. Frequently a printer is combined with the CRT unit. This allows users to select output from the screen for printing. When no hard copy is made, the display on a terminal is called **soft output**.

Some CRTs are **graphics display** units. They enable users to view shapes and drawings on the screen as well as characters of data. When such graphics CRTs are combined with a plotter, the user can obtain a hard copy of the visual display.

Figure 3.7 A dot matrix printer. The capability of printing graphics within a certain range is an advantage that dot matrix printers have over letter-quality printers. (International Business Machines Corporation)

Computer Output On Microfilm

Sometimes output needs to be kept for historical reference or legal reasons. Invoice files, student grade reports, medical records of patients, and police dossiers are examples of output that might be needed for future reference, although these files do not require frequent processing. When output is voluminous, storage can be a problem. In such cases, **computer output on microfilm (COM)** is an option.

The cost of producing COM is low and space requirements for storage are considerably less than storage for hard-copy reports. The initial investment for COM equipment, however, is high. The peripherals required for COM include a microfilm recorder and film developer. Another drawback is that retrieval and display of microfilm also requires special equipment—equipment that many persons find inconvenient and dislike using. At the present time, COM is cost-effective only when output volume is very large and the frequency of retrieval is very small.

Computer output on **microfiche** (a sheet of microfilm) is still another storage possibility. The advantages and limitations of microfiche are similar to those of microfilm summarized above.

Voice Output

Voice output is another output option. The equipment required reverses the process of voice analysis and recognition discussed earlier. Voice output requires voice synthesis. A specified vocabulary spoken by the human voice is broken down into digitized data and is stored. At the time of output, a computer selects the required words, draws the digitized data for these words from memory, and converts the data to sound through filters and amplifiers. Systems that digitize phonemes—the smallest units of speech, like the "m" of "mat"—are also under development, with the result that such computers can "speak" any word. These systems eliminate the need to store prerecorded words in memory.

Voice output is becoming more and more common. Most phone users have heard the following output message: "The number you have dialed has been disconnected." Many pocket calculators use voice output to give users totals. Some alarm clocks combine beeping with a message, such as "It is time to wake up." Voice output is also replacing many dials and display boards in factor-

Supplement 3.3 COM at TRW

When TRW, Inc. reorganized in 1981, an effort was made to reduce processing costs. At that time the company estimated that the cost of an impact-printed original page cost 12.5 cents; a high-speed, laser-printed page, 3.5 cents; and a microfiche of 270 pages, $1.37 (or 0.05 per page). Each duplicate microfiche cost 17 cents. The data processing department was producing some 8.2 million pages of output each month.

It was recognized that many departments in the company were interested in COM because of cost savings, but chose other output because the quality of COM was not satisfactory. Therefore, the company purchased new COM hardware, a Komstar 200 microimage processor (made by Eastman Kodak). In 1984, the data processing department generated more than three million frames a month on the Komstar processor and 80,000 duplicate microfiche on a Kodak Ektafiche duplicator, a 500 percent increase in COM volume.

ies and on machine control panels. How nice it will be to hear a pleasant, "Fasten your seat belt, please," instead of that annoying buzz! And computer-assisted instruction (CAI) is yet another promising application for voice output. It can be particularly effective in teaching and translating foreign languages. (For more information on CAI, see Chapter 9's discussion of computers in education.)

Eventually, input peripherals that recognize speech will be combined with output peripherals that synthesize speech. (Voice output is the easier design problem of the two.) Computers will then be able to understand a spoken question and give a spoken reply.

TELECOMMUNICATIONS EQUIPMENT

Although processing by computer is often measured in nanoseconds, users do not always receive the benefit of this speed because peripheral equipment operates at a much slower speed than the CPU. Data may backlog as a result of slow data entry equipment while the CPU stands idle. Sometimes slow output equipment is the bottleneck. In either case, such a system is **peripheral-bound**. Peripheral-bound systems are very common, and they are a major problem in processing today.

Time delays may also occur when input data stored on cards, tapes, or disks is transported to input equipment. In a similar way, the time required to move output from the computer to the user may be slow. Paper printouts, for example, create delays simply because of their bulk. The problem is accentuated when output is needed at a distant office, such as branch headquarters of a firm.

Telecommunications (the transmission of information by telephone lines, cable, microwave, satellite, or some other communication channel) is one method of speeding both the delivery of input and the distribution of output. Airline reservation systems use telecommunications. Onboard computers in the space shuttle communicate with NASA control via telecommunications. The following sections describe the interface equipment needed for a computer to receive and deliver telecommunication messages.

Equipment at the User's End

Users need a terminal and a modem when transmitting and receiving messages to and from a computer over a communication line. In addition, a multiplexer or concentrator may be added to facilitate telecommunication when several terminals are connected to the same line.

Terminals are used to input telecommunication messages. They may be keyboard terminals, optical scanning devices, card or tape readers, or any of the other input/output units described in this chapter.

Multiplexers Messages are transmitted to and from a distant computer through a communication channel. The speed of transmission and the capacity of the channel determine how quickly data flows. A **multiplexer** improves transmission efficiency by combining lines from terminals that have slow transmission speeds into one high-capacity transmission line, facilitating both transmission and reception of data.

Concentrators Some terminals operate less frequently than others. To prevent underutilization of transmission lines, a **concentrator** allocates a small number of channels to many users. Terminals are polled to see if they are ready to transmit or receive data; users may also request service. When all channels are engaged, users must wait their turn. How frequently each terminal is used, the average time spent per usage, and the cost of waiting by users wanting to transmit data but getting a busy signal—all these factors will determine the number of terminals per concentrator and the optimal number of output channels.

Modems Terminals produce **digital signals** (pulses representing the digits 0 and 1). When the telecommunication line transmits only **analog signals** (transmission in a continuous wave form, as in telephone line transmission), digital data must be converted to analog signals (see Figure 3.8). This process, called **modulation**, requires a digital-analog conversion device. The opposite conversion, or **demodulation**—from wave form back to pulses—is required when the digital computer receives the analog signal. The peripheral that performs conversion is a **modem**, a name derived from the terms **mo**dulation and **dem**odulation.

Ordinary phone lines are commonly used in telecommunications. Compact, portable terminals with built-in modems are currently available.

Equipment at the Computer End

Large mainframe computer systems generally include a **front-end processor** programmed to relieve the CPU of communication tasks. For example, a front-end processor receives messages, stores transmitted information, and routes input to the CPU according to preestablished priorities. It may validate transmitted data and preprocess this data as well. Another major function of front-end processors is to compensate for the relatively slow speed of transmission compared to the processing speed of the computer.

Front-end processors may also:

- Perform message switching between terminals.
- Process data when the teleprocessing load is low or absent.
- Act as multiplexers and concentrators.
- Provide access to external storage and other peripherals.
- Check security authorizations.
- Keep teleprocessing statistics.
- Accept messages from local lines with mixed modes of communications.
- Facilitate the use of the CPU by several users in a time-sharing system.

The exact responsibilities assigned to front-end processors differ from one system to another. The advantage of using them is that they handle communications responsibilities at less cost than the CPU. In addition, front-end processors are more easily maintained, programmed, and modified than CPUs.

Transmission Channels

Teleprocessing is a word used to describe computer processing that utilizes communications channels in connecting peripherals with a CPU or one computer with another. (See Figure 3.9 for an overview of a sample teleprocessing system.) The connection may be by telephone, wire, or coaxial cable. Data may also be transmitted by satellite, microwaves, or other means. Different physical transmission media can have vastly different data transfer-rate capabilities, which are measured in **baud** (bits per second). For example, telephones only transmit

Supplement 3.4 Fiber Optics

Alexander Graham Bell envisioned transmitting information via light energy. Two inventions of the 1960s have helped make that vision a reality: lasers and glass fibers. Lasers create intense directable beams of pure light. Glass fibers can be used in cables to transmit signals via light over long distances. These inventions led to the development of fiber optic technology for data transmission.

The advantages of fiber optic cables over copper wires traditionally used in telephone cables are many. Light frequencies are several orders of magnitude higher than the highest frequencies now used in the copper wires of computer communications. (Higher frequencies can carry more information). A single 125-micro diameter fiber optic cable (about the size of a human hair) can carry the same amount of information as 900 pairs of copper wires. In addition, signal loss is less, so that fiber optic signals need fewer repeater stations. Speed is improved as well. Fiber optic products can communicate from 19,200 to 38,400 bits per second over a 1,000-meter fiber optic cable. A 914-meter Texas Instruments EIA RS-232C cable (the maximum length for TI products) can carry 1,200 bits per second.

Other advantages include the following:

- Because fiber optic cables do not emit electromagnetic energy, they do not require shielding.
- Security is improved since it is almost impossible to tap fiber optic communications without detection.
- Fiber optic cables are suitable for electrically noisy environments. (They do not pick up electrical energy emitted by machinery, a problem with copper wires.)
- Glass fibers are small and flexible. They can withstand high temperatures.
- Buried fiber optic cables are virtually maintenance-free.
- Fiber optic cables can transmit all types of signals.

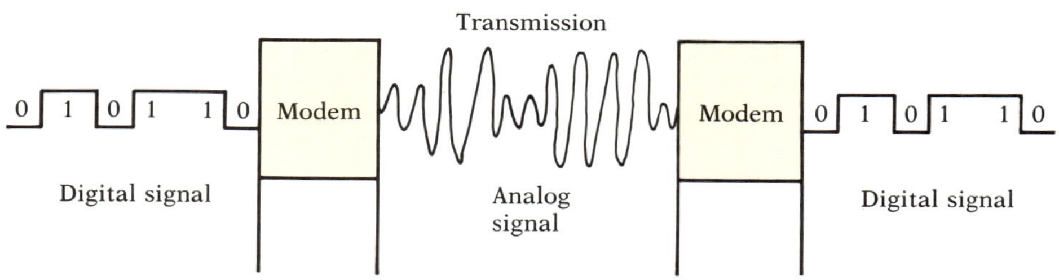

Figure 3.8 Function of a modem. Many transmission channels carry only analog signals. In order for a digital computer to utilize these channels during teleprocessing, a modem is needed. It modulates digital to analog signals when a message is sent, and demodulates (converts analog to digital) upon message receipt.

one to one million bits per second whereas satellites transmit at a rate of 60 to 1200 million bits per second.

Optical fiber is a new transmission mode that is becoming widely used. Glass that is half the diameter of human hair is made into a cable to provide a path for light. This new technology transmits data faster and with less interference than conventional cable. In addition, the material is lighter and less costly than copper wire. Glass fibers are gradually replacing copper wire in the phone network. When this conversion is complete, very high data transfer rates via the phone system will be available.

NETWORKS

Computers belonging to the same organization but located in different departments often need to share and exchange information. Sharing of peripherals can prove to be cost-effective for the organizations as well. Communication and efficiency can be similarly increased when several organizations within a community share computing resources.

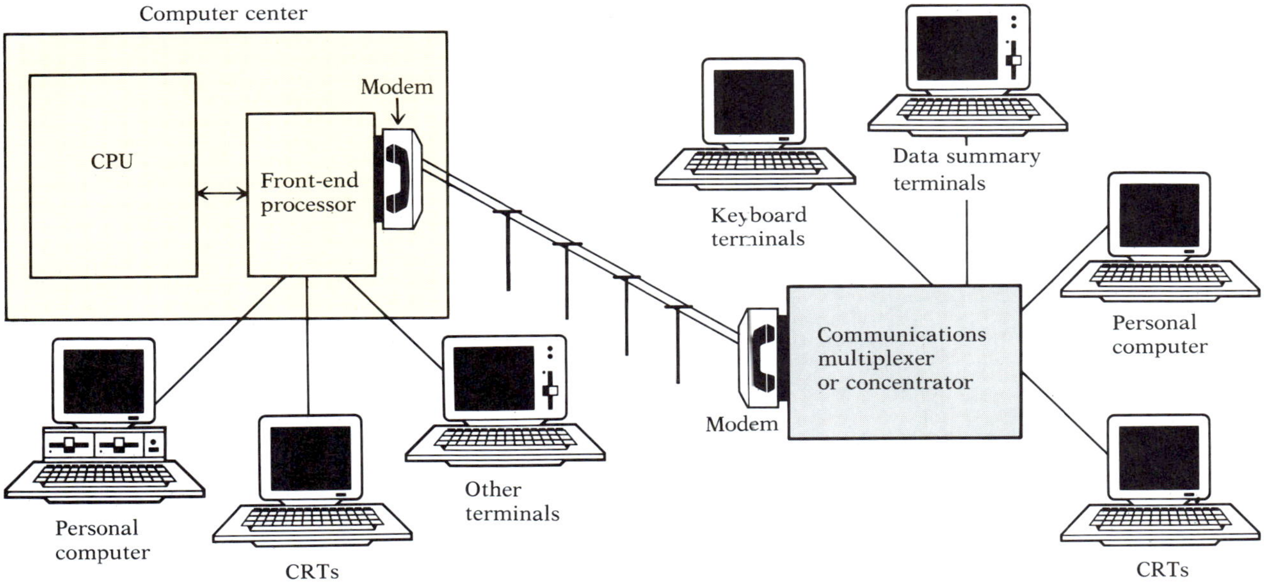

Figure 3.9 A sample teleprocessing system. A simple computer may serve both remote and on-site terminals. The front-end processor acts as an interface between slow-speed peripherals and the high-speed CPU. It also relieves the computer of communication tasks.

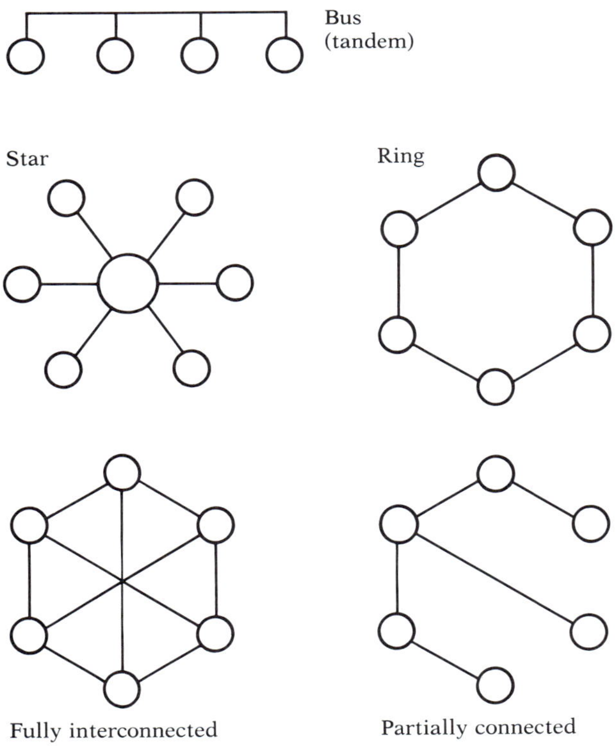

Figure 3.10 Sample networks. The design of a computer network varies from one organization to another. These are common network configurations.

All such sharing requires that computers (or computers and peripherals) be interconnected. If the sharing occurs in the same building, computers can be joined by cable. If it occurs in physically dispersed locations, connection by telephone lines is common. Whenever two or more computers are linked, a computer **network** is formed.

Figure 3.10 shows the most common configurations of networks. A **star network** has a centralized computer with links to dispersed CPUs. The problem with this configuration is that a breakdown of the central computer affects the entire system. Computers can also be connected in a **ring**. If one computer fails, the computer on either side can take on the workload or pass it to other computers in the network. The network can continue to function even with one computer down.

The network least affected by breakdown is an **interconnected network**. Of course, interconnections increase the cost of equipment and trans-

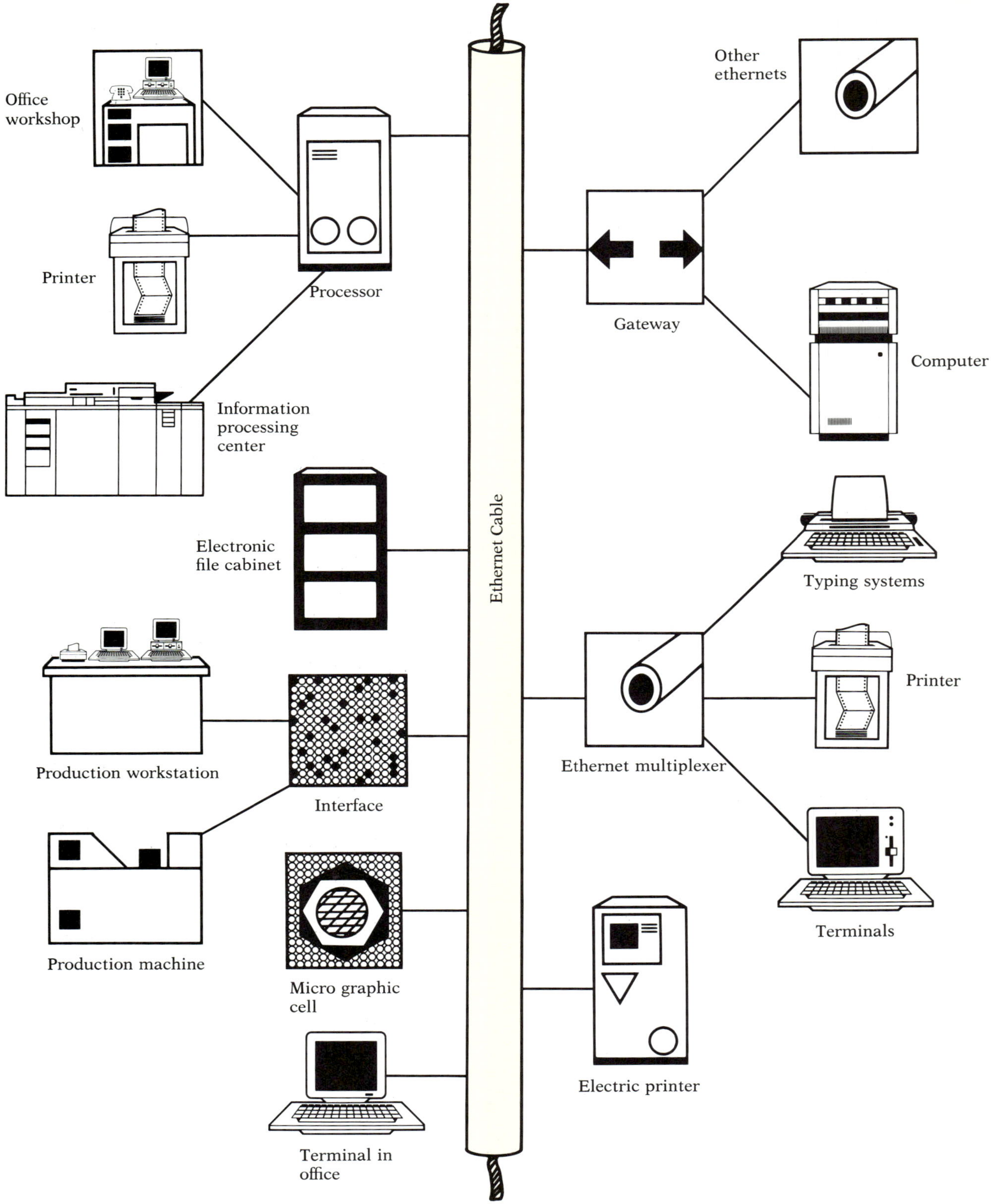

Figure 3.11 How Ethernet connects processors, peripherals clusters, and workstations.

mission lines. But sometimes the need for system reliability and backup justifies this cost. For example, a network of computers controls the space shuttle so that it can return from orbit even if an onboard computer fails. In a 1983 space mission, two of the airship *Columbia*'s five computers short-circuited as the *Columbia* was preparing to land, yet the plane had sufficient backup to land safely.

Hardware linked in a network must be compatible. Differences in speed, codes, and other design features will exist if the hardware has been manufactured by a number of companies. It must be possible to interface network components so that they interact with one another. Provisions must also be made to accommodate network users who have different security and backup needs.

Local Area Networks (LANs)

The term **local area network (LAN)** is used to describe interconnected computers and peripherals that are in close proximity. Cable is generally used in LANs. A number of companies sell such network systems. Wang-Net, developed by Wang Labs, utilizes the huge bandwidth of cable television networks. Xerox's Ethernet is one of the more popular network systems on the market. Many corporations use Ethernet to connect processors, clusters of peripherals, and workstations so that hardware, programs, and data can be shared by all departments (see Figure 3.11). With a local area network, top management can coordinate and control operations even though processing takes place at dispersed locations.

Linked LANs

Local networks can be joined to form a large network, like the network of linked resources shown in Figure 3.12. Once a network infrastructure exists throughout the country linking local LANs, many computer benefits realized only locally today will be available to the public nation-wide, and many new computer applications will be feasible.

For example, information found in newspapers, articles, books, and private reference services, such as the latest stock market quotes or suggestions on how to cure insomnia, will be available to every household with a home computer. (Teletex and videotex systems are discussed in Chapter 14.) Telemail (sending messages electronically from one computer to another) will be

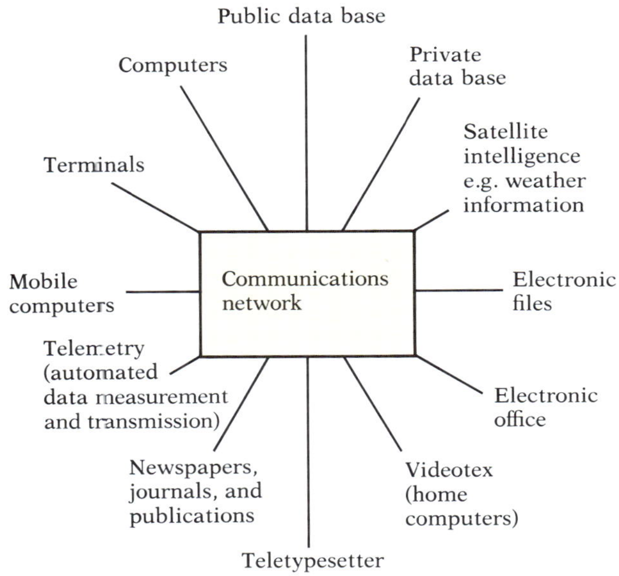

Figure 3.12 Linkage of computing resources. A communications network can be used to link a variety of computing resources. This figure shows sample network usage.

feasible for individuals as well as corporations (telemail is discussed in Chapter 7). Many of the chapters in Parts II and III of this book explore the potential of networks and describe the social implications of networking. The merger of communications and computers may have more impact on our future than any other scientific advance in this century.

SUMMING UP

Peripherals are needed for input, storage, and output of data. Figure 3.13 provides a summary of the various kinds of input, output, and storage peripherals.

Input peripherals include equipment to convert data onto a machine-readable medium, and equipment to read and deliver input to the CPU.

Data may be stored on magnetic tape, magnetic disks, magnetic drums, or other storage

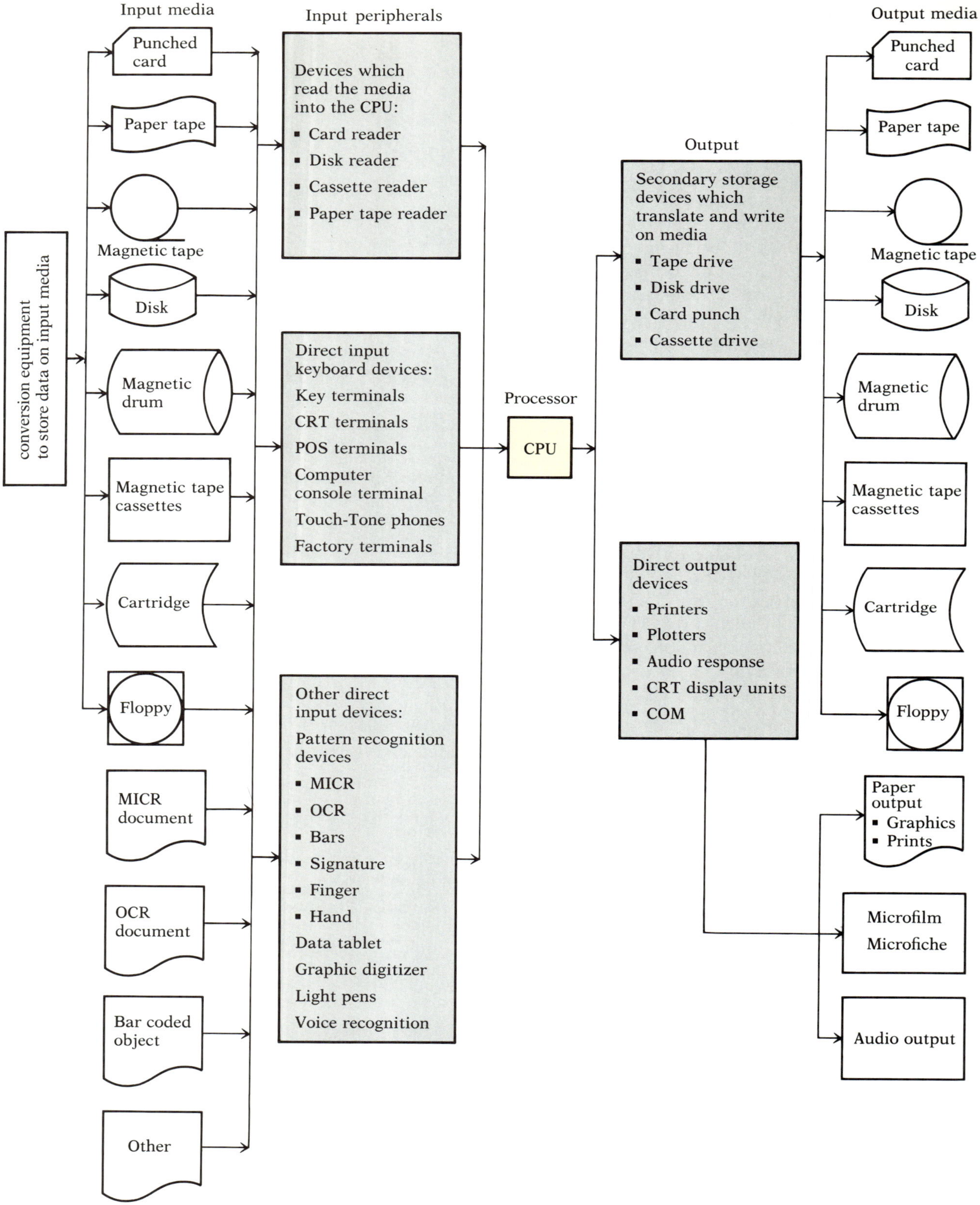

Figure 3.13 Summary of peripherals.

media. Peripherals are needed to record data on these media, to store the media, and to read the stored data when it is needed during processing.

Peripherals also deliver intermediate output to storage, or final output to the user. Output peripherals include printers, plotters, CRT display units, COM, and voice output devices.

When the user is remote from the computer, telecommunication equipment can be used to send input to the CPU and to receive output. This equipment includes terminals, multiplexers, concentrators, modems, and front-end processors. Telephone lines, telegraph, the use of coaxial cables, and transmission by microwaves and satellites are common transmission modes.

The integration of computing with telecommunications makes it possible to form networks of computers and data banks. It also facilitates implementation of distributed processing, a subject discussed in Chapter 19. Later chapters also examine computer applications for networks and the social implications of networks.

No attempt has been made in this chapter to identify equipment models, manufacturers, or prices. Furthermore, relatively few details on performance characteristics of peripherals, such as speed, storage capacity, or access times, have been included. This is because peripherals are designed for many purposes. Some are for large information systems, some for small, so that meaningful comparisons are hard to make. In addition, performance is improving with technological advances and prices are dropping. Any price/performance figures cited would be quickly outdated. When peripherals are needed, users must survey the market for hardware that fits their needs and conduct a cost-benefit study of appropriate models.

DISCUSSION QUESTIONS

1. What is currently the main constraint to computer performance? The CPU? Peripherals? Cite examples.
2. What factors influence the selection of peripheral equipment?
3. How would the selection of peripherals differ for online and OLRT (online real-time) systems?
4. What are the advantages and disadvantages of a computer network with telecommunications by satellite? Can the disadvantages be overcome with time and technological advances?
5. Discuss the factors that an organization must consider in choosing what type of telecommunications system to use.
6. What are some current trends in telecommunications?
7. What are the obstacles that prevent full exploitation of existing telecommunications technology?
8. Why are there more legal and regulatory problems with telecommunications systems than with on-site processing? What are the problems?

REVIEW QUESTIONS

1. Are peripherals essential to the operation of a computer? How do they contribute to the performance of a computer?
2. What is the difference between online and offline devices? Give three examples of each. What circumstances favor each?
3. What is an intelligent terminal? When would you use it?
4. What is the advantage of optical scanning devices over key input terminals? When should they be used?
5. Why are CRTs so popular? Cite five applications for CRT input terminals.
6. Compare the use of COM, printers, and CRTs for output.
7. Why is voice recognition equipment so expensive at the present time?

8. Give five examples of applications for voice input and voice ouput.

9. What purpose does external storage serve?

10. Compare the following storage media:
    a. floppy disks
    b. magnetic tape
    c. magnetic drum
    d. mass storage media

11. What is the difference between sequential processing and random processing?

12. What is a light pen? Why is it not universally used?

13. What functions do the following perform:
    a. modem?
    b. multiplexer?
    c. concentrator?
    d. front-end processor?

14. Contrast:
    a. modulation and demodulation
    b. analog and digital signals

15. What are the main components of a telecommunication system? Draw a diagram showing these components.

16. How do telecommunications contribute to computer processing?

EXERCISES

1. Describe the job of one computer user. List the peripherals needed by this individual and explain the user's teleprocessing needs. Draw a diagram showing how the components of the computer system for this user are interconnected.

2. Visit a computer room. Draw a block diagram of the hardware located in the room. Identify and label each hardware component in terms of devices for input, output, storage, processing, or multipurpose use.

3. Check the most appropriate storage device and processing mode for the applications listed below.

Application	Storage media		Mode of processing	
	Tape	Disk	Random	Sequential
Airline reservations				
Hotel nationwide reservations				
An auto dealer				
Accounting				
Contract calculations with buyer				
Instructor keeping grades				
University keeping grades				
University admissions				
University registration				
University computing for class				
University alumni				
Retailer point of sales credit checking				
Bank account status monthly ledger				
Wholesaler inventory				
Perishables				

4. You have been charged with the purchase of a peripheral for your job. Choose a peripheral that interests you. Specify your objectives and constraints, and list features you would like and features that you consider undesirable. Describe how you would go about selecting a model for purchase.

Selected Annotated Bibliography

References describing specific peripheral equipment would become outdated between the time this book is written and the time it appears. The fast pace of the computer industry, particularly with regard to peripherals, means that users must turn to recent periodicals for up-to-date information. Articles describing and evaluating models and features of peripherals frequently appear in *Datamation, Computer Technology Review, Mini-Micro Systems, Infosystems, Datapro, Data-World,* and similar publications.

Cakir, A.; Hart, D. J.; and Stewart, T. E. M. *Visual Display Terminals.* New York: John Wiley, 1980. This is a manual covering the following aspects of visual display terminals: ergonomics, use in workplace, design, health and safety features, and task organization.

Canning, Richard R. "A New Approach for Local Area Networks," *EDP Analyser*, vol. 19, no. 11 (November 1981), p. 14. A good survey of LANs with helpful classifications, descriptions, and comparisons of communication modes.

Dean, M. "How a Computer Should Talk to People," *IBM Systems Journal*, vol. 12, no. 4 (1982), pp. 424–53. This is an easy-to-read article on human-computer interaction. It discusses messages generated by programs for users and paths for successful interface.

Friend, David. "Graphics for Managers: The Distributed Approach," *Datamation*, vol. 28, no. 7 (July 1982), pp. 76–96. This article is more on graphics than distributed data processing. It discusses the characteristics of transaction and decision input data and how they can be expressed in graphics. It also examines the CPU and storage hardware needed for graphics representation and cost trade-offs of equipment.

Information Management, vol. 17, no. 4 (April 1983), pp. 18–38. This issue has a special section on microfilm, electronic filing, COM, and OCR. The discussion is both descriptive and prescriptive for the 1980s.

Murch, Gerald M. "Physiological Principles for the Effective Use of Color," *IEEE Computer Graphics and Applications*, vol. 4, no. 11 (November 1984), pp. 49–54. Guidelines for the proper use of color in visual displays are given. According to the author, the inappropriate use of color can seriously reduce the performance of information display systems.

Murray, William E. "Video Display Terminals: Radiation Issues," *IEEE Computer Graphics and Applications*, vol. 4, no. 4 (April 1984), pp. 41–44. The author, from the National Institute for Occupational Safety and Health, argues that the radiation levels from a VDU are well below occupational exposure standards and biological injury thresholds. This applies also to output devices and devices used for data entry.

Rodgers, Robert C. "Bar Codes–Automatic Production Cost Cutters," *Production Engineering*, vol. 29 (April 1982), pp. 46–50. Three types of bar code scanners are discussed: hand-held code pens, fixed position scanners, and moving beam scanners. Advice on selecting equipment is given.

Smith, Michael J. "The Physical, Mental, and Emotional Stress Effects of VDU Work," *IEEE Computer Graphics and Applications*, vol. 4, no. 4 (April 1984), pp. 23–37. There is evidence that VDU terminals affect the emotions and moods of users, cause eye stress and muscular aches and pains.

Scherr, A. L. "A Perspective on Communications and Computing," *IBM Systems Journal*, vol. 22 (1983). This issue has articles on X-25 (a telecommunications standard), teletex systems, token-ring networks, satellite communications controllers, SNA networks, videoconferencing, and network management of large computing services. An annotated bibliography of rare sources is included.

Tyler, Michael. "Touch Screens: Big Deal or No Deal," *Datamation*, vol. 30, no. 1 (January 1984), pp. 146–54. The author concludes that touch-sensitive screens are very exciting but whether they actually stimulate people to use computers is open to debate.

Wicklein, John. *Electronic Nightmare: The New Communications and Freedom*. New York: Viking, 1981. The author discusses the danger that social relationships will be adversely affected by telecommunication technology. For example, individual privacy may be threatened and poor nations may find themselves at the mercy of multinationals as a result of this technology.

Zarley, Craig. "The Wide World of Alternative Input Devices," *Personal Computing*, vol. 8, no. 4 (February 1984), pp. 129–37. The mouse, touch table, light pen, and voice command are discussed.

Telling a Computer What to Do: Programming Languages and Software

Computer programming as a practical human activity is some twenty-five years old, a short time for intellectual development. Yet computer programming has already posed the greatest intellectual challenge that mankind has faced in pure logic and complexity.

HARLAN D. MILLS

CHAPTER FOUR

Key Words

address
applications software
assembler program
assembler languages
binary digits
bits
canned programs
compiler
CP/M
fourth generation programming languages (4GLs)
high-level programming language
interpreter
language translation programs
machine-dependent
machine language
menu
MS-DOS
MSX
natural language
object program
operands
operating system
packages
portable
program
programmer
prompt
query language
software
source program
terminal-interactive language
UNIX

As discussed in Chapter 2, a computer processes binary digits. Data represented in English (or any natural language) must be translated into binary to be processed by computer. **Programs** (also called **software**) are the instruction sets that tell the computer what to do and the sequence of operations to be performed. They must also be translated into binary to be executed by the CPU.

This chapter describes how users communicate with a computer since binary is not appropriate for human communication. Much of the chapter is devoted to the evolution of programming languages. The chapter concludes with a discussion of the software required to make computer processing deliver the information users desire.

COMMUNICATING WITH A COMPUTER

Humans communicate in natural languages, such as English, French, or Japanese. We represent ideas in words, numbers (usually written in base ten), or symbols.

Natural languages are not meaningful to a CPU since computers only recognize **bits** (*bi*nary dig*its*) that can be represented by the flow of electrons in a circuit. Data and programs represented as words, base-ten numbers, and symbols can only be processed by computer when they are converted to the digits 0 and 1. This means that alphabetic and symbolic data must be given binary representations and that all decimal numbers must be expressed in binary as well.

Both hardware and software facilitate human-computer communication. As we learned in Chapter 3, input peripherals convert data into bits. Translators, which will be described later in this chapter, convert programs written in programming languages, such as FORTRAN, into **machine language**, the most elemental and direct of all programming languages.

Machine Language

When computers first appeared on the market, all programs were written in machine language, a string of binary numbers. Here is an example of three machine instructions to calculate total pay (regular pay plus overtime pay). In this example, a hexidecimal representation (a number system based on 16) is used instead of binary characters since the instruction in 0's and 1's would take too much space and be too confusing to the reader.

58AC010

- Address in memory where data (regular pay) resides.
- Register address where data is to be loaded (moved).
- Instruction to "load" (move from memory to register).

That is, the instruction 58 moves data (regular pay) from memory **address** C010 to register A. (The binary equivalent to 58AC010 is 0101 1000 1010 1100 0000 0001 0000.)

Now the computer must be told to add overtime pay that is stored in memory location C014 to regular pay in register A. The addition will change the data in register A to total pay (the sum of regular and overtime pay). This instruction is:

5AAC014

- Address in memory where data (overtime pay) resides.
- Register where overtime pay will be added to existing contents.
- Instruction to "add."

Finally, the computer must be told to store the result.

50AC018

- Address in memory for storage of total pay.
- Register where total pay now resides.
- Instruction to store.

As you can see from this example, writing programs in machine language has many drawbacks:

- The language is difficult to learn.
- There are many instructions to write—one for each machine command. Programming can become very tedious.
- The **programmer** (person who writes the program) must remember operation codes.
- The programmer must be knowledgeable about technical aspects of computers.
- It is necessary to keep track of memory locations and their contents. Contents keep changing. In the example just cited, the contents in register A switched from regular pay to total pay.
- Machine language is **machine-dependent**. In other words, each computer has its own machine language. The codes used are for the circuitry of a specific computer. A CPU designed by a different manufacturer may require the use of different codes. As a result, a program written in machine language will not be **portable** from one computer to another as a general rule. (A portable program can be run on more than one type of machine.)

In solving the problem total pay equals regular pay plus overtime pay, a representation of a machine instruction for an early computer, the IBM 1620, was as follows:

211400012002

This instruction has three parts. The first two digits represent the operation code (add, subtract, move data, and so on). In this example, code 21 represents "add." The data will, therefore, be channeled through circuitry that performs addition. (Other circuitry exists for other arithmetic processing operations.)

The second and third parts of the instruction are **operands**. An operand is what is to be operated upon and is identified in the instruction by an address. In this case, 14000 and 12002 are addresses where the operands are to be found. If the input data 120 (representing regular pay in dollars) were stored in location 14000, and the input data 30 (overtime pay) were stored in location 12002, the machine instruction 21140012002 would mean:

1. Find data stored in operand 1 (120).
2. Add it to data stored in operand 2 (30).
3. Store the result in operand 1 (150).

Figure 4.1 summarizes the way this machine instruction works.

Assembly Language

In an effort to simplify programming, **assembly languages** were soon developed. Whereas all instructions in machine language are numbers, assembly languages permit the use of abbreviations and mnemonic codes (for example, MP meaning "multiply" or C for "compare").

An assembly language instruction with the same meaning as the machine instruction 211400012002 cited earlier is:

A RGP OTP

Notice that the numeric operation code 21 has been replaced by the alphabetic code A for "add." Also notice that the address numbers have been replaced by names of data (for example, address 14000 becomes RGP for "regular pay"; address 12002 becomes OTP for "overtime pay").

Programs written in assembly language must be translated into machine language since computers do not understand alphabetic codes. This translation is done by an **assembler program** (also called an **assembler**). The translation process is illustrated in Figure 4.2. Programmers writing in assembly language need not worry about the translation process since the assembler is provided by the manufacturer of the computer and is internal to the computer system.

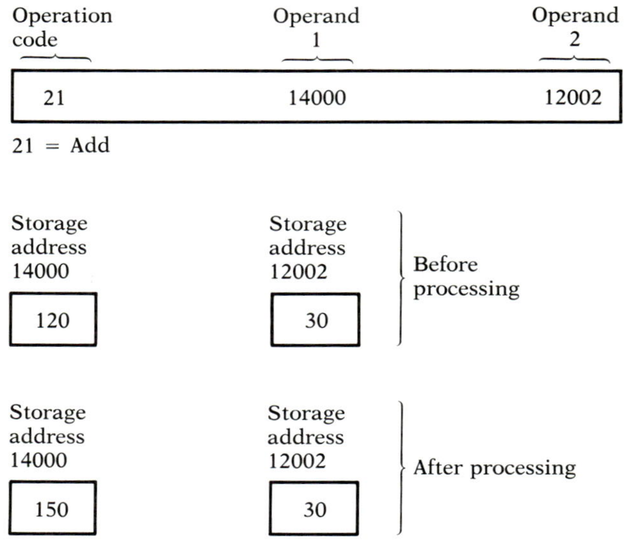

Figure 4.1 An example of a machine instruction. The instruction 211400012002 is value-independent. That is, the instruction tells the computer the address of values and what computation to perform on the stored values without ever stating what those values are. In the above example, two operands are identified. The instruction tells the computer to add the stored values and place the result as operand 1. Note that the operand in address 14000 becomes 150 after processing.

Assembly language programs are less difficult to write than programs in machine language since the need to remember storage locations and contents is eliminated. Furthermore, alphabetic operation codes are easier to remember than numeric codes. However, as in machine language, one instruction must be written for each machine command so that a large number of instructions must still be written. This makes programming tedious, repetitive, and error-prone. In addition, the alphabetic codes of the language depend on particular models of equipment. This means that in general, assembly language is nonportable.

High-level languages

Over the last twenty-five years, **high-level programming languages**—that is, languages closer to English—have been developed. These languages overcome most of the shortcomings of machine and assembly languages. An equivalent of the assembly language instruction A RGP OTP written in

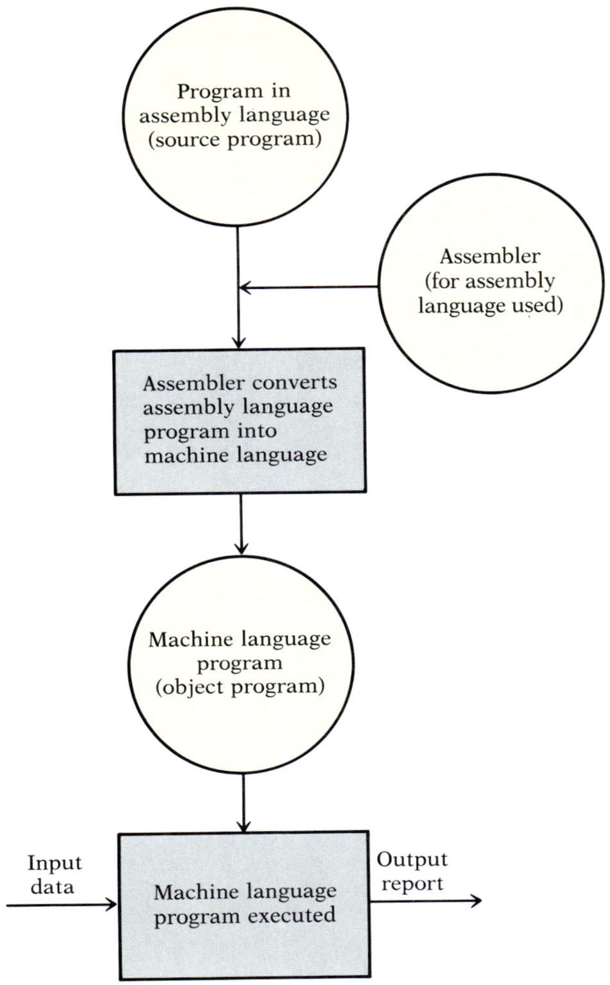

Figure 4.2 Assembly language translation process. Programs must be translated into machine language before they can be executed. When assembly language is used, this translation is done by an assembler as shown in this figure. Translation of a high-level language follows the same process, except that a compiler or interpreter makes the translation instead of an assembler.

COBOL, a high-level language commonly used for business applications, is as follows:

ADD REGULAR-PAY, OVERTIME-PAY GIVING TOTAL-PAY

or

PAY=REGPAY+OVTPAY

or

PAY=RGP+OTP

Before instructions are executed, they are translated into machine language by a program that is part of the computer operating system (we will take a look at operating systems later in the chapter). For high-level languages, the translation is done by a program called a **compiler** (or **interpreter**), as opposed to the assembler required to translate assembly languages into machine language. (We will learn more about assemblers, compilers, and interpreters later in the chapter.)

In many ways, high-level languages overcome the drawbacks of both machine and assembly languages. The computer keeps track of storage locations and contents, and operation codes are familiar symbols. Another major advantage is that few instructions are necessary. For example, when FORTRAN was developed in 1957, a set of forty-seven FORTRAN instructions equalled approximately 1000 machine language commands. Furthermore, high-level languages are portable, provided that the other computer has an appropriate compiler. In addition, these languages can be learned quickly and easily checked for errors. They also are much less tedious to write and modify than lower level languages. Better accuracy and increased speed of programming result.

Many high-level computer languages have been developed since the 1950s. See Supplement 4.1 for a description of common high-level programming languages, Supplement 4.2 for a comparison of features of many of these languages, and Supplement 4.3 for ways to express an English statement in sample languages.

Terminal Interactive Languages

All of the languages mentioned thus far require that the user be trained in programming. One needs to know the rules for data entry. The symbols and command structure required to process data and retrieve information from the computer system must also be mastered. Does this mean that every computer user must learn how to program?

When computers were first introduced, the answer to this question was "Yes." Computer use re-

Supplement 4.1 Common High-level Programming Languages

- *Ada.* Originally developed by the Department of Defense for use in embedded system applications in the military services. Used today for many other applications as well (for example, payroll). Named after Ada Augusta Byron, the Countess of Lovelace, considered by many to be the first programmer.
- *ALGOL (*ALGO*rithmic* L*anguage).* Designed by an international group of mathematicians, intended for use of those involved in scientific and mathematical projects. A modular, structured language used extensively in Europe.
- *APL (*A P*rogramming* L*anguage).* Conceived by Kenneth Iverson who worked at IBM to develop it. A powerful, interactive language for scientific and mathematical computations that can perform complex operations with a minimum of coding. Requires a large memory and a special keyboard. Available only on large- or medium-sized machines.
- *BASIC (*B*eginners* A*ll-purpose* S*ymbolic* I*nstruction* C*ode).* Developed at Dartmouth College for use with time-sharing systems. Easy to learn. Originally intended to be used by universities for instructional purposes, but has been adopted by many organizations for their data processing needs. Requires little internal memory and is, hence, available on most microcomputers.
- *C Language.* C language first appeared in 1983 and is often referred to as a portable assembly language. Used both by manufacturers and software developers for writing operating systems (for example, UNIX), utilities, and applications including the animation of the film *Return of the Jedi.* Used on small microcomputers as well as supercomputers like CRAY-2. Has many of the advanced, structured programming features found in Pascal.
- *COBOL (*CO*mmon* B*usiness* O*riented* L*anguage).* Designed for business applications with a large amount of input/output but few complex calculations. Machine-independent. English-like. Strong file handling capabilities. Required on all Department of Defense computers, which makes COBOL the most commonly available language on mainframes.
- Dialogue/Query: A class of high-level language often available with a database management system (DBMS). Used interactively for queries and quick retrieval of information from a terminal in a question-and-answer mode between the user and the system.
- *FORTRAN (*FOR*mula* TRAN*slating).* First commercial high-level language. Introduced by IBM in 1954 and designed primarily for scientific and engineering applications. Algebra-like, highly structured format. Not a good business language since it has limited ability to process alphabetic data and files.
- *GPSS (*G*eneral* P*urpose* S*ystem* S*imulation).* Designed by IBM. Graphic-oriented. Used for business simulation problems. Most appropriate for queuing.
- *LISP (*LIS*t* P*rocessing Language).* Developed in the 1950s. Has become the most widely used programming language for artificial intelligence and other symbolic applications. Its early inefficiency has been overcome through LISP systems with compilers and optimizers, and by "LISP machines" developed especially to run LISP.
- *Logo (Name derived from Greek word for reason).* Designed as a language suitable for children for use in a learning environment. Stems from LISP. Combines LISP's list processing capabilities with a syntax children can understand. Useful in introducing students to computer programming.
- *Modula-2.* Comparable to the procedures introduced by ALGOL and Pascal for structured programming, with the difference that Modula-2 is based upon the concept of modules that are either autonomous or embedded as submodules into larger modules.
- *Pascal.* Named after Blaise Pascal, French mathematician of the 17th century. Powerful, easy-to-learn language first developed to teach programming concepts but rapidly extended to business and scientific applications. Uses structured IF-THEN-ELSE, WHILE-DO, and REPEAT-UNTIL statements. Available on microcomputers.
- *PL/1 (*P*rogramming* L*anguage—version* 1*).* High-level language developed by IBM. Designed for general-purpose use but not used widely. An all-purpose, procedure-oriented language for both scientific and business applications. Has powerful features that make it good for systems programming. Facilities allow use of structured programming techniques. The large amount of storage required for compiler prohibits use on small computers.
- *PROLOG (*PRO*gramming in* LOG*ic).* Lends itself to inference-making and used extensively in artificial intelligence. Gained in popularity after the Japanese announced it as the language for their fifth generation computers.
- *RPG (*R*eport* P*rogram* G*enerator).* Problem-oriented language originally designed to facilitate the output of business reports. Easy to learn and use. Commonly used to rearrange and format reports and process files for accounts receivable, general ledgers, and inventory.
- *SIMSCRIPT.* A language used for general-purpose simulation.

Ada Countess Lovelace (1815–1852), collaborated with Charles Babbage on the never-completed "analytic engine," a prototype of the modern computer. (New York Public Library Picture Collection)

Supplement 4.2 Comparison of Common Programming Languages

	Ada	ALGOL	APL	Assembly language	BASIC	COBOL	FORTRAN	Pascal	PL/1	PROLOG	RPG	Dialog/ query
Machine-dependent			X	X								
Procedure-oriented	X	X			X	X	X	X	X			
Problem-oriented										X	X	X
English-like						X			X			X
"Structured"	X	X						X	X			
Mathematical/ scientific orientation		X	X				X					
Business-oriented						X					X	X
Multipurpose	X	X		X	X			X	X			
Good character manipulation	X			X	X	X		X	X			X
Interactive capability			X		X			X		X		X
Requires mainframe	X	X	X			X			X	X		
Standardized	X				X	X	X	X	X			

Supplement 4.3 Ways to Express an English Statement in Sample Programming Languages

Language	Instruction
English	The new value of the variable Y is the addition of a constant value of 4 to the currently existing value of Y
Ada	Y := Y + 4;
ALGOL	Y := Y + 4
An Assembly Language	MOVE Y ADD 4 RESULT TO Y
APL	Y ← Y + 4
BASIC	LET Y = Y + 4
C	Y + = 4;
COBOL	ADD 4 TO Y
FORTRAN	Y = Y + 4.0
LISP	(SETQ Y 4)
Pascal	Y := Y + 4
PL/1	Y = Y + 4;
PROLOG	Sum(Y, 4, Y),
RPGII	ADD Y AND 4
SIMSCRIPT	Y = Y + 4

Supplement 4.4 Pentagon Adopts Ada

The Pentagon has two types of software problems. The first is that programming complex military systems for the powerful and complicated computers of today is a difficult task. The second is that coordination of military hardware that runs with different languages is a practical impossibility. Military programs have been written in at least 300 languages.

Language standardization would help solve both problems. For the last ten years the Department of Defense has been working to produce a standard computer language for the Pentagon. This language, called Ada, was adopted as the official language of the Pentagon in June 1984. Ada will be mandatory for all military systems of the future. Defense contractors, however, may receive exemptions if their hardware is unsuited to Ada programming. The British defense ministry has also adopted Ada, and the language will be mandatory for English military systems starting in 1987.

American sales of Ada-based software (civilian and military) are expected to reach $900 million in 1986.

quired programming training. In recent years, however, **terminal-interactive languages** have been developed. These languages enable persons with no programming background to use computer systems for many routine tasks. Users have only to memorize a few codes and learn how to enter data on a terminal. Software is selected for a given task (such software is called an "application program," as we will see later in this chapter) and loaded into the computer. The user then follows a series of **prompts** (messages giving directions explaining how to proceed) displayed on the screen.

For example, a clerk in a warehouse that has computerized inventory records might find the following instruction on the terminal screen when processing a customer's order:

> Enter the item name, inventory number and quantity on order.

The clerk would then input—that is, type on the terminal keyboard—the requested data.

At other times, users may be asked simply to fill in the blanks or make yes/no choices. A **menu** may even be employed to solicit information from users. For example, should a clerk in a construction firm want a list of suppliers in Houston, the following might appear on the screen:

```
Do you want:
1. Names of suppliers located in
   Houston?
2. Names of companies supplying
   Houston projects?
3. Names of suppliers associated
   with Houston in some other way?
```

If the second choice is correct, the clerk simply types the number 2 on the keyboard. When further clarification is needed by the system, a new menu will appear, such as:

```
Do you want:
1. Electrical suppliers?
2. Plumbing suppliers?
3. Lumber suppliers?
4. Other?
```

The advantage of terminal interactive languages is obvious: a person with no knowledge of programming can use a computer for information retrieval. The individual may be totally unaware of the programming effort required to process and retrieve requested information. Nevertheless, every time a computer is used, it is operating according to instructions in computer software that are written in a computer language.

Query Languages

Query languages, designed for quick retrieval of information stored in the computer, are a type of terminal interactive languages. Unlike languages

Supplement 4.5 English and Query Language Equivalents

a. English:
Find employees working for Smith who make under $20,000.

b. SEQUEL:
```
SELECT NAME
FROM PERSONNEL
WHERE MANAGER = "SMITH"
AND SALARY < 20000
```

c. SQUARE:
```
    EMP       ('SMITH', <'20000')
NAME    MANAGER,SALARY
```

d. QUERY BY EXAMPLE:

PERSONNEL	NAME	MANAGER	SALARY
	P*	Smith	<20000

e. IQF:
```
(1) FROM PERSONNEL FILE
(2) FOR SMITH MANAGER
(3) AND FOR SALARY <20000
(4) LIST NAME
```

*P stands for print identifying desired output.

Although query languages use English, programmers must learn special codes, symbols, and format rules. Note the many programming differences between the programming languages SEQUEL, SQUARE, Query By Example, and IQF. There is no "best" language. Each has advantages and disadvantages.

discussed in the preceding section, however, query languages require some understanding of programming. Their code structures and rules for inputting data must be learned. An advantage of query languages is that many can carry on a dialogue with users requesting additional information when data entry is incomplete or when the computer does not understand the user's request. A query language is often used with a data base management system. (A data base management system is a set of programs that control the creation, maintenance, and utilization of data bases and data files. More on this subject appears in Chapter 5). See Supplement 4.5 for sample English instructions and query language equivalents.

Fourth Generation Languages

Fourth generation programming languages (4GLs) are another group of high-level languages. Their distinguishing feature is their ability to help automate the programming task.

To be more specific, 4GLs relieve the programmer of mundane portions of programming, such as the need to keep track of inordinate amounts of detail. They restyle the way in which the programmer specifies particular features of the program and, as a result, allow the programmer to think through the problem at a higher and more natural level.

4GLs work by employing a powerful set of commands telling the computer what to do. The user must first outline the problem. The computer then determines the structure of the problem from this outline and generates the necessary programming instructions to solve the problem. To utilize these languages, the user needs no formal background in programming. Indeed, it is estimated that 75 percent of all 4GL programming can be done by users with only two days of training. Specialist programmers are still needed, however, to handle complex applications and to fine tune the main nonprocedural code.

4GLs have English commands, are easy to use and support, simple to update, and portable from one computer to another. Almost all data base management systems (which are discussed in Chapter 5) use them. dBase II and 10/Base are examples of programs that use 4GLs. From the user's

Supplement 4.6 The Tower of Babel of Programming Languages

Programming languages have proliferated in recent years. One reason is that specialized languages have been developed for specific classes or types of problems. The diversity overwhelms users, forces programmers to learn many languages, and impedes the sharing of programs and the logic used to reach problem solutions.

The Tower of Babel as interpreted by sixteenth-century painter Pieter Bruegel. There was a time, according to the Bible, when people had one common language. They were able to cooperate and construct a tower whose top reached into Heaven. Angered by their arrogance, the Lord confused their speech, and cast down the tower. Without their common language, they were unable to maintain unity, and their attempts to reach Heaven were therefore frustrated. (Kunsthistoriches Museum, Vienna, Austria. Reprinted by permission.)

point of view, the languages are efficient. However, the languages are inefficient in their utilization of machine resources and computer time. This is because the computer's operating system must spend more time and effort converting 4GL commands into a set of specific machine language instructions than is required for lower level languages.

4GLs free users from their dependence on professional programmers since they provide users with a tool for writing many of their own programs. One immediate benefit has been to help organizations reduce programming backlogs. With further language research, the day may come when programming becomes completely automated, eliminating the need for programmers and programming languages altogether.

Natural Languages

At the present time a **natural language** like English and French can be used as a programming language, but only for a limited set of problems. Vocabulary is also restricted. Furthermore, natural language processing is costly and an inefficient use of computer time. Though users do not have to learn a programming language, they still must understand the function of computers and be able to formulate, organize, and analyze problems.

However, many of the limitations of natural languages for computer processing that now exist may be overcome in time. Indeed, natural language processing is the focus of much research, since it is recognized that users feel much more comfortable communicating with a computer in a language such as English than in a formal programming language. The Japanese have announced that natural language processing is one of the major goals of their fifth generation computers, which are currently under development and projected to reach the market in the 1990s.

Most of the natural language programs to date have been directed toward facilitating the user's interface with the computer. Standard messages and rules for constituting a natural language dialogue are stored in computer memory. The computer engages in a dialogue with the user in order to determine what information is needed. It is assumed that the user either does not know, or can't express, needs in terms that the computer understands. Here is a sample from a dialogue-oriented, interactive language that approaches natural language processing using Rendezvous, a system designed to customize applications for accounting:

```
SYSTEM (Words appear on CRT screen): IN
     ORDER FOR ME TO CREATE A BILLING
     PROGRAM FOR YOU I WILL NEED TO GET
     CERTAIN INFORMATION FROM YOU ABOUT
     WHAT YOU WANT. FEEL FREE TO ASK
     QUESTIONS AS WE GO ALONG. WOULD
     YOU LIKE YOUR SYSTEM TO BE
     TRANSACTION ORIENTED OR BATCH
     ORIENTED?

USER (Types on terminal keyboard): what
     is a transaction oriented system?

SYSTEM: IN A TRANSACTION ORIENTED
     SYSTEM AN INVOICE IS PRODUCED
     IMMEDIATELY WHEN AN ORDER ARRIVES.

USER: i want invoices to be produced
     just once a day at 5 p.m.

SYSTEM: DO YOU WANT A SEPARATE INVOICE
     FOR EACH ORDER OR DO YOU WANT THE
     ORDERS GROUPED BY CUSTOMER?

USER: separate invoices[1]
```

A major problem that arises with natural language communication is that users often have the illusion that the computer fully understands the problem when this is not the case. In addition, once users are familiar with the system, they tend to abbreviate their requests or express them in an ungrammatical form, which the computer cannot interpret. For example, input requests might be misspelled or include words not in the computer's lexicon of words. Requests for information may be inappropriate because the user has not mastered the structure of the program or data base. In addition, too many users assume that simply because the computer communicates in a natural language, the output is indisputably correct.

Researchers need to develop techniques to help users formulate problems so that they are computer-solvable. Although the problem of thinking as the computer thinks is inherent in the use of any programming language, the need to develop techniques to make this kind of problem formulation easier for users is particularly crucial for natural languages for the very reason that natural languages are so deceptively natural. Further research is also needed into techniques for evaluating computer solutions to problems and for testing them for correctness.

KINDS OF SOFTWARE

Computer programs fall into three broad categories: operating system software, translators, and application software.

Operating system software, the domain of computer professionals, functions as an interface between the user and the bare machine. The use of operating system software spares the programmer from having to acquire detailed knowledge of the internal operations of computer equipment. Although many users do not realize that operating programs exist, computers today could not function without them.

The second category of software required by computers consists of translator programs. These programs translate software written in higher level languages into machine code. The final category is applications software. These are programs that concern users most since they enable computers to

[1]G. E. Heidorn, "Automatic Programming Through Natural Language Dialogue: A Survey." *IBM Journal of Research and Development*, vol. 20, no. 4 (July 1976), p. 309.

do useful work. Each of these categories will be discussed in the sections that follow.

Operating System Software

Operating systems did not exist in early computers. Although computer hardware could be used to perform arithmetic and logic operations, people had to perform many manual tasks during the course of operations. For example, they had to ready input and output devices, determine the order in which jobs were run, and monitor the computer during processing. The manual tasks often caused extensive time delays. Furthermore, faulty output was often attributed to those operations performed by humans during job processing. It soon became apparent that the computer itself should take over many of the tasks performed by human operators. By the 1960s, operating systems were developed for this purpose.

An operating system is a collection of programs used by the computer to manage its own resources and operations. The programs function as a control system so that little or no human intervention is required during processing. For example, programs coordinate the flow of work done by peripherals and the CPU. Like a traffic manager working behind the scene, the software schedules jobs to be done, organizes them in an efficient sequence, and keeps a log of jobs accomplished.

Operating system subroutines also concern the physical location of data and the organization of data files. (You will learn about data organization and files in the next chapter.) They manage time sharing, telecommunications, and make it possible for several programs to share the same records. (A "record" is a collection of data relating to a specific topic.) In addition, many operating system subprograms provide services to users such as access and security control. Additional subprograms keep track of system use so that the efficiency of CPU utilization can be evaluated and users can be charged for computer time.

In short, the objectives of operating software are to maximize efficiency of operations, to minimize human intervention, and to facilitate the work of programmers in accessing data and peripheral equipment. Although operating systems will normally be supplied by the manufacturer or vendor of the CPU, systems programmers within an organization may modify the operating system to meet the organization's unique needs. Many computer centers are also acquiring data base management software to help organize and retrieve data in ways that are not possible with their existing operating systems.

Formerly, operating systems were written in machine language. This language was favored because of its processing efficiency. The disadvantage was that operating systems were not portable from one computer model to another. Today, importance is placed on the cost of writing and correcting programs, not on machine efficiency, since the cost of computer hardware has dropped while the cost of labor has risen. This explains, in part, why operating systems are now written in higher level languages. As a result, operating systems can be compatible with the processors of many manufacturers. For example, **UNIX**, developed by the Bell Laboratories, is an operating system used on many computer models. Unix is modular in its design, which means that users can add or remove some parts of the system to tailor it to their precise needs. Currently UNIX is being sold under a half-dozen names and is the operating system of over four dozen computer manufacturers. It is particularly suitable for microcomputers, but is also appropriate for larger computers. The supercomputer Cray-2 uses UNIX, for example.

Other popular operating systems are **MS-DOS, CP/M**, and **MSX**. Both MS-DOS and CP/M are mainly designed for single users of 8-bit and 16-bit microcomputers. One of the reasons many American companies favor CP/M is the large amount of supporting software available. MSX is the operating system used by more than ten Japanese computer manufacturing firms that hope to enter the American market with low-cost computers. It has been estimated that as many as 500,000 MSX computers have already been sold in Japan.

Language Translator Programs

Language translators are programs that convert instructions programmed in a language other than

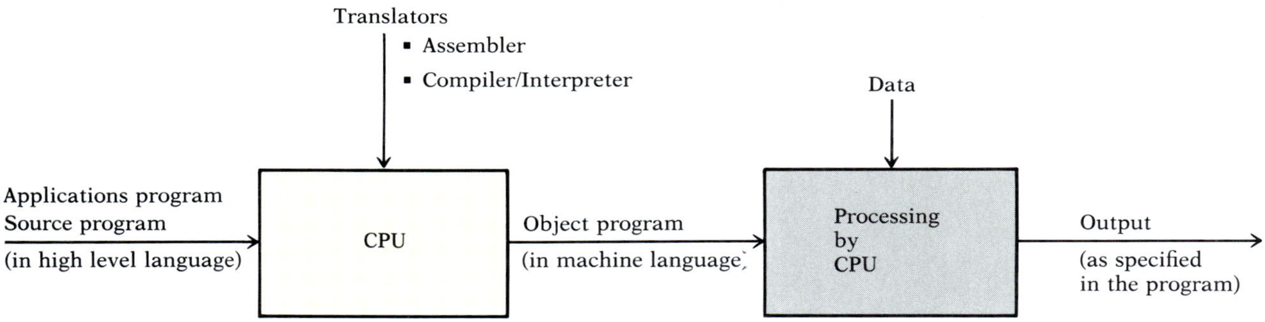

Figure 4.3 Relationship between source and object programs.

machine code, called a **source program**, into a program written in machine language, called an **object program**. There are two types of programs that make the translation. An assembler program translates assembly languages into an object program while a compiler (or interpreter) translates high-level languages into an object program. (Figure 4.3 illustrates the relationships between source and object programs and shows that the translation process goes on in the CPU.) Normally, there is one translator for each language. The translator usually resides on a magnetic disk. It is called into computer memory by special commands that precede the source program.

The difference between a compiler and an interpreter is a technical one. A compiler translates the entire program into machine language before the program is executed, while an interpreter translates each statement into machine language just before that statement is executed.

To illustrate this difference, consider the translation of a story from French to English. The story can be translated in two ways. Someone familiar with both languages may translate the story after several readings and spend time rephrasing and polishing the English. This is comparable to compiling a program. On the other hand, someone might translate the story word by word, without going back to correct sentence structure and awkward phrasing. An interpreter does this type of immediate translation. If the story were read again, the interpreter would make the very same word-by-word translation.

An advantage of interpreters is that they provide information helpful to programmers in the diagnosis of programming errors and problems. A disadvantage of interpreters is that they are less efficient than compilers because programs must be translated every time they are run. A compiled program, in contrast, can be saved on disk, so that it doesn't need to be recompiled each time the program is executed.

Applications Software

The third category of software is **applications software**. These are programs that enable a computer to do useful work, such as launching a satellite or keeping patient records for a dentist.

Since the majority uses computers to do standard kinds of processing, a single application program may serve many different users. A program for a common application, such as payroll processing, can usually be purchased from a software house along with documentation on the program. Such programs are ready for immediate use, although modification may be necessary. Even then, purchased software will usually save a user time and money since, as a rule, it is less costly to buy predeveloped programs (called software **packages**) than to develop custom programs in-house. Since the convenience of off-the-shelf software parallels that of canned food, packages are often called **canned programs** (see Figure 4.4).

Thousands of applications packages are on the market. The problem for an organization that wants to purchase a package, rather than develop customized software, is to find the right package for the work that needs to be done. A computer

Supplement 4.7 Sample Packaged Software

Many computer users lack the skills to write their own programs so they buy software packages. It's interesting to note that programmers as well as ordinary computer users often purchase packages since the cost of developing custom software is generally much higher than the cost of a package. The problem is locating appropriate packages. Thousands of packages are on the market, and the job of some computer analysts is to study product announcements and search through software manuals for packages for their organizations. Often packages need to be adapted to the special environment of the purchaser. Analysts and programmers will be assigned this responsibility. They will also be responsible for maintenance of the package. (Maintenance means keeping the program in satisfactory running condition.)

Packages exist for microcomputers, minis, and mainframes. Here is a very small sample of those available.

- *BEEF-UP.* Keeps track of weight and breeding of cattle. Helps breeders determine diet necessary to fatten cattle to desired weight.
- *CELLAR-MASTER.* Monitors the supply of up to 80,000 bottles of soft drinks, wine, and liquor.
- *FRIDAY!* A file management system designed for both 8- and 16-bit machines.
- *HURRICANE.* Tracks storms for meteorologists.
- *IMS.* A database management system for mainframes used to manage large and complex data bases.
- *MILLIONAIRE.* A game to teach students how to invest. Each player is given financial information and $10,000 to invest.
- *OFFIX.* Integrates filing with word processing.
- *SuperCalc.* A spreadsheet program used for financial and other tabular calculations.
- *TK Solver.* An equation-solving program.
- *WILL.* For will preparation without an attorney.

Booting up BEEFUP, a software package developed for controlling the weight of cattle. (St. Benedict's Farm)

analyst may be given the task of studying product announcements and searching through software manuals for packages that meet the organization's needs. Criteria for evaluating packages and a summary of the advantages and disadvantages of using packages appear in Figure 4.5. Supplement 4.7 gives brief descriptions of some of the many packages that exist for microcomputers, minis, and mainframes.

If a package needs modification after it is purchased, analysts and programmers will be assigned this responsibility. They will also be responsible for maintenance of the package. (Maintenance means keeping the program in satisfactory running condition.)

Part II of this book is devoted to the applications of computer software to a wide variety of fields, including business, government, education, and the arts. You will find more detail about the subject of applications programs in Chapters 8 through 14.

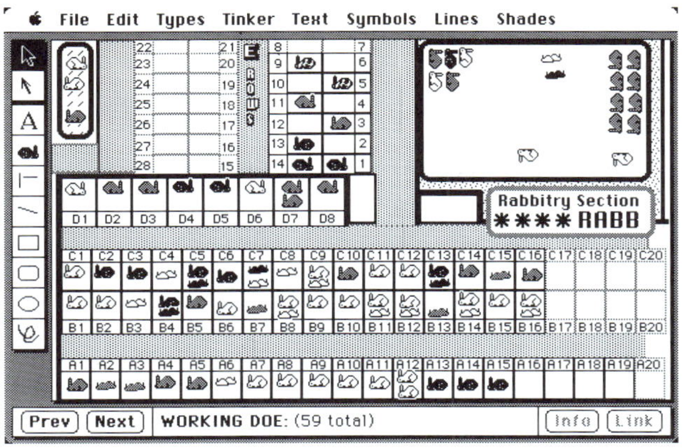

Figure 4.4 A display from a winning entry in a contest challenging the public to create new software for the Macintosh personal computer. This program aids rabbit breeders in increasing the productivity of their rabbit stock. (Telos Software)

SUMMING UP

While people speak and write in natural languages, computers process binary numbers represented as electronic signals. This means that both data and programs must be translated from natural languages into binary code before computer processing can take place.

The most elemental programming language is machine language. Although machine language is efficient in terms of computer runtime, the language is complex and difficult to learn. Languages closer to natural languages are easier to learn and faster to write in, but they are more costly to process and require more computer storage.

A large number of languages have been developed since computers were first introduced. Some require that the user be trained in programming. Others allow persons with no programming background to enter and retrieve data by following prompts that appear on the terminal screen. Language choice is limited to some extent by system hardware and the type of processing required. Factors like the required response time, who will be the user, and how often the program will have to be modified, have to be considered when a language is being selected. Supplement 4.8 is a comparison of generations of programming languages. A ranking of languages, from the authors' point of view, appears in Supplement 4.9.

Computer systems require system software to control the overall operations of the computer,

Advantages

Time is saved by the organization (compared to tailor-made system).

Time and worry over debugging reduced.

Cheaper because the development cost is distributed over many users.

Systems analysts, a scarce resource, are freed for other tasks.

Modification, if necessary, requires less commitment of resources than initial development.

Disadvantages or limitations

Programs for complex applications are often too generalized to be useful. When specific, they may need extensive modification to fit local needs.

Programs may require unavailable hardware.

Resistance to canned programs is common. Users prefer programs developed for their own special needs.

Purchase hampers the development of in-house program design and implementation capability.

Programs may not work as advertised.

Criteria for evaluating package

Quality and completeness of documentation.

Ease of installation.

Ease of use.

Vendor technical support.

Throughput.

Efficiency.

Amount of training required.

Figure 4.5 Software packages. Before deciding to purchase a software package, the package should be carefully evaluated. The advantages and disadvantages of packages in general should also be considered. A custom-developed program may better meet user needs. Many organizations formulate feasibility committees to study alternatives (for example, whether to purchase a package or develop in-house programs) when a new computer system is proposed.

Supplement 4.8 Comparison of Generations of Programming Languages

Generation*	Orientation/ characteristics	Examples	Uses
First			
Pre-1950s**	Hardware-dependent. Low-level.	Machine and assembly language.	For very frequent, highly efficient use, like compilers.
Second			
1950s	Hardware-independent. Higher-level language.	FORTRAN	Specially developed for scientific problems.
		BASIC	For scientific and business use.
		COBOL	For business use.
Third			
1970s–1980	Richer language.	PL/1	General-purpose.
	Greater options for user.	Ada	For computers that are embedded within military hardware.
	Oriented towards a wider range of problems.	Modula-2	Specialized applications.
Fourth			
1980s	Rule-based.	PROLOG (advanced version)	Appropriate for knowledge-based data systems (e.g., AI, CAD).
	Reduces complexity and economy of expression.	OPS5	For decision support systems.
	Nonprocedural.	FOCUS	
		RAMIS-II	
Fifth			
1980s–1990s	Does not mention the "how" (procedure of producing output) but the "what" of output.	Use.it	Used for automating system development, back-end processing, and to reduce time of developing and manufacturing new products.
	Defines the human/ computer interface.	TRANSFORM/IMS	

*Generations of programming languages do not correspond to the generations of computers.
**Dates represent early major developments.

Supplement 4.9 High and Low Level Language Spectrum

Language ranking is a subjective exercise. This spectrum represents the authors' view of language levels. Readers may disagree, particularly with the order in the high-level language category. In general, need and background will influence how one ranks a given language.

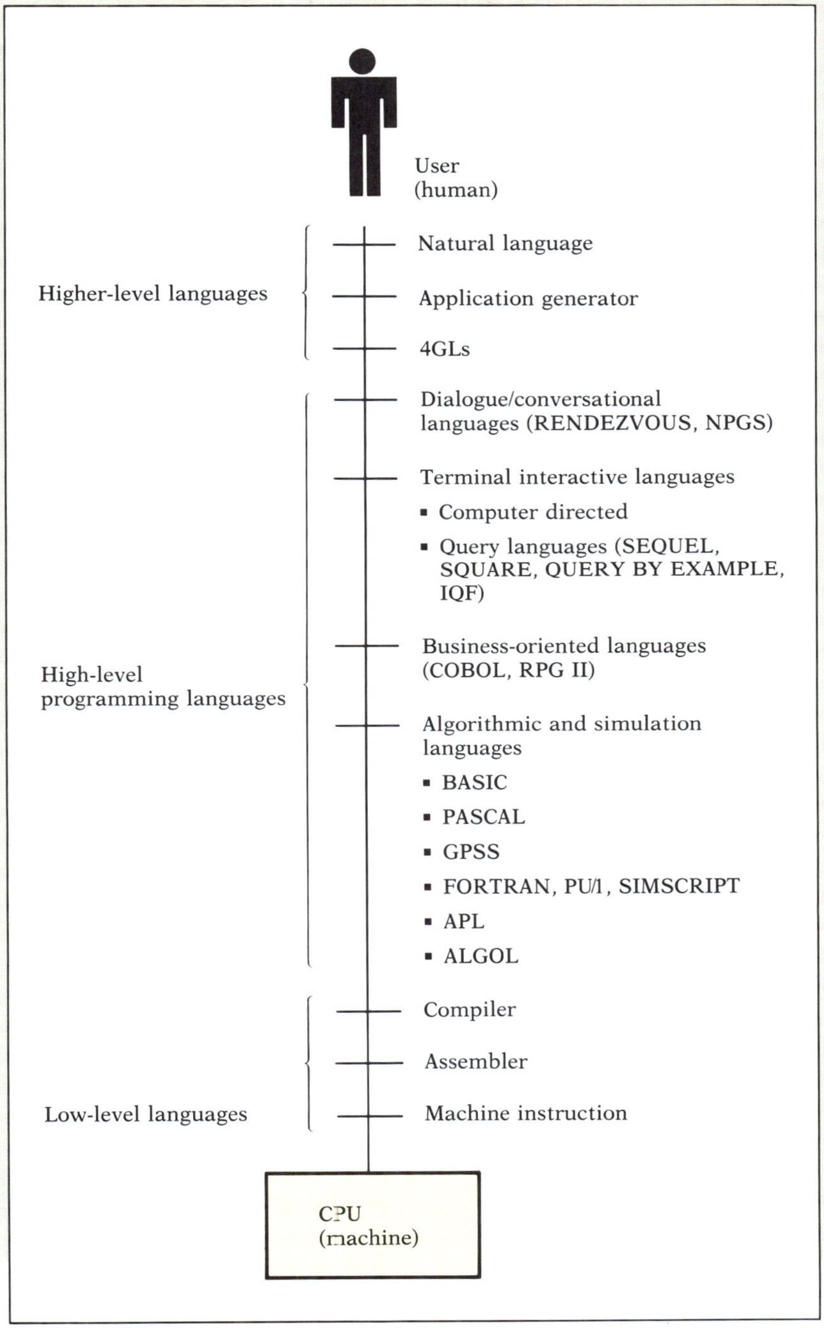

translation programs to convert programs into machine language, and applications software to enable the computer to produce useful work.

In coming years, software will become increasingly sophisticated but more user-friendly. That is, the computer will be able to do complex new tasks, yet the user will find that the equipment is easy to use and requires much less programming knowledge than is needed today. Software costs will rise, becoming a larger share of the total system cost (approaching 90 percent for large systems). More special-purpose packages will appear, and there will be more automation of the programming process. Future programming will be in languages close to English. Users will be able to enter input and generate output from a terminal in a conversational mode.

REVIEW QUESTIONS

1. What does a program do? Does every computer application require a computer program? Explain.
2. What is the difference between a natural language, such as English, and a formal programming language? Under what circumstances would it be desirable for programming languages to approach natural languages?
3. What are the advantages and disadvantages of:
   a. machine language?
   b. assembly language?
   c. high-level languages?
   d. fourth generation languages?
   e. natural language programs?
4. What is the difference between:
   a. an assembler and a compiler?
   b. a prompt and a menu?
   c. a compiler and an interpreter?
5. What are major categories of software?
6. Why are fourth generation languages considered an advancement over other programming languages?
7. What is an operating system? Why do you suppose that it is sometimes called the "underwear" system of hardware and software?
8. What is a software package? Why are packages purchased and where would you obtain one?
9. Would software packages be more appropriate for small or large organizations? Why? What are the limitations of software packages? What are their advantages?
10. What factors must be considered when selecting a programming language?
11. Why was using a computer more difficult before the advent of operating systems?

DISCUSSION QUESTIONS

1. Do you think that programming should be required for all administrators or business managers? Explain.
2. Comment on the following: "Computers are neutral and unbiased. They only do what they are instructed to do." Who, then, is responsible for a computer error?
3. Computers and information are neutral and amoral; it is the software that adds morality. Comment.
4. Why do we have so many programming languages? Why can't programming be standardized?
5. Should studying a programming language satisfy a university's foreign language requirement? If so, why? If not, why not?
6. Programming is essentially a human activity; it will never be automated. Comment.
7. Designing software is a creative human task; there is no limit to future software possibilities. Comment.
8. What is meant by "user-friendly" software? What features do you think user-friendly software should include?

EXERCISES

1. Do research on programming languages. Compare the advantages and disadvantages of the following:
   a. numerical and non-numerical languages
   b. high- and low-level languages
   c. BASIC and LISP
   d. Ada and C
2. Make a list of six different programs your computer center uses.
3. List the functions performed by an operating system. Find out this information by interviewing a systems programmer or reading an article on operating systems.
4. Interview a professional programmer and inquire why programs fail. Ask what can be done to avoid or prevent failure.
5. Interview a professional programmer. Make a list of the rewards and problems programmers experience in their jobs.
6. Design a short dialogue for a computer system that might appear on the screen to assist users in machine use. What are the friendly features?
7. Visit a computer software store. Select two similar packages and compare their features. Explain which you favor and why.
8. Compare the cost of buying a software package for a given application of your choice with the cost of writing a custom program for the same task. Other than price, what are the advantages and limitations of packaged software vs. custom software?

Selected Annotated Bibliography

Berard, Edward V. "Ada Steps Out," *Datamation*, vol. 29, no. 9 (September 1983), pp. 114–29. The author states that the characteristics that make Ada cost effective for military systems also make it attractive to the commercial software developer. What is lacking at present is the availability of validated, production-quality Ada compilers. This problem will be solved in time. Ada will affect more software professionals in the 1980s than COBOL did in the 1960s and 1970s.

Canning, Richard G., (ed.) "Query Systems for End Users," *EDP Analyzer*, vol. 20, no. 9 (September 1982), pp. 1–4. This article concentrates on software for human-machine interface. Menus, forms, command languages, free-form natural language systems, and multiquery systems are discussed. Criteria for evaluating end-user interface include comfort, helpfulness, efficiency, forgivingness, and ease in remembering procedures and codes.

Chapanis, A. "Computers and the Common Man," in R. A. Kasschau et al. (eds.) *Information Technology and Psychology: Prospects for the Future*. New York: Praeger Publishers, 1982, pp. 106–32. This article focuses on problems users have with software. The author believes that sensitivity to the needs of users and a willingness to develop computer software to meet those needs, rather than additional psychological research, will make computers a useful tool for everyone.

Martin, James. *Application Development Without Programmers*. Englewood Cliffs, N.J.: Prentice-Hall, 1982. The author does not predict or propose the elimination of programmers as the title suggests. Instead, he proposes approaches and tools to complement current application development methods. These include methods to help users develop their own applications and of purchasing software packages, consulting support for users, the development of 4GLs, systems prototyping, and the establishment of information centers. The author also discusses APL, NOMAD, MAPPER, DMS, and ADF.

McClennan, Stephen T. "The End of the Hardware Era," *Datamation*, vol. 30, no. 6 (May 1, 1984), pp. 122–34. McClennan is a professional journalist and Wall Street analyst. He argues that the future in computing lies in software and that the era of hardware is past.

PC World, vol. 1, no. 14 (Winter 1984/85). This is a special issue describing 1500 programs for the IBM PC and compatibles. This is just a sample of the number of packages available. One can purchase over 10,000 programs for Apple computers.

Sammet, Jean E. "An Overview of High-level Languages," in Marshall C. Yovits (ed.), *Advances in Computers*, vol. 20. New York: Academic Press, 1981, pp. 200–60. Jean Sammet also wrote a highly respected text in 1969 called *Programming Languages: History and Fundamentals*. This article discusses the relationship of languages to software technology and identifies programming trends.

Thiel, Carol T. "New Packages Spark Change," *Infosystems*, vol. 30, no. 3 (July 1983), pp. 44–46. This article is one of *Infosystems'* semiannual reviews of thirty-five categories of software packages. Database management systems, material requirements planning, teleprocessing, project management, decision support systems, spreadsheets, and functional applications, such as architecture, are among the topics discussed.

Wegner, Peter. "Programming Languages–the First 25 Years," *IEEE Transactions on Computers*, C-25, no. 12 (December 1976), pp. 1207–25. The author discusses thirty milestones in the history of programming. Thirteen milestones concern development. Evaluated are assemblers, FORTRAN, ALGOL 60, COBOL 61, ALGOL 68, SIMULA 67, and LISP. Ten milestones are programming concepts and theories, and the remaining seven concern software engineering technology. The article is descriptive with the technical portion separated so that it can be easily skipped. The author captures the sense of excitement and the enormous variety of activity that was characteristic of the first twenty-five years of programming.

Welty, Charles and Stample, David D. "Human Factors Comparison of a Procedural and Nonprocedural Query Language," *ACM Transactions on Database Systems*, vol. 6, no. 4 (December 1981), pp. 626–49. This article discusses two experiments testing the ability of subjects to write queries in two different query languages: SQL and TABLET. The experiment showed that subjects wrote difficult queries better using the more procedural language (SQL). A good bibliography of forty-three references is included.

Data—the Raw Material of Processing

Knowledge is of two kinds: we know a subject ourselves or we know where we can find information upon it.

SAMUEL JOHNSON

CHAPTER FIVE

Key Words

alphabetic characters	glance-check	numeric characters
code	information	output
common data base	input data	physical file
data	input documentation	physical organization
data bank	input manual	physical record
data base	key data element or key	record
database administrator (DBA)	linked files	symbols
database management system (DBMS)	logical organization	systems analyst
data element	machine-readable	transaction file
file	master file	value

Data, which consists not only of facts but also of observations and concepts, is a basic resource of computer processing systems. It can be compared to the raw material used in manufacturing—the raw material that becomes a finished product when processed. Processing by computer systems, however, consists of manipulation or interpretation by the CPU of **input data** (that is, data entered into the computer) as directed by software. The finished product, **output**, is **information**.

The quality of the information produced by computer processing is directly related to the quality of the input data. If the computer is given inaccurate input or if data is entered into the system incorrectly, the output produced by the system will be false. The popular saying that puts this truth in a nutshell is, "Garbage in, garbage out." It is for this reason that data must be collected, organized, and managed with care (see Figure 5.1).

This chapter opens with a description of how data is gathered, coded, and recorded on a medium that can be read by machine and then introduced into the computer. Collected data must also be organized logically and physically, so that it can be stored until needed for processing and so that it can be easily retrieved once processing begins. Both the physical and logical organization of data will be explained. The chapter closes with a discussion of how data organized in a structure called a **data base** is managed.

DATA COLLECTION

Data is usually represented as **alphabetic characters** (a through z), **numeric characters** (0 through 9), or characters that are **symbols** (such as $, %, ¢). For example, the number 24 is composed of numeric characters of data. It is a **value**: the fact or observation this value represents is called a **data element**. Also, 24 might represent "age of employee" or "pound weight of equipment." Sometimes the value of a data element is expressed in alphabetic characters. For example, HERNANDEZ may be the value of the data element "family name of employee."

Before data processing can begin, raw data must be input into the computer system. This means that a decision must be made about what data elements are essential to processing, and the values of these data elements must be collected. As in manufacturing, input needs depend on the out-

Figure 5.1 Printing out a letter. The computer saves an inestimable number of work hours by allowing the operator to perfect a document before printing it. (Hewlett Packard Company)

Table 5.1 Determining Input from Output

Output	Data required
Pay of John Smith, an employee paid by the hour.	Employee identification Wage rate Hours worked Tax rate: Federal State Health deduction rate Retirement deduction Social security deduction Other deductions
Value of Y where $Y = a + bx + cx^2$	a, b, c, and x

Processing begins with input and ends with output. But when determining an organization's data needs the sequence is reversed—output is studied first. From output, data that must be collected can be deduced.

put one expects to produce. By studying intended output, input needs can be derived.

Suppose, for example, that a university professor decides to program a computer to display the grades of students and to calculate the average, median, and range of exam scores. From this objective, the input can be deduced. The input must include (1) the array of scores (set or list) for each exam, and (2) a unique identification for each student (for example, name or social security number) associated with each score. In order to make the output meaningful, the course number for each array of scores should also be input as should the exam number (for example, first, second, or third midterm). Other examples of input determination from output appear in Table 5.1.

When a software package is used, data input needs are specified by the program. The user must enter data values for data elements requested by the program but does not have to go through the process of deciding what data is essential. When custom software is being prepared, a **systems analyst** is the professional who decides data needs. The analyst holds discussions with the user to learn what information the user expects the computer to generate. On the basis of these discussions, the analyst draws up output specifications. Once the output is formally stated, the analyst ascertains input specifications by a process of deduction.

Frequently, data required for computer processing is already in a data base belonging to the user and does not need to be collected again. If this is not the case, collection methods must be planned.

The use of forms is one way to collect data. For example, data on prospective employees, such as name, address, and phone number, can be collected on a job application form. Sometimes data values are collected from special labels, like the bar codes on grocery items (see Figure 5.2). Sometimes the required data is preprinted on documents, such as the routing codes that appear on the bottom of checks (see Figure 5.3). Logs can also be a source of data. A doctor may keep a log of patients treated, diagnoses, and drugs prescribed. An employee on an assembly line may log each completed task, time of completion, and equipment used. Data re-

0 12345 67890

Figure 5.2 The Universal Product Code (UPC). The UPC is a specialized code developed for retailing. The manufacturer's ID and the product ID are represented in each UPC symbol by a combination of black and white bars (the white being spacing) of different widths.

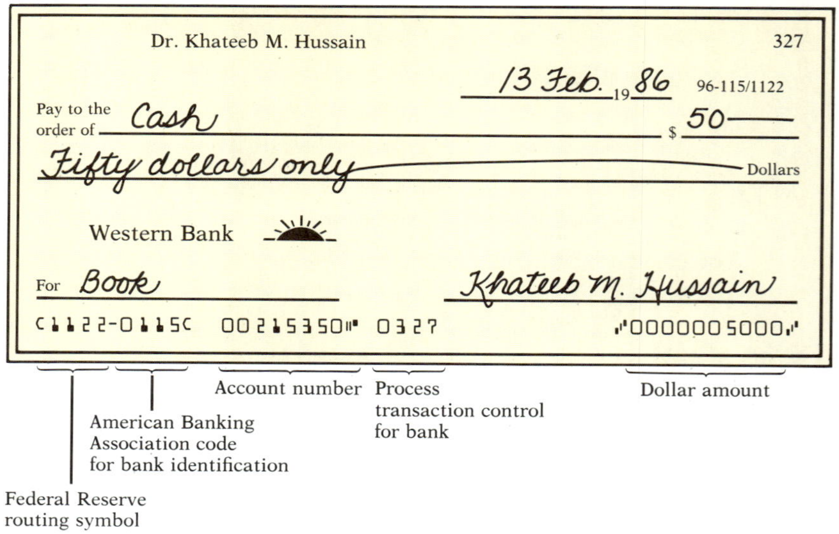

Figure 5.3 Codes on bank checks. Routing codes appear preprinted in magnetic ink in the lower left hand corner of checks. The dollar amount of the check is coded in the lower right-hand corner by bank clerks using special equipment after the check is cashed. This machine-readable data is then read by an input device called a *m*agnetic *i*nk *c*haracter *r*ecognition reader so that the data can be processed by computer.

corded in these logs may be subsequently used as data input.

Chapter 3 described the peripheral equipment that can be used to collect data, such as badge readers, terminals, optical scanners, and voice recognition equipment.

DATA PREPARATION

Collected data must be prepared for processing. Preparation depends on how the data will be input (for example, on cards, tape, or disk), the computing mode of the CPU, the equipment configuration of peripherals (offline or online), and output specifications. Coding, data conversion, and validation are the main activities in data preparation, as shown in Figure 5.4. Every computer system requires **input documentation**, which includes rules and procedures for data preparation. This documentation commonly appears in an **input manual**.

Coding

In computer processing, **codes** are frequently used to represent data. Numbers, letters, or symbols may serve as codes. One generally associates codes with secrecy, but they have other advantages as well. Codes shorten the length of data. Note the simplicity of this automobile code used by university police to identify cars registered to park on campus.

AEJ742 NM 82 W W S

- S: Classification of owner (S=student)
- W: Color (W=white)
- W: Type of car (W=station wagon)
- 82: Year of manufacture
- NM: State license issued
- AEJ742: License number

The use of such a code saves time when recording data on cards, tape, or disk so that the data can be read by machine and conveyed to the CPU. Codes also save time when data must be transmitted by telephone or some other communication channel. They facilitate classification of information and speed processing. In addition, less storage space is needed to store coded data.

Another advantage of coding is that codes avoid semantic vagueness found in much noncoded data. For example, many large organizations have two or more employees with the same name, such as Maria Hernandez. These employees may even have the same middle initial. This may cause errors during the processing of personnel data—for example, in payroll processing. If names are coded with each employee having a unique identification number, confusion in processing can be avoided.

The disadvantage of coding is that errors are frequently made in converting data to code. Computer programs can be written to check data against a list of acceptable codes so that nonexistent characters will be spotted. But a legitimate code used incorrectly will pass undetected.

The time saved by coding must be weighed against the possibility of introducing errors during coding and the time spent preparing and validating codes. Generally, the net savings in processing alone justifies coding.

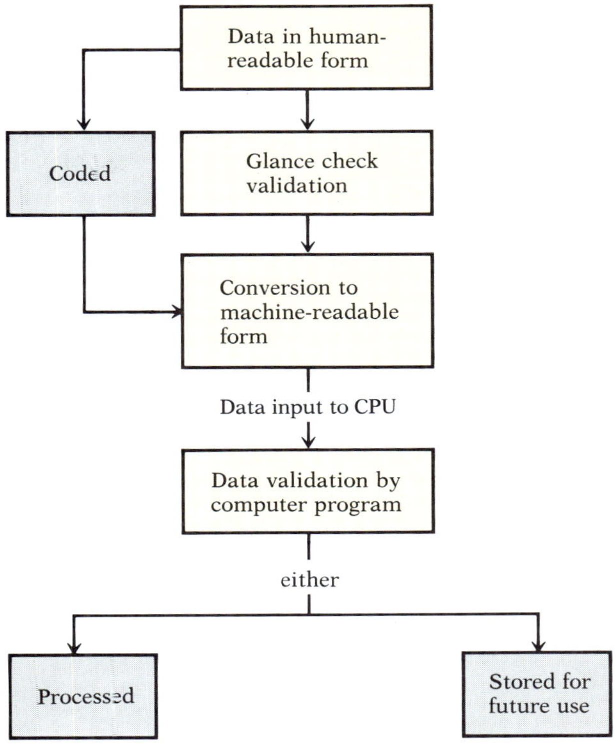

Figure 5.4 Data preparation.

Data Conversion and Input

Once data is collected, it must be made **machine-readable** (converted into a form that the computer can recognize and interpret) and input into the CPU. This is done by peripheral input equipment described in Chapter 3. For example, key-to-tape equipment converts data to magnetized spots on magnetic tape. A tape drive enters data stored on the magnetic tape into the CPU. Some input peripherals convert and input data in one step. This occurs when data is keyed on a terminal (see Figures 5.5 and 5.6).

Data Validation

Coded or uncoded data that is ready for input should be **glance-checked**. Errors like incomplete data (for example, blanks on forms) can often be spotted by alert clerks.

Data can also be validated by computer programs. For example, a program can be written to verify whether data has a prescribed length, such as nine digits for a social security number. If characters are missing, an error message will appear. A program might also check the format of input against input rules. One could check for numbers in names, or alphabetic characters in dollar amounts, for example. Sometimes a special check digit is added to a long string of digits at the time of data entry. The computer is then programmed to recalculate the digit during processing to ensure that no digits in the string have been transposed during data entry. An example of a check digit and how it is calculated is shown in Supplement 5.1. Bank identification numbers and account numbers generally include a check digit.

It is usually the people who use output who are responsible for deciding what data requires validation and what validation rules to apply. These decisions are important because failure to detect input errors results in faulty output. On the other

Figure 5.5 An input device that requires no keying. This electronic tablet recognizes a wide array of hand-inscribed data—script, checkmarks, or signatures—and is one of many available devices permitting alternative forms of data entry. (Inforite Corporation)

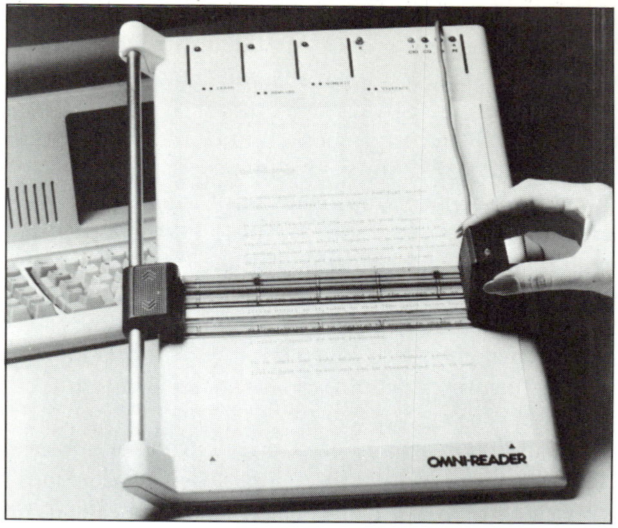

Figure 5.6 An optical reader. The reader scans typed copy and transfers the data directly into the computer with no keying required. (Oberon International)

hand, validation checks add to processing costs, so that it is best to keep such checks to a minimum.

Invalid data is usually the result of:

- Incorrect or outdated forms for data collection.
- Wrong data collected.
- Coding errors.
- Errors in data entry (the largest single cause of data error; for example, digit transposition when data is typed on a terminal).
- Operator errors during input (for example, mounting wrong tape).
- Errors in data handling (for example, lost data or incorrect sequencing).

ORGANIZATION OF DATA

Once data is collected for a data base (also called a **data bank**), it must be organized so it can be easily stored and retrieved. There are two types of data organization: logical and physical.

Logical Organization

Logical organization of data occurs at many levels. Data elements can be grouped into a logical association to form a **record** of data. For example, a customer record in a pharmacy will include patient name, address, telephone number, drugs purchased, dates that prescriptions were filled, refill limitations, and the names of prescribing physicians.

Related records are in turn grouped into a **file**. At the pharmacy in our example, a collection of all customer records would constitute a customer file. Figure 5.7 shows the relationship of student records to a student file at a university. An admission file, a course file, a space file, and an alumni file are other examples of university files.

Working files used for daily operations are called **transaction files**. A **master file** of all of an organization's transaction files is generally kept for

Supplement 5.1 International Standard Book Number (ISBN)

The publishing industry has adopted a 10 digit code to assist in order processing and inventory control. This code has four subfields consisting of a group identifier (national, geographic, or other grouping of publishers), publisher's prefix, title identifier, and check digit. A sample book in this code is 0-256-02990-3.

The check digit is used as a method of checking the accuracy of data input during book processing—for example, when a title is ordered by ISBN number. The check digit is based on a calculation using the other digits in the ISBN string. The computer recalculates this check digit every time the data is used in processing. If the computer-calculated check digit does not match the check digit that is in the input, an error message is printed.

There are many methods of calculating a check digit. Here is an example of Modulus 11, the system used in book codes.

0 - 256 - 02990 - 3

- 3: Check digit
- 02990: Title identifier *(Information Resource Management*, 1984, by Donna Hussain and K. M. Hussain)
- 256: Publisher identifier (Richard D. Irwin, Inc.)
- 0: National and geographic identifier (U.S.A.)

ISBN number	0	2	5	6	0	2	9	9	0
ISBN weights	10	9	8	7	6	5	4	3	2
Weighted values	0	18	40	42	0	10	36	27	0

(ISBN digits multiplied by ISBN weight)

Weighted total: 0 + 18 + 40 + 42 + 0 + 10 + 36 + 27 + 0 = 173

Smallest number to be added to total to make it divisible by 11 = 3

Check digit = 3

If the check digit had been calculated as 10, an X would have been used instead of the number, since only one character is assigned to the check digit.

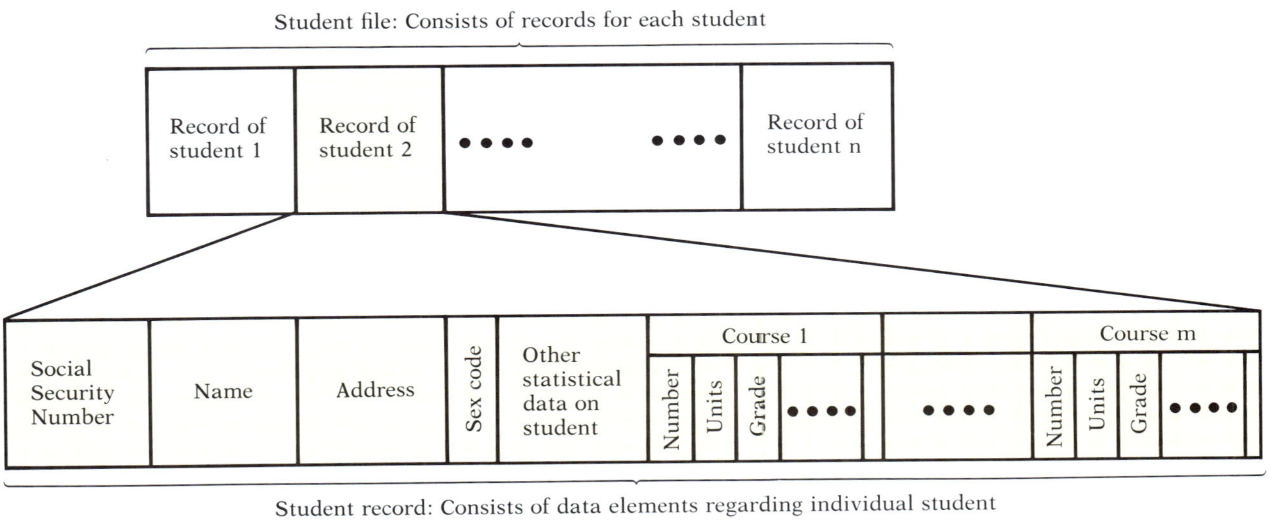

Figure 5.7 Relationship of student records to a student file. A file is composed of a collection of records. Data base design is planning what data elements to include in each record (logical organization), and how and where collected data will be stored (physical organization).

Supplement 5.2 Organization of Data: From Data Base to Bit

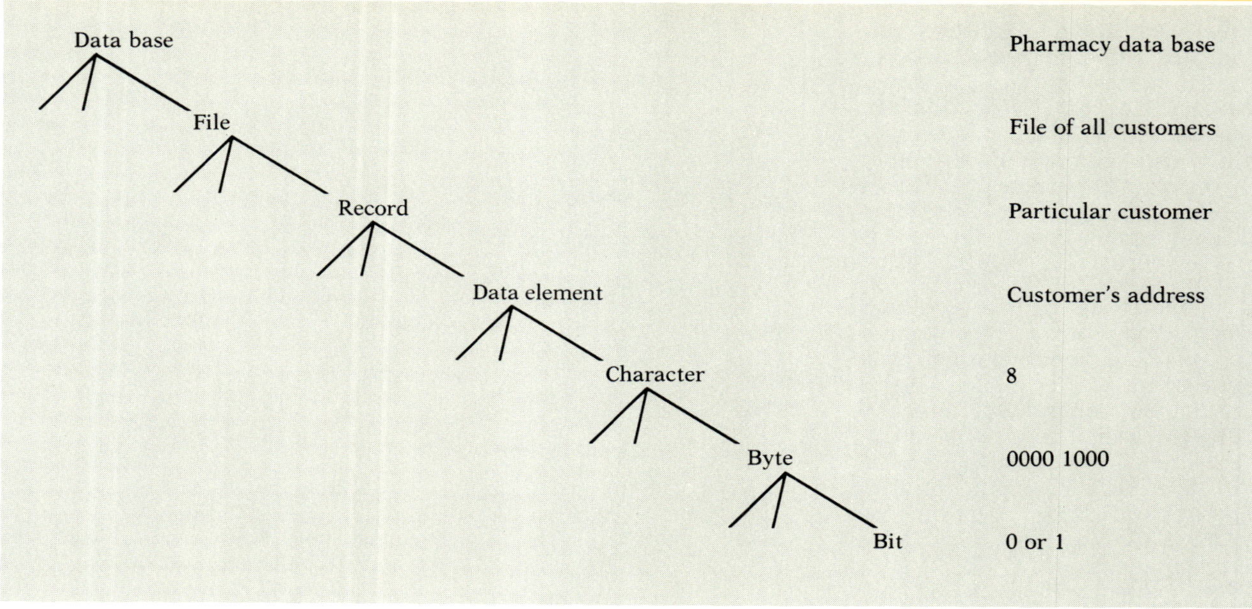

management and reporting purposes. Data on the master will be periodically updated from the transaction files. Some files, like address and code lists, are kept for reference purposes. Certain files are rarely accessed since they are kept for historical or legal reasons; criminal dossiers are an example of infrequently accessed files. Figure 5.8 illustrates the types of files commonly found in large organizations.

A data base usually has **linked files**. When files are linked, data stored in two or more files can be used during the processing of a single report. Let us imagine that a university is preparing a report that will compare the ACT (American College Test) scores of students with their grades at the university. Data for this report can be drawn from both the admission file (ACT score) and student file (grades) when these two files are linked. Linkage is possible when both files have one data element in common, called a **key** or **key data element**. Figure 5.9 illustrates the concept of linkage.

The advantage of linked files is that data, once entered and stored in a file, can be correlated with data located in other files. Without linkage, the storage of redundant data in the files of an organization may be necessary. For example, to produce the report mentioned in the preceding paragraph without file linkage would require the collection, coding, input, and validation of ACT data for the student file even though such data was already located in the admission file. Such redundancy can be costly.

Another advantage of linked files is that they create a pool of data—data that can be shared by a number of users for a number of purposes. The term **common data base** is used to describe data in this pool. An organization may have one or more common data bases. It may also have data that is excluded from a common data base because of its specialized nature. Indexes are used to keep track of the location of data elements in data bases.

Not all persons favor pooled data. In some organizations, individuals consider data their personal property and want to maintain exclusive use

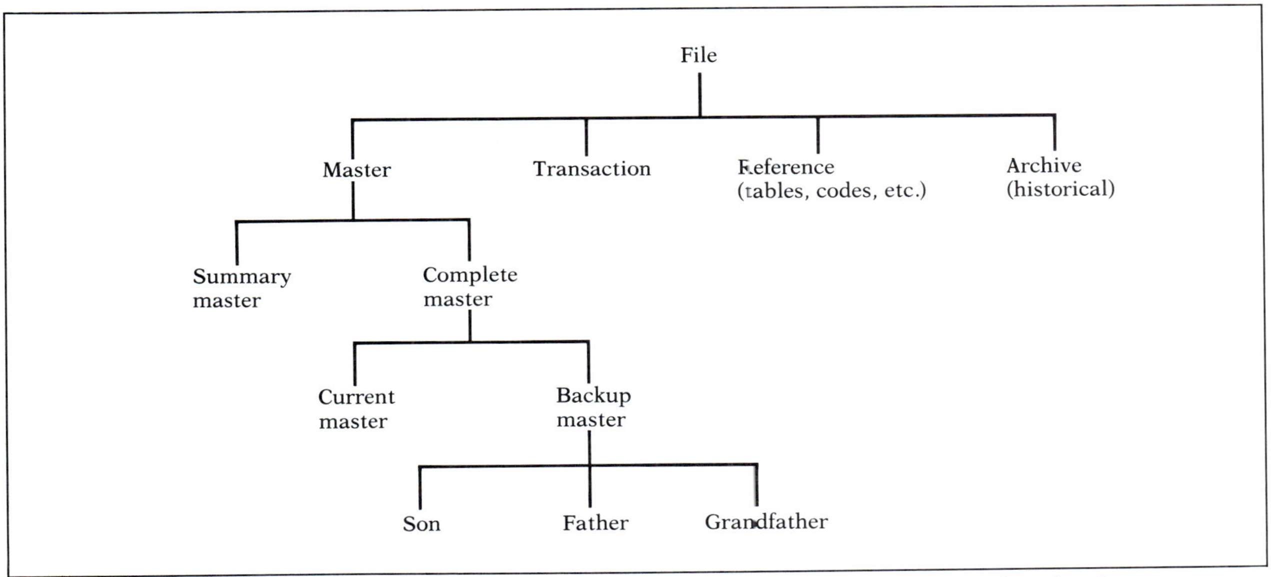

Figure 5.8 Types of files. An information system consists of many types of files as illustrated in this figure. Superceded master files are commonly retained as backup. Most organizations keep three levels of backup—the most recent superceded master and the two preceding masters. These three generations of backup are commonly called "son," "father," and "grandfather" files.

and control over that data. They do not want others to have access to their data files. They may also resent having to adopt standard procedures for data collection and data preparation. Standards are necessary when data is shared.

The logical organization of data into records and files is important because such organization determines the speed, cost, and efficiency of data retrieval and processing.

Physical Organization

Collected data must be stored until it is ready to be processed. Although forms, logs, and other types of source documents could be stored, data is usually converted to machine-readable form before storage. The **physical organization** of data determines what storage medium is used and where data is stored on that medium. Common storage media are cards, magnetic tape, and disks.

Long logical records of data may require many **physical records** (many tapes or disks). A grouping of physical records is called a **physical file**. Chapter 3 described storage media and storage peripherals for physical files.

DATA ADMINISTRATION

In organizations with large amounts of data, a computer specialist, called a **database administrator (DBA)**, is generally responsible for data base design, data quality, and controlled access to data files. DBA duties include the logical and physical organization of data described in the preceding sections. Backup and recovery of data in the event of system breakdown are also DBA concerns. So is data protection from theft or unauthorized disclosure. After all, data is a very valuable resource. Think of the worth of the formula for Coca Cola, designs for the next Ford car fleet, college entrance test questions, or information on the location of cruise missiles. Similar data of value can be found in most data bases. It's not surprising, therefore, that the security and privacy of data is a major DBA responsibility. (Security is the subject of

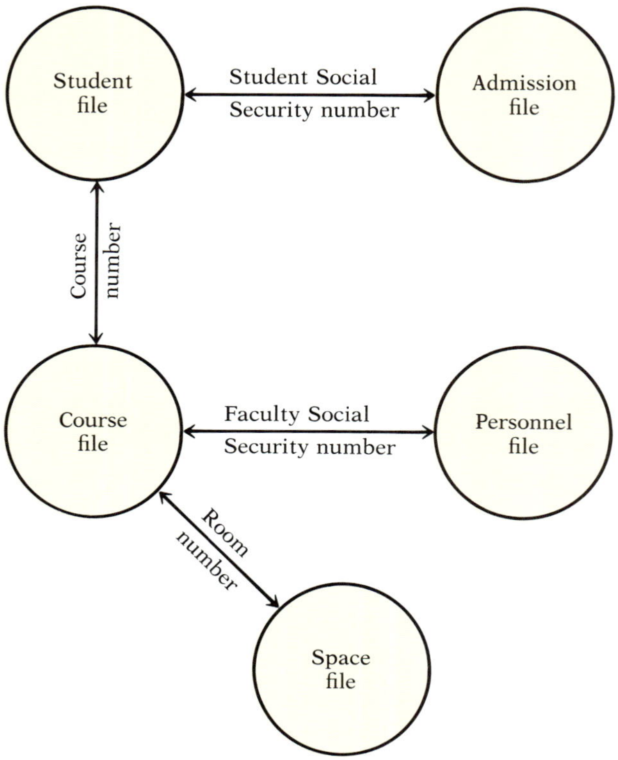

Figure 5.9 File linkage. Files are connected by linking data elements. In this example, data in the Admission File can be correlated with data in the Student File by using a student's social security number as a linking data element. Room Number is the linking data element between the Course File and Space File. Indexes keep track of the exact location of each data element in storage.

Chapter 6; the issue of privacy is explored in Chapter 15.)

Computer programs can assist in data base administration. Many such programs are part of the operating system of a computer. For example, "housekeeping programs" control utility routines, such as editing, dumping, and logging of files. In addition, sophisticated programs, called **database management systems (DBMS)** can be purchased to help with the organization and control of complex data bases. Not all computer systems require a DBMS, but some experts have predicted that by the late 1980s, 75 percent of data processing departments will be DBMS users.

SUMMING UP

Data is the raw material that becomes information when processed. Since the quality of that information is directly related to the quality of the data itself, the management of data is of importance in computer processing.

Data must be collected and prepared for processing (coded, validated, and converted into machine-readable form). It must also be organized in a logical manner to ensure processing efficiency. Related data elements are consolidated into records, related records are joined to form a file, and files are joined to form a data base. Linked data files constitute a common data base. Sharing data in a common data base reduces redundancy in data collection, and consequently minimizes time and effort in data preparation. Less storage space is also required.

Data must also be organized for storage on a physical medium until it is needed for processing. The storage medium must be selected, the peripheral storage device chosen, and the means of access to the stored data planned. This is called the physical organization of data.

Large organizations often hire a computer specialist, called a data base administrator, to manage their data. As data bases have grown in complexity, the need for sophisticated software to assist in the management of data has arisen. Data base management systems (DBMSs) help fulfill this need. Recently, the availability of DBMS programs for inexpensive minicomputers has made DBMSs feasible for small organizations. The main constraint is that many groups lack the organizational and technical expertise needed to implement such systems.

REVIEW QUESTIONS

1. What is data?
2. What is a data base?
3. Explain how the data needs of an organization are determined.

Supplement 5.3 Database Management System for Virginia-Wesleyan College

A number of administrative departments at Virginia-Wesleyan College track, classify, and schedule students. The same basic information is processed by all of these departments.

Recently a database management system was installed at VWC so that data bases could be shared by departments with the same data needs. Shared data avoids duplication of effort in data collection, validation, storage, and processing. The departments draw on and update information from online data files to keep track of student records, maintain the college catalog, produce class lists and grade reports, maintain alumni files, and for many other uses.

Students and faculty in the computer room. A DBMS contains information on students that all departments share and update as necessary. (Virginia-Wesleyan College)

Supplement 5.4 Data Base Helps Protect Whooping Cranes

To save the whooping crane from extinction, a Whooper data base is being designed consisting of 160 observation records by field biologists.

One of the uses of the data base will be to provide power companies with information on whether new power lines will pose a hazard to whooping cranes. (Power lines are the main threat to whooper survival once chicks are old enough to fly.) Formerly, a manual search through stacks of handwritten data was necessary to determine whether a proposed construction would endanger the birds. Using Infocen, a database management system, this information can now be quickly determined from the data base.

Another use of the base will be species management. Biologists will be able to follow the migratory routes of the cranes by compiling data about sightings in the base. They will also be able to monitor an individual bird's activities.

The DBMS allows a display of information in a variety of formats. For example, a list of information on one specific bird or all available data on all birds sighted in a specific state or refuge, can be called to the screen. Infocen can also provide requested statistical information, such as the sum, mean, standard deviation, and range of various age groups of cranes in specified locations.

4. Give three examples of data collection techniques.
5. What is the purpose of an input manual?
6. Why is data often coded? What are disadvantages of using codes? What costs are involved?
7. What is data validation? At what point in processing should validation take place? What resources are necessary to perform data validation?
8. What is the difference between the logical and physical organization of data?
9. What is the difference between a transaction and a master file?
10. What are the advantages of linked files?
11. Why isn't all data placed in a common data base?
12. Why does access to an organization's data base(s) need to be controlled?
13. What is the role of a database administrator?
14. What is a DBMS?

DISCUSSION QUESTIONS

1. What are some applications of bar codes in industries other than the retail industry?
2. Identify situations where optical scanning is a useful technique for data collection.
3. Comment on the following: Coding methods should be standardized within an organization, otherwise there will be confusion and inefficiency. Discuss ways in which coding methods can be standardized.
4. What would be the advantages of national and international standards in coding and data preparation? What purpose would such standards serve? Give examples. How could such standards be formulated?
5. Why is the privacy of data important? Is there a difference between data privacy and data security?
6. How can access to a common data base be controlled? Discuss problems of access control.
7. Under what conditions is a DBMS advisable?
8. Discuss problems of data management at your university or place of work.
9. What training and skills should a database administrator have?
10. Give examples from recent news stories of computer errors caused by the input of invalid data.

EXERCISES

1. Suppose that your instructor agreed to provide a computer report at the end of every class exam with statistics on student performance in the exam. For such a report, specify:
   a. the input needed
   b. how to collect the necessary data for the report
   c. how to validate the data input
   d. the physical media to be used for data storage
   e. the logical organization of the data base
   f. the key data element to link the data base with university student records
   g. how to define each data element in the data base
2. Find the ISBN number for this text. Decode it. The identifier for the country of publication is the first digit, the publisher identifier is the next three digits, and the title identifier is the next five digits. Compare this ISBN with the ISBN of another book. Which digits are the same? Which different? Why?
3. The last digit of the ISBN is a check digit. Find out the algorithm used for this book. Try the algorithm on another book by this publisher. Does it work?

4. Compare the UPC on a can of Campbell's cream of chicken soup with the code from some other product by Campbell. What parts of the codes are identical. Why? Which parts differ? Why?

5. List the transactions that you make that result in a computer record in your name. (Credit accounts at the university, at city hall, at a bank, and so forth.)

6. Construct codes for the following sets of data:

   a. an inventory of your property
   b. recipe collection for quick access to favorite meals
   c. records of financial transactions
   d. correspondence records

7. Get a copy of a computer record in your name. What information is included? How was the data collected? Is the data accurate? Does collection of this data violate your privacy? How would you go about correcting inaccurate entries?

8. Can the following errors be caught by validation? State the validation rule in each case.

   a. $93A2.4
   b. Dr. Smi4th
   c. $3 2.64
   d. WAGE $1686 per hour
   e. account number incorrect
   f. age incorrect by one year
   g. age incorrect by 100 years

Selected Annotated Bibliography

Adam, Robert G. "The Changing Fabric of Data Base Technology," *ICF Software Business Review*, vol. 12, no. 2 (February–March 1983), pp. 38–45. The author suggests that a DBMS affects the design of information systems, the selection of computers, the organization of data structures, the location of data, and the use of automated information. According to the author, data element dictionaries (not the DBMS) provide the "glue" that holds together the information resources of an organization.

Chorafas, Dimitris. *Databases for Networks and Minicomputers*. N.Y.: Petrocelli Books, 1982. This book has excellent coverage of the design, integration, and management of data bases. It is not as specialized as the title implies, and it includes sections on the role of the DBA.

Holland, Robert H. "The Executive Guide to Data Base Management Systems," *ICP Software Business Review*, vol. 2, no. 2 (February–March 1983), pp. 46–54. The author suggests that DBMS technology harnessed and integrated with other electronic technologies will produce 100-fold jumps in productivity in the next decade. A checklist of what to do to achieve such a productivity jump is included.

King, Judy M. *Evaluating Data Base Management Systems*. N.Y.: Van Nostrand Reinhold, 1981. This book describes DBMSs from the viewpoint of applications for an organization. The emphasis is on determining when to use a DBMS, how to justify costs, and how to implement them. The book is valuable, although it shows a bias toward IBM.

Kohn, B. *Secret Codes and Ciphers*. Englewood Cliffs, N.J.: Prentice-Hall, 1968. This is a small, delightful book with large print, many diagrams, and amusing illustrations.

Kroenke, David. *Database Processing*. Chicago: Science Research Associates, Inc., 1983. This book concerns data base fundamentals, their design, and implementation. Relational and CODASYL data models are discussed. A useful description of a DBA is also included. Appendixes discuss Data Language/I, TOTAL/IMAGE, and MicroRIM.

Martin, James. *An End-User's Guide to Data Bases*. Englewood Cliffs, N.J.: Prentice-Hall, 1981. Any data base installation that does not model its data in a logical form before doing the physical design is throwing money down the drain, according to Martin. Advice on how this modeling should be done is given in this book. Excellent chapters on ownership of data and considerations that affect machine performance are also included.

Pont, John W. "Collecting and Using Shop-Floor Data," *Infosystems*, vol. 32, no. 8 (August 1985), pp. 58–62. A good discussion of data collected on the floor of manufacturing plants to provide management with accurate and timely information necessary for the control of the production process.

Schultz, Gaymond. "An Intelligent Workstation Approach to Office Automation," *Mini-Micro Systems*, vol. 26, no. 6 (May 1983), pp. 193–204. This article is a technical discussion of one workstation used for data preparation.

Spiegler, Israel. "MIS and DBMS: Where Does One End and the Other Start," *Journal of Systems Management*, vol. 34, no. 6 (June 1983), pp. 34–42. The author classifies the purposes of information systems in four ways: data bank, prediction, decision making, and decision taking. He then examines how these purposes affect the data base, a DBMS, decision support systems, and management. Helpful diagrams are included.

Szewczak, E. J. "Two Approaches to Strategic Database Design," *Data Base*, vol. 14, no. 2 (Winter 1983), pp. 19–23. This article offers a descriptive and prescriptive approach to data base design. The underlying assumptions and tradeoffs in each approach are discussed.

Errors, Crimes, Breakdowns, and Calamities

Mistakes made while you wait.

SIGN ON COMPUTER CENTER WALL

CHAPTER SIX

Key Words

access directory	**hardware monitors**	**policy**
audits	**housing**	**protocols**
criminal intrusion	**law**	**separation of responsibility**
database management systems	**logs**	**software monitors**
data encryption	**packets**	**standards**
documentation	**password**	**testing and evaluation**
environmental conditions	**personnel policies**	**training**
handshake	**physical access controls**	**user feedback**

Speed and accuracy of electronic processing are two of the major selling features of computers. Computer circuits can perform hundreds of thousands of operations every second for days at a time without error, a record no human can match. But should an undetected error occur, that error can be compounded at an alarming rate because of the speed of the computer and the repetitious nature of its operations. As a result, even minor errors can have serious consequences.

To ensure the accuracy of computers, many different types of controls are needed. For example, monitors are usually installed to signal operators when equipment malfunctions. Programs are written to scrutinize data for errors that might lead to incorrect output. Additional common control measures will be outlined in this chapter.

In spite of controls, computer errors do occur. In one instance, a program that calculated savings account interest on thirty-one-day months cost a bank $300,000 before the mistake was detected. When Korean Air Lines Flight 007 was shot down in 1983 for intruding on Soviet air space and all 269 passengers were killed, the plane may have been off course because a crew member punched the numbers 139 instead of 149 into the plane's navigational system.

Processing errors are in fact seldom the fault of circuitry. For the most part mistakes are implicit in the data or result from human failures such as unsound programming logic, careless machine operation, or incorrect data input. Environmental factors may also cause errors to occur. Power surges, power failures, static electricity, or extremes of temperature and humidity can all affect computer performance. Although errors are usually unintentional, criminal activity that sometimes takes place can result in data distortion or the theft of processed information.

This chapter will discuss the controls through which computer systems can be protected from inadvertent errors, machine malfunction, and criminal intrusion. Measures to safeguard computing resources from natural disasters are also considered.

UNINTENTIONAL HUMAN ERRORS

Every computer run involves a large number of individuals. Analysts plan information systems and design processing procedures. Programmers write operating instructions. Clerks gather and input data. Operators load the computer and monitor processing. Data base administrators, security officers, supervisors, schedulers, librarians, technicians, and training coordinators serve as support personnel. Computer error or damage to computing resources can occur when any one of these individuals fails to act, acts improperly, or delays a

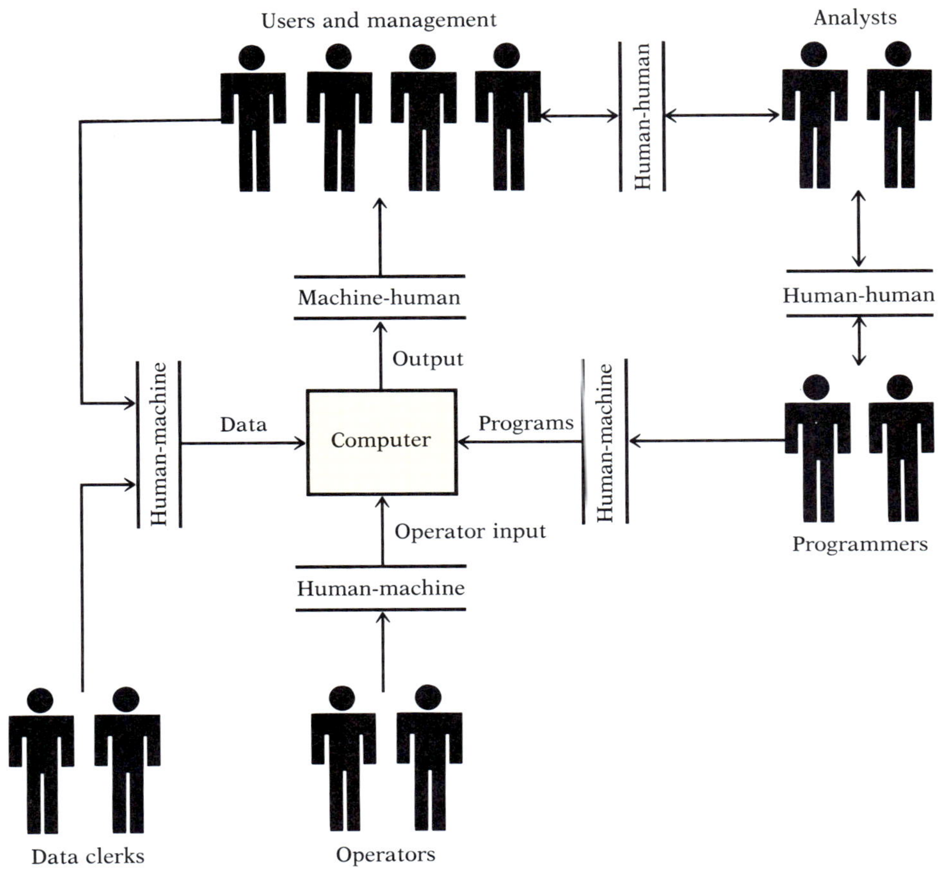

Figure 6.1 *Computer-human interaction.* Humans plan, design, and implement hardware and software. They are responsible for data input and interpreting output. Throughout processing, humans interact with the computer, making it vulnerable to human-induced error. Computer information systems can best be described as "human-machine information systems."

proper response. Figure 6.1 helps illustrate the importance of the human role in computer systems by showing that input/output, programming, and operations each involve human-machine interaction.

Control measures need to be initiated so that human mistakes are minimized, and those that do occur are caught and corrected. Managers and users must first decide which stages of processing need controls; that is, they must decide where mistakes are most common. They must then specify control standards; in other words, they must define what constitutes an error. Finally, the most appropriate procedures to identify and rectify blunders must be designed. The problem is to keep control costs low and yet minimize the risk of output error, of loss of data, or of damage to equipment.

Where Controls are Needed

Figure 6.2 illustrates where quality controls are commonly installed in computer systems to guard against unintentional human error. In this section, we will examine the purpose of controls at each location. In addition, we will describe the kinds of errors that can occur at each location when controls are lacking.

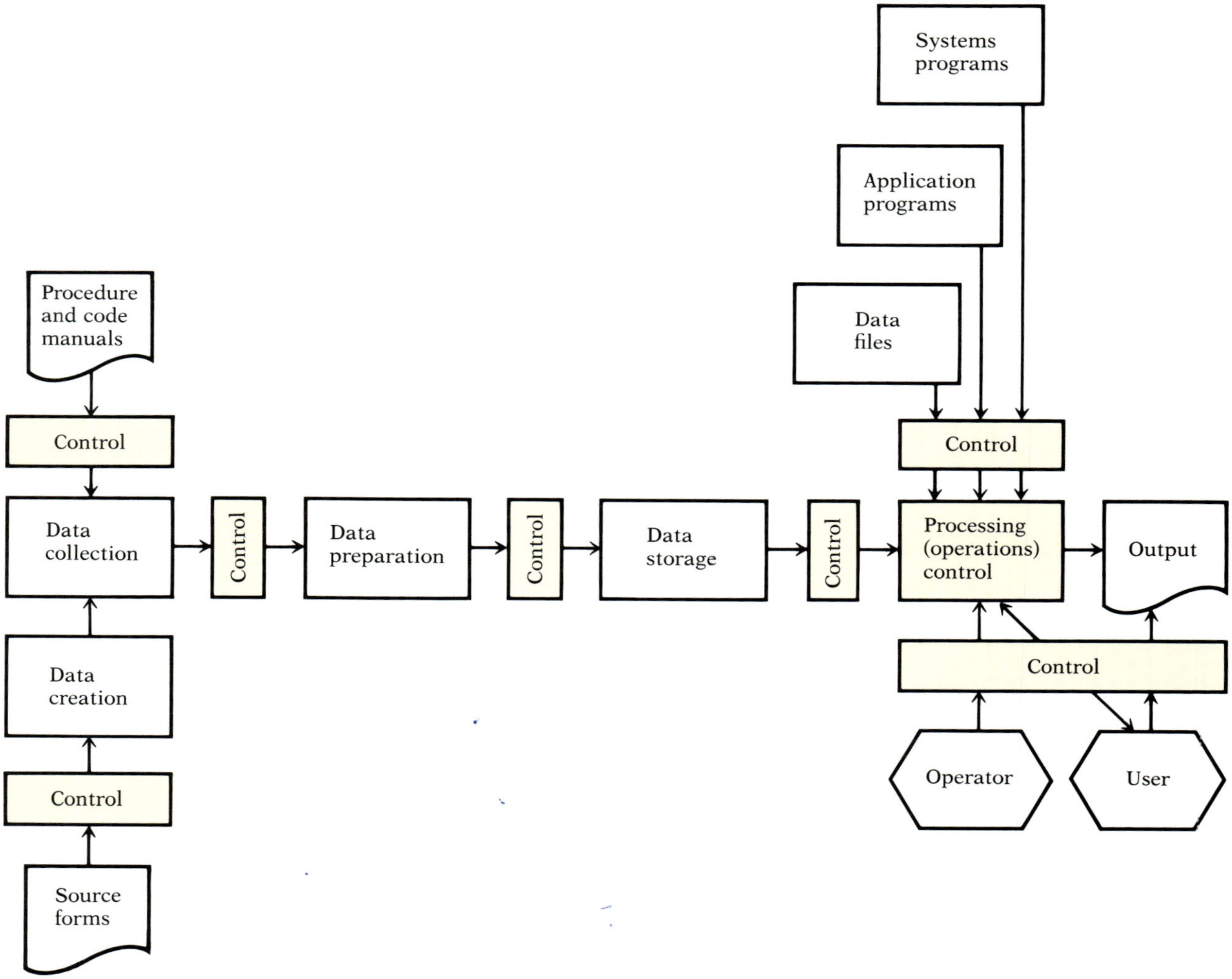

Figure 6.2 *The placement of quality controls.* This figure shows where control measures should be placed for error-free processing. It is up to users and managers to specify where controls are needed, to set control standards, and to allocate resources (monetary and personnel) for the implementation of controls. Usually, design of controls is the responsibility of computer personnel.

1. *Preparation of procedure and code manuals.* Controls are needed to ensure that user manuals are correct, complete, and unambiguous. Procedures must be designed for storing manuals so that they are available when needed, but only to authorized personnel. The code manual should contain needed codes but be free of redundant coding schemes.

Sample human error: An operator damaged a disk by mounting it incorrectly on new equipment. In this case, the operator had consulted the Operator's Manual, but it did not include directions for the new hardware. Lack of updated manuals was one cause of the damage. The operator was also at fault for attempting to mount the tape without first locating the needed documentation.

2. *Design of forms for data collection.*
The format of forms and directions for filling out forms should be monitored. For example, adequate space should be allowed for writing information, instructions should be easy to understand, and the sequence of questions should not invite misinterpretation. In addition, information already in the data base should not be requested unless changes in data element values are expected.

Sample error: A job application form requests name, address, birthdate, father's name, and date of high school graduation. Because of the order of the questions, a candidate entered the date his father completed high school instead of his own graduation date.

3. *Data collection and data input.*
Data should be verified for accuracy, completeness, consistency, reasonableness, and sequence. A check should also be made to see that values fall within a prescribed range.

Sample error: A misplaced decimal in an employee's rate of pay can result in a paycheck being issued for $146,987.00 instead of $1,469.87.

4. *Data preparation.*
Controls are needed to ensure that conversion of data to machine-readable form is error-free.

Sample error: In one firm, the code for equipment costing $20,000 was erroneously used to code the price of 50 manuals accompanying that equipment. This resulted in an inflated inventory value of one million dollars.

5. *File storage.*
Fireproof rooms with controlled humidity and dust levels should be designated for storage. Provisions should be made to clean tapes and disks. Access to files should be controlled. Regulations that govern file storage should identify who is responsible for files.

Sample error: An employee who was moving files to storage wedged a vault open but forgot to remove the wedge after the move was completed. Though the vault was fireproof, a fire swept through the open door and destroyed hundreds of tapes.

6. *Programming.*
Supervision of programming is needed to prevent the wrong algorithm, out-of-sequence instructions, poor documentation, or logic mistakes that can lead to faulty output.

Sample error: A hyphen omitted from a programming card caused a rocket being tested to head for Rio. It had to be destroyed in mid-flight at a loss of $18,500,000.

7. *Operations.*
Managers need to oversee operator training, daily processing, and equipment maintenance. Measures should be adopted to limit access to equipment to authorized personnel only.

Sample error: The running of an accounts payable program using an outdated price list cost one organization $100,000.

8. *Output.*
Although controls at earlier stages of processing should result in error-free output, mistakes that slip by can often be caught by output validation programs and sight checks by output clerks. Control procedures are needed to make sure that output is delivered on time to authorized users only. Online systems are vulnerable to loss or distortion of data during teleprocessing.

Sample error: A university, which generates semester grade reports by computer, mailed one student 14,000 copies of his grades. An untested program was responsible for this duplication, but an alert operator should have caught the mistake. Likewise, output clerks and persons responsible for the mailing should have noted the error and stopped the mailing.

Solutions To Control Accidental Errors

All organizations with computer systems take measures to protect their output from inadvertent human error. But since users have different goals, priorities, and financial resources, controls vary widely from one organization to another. The following list includes common measures to control human mistakes.

1. *Standards.*
   Standards define acceptable quality levels. Without quality guidelines, employees may not realize that their work is unsatisfactory.

2. *Policies.*
   Organizations should have **policies** that state do's and don'ts. For example, a policy forbidding duplication or copying of manuals will control the number of manuals in circulation. An exact count is important to ensure that all are collected and revised when updating takes place.

3. *Documentation.*
   Documentation is the recording of information. Procedures should be adopted for creating, collecting, organizing, storing, citing, and disseminating all documentation having to do with the computer system so that employees have the information they need to perform their assigned duties.

4. *Testing and evaluation.*
   Manuals and forms can be tested by sample user groups for clarity of directions and ease of use. Procedures should also go through **testing and evaluation** to ensure their efficiency and effectiveness before they are adopted. Computer software can be written to validate input data and output. Test data should check the algorithms and programming instructions of new software.

   Employees should be motivated to double-check their own output, and supervisors should oversee all work. Regularly scheduled performance evaluation should help identify weaknesses in the system before errors become chronic.

5. *Monitors.*
   Hardware monitors (equipment with sensors) and **software monitors** (programs that are part of the operating system) can be installed to oversee operations. They can signal an operator when equipment malfunctions or when errors occur—for example, when data bits are lost during the transfer of data from internal memory to the CPU.

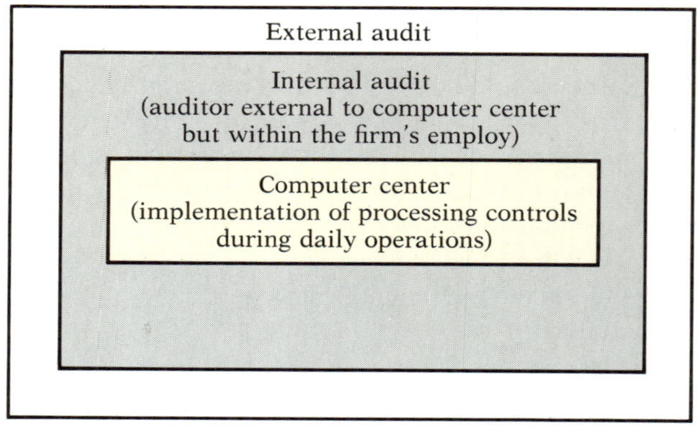

Figure 6.3 Auditing levels. Auditing can occur at three levels but all three levels may not be necessary. When deciding frequency of audits and depth of coverage, an organization should evaluate potential magnitude of loss if errors occur, the probability of criminal intrusion, and the degree to which the system is exposed to both errors and criminal intrusion.

6. *Logs.*
   Logs keep track of data, files, and activities in progress. Logging is particularly useful when events must take place in a given sequence.

7. *Database management systems.*
   Database management systems are computer program sets that control the creation, maintenance, and utilization of data bases and data files. They are very effective in minimizing human error when large and complex data bases are in use.

8. *User feedback.*
   Procedures that allow users to participate in the evaluation of computer systems are helpful. Many mistakes are caught by users. In addition, users can often make valuable suggestions regarding ways to upgrade the quality of output. **User feedback** can contribute to quality control.

9. *Audits.*
   Computer auditors have two functions. They check to see that controls exist to protect equipment and data, and they check to see that processing follows established procedures and decision rules. Most computer departments assign a staff member to audit processing during daily operations. Program

Error	Cause	Solution
Wrong procedure or code used	Manual incorrect	Pretest manual Improve updating procedures
	Language of manual inappropriate to user	Have manual prepared by qualified technical writers Have manual tested by users
Forms filled incorrectly	Format poor	Have user groups pretest forms
Data collection inaccurate	Carelessness	Improve employee training Glance-check data Implement validating programs during processing
Data lost	Carelessness	Log all data
Incorrect operation	Ignorance	Upgrade personnel selection, training, and procedure testing
Incorrect solution	Wrong algorithm or out-of-sequence instruction	Upgrade selection and training of programmers Establish standard programming procedures Implement team audits Implement tests: desk check, manual check, run test data, compare historical results, cross-check totals
Inaccurate output	Failure to catch human error at earlier processing stages	Implement validation programs Implement audits Perform sight check

Figure 6.4 Sample human errors and recommended control solution

audits are usually the responsibility of a team of programmers. Audits may also be performed periodically by someone from another department. Most companies hire external auditors for a third level of control as well. Figure 6.3 illustrates these different levels of auditing.

10. *Hiring and Training.*
Qualified and well-trained employees make few mistakes. Many organizations have improved their computer operations by adopting personnel policies to attract competent applicants and by introducing in-house **training** programs for workers.

Figure 6.4 summarizes common human errors and recommends control solutions.

HARDWARE MALFUNCTION AND BREAKDOWN

Despite the many ways in which people can introduce errors into computer processing, people are not always responsible for computer error. Sometimes faulty output can be attributed to hardware malfunction or breakdown. (If caused by poor maintenance and service, even malfunction and breakdown can be attributed to humans. Sometimes **environmental conditions** can be a factor. For example, a power surge may cause the speed of a tape drive to be altered as data is being recorded. This creates a problem when data on the tape is subsequently read. Since computers are sensitive to surrounding electrical fields, adverse conditions of static electricity can cause the loss of whole disks of data. The disruption of power when a computer is running can wipe out computer memory as well. Changes in room temperature and humidity can cause damage to hardware parts as they expand and contract.

Fire, smoke, and water can also damage computer facilities. So can acts of nature, such as earth-

Supplement 6.1 Poorly Written Documentation

The following is a sample from a user's manual:

> Diskettes: Handle diskettes carefully. Protect them from direct sunlight and extremes in temperature. Safeguard them from dirt, dust, and fingerprints. Keep diskettes in their protective sleeves when they are not in use. Turn on the computer before inserting a diskette.

The above directions were tested on sample users who had never worked with computers before. Many of the testers interpreted the directions to mean that the plastic diskette had to be removed from its paper covering in order to be inserted in the computer. Some of the individuals tore off the cover; others used scissors or letter openers to remove the paper. Still others grabbed the plastic at the center hole and pulled.

After the test, the manual was amended. The revised manual showed a picture of a diskette identifying its protective cover and storage envelope. The new directions read (in part) as follows:

> Diskettes are enclosed in a permanent, protective paper cover. Do not remove this cover. When the diskette is not in use, place it in a removeable storage envelope for additional protection.

quakes, hurricanes, windstorms, or lightning. An excessive snowfall caused the roof of one computer center to collapse.

Control Measures to Protect Hardware

Many controls to safeguard hardware can be built into the **housing** of computer equipment. For example, computer centers can have earthquake-proof foundations, fireproof vaults, locks and window grills, alarms and panic buttons, smoke detectors, and automatic fire extinguishers. Electric static mats can be placed in front of equipment; power pack devices can dissipate electric surges before they reach equipment; and portable generators can provide power during blackouts. It is important that employees are drilled in emergency procedures. They should also be motivated to follow, rather than short-cut, security procedures.

While nothing can prevent natural disasters, losses can be reduced through insurance, and **downtime** (time the computer is out of service) can be minimized through recovery planning. Most computer centers store backup files in a distant location. Many companies make an arrangement with another organization to process their data in the event of total system collapse. Safeguards are essential because downtime can be crippling to a company. Research by the University of Minnesota suggests that even 10 days after a big corporate computer failure, a firm would be operating at only a tenth its normal level of business.

ERRORS AND LOSS RESULTING FROM CRIMINAL ACTIVITY

Unintentional mistakes and equipment malfunction are not the only sources of computer error. Error caused by **criminal intrusion** into computer systems is a problem as well. Data needs to be protected against fraudulent changes, destruction, theft, and unauthorized disclosure.

Consider the billions of dollars involved in daily processing by computer. Every two to four hours, an estimated $845 billion is transferred electronically through computer networks. A person who taps into a computer can embezzle large sums of money. In one such case, an employee of Security Pacific National Bank got access to a money-transfer code and stole ten million dollars from the bank.

Data of a personal nature that is stored in a computer, such as health records and credit ratings, also needs protection. So does sensitive and proprietary information kept in computer memory. The theft of trade secrets, for example, can ruin a company's competitive advantage. Think of the

Supplement 6.2 Credit Bureau Sued for Lax Security

A suit against TRW, the nation's largest credit rating firm, was filed in 1984 by Burt Mazelow in order to force the company to tighten its security. Mazelow became concerned about TRW security when he examined his credit files and found an inquiry from an auto dealer from whom he had never sought credit. Are persons browsing through TRW credit files without authorization? Mazelow thinks so. He claims that TRW favors ease of access to credit files for clients when the emphasis should be tight security to protect consumer records.

According to Gary Sodikoff, one of Mazelow's attorneys, "TRW has not kept pace with the industry in terms of what can be done. . . . Because TRW has the legitimate right to gather the information, it has to secure it."

TRW believes that its security is adequate. The company claims that careless use of passwords by clients is the problem. In one instance, an access code was simply taped to a client's terminal, permitting anyone to walk up to the terminal and use the code to obtain private information. When carelessness of this nature is called to the attention of TRW, companies risk losing their subscriptions to TRW's records.

The Mazelow court case will address an important issue: What is the responsibility of computer users regarding security of computer files?

Source: Peggy Watt, "Credit Bureau Sued on Security," *Infoworld* (December 3, 1984), p. 18.

value of formulas for petrochemical products. Advance knowledge of a competitor's new line (for example, Yves Saint-Laurent's spring fashions) or tampering with records (for example, altering student grades) can be harmful as well. Mervyn's department store was cheated out of $250,000 in merchandise by an employee who gained access to the store's computer to create phony credit card accounts. In 1983, ten Milwaukee youths were arrested for using home computers to gain access to a computer at the nuclear weapons research lab at Los Alamos, New Mexico. Although the accessed computer was not one used for processing classified information, such an event certainly raises the issue of how safe computer systems really are. System security is an issue that is receiving much attention in computer circles and in the popular press today.

Where Security Is Needed

Each stage of processing needs controls; that is, measures must be adopted to protect manuals, forms, files, and output. Data collection, data preparation, programming, and operations must also be monitored. Failure to install controls can lead to the kinds of problems listed in Supplement 6.4.

Estimates of annual losses resulting from malice range from 100 million to 3 billion dollars. In a 1984 Computer Crime Task Force survey conducted by the American Bar Association, over 25 percent of the respondents reported "known and verifiable losses due to computer crime during the last twelve months"—losses that ranged between $145 and $730 million. (Per respondent, reported losses ranged from two million dollars to as high as ten million dollars.) An accurate assessment of total losses due to computer crime may never be achieved since many crimes are undetected. (Approximately 28 percent of the Bar Association survey respondents reported no available system to monitor or estimate the value of their computer crime losses.) Furthermore, many organizations do not report computer crimes because they are embarrassed that their security has been breached and fear that publicity will lead to loss of confidence in their management by the public.

Protection Against Malice

Most of the control measures cited earlier in this chapter help protect computer systems from computer crime. But a number of measures specifically guard against criminal activity. **Physical access controls** (see Figures 6.5 and 6.6), which restrict a computer facility to authorized personnel, are one such measure. These controls may begin with perimeter security; that is, the property where the

Supplement 6.3 Fire at Postal Service Headquarters

On October 15, 1984, a four-alarm fire broke out at the headquarters of the U.S. Postal Service (USPS) in Washington, D.C., damaging its data communications network. The network links six data centers to 350 locations through dedicated circuits. Because of disaster recovery planning, the post office was able to restore network service within thirty-six hours. Recovery consisted of a replicate telecommunications node established in temporary offices near the headquarters. A team of USPS staff and vendors worked round the clock to make this node operational.

USPS was less well prepared for smoke and soot damage caused by the fire. Diskettes used in the 1200 desktop personal computers at the headquarters were contaminated by fine grit from the fire even when stored in desks and filing cabinets. Many were warped by the fire. Few users had backup copies securely stored in fire-safe locations.

Before the personal computers could be put back in service, each had to be cleaned and certified as operational. Fortunately, USPS mainframes were not involved in the fire. They are not located in Washington, but at a computer center in Raleigh, North Carolina.

Supplement 6.4 What Lack of Controls Costs

- Lack of controls over manuals enabled a college student, who had picked up discarded operations manuals from trash cans, to learn how to direct computers at Pacific Telephone to deliver telephone equipment to specified locations. The student then collected and sold the equipment. In many instances, the student sold the equipment back to the company from which it was stolen.
- Computers have been shot, short-circuited with metal objects, and doused with gasoline and set afire. Such acts of vandalism can occur when access to hardware is not restricted.
- Lack of controls over the dispensing of forms enabled a Blue Cross/Blue Shield claims examiner to mail forms to his relatives who filled them in with real names and policy numbers and defrauded the system of $128,000.
- Sometimes individuals are challenged simply to "beat the system." In Oregon, an eighteen-year-old used a remote terminal to gain access to the computer of the Department of Motor Vehicles, and then put the system into irreversible disarray just to illustrate its vulnerability. Files had to be recreated from scratch.
- The University of California charged a fifteen-year-old boy with felony, grand theft, and vandalism for using 200 hours of unauthorized computer time worth about $10,000. The boy had accessed the university's computer from a second-hand terminal costing $60.

Supplement 6.5 Tape Theft

A software systems engineer, Wei Chen Yen, was arrested in 1984 by Palo Alto, California police and charged with burglary and illegally copying computer tapes. The engineer, a former Hewlett-Packard (HP) employee, allegedly stole the tapes from HP corporate offices, intending to use them on hardware at his new company, Axion, Inc. When Yen discovered that the tapes were incompatible with Axion's system (the tapes contained UNIX source code), he attempted to reformat the tapes at HP, using a false name to slip past security guards. An HP tape custodian detected that something was amiss when Yen logged on to an HP computer. The custodian alerted security guards, who confiscated the tapes and ejected Yen from the building.

According to police, data on the tapes could have been sold in the black market for millions of dollars. The tapes themselves were worth more than $44,000 in licensing fees to AT&T and the University of California at Berkeley for the UNIX version on the tapes.

Supplement 6.6 Just How Secure Is the Pentagon?

The term "hacker" was originally coined to identify someone who enjoys working with computer systems. Recently, however, the term has taken on an ominous meaning. It has become associated with malicious or inquisitive meddlers who try to use deceptive or illegal means to gain unauthorized access to computer systems. Often these meddlers are teenagers who enjoy matching wits with the "establishment."

In July 1985, a series of arrests of teenagers were announced by Prosecutor Alan Rockoff. Seven teenagers, who used codenames such as Beowulf and Vampire, had penetrated "direct lines . . . into sensitive sections of the armed forces," according to Rockoff. He considers it the most serious breach of computer security since a Los Angeles college student penetrated a computer network linking research firms to the Department of Defense. In 1984, computers at Marshall Space Flight Center in Huntsville, Alabama were entered illegally on several occasions. Some information was destroyed and service disrupted as a result. Investigation by the FBI led to the raid of four Huntsville homes and the confiscation of personal computers believed to used by four boys, ages 13 to 16, to gain access to the computers.

The FBI hopes the federal government will take an aggressive position in prosecuting cases. Lawmakers are now considering a plan to make it a federal crime to commit any computer fraud involving $5,000 or more. Also, a number of federal agencies are working to make telephones and computers more secure from invasion by hackers.

Figure 6.5 An example of physical access security control. Use of this computer is limited to personnel with access to keys to the machine. (MicroComputer Accessories, Inc.)

Figure 6.6 Another example of physical access control. This key device keeps unauthorized personnel from using the computer's telecommunications capabilities. (Cermetek Microelectronics)

Figure 6.7 Sample access directory. This printout from an access directory stored in computer memory is sorted by user identification number. The CPU can use information stored in access directories to determine who is authorized to use the computer, when they can use it, for how long, from what terminal, and for what purpose.

User identification: 076-835-5623
Access limitation: 13 hours (of CPU time for current fiscal year)
Account No: AS5842

Data elements	Type of access	Security level	Terminal number	Time lock
Customer No.	Read	10	04	08.00–17.00
Invoice No.	Read	10	04	08.00–17.00
Cash receipt	Read/Write	12	06	08.00–12.00

computer center is located may be protected by measures like fencing, alarms, cameras, lighting, a security force, patrols, and local police surveillance.

Physical barriers may also be installed at the computer center itself. Windows in the building may be barred and all exterior doors to the building kept locked and monitored by alarms, except for the lobby entrance where a security guard checks the authorization of people entering the building. TV monitors may watch entrances and motion detectors may be placed in sensitive areas. It is common practice to locate computer equipment in the most secure part of buildings, away from outside windows. A vault may be used to store data and files during nonworking hours.

Restricted entrance to computer equipment is another type of physical access control. Centers with tight security permit only operators, security officers, maintenance engineers, and system programmers in the computer room. These persons are required to wear badges and pass through a security station. Visitors are generally required to sign in and must be escorted by the persons they have come to visit.

To protect systems from employees with criminal intent who are bona fide computer users, an **access directory** stored in computer memory is customary (see Figure 6.7). Security codes needed to process specific data elements or files are listed in the directory. Before a job request is run, the CPU checks the directory to make sure that the user is authorized to use the programs and data required for the job. In other words, the codes restrict users to their work domain, preventing access to the files of others. Directories may also be used to specify which terminals can access the data base, the time of day access is permitted, and type of access, such as "read only" (meaning that files can be read by the user but not modified). The use of secret **passwords** is still another control technique to limit access to data and files.

Teleprocessing adds to the problem of maintaining security. It is hard to restrict terminal use when terminals are scattered in remote locations. Moreover, data is subject to intrusion as it is transmitted over telecommunication lines to and from the CPU.

A number of sophisticated security techniques have been developed to protect the confidentiality of data during transmission. The implementation of **protocols**—that is, rules, conventions, and procedures governing computer access and user identification—is a major means of protecting system security. For example, a secret signal, called a **handshake**, may have to be received by the CPU before processing can begin. This prevents individuals from pretending to be legitimate users of the system when they are not.

Another common measure to prevent message interception is **data encryption**, or the coding of data. Encryption makes the data incomprehensible should wiretapping take place. In addition, security can be served by subdividing data messages into **packets** for transmission at different times of the day by a variety of routes.

Since studies show that employees within an organization are as likely to breach computer security with malicious intent as outsiders (see Table

Table 6.1 Identity of Known Perpetrators of Crime

		Number of respondents*	Percentage of total (160)
Perpetrator not identified		62	39
Individuals within the organization		125	77
a. Executives, managers not directly involved with computers	21		
b. Computer operations supervisors	22		
c. Computer programmers, software personnel	67		
d. Nonsupervisory computer operations personnel	42		
e. Nonsupervisory personnel not directly involved with computers	40		
f. Other	18		
Individuals outside the organization		73	45
a. Competitors	16		
b. Customers/clients	11		
c. Outside consultants	22		
d. Individuals with no prior relationship with organization	37		
e. Other	16		
Total number of respondents =	160		

*Some reported crimes involved more than one individual. Some respondents reported more than one crime.

Source: Task Force on Computer Crime, Section of Criminal Justice, American Bar Association. *Report on Computer Crime*. Washington, D.C.: American Bar Association, June 1984.

6.1), the **personnel policies** of an organization are very important. An organizational principle that contributes to computer security is **separation of responsibility**. Computing can be divided into five basic functions: programming and system development; handling input media; operation of data processing equipment; documentation and file library; and distribution of output. Under the principle of separation of responsibility, work assignments are designed so that employees do not have duties that cross these functional lines. For example, a person who helps develop a system does not operate it and certify results; a programmer who writes software does not input data and run the program. Separation of responsibility serves as a deterrent to crime because a given job must pass through many hands, and there can thus be many independent checks for accuracy and possible fraud.

In small organizations, separation of responsibility may not be feasible. However, the principle should be followed whenever possible.

Care should also be taken in screening job applicants and in the supervision of employees. Workers should be technically competent and also trained in the vulnerability of computer systems. Awareness of the dimensions of computer crime can lead to more cautious use of computer resources.

In addition, employers should formulate and publicize conduct codes. They should encourage the formulation of ethical standards for computer users and professionals, and they should also provide forums for discussion of what these ethical standards should be. The Council of the Association for Computing Machinery and the Data Processing Management Association have adopted guidelines for professional conduct in information processing. The British Computer Society also has a code of conduct to which members are expected to subscribe. Other computer organizations, such as the

American Federation for Information Processing Societies, have encouraged the development of codes of responsibility. Of course, codes can contribute to system security by serving as a framework for professional conduct, but they cannot be expected to eliminate ethical problems in computing altogether. Other professional groups with long-standing disciplinary procedures and enforcement mechanisms, such as the American Society of Civil Engineers, consider hundreds of ethical complaints every year.

The **law** can be another deterrent to crime. Unfortunately, legislatures move slowly. In a field as dynamic as computer science, the law simply hasn't kept pace with technological advances. As a result, a potpourri of statutes govern computer operations. More than forty sections of criminal code can be cited to provide sanctions for computer-related criminal conduct. Other applicable laws include the Wire Fraud Act, the Bank Fraud Acts, the Privacy Act, the Securities and Exchange Commission Insider Trading Rules, and the Foreign Corrupt Practices Act.

In 1984, Congress did pass the Small Business Computer Crime Prevention Act. This act sets up a task force to investigate computer crime in small businesses and to recommend preventive measures. Congress also attached computer crime amendments to a 1984 budget resolution. These amendments make it a federal crime to gain unauthorized access either to data stored in computers by the federal government or to financial data protected by federal privacy statutes. However, private sector computer use other than financial data processing is not covered.

Efforts to pass comprehensive federal legislation dealing with computer fraud and abuse have been unsuccessful. The Federal Computer Systems Protection Act of 1979 (House of Representatives bill 1092) has been in committee for five years without reaching the floor of Congress for a vote. This bill defines four broad categories of criminal activity:

1. The intentional introduction of false data into a computer.
2. The use of computer facilities for unauthorized or illegal purposes.
3. The alteration or destruction of a computer, its information, or files.
4. Electronic burglary of money, financial instruments, property, services, or valuable data.

A bill of this nature would serve as an important mechanism for the prosecution of computer-related crimes.

Twenty-six states have enacted statutes against computer abuse and misuse. In Florida, for example, the Computer Crimes Act of 1981 defines two types of computer crimes: an offense against intellectual property and an offense against authorized computer use. Persons who willfully modify or destroy data, programs, or supporting documentation without authorization are guilty of a felony. So are persons who deny an authorized user access to computer system services. In many other state statutes, however, computer crimes are only misdemeanors, somewhat lower on the scale of offenses than drunk driving.

The widespread use of personal computers makes information systems more vulnerable to security infractions than in the past since every terminal and microcomputer has the potential to infiltrate information networks. In addition, the opportunities for system intrusion are increasing because the number of computers is increasing, applications are expanding, and data bases are growing. The protection of computer systems against criminal activity is a major problem in computer processing today.

HOW MUCH CONTROL IS NECESSARY?

Control measures are expensive. The services of analysts and security experts are needed to design controls. It takes both equipment and personnel to implement controls. Furthermore, controls can delay or impede the work of employees, causing dissatisfaction and loss of morale.

When planning computer system controls, organizations must analyze their vulnerability to er-

Supplement 6.7 Security Rating Guidelines for the Federal Government

The *Trusted Computer System Evaluation Criteria* was published in August 1983. This publication culminates a ten-year study to develop a set of basic requirements and classes for evaluating computer system security controls for the federal government. According to the report, federal agencies should take the following measures to secure their computer systems:

1. Security policy should be defined and enforced.
2. Data should be classified regarding the level of security needed so that security policy can be enforced.
3. Policy should state who is authorized to access information and related processes.
4. Security actions should be recorded so that responsibility for security can be determined.
5. Security systems should be designed so that security hardware and software can be independently evaluated.
6. Security mechanisms should themselves be made secure.

The publication identifies four classes of secure systems since it is recognized that not all systems require the same degree of security. In addition, the publication presents guidelines for system evaluation. These guidelines specify the level of experience for personnel evaluating system security and formal training requirements. The document also recommends types of security tests to run and how much time should be spent in the testing phase.

Access control	Physical controls	Processing controls	Organizational controls	Deterrents
Authorization/ authentication (e.g., passwords, cards) Hardware locks Logging access Time locks Librarian control of: Data Programs Documentation	Vaults Fire extinguishing equipment Physical restrictions to: Peripherals Libraries CPU	Transformation of data Ciphering/ deciphering Validity checking Control totals Form control Procedure control Backup: Equipment Personnel Audits	Separation of duties Rotation of duties Bond personnel Identify disgruntled personnel Train personnel Remove conflicts of interest Disaster insurance Background check Appoint control and security officer Security education of employees and users Installation of accountability controls	Laws Severe sanctions for employees involved in computer-related irregularities Prompt referral of suspected illegal activity to law enforcement authorities

Figure 6.8 Steps taken to prevent and deter computer crime.

ror, criminal intrusion, and breakdown. They must also assess the cost of potential mistakes, fraud, or damage. Unfortunately, there are no simple rules of thumb to aid organizations in risk assessment, and there are no foolproof techniques for identifying error or criminal activity. Usually organizations adopt the measures listed in Figure 6.8 to protect their computer facilities. When errors become apparent or system intrusion takes place, additional controls are usually implemented.

Controls are a major managerial headache today. As Figure 6.9 suggests, organizations must engage in a never-ending cycle of planning, imple-

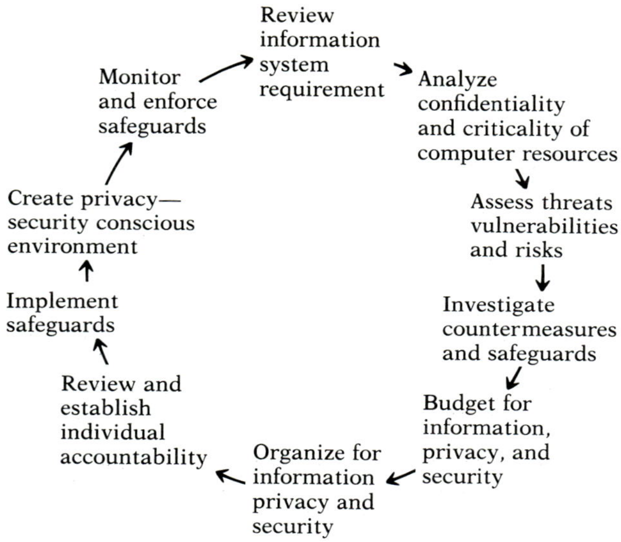

Figure 6.9 An overview of the process of making a computer system secure. System security is a never-ending cycle of planning, implementing, monitoring, and evaluating controls.

menting, monitoring, and evaluating controls. The computer industry recognizes the importance of the issue of system security. Much research effort is currently underway to devise improved methods of error detection and better ways to protect data and hardware. (The issue of data privacy, which is closely related to system security, is discussed at length in Chapter 15.)

SUMMING UP

Human errors should be detected and corrected when information is processed by computer. Protective measures should also be installed to minimize damage in the event of fire, lightning, or natural disaster. In addition, security measures are needed to protect computer systems from unlawful intrusions. It is estimated that computer crime is increasing at an estimated annual growth rate of 400 percent.

Common incidents of computer crime include crimes where the computer or system components are *objects* of the crime. This includes destruction, alteration, or theft of hardware, software, and data. Sometimes computers are *instruments* used to perpetrate crime. For example, a terminal might be used to commit fraud, extortion, blackmail, or embezzlement. A third category of crime is unauthorized *use* of an organization's computer for personal activities. A different security response is required to counter each of these activities.

Supplement 6.8 Rules to Live By: College Prof Devises 15 Irrefutable Laws of Computer System Operation

1. Any computer program that runs well is obsolete.
2. A good computer program is always accompanied by extremely bad documentation.
3. The value of a computer program is inversely related to the weight of its output.
4. Program complexities always grow to exceed the capabilities of the programmer responsible for it.
5. Any time a system appears to be working well, something has been overlooked.
6. What you don't do is always more important than what you do.
7. In any computer program, constants should always be treated as variables.
8. Investments in system-reliability products always exceed the probable cost of errors they are designed to avoid.
9. The problem is not that computer salespeople are not knowledgeable, it's that most of what they know isn't true.
10. If a system requires "n" number of spare parts, there will always be "n − 1" parts in stock.
11. Major software revisions are always requested after system installation is completed.
12. Installation and operating instructions are always discarded with the shipping cartons.
13. Any component part requiring the most frequent service or adjustment will be the least accessible.
14. Undetectable errors are infinite while detectable errors, by definition, are finite.
15. Nothing is impossible for the person who doesn't have to do the work.

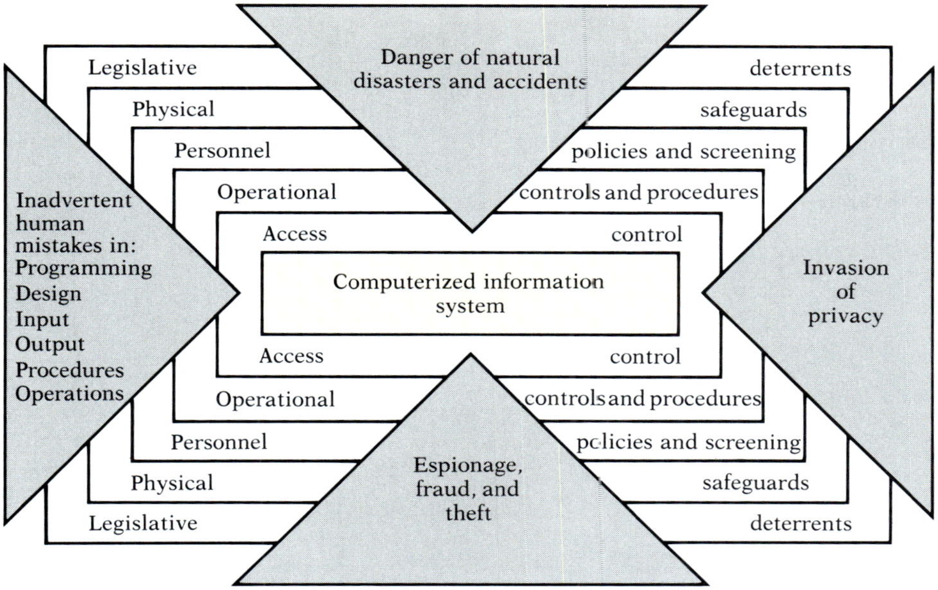

Figure 6.10 *Layers of protection.* An information system is vulnerable to many types of threats to accuracy and system security. Many layers of protection are needed to counter these threats.

Sample controls to ensure the integrity and security of computer systems fall into five general categories:

1. Physical safeguards.
2. Personnel screening and policies.
3. Operational controls and procedures.
4. Access controls.
5. Legal deterrents.

One can envision these safeguards as layers of protection, as illustrated in Figure 6.10.

The problem with controls is that they are costly. Controls can also interfere with work and adversely affect employee morale. An organization must weigh the risk of inaccuracies and breakdown against the cost of implementing controls. The amount of sensitive and proprietary data processed should be taken into consideration. So should the right of clients to privacy.

Unfortunately, all known protective mechanisms against crime can be broken, given enough time, resources, and ingenuity on the part of felons. Perhaps the major objective of security systems should be to make intrusion too expensive (in equipment costs and risk) and too time-consuming (in planning effort and time needed to actually breach safeguards) to make attempted violations worthwhile. The passage of comprehensive laws defining computer crime might serve as a deterrent to crime and would assist in the prosecution of computer felons. At present, computer-related cases are generally prosecuted under laws written for other purposes.

REVIEW QUESTIONS

1. Comment on the statement: A computer system adds to the probability of errors, fraud, and destruction of data and information.
2. Comment on the statement: Computers never make mistakes. People do.
3. What are some of the common causes of er-

rors in computer systems? Classify them regarding:
   a. source
   b. motivation
   c. importance
   d. difficulty to trace
   e. difficulty to correct

4. Can error-free data be guaranteed? Can error-free results be guaranteed? Explain your answers.

5. Identify control points where measures should be taken to ensure security of data. Explain what measures you would require and why?

6. How can careless errors be reduced?

7. Describe the types of crimes perpetrated against computer systems. What are some common abuses of computer systems? How can crimes and abuses be prevented?

8. Can a computer system ever be completely secure? What are the tradeoffs in costs? What are the social and nonmonetary costs?

9. Should computer operations be audited? If so, at what level or levels?

10. What do you understand by the expression, "Garbage in–garbage out"? Why is this expression associated with computers when computers are also known for their accuracy?

11. What is separation of responsibility?

12. How can the setting of standards contribute to quality control?

13. Describe types of controls to protect computer resources from adverse environmental conditions?

14. How does an organization know when controls are needed? Who decides how much control is necessary? Who designs and implements controls?

DISCUSSION QUESTIONS

1. Give two examples of unexpected results that might be produced because of:
   a. malfunction
   b. mistakes
   c. fraud
   d. theft
   e. sabotage

   How might security be improved to prevent incorrect results caused by each of the above?

2. Describe five situations in which personal identification might be required before access to a computer is granted. In each case, what security methods would you recommend?

3. What makes particular organizations more vulnerable to security violations than others? How can this vulnerability be reduced, if not eliminated?

4. What would you do if you suspected a fellow employee of being a computer criminal? Should your action depend on the organization where you work? Would your action differ if you were working in a:
   a. bank?
   b. retail store?
   c. multinational firm?
   d. insurance company?
   e. library?
   f. hospital?

5. Do you think computer professionals should adopt a code of ethics? What should be included in the code?

6. Are laws in the United States adequate in discouraging and punishing:
   a. computer crime?
   b. privacy violations?

   What laws relating to computer crime do you think should be given priority in Congress?

EXERCISES

1. Prepare a code of ethics for computer professionals.

2. Research computer crime bills that are currently before Congress. What are arguments for and against the bills? Do they have a

chance of passing this session of Congress? What is the position of the White House?

3. Interview a computer user. Make a list of computer errors the user has experienced. Discuss ways these errors could have been avoided.

4. You have been appointed director of a computer center to process all administrative reports for a university (e.g., payroll, grade reports, registration, grounds maintenance, fee collection, etc.) List security measures you would install. What would these measures cost? Is the cost worth the benefit?

5. Report on a recent case of computer crime reported in the press. Who participated? Why? What losses occurred? How was the crime detected? How could it have been avoided?

Selected Annotated Bibliography

Computer, vol. 16, no. 7 (July 1983), pp. 10–95. This is a special issue devoted to computer security. S. R. James, Jr., and P. G. Neuman present an excellent introduction to new technologies. C. E. Landwehr discusses the best technologies available as well as projects for trusted systems under development. Other articles are on the following topics: securing a distributed system, statistical data bases, multilevel systems, and multiprocessor microcomputers.

Gillard, Collen and Smith, Jim. "Computer Crime: A Growing Threat." *Byte*, vol. 8, no. 10 (October 1983), pp. 398–424. The proliferation of home computers facilitates illegal access to small business computers and corporate mainframes, according to the authors. Yet the potential for damage remains. Documented cases of computer crime are discussed as well as the technical requirements of a secure system.

Howe, Charles L. "Coping with Computer Criminals." *Datamation*, vol. 28, no. 1 (January 1982), pp. 118–28. According to the author, "Too often MIS managers concentrate on hardware and software rather than on personnel as a means of checking computer abuse." Howe outlines a plan for security against fraud, including means to thwart theft of computer time.

Hsiao, David L.; Kerr, Douglas S.; and Madnick, Stuart E. *Computer Security*. New York: Academic Press, 1979. This book is a superb guide to the extensive literature on security. Each chapter has a postscript that reviews the literature relevant to the chapter, followed by references, including annotated bibliographies. A total of 720 references with 353 annotations are included in the text. The book is tutorial in approach. A good chapter on privacy is included. Throughout the book areas for future research are identified and discussed.

Menkus, Belden. "The Problem with 'Errors'." *Journal of Systems Management*, vol. 34, no. 11 (November 1983), pp. 11–13. The author argues that understanding errors is the first step in eliminating them. He then defines errors, classifies them, and discusses ways to reduce them.

Parker, Donn and Mycum, Susan. "Computer Crime." *ACM Communications*, vol. 22, no. 4 (May 1984), pp. 312–15. Two professionals in the field discuss the nature and future of computer crime.

Sardinas, Joseph; Burch, John G.; and Asebrook, Richard. *EDP Auditing: A Primer*. New York: John Wiley, 1981. This is an introduction to EDP auditing. Discussed are tagging, tracing, computer-assisted audit techniques, audit software, Integrated Test Facility (ITF), and Parallel Test Facility (PTF). There are also good sections on controls for operations, administration, documentation, and security.

Summers, R. C. "An Overview of Computer Security," *IBM Systems Journal*, vol. 23, no. 4 (1984), pp. 309–25. Included is a discussion of motivations for security measures, security strategies, security models, and specific technical and administrative measures for promoting security.

Task Force on Computer Crime, Section of Criminal Justice, American Bar Association. *Report on Computer Crime*. Washington, D.C.: American Bar Association, 1984. This report presents results of a survey distributed to approximately 1000 private organizations and public agencies on the subject of computer crime.

Ware, Willis. H. "Information Systems Security and Privacy." *ACM Communications*, vol. 22, no. 4 (May 1984), pp. 325–27. This article discusses the nature of privacy, the "people threat," the question of leadership, and the need for a national commission to study problems related to privacy and security.

Weber, Ron. *EDP Auditing: Conceptual Foundation and Practice*. New York: McGraw-Hill, 1982. The author focuses on the framework for control and the techniques of evidence collection, and explains how evidence itself should be evaluated. It is the author's premise that a good auditor must be better at business than clients. Many detailed and technical aspects of EDP control are discussed, such as concurrency, cryptography, kernel programs, data dictionary, and rollbooks.

Computer Applications

Computers are used in a wide range of vocations. The purpose of Part II is to show how society benefits from such use. Part II describes sample computer applications in offices (Chapter 7), factories (Chapter 8), educational institutions (Chapter 9), medical facilities and sports (Chapter 10), the arts (Chapter 11), government and politics (Chapter 12), and scientific endeavors (Chapter 13). The use of microcomputers at home and at work is also discussed (Chapter 14).

While reading this part, keep in mind the advantages of computers outlined in Part I, such as speed, accuracy, and reliability of information processing combined with low cost for large-volume data handling. But don't forget that many things can go wrong with computer systems. Software may not be available or may be poorly designed so that output does not meet user needs. Data may be unobtainable or too costly to collect. Unintentional human mistakes on the part of programmers, operators, analysts, system engineers, and users can lead to faulty output or cause hardware to malfunction or break down. Errors and loss can result from criminal activity. Not every user of computers is a satisfied one.

This word of caution is necessary because Part II presents the benefits of computer use without dwelling on problems that may prevent realization of expected benefits. Readers will learn how computers contribute to the solutions of problems and how they improve decision making. The part will help explain how modern society has become dependent on computers for the delivery of goods and services.

PART TWO

Administration and the Electronic Office

Our two greatest problems are gravity and paper work. We can lick gravity, but sometimes the paper work is overwhelming.

WERNER VON BRAUN

CHAPTER SEVEN

Key Words

cell	**electronic office**	**teleconferencing**
critical path	**implementation**	**telemail**
decision support system (DSS)	**multimedia center**	**training**
electronic mail	**second generation spreadsheet**	**word processing (WP)**
electronic mailbox	**shell document**	**workstation**
	spreadsheet	
	superspreadsheet	

Organizations have features in common regardless of the work they do or their size. For example, all organizations order supplies, process payrolls, and prepare tax returns. And all organizations must generate letters, make forecasts, prepare budgets, schedule activities, bill clients, and control inventories. What is more, this type of paperwork must be done not only in business firms, but also in research labs, dance troupes, hospitals, government agencies, schools, circuses, and scouting clubs as well.

This chapter will describe how a computer can contribute to the efficiency of running an organization. Our first topic is the use of computers for administrative data processing, including word processing. Next we discuss the use of computers for organizational planning and control. The chapter concludes by describing the typical system components found in an electronic office. While the computer applications described in this chapter are relevant to all types of organizations, later chapters will focus on computer systems for specialized purposes, such as the use of computers in manufacturing, education, health services, government, and the arts.

ADMINISTRATIVE DATA PROCESSING

In Chapter 1 we saw that early computers were designed to solve scientific and engineering problems. Data processing for business applications developed rapidly, however, and soon outstripped science as the major computer use. One reason for this is that much office work involves the routine processing of records, orders, and payments, and such repetitive tasks can be easily programmed. Repetitive work can also be done more accurately and much faster by computer than by clerks, and at less cost per transaction for large volume processing. An estimated 52 percent of the U.S. work force is engaged in office work and 40 to 50 percent of the operating expenses of most organizations are for office costs. Cost-conscious administrators favor computer use for data processing as a way of reducing these percentages.

The first administrative use of electronic data processing was for accounting and finance. Programs were written to automate billing, payroll, general ledger, and purchasing. In addition, computer storage of records like personnel files and inventory lists soon replaced conventional record keeping. Computerized record keeping improves upon conventional record keeping in several ways: access is easier, retrieval is faster, updating is more convenient, and the amount of storage space required is reduced.

Today, software is available for most business functions. Supplement 7.1 lists only a limited sample of the kinds of administrative tasks for which programs are commonly used. Keep in mind

Supplement 7.1 Some Administrative Tasks for Which Programs Are Commonly Used

accounts payable	credit checking	materials procurement
accounts receivable	equipment inventory	operations research models
asset accounting	facilities control	ordering
auditing	financial reporting	project control
billing	forecasting	property management
budget analysis	funding	regulatory reporting
capital budgeting	invoicing	scheduling
cash disbursements	inventory control	tax accounting
check writing and reconciliation	job costing	tax analysis
cost accounting	market analysis	warranty administration

that programs to perform these tasks are used widely by organizations that have nothing to do with commerce. In all likelihood, the Sierra Club, the Red Cross, the Baptist Church, and your public library use such programs, as do most organizations that can afford a computer.

The programs listed in Supplement 7.1 are primarily accounting programs for processing numerical data. For example, an accounts receivable program might be used to generate finance charges or to provide automatic input of recurring charges; an accounts payable program can generate reports of anticipated cash flow by date. In addition to such numerical processing, all offices need to process words: that is, offices need to generate correspondence, memos, reports, advertising copy, publicity, minutes, contracts, and forms. It was only after computers gained acceptance for numerical processing that hardware and software for word processing was developed. Today, however, word processing is the computer application most widely used in offices.

WORD PROCESSING

Word processing (WP) can be defined as the use of electronic equipment to write, edit, store, retrieve, display, transmit, and print text. An overview of word processing appears in Figure 7.1. A terminal keyboard replaces a conventional typewriter; typed words are displayed on the CRT screen. The advantage is that the user can make corrections and revisions without having to retype an entire page. Words can be deleted, sentences can be added, and whole paragraphs can be moved or rearranged when the user presses special keys or types simple codes. Once the text is put into its final form, it can be stored for later retrieval, transmitted electronically to another CRT screen, or converted to hard copy by a printer.

Another advantage of word processing systems is that they allow you to format documents automatically. Word processing software will, for example, center headings, add page numbers, and set margins and tabs. The user keys in printing instructions to establish the number of lines per page, spacing (single or double space), and the line on which typing is to begin. Some systems will hyphenate words at the end of lines according to syllable division rules stored in computer memory. Others will highlight words on the screen that do not appear in a stored dictionary, alerting typists to a possible spelling error.

Word processing is particularly useful when form letters must be sent. To create a form letter, the user first types a basic **shell document** containing text that will stay the same for all letters. What happens next depends on the word processing system. In some, a code is used to mark the spots where items need to be inserted in order to

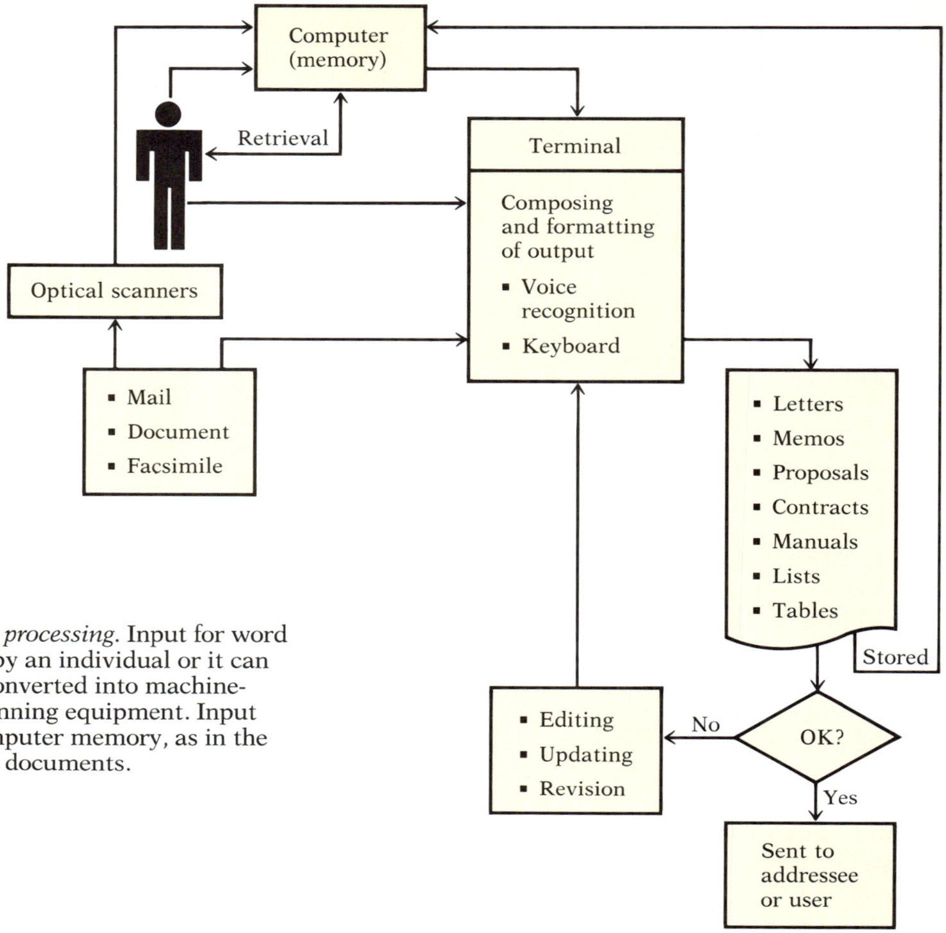

Figure 7.1 Overview of word processing. Input for word processing may be keyed in by an individual or it can be printed material that is converted into machine-readable form by optical scanning equipment. Input may also be drawn from computer memory, as in the case of form letters and shell documents.

customize the form letter—items such as name, address, or amount of payment due. Then a separate document is prepared that contains only the variable data to be filled in. The computer will merge the shell document and the fill-in parts at the time of printing. This process and an example of the resulting individualized form letters is shown in Figure 7.2. Notice, for example, how the client's name is placed in the salutation. The same principle of shell documents and variable pieces of information can be used in the preparation of reports and contracts.

What makes word processing different from use of electronic typewriters? One difference is that word processing allows users to extract sentences and entire paragraphs from a computer data base to create a document. Another difference is that a word in a stored document can be located and changed each time it appears in the document by a simple command. This feature is useful, for example, when the name of a client is misspelled or needs to be changed in a contract prepared on a word processing system. A word processing system can also be instructed to pick out from an address list stored in memory only those clients in a particular zip code area and to generate a given letter only to them. The system may also be directed to print the letters and envelopes with a special font chosen from a large variety of styles and sizes. Yet another useful feature distinguishing word processors from electronic typewriters is that a word processing system can keep track of the time spent

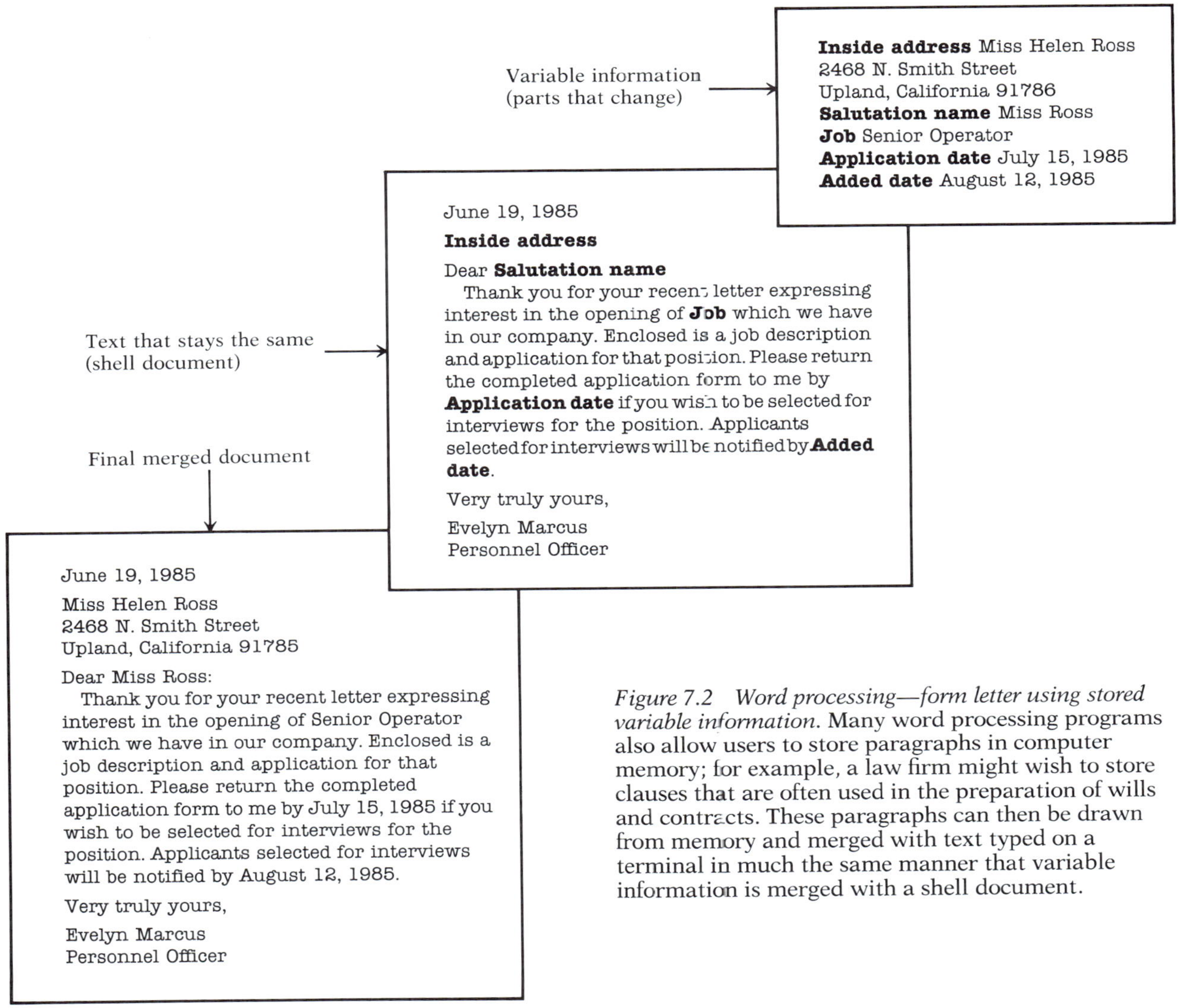

Figure 7.2 Word processing—form letter using stored variable information. Many word processing programs also allow users to store paragraphs in computer memory; for example, a law firm might wish to store clauses that are often used in the preparation of wills and contracts. These paragraphs can then be drawn from memory and merged with text typed on a terminal in much the same manner that variable information is merged with a shell document.

on each job to facilitate charging customer accounts for service. This feature is particularly valuable for law and consulting firms.

Several companies are currently working on word processing programs that will not only type and reproduce a document, but help compose it as well. For example, Wang has recently bought electronic reproduction rights to the *Random House Dictionary* and *Thesaurus*, and to dictionaries from French and German publishers. Wang plans to give users the option of asking for a definition, a range of synonyms, or foreign language translations of a particular word or phrase. Other companies are working on software that will offer the user alternatives to stylistically awkward passages. Such programs might identify archaic expressions, commonly misused phrases, and certain types of grammatical errors.

ELECTRONIC MAIL

Word processors can be connected to one another by telecommunications equipment. This means that messages can be transmitted from one termi-

Supplement 7.2 Word Processing Fonts

This is
an example of comput-
erized typesetting using TEX, a
program developed by Don Knuth at
Stanford University. TEX is widely used
for letters, technical papers, catalogues, concert
programs, and books. TEX's forte is mathematics:

$$\sum_{i=1}^{\infty} \frac{1}{2^i} = 1, \quad \{\underbrace{\overbrace{a,\ldots,a}^{k\ a\text{'s}},\overbrace{b,\ldots,b}^{l\ b\text{'s}}}_{k+l\text{ elements}}\}, \quad \sqrt{1+\sqrt{1+\sqrt{1+x}}}.$$

TEX produces identical results on different computer systems and the output may be printed on a variety of different printers. As many as 256 different fonts may be used for a single document. These include **boldface** *text italic math italic* CALLIGRAPHIC `typewriter` *slanted roman* sans serif *sans serif slanted* unslanted text italic $\epsilon\lambda\lambda\eta\nu\iota\kappa\alpha$ *`slanted typewriter`* **sans serif bold**, and, of course, in many different sizes.

TEX TEX TEX TEX TEX TEX TEX TEX TEX TEX TEX TEX TEX TEX TEX

nal to another, eliminating the need to print output, to address, stuff and stamp envelopes, and to depend on interoffice or conventional mail delivery. **Electronic mail** (also called **telemail**) therefore saves time and reduces the work of clerks.

When electronic mail is sent over long distances, telephone lines are the communication channel generally used. Coaxial cable is common for systems linking offices within one company. In 1985, an estimated 31 percent of electronic mail was intercompany; 44 percent was interoffice.

The term electronic mail is also used to describe transmission of messages to a central computer that serves as an **electronic mailbox**. Memory space called a "mailbox" is reserved for authorized persons. When a message is received, the computer stores it in the mailbox of the intended recipient. Usually a signal like a blinking character on a CRT screen alerts the user that a message has arrived.

Mailgram, a joint venture of Western Union and the U.S. Post Office for overnight delivery of messages, is another mode of electronic mail. Western Union has also introduced Easylink, a service that enables subscribers to send messages between Easylink connections and telex machines and to thereby communicate with one another in a conversational mode. Still another variation is Datapost, a message service with a network of computers in major cities. With Datapost, messages are transmitted electronically to the computer nearest the intended recipient, and then printed and given to the post office for next day delivery. MCI Mail is also a major electronic mail vendor. MCI offers all major delivery methods: electronic mailboxes, a four-hour courier service to deliver a printout of a message in major cities, and overnight courier delivery.

At the present time, electronic mail is used predominately for telegrams, memos, and short office messages. As more and more people begin to use computers in their homes and offices, however,

Supplement 7.3 Savings through Electronic Mail

In 1982, USAA General Indemnity Co., an auto insurer, began an office automation program. Electronic mail was one feature of the program. In a pilot study, it was determined that electronic mail functions resulted in:

- An 80 percent cut in time spent on the telephone
- A 50 percent reduction in the amount of paper for interoffice memos
- A 94 percent reduction in use of interoffice mail
- A 61 percent drop in the number of copies being made.

Robert McDowell, who spearheaded the program, estimates that 75 percent of the internal paper that organizations create could be cut by use of electronic mail.

the use of electronic mail will undoubtedly expand. One reason people are turning to telemail is frustration with the slowness of conventional mail and the rising cost of telephone service. In addition, the burgeoning development of telecommunications networks for message transmission between distant computers is improving customer service, making electronic mail more attractive to customers than in the past. In the future, new developments in interface technology can be expected to resolve problems of equipment incompatibility that now hamper the exchange of messages between computers made by different manufacturers. All of these advances in telecommunication technology should cause costs to drop, thus increasing the demand for electronic mail services.

TELECONFERENCING

Teleconferencing is a method of electronic communication that permits interactive exchange between two or more persons through their terminals. With electronic mail, a message is delivered instantaneously to an electronic mailbox, but there may be a delay before the intended recipient collects it. Teleconferences eliminate this time lag since participants are waiting to respond to messages that are sent to the terminal screens of linked workstations, or between computers in conference rooms that may be as close as a few blocks or as far apart as a continent. Often the terminals of conference participants serve as electronic flip charts enabling the participants to access specially prepared conference materials from a data base.

The computer equipment used determines the type of messages that can be sent between conferees. A typical message requires 500 bits; a document page in facsimile form, 200,000 bits; a newspaper-quality photograph, 100,000 bits; and a television frame, 1 million bits. A special kind of teleconference called a videoconference, whereby people can confer via the transmission of television pictures and sound, is also technologically feasible. The problem is that the huge amount of data-carrying capacity required for videoconferencing makes the cost quite high. For example, in 1985 a one-hour call between Washington and New York using AT&T's "picturephone" videoconferencing service cost $400. AT&T and competing vendors hope to eventually develop videoconference systems that will cost little more than a long-distance telephone call.

Teleconferencing saves travel time and travel costs. However, many administrators believe that interpersonal relationships are important when conducting business and, therefore, they prefer live meetings. In addition, many people who work in organizations like to break their daily routine by visits to other cities. The cost of teleconference equipment is also a consideration. Atlantic Richfield recently spent $20 million to upgrade its teleconferencing capabilities. Not many organizations have the financial resources for such an expenditure.

THE USE OF COMPUTERS IN CONTROL AND PLANNING

As you may have gathered from this chapter's discussion of the electronic office, the use of computers for administrative functions affects all levels of personnel in an organization. The work of filing clerks and typists is changed by word processing. The work of bookkeepers and accountants is dramatically altered by financial programs. Managers, in addition to using word processors and financial programs, often use telemail and participate in teleconferences.

All of the uses of computers we have discussed so far in this chapter are operational uses: that is, applications involving day-to-day operations. Let us now consider how computers assist administrators in the broader and often more abstract activities of control and planning.

Sample Control and Planning Programs

In general, problems that are structured lend themselves to computer solutions since such problems can usually be quantified and solved by the decision rules that computers follow. Many problems in administrative planning and control, however, are poorly defined or poorly structured, and so they do not lend themselves to solution by program. The solutions to such problems, which are called "wicked problems" by many computer professionals, depends on the intuition, judgment, and experience of administrators, none of which can easily be translated into decision rules. As a result, computers can contribute to a much lower percentage of problems in the sphere of control than in the sphere of operations. There are even fewer computer applications in planning.

Nevertheless, computers do contribute to the fields of control and planning. Two common kinds of control programs do regulatory reporting and credit checking. Software is also commonly used to manage inventories and evaluate processes.

One especially prevalent form of process evaluation is project scheduling. Two important computerized project scheduling techniques are called PERT (Program Evaluation Review Technique) and GERT (Graphic Evaluation Review Technique). GERT and PERT serve to establish which activities must be completed before others can begin when planning a project. They also calculate the **critical path**—that is, the set of activities where delay retards the entire project. This information is needed to identify the activities that must be carefully monitored and controlled and to determine how long the project will take. PERT allows three types of time estimates: optimistic time, pessimistic time, and most likely time. One of the advantages of GERT is that planners can specify the probability of alternative paths. The time of completion is then calculated with probability associations.

The need for computerized project scheduling can be illustrated by the following example. Suppose that a new computer system is being developed. The project will involve many activities including a feasibility study, specification of system requirements, design (including design of models, standards, tests, programs, procedures, controls, input, files, forms, and output), programming, acquisition of equipment, reorganization of departments, installation, testing, personnel training, and conversion. An IBM manual lists 222 activities for the installation of equipment alone.

Clearly, the manager of a project of this size would benefit from a computer program to schedule human and financial resources. Information provided by the program would answer questions such as: When will programmers be needed? When should equipment be acquired and installed? Which activities will be affected if wiring is not completed by electricians on schedule? Suppose there is a month's delay in delivery of storage devices: how will the entire project be delayed as a result? What additional costs will be incurred by the delay?

An electronic **spreadsheet**, the equivalent of an accountant's worksheet, is another sample planning application. Before the advent of computers, accountants commonly used a large sheet of ledger paper with a set of categories across the top and another list of categories down the left margin to organize information and show relationships between fiscal data in a readily understandable format.

An electronic spreadsheet displays an empty "matrix" or grid on the computer screen. Each

A1

	A	B	C	D
1	OFFICE		5	OFFICES
2	REFURBISH			
3	PROJECT			
4				
5	ITEM	COST	QTY	TOTAL
6	----------	----------	----------	----------
7	DESKS	200.00	5	1000.00
8	CHAIRS	129.95	10	1299.50
9	FILES	69.00	5	345.00
10	TABLES	76.00	5	380.00
11				----------
12				3024.50
13	LABOR	10.50	7.5	78.75
14				----------
15		ESTIMATE		3103.25
16				
17	AVERAGE PER/OFFICE			620.65
18				

Source: Intro-Calc Spreadsheet from *Using Computer Applications: Intro-Software* by Fredric Beisse, Burgess Communications, 1986.

Figure 7.3 Sample spreadsheet.

	ACTUAL FY1985 Q1	ACTUAL FY1985 Q2	PROJECTED FY1985 Q3	PROJECTED FY1985 Q4	PROJECTED FY1985 Year	PROJECTED FY1986 Q1	PROJECTED FY1986 Q2	PROJECTED FY1986 Q3	PROJECTED FY1986 Q4	PROJECTED FY1986 Year
Net Revenue	1154052	1083407	1261800	2379754	5879013	1222735	3587931	4644702	6387702	15843070
Cost of Revenue	740112	667655	741013	1390631	3539441	686802	2084616	2751817	3850462	9373697
Gross Margin	413910	415572	520787	989123	2339572	535933	1503315	1892885	2537240	6469373
Operating Expenses										
Sales and Marketing	143241	174296	173411	852395	843348	406483	470363	460810	487948	1825604
Engineering	84717	97602	100944	190380	473643	61137	179397	232235	319385	792154
Customer Service	18348	7849	25236	47595	99028	36682	107638	139341	191631	474292
General and Administrative	119739	128432	130000	140000	518171	175000	200000	200000	200000	775000
Total	366045	408179	429591	730370	1934185	679302	957391	1032386	1198964	3868050
Income from Operations	47865	7573	91194	258753	405387	-143369	545917	860499	1338276	2601323
Interest Income (-Expense)	-17163	-7573	-13294	-11283	-49385	15461	12411	6786	14286	48944
Other Income (-Expense)	0	0	-170	-5411	-7121	0	-8608	17346	-27051	-53005
Income Before Taxes	30702	0	76195	242054	348951	-127908	549720	849939	1325511	2597262
Provision for Taxes	0	0	0	0	0	0	0	0	0	0
Net Income (-Loss)	30702	0	76195	242054	348951	-127908	549720	849939	1325511	2597262
PERCENT TO NET REVENUE:										
Cost of Revenues	64	62	59	58	60	56	58	59	60	59
Gross Margin	36	38	41	42	40	44	42	41	40	41
Operating Expenses	32	38	34	31	33	56	27	22	19	24
Income from Operations	4	1	7	11	7	-12	15	19	21	16
Interest (-Expense)	-1	-1				1	0	0	0	0
Net Income	3	0				-10	15	18	21	16

Figure 7.4 Spreadsheet application: projected statement of income.

intersection of a vertical column and horizontal row is a **cell** in which a value can be placed. As Figure 7.3 shows, particular rows and columns are identified by the type of information in them. A value may be directly input into a given cell by the user or it may be generated by computer based on a formula that depends on values in other cells. For example, in Figure 7.3, the value in cell *B5* is calculated by adding the values in *B2*, *B3*, and *B4*, all of which are input by the user. Once the relationships for calculating values in the matrix have been specified by the user and once any data that is to come from outside the program has been input, the spreadsheet program will direct the CPU to perform the calculations according to the appropriate formulas and to place the results in the appropriate matrix cells. While Figure 7.3 shows simple spreadsheet relationships, Figure 7.4 is an example of a spreadsheet put to a typical use: namely, the creation of a projected statement of income.

A computer program that does spreadsheet calculations replaces the drudgery of manual ledger sheet calculations and eliminates human errors. The computer can also make the calculations faster than a human. Furthermore, the computer allows a person to ask "What if?" questions like "What if overhead increases by five percent?" Or "What if depreciation were X instead of Y—how would the change affect net profits?" The spreadsheet program will calculate a whole set of values in response to such questions, projecting different scenarios based on variables input by the user.

In an electronic office, spreadsheets are commonly used for preparing budgets, evaluating proposals, comparing alternatives, and measuring results. A spreadsheet can aid administrators who want to know how a change in the rate of inflation or a change in interest rates might affect the financial situation of their organization. An entrepreneur who wishes to open a restaurant can simulate the capital requirements, fluctuating food costs, growth of clientele, pricing policy, and cash flow in order to estimate how much money is needed to launch the business. A newspaper publisher can forecast the circulation levels required for a range of projected selling prices and advertising revenues.

Spreadsheets are also used to determine cash-flow status, to make currency conversions, to prepare income statements and expense reports, to make payroll projections and mortgage calculations, to generate price lists, and to analyze job cost. It should be noted that spreadsheets have applications at the operational level as well as planning and control applications. They are useful whenever tabular (that is, grid or matrix) calculations have to be made.

Spreadsheet programs are generally purchased as packages. A mainframe or minicomputer is no longer necessary to run a spreadsheet; today spreadsheet programs can be purchased that run microcomputers. Lotus 1-2-3, SuperCalc, VisiCalc, and the more advanced versions of these programs are examples of commonly used spreadsheets. Recent spreadsheet packages are so much more powerful than earlier versions that they are called **superspreadsheets** or **second generation spreadsheets**. One benefit of many superspreadsheets is the condensation of commands that formerly required many keystrokes into one- or two-key commands. Other features may include online help prompts, varied column width, graphics, and the use of "windows" to enable users to look at different parts of the file simultaneously.

Decision Support Systems

Often, decisions that cannot be totally automated can be reached by having the human user interact more extensively with the computer than is normally the case when applications programs are used. Many problems in control and planning can be solved in this manner. Programs dedicated to such problem solving are called **decision support systems (DSSs)**. Decision support systems are valuable when either the model, the data, or both prove inadequate by themselves because the problem's solution requires judgment and subjective analysis. (For example, a computer can be used to identify staffing needs for a given project, but not to identify which employees to transfer to the project to ensure a compatible team.) Conversely, decision support systems are also useful when the size of the problem or its complexity requires more than managerial judgment. In both situations, a human using a computer can arrive at a more effective solution than a human without computer aids or than a program or set of programs could without more extensive human intervention.

There are many DSSs on the market today. Sample application areas include financial structuring, manpower leveling, sales forecasting, design simulation, scheduling, inventory optimization, acquisition analysis, and decision-tree analysis. STRATANAL, useful in planning corporate strategies, is an example of a DSS program. GIDS (General Intelligent Decision System) has the ability to comprehend English-like queries and to subsequently formulate models. (A model is a representation of a system that attempts to relate some of the variables in the system in a meaningful way so that an increased understanding of the system is attained.) AIDS (An Interactive Decision

System) rationalizes the judgmental process on a broad range of topics.

Decision support systems are particularly useful when the problems in question have the following characteristics:

- Solutions are open-ended (that is, there is no single correct answer).
- Problems can be factored and tackled incrementally.
- Limited human patience is a consideration.
- The data or other factors in the environment are rapidly changing.
- The decision maker's perception is also changing over time.
- The problem is complex and needs raw data analysis, transformations, projections, and so on.
- Decisions must be made rapidly.

Although problems at the operational level may meet these criteria, a DSS is generally used for the more abstract and multifaceted sorts of decisions that must be made in planning and control.

Multimedia Centers

Multimedia centers have been established in many organizations to facilitate planning and control. These centers borrow the concept of the "war room" from the military. They are information and communication centers using computer technology.

The typical multimedia center will have on-line, real-time terminals for information processing and retrieval. CRT screens with graphic and color capabilities may be available. The center will be used to run mathematical and statistical models for decision making. For example, computers at the center might be used to simulate "What if?" questions when strategies are planned. Or the center might be used to simulate results if the sequence of activities in a major project were altered. Some centers have teleconferencing capabilities, closed circuit TV, training videotapes, and special output equipment, such as plotters. Equipment placed in a multimedia center will naturally depend on the needs of the organization served.

THE ELECTRONIC OFFICE

As a result of the automation of many of the administrative functions required to run an organization, we now have **electronic offices**. An electronic office is one that uses computer technology to:

- Handle correspondence and office communications
- Capture, file, process, and retrieve information
- Facilitate (or replace) administrative paper work, and
- Provide assistance in decision making.

Benefits include higher office productivity, more detailed and more easily accessed data and information, and faster communications both within and between organizations at lower cost. In addition, the quality of administration in an electronic office often improves. Figure 7.5 shows how communication within and between electronic offices takes place.

Both hardware and software go into the making of an electronic office. Since the environment and financial resources of organizations differ, equipment configurations and programs will vary from one organization to another, as will components from one workstation to another. (A **workstation** is simply a self-contained work area that includes electronic resources.) For example, secretaries may require only a keyboard terminal while a manager may need a push-button terminal with voice input/output capabilities and a light pen. Employees may have individual workstations or workstations may be shared by several users (see Figure 7.6).

Electronic Office Hardware

Hardware components for electronic offices include devices for data creation and capture, processing, output, copying, and distribution. For

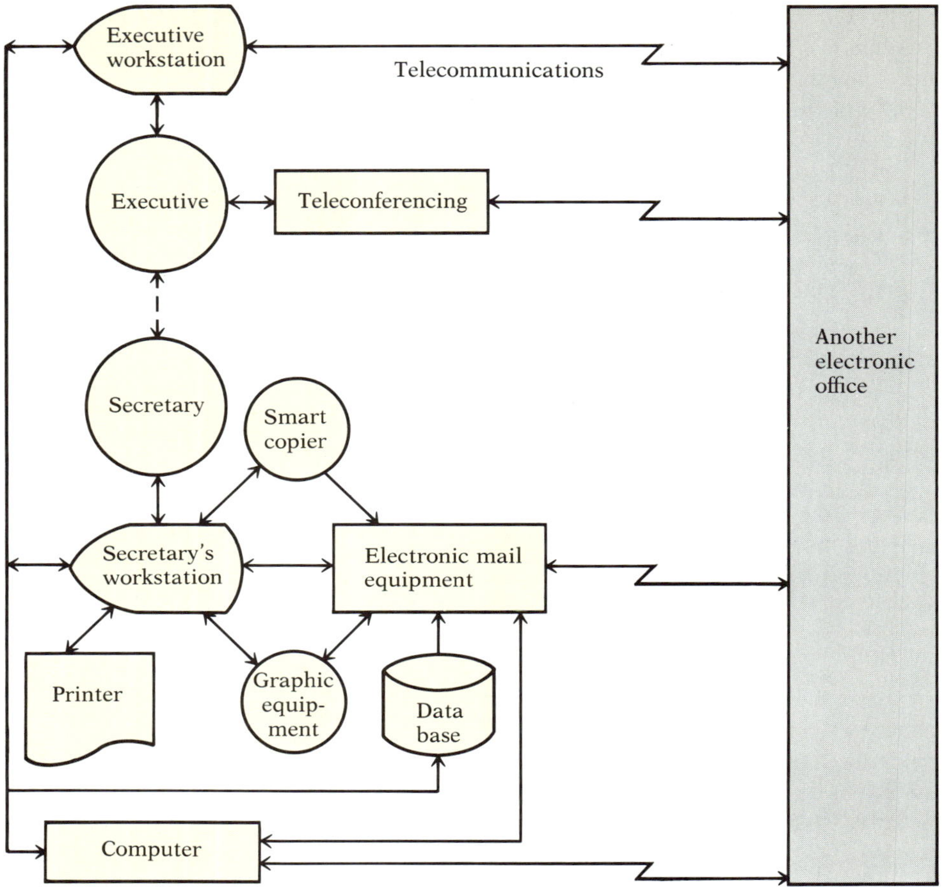

Figure 7.5 An electronic office. In an electronic office, interaction between secretaries and executives will be largely through the intermediary of a computer. Communication between offices will be by electronic mail. Teleconferencing is another mode of communication between individuals in offices remote from one another. All these applications will use a telecommunications network.

example, online terminals with a dialogue or interactive mode can be used to create data. Optical scanners can be used to capture data. A CPU processes data, a CRT screen can display results, and communications equipment can distribute output to terminals or computers in remote locations. The use of telecommunications means that office workers can share a CPU and peripherals when their workstations are located on several floors of a building, or miles apart. Employees may even work on terminals in their own homes. (Telecommuting, which involves working at home using a computer and telecommunications equipment to transmit completed work to a central office, is discussed in Chapter 17.) The various hardware components used in an electronic office and their functions are listed in Figure 7.7.

The components in an electronic office can be multipurpose; that is, they can serve clerks for correspondence and managers for project control, forecasting, and planning as well. It should be noted, however, that hardware does not exist for all administrative functions. Though managers can use computer-aided instruction to practice speed reading, they still must spend time reading and assimilating reports. Likewise, the need for meetings will never be totally eliminated. Furthermore, no equipment is appropriate for making personnel

Figure 7.6 An electronic office. Each workstation is a separate data terminal adapted to the particular tasks performed by the individual worker, and all are linked to the firm's central computer. (Burroughs Corporation)

evaluations or hiring and firing decisions. In short, we still do not have machine equivalents for the intuition and experience of most administrators and managers.

Electronic Office Software

Software for an electronic office must be easy to use since all personnel will deal directly with computers. Fortunately, much modern software does not require that users be experienced in programming or knowledgeable about computers. Such software avoids complex sets of commands, employs English-like languages, and is tolerant of errors. The development of query languages, described in Chapter 4, will be valuable in electronic offices of the future. They will help staff determine what information is needed and will retrieve that data automatically from the data base, saving users from having to specify retrieval procedures (see Figure 7.8).

A Day of Work in an Electronic Office

To show how the components of an electronic office affect office work, let us follow a hypothetical administrator, Adams, throughout a work day. All of the information technology described in this sce-

Supplement 7.4 Sample Electronic Office Hardware

This IBM equipment is basically a copier/printer machine, but it is capable of performing a number of office functions. For example, it can receive input from mag cards, terminals, and other communicating computers or information distributors. This input can then be combined to create original documents.

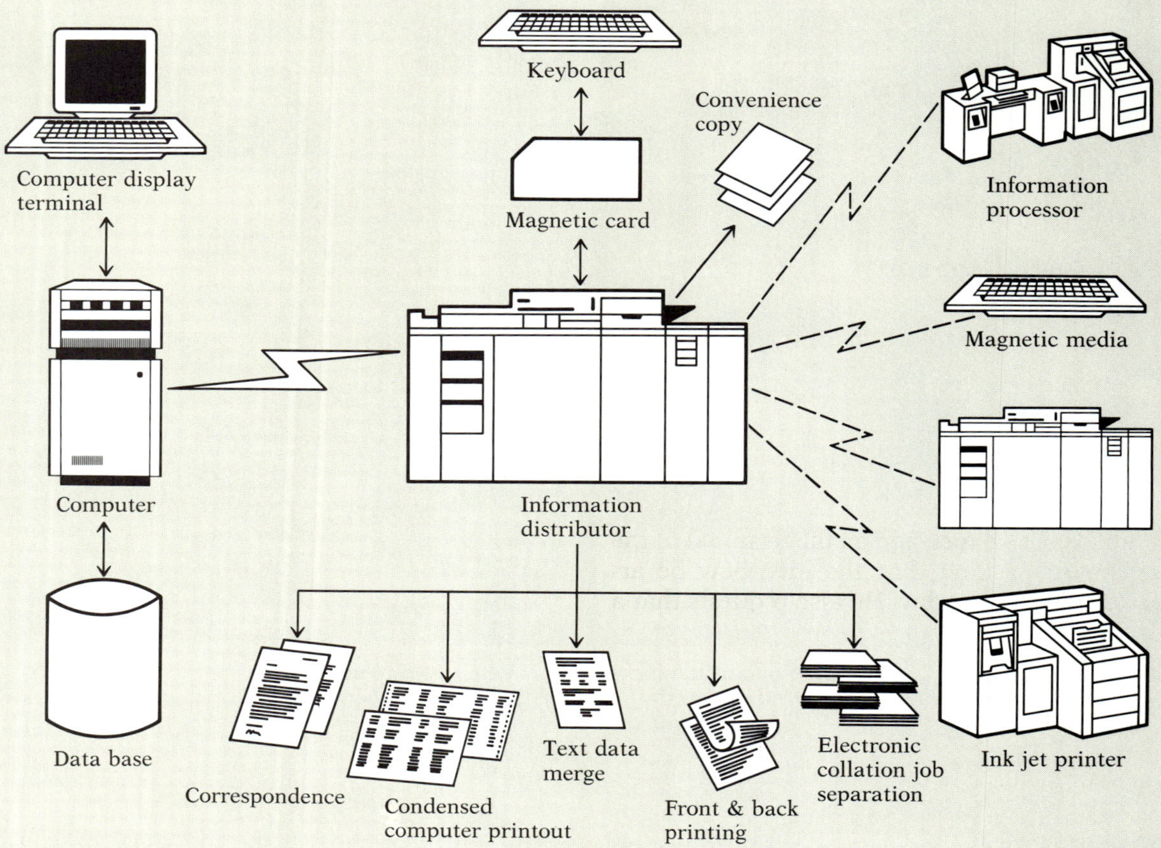

nario is currently available. Failure to use it can be traced to economics (that is, the price of hardware and software), organizational factors (that is, the need to reorganize departments and restructure jobs), and simply to human resistance to computers.

Upon arrival at work, Adams first checks the day's calendar. This is displayed on Adams' CRT screen once a coded command is keyed on the terminal keyboard. Next, Adams types in a request for a list of correspondence, which is displayed as a menu. The letters may be ranked in order of importance by Adams' secretary according to rules Adams has previously specified. Letters are chosen for display on the screen and their contents read. Short responses that can be delivered by telemail are keyed online. Others may be drafted by Adams on a word processing program.

A letter from Mary Williams requests an inter-

Data creation and capture	Processing	Output	Copying and distribution
Computer console	Routine software	Printer	Electronic mail
Keyboard terminal	Scheduling capability	Plotter	Intelligent copiers
CRT terminal	Indexing systems	CRT display units	Smart facsimile devices
POS terminal	Retrieval systems	COM	Automatic typesetting
Light pen	Personal calendar system	Audio	Teleconferencing
Voice recognition unit	Information packaged services (for example, on industry status, stock market, newspapers, journals)		Integrated communication of data, word, voice, graphics, and images
Graphic unit	English-like query languages		Networks access internal external
Data tablet	Interactive languages		
Telephone	Interactive graphics		
Pattern recognition unit	Bibliographical search capability		
Micrographic reading equipment (for microfilm and microfiche)	Word processing		
OCR	CAI (Computer-assisted instruction)		
Card reader	Decision support systems		
Tape reader			

Figure 7.7 Components of an electronic office.

view. Adams keys a message on the terminal to the office secretary asking that the interview be arranged for later in the day. He also requests that a meeting of all department heads be arranged for Thursday afternoon or Friday morning. The meeting will be set by a scheduler, a program that scans the calendars of the department heads, choses a time when all are free, schedules a time and place for the meeting, sends a message about the meeting to each head by telemail, and automatically updates their calendars.

Adams then keys a request for a list of jobs to be done. Included in the list is a message from the department of project control stating, "Project B85 Activity 10-15 due for completion yesterday, off schedule." Adams displays the PERT chart on the screen, locates activity 10-15 on the critical path, and retrieves the name of the employee responsible (James) from a menu for the PERT program. A message requesting an explanation for the delay is prepared using word processing and delivered to James by telemail.

Next Adams is alerted to the receipt of an urgent communication by a two-star flash on the screen. A one-star flash is for less pressing messages, such as "Meeting with Williams OK for 15:30 today." A buzzer and screen announcement interrupt work at 9:55, reminding Adams of a telecon-

Figure 7.8 A translation device. This machine acts as a go-between, transferring data among otherwise incompatible word processors and personal computers. (Telentry Systems)

ference he has scheduled for 10:00. Reports and documents needed for the meeting have been automatically retrieved and transmitted to the teleconference room, with hard copies preprinted as previously specified.

After lunch, Adams calls correspondence prepared by the secretary to the screen and makes changes where necessary. Adams' terminal is linked to the organization's data base so that Adams is able to obtain accounting and financial information, current news reports, directories, and other pertinent information simply by entering commands. A list of outstanding tasks keeps Adams informed of jobs that require attention, but priorities are decided by Adams, not by the computer.

Note that the electronic office is paperless. In addition, no jangling telephones or drop-in visitors interrupt Adams. When important communications arrive, Adams is alerted, but receipt of the messages can be delayed until convenient. Little time is lost waiting for files to be located or reports typed. Travel time has been saved by the teleconference. In conventional offices, 35 percent of an administrator's time is spent on the telephone, responding to correspondence, and travelling. An increase in productivity in any one of these areas represents a significant saving and releases time for more creative work.

The all-work atmosphere of an electronic office requires self-discipline. Communication between coworkers is accomplished by electronic means, minimizing foot traffic between offices. This reduces informal socializing that usually accompanies face-to-face contact. People who work in an electronic office must be both willing to interact with machines and also knowledgeable about the limitations and capabilities of those machines. The implementation of electronic technology requires a major adjustment in the skills, work habits, and attitudes of office personnel (see Figure 7.9).

Figure 7.9 Punching in. Data from this computer terminal goes straight into the data base used by the accounting office, making time clocks, time cards, and manual ledgering obsolete. (NCR Corporation)

Implementing the Electronic Office

Office automation requires capital investment in hardware, the allocation of resources for software, the redesign of office space, organizational changes, and managerial planning to ensure a smooth transition into the new environment. (See Figure 7.10 for a more detailed list of considerations involved in implementing an electronic office.) In many organizations, **implementation** of computer technology in the office proves more difficult than implementation of functional applications, such as manufacturing systems. On the factory floor, employees are fairly homogeneous. In an office, there is a wide range in the levels of education and experience and in the status of personnel. There are young clerks with no more than a high school background and highly paid executives with years of administrative experience. Obviously, these employees differ in their approach to computers and in the use to which they will be putting computers in their jobs. The configuration of hardware/software for each office workstation will have to be planned with these differences in mind.

Training in the use of an electronic office is also part of implementation. Again, the diverse nature of office staff presents a problem since each group of users needs a different type of training. One of the goals of training should be to help overcome resistance to computer technology. Many companies

Systems considerations	Environmental considerations	Organizational considerations
Indexing Directory maintenance Filing and retrieval subsystems Text and file transmission protocols Security and privacy of data protocols Integration of electronic data processing, WP, and telecommunications Short-term plans within long-range system plan Capital investment	Space Reorganization Aesthetics Noise reduction Security	Changes in job content Changes in supervisory relationships Displacement of personnel Unemployment Training Human factors: Fear of work invisibility Resistance to change Fear of machines Social isolation

Figure 7.10 Implementation considerations. The technical aspects of electronic office implementation are the responsibility of computer professionals. Many features of office automation should be available to all employees in the organization, not just office personnel; for example word processing and electronic mail.

Table 7.1 Projected Characteristics of Typical Office Workstations in the Future

Characteristic	1984	1986	1996
Memory:	256K to 512K	512K to 1MB	2MB and up
Processor:	16-bit (8088)	32-bit (286, 68020, etc.)	64-bit (?)
Display:	Mono	Bit-map or color	Bit-map, color, high resolution, flat
Storage:	Dual floppy to 10MB hard disk	10MB hard disk	10 to 50MB hard disk
Software:	Individual and integrated packages	Integrated	AI expert Customized interface and customized functions

K=1024 memory locations
MB=Megabyte
Source: Courtesy of Amy D. Wohl, Advanced Office Concepts Corporation

encounter strong opposition when they attempt to alter the traditional secretary-boss office structure. When McGraw-Hill first attempted to introduce an electronic office, for example, resistance was so intense that the company was temporarily forced to withdraw implementation plans.

The Results of Implementing the Electronic Office

Where office automation has taken place, the results have been impressive. According to one study, executives who have implemented electronic office technology feel that enhanced decision making is the prime benefit. Higher managerial and clerical productivity, an improved competitive position,

Table 7.2 Clerical Activities in a Traditional Office and their Electronic Equivalents

Traditional office	Electronic office
Writing	Word processing (key data)
Taking shorthand	Word processing (voice input)
Typing	
Proofreading	
Copying and duplication	Word processing
Filling out forms	
Checking documents	
Mail handling	
Bulk envelope stuffing	
Collating/sorting	Electronic mail
Pickup and delivery	
Dispatching	
Looking for information	
Filing	Information retrieval system
Pulling files	
Scheduling meetings	Specialized software
Calendar update	
Calculating	Data processing
Telephone	Smart telephone
Reading	(No electronic alternative)

and the ability to pinpoint managerial accountability were also listed as benefits.

At IBM, experience with electronic offices in two divisions over a four-year period has led to the following observations:

1. An electronic office improves the quality of office services.
2. Operations are more efficient, with a savings of 5.25 percent in the time of the principal (manager or professional user) and a 15 to 34 percent savings in secretarial time.
3. Five to ten hours of individual instruction given to new employees reduces their frustration with electronic components and provides them with the background they need to follow regularly scheduled training courses.
4. Users develop personalized work routines that give them the feeling that the system is responsive to their special needs.
5. Users are able to cope with the new tools of an electronic office and to incorporate these tools into established work patterns.
6. Enthusiasm grows as computerized aids increase in numbers and sophistication.

SUMMING UP

Paperwork and red tape have been the bane of organizations in the past. In the last decade, administrative office work has become more voluminous than ever. One reason is the realization that intelligent decision making requires data collection and analysis and that better tools for data reporting, collection, and analysis now exist. Another reason for the increase in office work is that the government is demanding more regulatory reporting. The rise in work load has occurred at a time of rising wages, giving impetus to office automation. The steady drop in the price of minicomputers, terminals, and storage devices coupled with the development of word and image processing technology has led to a viable alternative to the conventional labor-intensive office: the electronic office. office.

Today, terminals replace typewriters in many offices. Messages are sent by electronic mail. Routine tasks, like payroll processing, are commonly done by computer. Optical character readers (OCRs) scan documents and correspondence while computerized storage and retrieval systems reduce the need for filing cabinets. The response time in decision making has been reduced as has the amount of paper involved with office work.

Despite the benefits of automation, however, office workers often resist the introduction of new technology. They are afraid of change and unwilling to disrupt the status quo, fearful that they might loose their jobs or become subservient to machines. To avoid upsetting traditional work patterns and relationships in the office, administrators may not in fact implement information technology even though they recognize its value. Cost is also a factor that slows the installation of electronic office equipment. Although automation speeds information processing and should reduce operating expenditures in the long run, a large capital investment for equipment and software is required. Many organizations lack the financial resources for such an investment.

One solution is to implement office automation slowly, starting with a single application such as a word processor and then adding other pieces as financial resources become available. Small units of change are also less threatening to employees than major changes and evoke less resistance.

This chapter has discussed how computerization can assist administrators at operational, control, and planning levels. Not all administrative problems have computer solutions. But given the present state of the art, approximately 80 percent of decision making in areas such as accounting and finance can be accomplished through computer programs. A much lower percentage of work is programmable in areas like planning and control, where many problems do not lend themselves as easily to the problem-solving processes used by computers.

The electronic components described in this chapter can be used for purposes other than administration. For example, teleconferences can serve researchers at different hospitals working on a cure for herpes. Messages can be sent by telemail between parents and distant children if both have computers linked in a telecommunications network. Word processing is used by students to write term papers and by reporters to file stories for the evening news. Control and planning programs can be applied in factories to analyze and improve production, in banks to perform financial planning, and in the army to plan staffing.

A great many other applications could be cited. In the chapters that follow, special uses of computers will be described in fields such as manufacturing, government, and medicine. This chapter has been written to describe administrative uses for computers that are common to all organizations regardless of their field of endeavor.

REVIEW QUESTIONS

1. What is the difference between data processing and word processing?
2. What advantages does word processing have over a conventional typewriter?
3. What factors will promote growth of electronic mail?
4. List advantages and disadvantages of teleconferencing.
5. How can computers be used in planning and control? What types of problems in these areas are ill-suited to information technology?
6. What is an electronic spreadsheet? How can it be used?
7. What is a decision support system? When are such systems helpful?

8. What is the function of a multimedia center?
9. Describe typical components in an electronic office.
10. Discuss functions in offices that computers cannot perform well.
11. List the advantages of a desk terminal or minicomputer in an office over traditional office systems. Examine these advantages from the viewpoint of a:
    a. secretary
    b. clerk
    c. office manager
    d. executive
12. How can a computer assist in the following areas:
    a. correspondence?
    b. information storage, filing, and retrieval?
    c. text production, such as preparation of manuals?
    d. conferences?
13. Describe problems to be solved when implementing an electronic office.
14. Describe common applications for spreadsheet programs.

DISCUSSION QUESTIONS

1. Is electronic mail an option of the U.S. Postal Service? Should it be? What problems are involved?
2. Will advances in electronic office technology eventually make the use of paper obsolete for office purposes (for example, letters and office documents)?
3. What are some of the unique problems of an electronic office? What human issues need to be resolved? How might the electronic office be structured so as to retain human interaction? That is, how can impersonality be avoided?
4. Some persons claim that computers, especially home computers used for office work, will create new office jobs. Others claim that computers will cause unemployment among office workers. Which claim do you think is true? Justify your answer.
5. Discuss the following statement: The computer will remove tedium and monotony from offices and make office work more creative, stimulating, pleasant, and easy.
6. If workstations were being designed for you as an administrator and for your administrative assistant, what features (hardware and software) would you want included?
7. Can information technology help improve the quality of decision making in the office? How? Give examples.

EXERCISES

1. Use a word processor to:
    a. compose a letter using stored paragraphs in computer memory
    b. to change the tense of a letter
    c. to check spelling of text
    d. to add a footnote to text
    e. to increase margins
2. Interview a user of a word processor who participated in selecting the system. List the criteria used in selecting both hardware and software. Who made the final decision? How? Has the system proven satisfactory? What mistakes were made that could have been avoided?
3. Interview a salesperson or a vendor of office automation. List the advantages and limitations of a product this vendor sells. Compare that product with one offered by competitors by studying advertising literature provided for the consumer.
4. Do a cost analysis for the purchase of word processing equipment and software for family use. Now estimate the benefits, both direct and indirect. Calculate the benefit–cost ratio of the acquisition.
5. Assume that you budgeted $5000 for a home computer. What computing system would you acquire and why?

6. Use a spreadsheet program for a problem in your field.
7. List some common spreadsheet programs. Compare their features.

Selected Annotated Bibliography

Antonoff, Michael. "The New Spreadsheets," *Personal Computing*, vol. 9, no. 11 (November 1985), pp. 107-117. Enhancements to spreadsheet programs are described. A buyers guide to stand-alone spreadsheets and spreadsheet publishers is given.

Cohen, A. and E. "Computers: Ergonomics and the Electronic Office," *Architectural Record*, vol. 107, no. 11 (September 1982), pp. 45 ff. The source of this article is of interest—an indication that office automation is affecting all disciplines.

Denise, M. Richard. "Technology for the Executive Thinker," *Datamation*, vol. 29, no. 6 (June 1983), pp. 206–16. This article touches on a broad range of topics including software functions to satisfy management needs, software solutions, modeling languages, packages for DSS, the integration of decision support, and the implementation and audit of decision support systems.

Connell, John J. "Is There an Office of the Future?" *Management Technology*, vol. 1, no. 5 (May 1983), pp. 22–31. A major educational effort is needed at all levels of management to explain office tools that improve productivity. These tools will change over time. The term "office automation" is inappropriate, according to the author, since many office workers see their work as creative, not something to be automated.

Giuliano, Vincent E. "The Mechanization of Office Work," *Scientific American*, vol. 247, no. 3 (September 1982), pp. 148–64. The author believes that electronic processing to replace paperwork is inevitable. A major factor is that the cost of computer processing is dropping substantially. Giuliano argues that productivity, job satisfaction, and service to the customer will be improved by office mechanization.

Heinmiller, Robert. "Use Electronic Mail: Save Time and Money, Get More Work Done," *Industrial Research and Development*, vol. 25, no. 6 (June 1983), pp. 83–85. The author of this article is the president of a company specializing in electronic mail.

Husbands, Bernard. "Electronic Mail—Applications for Management," *Journal of Systems Management*, vol. 33, no. 8 (August 1982), pp. 6–8. The author suggests how the conference table can be turned into either an electronic forum, or, if things go wrong, "a battlefield of personalities, a wasteland of productivity, and a cemetery of unvoiced ideas."

Jaffe, Louis. "Convenient Conferences," *Popular Computing*, vol. 4, no. 5 (March 1985), pp. 88–94. Online meetings break barriers of time and distance. The benefits of teleconferences are discussed, as are forms of conferencing with various services like The Source, Compuserve, and EIES.

Lasden, Martin. "Make Room for Executive Workstations," *Computer Decisions*, vol. 14, no. 12 (December 1982), pp. 116–26. This article puts to rest many of the arguments given against the use of computers by executives. It also gives suggestions for encouraging top-level managers to use computers.

Makhoff, N. "Local Data Nets: Untying the Office Knot," *Spectrum*, vol. 18, no. 4 (April 1981), pp. 57–59. Contains good charts of some of the available local area networks and their relationship to office automation.

Mandela, Audrey. "Electronic Express," *Popular Computing*, vol. 4, no. 5 (March 1985), pp. 82–88. Sourcemail, EMAIL, MCI Mail, and EasyLink are among the services compared.

Mankin, Don; Bikson, Tora K.; and Gutek, Barbara. "The Office of the Future: Prison or Paradise," *Futurist*, vol. 16, no. 3 (June 1983), pp. 33–36. The authors believe that management, not technology, determines working atmosphere. This issue also has three other recommended articles on the office of the future, telecommuting, and shopping for the office computer.

McCartney, Laton. "Teleconferencing Comes Down to Earth," *Datamation*, vol. 29, no. 1 (January 1983), pp. 76–81. According to the author, "The new technology is not just for top companies with enormous budgets. There is now a variety of modest-priced options and approaches open to the user." These options are discussed. The article includes a graphic layout for a sample system.

Olson, Margrethe and Lucas, Henry C., Jr. "The Impact of Office Automation on the Organization: Some Implications for Research and Practice," *ACM Communications*, vol. 25, no. 1 (November 1982), pp. 838–47. Eighteen research propositions on the nature of the changes in work are discussed. The effect of such changes on individuals, groups, and organizational structures is examined. This thought-provoking article is for the serious reader.

Rhyne, Lawrence C. "Strategic Information: The Key to Effective Planning," *Managerial Planning*, vol. 32, no. 4 (January–February 1984), pp. 4–11. Discussed are different types of information needed for various types of planning (for example, budgeting, long-range planning, strategic planning). Good tables are included.

Rockart, J. F. and Treacy, N. E. "The CEO Goes On-Line," *Harvard Business Review*, vol. 60, no. 1 (January–February 1982), pp. 82–88. This article gives examples of chief executive officers going online. The authors think this is a trend that will continue, and they offer reasons why.

Strassman, P. A. "The Office of the Future: Information Management for the New Age," *Technology Review*, vol. 82, no. 3 (January 1980), pp. 54–65. Most of the uses for office automation to help clerical staff have already been discovered. This article suggests how office information can aid managers and technical/professional workers.

Thierauf, Robert J. *Effective Management Information Systems*. Columbus, Ohio: Charles E. Merrill Publishing Company, 1984. This book combines a theoretical and practical look at effective management information systems. Chapters 12 through 15 discuss marketing, manufacturing, accounting and finance, and personal subsystems.

Walsh, W. A. "Clustered Systems Integrate Information," *Word Processing and Information Systems*, vol. 18, no. 10 (October 1981), pp. 21–34. One message of this article is that you do not have to be discouraged if your system is not totally integrated. Partially integrated systems also have great utility.

Smart Products, Robots, and Automated Factories

The real cause for dread is not a machine turned human, but a human turned machine.

FRANZ F. WINKLER

CHAPTER EIGHT

Key Words

automated factory

collage

computer-aided design (CAD)

computer-aided design and drafting (CADD)

computer-aided design/computer-aided manufacturing (CAD/CAM)

computer-integrated manufacturing (CIM)

factory-wide management information system (FMIS)

firmware

growth path

growth stages

image mixing

material requirements planning (MRP)

Nolan curve

numerical control (NC)

process control (PC)

robot

robot self-regeneration

smart products

system integration

vision system

Computer technology plays two unique roles in manufacturing. First, microprocessors can be added to items during their manufacture to create products with "intelligence," goods commonly called "smart products." Second, computers can also be used as a tool in the manufacturing process itself—for example, in numerical control, process control, and computer-aided design. Both roles are discussed in this chapter.

Computers are also used, of course, in the head office of every factory to handle correspondence, place orders, regulate inventories, keep accounts, pay bills, and generate reports. The role of computers in such office activities has been described in the preceding chapter. In addition, factory managers employ decision support systems, also discussed in Chapter 7, in production control and planning.

Computer-integrated manufacturing is the direction of the future. This means linking computerized production subsystems to one another, and then integrating production with information systems in accounting, marketing, and other functional areas. A discussion of system integration and the relationship of integration to growth brings this chapter to a close.

SMART PRODUCTS

Smart products are products manufactured with embedded microprocessors. These products sense variables in the environment, compute, make choices, store information, and control and time specific activities. For example, a microprocessor built into a postal scale can determine the exact postage required for a weighed package once the destination is keyed by an operator or read by an optical scanner.

Software for smart products is stored in read-only memory (ROM), a chip containing a special electronic circuit that is designed to store instructions permanently. Users enter commands to activate the programs stored in ROM. Such programs are called **firmware** because they perform the function of software but are as permanent as hardware. Some smart products are sold with a number of firmware cartridges; by switching cartridges, the user can alter what the microprocessor does. Video game cartridges are examples of such firmware cartridges.

Supplement 8.1 lists some sample products that are enhanced by embedded microprocessors. To improve product performance, manufacturers are adding embedded microprocessors to a wide range of existing consumer and industrial products. Totally new products incorporating microprocessors are being introduced as well. Think of all the new electronic games and educational toys available on store counters. High development cost, not lack of technology, is the principal marketing constraint. Sales must be voluminous to

Supplement 8.1 Some Examples of Smart Products

- *Smart taxi meter.* Keeps track of charges for as many as five persons sharing a cab even when passengers are travelling to different destinations. The meter automatically adds luggage handling charges to each bill.
- *Smart thermostat.* Automates control of heating, ventilation, and air-conditioning systems. To prevent energy surcharges during peak demand periods, the thermostat is programmed to switch systems off for short periods of time when energy demand reaches a predetermined level.
- *Smart crane.* Includes a microprocessor-based monitoring system that computes safe machine operation based on data supplied by the operator. A load chart stored in memory computes variables, such as safe boom acceleration and hook load. The operator can enter constraints like the location of a power line or wall to be avoided. The range of the crane will be restricted accordingly.
- *Smart TV.* Enables viewers to program entertainment for an evening. The correct channel for each program will be automatically selected. Captions for the deaf, transmitted in code and not visible on ordinary TV sets, can be decoded and displayed at the bottom of the screen. Favorite programs can be recorded and stored for later replay.
- *Smart camera.* Focus is set by an embedded microprocessor after distance to the subject being photographed is calculated using sonar technology. That is, the camera emits ultrasonic waves, and the length of time it takes for these waves to reach the subject, bounce off, and return to the camera is used by the microprocessor to calculate distance. Camera focus is then automatically adjusted. (More than one microprocessor may be used in a single camera, each performing a different function.)
- *Smart watch.* The wearer can enter dates of importance, such as birthdays and anniversaries. The watch will flash a reminder when each date arrives.
- *Smart calculator.* A sequence of instructions can be programmed for execution when a given key is pressed. Special-purpose calculators are available for realtors, financial agents, persons planning diets, airline pilots, race track betters, and so forth. These calculators will perform square roots, logarithms, and other trigonometric functions in a preset sequence according to the use for which the calculator is designed.
- *Smart car.* Microprocessors in an automobile can be used for control of emissions, engine operation (for example, air-fuel mixture, ignition timing), door locks, theft deterrent alarms, air conditioning, belt buckling, braking, skidding, and speed control. Other uses are vehicle diagnosis, collision avoidance, maintenance analysis, and vehicle performance analysis.
- *Smart materials handler.* Uses sensors to inspect certain materials passing on an assembly line. If materials are upside down or at the wrong angle for the next assembly stage, robot arms will correct the position. Materials can also be scanned and X-rayed in search of structural defects, such as air bubbles, and removed if they fail to meet manufacturing specifications.

cover the expense of smart product development. Or a number of uses for a given microprocessor must be found so that it can be embedded in a variety of products. For example, a smart clock might be programmed as an alarm clock, embedded in a thermostat to turn on household heat at a given hour, or added to a household security system so that doors can be locked automatically and alarms activated at a preset hour (see Figures 8.1 and 8.2).

Obviously, smart products will sell only if the price is right. Manufacturers must assess customer preferences and needs, be innovative in product design, and keep costs competitive to succeed in the smart product marketplace.

ROBOTS

Robots are machines composed of sensing devices, links, and joints that have been designed to perform specific manual tasks. Robot action may be directed by one or more embedded microprocessors, in which case the robot fits the classification of a smart product. Or a supervisory computer may direct and coordinate the performance of many robots. Figure 8.3 shows robot components and describes how robots work. A robot arm is illustrated in Figure 8.4.

Robots are most effective in structured and highly repetitive jobs. In factories, they are used to spray paint, machine parts, pack cartons, and shelve merchandise by matching product codes with shelf codes. They load and unload furnaces and presses, oblivious of the heat. They spot-weld and assemble goods, and then inspect their own work. A major user of robots is the automobile

Figure 8.1 Computerized sushi. The customer in this Tokyo restaurant can make selections from a computerized menu without having to order from a waiter. (Mark Chester)

Figure 8.2 A sushi-making robot. The robot can make 1200 standardized pieces of sushi in an hour. (Mark Chester)

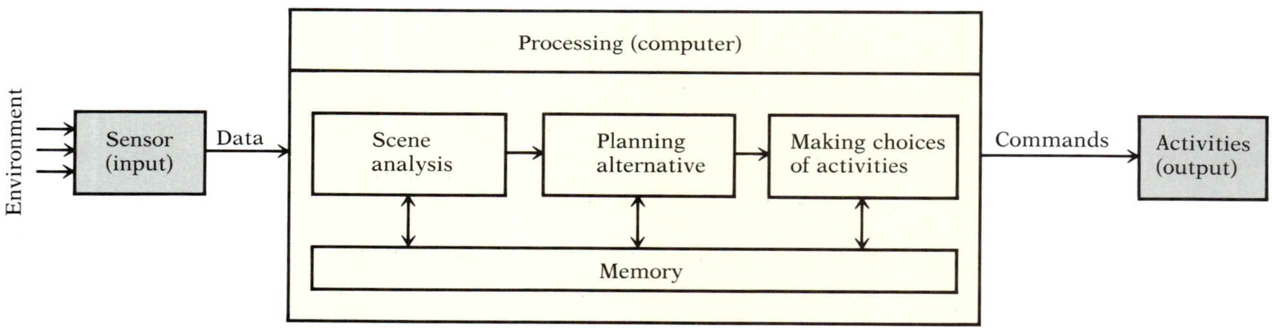

Figure 8.3 Components of a robot. Data is collected on the environment through a sensor. This input data is then processed by a computer to determine a course of action. Information stored in memory regarding operational steps for given conditions is used in the processing. Artificial intelligence techniques can also be incorporated to analyze the data and choose the best operation alternative. The actual choice of action is translated into commands to direct an actuator, the robot arm that performs the chosen activity.

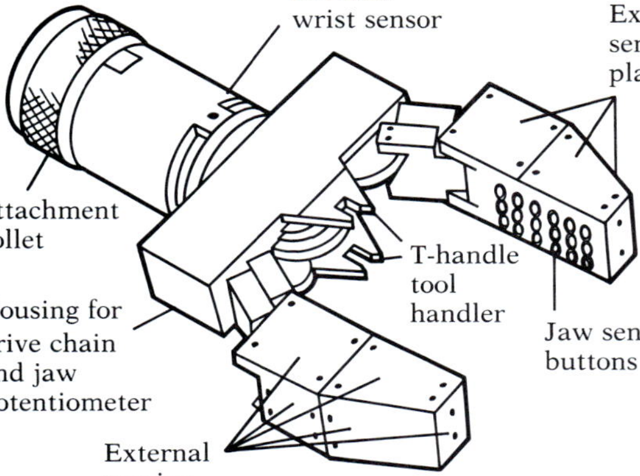

(Courtesy of Systems Research International)

Figure 8.4 *Arm of a robot.* Robots can be activated by toggle switches, push buttons, joysticks, handlebar controls, or instructions from a keyboard. Some robots also have voice recognition software that enables them to follow spoken commands such as, "Go higher," "Repeat last step," or "Turn right." One application for voice recognition: controlling the movements of a firefighting robot at the scene of a fire.

industry. According to a report by International Data Corporation, the industry purchased 60 percent of the robot market in 1984. The tasks assigned robots by car manufacturers are painting, arc welding, spot welding, materials handling, and loading/unloading, as shown in Figure 8.5.

Speed, accuracy, reliability, and increased productivity and quality are all advantages of using robots in manufacturing. For example, a robot can bore holes accurate to 0.0002 inch with a reliability factor of 97 percent at ten times the speed of a human operating a drill. In addition, robots can operate in environments hostile to humans, such as outer space, and safely handle both toxic chemicals and radioactive substances. Unlike people, robots can perform efficiently in temperatures from 40° to 120°F and can handle 2000 pound loads. For instance, at International Harvester, a robot places harrow discs in a hearth for tempering, and then removes them while they are white hot. From management's perspective, furthermore, robots are appreciated because they do not report late for work, complain about unpleasant tasks, take coffee breaks, or get sick or tired. They can work three shifts in a row without a union complaint and never demand pay hikes or rally against management.

Cost is also a factor favoring the use of robots in manufacturing. In the automobile industry, the expense of a robot is approximately $5.50 per hour, in contrast to union labor of roughly $18.50, including wages and benefits. It's no wonder, therefore, that blue collar workers are losing jobs to robots. Some experts predict that robots will eventually replace 65 to 75 percent of the current factory work force.

Although the robotics industry is relatively new, sales are already formidable. The 1985 market should be $214 million, up from $68 million in 1980. Many U.S. corporations that foresee heavy reliance on robots in the future are starting to manufacture robots for internal use. IBM, General Motors, and Bendix fall in this category. Actual expenditures on robots are therefore higher than sales figures indicate.

The reasons why growth in the field of robotics has been so explosive include:

- The dramatic reduction of the price of microchips.
- Rising wage scales of workers and increased fringe benefits, which makes investment in robots economically viable.
- Improved technology resulting in robots that are more intelligent and better able to perform a wide variety of activities.
- Competition among robot manufacturers, which has led to lower prices and spurred the development of innovative robots, ultimately resulting in increased sales.

Despite their growing popularity, however, robots are still limited in their usefulness. One reason is that most robots lack flexibility. They are programmed to perform precise movements in a precise sequence. If a part on an assembly line is out of position when it passes a spot-welding robot, the weld may take place in the wrong location. In

Supplement 8.2 Robots at General Dynamics

The F-16 fighter plane, built by General Dynamics, has over 200,000 fasteners. Each of these fasteners must fit in needs a hole to fit in a hole. These holes are made by computer-controlled robot drills that do the work with efficiency, speed, and accuracy. Drilling holes on wing panels, a task that formerly took thirty hours of labor by hand, now takes only three and a half hours. Mounting-hole tolerances are accurate to within 0.0002 inches. Though each robot costs about $150,000 per workstation, the company estimates that its payback period is two to two and a half years per robot.

The robots are programmed by guiding them through the motions of their tasks, step by step. The coordinates of key positions are entered in a program-entry terminal and stored in memory. The robot can then repeat the routine any number of times. A special feature of the robots is their ability to sense when a drill bit is worn. When this occurs, the robot is programmed to change the drill tooling before drilling is resumed.

General Dynamics also uses robots to feed lengths of tubing into deburring machines, an extremely monotonous task. Per shift, robots deburr between 600 and 1000 tubes, compared to 150 to 300 per shift by human counterparts.

order to correct problems of this nature, robots require sensory capabilities. Robots in the future may incorporate vision systems, a sense of touch, and hearing. They may also have nonhuman sensory capabilities, such as infrared sensors, sonar, ultraviolet sensors, or radiation detectors.

At the present time, **vision systems** for robots are given high priority by most manufacturers. Some vision systems under development involve capabilities as simple as verification of an object's presence. Others involve capabilities as complex as sorting and selecting specific parts from a random mix. All vision systems work by using cameras and then coding the image into bits for computer analysis. Researchers are trying to develop ways to filter out all but essential parts of a picture. They are also looking for methods of reducing the number of bits needed to interpret a visual image.

Consight, a vision system of General Motors, employs an array of 100 by 100 light-sensitive elements to produce a black-and-white image. Each element is assigned a number between 0 and 63 to represent light intensity of that portion of the picture (0=black, 63=white, with shades of gray in between.) The 10,000 numbers constitute the digital picture to be analyzed. One way the robot can identify what the digital picture represents is by comparing it with digitized images stored in computer memory.

If a vision system is incorporated in a robot that must lift and position parts on an assembly line, the next requirement is to program the robot so that it knows how to pick up and move parts it "sees" on the conveyor belt. One method is for the computer to find edges, recognized by a sudden change from light to dark. This information, added to a model stored in the program of outside boundaries and holes, can be used to compute the position and orientation of the part. This computation, in turn, gives the computer the information it needs to control the lifting and positioning movements of the robot arm.

In the future, we can expect more complex robots that have, for example, many arms working in concert. In addition, robots may integrate sensory capabilities with artificial intelligence, which will enable them to make limited decisions. For example, the robot might then be able to determine whether a damaged part on an assembly line should be repaired or discarded, or when to turn itself off. **Robot self-regeneration**—that is, the use of robots to manufacture robots—may soon be the norm. Fifth generation computers may use artificial intelligence to improve both robot design and the design of machines used to produce robots.

An area of research that should not be neglected is how to balance high technology with human values and how to utilize robots without creating social turmoil because of labor displacement. Chapter 17 of this book discusses problems of unemployment as we move from our

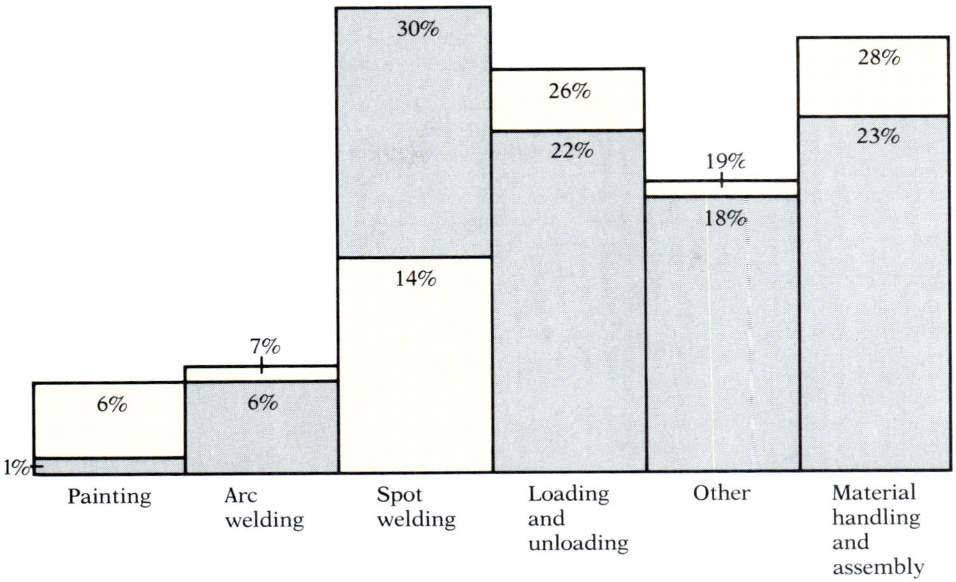

Figure 8.5 Robot use in the automobile industry

present labor-based industrial society to an automated, postindustrial future.

PROCESS CONTROL

Process control (PC) is the use of computers to monitor a continuous activity, such as the production of chemicals or the generation of electricity. In process control a whole *process* is automated, whereas robots and smart products automate only single activities or sets of activities.

Process control works in the following way. First sensors collect information on key variables at timed intervals (for example, temperature, pressure, or production rate). The computer then compares this information with predetermined acceptable tolerance limits stored in memory. When tolerance limits are violated, the computer determines what corrective action is necessary based on given conditions. It then directs an actuator to make necessary adjustments (for example, to close valves if pressure is too high). The corrections made are then monitored by the sensors and the process reevaluated by the computer in a new control cycle. This sequence of events is illustrated in Figure 8.6.

Process control requires an online, real-time computer. Though many processes may be controlled by a single computer, microtechnology has reduced computer costs so much that many factories now dedicate a computer to each function that needs to be controlled. In an automated system, a number of dedicated computers will be under the control of a supervisory computer, which in turn will be governed by a scheduling computer. A schematic representation of such a hierarchy appears in Figure 8.7. Supplement 8.3 lists some process control applications.

NUMERICAL CONTROL

Numerical control (NC) is another automation technique. In contrast to process control, numerical control provides automation of discrete operations. It involves the use of computers to control specific functions in a production process, such as boring, milling, planing, and pressing. In numerical control, numeric data representing machine instructions is recorded on cards, tape, or floppy disks. Preparation of these instructions can take place on offline equipment. The instructions are subsequently fed into a computer, which interprets them and generates the appropriate impulses to

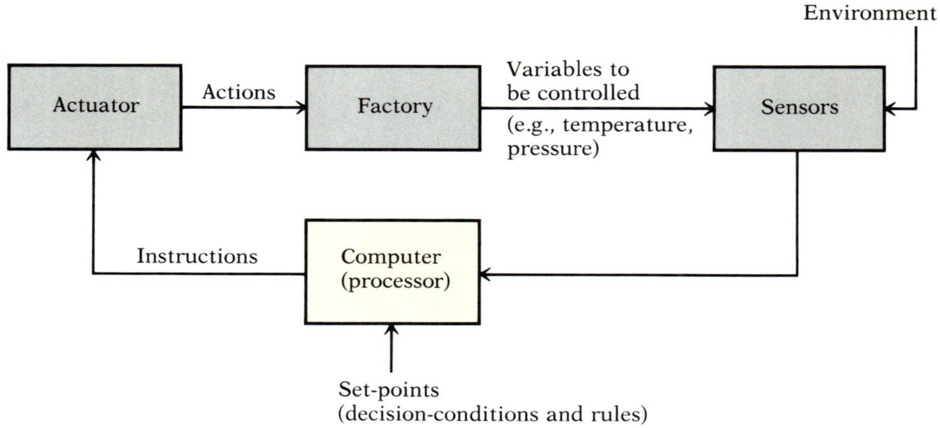

Figure 8.6 Components of process control. Three components are necessary to control a process: sensors, a processor, and an actuator. Sensors input data on the environment and the process itself. A computer then relates this data with set points (decision conditions and rules) drawn from memory. It is the programming that specifies what action to take under given conditions. The computer derives appropriate action rules during processing and directs the actuator to implement the rules.

Supplement 8.3 Process Control Applications

Production center	Input	Sample output
Pharmaceutical factory	Mould	Penicillin
Plastics factory	Ethane (gas)	Polyethylene (plastic)
Rubber factory	Butane + benzine	Rubber
Resource recycling	Domestic garbage	Fertilizer Mineral resource Energy
Glass production	Silica + additives like sodium	Glass
Food factory	Crude oil	Synthetic steak
Petroleum refinery	Oil	Gasoline
Steel mill	Coke, coal, and iron	Steel wire
Bakery	Flours, yeast, butter, and other ingredients	Bread

govern the movement of machine parts. Figure 8.8 diagrams this process.

An example of a numerical control machine commonly used in manufacturing is an NC drill. A computer controls the positioning of materials to be drilled as well as the selection and operation of drilling tools. To bore a large hole, for example, a series of small holes must be drilled. The computer determines the number of small holes needed and their drilling sequence. It also positions the drill by three coordinates and regulates the rotation speed and feed rate of the drill. The computer will calculate and adjust for tool wear as well. The precision with which the drilling is done and lack of human intervention required make such an NC machine invaluable.

When numerical control machines were introduced in the late 1960s, a large, centralized computer directed the operation of many tools and other production equipment. Priority conflicts and delays were frequent since the single computer was often overburdened and subject to breakdown.

Today, many factories dedicate a small computer to each production machine. Microchip technology, which has reduced the price of computers, makes dedicated systems economically feasible. Usually a central computer schedules operations and monitors the dedicated computers.

We can expect improvements in numerical control in the future. For example, diagnostic packages are being developed to ensure that oper-

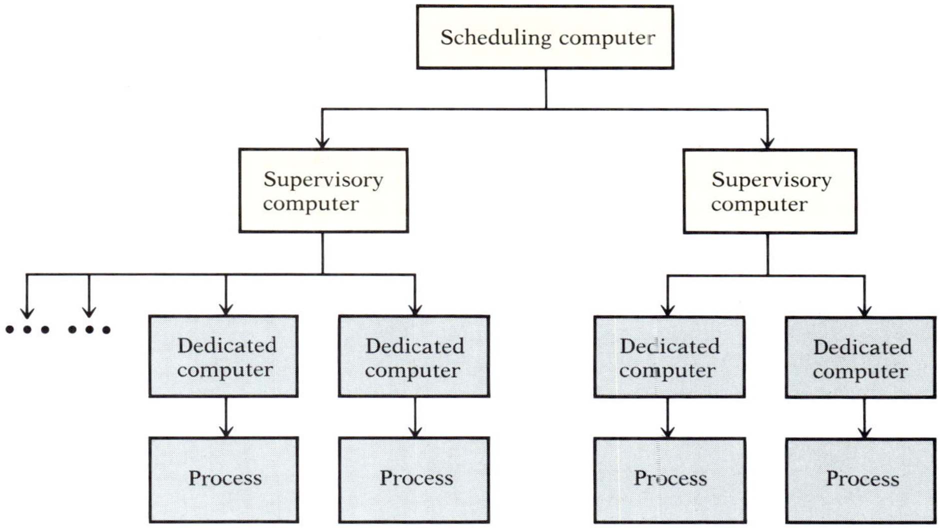

Figure 8.7 Hierarchy for process control. Dedicated computers for a number of processes can be coordinated by a single supervisory computer. In a large factory with many computers dedicated to process control, several supervisory computers may be needed. A scheduling computer will coordinate the activities of these supervisory computers.

ational steps are performed in the proper sequence and on schedule; software for new applications is being written; and better NC architecture is being researched.

COMPUTER-AIDED DESIGN

Computer-aided design (CAD) is another application of computers in manufacturing. In computer-aided design, a CRT tube replaces the engineer's drawing board. The computer can be used to produce conventional engineering drawings, to make design calculations, and to simulate operation of the device being designed. In other words, CAD gives the engineer a working model, not just a static drawing.

CAD is used not only for original product design, but also to make changes in response to factors such as revised contract specifications or altered marketplace preferences. Firms claim that they have a competitive edge using CAD because it improves design quality and reduces the labor and time required for product design. If computerized equipment is used in drafting as well as design, the term **computer-aided design and drafting (CADD)** is employed.

CAD is an application of computer graphics, a subject discussed in Chapter 11. CAD software will store an image and also store the instructions to create that image. This makes it possible to mag-

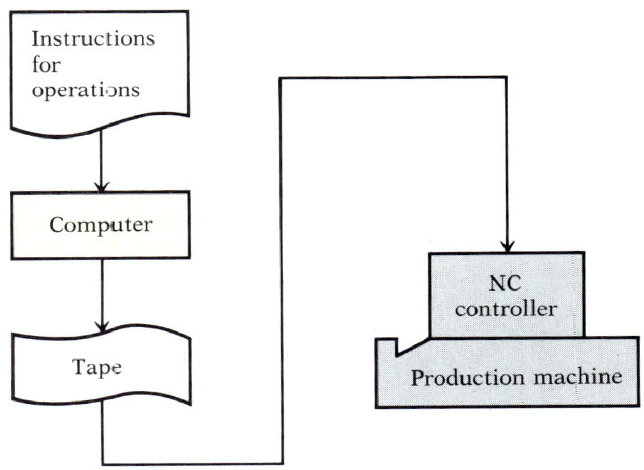

Figure 8.8 Numerical control. The computer is programmed to generate numerical data on tape representing machine instructions. If this computer is not online with a NC controller, the tape will have to be physically transported to the production machine room. There it will be used as input to a dedicated NC controller, which is attached to the NC machine as in this illustration, or loaded in a computer that controls several production machines.

Supplement 8.4 Numerical Control at General Electric

General Electric has a $16 million flexible machining system in its diesel engine production plant. This system includes nine numerically controlled machine tools, with over 500 cutting tools stored within these nine machines. The system also includes an automated transporter to move frames among twenty-one load/unload stations and a DEC PDP 11/44 computer that directs and tracks activities of the automated system.

Using production requirements specified by management, the DEC computer calculates the sequence of parts to be loaded/unloaded for maximum productivity. Parts are delivered by the material transporter to the machine tool able to handle needed machining operations in the shortest time. The DEC computer then downloads the machining program to the tool's NC controller. Thereafter, the DEC computer initiates the program.

This flexible machining has resulted in a 240% boost in employee productivity. Machining sequences that formerly took seventy workers sixteen days to complete are now done by four in just sixteen hours. Should the automated system fail, tools can be made to work in a local, independent mode.

nify a small section of a drawing 10 or even 1000 times its original size. Textures can be added by a method called **collage**. A mix of texture and color, called **image mixing**, can give a screen design the illusion of a three-dimensional figure. Advanced CAD versions utilize high-level language programming statements for moving, scaling, and rotating figures. In addition, a light pen can be used to draw on the screen with shapes geometrically corrected by the computer (for example, a circle can be drawn accurately for a given radius, or a hand-drawn line can be straightened).

CAD software can also be combined with other program packages, such as a program with a library of standard geometric components (also called "base parts"). Designers can use these base parts in a variety of design situations simply by modifying line lengths and arc radii (Figure 8.9 shows an example of a CAD modification of a base part.) A designer can then perform a variety of calculations to determine weight, volume, or cost of the new part when manufactured. These calculations could also be made for substitute materials—for example, for aluminum instead of steel. Another feature found in some CAD software is the ability to generate a three-dimensional graphic model from design specifications.

The intelligence that makes CAD systems able to perform such transformations resides in the software. Although approximately 1600 CAD programs developed under NASA funding are in the public domain, many manufacturers prepare their own programs. In addition, graphics packages are available from software houses. Despite the high cost of CAD equipment and software, many firms believe that increased productivity makes CAD cost-effective.

As might be expected, the computer industry itself is one of the major users of CAD systems. For example, CAD was used in developing large-scale integration of computer circuits. In other industries, CAD has been used in a variety of ways, some examples of which are listed in Supplement 8.5.

Since computer-stored data that defines a design is precisely the same data needed for various manufacturing purposes, computer-aided design and numerical control can be integrated, as outlined in Figure 8.10. Integration of CAD with a manufacturing process is called **CAD/CAM (computer-aided design/computer-aided manufacturing)**. Data bases of engineering designs that are part of CAD/CAM systems can also serve persons with planning, purchasing, and inventory control responsibility.

The cost-effectiveness of CAD should improve as advances are made in computer technology. The turn-around time from design to production that is possible with CAD systems should also be reduced in the future. But CAD places a new burden on designers: they now require knowledge about

Supplement 8.5 Some CAD Applications

To design and proportion bottle shapes; perform modeling and volume calculations for bottle molds; generate tooling of fixtures, jigs, and pumps; and prepare engineering drawings for bottle molding and manufacturing.

To generate technical illustrations, both two-dimensional and three-dimensional, for instrument housings, assemblies, schematic and wiring diagrams, and to generate layouts for use in technical manuals of an electronics company.

To perform the mechanical design and layout of gear boxes, axles, springs, drive shaft, and so forth, for the undercarriage of truck models.

To produce high-quality, accurate engineering drawings for sheet metal parts, electrical schematics, wiring diagrams, and control panels.

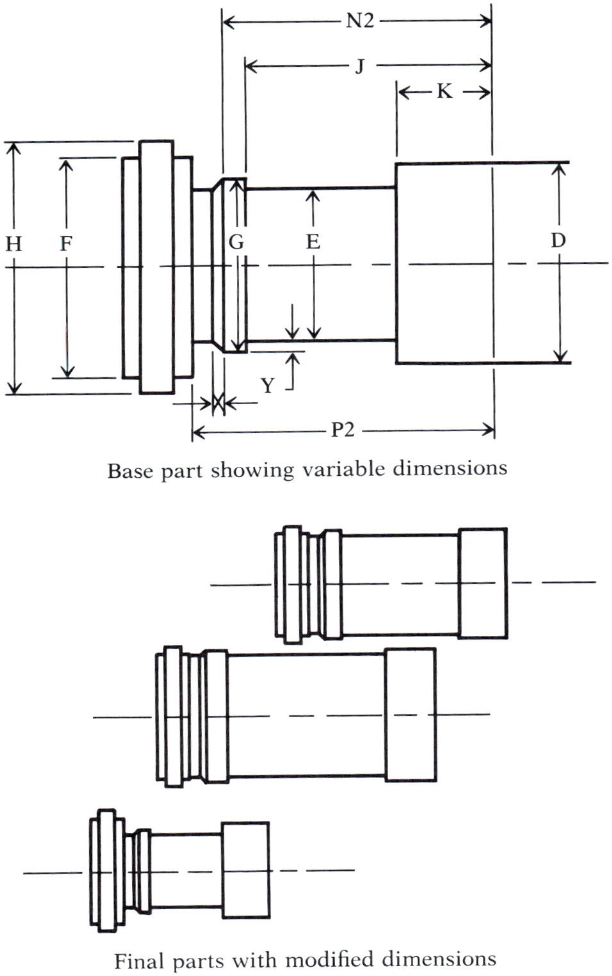

Figure 8.9 CAD modification of a base part. The base part in this figure can be modified by a CAD program to create final parts that look like those illustrated. The program user can make these changes with a few simple commands using the relationship of the dimensions of the base part that are stored in the system.
Source: Gerber Systems Technology, Inc.

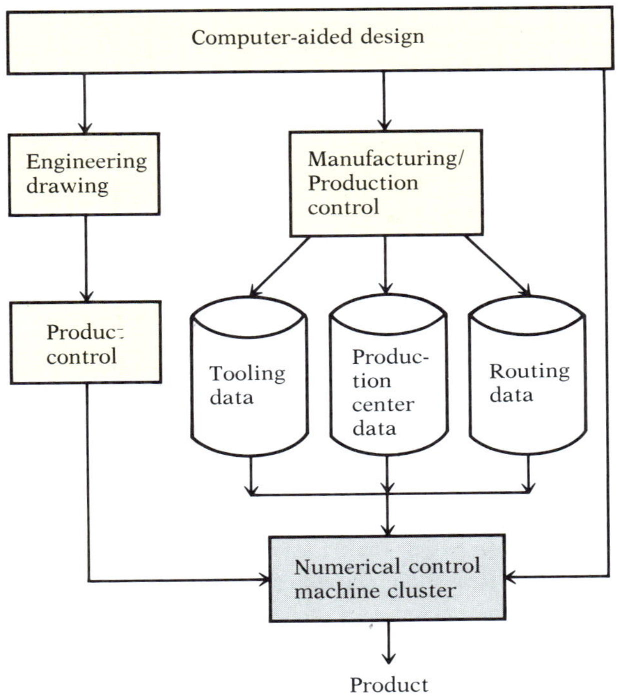

Figure 8.10 Integration of CAD with NC. When a device designed by CAD is ready for manufacture, the computer can be programmed to produce codes necessary for numerical control of the machines that will be used in the product's manufacture. Routing data (that is, the sequence of operations) is prepared by manufacturing control. So are machine and work center requirements (that is, which machines in which work centers will produce the product), and tooling data (that is, what tools are needed for each production stage).

computers. They must understand computer capabilities and limitations. They must also be able to structure design problems so that they can be solved by available data and software. As with all new technology, it will take time before the full benefits of CAD can be exploited.

AUTOMATED FACTORIES

The automated factory is the wave of the future (See Figure 8.11). Not only does it combine all the kinds of computer support to manufacturing that we have discussed so far in this chapter, but it also integrates these production-related applications with the data processing systems used for business functions like accounting, planning, and inventory control (the role of computers in administration was the subject of Chapter 7). An automated factory can be defined as including the following:

- Computer-aided design and drafting (CADD).
- *Computer-aided manufacturing (CAM)*. This includes numerical control, process control, and use of robots.
- Use of computers in costing, sales management, inventory control, planning, and other business aspects of manufacturing. These functional systems may be independent of one another. However, linkage of functional systems allows information stored in files to be shared and correlated by many programs for many purposes. A **factory-wide management information system (FMIS)** consisting of linked functional subsystems should be the goal.

Figure 8.11 A robot with a light touch. This robot arm can pick up a 2.5-lb. manufacturing component, but it can also grasp a raw egg without breaking it. (Ford Motor Company)

Figure 8.12 shows how the market for data processing products in each of these areas is growing. In the future, automated factories will utilize computers to coordinate all automated factory systems. When this occurs, we will have **computer-integrated manufacturing (CIM)**. This concept, illustrated in Figure 8.13, can be expressed by the following formula:

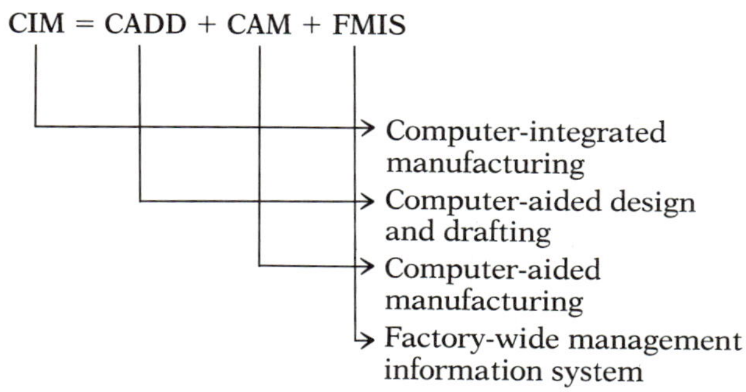

Efficient as computer-aided manufacturing is, however, it will take time and effort before the concept can be implemented on a broad scale. The reason is that plant floor automation, design automation, inventory and parts control automation, and office automation have evolved as separate disciplines. At the moment, communication between computer equipment from different manufacturers is often impossible. Protocols for computer communications are lacking. At General Motors, for example, where more than 40,000 intelligent devices are used on car production lines, only about 15 percent of the machines talk to each other. The company recognizes that compatible computer equipment is needed to manufacture cars efficiently. Rather than wait for the evolution

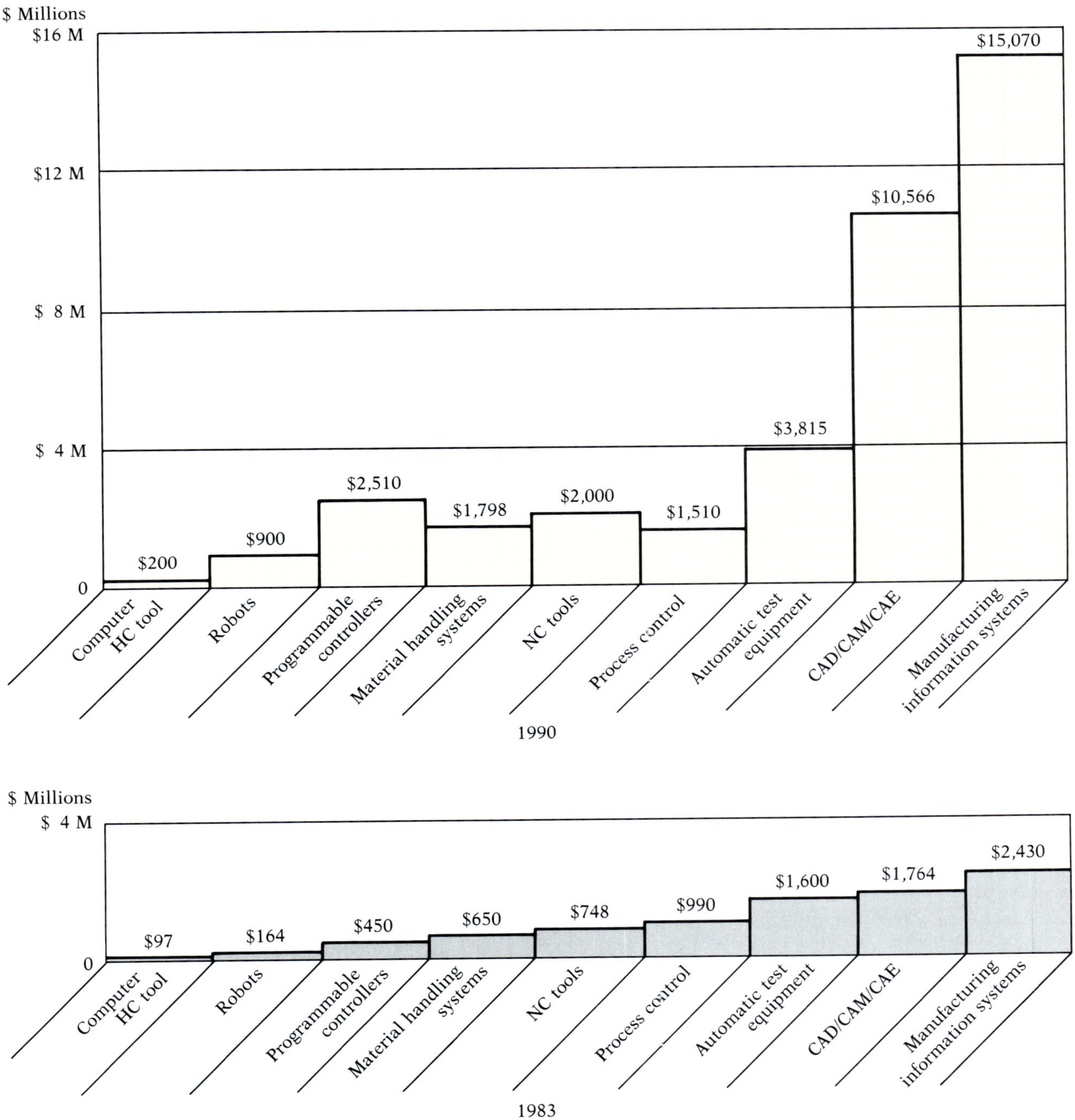

Figure 8.12 Factory Automated Systems—Worldwide Shipments, U.S. Manufacturers

of standards, General Motors has decided to create its own protocol for computer communications. This protocol, called MAP (manufacturing automation protocol), may become an industry standard. Corning Glass, Goodyear, Nabisco, Philip Morris, Procter & Gamble, and Scott Paper have

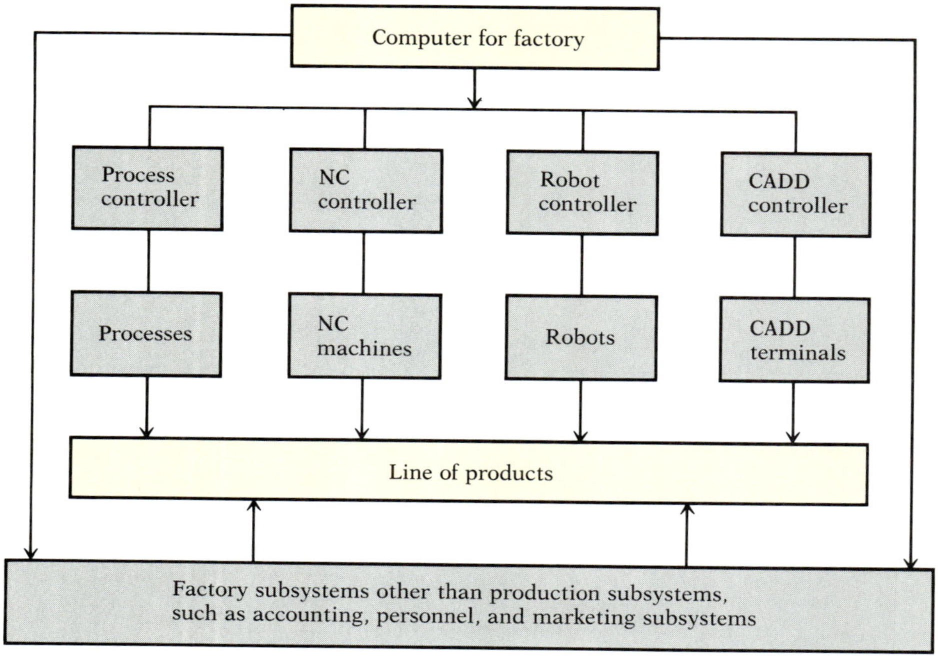

Figure 8.13 Computer-integrated manufacturing. This schema represents CIM, the integration of all computer applications in a factory. In the future, few blue collar workers will be needed in manufacturing. Instead, skilled white collar personnel will be used to monitor operations at a console and repair machines that malfunction.

shown interest. IBM and General Electric plan to use MAP systems in their own plants.

The primary argument in favor of factory automation is that it increases productivity. At a time when the U.S. industrial lead is being challenged by foreign nations with lower wage scales, most American manufacturers believe that they must automate to remain competitive. The main disadvantage is that factory automation disrupts the labor force. The social impact of computers on employment is discussed in Chapter 17.

AN EXAMPLE OF FACTORY INTEGRATION: MATERIAL REQUIREMENTS PLANNING

Material requirements planning (MRP) is an integrated computer system used by many manufacturers. Information stored in a large number of files is used to calculate materials needed to manufacture each production item. The information is also used to order materials and schedule their arrival so that materials are available when needed but not held in storage for a long duration. This reduces inventory costs.

Figure 8.14 is a representation of MRP showing linkage for files. Let us illustrate the value of such a system for materials planning during the manufacture of cars. The number of back orders in the order master file, along with projected orders input by the manager, can be used by the MRP system to determine the number of cars to be manufactured. The shop-floor control subsystem provides information on whether some of the needed cars are already in production. Data on car components that is stored in the product structure file will be used to determine what raw materials are needed if additional cars are to be manufactured. Whether these materials need to be ordered or already exist in inventory will be determined from inventory data in the inventory subsystem. When supplies must be ordered, the procurement subsystem will be referenced to determine where to place orders for raw materials, and the computer will initiate the orders automatically. The master production

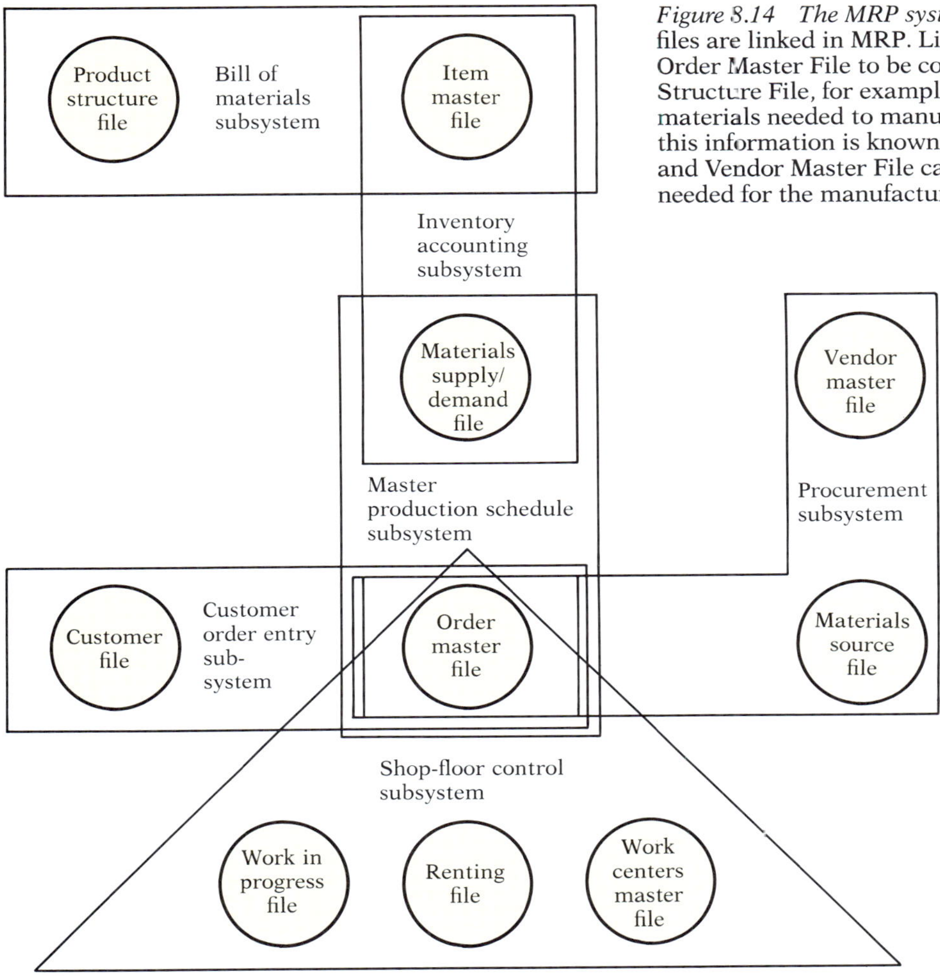

Figure 8.14 The MRP system. Many subsystems and files are linked in MRP. Linkages allow data in the Order Master File to be correlated with the Product Structure File, for example, in order to determine materials needed to manufacture items on order. Once this information is known, the Materials Source File and Vendor Master File can be used to order materials needed for the manufacture of the desired items.

schedule subsystem will be used to determine delivery dates for ordered materials.

In other words, the MRP system makes sure that materials are on hand when they are needed. Without such a system, materials planning is done manually by office personnel who work much more slowly and with much less accuracy than the computer.

Note that the integrated subsystems in Figure 8.14 include inventory accounting, production scheduling, shop floor control, procurement, customer order entry, and bill of materials. An advanced version of MRP, called MRPII, has two additional features: capacity planning and execution of work orders. It can be implemented company-wide, and it standardizes interdepartmental transactions, enforces a master production schedule, and reduces waiting time for finished jobs. An MRPII system will prepare reports on production hours and production units. It will even simulate daily operations to identify potential bottlenecks.

MRP reduces purchasing problems. Shortages of goods are uncommon, inventory costs are reduced, and engineering changes are easy to accommodate. Furthermore, less time is required to calculate material requirements. Finally, MRP makes for greater efficiency because it means that three-month projections are feasible, in contrast to the monthly projections common when requirements are calculated manually.

The main disadvantage is that MRP requires careful handling of bills and supply orders. Often inventory managers and material planners, the persons MRP is designed to help, resist use of MRP because of the discipline this computerized technique requires. Cost is also a constraint. Most firms that have implemented MRP, however, find the system extremely helpful and well worth the cost.

GROWTH PATHS

In factories or other organizations, information systems grow when new programs are developed and when system integration takes place. The areas where growth occurs and the order in which new systems are developed, called a **growth path**, is a management decision. Requests by employees for new programs are weighed against the recommendations of computer specialists. Often the developmental priorities of these two groups differ. For example, departments that will be using the new systems want the systems to have tangible payoffs and frequently demand systems to match those of competitors. Computer professionals, on the other hand, generally give priority to programs that affect the work of a large number of employees and favor projects that lead to system integration.

The size and configuration of existing computer systems may constrain growth. The state of technology may also be a constraint. How quickly employees in an organization can absorb new computer technology is an additional factor in the growth of systems.

Computer scientists who have studied information system growth in manufacturing concerns and other types of organizations have noted that growth in electronic data processing expenditures is an S curve. At the beginning, there is the slow acquisition of knowledge and skill that are required to utilize new technology, so that expenditures are low. This is followed by a period of rapid learning and implementation of that technology. At the end of the cycle, there is a slowdown in system growth leading to a final plateau. Richard Nolan, who has written extensively on growth, divides this learning curve into four **growth stages**:

1. Initiation of electronic data processing.
2. Expansion (adding new systems and subsystems to automate additional functions, such as new marketing, finance, or production applications).
3. Formalization of control (development of procedures and techniques to monitor, evaluate, and redevelop systems that prove unsatisfactory).
4. Integration (subsystem linkage).

The **Nolan curve** is illustrated in Figure 8.15. Note that a second S curve is superimposed by Nolan, starting at the period of time during which formalization of control is taking place. This second curve represents the assimilation of database technology: that is, the assimilation of the techniques for administering large and complex data bases that are developed as systems grow. A database manager may be hired, data bases may be restructured to allow sharing, and database management system software may be implemented to monitor database use, to control data access, or to protect data independence.

It is not until Stage III, according to Nolan, that the need for database technology becomes acute. The assimilation of this technology also follows the S learning curve, beginning with slow acquisition of knowledge, then rapid learning and implementation, followed by a learning plateau. Nolan names the growth stages that result.

5. Data administration, and
6. Maturity.

Of course, curves in Figure 8.15 are theoretical. In actual practice, growth will vary from one organization to another depending on management style, the firm's infrastructure, and its financial

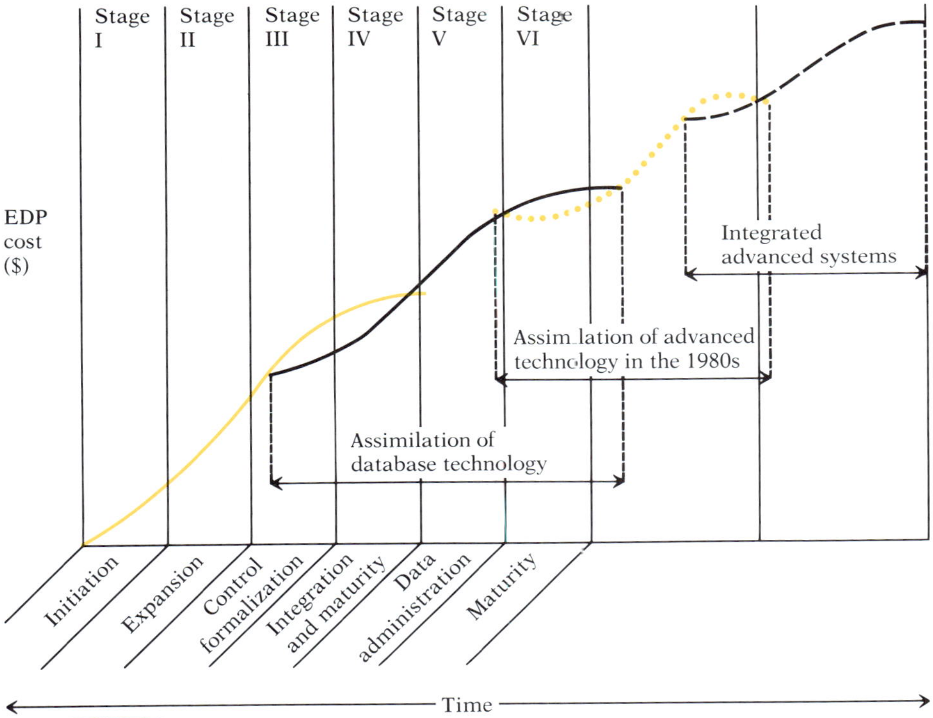

Figure 8.15 Nolan's growth curves. Advanced computer applications means adding an additional growth curve to Nolan's two curves (see dotted line). In manufacturing, this third curve represents CIM, the integration of all computer systems within a factory. Yet another curve is in the making: a curve representing the merger of telecommunications with information processing and the advent of integrated, advanced computer systems incorporating artificial intelligence.

resources. Background knowledge and experience of employees with computer systems will also have a bearing. A company may be in the first stage of growth in implementing word processing, but in the fourth stage in its applications for production, such as CAD, process control, or numerical control.

Can computer systems leapfrog over stages of growth? This can occur if management, analysts, and users have had experience with computer systems while they were working in other organizations. But leapfrogging is inadvisable in most cases. There is a limit to the ability of an organization to absorb technology. It takes both learning and experience to implement computer technology effectively. It is generally necessary for a firm to absorb the lessons it will learn as new equipment and software are added at each stage of growth before it can effectively operate and manage sophisticated integrated computer systems. This is as true, moreover, for organizations in other segments of the economy as it is for manufacturing.

SUMMING UP

Computers have many roles in manufacturing. Microprocessors can be embedded in products on the assembly line so that the manufactured goods can sense the environment, compute, and make desired logical decisions. These smart products have many industrial applications; for example, robots which are a type of smart product, are used extensively in welding and painting. In addition, many consumer goods with "intelligence" are now for sale, including smart cameras, smart calculators, and smart clocks.

Supplement 8.6 Growth Stages of Computer Applications in Manufacturing

Stage I	Stage II	Stage III	Stage IV	Stage V	Stage VI
Initiation of decentralized jobs	Proliferation of applications	Consolidation of application Some networks	Selected data base application Individual networks	Integrated data resource management Integrated switched networks Satellite transmission Integrated voice data, facsimile, text editing	
Initiation of: Payroll Accounts payable Accounts receivable	Initiation of: Budgeting Cash Management Inventory Materials control Marketing Order processing Purchasing Stores control	Initiation of: Cost analysis Scheduling Financial and capital investment planning Personnel	Initiation of: DSS OLRT CAD Process control Numerical control	Initiation of: Electronic office DSS for strategic planning Advanced robots and CAM Word processing Personal computing	Refinement of: Text management CAI Heuristic modeling
Selected reduction of cost and labor-intensive jobs	Initiation of: Data base and telecommunication Minis and micros			Integration of data base, telecommunication with minis and micros	

Nolan's theory of growth is not limited to computers in manufacturing. A similar chart could be prepared for computer use in government, medicine, transportation, and other segments of the economy.

Computers can also be used in factory automation. They can control how machines operate on the factory floor (numerical control) and can monitor manufacturing processes (process control). They can assist in the design and drafting of new products as well (CADD). In the future we may achieve computer-integrated manufacturing (CIM). CIM is the integration of computer systems in order to link the automated production processes with the automated offices that are responsible for the business activities of the factory. In other words, through CIM the business side and the production side of an organization are linked in an integrated and maximally efficient whole.

It should be noted that CIM is a new term and is not uniformly defined by all of its users. In this text, CIM means *total* systems integration. (Lack of common definitions is a major communication problem in computer science. New terms and a flood of acronyms are constantly being introduced, as readers of this chapter may have noted with dismay.)

The use of computer systems in manufacturing generally follows the growth stages postulated by Richard Nolan. The introduction of computer technology proceeds slowly; during this period users are acquiring knowledge and skill in implementing that technology. Rapid learning and growth of electronic data processing expenditures follow as a knowledge base is established and a large number of applications are developed. There is then a slowdown of growth as the number of useful applications of the computer systems reaches its maximum. Finally the S plateaus when the system has been fully absorbed into the manufacturing facility and new applications are developed only at a slow rate, if at all.

Nolan's curves apply to all computer applications, not just to use of computer technology in manufacturing. The same S curves occur when offices are computerized or when computers are used in medicine, sports, government, or science. As you read chapters that follow, keep Nolan's theory of growth in mind. It provides a useful foundation for understanding the applications of computer technology and the social problems which arise as that technology is assimilated.

REVIEW QUESTIONS

1. What is a smart product? Give examples. What limits the number of smart products on the market?
2. Give reasons why a factory manager may replace human workers with robots. For what types of tasks are humans irreplaceable?
3. What makes robots economically viable in factories today?
4. What is the difference between:
   a. numerical control and process control?
   b. CAD and CADD?
5. How can numerical and process control be used to automate production? What industries and tasks are most appropriate for each type of control?
6. What constitutes an automated factory? Do fully automated factories exist today?
7. What is the effect of CAM on:
   a. productivity?
   b. competitiveness?
   c. unemployment?
8. What is the meaning of system integration?
9. How can basic functions in a manufacturing concern be integrated?
10. What are the stages of growth of computer systems? Is it necessary to follow all of the stages in sequence? Why must a manufacturing concern go through stages of growth outlined by Nolan when automating a plant?
11. What is the shape of the growth path for computer systems? Is the same growth path followed for all applications within a factory or does each computer application have a unique path?

DISCUSSION QUESTIONS

1. Discuss functional applications of computers in manufacturing in:
   a. design of product
   b. manufacture of product
   c. testing of product
   d. control of manufacturing process
   e. performance of product
2. What are the implications of CAD for the manufacturing process?
3. How can robots be used in
   a. a house?
   b. an office?
   c. manufacturing of a part?
   d. an assembly plant?
   e. a continuous industrial process?
4. There are more industrial robots in Japan than in the United States, yet some of those are manufactured from U.S. patents. Why is this the case? What limits robot use in the United States?
5. What are the economic and social implications of industrial robots?
6. What is the potential of CAD in industry in the United States? How will CAD use vary between industries? Why will this variance exist?
7. Briefly describe smart products not mentioned in this chapter that are available on the market.
8. What are the advantages and disadvantages of system integration?

9. Can systems integration be achieved during operations after experience is gained with the system or should it be planned in the stage of system design?

10. Is it desirable and practical to plan and strive for total system integration in factories? Why?

11. What is needed to achieve an integrated system?

12. Does CAD help or hinder creativity?

EXERCISES

1. Visit a factory. List the applications of computers in that factory. If you are a photographer, make a photo essay of factory computer use.

2. Identify a situation in your field in which a robot would be helpful. List specifications for the robot for a purchasing agent. Tell what the robot must do and must not do. Also consider constraints such as size, cost, materials, and so forth.

3. In each of the following situations, identify the type of computer equipment that should be used to automate:
   a. a petroleum refinery
   b. gardening
   c. picking up the newspaper from the front lawn
   d. furniture design
   e. painting
   f. cutting cloth for a suit

Selected Annotated Bibliography

Albus, James S. "Robots in the Workplace: The Key to a Prosperous Future," *Futurist*, vol. 17, no. 1 (February 1983), pp. 22–27. According to Albus, robots will become cheaper and more sophisticated. They will increase productivity and quite possibly make all of us rich. When? Over the next two centuries, although many changes will take place by the 1990s. Another article in this same issue, "The Potential Impact of Robots," discusses the displacement of humans and the changes such displacement will bring to our social structure.

Argote, Linda; Goodman, Paul W.; and Schkade, David. "The Human Side and Robotics: How Workers React to a Robot," *Sloan Management Review*, vol. 24, no. 3 (Spring 1983), pp. 31–41. This case study of one factory focuses on workers' psychological reactions to robots and the emotional stress employees experience when robots are used.

Ayres, Robert U. and Miller, Steven M. *Robotics: Applications and Social Implications*. Cambridge, Mass.: Ballinger, 1983. Issues discussed include current and future applications of industrial robots; the role of robots in underground mining, space, and undersea exploration; job displacement; and the effects of robotics on the economy.

Beavers, Alex N., Jr. "Factory Automation," *Mini-Micro Systems*, vol. 15, no. 12 (December 1982), pp. 222–29. Beavers states that the need to boost productivity has forced companies to automate and integrate design engineering with machine control, process control, and management information systems. Excellent diagrams support this short but meaningful discussion.

Clark, Mike. "MRPII and the Small Manufacturing Company," *Manufacturing Engineering*, vol. 92, no. 1 (January 1984), pp. 62–64. The author argues that the size of a company appropriate for MRPII depends on how tightly the company is able to structure its production process.

Computer Technology Review. This journal, started in 1980, has a subtitle: *The Systems Integration Sourcebook*. The magazine publishes articles on the integration of subsystems, including architecture, human interface, software, communications, control, and devices.

Foulkes, Fred K. and Hirsch, Jeffrey L. "People Make Robots Work," *Harvard Business Review*, vol. 62, no. 1 (January–February 1984), pp. 94–102. Introducing robots successfully to the workplace depends largely on management decisions: how soon, where, who needs robots, and how many.

Groover, Mikell P. *Automation, Production Systems, and Computer-Aided Manufacturing*. Englewood Cliffs, N.J.: Prentice-Hall, 1980. This book surveys various topics on the subject of production automation and related systems. These topics include numerical control, industrial robots, computer-aided manufacturing, process monitoring and control, group technology, and flexible manufacturing systems. The author also discusses the concept of combining automated flow lines with numerical control machines.

Hudson, C. A. "Computers in Manufacturing," *Science*, vol. 215, no. 4534 (February 12, 1982), pp. 818–25. This article discusses computer evolution, manufacturing automation, robotics, fostering innovation, human factors engineering, and the sociological impact of automation.

Inglesby, Tom. "New CAD/CAM Entries Have Designs on the Future," *Infosystems*, vol. 29, no. 11 (November 1982), pp. 56–62. The author reviews the entry of mainframe manufacturers into the exploding market of CAD/CAM systems, although manufacturers of specialty systems are still very competitive. The beneficiaries of this competition are the designers of industrial and commercial products.

Johnson, J. "Pushing the State of the Art," *Datamation*, vol. 28, no. 2 (February 1982), pp. 112–17. CAM-1, an organization composed of hardware manufacturers, persons from software houses, and CAD/CAM practitioners, is discussed. CAM-1's goal is the push-button factory: a completely computer-operated factory in which products are designed and simulated by computer.

Lerner, Eric K. "Computer-Aided Manufacturing," *IEE Spectrum*, vol. 18, no. 11 (November 1981), pp. 34–39. Lerner discusses the use of CAM in a flexible machining system (FMS). He evaluates CAM limitations in this context, including the lack of versatility, the heavy burden of maintenance, the difficulty in automating assembly, the need for large investments, and market uncertainty. According to Learner, FMS workers in Japan are having to work faster to keep up with new computerized machines.

Newman, P. S. "Towards an Integrated Development Environment," *IBM Systems Journal*, vol. 21, no. 1 (1982), pp. 81–107. The author proposes an approach to systems integration and recommends consistent development and execution as solutions to problems of cost control and effectiveness of applications. The article includes a discussion of system description languages, very high-level languages, application generators, and new data models. There is also an excellent bibliography containing sixty items.

Thompson, Harry B. "CAD/CAM and the Factory of the Future," *Management Review*, vol. 72, no. 5 (May 1983), pp. 27–28. This article discusses how CAD/CAM in a computer-integrated manufacturing environment will change the way businesses are planned, organized, and managed. The article is written from management's perspective.

Computers for Teaching—Teaching About Computers

The future is a race between education and catastrophe.

H. G. WELLS

CHAPTER NINE

Key Words

authoring languages	copy-protected formats	problem solving
authoring systems	computer literacy	programming
backward recycling	discovery	role-playing games
CAI software	drill-and-practice	simulation
computer-assisted instruction (CAI)	frame	stimulus response sequence
computer-based learning (CBL)	host	tutorial
computer-managed instruction (CMI)	modeling	user friendly
	network	workstations
	network controller	

What role do computers play in education? They can be used for instruction, and they can perform many administrative tasks involved in running an educational institution. Word and data processing assist students with assignments. Because computers are able to store vast amounts of information in data bases, computers can also serve as an information resource and research tool. In fact, whole libraries of information may soon be on tape and disks, replacing conventional books on library shelves.

Although computers contribute to the educational process, they have also added to the responsibilities of teachers. Today, mastery of the three R's is no longer sufficient; schools must teach computer literacy as well. Students must be introduced to hardware and software. They must be taught about the potential and limitations of computers and be made aware of the social and ethical implications of widespread computer use. This means that teachers need to learn about computers themselves and educational institutions must add computer science courses to their curricula.

Computers and education is the theme of this chapter. We will approach this theme from a variety of angles, touching on computer-assisted instruction, the computational use of computers in the classroom, computer-managed instruction, computers as an educational resource, and computer literacy.

COMPUTER-ASSISTED INSTRUCTION

The term **computer-assisted instruction (CAI)** is used when a computer is a teaching aid, a proxy for a human tutor. CAI software is purchased as a package or written by the classroom teacher. The programs present subject material on a CRT screen. Then students are tested by the program on their mastery of the material. Correct answers are rewarded, usually by means of a comment on the screen such as "Well done." Incorrect responses trigger a beep or some other error signal. (One program for young children displays a sad face when answers are wrong. Another shows a fire-breathing dragon.)

This type of **programming** is essentially a **stimulus response sequence**, providing fast positive reinforcement for the right answers. According to B. F. Skinner, a renowned psychologist, such immediate feedback is an important factor in motivating students to learn. A well-written program should lead the student to select the correct answer 90 percent of the time.

Programs for CAI can be written in a variety of modes.

Supplement 9.1 The Oregon Trail, A Simulation Program

Oregon Trail is a simulated 2040 mile journey to Oregon from Independence, Mo. by covered wagon by a family of five. Players start with $900 with which to purchase the wagon, oxen, and supplies, including ammunition, for the trek. En route, they encounter Indians, bandits, lightning, snakebites, earthquakes, and other hazards. The aim is to arrive in Oregon before succumbing to calamity. One dire possibility: starvation because the money has run out.

Is this learning or simply game-playing for fun? According to teachers who use the program, pupils identify with the pioneers after playing the game and have a far better understanding of their hardships than they have after simply reading about the trip in a social studies book. The simulation serves as a supplemental teaching aid to reinforce and extend concepts being taught in the classroom.

1. In the **tutorial** mode, new concepts are presented followed by questions. An incorrect answer will lead to **backward recycling**; that is, additional **frames** (screen displays) on the same subject. These will not be repetition of the original frames but supplementary material on the same concepts but differing in detail, pace, and sequence. A flowchart of backward recycling appears in Figure 9.1.

2. The **drill-and-practice** mode assumes that the skill in question is known but that repetition is necessary to master the skill. Drill and practice is particularly helpful in subjects like mathematics, spelling, and foreign languages.

3. The **discovery** mode fosters new insights by presenting information and asking the student to draw conclusions. The discovery mode may state a principle and then ask pupils to choose a fitting example, or give an example from which a generalization or rule must be drawn.

4. The **problem-solving** mode requires students to think by making them apply concepts that they have learned to problem solving.

5. The **modeling** mode represents a process or system mathematically and lets students change variables so that an increased understanding of the process or system is attained.

6. **Simulation** or **role-playing games** allow students to explore relationships in real-life situations.

Which CAI mode is appropriate depends, in part, on the subject matter and, in part, on the grade level of the students who will be using the program. CAI can be designed for preschoolers, elementary pupils, high school and university students, or adults who need special training at home or on the job. Sometimes programs are customized for persons with learning disabilities. One of the aims of CAI is to individualize instruction. It is the programming that determines whether this objective is met.

Both students and teachers benefit from CAI. The computer can compensate for teacher shortages by assuming some of the academic load; more time in the classroom for human teachers to engage in one-on-one tutoring often results. In addition, CAI learning can be self-paced. Well-programmed software also provides students with immediate acknowledgement of correct answers and supplementary work when mistakes are made—feedback that is often delayed in other learning situations. Just using a computer motivates many students to learn. They enjoy the interactive nature of computer instruction and many benefit from the computer's unlimited "patience" and attention to their individual learning problems. Furthermore, the student can experiment with concepts in ways that would be too costly or too risky in actual practice; for example, a chemistry experiment that could lead to an explosion in the lab can be simulated safely on a computer (see Figure 9.2).

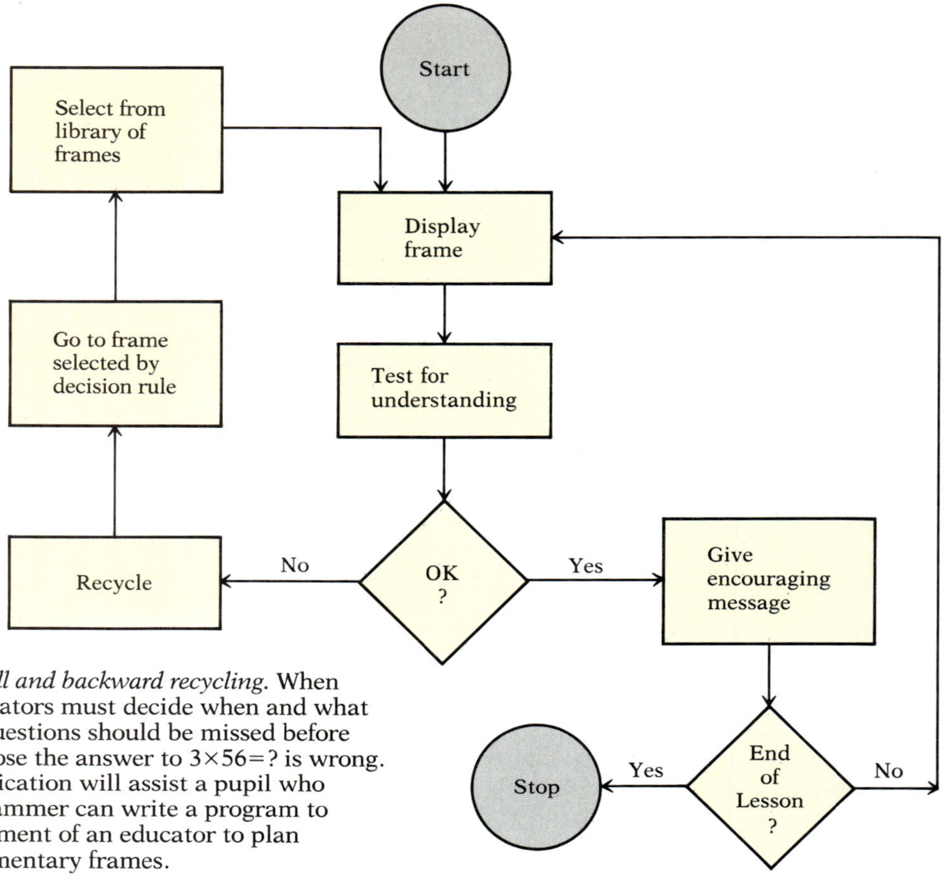

Figure 9.1 Flowchart for drill and backward recycling. When writing a CAI program, educators must decide when and what to recycle. How many test questions should be missed before recycling is desirable? Suppose the answer to 3×56=? is wrong. What type of drill in multiplication will assist a pupil who makes the mistake? A programmer can write a program to recycle, but it takes the judgment of an educator to plan recycling and design supplementary frames.

Figure 9.2 Computer-assisted instruction. Students can perform safe experiments in the lab, and use computer simulation for costly or risky experiments.

CAI Programming

Programming is the key to the success or failure of CAI. We know that computers can engross children for hours at a time; the popularity of computer games and video arcades is evidence of this. The fact that CAI has been unable to sustain student interest in the past cannot be blamed on the medium of instruction (computer hardware) but on how learning has been presented (computer software).

Until recently, **CAI software** was written by programmers. Teachers may have designed the CAI logic and made content decisions, but logic and content were translated into program statements by computer professionals. Too often, flat, boring software resulted. In part, the programming languages used, BASIC and Pascal, were at fault. These general-purpose languages are simply not well suited for CAI. The selection of CAI software was limited, and available packages were primarily drill-and-practice or textbook substitutes.

Supplement 9.2 Chemistry Simulation

TRS-80 Chemistry Lab is a Radio Shack program that lets secondary students simulate chemistry experiments in six topics: kinetic theory, Charles' law, Boyle's law, conductivity, solubility, and titration. Though not intended to replace experimentation in a real laboratory, the program does have certain advantages. It allows students to see the results of an experiment again and again. Furthermore, the computer can help collect, graph, and analyze data produced by experiments.

In the titration simulation, students choose a basic solution and a quantity of an unknown acid. A filled beaker and buret appear on the CRT screen. The student uses the down-arrow key to add drops of the base to the acid. The solution changes color on the screen when the solution has been titrated just as it would if an indicator were used in the laboratory.

Data for the titration next appears on the CRT screen along with the equation used to calculate the molarity (concentration) of acid for this titration. This information is used by the student to solve for the molarity of the acid.

Nevertheless, several well-respected sources for instructional software have been in existence for some time. CONDUIT, a nonprofit organization that promotes the use of computers at the university level, is one. The PLATO project at the University of Illinois, which has developed programs for elementary through college-level students, is another. Although many consider PLATO the most successful CAI project to date, cost is a limitation since programs are implemented on a large, time-sharing computer system. When the project was begun in 1960, it seemed obvious that a single centralized mainframe computer serving hundreds of remote terminals would be most economical. In the interim, inexpensive microcomputers have reached the market. Decentralized CAI is now a cheaper alternative under certain conditions.

Advances in technology today enliven instructional programs. Color and computer graphics, including figures that rotate and move, add interest to the CRT screen. Computers can voice comments, even joke with pupils, to encourage student involvement. Computers have also become **user-friendly**; that is, systems are designed for persons with little background in computer technology. Only minimal instruction is required to operate a user-friendly system. Help prompts appear on the screen and the use of menus eliminates the need for programming knowledge on the part of CAI users.

Furthermore, new languages have been developed, such as the extended version of Pascal called UCSD Pascal. These languages make it easier to process words, clauses, sentences, lines, curves, and also student answers; the overall effect has been to improve CAI software. LOGO is another language favored for CAI instruction because its graphics capabilities allow the user to draw pictures and animate figures, features that appeal to students. LOGO is so easy to learn that children themselves can become LOGO programmers. At the same time, the language is complex enough to do sophisticated procedural programming. A popular use of LOGO by children is programming to control the movements of a turtle pictured on the CRT screen. In trying to make the turtle move, children learn important principles in programming and concepts in mathematics, physics, and geometry as well.

Authoring systems have also been introduced to the market in recent years. These systems help teachers write programs for the specific learning needs of their classes. The program AUTHOR designed to help program a lesson, is one example. QUICKQUIZ, which guides teachers through ten easy steps to program a test, is another.

Authoring languages, which allow the instructor to forget about the technicalities of programming and instead concentrate on the information being programmed, have been developed as well. PILOT fits this category. It is a dialog-oriented language, has a simple syntax, and handles words and text easily. This language can be learned in several hours by people who have no prior programming experience.

Further language research is still needed, however. Once teachers have access to powerful, easy-

Supplement 9.3 Sample CAI Programs

- *Preschool*

Reading readiness. Provides drill on shape recognition, capital letter discrimination, the order of the alphabet, and matching capitals with lowercase letters.

- *Elementary School*

Spelling. Computer pronounces words to be spelled, student types words on terminal, computer corrects answers.
Vocabulary. Combines pictures and text on the screen with words voiced by the computer.
Reading. Includes read-along cassette with computer exercises on content and vocabulary.
Social studies. Simulates process of getting elected to a government office.

- *High school*

Algebra. Provides problem-solving practice, with twenty-four different levels of difficulty for each series of problems.
Foreign language. Helps create and edit text in French, Spanish, and other languages.
Biology. Used to design DNA molecules. Another program will analyze and graph the rate of enzyme reactions as a function of substrate concentration, enzyme concentration, pH, and temperature.
Art. Helps to create computer graphics, animated pictures, posters for theatrical productions, and charts for science courses.

- *University*

Business School. Simulates portfolio investment to teach financial management.
Computer Science Department. Teaches how to program in BASIC.
Statistics. Presents solutions from which student derives the Pascal triangle for binomial coefficients.

- *Adult*

Factory. Shows employees how to operate and maintain equipment. Simulation allows trainees to manipulate control panels and see what happens when machines are incorrectly operated.
Business. Teaches company employees how to comply with fair employment laws in recruitment, selection, placement, promotion, transfer, discipline, and discharge.
Pharmacy. Provides information on new prescription drug products.
Airlines. Tests and manages transition training for pilots being upgraded from one type of aircraft to another.
Home. Coaches for high school equivalency exam.

to-learn languages that really resemble language as it is spoken, the number of creative, pedagogically sound programs should increase since more educators will be able to write programs on their own. This is not to suggest that good CAI materials will ever be easy to write. Many educators who have worked in the field of programmed learning say that it is harder to develop good CAI materials than to write a textbook. Features that should be incorporated in CAI software are listed in Figure 9.3.

The Potential of CAI

Although educators agree that CAI can be an effective learning tool, few applications of CAI have undergone rigorous experimental examination. The claim that CAI produces accelerated skill acquisition over traditional learning methods is controversial. Nevertheless, because most educators recognize that there are benefits from instructional computing and also believe that it is only a matter of time before computers become commonplace in the classroom, they support efforts to develop improved CAI software and to train teachers in computer use.

In classrooms of the future, each student may have a desktop terminal served by a **host** mainframe, mini, or microcomputer and a **network controller**, as illustrated in Figure 9.4. Their function will be to send instructional software to student stations and to transmit programs from one student terminal to another. Such network configurations facilitate rapid, organized, and inexpensive storage and retrieval of programs. Another advantage is that all teachers in a building can schedule classes for CAI simultaneously without having to worry whether a needed program is available. The fast transfer rate of a network allows the loading of different programs for different groups without significant delays.

An alternative classroom configuration that is becoming increasing popular is desktop, standalone microcomputers. Though microcomputers lack the computing power of minis and mainframes, they are less expensive and have adequate computing capability for many CAI programs.

- *User-friendly.* System easy to operate and frames easy to use. System provides help prompts. Messages of encouragement given to users.
- *Well-organized material.* Frames in logical sequence. Concepts introduced in modules to facilitate learning, with modules becoming progressively more difficult.
- *Reinforcement provided.* Correct answers rewarded. Wrong answers identified in a manner that does not discourage or demean the user. Supplementary material provided when errors indicate the need for more practice frames.
- *Branching capability.* Allows pacing to be adjusted to individual student abilities. Allows backtracking for more practice or skipping ahead when student demonstrates mastery of concepts.
- *Tolerant system.* Will accept minor input errors or incorrect procedures. For example, "Yas" might be accepted for "Yes."
- *Feedback provided.* User immediately informed of correct/incorrect answers and given periodic progress reports.
- *Flexible system.* User able to enter or exit at any time. Able to choose mode (for example, drill or tutorial) and free to take tests upon request.

Figure 9.3 Desirable features of a CAI program.

The Problems of CAI

Critics of CAI argue that we simply do not yet know enough about learning to automate the learning process and that other instructional techniques may be more effective. In addition, some socialization development may be sacrificed since CAI is impersonal. Critics also claim that the taxpayer's dollar is being wasted by the way computers are often used in schools at the present time; that is, for drill and practice and as a substitute for flash cards and work books. At a time of shrinking school budgets, this kind of underuse of computers is indeed hard to justify.

A problem that limits CAI implementation is that many school districts do not have the money to computerize. Although the cost effectiveness of CAI in itself is improving, one must not forget the expense of course development, teacher training, and overhead costs like electricity and space. The current cost of hardware and software for CAI instruction, based on a 2000-hour year and using a $2000 microcomputer system, works out to only twenty-five cents an hour. But for every dollar spent on hardware, two or more must be spent on support.

Effective implementation of CAI means that teachers must be trained to use computers. This raises questions such as the following: Will all teachers be required to take computer courses for certification in the future? Who will pay for computer training of teachers already accredited? (It is estimated that only 10 percent of the educational community has been motivated to participate in computer courses on their own.) Some teachers dislike machines and resist the introduction of computer technology in their classrooms. How will this resistance be overcome?

Another issue to be resolved with widespread implementation of CAI is control over CAI content. Will control lie with persons who design and write programs? Will these persons be educators or computer technicians? Will schools in the future shape their curricula according to available CAI materials? It is possible that unstructured disciplines that do not lend themselves to programming may cease to be taught.

Finally, there is the problem that the selection of CAI software for school use is still limited. One reason for this is that many software houses place more emphasis on developing programs for the home education market than for the school market because the former is much more lucrative. In 1983, consumers spent $94 million on educational programs for the home. During the same period, the schools spent only $55 million.

At the same time, software piracy sometimes practiced in the schools can make it difficult for software houses to recoup program development costs. School districts commonly buy a single CAI program, and then make copies for classroom use. Some teachers even distribute free duplicates to students. One result of such software piracy is to limit the development of new CAI programs, since software houses are reluctant to invest in a market where the return on investment is not what it should be.

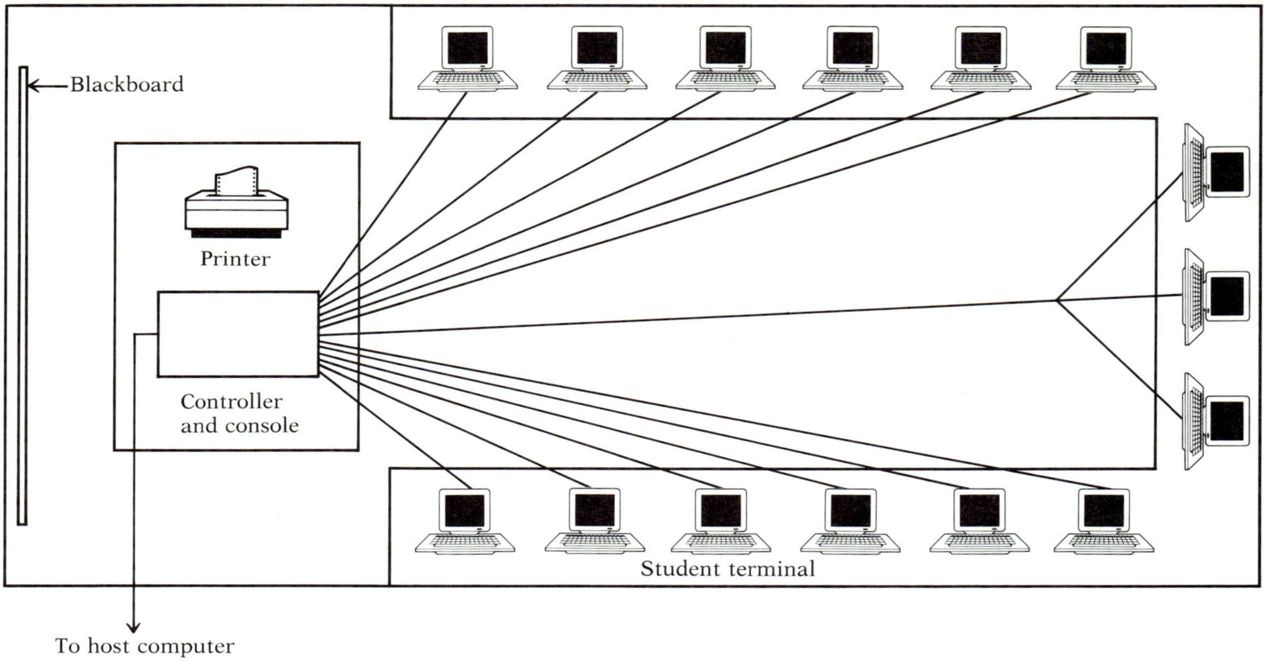

Figure 9.4 Sample classroom terminal configuration. Each of the terminals (or computers) in this drawing is connected to a microcomputer, mini, or mainframe host computer. A single library of programs can serve many workstations in this configuration. An alternative is the use of stand-alone microcomputers for each student.

To protect CAI investment and counter illegal copying, many software houses are using **copy-protected formats** (that is, disks that cannot be copied with standard equipment). The disadvantage of copy protection is that it prevents teachers from making the legitimate backup copies needed to replace worn or damaged diskettes. Another remedy is to sell a license permitting unlimited copies to schools.

More educators might program software for the schools if they were better paid for their efforts. Perhaps program authors should get royalties. Computer manufacturers, software houses, and traditional textbook publishers that market CAI software may have to devise new fair-payment authoring schemes to attract more talent to the educational software market.

In spite of these problems, the use of teaching computers will undoubtedly increase in the future. New languages for CAI and hardware with expanded capabilities, such as the ability to make inferences, are currently under research. Technology has a momentum of its own. Let us hope that educators master computer technology and learn to apply it to learning so that instruction will be enhanced and individualized by CAI in the years to come.

COMPUTER-MANAGED INSTRUCTION

An application that complements programmed learning is **computer-managed instruction (CMI)**. In CMI, the computer serves to oversee instruction and to direct students to learning resources (see Figure 9.5). For example, assignments, bibliographies, extra-credit activity lists, film and record inventories, and study question banks might be stored in computer memory. Tests might also be stored so that students can take exams at their own pace. Computer programs can save teachers time by grading homework, summarizing test results, plotting test score curves, statistically analyzing each student's performance, analyzing responses to each test question, and keeping a record of student grades—all tasks that frequently occupy much of a teacher's time. Programs can also be written to draw questions from a multiple-choice data base to format a test.

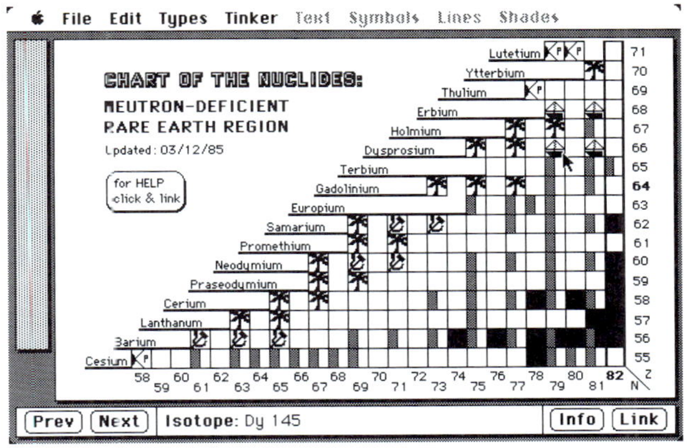

Figure 9.5 Zooming in on organized information. The operator uses a mouse to select (see pointer on line 66) the element of the display for clarification. A click of the mouse shows a further category of information linked to the initial element. (Apple Computer, Inc.)

COMPUTERS AS A RESOURCE FOR STUDENTS

Information stored in computer data bases can be a learning resource for students comparable to the storage of knowledge in a traditional library. The difference is that computer programs, rather than library check-out systems, retrieve the information. The data base may be purchased as part of a package (for example, a spelling dictionary that is part of a word processing package); developed by students and professors for their particular needs; or it may belong to a remote data base service accessed through a computer network. (Chapter 14 discusses remote data base services.)

In many other ways as well, computers have become a necessity to students in a wide range of disciplines at the university level. In the sciences, students make use of the computational power of computers in a variety of ways. For example, computers can be used by agriculture students to trace breeding characteristics in animals. Engineering students use computers to make complex calculations when designing a bridge; astronomy students may use computers to calculate the path of a comet, while physics students might use a computer to calculate forces on a body involved in a collision. Computers can also simulate mathematical models in order to answer "What if?" questions. What will happen to a given petroleum product if input or process variables change? How will weight, performance, and gas consumption be affected if the design of a car bumper is altered?

But it is not only the computational power that is valuable to students. Computer graphics assist students in visualizing three dimensional space. Figures on a CRT screen can be scaled, rotated, and looked at from different directions. This feature is particularly beneficial to architecture and engineering students.

In addition, the word processing ability of computers is becoming indispensible to students writing term papers and dissertations. The ease with which rewriting can be accomplished saves time, effort, and much frustration, especially if students are poor typists.

Because computers have become part of the educational experience on college campuses, many universities require their students to purchase microcomputers. Sometimes the model is specified. At Clarkson University, for example, all incoming freshmen are issued a Zenith Z-100 that is financed by a charge of $400 added to each semester's tuition. Drexel and Dartmouth require that all freshmen have access to a Macintosh. Universities commonly negotiate hardware discounts for students even on campuses where computer ownership is not required. Manufacturers give discounts because they believe that they are "seeding the market," creating loyal customers who will make future purchases and recommend their products to future employers.

The problem with required ownership is that a single computer may not meet the specialized needs of students in all fields. Furthermore, many upper division students need the computational capability of a mainframe, not a microcomputer. Another disadvantage is that technology is moving

Supplement 9.4 Apple University Consortium

In 1984, 23 American universities were members of the Apple University Consortium. An estimated 50,000 Macintoshes had been sold to faculty, students, and staff at consortium schools at a discount. The price break is one advantage of joining the consortium. Another is that the microcomputers are now readily available for course work and research at member schools. The universities plan to share software and market their own Macintosh programs as software is developed on campus. Apple believes that it will benefit from such campus software development by discovering new applications for Apple products.

The only possible losers are competitors and local Apple retailers who cannot match the consortium's discount. But perhaps both will later benefit. It is possible that students and faculty will outgrow their Macintoshes and become future customers.

*The members of University Consortium are Boston College, Brigham Young, Brown, Carnegie-Mellon, City University of New York, Columbia, Cornell, Dartmouth, Drexel, Harvard, Northwestern, Princeton, Reed, Rice, Stanford, University of Chicago, University of Michigan, University of Notre Dame, University of Pennsylvania, University of Rochester, University of Utah, University of Washington, and Yale.

so fast that a given micro may become obsolete even before a student graduates.

As an alternative to individual computer ownership, many universities provide computer **workstations** for students. Brown falls into this category. This university plans to have 10,000 workstations in operation by 1989. Workstation computers may be stand-alone microcomputers or belong to a computer **network**. The University of Houston has announced plans to build a $70 million, 4500-terminal computer network on its campus. A network at Reed is being planned that will link all campus computers, from mainframes to Macintoshes.

Network projects are very expensive. The cost is generally shared by manufacturers, institutions, and students. Manufacturers offer a discount, while the university itself absorbs part of the cost and generally passes on the rest to students in the form of a user's fee. The latter can be an hourly rate or a semester charge. For example, engineering students at the University of Michigan pay a usage fee of $100 per term. At Houston, Digital Equipment Corporation is granting the university up to $35 million in hardware and technical assistance. The remaining cost of their network will be acquired by the university through fund raising, legislative appropriations, and other sources.

For the most part, students are receptive to the use of computers as a learning tool. They value the information processing capabilities of computers and recognize that professionals in all fields will soon make use of computers in their work. Most students want computer experience before they enter the job market.

COMPUTERS IN EDUCATIONAL ADMINISTRATION

Most of the business applications of computers described in Chapter 7 take place in schools and universities as well, where functions like payroll, purchasing, and budgeting may be computerized.

Storage and retrieval of student records is another important use of computers in educational institutions. At universities, student records are created from personal information collected by admission applications. Additional data is added at registration (for example, campus address and courses in which a student is enrolled). By the time a student graduates, the record will contain a complete listing of courses taken, grades earned, honors received, and degrees awarded.

Records of registration and fee payment are also commonly put online. So are library transactions. Most campus bookstores order and process educational materials and keep inventory records by computer. In addition, computers may be used to edit and store university catalogs, keep records on alumni, handle a university's investment portfolio, plan facilities, administer financial aid programs, schedule classes, control inventory, and so on.

Various departments and organizations on campus may use computers administratively as well. School yearbooks, newspapers, and literary magazines, for example, often use word processing facilities; football coaches may use computers to help scout opponents; basketball coaches to keep game statistics. It is more than likely that meal planning and food management at the school cafeteria will be computerized.

SDI (Selective Dissemination of Information) is a computer system that helps keep professors professionally up-to-date. A profile of subjects of interest to individual instructors by key words is stored in a computer. When new materials are processed by library staff, they are coded by key words. The computer matches acquisition codes with the profiles and automatically notifies persons of receipt of materials in their fields of interest.

COMPUTER LITERACY

Thus far, this chapter has focused on computers as an educational tool and resource. In addition to these benefits, however, computers have also placed a demand on education and on society as a whole: namely, the demand that people learn how to use them. Because knowledge about computers has become essential in contemporary society, educators must plan and implement programs to promote **computer literacy**.

What is "computer literacy"? The term is often used as a buzzword but has no universally accepted definition. One way to define computer literacy is to say that it encompasses three kinds of knowledge:

- Knowledge about the technology involved in hardware and software and about how computers and computer systems work.
- Knowledge about capabilities and limitations of computers in application areas. Theoretical knowledge should be supplemented by experience using programs and operating computer equipment.
- Knowledge regarding the social implications of computers.

Often the ability to program is considered essential to computer literacy as well.

Although school systems will have to assume the major responsibility for preparing students to live in a computerized society, formal schooling is not the only way to teach computer literacy. The following sections describe how schools, employers, community organizations, and private concerns can all contribute to public understanding of how to use computers and of their potential.

School Literacy Programs

Computer literacy is easier to acquire if children begin learning about computers at an early age. The use of CAI in the classroom is one way that young children can gain familiarity with computers. In addition, many elementary schools have successfully taught programming to children ages five to ten. Learning to write a simple game program can teach a child some fundamental programming concepts such as selection, branching, iteration, and nesting.

Since many persons end their formal schooling at the secondary level, high schools should accept the major responsibility for making the general public computer literate. Students at this level should, first of all, gain experience with input/output operations. (It is estimated that by the end of this century, more than two-thirds of the work force will have direct daily contact with computers and every adult will encounter transaction terminals in department stores, banks, and supermarkets.) Many educators also recommend that students be introduced to programming languages, gain familiarity with text editors, have experience with online data bases and information utilities over telephone lines, use computers to control and monitor laboratory experiments, and learn to utilize the sound and graphic capabilities of computers to express themselves in the arts. In addition, high schools should provide a forum for discussions regarding the social implications of widespread computer use.

In the future, the role of post-secondary institutions (that is, junior colleges, colleges and universities, and graduate and professional schools)

Supplement 9.5 Should the Federal Government Subsidize Computers in the Schools?

The cost of computer hardware and software is delaying the introduction of computer education in elementary and secondary schools across the country. To help school districts finance computer literacy programs, legislation has been proposed that will provide tax incentives to firms donating computers to schools. In California, 11,000 computers were donated by various microcomputer manufacturers in fifteen months following passage of such a law in 1983. In 1984, no fewer than eight pieces of legislation were before both houses of Congress regarding Federal support of computer literacy programs.

Those who favor federal tax incentives for computer donors believe that computer literacy should be part of public education. The taxpayer dollar will be purchasing needed equipment at a bargain price.

Opponents claim that the impact on tax revenues of such legislation will be costly. The joint Committee on Taxation in Congress estimated in 1983 that H.R. 701, "The Computer Contribution Act of 1983," would cost about $60 million if implemented. According to critics, such a bill amounts to a subsidy to computer manufacturers and free advertising to a captured audience. They fear that tax incentives might also lead to overproduction of computers. In addition, it is possible that school districts might be tempted to accept equipment that is not really well suited to their needs. Would it not be wiser, critics suggest, to first learn more about the learning process itself before Congress subsidizes the replacement of human teachers by computers?

The provisions of bills before Congress vary in details. Some include incentives to donate hardware to vocational schools and museums as well as to public schools. Others allow tax write-offs for software, humidity/temperature control systems, and even special furniture. There are also differences in deductions allowed, period of deduction, and requirements regarding features such as languages, storage, and warranty. Debate on these bills centers on this question: Are government-supported computer literacy programs in the long-term public interest?

may be to provide the training needed for jobs in computer operations, programming, and system analysis. People who will work in these areas need knowledge about data structures, operating systems, compilers, logic design, and other technical aspects of computer science—knowledge not required by the general public. At the present time, however, universities do, of course, teach basic computer literacy courses as well. (This book has been written to be the text for such a course.) As the public schools integrate microcomputers in the classroom and teach more about computers at the elementary and secondary level, the need to teach basic computer literacy at the college level should vanish.

On-the-Job Training Programs

Many companies are committed to computer literacy programs for their employees. They recognize that they cannot automate their offices or place microcomputers on the desks of workers without planning the transition carefully. Teams are being organized by management to formulate computer literacy requirements and plan computer-related courses for staff. Sometimes literacy training is done in-house. Sometimes outside consultants and vendors are contracted. Industry is already beginning to use CAI techniques in regular training, as shown in Table 9.1. This, in itself, is contributing to the level of computer literacy in the public at large. The computer is becoming an increasingly popular instructional tool among industrial trainers. According to a survey by the magazine *Training/HRD* in 1980, only 9 percent of the respondents owned CAI equipment. A similar survey made in 1983 revealed that 18.3 percent of the nearly 1000 respondents had such equipment. More than 50 percent of the trainers who had not yet been able to fit CAI into their budgets and curricula indicated that they regard computer-based learning as a desirable instructional format.

Employers can draw on the resources of many institutes and firms dedicated to computer literacy training. These will organize workshops, distribute films, or design, script, and produce training programs to fit the specific training needs of their clients.

Table 9.1 Industry Groups Using CAI

Group	Percent using CAI
Educational services	36.4
Financial institutions including real estate	27.4
Non-profit organizations	21.6
Business services	19.7
Wholesale trade	18.4
Construction	15.7
Transportation, communications, utilities	15.2
Health services	14.9
Retail trade	14.0
Oil drilling and mining	12.9
Manufacturing	12.7
Hotels, food services	12.3

Adapted from: "Trainers Boost Computer Use," *Training/HRD*, vol. 20, no. 1 (January 1983), p. 68.

Literacy Programs for the Public

The media represent a major source of information about computers. Educational TV channels, in particular, regularly schedule programs on computer technology. Computer articles directed to nonprofessionals appear almost daily in the press. More specialized information appears in trade journals and scientific magazines. Supplement 9.6 lists the ten top computer magazines in 1985.

Libraries in many communities provide microcomputers for public use and sponsor computer literacy workshops. For example, ComputerTown USA, which is funded by the National Science Foundation and is located in the Menlo Park Public Library, sponsors seminars and provides equipment for hands-on computing experience. It has helped other groups start similar centers by providing resource information and "how-to" materials. Affiliates exist in commmunity centers, senior citizen centers, scouting clubs, other libraries, and a wide variety of organizations across the country.

Supplement 9.6 12 Top Computer Magazines (By Circulation in 1985)*

Title	Year of first issue	Audience	Circulation (rounded to thousands)
Personal Computing	1976	Business persons	541,000
Byte	1975	Small system users	395,000
Family Computing	1983	Hobbyist	383,000
Compute!	1979	Computer professionals	373,000
Compute!'s Gazette	1983	Commodore computer owners and users	303,000
Lotus	1984	Managers & professionals using Lotus and other software	300,000 (nonpaid)
PC World	1982	Owners of IBM PC and compatibles	277,000
Popular Computing	1979	Hobbyist	268,000
Creative Computing	1974	Business persons	250,000
PC	1982	Owners and users of IBM standard microcomputers	222,000
Online Today	1981	Business and consumer subscribers to CompuServe Information Services	185,000
Run	1984	Commodore computer owners and users	185,000

*Figures from 9/27/85 issue of SRDS-Consumer Publications.

In many cities, museums provide computer education. In Washington, D.C., for example, the Capital Children's Museum opened a center in 1981 with twenty Atari 800 micros to provide hands-on computer experience to visitors, a model now being followed by other museums throughout the country.

The interest of the public in computers has led to programs for vacationers that combine learning about computers with relaxation in resort areas. For instance, computer classes are offered on the *Mississippi Queen*, at twelve locations of Club Med, aboard a sailboat cruising in the Caribbean through a group called Micro People, and in the Green Mountains of Vermont at Smugglers' Notch. At Lake Tahoe, vacationers can combine a half day of computer instruction with a half day of golf or tennis, followed by an evening party with electronic games. Computer holidays are available for children as well as adults. National Computer Camp, with camps in several locations, caters to youngsters ages nine to eighteen.

This list is by no means complete. The best way to find out about computer literacy programs in your community is to check with your local schools, computer vendors, and libraries.

SUMMING UP

The growing use of computers in society means that a new subject, information technology, must be added to the curriculum of schools. Computer literacy is becoming as important as basic reading and writing skills in the modern world.

Fortunately, computers themselves can be a mechanism for teaching information technology. CAI software can teach about computer components and how to program. Computers can facilitate the administration of computer literacy programs and computer data bases can store bibliographical data on the availability of computer literacy materials. Obviously, the contribution of computers to learning is not restricted to the field of computer science. In most subject areas information technology can contribute to learning in similar ways.

The umbrella term **computer-based learning (CBL)** encompasses computer-aided instruction (CAI), computer-managed instruction (CMI), and the use of computers as a learning resource. CBL can contribute to the efficiency of running an educational institution and assist human teachers in the classroom, helping schools face the problem of reduced teaching staffs and larger class sizes. Electronic media allow self-paced learning and flexible scheduling of the time of instruction. CBL can also contribute to learning at work or at home.

Information technology by itself, however, cannot solve all educational problems. There are many institutional and societal barriers that prevent the full realization of the educational potential of computers. These barriers are, first of all, institutional, in that curricula and classroom organization must be adjusted to allow for computer use in schools. Second, the shortage of teachers with computer training limits both the use and production of CBL materials. Third, the newness and the uncertainties of the educational marketplace have kept a lid on the development of good CBL software. Fourth, cost has been a factor. Although the price of computer hardware and software has been dropping steadily, computer technology is still too expensive for many school districts, colleges, individual students, and for other organizations that might teach people about computers. The fifth obstacle to the realization of the educational potential of computers is simply skepticism about long-term effects. Many educators believe that we do not yet understand sufficiently the nature of learning and they are therefore hesitant to endorse adoption of information technology in schools. Finally, the fear of some teachers that they will be replaced by computers can cause resistance to the implementation of computer technology. What is more, negative teacher attitudes towards computers can be transmitted to students, causing them to resist classroom use of computers as well.

REVIEW QUESTIONS

1. What is CAI? When is use of CAI appropriate? What are the advantages and disadvantages of CAI?

2. What is the fundamental principle of learning used by most CAI modes? How would you adapt this principle to CAI software for different age groups?

3. Describe the following CAI modes and give examples of each:
a. tutorial
b. drill and practice
c. discovery
d. problem-solving
e. simulation
f. modeling

4. How have advances in technology contributed to recent improvements in CAI?

5. What is the difference between:
a. authoring systems and authoring languages?
b. CAI and CMI?
c. use of stand-alone microcomputers and network systems for CAI?

6. Why has implementation of CAI in the schools been limited to date?

7. In what ways can computers assist university students with their studies?

8. How should computer literacy be taught? Recommend programs for:
a. schools
b. on-the-job training
c. adult education

DISCUSSION QUESTIONS

1. How should "frames" in a CAI environment differ according to the CAI audience?

2. What conditions are necessary for successful CAI? Which is most important: hardware, software, or people?

3. Should government (federal or state) promote CAI? How?

4. Will CAI improve the quality of education? Explain.

5. What are the social implications of widespread implementation of CAI?

6. What legal protection for CAI software would you recommend?

7. What measures should be taken to promote improved quality of CAI software?

8. Do you think that every university student should be required to own a microcomputer? If so, why? If not, why not? Or should universities provide access to microcomputers as a service?

9. How have computers affected your university career? Have they contributed to your learning or been primarily used for administrative functions? Explain.

10. Do you agree with this book's definition of computer literacy? How would you define the term?

11. Who should be responsible for computer literacy of the general public? Schools? Government? Employers? Computer professionals? Justify your answer.

12. Describe the use of computers in one of your classes. Include use of both students and instructor.

13. If you were taught by CAI, would you miss contact with fellow students in the classroom?

14. What should be taught about computers at the following levels:
a. primary school?
b. secondary school?
c. post-secondary educational institutions?

15. What are some of the problems regarding implementation of computer literacy in schools? How can they be overcome?

16. Will computers fundamentally affect the:
a. content of the curriculum?
b. format of teaching?
c. student-teacher relationships?
d. student-student relationships?
e. relationship of government to education?
If so, how?

EXERCISES

1. Discuss the definition of computer literacy with fellow students, friends, and family. List their definitions. Why do they differ?
2. Design a small CAI module for one of the following:
   a. teach multiplication
   b. teach a simple algebra concept
   c. teach about a historical event
   d. teach a philosophical concept
3. Imagine that you are given $5,000 to buy educational software for family use. Make a list of software you would purchase. Explain what sources of information you used and how you evaluated the products you selected.

Selected Annotated Bibliography

Bell, Trudy. "Computer Literacy: The Fourth R," *Personal Computing*, vol. 7, no. 5 (May 1983), pp. 43–71. Bell argues that computer skills are just as important for a child as reading and arithmetic. Bell has advice for parents on how to use personal computers at home.

"Computers in Education," *TRS-80 Microcomputer News*, vol. 4, no. 8 (September 1982), pp. 8–12. An overview of the entire Radio Shack curriculum for public shools.

Evans, Christopher. "An Invitation to the (Near) Future," *Today's Education*, vol. 71, no. 2 (April–May 1982), pp. 12–15. The focus of this article is computer technology in the next two decades. A good look at the ethical implications of computerization.

Green, John O. "Artificial Intelligence and the Future Classroom," *Classroom Computer Learning*, vol. 4, no. 6 (January 1984), pp. 26–31. This is a daring attempt to predict how AI will be applied in the classroom of the year 2001.

"Group Charges 'Microcomputer Overkill.' " *Training/HRD*, vol. 19, no. 12 (December 1982), pp. 9–10. This brief article gives examples of typical taxpayer complaints against CAI and computer classes in schools.

Interface: The Computer Education Quarterly. This is a journal dedicated to the computer in education. Many articles on computer literacy appear in this quarterly.

Meierhenry, W. C. "Microcomputers and Adult Learning," *Training and Development Journal*, vol. 36, no. 12 (December 1982), pp. 58–66. This is an excerpt from a book with the same title. The author suggests that with appropriate microcomputers and programs, the number of dropouts in adult education courses should decrease.

Mroz, Henry and Lawner, Harvey. "Realizing the Educational Potential of Computers," *T.H.E. Journal*, vol. 11, no. 8 (May 1984), pp. 107–10. Partnership between a school district in Massachusetts and a nearby university in using computers led to establishing a masters and doctoral program in instructional technology.

Office of Technology Assessment. "Information Technology and Its Impact on American Education," *Computers and Society*, vol. 12, no. 3 (Summer 1982), pp. 7–12. An excellent summary of the government's assessment report, this article discusses the information society, barriers to information technology, and policy issues and options that educators must resolve.

Papert, Seymour. *Mindstorms: Children, Computers, and Powerful Ideas*. New York: Basic Books, Inc., 1980. Describes what children can do and have done with computers using CAI.

Popular Computing, vol. 3, no. 13 (Mid-October 1984). This is a special issue of *Popular Computing* devoted exclusively to education. Included are articles on computer use for educational purposes at home, in the public schools, and at college.

Selden, Paul H. and Schultz, Norman L. "What the Research Says about CAI's Potential," *Training/HRD*, vol. 19, no. 11 (November 1982), pp. 61–64. Among the findings discussed is how skill acquisition by CAI compares with learning by traditional methods. The authors conclude that there are sound reasons for optimism regarding the contributions of CAI. The authors note that CAI is becoming increasingly cost-effective as a result of advances in technology.

Senter, Joy. "Computers, Technology and Education," *Educational Forum*, vol. 36, no. 1 (Fall 1981), pp. 55–64. Discusses cost and both the social and legal implications of using CAI and CMI.

Stoan, Stephen H. "Computer Searching: A Primer for the Uninformed Scholar," *Academic*, vol. 68, no. 6 (November/December 1982), pp. 10–15. This excellent article discusses the importance of both the searcher (librarian) and the user (person with subject expertise) in identifying relevant search keys.

Watt, Dan. "Learning With Logo," *Classroom Computer News*, vol. 3, no. 5 (April 1983), pp. 40–45. Suggests ways to use LOGO for children and adults. This issue also includes three other articles on LOGO, including a beginner's guide and a futurist view of LOGO.

In Sickness and in Health: Computers for Medicine and Sports

The machine does not isolate man from the great problems of nature but plunges him more deeply into them.

ANTOINE DE SAINT EXUPERY
Wind, Sand, and Stars

CHAPTER TEN

Key Words

biofeedback system	hospital information system	positron emission tomography (PET)
biomechanics	judging	privacy invasion
cataloging	lab test	scoring
computerized axial tomography (CAT)	magnetic resonance imaging (MRI)	scouting
computerized treadmill	Massachusetts General Hospital Utility Multiprogramming System (MUMPS)	Selspsot motion analysis system
data capture	medical data base	shared service
dynometer	national integration	Shared Medical System (SMS)
electronic hospital	nutrition	statistical sports package
electronic office	patient monitoring	system integration
expert system	patient record	timeliness
facilities management	pharmacy computer system	training
force platform		

Information technology helps physicians tend the sick in a variety of ways. Computers are used to process medical data, to assist doctors in diagnosis, and to monitor patients. Most aspects of hospital administration have been computerized. This includes admission and discharge procedures, lab analysis, and dispensation of drugs. Microprocessors are embedded in surgical tools and equipment for the disabled. In addition, computer systems can give doctors instantaneous access to information stored in medical data banks—for example, information on availability of a rare type of blood at a distant blood bank. These and other medical applications of computers are discussed in this chapter.

Public health includes the prevention of illness, another role for information technology. For example, computers can plan diets and monitor physical fitness. Athletes, in particular, are interested in these computer applications. The chapter closes with a look at the use of computers in athletic training and sports administration.

AT THE DOCTOR'S OFFICE

The role of computers in health care often begins the moment a patient enters a doctor's office. Before being examined a patient may be asked to fill out forms that are used to create a document called a **patient record**, which the doctor references, and adds to, during examinations. Information from the record will subsequently be used in billing. Today, patient records are commonly stored and processed by computer. (See Supplement 10.2 for a sample patient record.)

Computers can also be used to capture data for records. During such **data capture** sessions, the patient is generally seated at a terminal and keys answers to questions that appear on the screen. A light pen can register answers on a touch-sensitive screen. One such system shows a picture of the human body and asks patients to point to the areas that hurt.

Computer systems for data capture save time for the staff in a doctor's office. (An estimated 50 percent of a nurse's time is spent obtaining information from patients.) Even more important, the information given the computer is often more ac-

Supplement 10.1 Assistance in Healing

An early medical symbol was a staff with a serpent winding around it. The ancients credited serpents with magical healing powers. The staff belongs to Asclepius, a legendary Greek physician, so skillful that Zeus made him god of medicine.

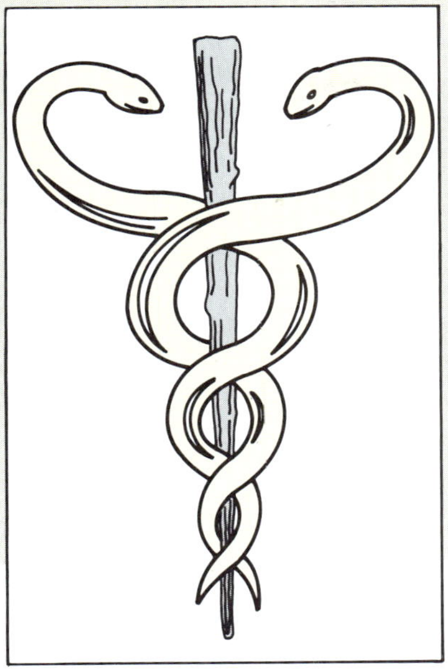

Magic and the spirit world have long been associated with healing. Today, computers have given doctors new power in their treatment of patients: the power of information technology.

curate than information collected by humans. Why? According to studies, many patients like the impersonal nature of a machine when responding to health questions of a sensitive nature.

Many medical offices use computer systems for other administrative functions besides record keeping—for example, for budgeting, asset accounting, purchasing, tax preparation, inventory control, and generation of reports such as those required by the government on medicare and welfare patients. Word processing is used for correspondence. Many specialists employ teleconferencing for consultation and teaching. Features of the **electronic office** described in Chapter 7 may soon be the norm in medical offices throughout the country.

AS AN AID TO DIAGNOSIS

Another contribution of computers to the field of medicine is the growth of medical data bases that contain information on diseases and treatment. These data bases can be accessed by physicians using remote terminals. Finally, computer programs called "expert systems" help doctors in their treatment of certain types of medical problems.

Computers can also be used as a diagnostic tool by medical pathologists, radiologists, and other specialists. For example, we now have CAT scanners and other kinds of imaging equipment that allow doctors to see inside the body and find out about biochemical processes in ways not possible in the past. The vast amount of data generated by imaging equipment is processed by computer. With manual processing, analysis of the data would require days or months, with results too late to be of value.

Let's take a brief look at each of the various ways in which computers assist doctors in diagnosing illness.

Medical Data Bases and Expert Systems

Once a doctor has completed a physical examination of a patient and test results have been received, a diagnosis will be made. Often doctors use a medical library or consult with one another on difficult cases. Both of these resources have elec-

Supplement 10.2 Dental Patient Record

This dental record includes personal data of patient (name and address), date of visit, treatment code (21, 24, 26, and so on) patient number and name (dependents might be listed on this record), transaction number, code and a description of treatment provided, charges for dental services, payment, form of payment, balance due, and an account summary. The record is stored on a disk and updated through a computer terminal. For most office purposes, the record is accessed on a terminal screen, although a hard copy can be printed if one is needed.

W.A. Winters D.D.S,P.A. JUL 25, 1985 PAGE

TRANSACTION LIST FOR: JOHNNY B. DOE FROM: 01/01/80
25800-101 123 MAIN STREET TO: 07/25/85
PHONE: LAS CRUCES, NM 88001

DATE	DR	PT#	NAME	TR#	ADA	DESCRIPTION	AMOUNT
40985	6	25300	DOE, JOHNNY B.	21	110	INITIAL ORAL EXAM	10.50
40985	6	25300		24	270	BITEWING X-RAYS (2)	8.35
40985	6	25300		26	1110	PROPHY-ADULT	16.70
40985	6	25300		2	0	PAYMENT-CHECK	35.55
61185	1	25300		36	2150	AMALGAM 2 SURF-P	38.75
61185	1	25300		36	2150	AMALGAM 2 SURF-P	38.75
61185	1	25300		72	7110	EXTRACTION	21.00
61185	1	25300		2	0	PAYMENT-CHECK	98.50
70985	1	25300		47	3330	ROOT CANAL - THREE	167.80
72485	1	25300		84	0	BILL INS CO	

TOTAL CHARGES = 203.35 TOTAL PAYMENTS = 35.55

FROM: 01/01/85 TO: 07/25/85

ACCOUNT BALANCE FOR JOHNNY B. DOE AS OF JUL 25, 1985

CURRENT	30 - 60	60 - 90	OVER 90	TOTAL
167.80	0	0	.0	167.80

tronic equivalents. For example, the information on illnesses and diseases found in a conventional library can be stored in a **medical data base**. Doctors with office terminals and a telecommunications link to such a data base can call medical information to their screens. For instance, should an unusual disease be suspected, the doctor could use the base to retrieve a list of symptoms or drug options for treatment.

Expert systems are an electronic equivalent of consultation with a specialist. An expert system is a program prepared by a physician with expertise in a given medical domain. The software is a diagnostic tool for doctors. Questions appear on the terminal screen asking the user (the doctor who needs advice) about the patient, such as age, sex, test results, symptoms, and medical history. This information is then processed by the computer and a diagnosis suggested based on decision rules stored in computer memory.

In traditional practice, a doctor makes diagnoses on the basis of decision rules and information learned at medical school and gleaned from experience. Unfortunately, human memory is fallible: doctors may not remember, or may remember incorrectly, the rules and information they have learned. With the vast amount of new information that is coming to light through medical research and practice every year, the problem of retaining and mentally organizing medical knowledge has increased dramatically. The potential advantage of using an expert system to assist in diagnosis is that more information can be stored in computer memory than in human memory, and that information can be retrieved quickly and accurately.

Expert systems are still by no means sophisticated enough, however, to substitute for the clinical judgment of an experienced doctor. There are at least two important reasons for this. First, the information involved in challenging medical cases is often ambiguous and incomplete, and this kind of input, of course, limits the accuracy of the diagnosis that the expert system can generate. Second, no expert system yet designed can deal with the vast network of causal relationships in disease processes unfolding over time the way an experienced human observer can. For these reasons, expert systems are currently useful primarily in reminding doctors and researchers of diagnoses that should be considered and in suggesting additional data that might be of value, such as new medications. (The data base in the expert system must, of course, be constantly updated and checked to ensure that the information is current and still accurate.)

Despite their limitations, expert systems are an exciting medical application of computer technology. Chapter 16 will describe expert systems as a branch of the field of artificial intelligence and will describe how one expert system for medical diagnosis, a system called MYCIN, works.

Imaging Devices

Computerized imaging equipment is contributing to a revolution in medicine. We now have a device called a **positron emission tomography (PET)** scanner that measures the radiation emitted by a patient who has ingested sugar tagged with a radioactive element. As the sugar is digested by brain cells, particles called positrons are emitted which collide with electrons to produce gamma rays which can be measured by the device. The radiation information is then processed by the computer which produces a picture of the brain at work. The output is a color display that tells physicians what parts of the brain are functioning when the patient raises an arm, listens to music, or engages in other activities.

Doctors are already beginning to identify how PET scans vary among persons with different psychological illnesses. They can use the scans to spot epileptic brain lesions and to screen epileptic patients for surgery. The scans can also be used to detect minute changes caused by brain cancer or multiple sclerosis and to identify what parts of the brain are involved in diseases like Alzheimer's. Another usage of PET technology has been to image opiate receptors, those parts of brain cells that appear to be involved in the transmission of pain-killing substances. It may eventually be possible to help block chronic pain as a result of research using this new image technology.

PET technology is used primarily for research into the basic biochemistry of the brain. To date, clinical applications of the technology have been limited. The high cost of PET devices (about $3 million per unit) and the cost per scan (about $1000) are reasons why the equipment is not commonplace. Recently the National Institutes of Health, which has financed most of the 15 PET units in this country, withdrew its support to all but a few centers.

The **computerized axial tomography (CAT)** scanner is perhaps the best-known new imaging device. This equipment takes X-rays of the patient's head from many angles. Since the density of the brain determines how much radiation is absorbed, a picture of the brain can be constructed by computing the difference between the total radiation and the absorption of the X-rays as they enter the head using data collected by the machine's sensors. This mathematical difference, calculated by computer, becomes the basis for a detailed cross-sectional image of the brain.

Supplement 10.3 Taking the Guesswork Out of Surgery

Visualization of an image plays a particularly important role in aiding a radiologist to diagnose a disease, and a surgeon to plan surgery. Up until now, the physician has had to construct a three-dimensional "mental image" of an anatomical region of interest from a series of two-dimensional x-rays, CAT scans, or NMR images. This process is often difficult and time consuming, with increased chance for misinterpretation of vital clinical data.

While CAT scanners have given doctors a good view inside the body, the pictures show only thin slices of, say, an elbow; trying to see a whole elbow has been likened to trying to picture a loaf of bread by looking at each slice! According to Dr. Jeffrey Marsh, a leading figure in computer-aided plastic surgery at Washington University Medical Center in St. Louis: "Unfortunately, patients don't come in slices; craniofacial surgery is definitely a three-dimensional problem. But after the physical examination, you'd never see your patient in 3-D again until he or she was on the operating table."

A number of companies are finding solutions to this problem through computer-graphics programs that can take the data generated by the CAT scanner and reconstruct it into a whole image. One product is the CEMAX-1000, a 32-bit interactive computer graphics workstation manufactured by Contour Medical Systems of Mountain View, California. The system is a stand-alone image processor that rapidly displays and reformats two-dimensional CAT scanner slice images and constructs 3-D representation of these images. The 3-D representation is built by stacking multiple planar representations, or slices, taken from a computerized axial-tomographic system. The system enables the operator not only to display, manipulate, and alter the 3-D image on a high-resolution screen, but also to request that Contour create an actual physical model using a proprietary computer-controlled process. By reformatting the CEMAX-1000 data, a file of cutting tool positions drive a numerically-controlled milling machine for custom design of patient models and implants, in short, "designer bones." Objects of considerable complexity can be accurately generated without the need for detailed cutting of individual slices; the finished implants are accurate with 2 percent.

CEMAX-1000 and similar systems are proving useful in a variety of clinical areas, including diagnostic and therapeutic radiology, preoperative planning, and surgical simulation in specialties such as orthopedic, and plastic and reconstructive surgery. Time spent in surgery is often reduced, in some cases up to a 50 percent reduction.

CAT scans can be used to locate brain tumors, in many cases eliminating the need for painful tests or exploratory surgery. The machines can also help reveal potential health problems before they become acute. For example, the narrowing of blood vessels can be observed before the constriction become a life threat. The machines also play a role in neurosurgery. By using information about the patient's brain and head derived from a scan, the computer can plot the best surgical strategy for the treatment of brain tumors.

Unfortunately, a CAT scan, like PET technology, is costly. The equipment can cost $4 million a unit. The patient pays about $350 for a scan.

Magnetic resonance imaging (MRI) is still another new technique used to aid doctors in the diagnosis of brain problems. A magnet is used to make the nuclei of hydrogen atoms in the brain spin and line up in the direction of the magnetic field. A radio wave, tuned to this frequency, can give these nuclei extra energy. When the wave is turned off, energy is released. It is data on this energy release collected by sensors that is processed by a computer to produce a visual image of the brain.

One advantage of MRI technology is that a tumor that is hidden by bone on a CAT scan will clearly show. The damage of certain diseases, such as multiple sclerosis and plaques (hardened tissues) is also more clearly visible with MRI than with other imaging techniques. A disadvantage is that the magnetic field of the machine can jam heart pacemakers, interfere with radio transmission, and cause the metal in artificial joints to heat. As a result, many patients are not candidates for MRI scans. Moreover, the equipment must be housed in a sealed room away from hospital equipment that is sensitive to magnetic influences. An-

Supplement 10.4 Reporting Lab Test Results by Computer

The vast amounts of clinical and laboratory data that doctors must analyze in treating patients may be difficult to organize. For example, laboratory test data is usually recorded on single lab slips. When a patient is hospitalized for a long period of time, information from the slips may be copied onto charts showing test results listed in sequence. But preparation of the charts is time-consuming and subject to copy errors. Moreover, only a limited time span can be represented on each chart, making it harder for the physician to scan the data when searching for abnormal results and attempt to recognize trends.

When lab results are entered directly into a computer, all of these problems are eliminated. There are no copy errors (although input errors may, of course, occur) and the computer can be programmed to recognize test results that rise or fall outside normal bounds. Storing results in the computer can also enable the physician to review the data from different perspectives by, for example, asking the program to select and display all laboratory data for particular periods of time. In the treatment of burn victims at the U.S. Army Institute of Surgical Research, a graphics program is used to supplement standard tabular display of laboratory tests results. The color graphs help the doctors interpret lab test results. A few keystrokes will give values of sodium, potassium, blood urea, nitrogen, creatinine, glucose, and bicarbonate for the past seven days.

Similar graphics systems have been developed to represent data about patients for other purposes, including respiration therapy, drug treatment, nutritional care, and physiological monitoring. Graphics systems are also used as an aid in the performance of surgical and nursing procedures.

other disadvantage is the expense of MRI technology. An MRI installation costs from $1 to $4 million; a scan can cost the individual patient about $850.

Although the medical community is excited about the potential benefits of PET, CAT, and MRI technology, the purchase of imaging machines has become the subject of political controversy. Spiralling medical expenses can be attributed, in part, to the cost of such technology. Are we raising the price of health care beyond the reach of many of our citizens by installing such machines? What role should the government play is subsidizing PET, CAT, and MRI research? Politicians are debating whether money spent for space-age diagnostic machines can be justified when we have so many pressing needs for the taxpayer dollar. They question whether Medicare should reimburse hospitals for the scans. There is also the issue regarding how information produced by imaging technology will be used. Will people who have "brain profiles" which deviate from the norm be identified and penalized by schools and employers as intellectually deficient?

Health care has always had social, political, and ethical ramifications. Now that computer technology has entered the medical domain, the issue has become even more complex.

IN THE LABORATORY

Before a doctor can make a diagnosis, **lab tests** may be required. Lab tests usually involve numerous steps, such as adding, mixing, centrifuging, heating, and cooling. Computer programs have been developed to control these steps. Once the procedure is complete, the computer will record and analyze results by comparing them with given norms stored in computer memory. From a single drawing of blood, for example, a computer can test for hemoglobin, hematocrit, glucose, BUN, creatinine, sodium, potassium, chloride, total CO_2, uric acid, calcium, phosphorous, protein, albumin, globulin, A/G ratio, cholesterol, triglycerides, bilirubin, phosphate, and make a white and red blood cell count. Computer controlled monitoring of such tests ensures their reliability. Furthermore, errors in interpretation of results are less likely since the computer can automatically make adjustments for

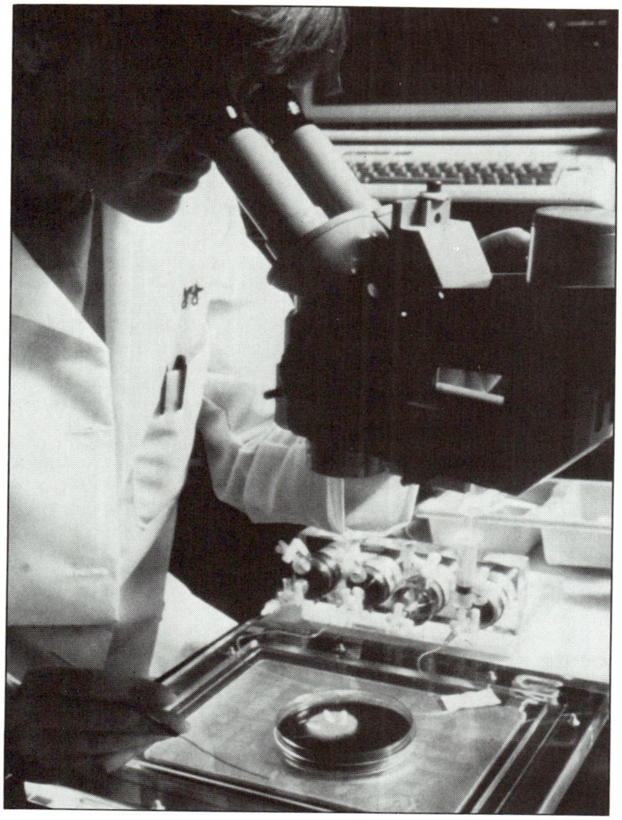

Figure 10.1 Analyzing a culture. Medical researchers use computers to facilitate laboratory work, increasing reliability, timeliness, and accuracy. (Apple Computer, Inc.)

age and sex of the patient or for any other factor that might be critical in the evaluation of test data. (See Figure 10.1.)

In testing, **timeliness** is crucial. A patient's life may depend on the speed with which test data is processed and results delivered to attending physicians. When a computer network connects the lab with terminals of doctors and nursing stations—for example, in intensive care hospital wards—telemail can be used to deliver lab reports. Terminals may even beep until someone acknowledges receipt of the message. Often test results are displayed as charts or graphs on terminals with graphic capabilities. Such displays facilitate interpretation of lab report information.

Another use of computers in the laboratory is to monitor lab operations. Computers can be used to generate a variety of reports to help make labs more efficient and precise. For example, unfinished procedure reports might be processed to identify lab work that is overdue, abnormal value reports might be processed to identify test results that fall outside the "normal" range, or turn-around time analysis reports might be processed for use in evaluating lab procedures. Computer output might also be a lab summary report listing work done in the lab each day.

In a hospital environment, lab computer systems can produce morning reports and patient chart summaries. A daily report can be prepared showing the work ordered by each physician. Of course, the type of lab reports generated by computer will depend on hardware and software at a given installation. This, in turn, will depend on the financial resources of the lab and the environment it serves.

IN THE PHARMACY

The prescription the pharmacist fills for you when you leave the doctor's office can require a lot of paperwork. Pharmacists must prepare labels and receipts, process insurance claims, file prescriptions, and check patient records for allergies, interactions, and misuse. In addition, prices must be calculated, billing records must kept up-to-date, and inventories must be managed. Every pharmacy must submit Drug Enforcement Agency reports on controlled substances (like morphine and heroin) and prepare tax returns. Paperwork is endemic in pharmacies as in other types of organizations.

As might be expected, **pharmacy computer systems** are now on the market. Many are designed to perform routine time-consuming tasks like those listed above. They claim to increase productivity and reduce both pharmacy errors and costs. In addition, computers can enhance service. For example, programs are available that provide information for customer counseling on issues like generic substitutions for name-brand drugs (generic drugs are generally cheaper). Furthermore, computers can be used to generate a wide variety of reports with information druggists could not easily access in the past. These include:

- Daily prescription audit
- Insurance profile
- Doctor activity list
- List of prescriptions by selected doctor or selected drug
- Drug reorder notification
- Drug components
- Monthly and year-to-date revenue summary

HOSPITAL INFORMATION SYSTEMS

While the use of computers in hospitals is growing, **hospital information systems** are years behind their corporate counterparts because hospital administrators in the past have been much less receptive to computer technology than the business community.

Supplement 10.5 lists common hospital computer applications. Although many of the programs on this list are for hospital administration, computers have clinical uses in hospitals as well. For example, information technology is commonly used for **patient monitoring** in postoperative and intensive-care wards. Sensors measure patient variables such as skin temperature and internal temperature, heart rate, cardiac output, venous pressure, and respiration rates. When values of these variables fall above or below an acceptable range for the patient's condition (acceptable values are stored in computer memory), the computer flashes a signal to the nurse on duty. Sometimes the computer itself is programmed to initiate corrective action. For example, software might activate a pump to infuse a diuretic agent if the patient's urine output falls lower than a predetermined level. Because of microtechnology, many patient monitors have become portable. Thus a patient might wear a computerized monitor to analyze electrical signals from the heart. (See Figure 10.2.)

Two sources of hospital software exist. A hospital can develop its own specialized programs, or it can obtain more generic programs from software vendors. Hospital packages have been marketed commercially for over twenty years.

A special computer language has been devised

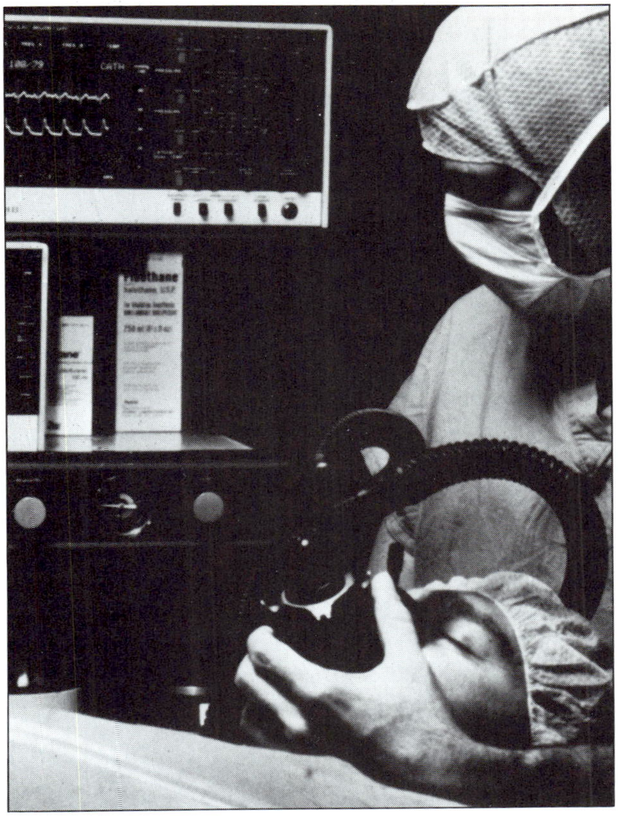

Figure 10.2 During surgery. An anesthesiologist uses a computer to monitor and update vital signs and dosages and to centralize the display of information for easy viewing. (Gould Electronics, Inc.)

to assist hospitals in writing their own programs. This language is called **MUMPS (Massachusetts General Hospital Utility Multi-Programming System)**, a language that includes operating and data base systems. MUMPS can be easily modified and allows clinicians to converse with the machine. The language has been chosen by programmers at thirty-five Veterans' Administration hospitals. These hospitals are developing modular software for piece-by-piece implementation as they add to their computing capacity and install more terminals. The modular software planned includes data

Supplement 10.5 Common Uses of Computers in Hospitals

General ledger accounting	Insurance claim processing	Accounts receivable
Purchasing	Inventory control	Food and beverage inventory
Billing	Pharmacy	Patient admission and discharge
Medicare reporting	Supplies	Room assignments
Budget modelling	Hospital equipment	Patient listing
Fund raising	Maintenance control	Scheduling
Asset accounting	Planning	Nurses
	Personnel records	
	Payroll processing	

systems for registration and admissions, for patient profiles, for lab and pharmacy management, and for patient-data lookup.

Some hospitals contract **facilities management** firms to operate and manage in-house data processing systems rather than hire computer expertise of their own. Another option is to contract **shared services** like **SMS (Shared Medical System)**, a service that enables a hospital to benefit from information technology without owning its own large computer or data base. Resources like programs for hospital-wide data collection, automated departmental support, financial management, and pharmacy management, are accessed through a computer network and shared with other hospitals. SMS uses on-site minicomputers for local processing while terminals access the shared mainframe system.

INTEGRATION OF HOSPITAL SYSTEMS

Today, the hospital industry recognizes the value of **electronic hospitals** with **system integration**. There is increasing awareness that data, once captured, should be accessible to all departments. Moreover, doctors want to be able to read patient monitors from distant terminals. They would like to eliminate paperwork by using terminals stationed throughout the hospital to enter orders for lab tests, special diets, and prescription drugs.

Hospital systems are being implemented to integrate health care computer applications from patient admission to discharge. Several factors have given impetus to this integration. First, there has been a rapid increase in the volume of record keeping required by hospitals in order to comply with recent government regulations. These regulations have been imposed by federal and state agencies in an effort to monitor and control escalating medical expenditures. Hospital administrators recognize the benefit of record keeping by computer. In addition, more stringent control on the cost of each unit of service is being imposed by funding agencies such as Medicare. The integration of financial data with patient care data by hospitals is necessary to perform the cost accounting required.

A second factor in the movement toward integration of hospital computer systems is that public outcry over health costs is causing many hospitals to reexamine the efficiency and effectiveness of hospital procedures. Administrators are finding that better service at less cost can be provided if integrated computer systems are installed.

Third, because well-planned integrated systems are flexible, they facilitate the introduction of new hardware and software modules. Hospitals can add new applications as they perceive the need for them or when finances permit.

Hospitals differ from one another in size, services, and financial resources. Not every hospital can afford a comprehensive hospital information system. Nor is computerization of every department necessarily cost-effective. But even smaller hospitals with limited budgets are beginning to make long-range plans for extensive use of computers and for the integration of hospital computer systems.

Supplement 10.6 Cost Accounting in Hospitals

Thirty-eight percent of hospital income (over $40 billion) comes from Medicare. In the past, Medicare audited payments to hospitals for treatment of Medicare patients but did not dictate how hospital charges were assessed.

In 1984, the federal government, determined to cut rising health-care expenditures, revised its method of reimbursing hospitals for Medicare costs. It has established fixed prices for treatment of Medicare patients based on 476 diagnosis-related groups, classifying patients by age, needed medical procedures, and standard length of stay. If a hospital spends more on Medicare, it must absorb the loss.

This change means that hospitals must be efficient in cost accounting in order to determine where their costs exceed government allowances. Cost of each unit of service is also needed in planning hospital economies. An integrated hospital computer system is well suited to this type of accounting task.

Doctors are responsible for 75 percent of hospital costs. They are the persons who order X-rays, lab tests, drugs, therapy, and special services. So cost accounting requires hospital administrators to monitor doctor's orders. Which doctors exceed hospital norms in drug expenditures? In calling for expensive tests? Doctors resent such administrative scrutiny. They fear that they may be harassed by administrators who care more for numbers on a balance sheet than quality patient care. They also believe that government bureaucrats are not qualified to interfere in patient care. The concept of patient classification and fixed cost for treatment is the antithesis of good medicine, according to many physicians.

Hospital cost accounting is more than dollars and cents. It raises medical issues such as, "Who is responsible for deciding the level of care for Medicare patients?"

A Sample Integrated Hospital System

A variety of hospital information systems are currently on the market. We will now examine the features of a sample advanced integrated system that includes a communications network extending to all departments and nursing stations.

One major subsystem of this sample system is dedicated to processing admissions, discharges, and transfers (ADT). Since online terminals are located in all departments, patients can be admitted to the hospitals by the emergency room and out-patient clinics as well as by admissions staff. No matter where patients are admitted, clerks are prompted by the system to gather needed admission data from the patient. If patients have been hospitalized in the past, admission information will be drawn from their records in computer storage, so that only updating is required. The ADT system keeps a count of the patients currently in the hospital and is able to assign beds.

A second feature of this integrated system is that services and lab tests given the patient can be entered by hospital staff on any terminal in any building in the hospital complex. (See Figure 10.3.) The lab and pharmacy subsystems determine the charges, automatically add them to the patient's account, and update the patient's medical record. Yet another management subsystem handles the staffing and scheduling of nurses and generates statistics to keep track of workload trends.

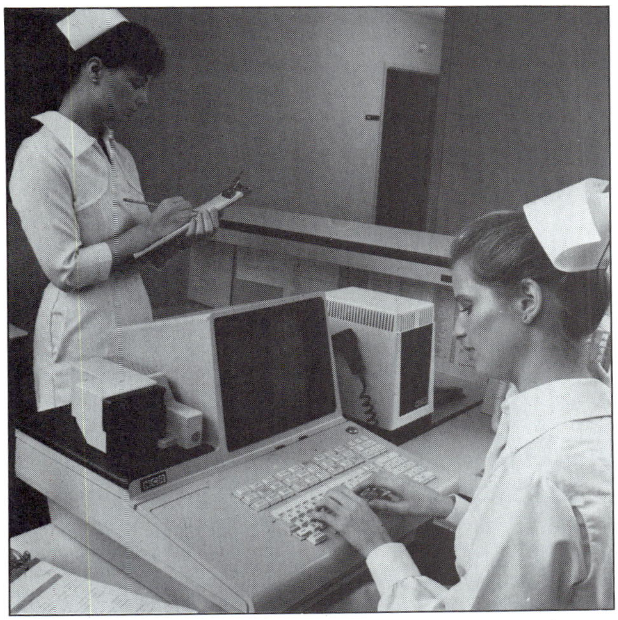

Figure 10.3 At a nursing station. With the general-purpose terminal, nurses and doctors can update patient charts at a central location. (NCR Corporation)

Supplement 10.7 HELP—An Expert System

Originally, HELP, an expert medical system, was designed to aid nurses in a cardiac unit at a time of crisis. Under the direction of Dr. Homer Warner, a team of doctors programmed a computer with a data base of expert knowledge regarding heart disease. Over the past fifteen years, subsystems have been added. Today, HELP has 4000 modules of expertise. Because of its large data base, massive storage capacity and extensive hardware is required. Six Tandem Computer Inc. Nonstop II CPUs (with 1.3 billion bytes of disk storage) are required for HELP at The Latter Day Saints Hospital in Salt Lake City.

HELP links the hospital's testing facilities, pharmacy, and patient rooms. It also integrates all the hospital's computer applications from record keeping and accounting to patient care. Once preliminary data about a patient is in the system, HELP will suggest what tests to run. If medication is ordered, the HELP system reminds the doctor of potential dangerous side effects and may even recommend a change in dosage because of data in the patient's record.

Physicians benefit because HELP gives second opinions and fast responses to technical questions. Of course, doctors need not accept HELP advice. But many do. According to Dr. Warner, about 80 percent of HELP recommendations are adopted by physicians who interact with the system.

Our sample integrated hospital system also enables doctors to retrieve medical records, key orders, and request answers to questions from any workstation. With COSTAR (**CO**mputer-**ST**ored **A**mbulatory **R**ecord), a medical data base system, a doctor might have the following interaction at a terminal:

```
WHEN SEX = MALE
     AND AGE OVER 50
     AND CODE = HYPERTENSION
     AND PROVIDER = JONES
     AND DATA AFTER TODAY - 3 YEARS
LIST NAME
```

Within seconds a list of all male patients over fifty diagnosed in the past three years by Dr. Jones as having hypertension would appear on the screen. This information might be useful if the doctor wanted to review medications prescribed or case histories in order to treat another patient in the same category.

Linking files in an integrated system means that redundancy in data collection and data storage can be eliminated. More important, information is readily available to hospital personnel when needed. For instance, checkout is facilitated since a complete listing of services performed by a patient has been recorded online. The patient's bill can be prepared in seconds. Before computerization it often took months after a patient was discharged to process all of the paperwork for billing.

National Integration

In Great Britain, Israel, Australia, and New Zealand, information stored in one hospital can be accessed by another. Intrahospital system integration in these countries is facilitated by the fact that these countries have comparatively small populations as well as by the fact that all of them have nationalized health systems. The technology required for national integration of hospital systems is the same as that used to integrate systems within a single institution, except that the type of communications network and method of telecommunications may differ. (See Figure 10.4 for examples of facilities that might be integrated in a national medical network.)

National integration of medical systems has several advantages. One is that physicians treating a patient who has fallen ill or been injured away from home have online access to that patient's medical records. Doctors can also call family medical records to their screens, even though the records may be stored in a remote data base. This can be helpful when a hereditary problem is suspected.

Yet another advantage of national integration

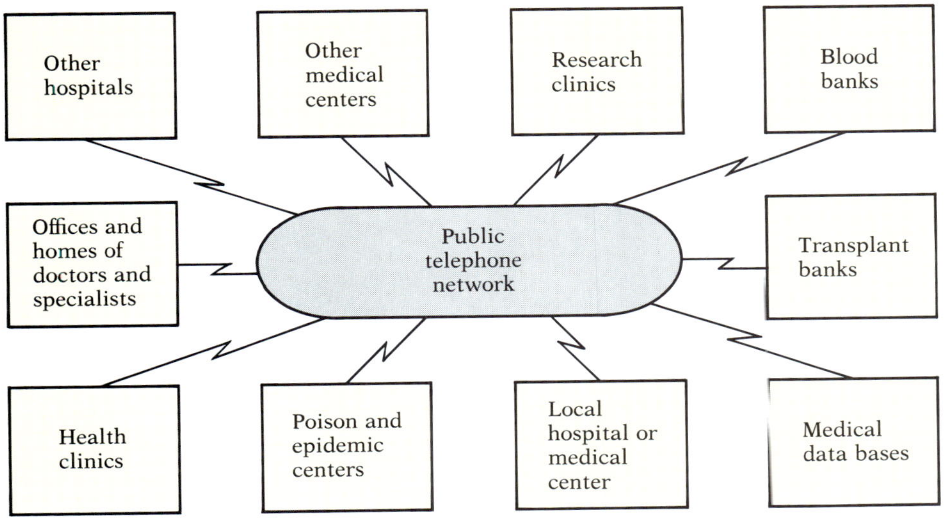

Figure 10.4 A national medical network.

of medical systems is that instant information regarding organs available for transplant is accessible to every physician. This information can, of course, save a patient's life.

Finally, the access to case histories afforded by national integration can help researchers find new cures. The depth and diversity of the information in such a system allows researchers to study particular subgroups in a population and in general to look at data from a wider variety of perspectives than they could if this data were scattered throughout many data bases or not systematically collected at all. Health records that are already computerized also save researchers time.

The reason why hospitals in the United States are not nationally integrated is not the lack of technology. Indeed, the national medical system in New Zealand runs on American computers and was designed by a U.S. consulting firm. The reasons for this lack of integration are of a more complex social nature. The medical profession has argued that patient records should be considered propriety data, and many Americans agree. Medical data, it is argued, does not belong in the public domain. The fear is that personal information will be misused and that integrated computer systems will jeopardize the relationship of trust between patient and physician, a relationship that is essential to treatment. The problem of **privacy invasion** is not limited to medical computer systems; many other types of computer applications threaten personal privacy as well. Chapter 15 discusses privacy concerns at greater length.

MICROTECHNOLOGY FOR THE DISABLED

The ability to etch the integrated circuitry of a complete processor on a single chip, which has contributed to embedded control devices in industrial equipment and household appliances, has revolutionized prosthetic devices for the disabled as well. As a result of advances in microtechnology, the "Utah arm," an artificial limb, can pick up signals from electrodes placed over shoulder muscles and lift four pounds when locked into place. Microprocessor-controlled artificial legs work on the same principle, picking up muscle signals from the user's thigh and hip.

For the paralyzed, robot arms that respond to voice signals handle eating utensils, move objects, and turn pages of a book. Engineers are working on a mobile robot mounted with a video camera. A person confined to bed can watch the robot's movements on a television monitor and direct its movement by voice commands. When perfected, the robot will be able to do errands for the handicapped, like bringing a snack from the kitchen.

In 1983, Nan Davis, paralyzed from the rib

Supplement 10.8 Case Study: Stamford Hospital

Stamford Hospital in Stamford, Connecticut is a 320-bed, private, nonprofit hospital. Dissatisfied with its data processing, hospital management hired a consultant to draw up a five-year computerization plan. According to the plan, basic financial computer applications would be implemented in the first three years and clinical applications would also begin in this time frame. The ultimate goal—a complete "order entry" system: that is, the hospital wants to be able to enter all medical orders by terminal (diet, tests, medicine) to eliminate paperwork. In addition, it wants to automate bill preparation for these orders.

The local network chosen for implementation at Stamford Hospital was ARC (Attached Resource Computer) produced by Datapoint Corporation of San Antonio, Texas. Medical Scientific International Corp. (MSI), a firm specializing in hospital systems, was selected to put together software.

In 1983, at the end of the first three years of the plan, Stamford had twelve processors, fourteen printers, and forty-one terminals on its ARC network. Three pieces of lab equipment, a card embosser, and an optical character reader were also part of the system. System components are connected via coaxial cable.

Most of the software has been purchased from other hospitals, although MSI has rewritten the programs to make them compatible with MSI systems. Implementation has proceeded smoothly. According to hospital officials, the new system is vastly superior to the old yet costs less. In spite of inflation, the hospital budget three years into the project was no greater than at its start.

cage down, took a few steps with the aid of a portable computer. Her leg muscles were electronically stimulated by the computer in the sequence needed to make a coordinated step. Movement was controlled by a pattern recognition system that uses level detectors to determine body and leg position in relation to the floor. Sensor information was processed by the computer to determine which muscles to stimulate next.

The manufacture of computer equipment that can be activated by slight movement, breath, or pounding to control terminal keyboard functions also benefits the disabled. A cerebral palsy victim who cannot speak or type might use such a keyboard to choose letters to spell out words on a terminal screen. In some cases, adaptive devices enable persons with limited motor control to become trained as programmers and to hold programming jobs.

We now have a bionic ear that promises to bring sound to 70 percent of the deaf who do not benefit from hearing aids. A microphone is worn around the ear connected to a microprocessor. This microphone turns sound waves into electrical impulses and transmits them through implanted wires in the inner ear to the auditory nerve. There is also an implantable programmable infusion pump on the market. The pump, which is surgically inserted in the patient's abdomen, delivers insulin to diabetics throughout the day. With proper communications equipment, a doctor can transmit altered dosage instructions over the telephone.

These are just a few medical applications being pioneered for microprocessors that will revolutionize health care for the disabled in coming years. Clearly, **microtechnology** can contribute to greater independence **for the disabled** and should help them lead richer lives.

COMPUTERS FOR HEALTH

Preventative medicine and various branches of public health are growing fields in which computers can play an important role. Software packages for diet analysis and menu planning are on the market for anyone with an interest in good nutrition, including physicians, home economists, parents, and athletes. The impetus for computer use to monitor and improve physical fitness has in fact come primarily from athletes and coaches.

Nutrition Software

A number of programs on the subject of **nutrition** are being marketed for health professionals and for home use. Most of these programs work in basically the same manner. A record of food consumed over a period of time is entered on a terminal. The computer then analyzes the nutrient content of the food intake and compares it with U.S. Recommended Dietary Allowances or other preestablished standards to determine whether a change in diet is advisable. Supplement 10.9 shows an example of nutrition software in use. Some programs allow the user to modify the minimum and maximum allowances set by the program. For instance, if a person is on a low cholesterol diet and must eat less than 250 milligrams of cholesterol per day, this requirement can be entered. The program will list foods that cause this limit to be exceeded.

Some nutrition programs assist in menu planning. When the user enters the appropriate information, the program will calculate calorie guidelines for safe weight loss and then suggest menus for dinners that fall within the dieter's caloric quotas. Foods suitable for a special diet might also be suggested. For example, a user might obtain a list of foods rich in iron. One program calculates energy spent (calories burned) for 26 physical activities to help users determine calorie intake needs. This feature is of particular value to athletes who need to consume far more calories than average when engaged in strenuous training.

Athletic Training

Biomechanics is the application of mechanics to biological systems. Information technology today contributes to the field by helping researchers analyze how the body moves. Biomechanics research has medical applications; for example, the identification of improper walking techniques might be an indication of physical maladies. (See Figure 10.5.) But biomechanics has had the greatest impact, to date, in the training of athletes. Biomechanical engineers study sports techniques and then design hardware and software to help athletes develop their muscles so that they can perform at their peak.

One of the methods used to analyze athletic form begins by filming an event. For most sports, 100-frame-per-second film suffices. The film is then projected onto a large digitizing tablet (a grid dotted with thousands of coordinates). A researcher uses an instrument to enter specific coordinates from the image in each frame into a computer—

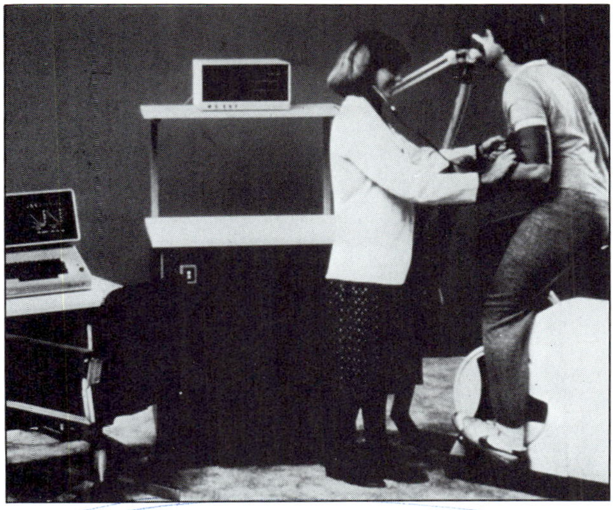

Figure 10.5 The pulmonary exercise lab. This computerized system combines capabilities for exercise testing and spirometry (measurement of air entering and leaving the lungs.) (Gould Electronics, Inc.)

coordinates, for example, marking the position of the toe, heel, hip, and shoulder points. A series of stick figures drawn from the digitized data is then projected as a graphics display representing the athlete's movement. In the case of a weight lifter, the figures could be utilized to spot errors in form by observing the trajectory of the bar, the lifter's center of gravity, and arm and leg positions.

A study of digitized figures of one marathon runner revealed that one foot was rolling inward too much, a common problem among distance runners. After pinpointing the problem, a series of exercises were prescribed to strengthen the muscles on the inside of the foot. Four months later, filming showed that the rolling had been cut in half.

Since biomechanical principles are still not well understood, coaches are not yet sure how to utilize all of the data they are gathering. In 1983, films were made of the eleven best swimmers in the country. Their fingers, hands, and hips were digitized to measure acceleration and stroke patterns.

Supplement 10.9 An Example of Nutrition Software

ITEM	FOOD NAME	PORTION	SERVING	AMOUNT
327	BREAD-CRACKED-WHEAT	1 SLICE	200%	50.0 GM
160	TUNA SALAD	1 CUP	200%	410.0 GM
50	MILK-FLUID WHOLE-3.3% FAT	1 CUP	150%	366.0 GM
600	CARROT-RAW-SCRAPED	1 CARROT	200%	144.0 GM
273	ORANGE-RAW-ALL VARIETIES	1 ORANGE	100%	131.0 GM
318	WATERMELON-RAW-W/ RIND	1 WEDGE	100%	926.0 GM
724	SOUP-CHICKEN NOODLE-F/MIX	1 CUP	150%	360.0 GM

NUTRIENT VALUES (%RDA)

KCALORIES	1372 KC (68%)	RIBOFLAVIN	1.51 MG (125%)
PROTEIN	84 GM (190%)	NIACIN	25.4 MG (195%)
CARBOHYDRATE	125 GM (- %)	VITAMIN B6	1.83 MG (91%)
FAT	60.5 GM (- %)	FOLACIN	126 UG (31%)
FIBER	5.14 GM (- %)	VITAMIN B12	1.3 UG (43%)
CHOLESTEROL	190 MG (- %)	PANTO- ACID	4.14 MG (75%)
SATURATED FA	16.4 GM (- %)	CALCIUM	711 MG (88%)
OLEIC FA	16.1 GM (- %)	PHOSPHORUS	1137 MG (142%)
LINOLIC FA	14.1 GM (- %)	TRYPTOPHAN	259 MG (158%)
SODIUM	3266 MG (148%)	THREONINE	878 MG (201%)
POTASSIUM	1832 MG (48%)	ISOLEUCINE	1004 MG (153%)
MAGNESIUM	224 MG (74%)	LEUCINE	1470 MG (168%)
IRON	10.4 MG (57%)	LYSINE	1665 MG (254%)
ZINC	3.01 MG (20%)	METHIONINE	400 MG (107%)
VITAMIN A	20350 IU (508%)	CYSTINE	183 MG (107%)
VITAMIN D	153 IU (76%)	PHENYL-ANINE	822 MG (179%)
VITAMIN E	7.92 MG (99%)	TYROSINE	742 MG (179%)
VITAMIN C	115 MG (191%)	VALINE	1085 MG (142%)
THIAMIN	.9 MG (90%)	HISTIDINE	429 MG (- %)

PERCENTAGES BY CALORIE (4:4:9)
PROTEIN: 24% CARBOHYDRATE: 36% FAT: 39%

The program also displays the information graphically, a sample of which follows.

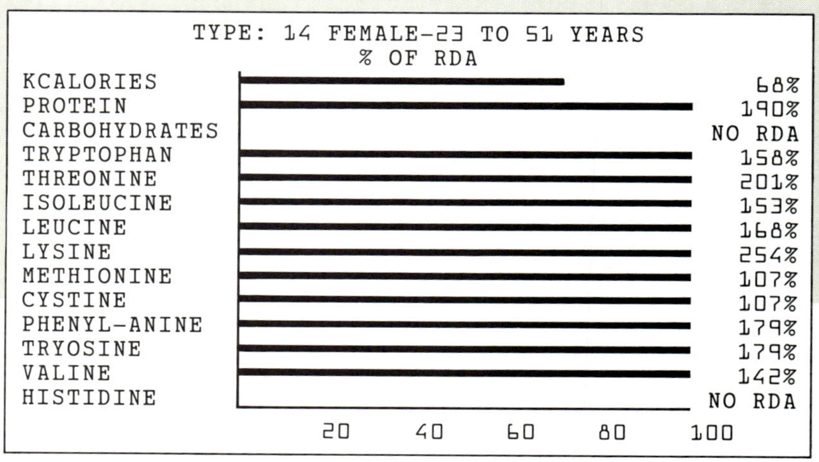

Since no one yet knows what the perfect stroke is, the data is being used to analyze how swimmers generate propulsion.

There are many other interesting examples of computer technology being used in athletic **training**. The **Selspsot motion analysis system**, for instance consists of small, light-emitting diodes attached to specific points on an athlete's body. Cameras detect infrared waves produced by the diodes, which are turned on and off successively by an "administrative unit." This unit also coordinates the camera sampling. Data produced by the cameras tracing the position of each diode is used by the computer to generate stick figures on a computer screen. Two or more cameras can give three dimensional data on parameters such as position, velocity, acceleration, center of mass, and body angles.

Another device called a **force platform** monitors the techniques of skiers, dancers, and track competitors. This device, which looks like a bathroom scale, can reveal how much body weight is on each leg or whether an athlete is breaking stride. Just a slight hesitation before a high jump, unnoticeable to the human eye, can be detrimental to performance. A related device is the **dynometer**, which measures mechanical force. It can be connected to a computer to analyze muscle strength on a single joint movement, or to measure dynamic force or fatigue characteristics. (See Figure 10.6.)

More widely known is the **computerized treadmill**, which helps athletes evaluate the effectiveness of their training programs. It can measure physiological factors such as heartbeat, respiratory rate, and oxygen intake on a cardiac/pulmonary monitor.

Finally, even more general in application are computerized **biofeedback systems**, which aid athletes in their psychological preparation before events. In a computerized biofeedback system, electrodes monitor muscle tension, brain waves, breathing, and heartbeat of the athlete. The computer collects and stores the information, which is then used to determine whether the athlete is relaxed or needs to concentrate more. One psychologist has discovered that top rifle shooters have a significant cardiac deceleration before firing. He has employed biofeedback techniques to teach other shooters to relax, and this has resulted in a significant improvement in their scores.

The advantage of training devices such as these is that athletes have an objective analysis of their strengths and weaknesses, in contrast to performance analysis in the past, which was based largely on guesswork and intuition. In addition, the instantaneous nature of the feedback generated by these devices helps athletes improve their skill and drop bad habits quickly, thereby maximizing physical potential.

Figure 10.6 An "electrodynogram" system. Hardware and software for doctors, physical therapists, bioengineers, and others that records and analyzes biomechanical information related to a person's gait. The system can gather the data as the subject freely moves about. (Langer Biomechanics Group)

COMPUTERS FOR SPORTS ADMINISTRATION

While we're on the subject of sports, let's take a look at some of the ways in which information technology contributes to the administration of athletics.

Supplement 10.10 High-tech at the Olympics

The 1984 Summer Olympics in Los Angeles brought together a field of world-class athletes. Management of the games depended on the high technology of world-class computers. Computers captured, recorded, compiled, listed, summarized, classified, analyzed, number-crunched, stored, retrieved, and reported information on every aspect of the competition from the early planning to final cleanup.

Here is a partial list of ways information technology helped the Olympic Committee stage the games.

- Route planning and scheduling of the eighty-two-day, 8700 mile Olympic torch relay was assigned to computers. They calculated distances between cities and estimated running times. They kept track of runners and sponsors, processed financial records of money raised by the relay, and determined who would pick up the torch where, when, and from whom.
- Distribution of tickets and ticket inventories were managed by computer.
- Personal computers were used for budgeting, purchase orders, payroll, and accounting. An investment portfolio of donation money was also processed by a personal computer.
- Accreditation and security were computer responsibilities. Computers kept track of people scheduled in events, kept lists of access rights to specific areas, issued badges, and provided up-to-date security information to guards.
- Computers managed a complex transportation system to move 8200 media representatives, 10,000 athletes, and another 10,000 coaches and trainers to and from events at 30 locations.
- Computers scheduled the work of more than 50,000 people (both paid and volunteer personnel) in the Olympic villages and venues.
- An audio distribution system digitized phone messages so that anyone with an authorized password could call in for a message. Another communication system was for electronic mail. Approximately 2000 terminals, each with its own printer, were located at Olympic venues, administrative buildings, and press centers. This system interfaced with the international telex network so that reporters could file a story from any of the electronic mail terminals for instant transmission to their home offices throughout the world.

Construction time and price projections, training site scheduling, room assignments, allocating of phones and copy machines, athletic profiles, timing, paging, judging, score keeping—the list of Olympic computer uses could go on and on. Though backstage, computers gave a first-class performance.

Statistics

All coaches want specific information about how their players and teams are doing. Today, coaches rely on microcomputers to tabulate, process, and analyze game statistics following each sporting event. One basketball program for a microcomputer will process eighteen variables, such as field goals attempted, completion percentages, offensive rebounds, total rebounds, assists, steals, turnovers, blocked shots, and fouls. Sometimes a coach wants a minute by minute analysis of a game; sometimes a comparison of an individual's performance against the player's own season figures is the objective.

In general, **statistical sports packages** are user friendly—that is, they are designed for easy access to information for people with no previous background or experience with computers. The low cost of microcomputers means that many teams and school athletic departments, and even individual coaches, have been able to start using such packages.

Scouting

In preparing for competition, many coaches **scout** their opponents in order to identify patterns and tendencies of play. They attend games of their rivals to analyze their performance and collect statistics and study game films. Performance data is then entered into a microcomputer data base. Programs that draw on this data serve as the basis for game plans. For instance, the computer might be programmed to print out a passing-zone chart for football indicating the number of passes thrown by an opponent into each of ten field zones. A "hole chart" might present frequency, percentage, and total yardage gained through each hole in the line. A running-plays chart could list the frequency, percentage, total yardage, and average yardage of running plays. Such precise information on an op-

Supplement 10.11 Mini at the Marathon

Results of overall standings, placement by age and sex, and run times of 17,000 participants were compiled within hours at the 14th New York City Marathon, thanks to a mini. In previous races, the final tabulation of results and notification to participants took from three days to one week.

Here is how the computerized system worked. Race officials recorded times of runners as they crossed the finish line, then steered runners down a chute in order of finish. At the end of the chute, the bar-code identification number carried by each runner was removed by officials and subsequently sent in batches to a trailer where the numbers were read by a Computer Identics Corp. FCP22A scanner. A Qantel Corp. System 64 linked to two high-speed printers took over from there. It compiled results from time sheets and placement order. It also prepared postcards to participants showing their time and place of finish.

ponent's offensive attack can be used by the football coaching staff to plan blocking schemes and specific backfield actions.

Timing and Scoring

Both athletes and spectators want instantaneous final results at the conclusion of a sporting event. In many sports where hundredths of a second separate competitors, the human eye cannot judge who has won the event, much less keep track of the order of finish.

We use electronics today in both **judging** and **scoring** athletic events. We have special devices to link the starter's gun with photo-finish cameras and electronic touchpads. Calculators determine results by a trigonometric formula for shotput, discus, and javelin throws. A slide carriage trained on an optical detector measures jumping events down to as little as two millimeters. A computer is used to calculate diving results based on a formula which incorporates a score for level of difficulty and judges scores. It also speeds the averaging of marks given by judges at gymnastic meets and can immediately flash results on a scoreboard.

Many stadium scoreboards are now computer-controlled. Some allow pictures, player information, and messages to be displayed as well as important game statistics and scores.

Cataloging and Other Activities

A computer can be used for **cataloging** of almost any kind of sports information: names, addresses, eligibility records, schedules, game results, injury reports, locker assignments, awards lists, and handicaps. Computers can handle ticketing, store athletic profiles, plan budgets, process payrolls, inventory equipment, and facilitate the order of supplies. Professional sport teams are a business—a business that can take advantage of computer technology for all of these functions and those described in Chapter 7.

SUMMING UP

We all aspire to good health. Computers are making major contributions not only to care of the sick but also to better nutrition and improved physical fitness. Doctors have instantaneous access to information on patients, diseases, treatment, and drugs using information technology. They can draw information from distant data banks and expert systems, or consult with colleagues using teleconferencing and telemail when their terminals are part of a communications network. We now have computer imaging techniques to help doctors and researchers study the body, and microprocessors embedded in prosthetic devices to aid the disabled. In addition, computerized laboratory equipment processes complex medical tests with speed and accuracy—tests not feasible when data had to be collected by humans and processed by hand. Hospitals benefit by computerized record keeping and the integration of medical subsystems.

The impetus to improve physical fitness by using computer technology has come from persons in sports. They are cooperating with engineers and computer technicians to develop hardware and software to measure muscle strength and monitor athletic performance. The technology spillover should affect the general public as well. We will benefit by the knowledge athletes are acquiring on biomechanics and nutrition, and we will have better tools to measure, evaluate, and plan physical therapy for the injured.

Use of computers in medicine raises many ethical questions. Is it in the public interest to spend money for computerized medical services? Many persons see no improvement in patient care as a result of computer technology even though everyone is aware of skyrocketing medical costs that can be attributed, in part, to this technology. Will computerization make health care so expensive that only the rich will be able to afford professional treatment?

Who is responsible for the consequences of a medical mistake made by a computer, such as an inaccurate test result leading to a death because of faulty programming? How can a patient's right to privacy be secured when online terminals can access patient records from any department in a hospital?

We must address the impact of computers in sports as well. Will high-tech result in remote electronic stimulation of muscles and force-thrusting devices in the shoes of runners during a race? We disapprove when steroids artificially strengthen muscles. Why should we accept microcomputers if their use has the same effect? Will sport become competition among biomechanical engineers instead of a natural performance?

Technology solves many of the problems that confront society, but not without creating new issues to be resolved.

REVIEW QUESTIONS

1. Describe how computers assist in data capture and processing medical records.
2. What features of an electronic office can be used in:
   a. a doctor's office?
   b. labs?
   c. pharmacies?
   d. hospitals?

   For what purpose can electronic equipment be used?
3. How have computers contributed to medical testing?
4. What administrative functions in a lab can be done by computer?
5. How can medical data bases assist a doctor?
6. What is an expert system in medicine? What purpose does it serve?
7. List activities in a pharmacy that can be computerized.
8. Compare:
   a. MUMPS vs. packaged hospital systems
   b. independent hospital programs vs. integrated hospital information systems
   c. expert medical systems vs. consultation with a specialist
   d. computerized hospital system vs. noncomputerized processing of hospital data
   e. traditional pharmacy vs. computerized pharmacy
9. What factors have contributed to the integration of hospital systems?
10. Describe how computers assist in patient monitoring.
11. Discuss how computer technology is being used to assist the disabled.
12. How can software contribute to diet planning?
13. How does biomechanical training benefit athletes? Describe examples of hardware/software that have been developed to assist the athlete.
14. How can computers be used in sports administration for:
    a. keeping statistics?
    b. scouting?
    c. timing?
    d. coaching?
    e. training?

    What other tasks can computers perform to assist coaches and athletic directors?

DISCUSSION QUESTIONS

1. How does a hospital information system compare to an information system used in a business, such as an insurance company? Can it perform many of the same tasks? Explain.
2. As a patient, would you want your medical record accessible to all hospital departments? How can your privacy be protected?
3. Who should be responsible for ensuring that hospital records are complete and up-to-date? How can patients be sure that their medical records are accurate?
4. Do you think hospital computer systems dehumanize patient care? What can hospitals do to make patients feel that they are special individuals, not merely a statistic?
5. If given a choice, would you prefer to give your medical history to a nurse or enter it in a computer terminal? Explain the reasons of your choice.
6. If you were given responsibility for planning the integration of hospital files, where would you begin? Which files would you integrate first? Explain your reasons.
7. Do you favor national integration of hospital information systems? Why?
8. Who should be responsible for computer error in a doctor's office, lab, or hospital? How can errors be avoided?
9. Discuss the implications of computer diagnosis from one of the following points of view:
   a. moral b. ethical c. legal
10. Do you believe that computerized hospitals will improve health care of patients? Explain.
11. Can the increase in the cost of health care as a result of computer technology be justified?
12. Is it in the interest of society to limit technological innovation in medicine? Explain your answer.

EXERCISES

1. Interview a doctor who uses computers in private practice and in the hospital. Record these uses. What benefits does the doctor gain through computer use?
2. Research how each of the following are used in your favorite sport.
   a. mainframe computer
   b. microcomputer
   c. hand-held computer
   d. microprocessor
3. Visit a friend who is hospitalized. List the ways in which computers have aided in the health care of your friend.
4. Research ways in which computers aid the handicapped. Limit your research to products developed in the last two years.

Selected Annotated Bibliography

Arlt, S. "10 Steps To Establish Athletic Computer Systems," *Athletic Director*, vol. 13, no. 4 (December 1983), pp. 1–2. Describes administrative and training applications of computers.

Ash, Dr. Stephen R. "Developing A Patient Database on a Microcomputer," *National Report: Computers and Health*, vol. 4 (July 15, 1983), pp. 7–12. A data base of patient records and clinical facilities helps doctors in their treatment of patients and evaluation of therapy. This article describes a small portable system.

Barlow, Mike. "A Computer Cure For a Doctor's Dilemma," *Personal Computing*, vol. 7, no. 4 (April 1983), pp. 211–15. A personal computer is the medicine a doctor needs to keep track of patient accounts. This is a case study with specifics on equipment, cost, training, and productivity.

Barrett, Charles N. "Preoperative Planning with Interactive Graphics," *Computer Graphics World*, vol. 7, no. 3 (March 1984), pp. 11–18. Computer graphics help physicians visualize plastic or reconstructive surgery.

Cherry, Laurence and Rona. "Another Way of Looking at the Brain." *The New York Times Magazine*, vol. CXXXIV, no. 46, 435 (June 9, 1985), pp. 56–120. This article discusses in detail imaging techniques like CAT, MRI, and PET now being used in medicine and research. The article also deals with the implications of the use of expensive high-tech equipment for society as a whole.

Chin, Kathy. "America's High-Tech Olympians," *InfoWorld*, vol. 6, no. 31 (July 30, 1984), pp. 22–27. This article describes how microcomputers are used in the training of athletes.

Davis, Dwight B. "Sports Biomechanics: Olympians' Competitive Edge," *High Technology*, vol. 4, no. 7 (July 1984), pp. 34–41. A superb article on the application of engineering principles and on the modeling of human motion in order to analyze and improve athletic techniques of exercise and training.

Dean, Andrew G. "EPIAID," *Byte*, vol. 10, no. 10 (October 1985), pp. 225–33. EPIAID, a set of experimental microcomputer programs, is being developed to provide better tools for field epidemic investigation. This article describes many of the facilities of EPIAID and the present status of this expert system.

Evans, James R. et al. "Play Ball!—the Scheduling of Sports Officials," *Perspectives in Computing*, vol. 4, no. 1 (Spring 1984), pp. 18–29. Computer-based assignment and matching techniques aid in scheduling referees and umpires for professional and collegiate athletic contests. *Perspectives in Computing* is an IBM publication.

Fell, Peter J. and Skees, William D. *The Doctor's Computer Handbook*. Belmont, CA: Lifetime Learning Publications, 1984. This book describes how to computerize a doctor's office, telling advantages, disadvantages, and pitfalls.

Mareena, Thomas. "Computerizing the Medical Profession," *Popular Computing*, vol. 3, no. 12 (October 1984), pp. 88–92. Until recently only large medical clinics and groups of doctors could afford computer technology. Today, microcomputers can be afforded by all doctors. Billing, diagnostic programs, and medical data bases are explored.

Miller, J. "How A Computer Can Help You," *Athletic Journal*, vol. 63, no. 9 (April 1983), pp. 30–31. Miller describes how the high school athletic director can use a microcomputer.

Mishelevich, David, and Van Sluke, Don. "The IBM Patient Care System: An Overview of its Software," *Data Base*, vol. 11, no. 3 (Winter-Spring 1980), pp. 64–75. A technical presentation well supported by diagrams.

Physicians and the Computer. This is a journal started in 1983 devoted to the use of computers in the doctor's office. It is for microcomputer users more than users of large mainframes or shared systems and does not include hospital applications. Articles are devoted to hardware, software, office management, and education.

Rudy, D. "Biomechanics—How Computers Extend Athletic Performance to the Body's Far Limits," *Popular Science*, vol. 22, no. 1 (January 1982), pp. 58–60. Discusses how the computer and human can join together to increase an athlete's physical capabilities.

Starr, Paul. *The Social Transformation of American Medicine*. Basic Books: New York, 1982. A definitive social history of the medical profession in America, with special attention paid throughout to the costs of health care and to show how this and other factors will affect the nature of health care in this country in the future.

Stern, Nancy and Robert. Chapter 10, "Computers and Heath," *Computers in Society*. Englewood Cliffs, N.J.: Prentice-Hall, 1983. This chapter is devoted to computers and health. It has illustrations, a list of key words, and questions. It discusses hospital information systems, medical information systems, computers as a diagnostic tool, and computers in medical research, among other topics.

Trappl, R. "Computer Psychotherapy: Is It Acceptable, Feasible, Advisable?" *Cybernetic Systems*, vol. 12, no. 4 (October–December 1981), pp. 385–94. A concise and intriguing examination of the subject, including the patient's viewpoint. Discusses both technology and ethics.

Ward, Bernie and Mareman, Thomas. "Olympics," *Popular Computing*, vol. 3, no. 10 (August 1984), pp. 97–109. The authors review the use of computers in the 1984 Olympics, including biomechanical training, financing, coordination, logistics, and communications.

(clockwise from top left) ▪ Today's "clean," paperless workspace, the electronic office ▪ Herman Hollerith's revolutionary data processing machine ▪ This megabit chip is smaller than a dime and can store over one million bits of information. ▪ Each silicon chip in this thimble has been etched with a miniaturized circuit.

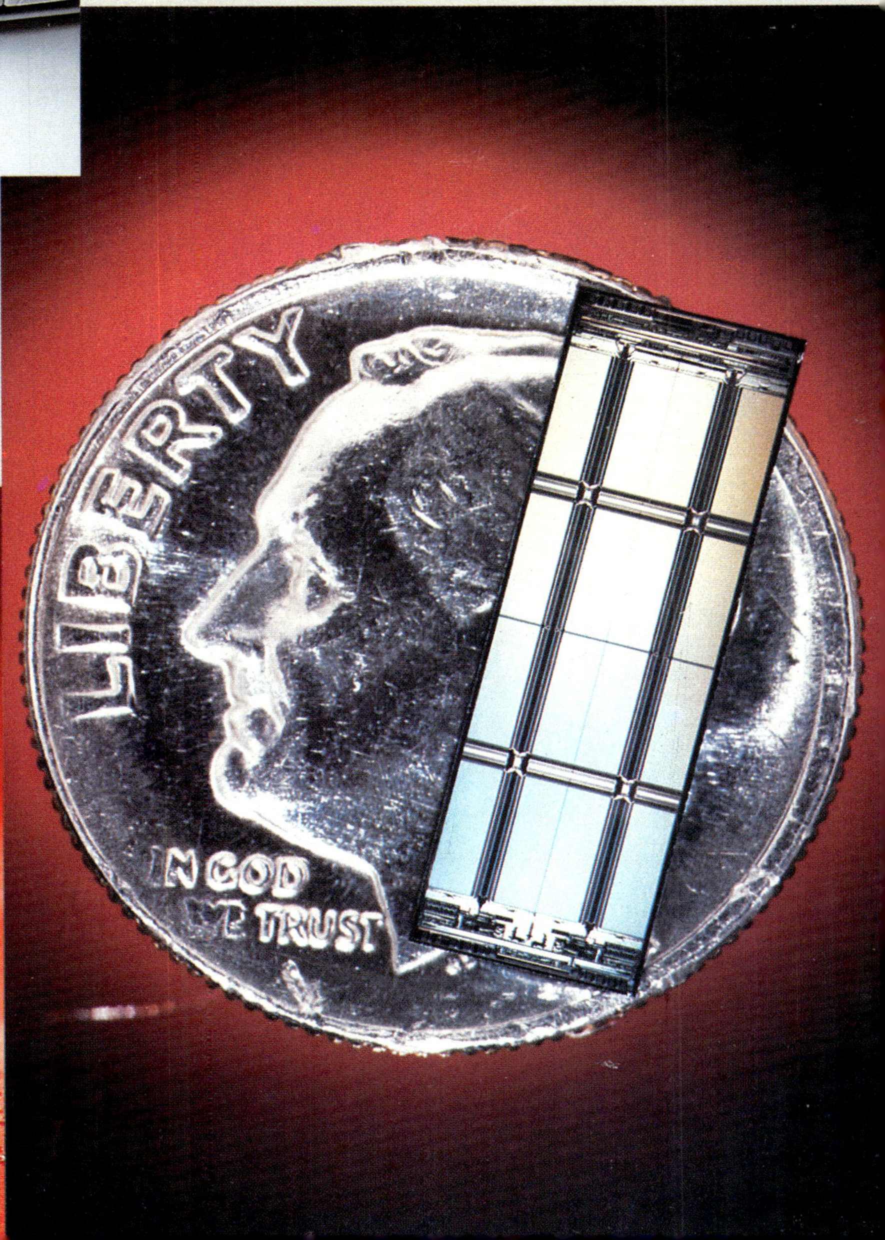

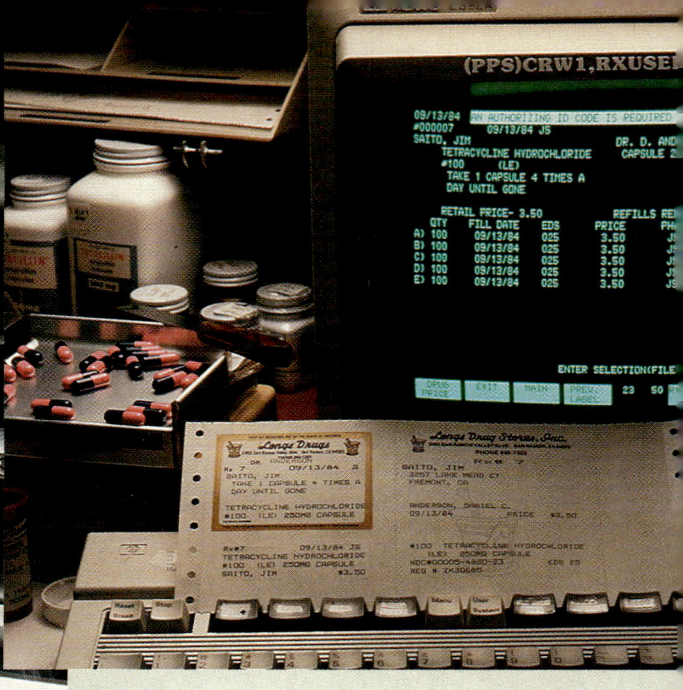

(clockwise from top left) ▪ A technician inspects diskette coating operations. ▪ Computers help to maintain inventories in large drugstores. ▪ A terminal for a home system can control environmental temperatures, appliances, security, and a message center.

(clockwise from top) ▪ Color plotters can produce complex engineering drawings. ▪ Using a bar code reader in inventory control ▪ Computer circuit boards are produced in countries all over the world.

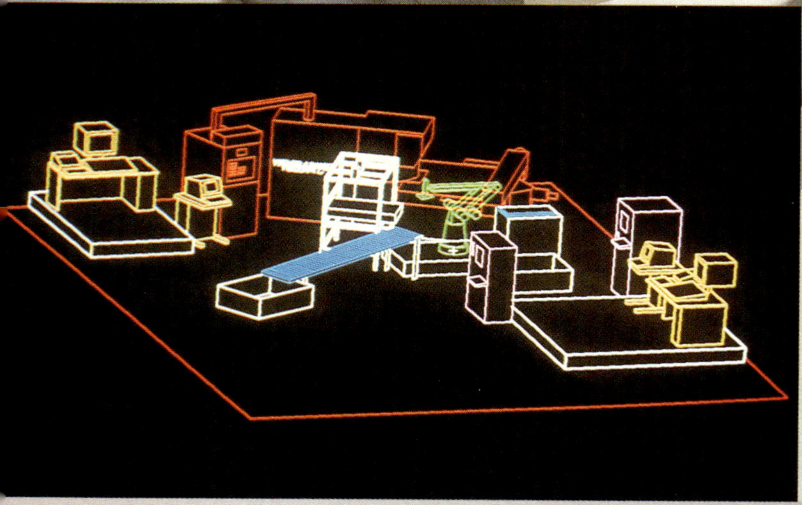

(top to bottom) ▪ *Optical disks for ROM data storage offer higher area densities than magnetic disks.* ▪ *This program produces a three-dimensional color graphics display.* ▪ *A miniaturized ten-megabyte hard disk drive replaces bulkier devices of equal capacity.*

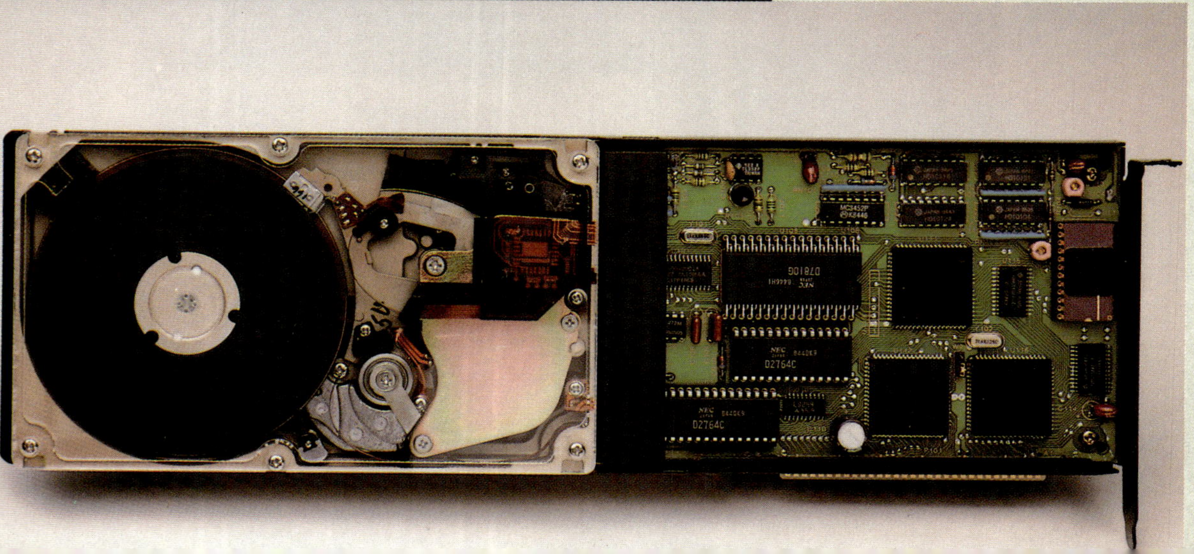

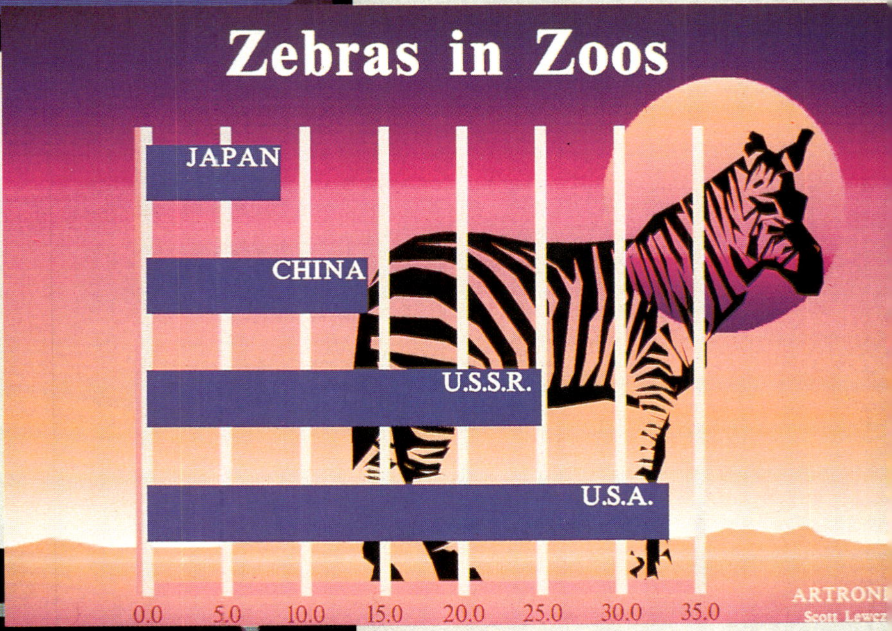

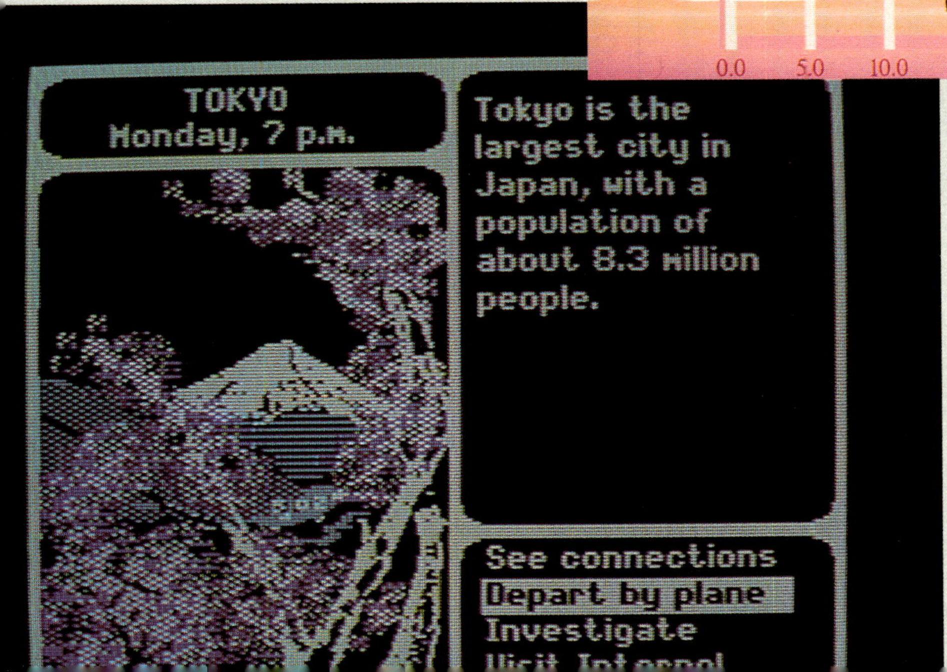

(clockwise from top left) ▪ *The player learns to interpret financial news in order to play the market in this software game—it simulates the real-life experience of playing the market.* ▪ *Advanced graphics programs can "paint," label, and chart data with more sophistication than earlier programs.* ▪ *An interactive geography program combines visual imagery with text information.*

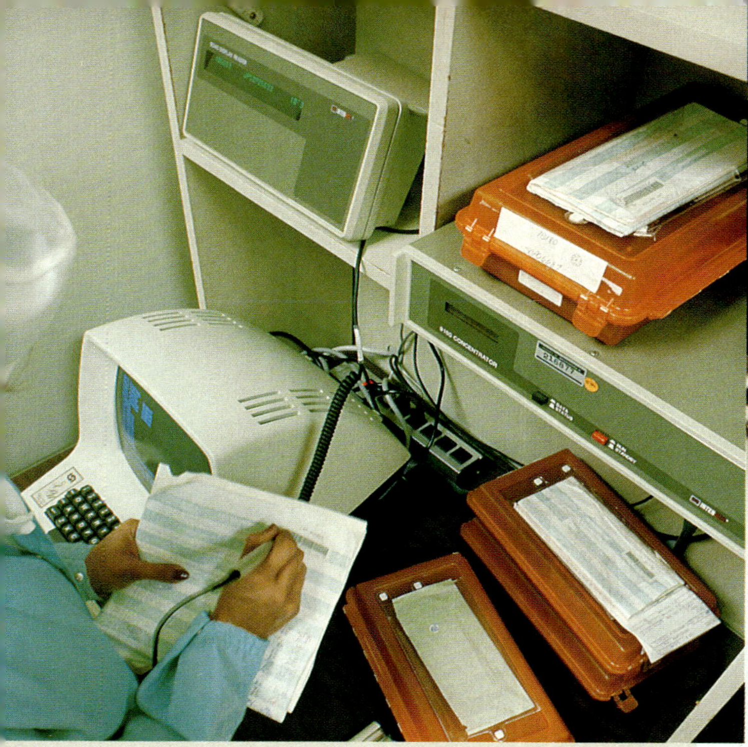

(clockwise from top left) ▪ *Entering data with a scanner wand* ▪ *By moving the digitizer over an image and entering the proper coordinates, the stored data can be used to recreate or manipulate the image.* ▪ *Transferring data into a wristwatch computer* ▪ *The touch-screen makes the computer respond to the pressure of a fingertip.*

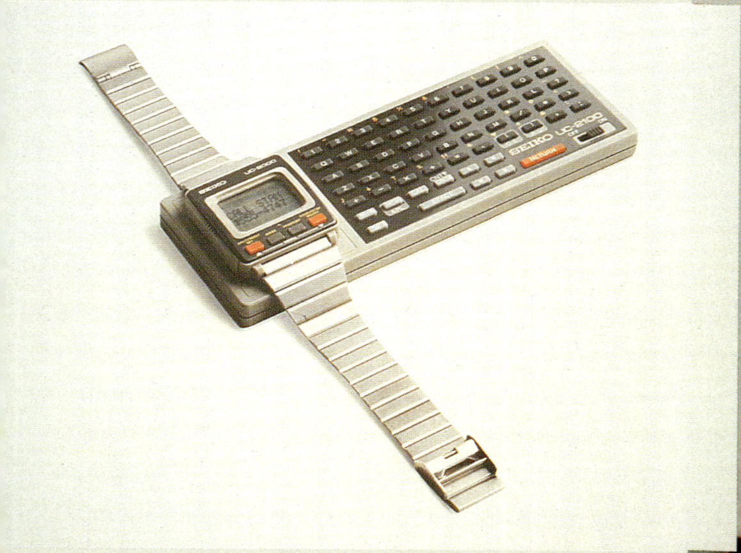

(clockwise from right) ▪ *A computerized security system* ▪ *New Jersey Prosecutor Alan Rockoff amid evidence collected against hackers who violated credit records and military files* ▪ *This software key limits the use of the program disk to keyholders without locking up the hardware.*

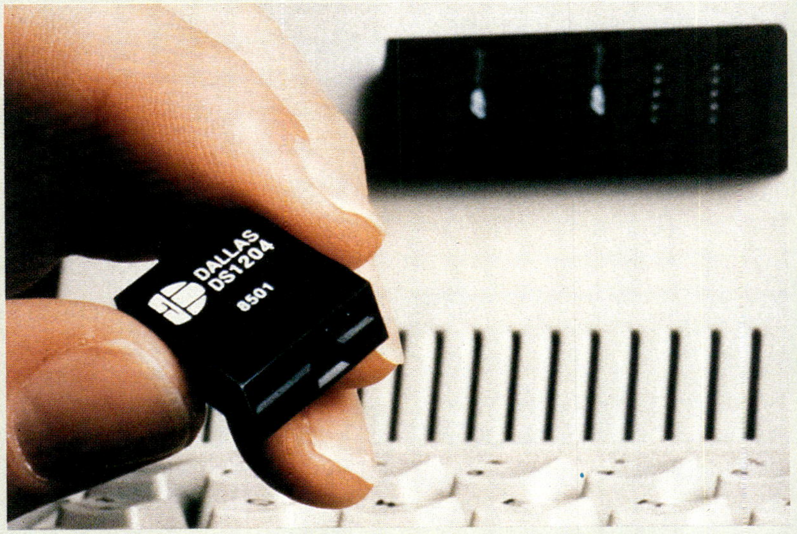

(clockwise from top) ▪ Four workstations can be linked to a central computer system. ▪ Some terminals can notify the sender than an electronic message has been received. ▪ Updating and recalculating data can be done quickly during a meeting. ▪ Computers lend themselves to a variety of jobs, even in small offices.

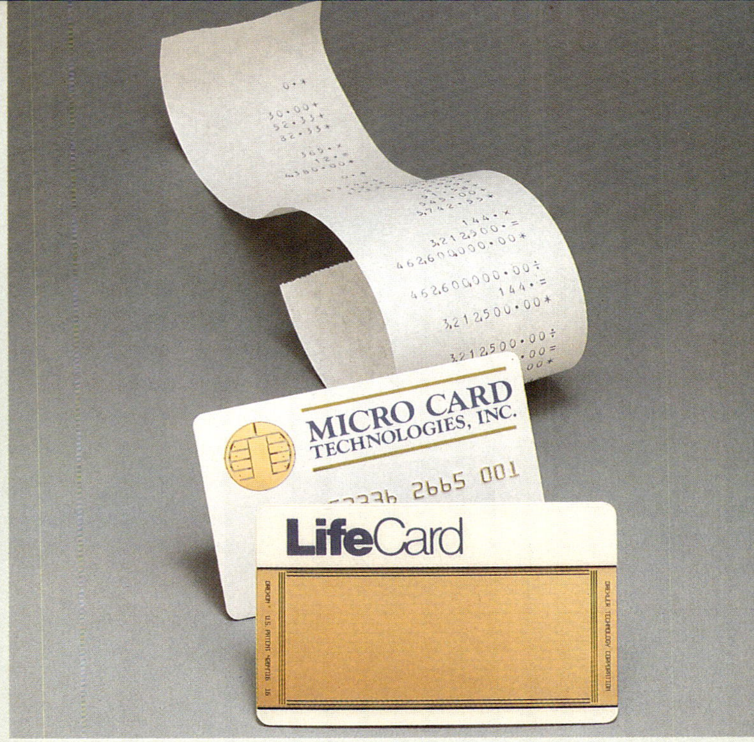

(clockwise from top left) ▪ *Robots can be adapted to delicate tasks such as picking up pieces of tofu (bean curd).* ▪ *Micro Card and LifeCard, card-sized carriers of credit and medical information* ▪ *An engineering drawing produced with computer-aided design program* ▪ *A robot arm used in a manufacturing operation*

(clockwise from left) ▪ Computers can be of significant help to students. ▪ This portable computer can be carried in a backpack or a briefcase. ▪ Continuing education for upper-level management is essential to the implementation of technological developments. ▪ Scholarly research can be supplemented with electronic data-search methods. ▪ With computers, geologists have more detailed information available for projections.

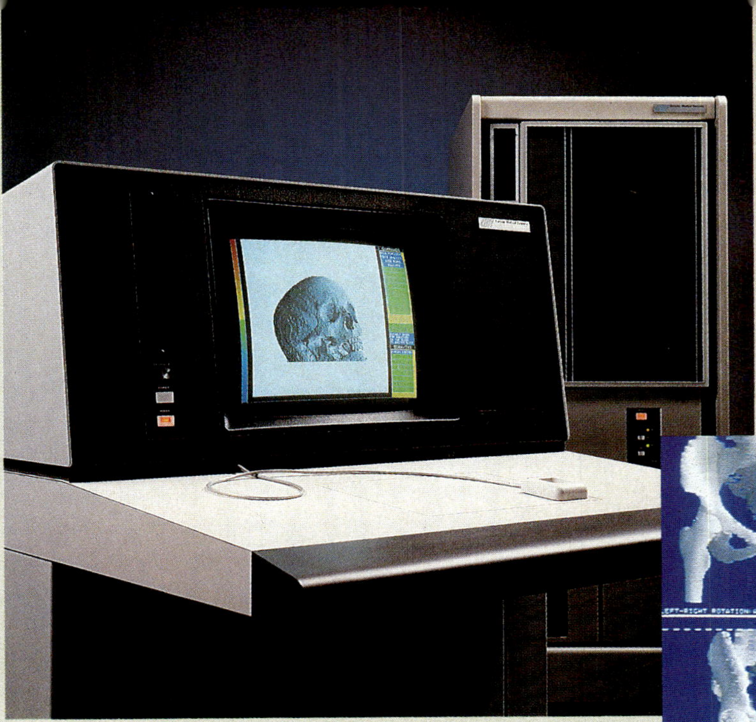

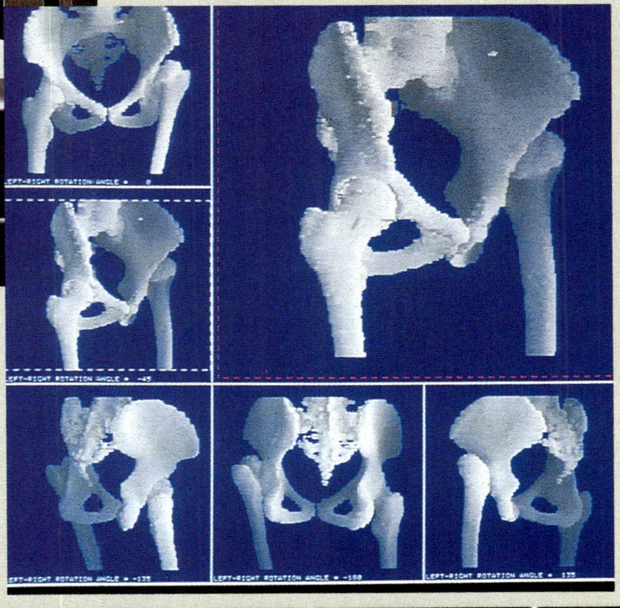

(clockwise from top) ▪ A computer with reformatting and three-dimensional reconstruction capabilities used by radiologists and surgeons ▪ The image can be rotated to various angles for complete analysis. ▪ CAT scanners can give precise images of the body's soft tissues.

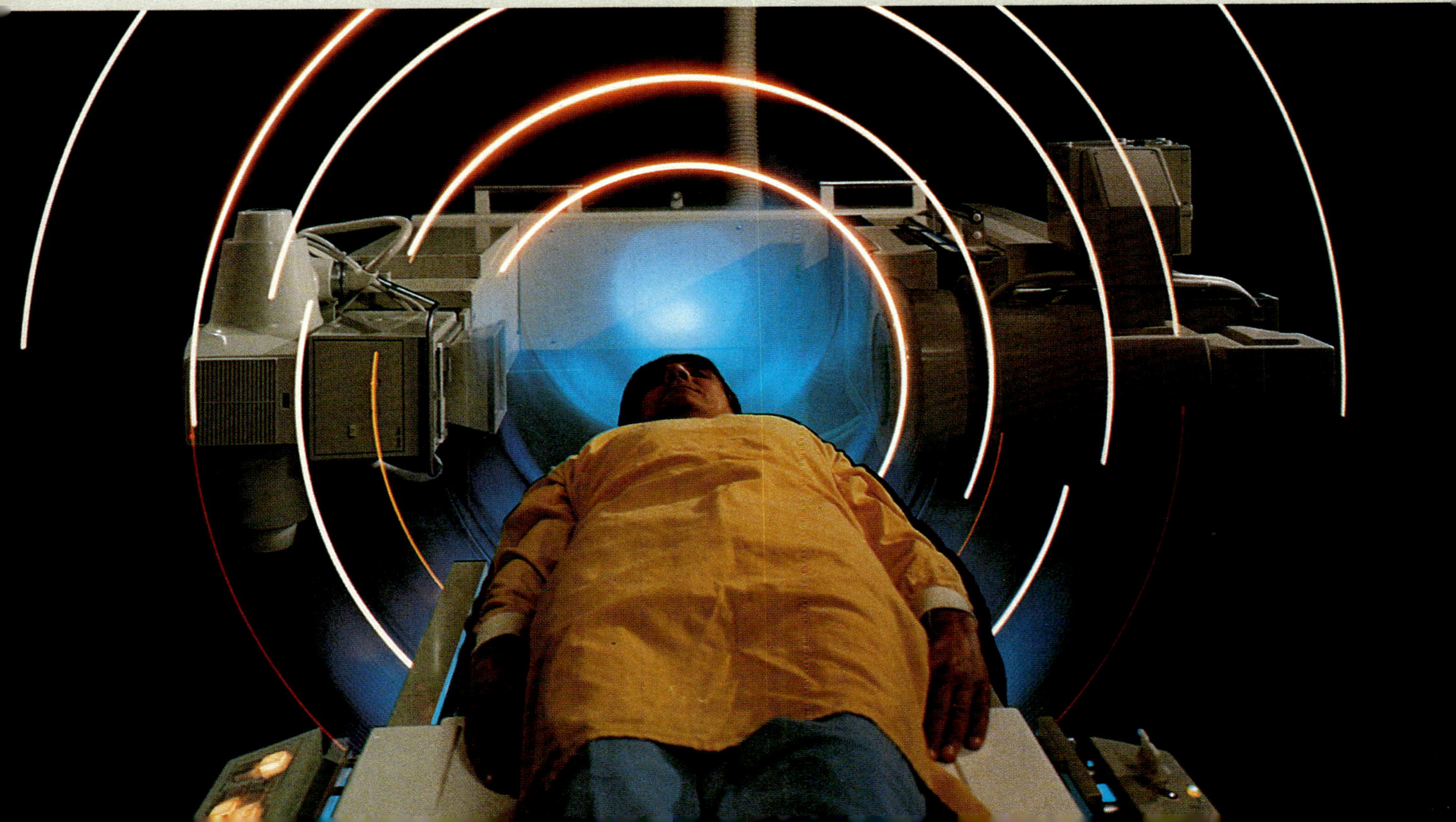

(clockwise from top) ▪ *Collecting vital statistics from a healthy orangutan at the San Diego Zoo.* ▪ *A programmable running shoe interprets distance, time, speed, and other information.* ▪ *The Red Cross uses a personal computer and a laser reader to verify blood-type labels.*

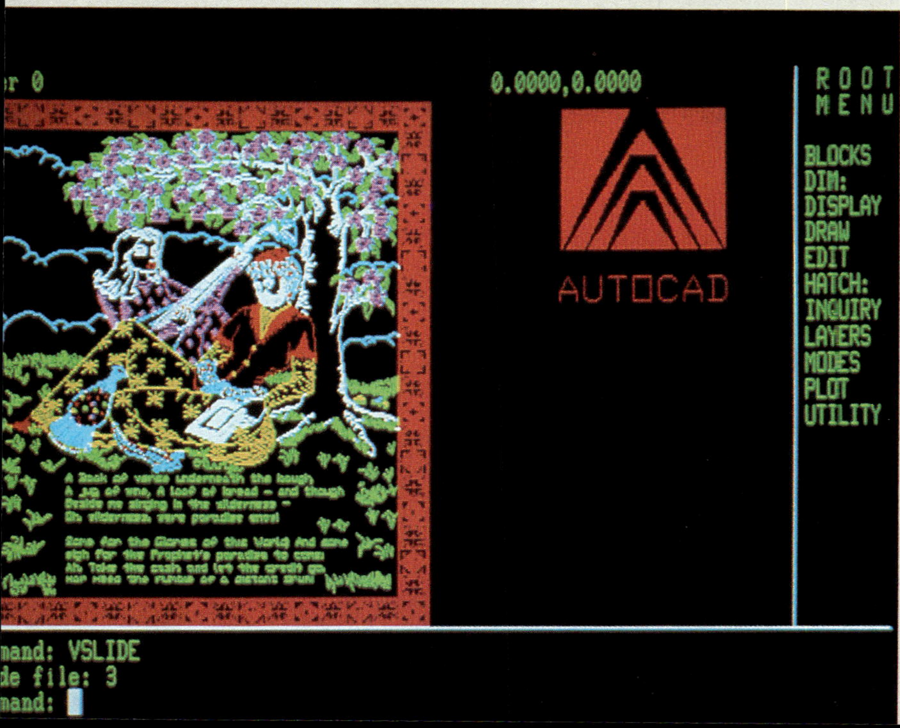

▪ *(top) This Japanese-made robot can read sheet music and play what it sees.* ▪ *(bottom) Art and text can be combined with some programs.*

▪ *Three examples of the computer used as an artist's tool: in some cases, the artist might expose an underlying structure.*

- *Three examples of the computer used as an artist's tool: in some cases, the artist might expose an underlying structure.*

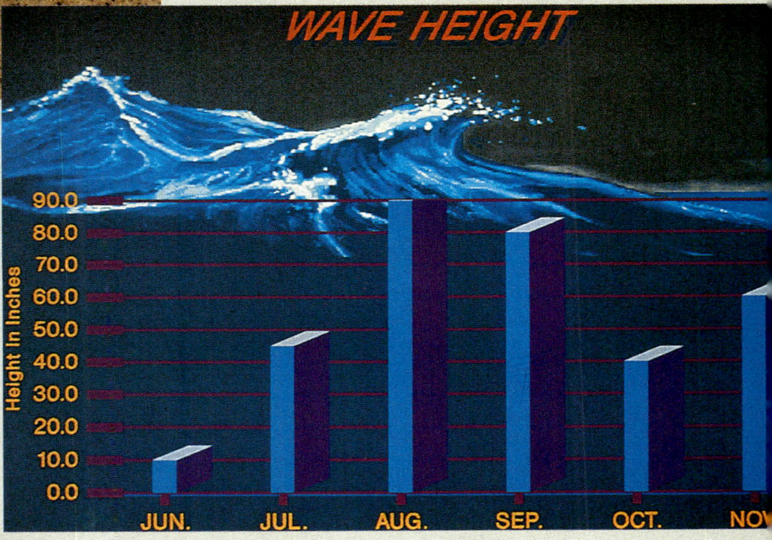

▪ *(top) The Prowler, a robot for military and civilian security enforcement* ▪ *(middle) A bar chart combined with a graphic image.* ▪ *(bottom) Police dispatchers using a computer for communications.*

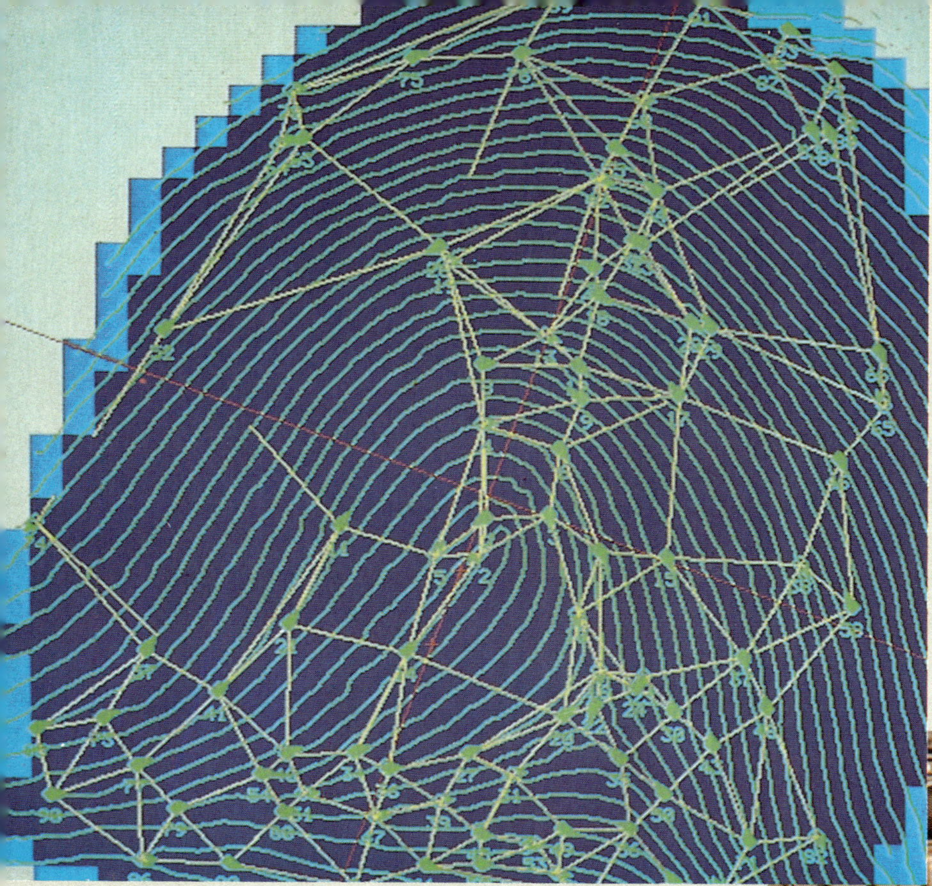

(top to bottom) ▪ *California's automated fingerprint identification system took only three minutes to match prints leading to the arrest of a suspect in the Night Stalker case.* ▪ *Defense agencies may use a telecommunications network including satellites, microwaves, electronic switching, and local transmission lines.* ▪ *The conductor on a Japanese train can contact the dispatchers via radiotelephone.*

▪ *A series of computer-generated, manipulated, or enhanced images (clockwise from top left):* ▪ *large-particle model with four light sources* ▪ *reflections on the surface of metallic objects* ▪ *shadows on a solid model with two light sources*

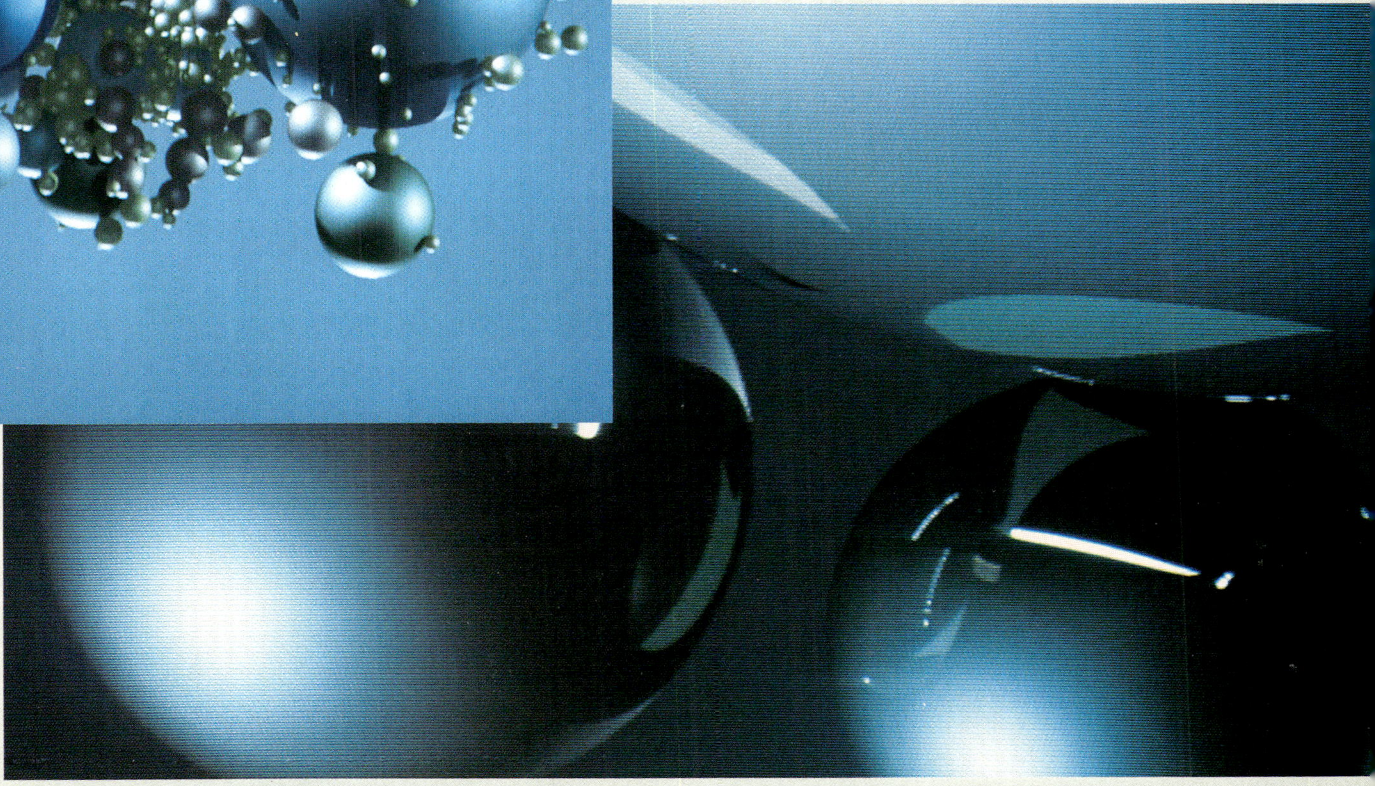

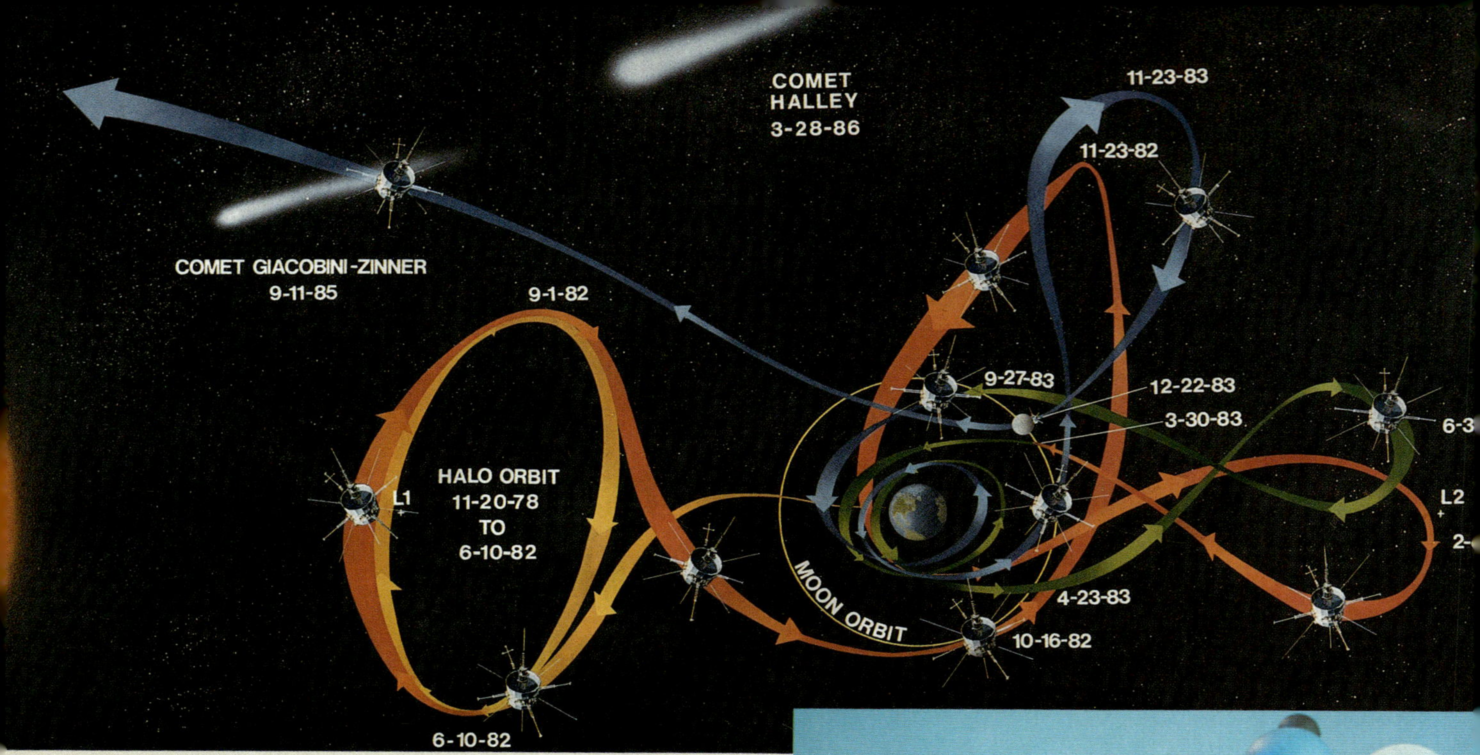

▪ *More computer-enhanced images (clockwise from top):* ▪ *an image of the comet Giaccobini–Zinner indicating relative brightness (red is brightest)* ▪ *an aggregate of particles with eight light sources* ▪ *a wheel and suspension apparatus*

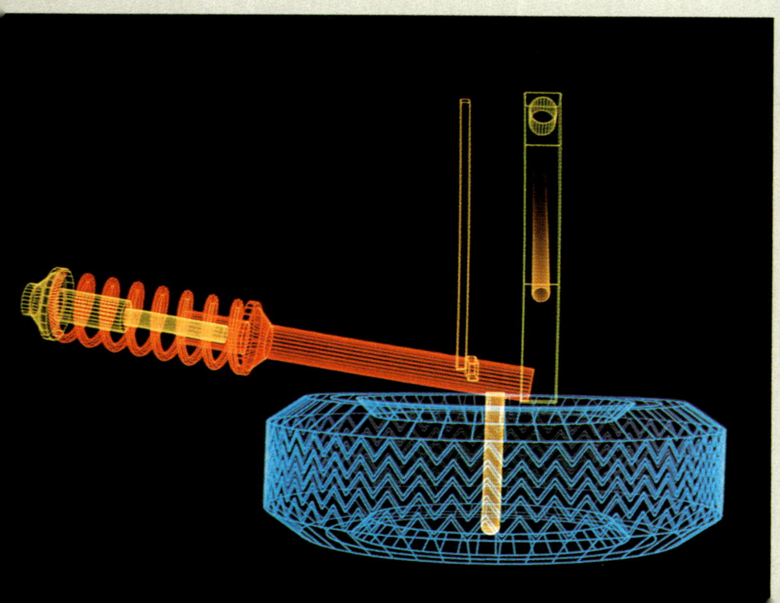

(clockwise from top) ▪ Encoded on special strips, data can be read from the printed page by an electro-optical scanner. ▪ A computer can govern a home-control system. ▪ The instrument/diagnostic panel for an automobile dashboard

▪ *(top) This businesswoman is a computer consultant and instructor for other small businesses.* ▪ *(bottom) A data-search on wildlife in East Africa helped these photographers plan their photo safari.*

(clockwise from top left) ▪ *The optical scanner inputs information from typewritten copy.* ▪ *These images appear to be three-dimensional and can be manipulated easily to produce an animated sequence.* ▪ *An artist (the model) sketched by an artist (the robot)*

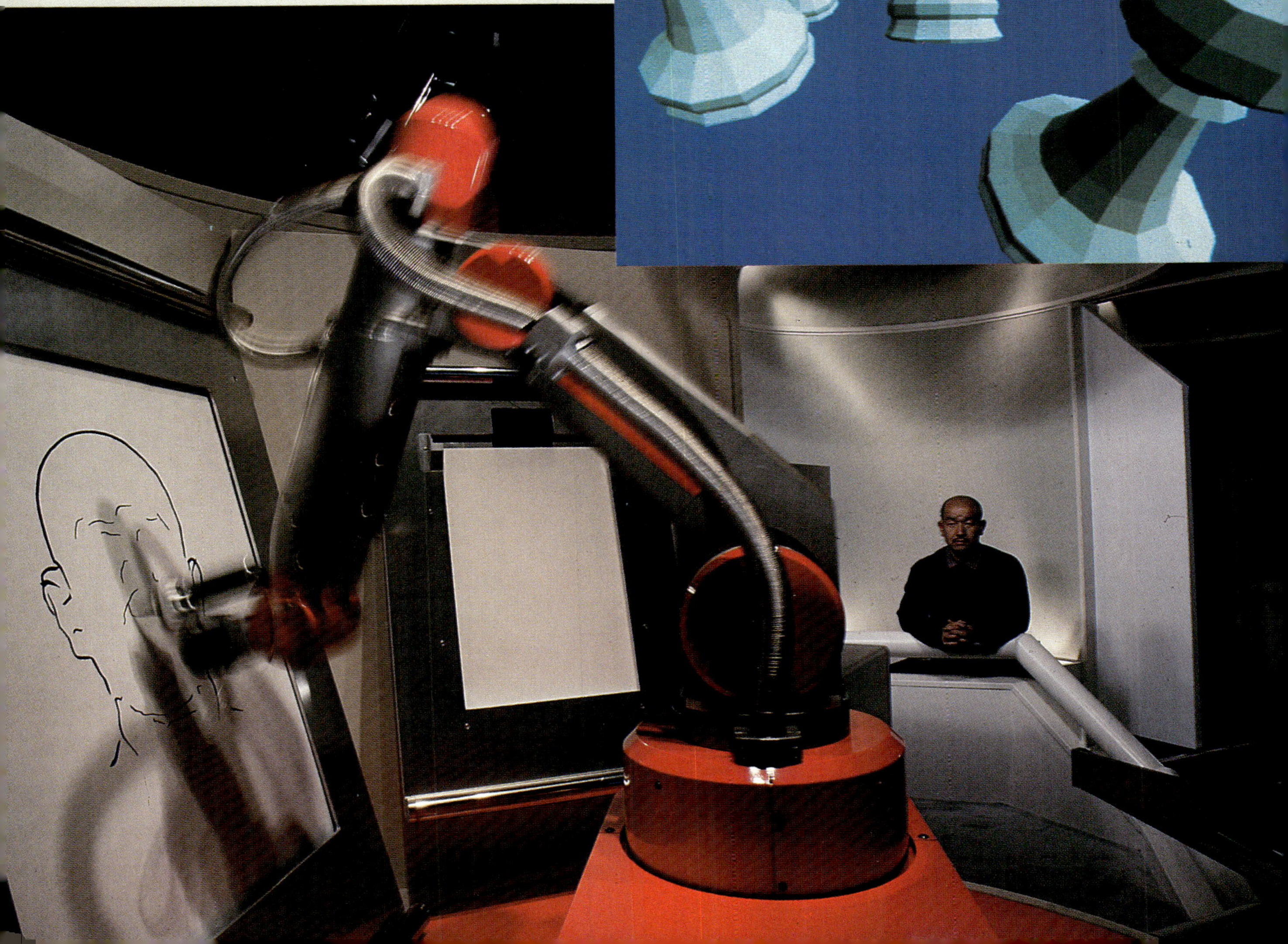

(clockwise from top left) ▪ *Technicians oversee automated procedures on an assembly line.* ▪ *Terminal for the computer at the main Hewlett-Packard parts center* ▪ *One employee and a computer can track inventory and sales for a multitude of items in this department.* ▪ *This small business uses a computer to keep track of items coming in for service.*

(top and right) ▪ *The microprocessor embedded in the card, stores, processes, and analyzes data, keeping the cardholder's account current.* ▪ *This automated teller machine (ATM) dispenses bills in five denominations plus exact change. It can also authorize the cashing of checks.*

(left to right) ▪ *Many aspects of international travel have been improved by computerized data processing and telecommunications.* ▪ *The passbook printout of an American computerized finance system adapted for Japan* ▪ *A Japanese ATM*

(clockwise from top left) ▪ The software on this computer helps bookstore customers find books, and can recommend books based on preferences customers enter into the system. ▪ Computers permit access to the world's electronic libraries ▪ The electronic newspaper ▪ The electronic sports reporter

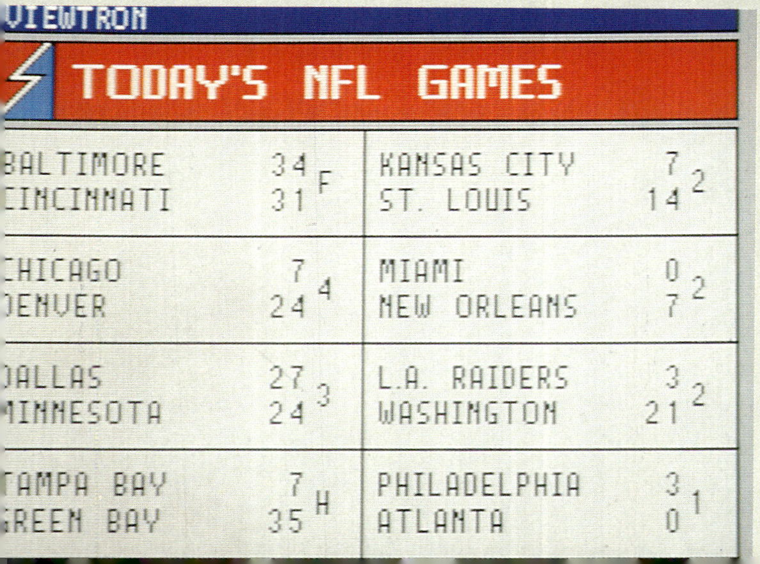

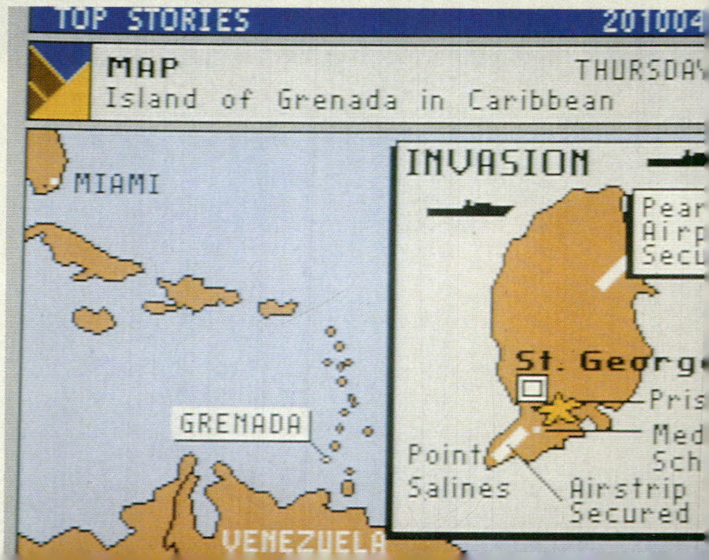

The Cultured Computer

Please be sure the electronic signal on your watch or pager is switched off before the concert begins.

SAN FRANCISCO SYMPHONY PROGRAM NOTES

CHAPTER ELEVEN

Key Words

analog synthesizer	digital recording	preset
animation system	digital synthesis	real-time
computer art	digital-to-analog converter	research
computer-controlled camera	frame buffer	sequencer program
computer-generated art	graphics	sound editing
concordance	graphics tablet	sound waves
computer-generated art	image synthesis	synthesizer
delayed playback	light pen	word processing
	move-generation system	

Computers are helping to bridge the gap between the humanities and the sciences. The computer's ability to manipulate, analyze, and store information serves musicians and biologists, historians and chemists, writers and mathematicians. The technology that provides artists with a new medium for expression is the same technology used by engineers to design machine parts. Indeed, technological advances in hardware and software are beneficial to people in most fields of endeavor.

This chapter will discuss the use of computers by artists and others who work in the humanities, with an emphasis on literature, music, art, film, and dance. (While computers are used to train young artists in the fundamentals of their art, computer-assisted instruction will not be covered here. Refer to Chapter 9 for a full discussion of CAI techniques.) This chapter will also include a look at the technology of computer sound synthesis and computer-generated graphics.

COMPUTERS AND LITERATURE

In the field of literature, computers can contribute to the mechanics of writing and to literary research. Programs are also being developed that enable computers to write stories and poetry.

The Computer as a Writing Tool

For writers, **word processing** is invaluable. Writers who master a few basic keystrokes and commands discover that they no longer have to focus on the mechanics of putting words on paper. They can concentrate on ideas and ways of expressing those ideas instead.

It is easy to delete, rearrange, and rewrite text with a word processor. There is no laborious crossing out, erasing, or retyping to slow the creative process. A clean text, with no sentences scribbled between the lines or in margins, can always be viewed on the screen. Different versions of a passage or chapter can easily be created through file merges or block moves and then printed out and compared. (See Chapter 7 for a more detailed discussion of word processing.)

In addition to their role in revolutionizing the process of putting words down on paper, many word processors come with spelling-check routines. Programs that will perform a grammatical and stylistic analysis on a piece of text in order to identify errors and make suggestions for improvement are also available. Even experienced writers can often benefit from these supplementary products. It should be noted, however, that programs that correct grammar and style are most appropriately applied to certain kinds of expository writing and cannot in themselves produce good writing. The reason for this is that a stylistic program assesses prose from a finite set of rules for good style, whereas a human takes a variety of subtle factors like context, audience, and purpose into account in making stylistic decisions.

Finally, computers play an increasingly important role for authors because many publishers now accept (and some even demand) that authors submit their work on disks rather than as hard copy manuscript. Electronic printing from disk to book, eliminating the intermediary step of typesetting from hard copy, is becoming the norm. (This text is an example of electronic composition.)

Literary Research

One way to analyze an author's work is to prepare a **concordance**, an index of every word in a work with reference to passages in which they occur. This is a task well suited to a computer. Once text is input in machine-readable form, it can be manipulated in a fraction of the time required for manual processing.

The computer can also be used to study an author's style. It can determine average length of sentences, evaluate word choice and word patterns, and analyze the use and arrangement of various linguistic features. Such studies can establish the author of a given work. For example, this technique was brought to bear in a 150-year-old controversy regarding the book of Isaiah in the Bible. Could chapters forty through sixty-six have been written by someone other than the prophet Isaiah, as many scholars contend? Style comparisons of the two parts of Isaiah were made on a computer by a doctoral student at Hebrew University, Dr. Yehuda Radday. Every test suggested that the text from chapter forty onward was written by an entirely different person than the writer of chapters one through thirty-nine. Using advanced statistical methods, Radday showed that the probability of both parts having the same author was one in 100,000.

Computer as Author

A number of game programs have been developed to produce computer novels. Text that is drawn from a basic plot stored in the game program is displayed on the screen. The user is then given a role in determining how the story unfolds. For example, the user can type in a piece of dramatic action like "Pick up the bomb and put it in the mailbox." The machine will advance the story line from that point with snatches of dialogue and descriptions of places and people. This interactive fiction has the potential of moving in literally thousands of directions.

Can such fiction on a floppy disk be classified as literature? To date, the characters generated in such stories have been two-dimensional, and the plots and writing sophomoric. But as this technique is developed, might a new literary form evolve?

At Allegheny College students in a course called "BASIC Poetry: The Computer as Poet" programmed a computer with basic language skills: parts of speech, word functions, pronunciation codes for words stored in computer memory, rules for syllabic weight, number of stressed syllables and their locations in given poetic forms, the poetic forms themselves (for example, sonnets or quatrains) and so forth. The computer was then instructed to:

- Choose a form.
- Set length of line, meter, syntax, and stanzas according to the conventions of the form.
- Draw words from a data array to create a finished product.

The computer succeeded in writing some poetic lines with words joined in imaginative ways. (See Figure 11.1 for a sample.) But the results could not be called "poetry."

What was lacking? Students found that they did not know enough about the English language to program the computer with writing fundamentals. They also wanted a better understanding of the elements of good poetry and more programming skill to bring to the project. They recognized that the computer certainly has the potential to manipulate the language of sensory images but they were troubled by the concept of computer as poet. Is the manipulation of language "poetry" if it does not

A Day in a Time

The sunrise is coming, breathing but secret,
Singing or weeping its joy or its terror;
The planet's impulse is this night's gift:
Tender, wicked, knowing, now forgotten, now treasured,
Sometimes buried, sometimes remembered, always grasping
As we are compelling earth and thighs and fields of violets
And the curse and the melody of our own insistent blood;
For this sunset is ours, our vow, our fortress,
Veering but staying, devouring worlds enormous and sure.

*Source: Alfred Kern, "GOTO Poetry," *Perspective in Computing*, vol. 3, no. 3 (October 1983), p. 45.

Figure 11.1 Poetry written by computer at Allegheny College.

express a deeply *felt* emotion or idea? Is poetry a reflection of the poet or simply the words on the page? If poetry is the latter, we may indeed have computer-created verse that qualifies as poetry in the future.

COMPUTERS AND MUSIC

Sound consists of vibrations in the air, and music is an art form using sound. The link between computers and music is that it is possible to generate sound electronically. Electronic impulses, when amplified and run through a speaker, cause **sound waves** (air vibrations). A **synthesizer** is a device used to generate these electronic impulses. Synthesized sound waves can be made to vary in pitch, timbre (quality of sound), loudness, and duration. They can be made to resemble a musical instrument or to imitate a noise, such as the whistle of a locomotive.

How is this done? A sound is made up of many characteristics. "Pitch," for instance, is determined by the frequency at which a sound wave fluctuates. Most musical tones are composites of several related frequencies, called "harmonics." The relative strength of the harmonics determines an instrument's "timbre." Finally, "loudness" is directly related to the amplitude (breadth) of the wave. Musical tones vary in loudness over time. For example, a guitar produces tones that rapidly rise and fall in amplitude, whereas a flute's tones have a longer attack time and can be sustained. The term "amplitude envelope" is used to describe the attack time, initial decay time, sustain time, and final release time of a note.

When an instrument plays a note, what you are actually hearing is the envelope of that waveform plus the harmonics of that form. All of the characteristics of the waveform can be represented by an electronic signal. The contribution of the computer is that it can give a composer or performer control over the characteristics of a signal being synthesized.

Sound Synthesis

There are two types of sound synthesis: analog synthesis and digital synthesis.

An **analog synthesizer** generates electronic impulses by a device known as an "oscillator." (The oscillator might be compared to the strings of a violin.) The impulses are then modified by filters for resonance. (In our analogy, the body of the violin provides such resonance.) When an analog synthesizer is played, the oscillators and filters must be individually adjusted to produce the desired sounds. A computer program can provide instructions for this adjustment.

In **digital synthesis**, sound is modeled by a stream of binary numbers from a computer instead of being produced directly by an oscillator. The computer is instructed on the basic note and quality of sound the user desires by a program. The shape of that sound wave (the envelope and har-

Supplement 11.1 Program That Simulates the Ringing of Chimes

```
100 REM  **** CHIME SOUND ****
110 REM
120 N=17  :REM Tone Generator Address
130 GOSUB 1000  :REM Clear All Outputs
135 REM
140 REM Set Tone 1 to 679 Hz
150 OUT N,140  :OUT N,5
160 REM
170 REM Set Tone 2 at 694 Hz
180 OUT N,170  :OUT N,5
185 REM
190 FOR T=0 TO 11  :REM Strike Chime 12 Times
200 FOR A=145 TO 159  :REM Loop to Generate Attentuation Steps
210 OUT N,A  :OUT N,(A+32)
220 FOR Q=0 to 65  NEXT Q  :REM Delay While Sounding Chime
230 NEXT A
240 NEXT T
250 REM
1000 OUT N,159  :OUT N,191  :OUT N,223  :OUT N,255
1010 RETURN
```


monics) is represented mathematically as part of a wave table loaded into the computer with the program and stored in computer memory. The computer scans the table many times a second, and the rate of the scan determines the frequency. As a result, a continuous stream of 8-bit words (each equal to two bytes) is generated, and this stream describes the waveform specified by the program.

Converting the stream of binary numbers in digital synthesis into sound requires an integrated circuit board containing one or more **digital-to-analog converters**. These change the sequence of binary words sent by the computer into a continuous voltage wave, an analog signal. This analog signal passes through a filter, is amplified, and run through a loudspeaker in the same manner as a signal from an analog synthesizer. (See Figure 11.2 for an illustration of digital synthesis.)

In microcomputer-based systems, floppy disks load a master file of instrument sounds, called **presets**, into the computer. Each preset will specify waveforms and amplitude envelopes for given instruments, such as pipe organ, trumpet, strings, clarinet, and sax. More complex systems allow musicians to design waveforms of their own.

To sum up, then, the difference between digital and analog synthesis is that all the manipulation in digital synthesis is occurring in the realm of numbers, whereas in analog synthesis the sound is continuous voltage being changed by various filters.

All aspects of analog synthesis are reproducible in digital synthesis. Thus, the amplitude and timbral characteristics of instruments can be constructed in computer software to duplicate the functions of analog synthesizers. Only the human voice is difficult, if not impossible, to reproduce with synthesis.

Types of Computer Music Systems

Analog and digital computer music systems can be of two types: delayed playback or real-time. In a

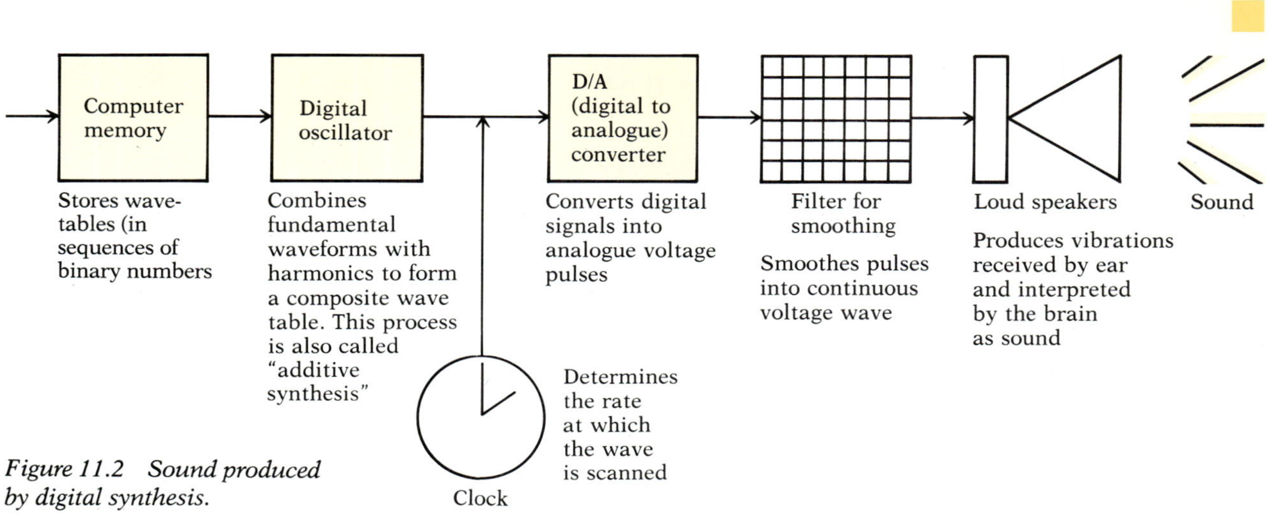

Figure 11.2 Sound produced by digital synthesis.

delayed playback system, a user types musical notation into a computer. Apple's Macintosh, for instance, uses a mouse to allow you to move symbols representing clefs, notes, rests, time signatures, chords, and even ties, beams, and note ornaments to a blank manuscript on the screen. The computer can then be instructed to play the composition.

In a **real-time** system, the user plays on a synthesizer keyboard. A pressed key tells the computer to generate a tone of the appropriate pitch by scanning the wave table at the corresponding frequency. Because of the speed of computer processing, there is no perceptible delay before sound is produced.

Computer Music for the Professional

The computer lets musicians experiment with sound by designing new waveforms. No longer is the composer restricted to the timbre of conventional instruments. In addition, a composer can control music in space by placing speakers throughout a concert hall, providing a new dimension to music for the listening audience.

Computers facilitate the mechanics of composition as well. Software allows compositions keyed into the machine to be displayed in conventional notation on the screen. Notes, accents, clefs, and time and key signatures can be inserted or deleted with ease. A computer will also store music that is improvised on the keyboard, for instance, as it is being played and then transcribe the music at the touch of a switch. The score can be played back so that the composer can hear the composition as soon as it is written with no need to wait until musicians are assembled for a live performance. What is more, the score can be stored for later recall or can be printed as sheet music with accuracy, either in individual instrumental parts or as a whole.

Digital recording is used to produce high-quality tapes and records of professional performances. Even personal computers, using a **sequencer program**, can be converted into a recording studio. A musician can orchestrate a multipart musical arrangement by layering instrumental parts on top of those previously stored in memory using such a program. During playback, any parameter of the sound can be altered (for example, vibrato, envelope, volume) while the same note is kept on file. The system can also automatically transpose the composition into a different key.

Computer music systems are ideal for radio programs, commercials, and sound tracks of movies because of the control they provide. Precise timing can be worked out for dialogue cues, music, and sound effect sequences, and these sequences can be altered or repeated at will.

Computer-assisted instruction for music education is another application of computer music systems. CAI can teach sight reading, the identifi-

Supplement 11.2 A Computer for Music Research

Dr. Franklin B. Zimmerman, professor of music at the University of Pennsylvania, is using a computer to create an index of baroque composers. This is done in three steps. First, a thematic index of first lines is being compiled. (According to Zimmerman, the theme of most works is revealed in the first ten tones.) Next, thematic usage and borrowing is traced. Finally, the computer is used to analyze the stylistic "fingerprints of melodics" to help determine authorship.

cation of instruments by sound, rhythm concepts, harmony, and the fundamentals of composition. The ear can be trained to single out the bass line in a composition or trained to recognize pitches. The principles of musical notation can be drilled and the phraseology of different composers compared. A simple accompaniment can be keyed for an instrumentalist to use during practice. This is only a sampling of potential educational uses of computer music systems. Some educators believe that children of the future will receive all of their basic music instruction on a computer.

Computer Music for Entertainment

In the past, the ability to perform music required hours of practice to develop playing skill. With a computer music system, no manual dexterity is needed to create music. Notes can be keyed in slowly, one at a time, and then played back by the computer at whatever speed the system user specifies. In addition, no knowledge of musical notation is required. One can experiment with the production of sound without being able to read a music score. The computer can bring the pleasure of music making to people who have not had formal music instruction or years of practice.

Microcomputer-based music systems are still in the early stages of development. Computer analysts expect a fast growing home entertainment market as sound improves and easy-to-use software is packaged. Already the systems have become quite inexpensive and flexible. Their modular nature means that new technology can be added without making the main components obsolete.

The Computer as Composer

A computer can be programmed with the procedures of music composition and principles of melody and harmony, then instructed to compose music. The program might specify that the music imitate the style of Bach or Beethoven. But more often, the aim of people who experiment with computer-generated music is not imitation but the creation of original contemporary compositions. (See Figure 11.3.) The sound medium (digitized electronic sounds) and the techniques for designing musical artworks differ from the past, but the goal of the programming artist is the same as that of most composers: to create an aesthetically pleasing or harmonious mix of sounds. It is the listener who will evaluate computer music and assess its merit. Only time will tell whether computerized compositions will form a significant contribution to the world's music literature.

Figure 11.3 Musical composition on a computer. Stewart Copeland with the computer instrument he used in composing the score for "Lear." (San Francisco Ballet)

THE VISUAL ARTS

Human interaction with a computer can result in a creative product called **computer art**. The vision of the artist is displayed on a CRT screen or is placed on paper by a printer or plotter.

To create computer art, the idea of the artist must first be described to a computer. Input hardware is used for this purpose. The computer must also be programmed with instructions that allow the artist to manipulate and experiment with the original idea. It is the software that allows the artist to add color and texture to an input image or rotate, magnify, distort, enlarge, or transform it through an interactive process with the machine. Finally, hardware is needed to display changes as they are made and to produce the end product.

Special devices used for computer **graphics** are at the heart of the whole enterprise of computer art. Although graphics programs exist for home computers, graphics workstations capable of producing illustration-quality art are expensive, costing $50,000 or more in the early 1980s. In general, such graphics systems are owned by companies in the field of commercial art. The cost factor means that most individual artists have not had an opportunity to experiment with sophisticated graphics hardware and software.

Graphics Input Hardware

A **light pen** is a device for drawing on a CRT screen. This cigar-shaped instrument has a photo-sensitive cell hardly larger than a pinhead at one end. The cell detects light coming from special position-reporting patterns on the screen. The *x-y* coordinates of the position being touched are then sent to the CRT screen. When the light pen is drawn across the screen, software tracks the motion of the pen on the screen and a line is drawn along the pen's path.

A mouse controlling a cursor on the screen can also be used in drawing. Some CRT screens are touch-sensitive, so that the artist's finger can serve as a drawing tool. Sometimes keyed instructions will result in a drawing. For example, if the artist keys in a radius, software will draw a perfect circle with that radius on the screen. In addition, images can be stored in computer memory. A few keystrokes will bring a representation of Michelangelo's David to the screen if the image is in the computer's data base.

Another input device is a **graphics tablet**, which looks like a drawing board covered with a grid similar to that of graph paper. A picture or drawing put on the grid can be digitized by placing a special pen at different points of the drawing. A button pushed to record each location conveys the coordinates to the CPU. (Digitizing the figure of an athlete from a frame of film, a process described in Chapter 10, is done in the same manner.)

Images captured by TV cameras can also be processed by computers. Computer portraits for T-shirts at a shopping mall are an application of this technique. NASA uses such image processing to analyze data filmed by satellites in space.

Graphics Output Devices

Graphics output can be projected on a CRT screen. The quality of the image depends on memory space in a **frame buffer**, the hardware that determines the color and intensity of each point in the screen image. More points on the screen increase the amount of detail that can be displayed but also increase memory requirements. A video display comparable in quality to a color TV broadcast requires more memory than current microcomputers have available.

Printers and plotters, which were described in Chapter 3, can be used to produce hard copies of graphic images.

The Computer as an Artist's Tool

A popular application for computer graphics has been video games. Computer-aided design, discussed in Chapter 8, takes advantage of graphics hardware and software for the production of engineering drawings and blueprints. Architects use drafting packages for the preparation of building plans. Many different types of programs incorporate graphics features, such as pies, graphs, and other visual images, for the presentation of information commonly stored in tables. For example, a graph might illustrate the growth of profits or the fluctuating body temperature of a hospital patient.

Supplement 11.3 Graphics Used for Strip Mine Reclamation

Sculptor Robert Mallary and colleagues at the University of Massachusetts are applying the graphics capabilities of computers to an aesthetic, engineering, and environmental problem: land reclamation. In the process of mining for coal, land surface material is removed. This "overburden material" seldom fits compactly back in place because it is churned up during removal, a process that makes it swell in volume.

Mallary would like to sculpt the land using this overburden to give the land artistic shape. (Most overburden is bulldozed into unattractive mounds.) He uses computer graphics to design, simulate, and test design options. One advantage of computers used for this purpose is that programs will take a given design and shrink or expand it until all of the overburden is accommodated.

Computer-generated drawings are found in commercial advertisements, logos, letter heads, art for reports, and other business-oriented documents.

Graphics software for the home entertainment market is also popular. Users can start with a blank screen and draw an original work or modify an image created by a professional artist that has been stored in memory. They can experiment with textures, color, shadows and outlines, drag one image on top of another, alter proportions, and even color over an existing pattern to produce a blend of the old color with the new.

In each of these applications, the advantages of graphics hardware and software are that they:

- Help users express ideas visually. The final artistic work may be computer output, or the idea may be transferred to some other media, such as clay, weaving, or sculpture.
- Allow users to make real-time changes as they experiment with images.
- Remove many tedious aspects of an artist's job. A single image may be stored, repeated, enlarged, moved, viewed from a different angle, rotated, or changed in a variety of ways.

The creative artist engaged in noncommercial art benefits from these same features. Although the quality of computer-generated fine art to date has been uninspiring, the medium is still new. The work that is being done in the field is comparable to experimentation with graphic images produced mechanically and photographically in the early decades of this century. As artists explore ways to render visual forms on a computer, they will learn the limitations and strengths of this new artistic mode. Aesthetic investigation has to take place before artists can begin to employ the computer in their own creative ways.

The Computer as Artist

Computer-generated art has appeared in many museums around the country. Some of the art is a graphic rendition of mathematical formulas or geometric variations. Some is experimentation with electronic signals. Some is produced by programming the computer with basic principles of drawing.

Visitors at the San Francisco Museum of Modern Art may have seen Arron on display. Arron is essentially a computer programmed with the principles of drawing. A small metallic contraption that vaguely resembles a toy truck is placed on a large sheet of paper spread on the floor. Its movements controlled by a DEC PDP 11/45, the device makes line drawings as it wanders over the paper. The observers of this art are the ones who give meaning to it, seeing landscapes inhabited by creatures and so on even though Arron has no knowledge of the world and has been programmed with only basic drawing fundamentals.

Can designs created by step voltages and frequency variations qualify as art? Do the meanderings of Arron belong in a gallery with Van Gogh and Monet? To really answer this question, one must first address more basic questions: What is art? What is beauty? Computers are challenging

Supplement 11.4 Art for the Ages

Works of art, like all material things, are subject to the ravages of time—to erosion by chemical and physical processes. The preservation of what we have now and the restoration of what has already been lost is a major problem to art experts and other concerned professionals. Recent experiments in digital image processing being conducted at the IBM Scientific Center of Rome may provide some solutions to our present dilemma.

Simply stated, digital image processing is based on the reasoning that a work of art—a painting, for example—holds "information," that the information can be "coded" using numerical symbols and may later be "decoded" and reproduced.

To understand how a painting is encoded or "digitized," one must first examine the concept of color. Any color perceived by the human eye can be simulated by various mixtures of the primary colors of red, green, and blue. By using optical filters to record the levels of red, green, and blue light reflected by a painting, one can digitize or make a record of that color.

The painting itself is coded by first setting the image on a grid. Each square of this grid may have sidelength of only 0.1 millimeter. These squares called pixels (for picture elements) contain uniform hues, making it possible to assign to each pixel a series of numbers representing the hue it contains.

A typical painting of one meter square may contain one hundred million pixels. If ten bits of data are used to encode each pixel, it would require a total of three thousand million bits for the entire painting. This information could be contained on one optical digital disk no larger than a long-playing high-fidelity record. Once coded, a painting may be reproduced or "decoded," by means of a television monitor.

In 1983 IBM, in conjunction with the Laboratory for Restoration in Florence, began experiments to aid in the restoration of important works of art damaged in the 1966 flood in that city. These experiments take digital image processing a step further. Using an IBM 7350 Image Processing System, images are digitized and the resulting data processed. Based on a method called "chromatic selection and abstraction," the hues are coded numerically and an "average neutral hue" arrived at. With this information as a guide, an artist can render an almost perfect restoration of a damaged masterpiece.

Although we still cannot hope to physically preserve a painting indefinitely or restore one to its original state, the "information" contained in such a work can be saved. These new applications of computer technology to the arts are important steps toward the preservation of our cultural and artistic heritage.

the way we perceive the arts as well as challenging artists by providing a new medium of expression.

FILM

Computers are behind the scenes in the film industry, expanding artistic capabilities of movie makers. In addition, sound editors, camera operators, and animators are relieved by computers of many time-consuming tasks in film production. Here are some of the ways computer technology contributes to sound and visual effects in films.

Sound

One of the first applications of computers to film was in **sound editing**. Since the early 1970s, computers have been used to synchronize background noises, dialogue replacement, and dubbing with visual images that appear on the screen. Most of the sound that is ultimately used in a film is not recorded when a film is shot, since sound needs to be more tightly controlled than is possible on location.

Today, in a studio a computer-based controller will cue actors when to voice their lines in a scene and pace them through it in synchronization with the film. Dialogue and sound effects can be digitized and stored on disks, and then instantly called upon when needed. The computer combines a sound effects library with an editing machine in a single system. Furthermore, before being committed to the physical film, sound and image can be coordinated inside computer memory. The advantage of this is that the sound editor can make decisions about the most appropriate effects and preview the synchronization before committing sound to the film.

Camera Control

Computer-controlled camera platforms today provide filmmakers with precise positioning. The movement of a camera rig can be programmed with the operator defining points for the filming sequence via a keyboard. As the camera moves, the computer will make automatic camera adjustments for focus and lens settings.

Computer-controlled cameras have many other advantages as well. For instance, the software often contains safety checks and warnings to prevent damage by the cameras to props or injury to people. An instant replay system can simulate a take on video before the actual film is exposed so that camera operators can check angles and lighting. Combinations of camera movements, film speeds, and exposures can be recorded and the information stored. Should a retake prove necessary, this information can be drawn from memory and the camera automatically repositioned in exactly the same location with the same camera settings.

Animation and Special Effects

Most readers will associate animation with Walt Disney. Long before computers, Donald Duck was brought to life by a process called "cel animation." Artists drew image after image of Donald with slight variations and the images were filmed in sequence, one image per frame of film. When projected at twenty-four frames per second, the character appeared to move as a result of the variations from one frame to the next.

Today, computerized systems simplify the artist's task. The artist need only draw a key frame and let software called a **move-generation system** do the rest. If three views of an object are drawn (top, front, and right side, for example) and digitized for computer storage, the processor can rotate the image, view it from different angles, and manipulate it for the animation camera.

Computer **animation systems** are interactive. They allow film artists and editors to evaluate and direct the action of the animation. Real-time systems allow the animation to be mixed with standard video signals. Both prerecorded video takes and live action filmed in a studio can be integrated with the animation. In addition, animated motion can be given to any element in a picture. This latter technique is often employed when filming commercials.

Computer graphics are also used to create special film effects. *Tron* (1982) was the first feature film to use computer-generated imagery as a background for live actors. But only a few sequences, less than five minutes on screen, utilized graphics techniques. By the time *The Last Starfighter* was released in 1984, many advances in graphics technology had taken place. The film included twenty-five minutes of imaginary landscapes with highly realistic features. These included shiny reflective surfaces such as polished metal and the billowing of flames and clouds synthesized on a computer. It is expected that computer-generated images will eventually replace many costly movie sets and scale models in film making.

The impact of **image synthesis** is not limited to films for entertainment. The techniques are being applied to computer-aided design in manufacturing, medical imaging, and molecular design as well. Architects are beginning to use computer animation to let clients "walk through" their house plans before the foundations are laid. Manufacturers use animation techniques in films to train employees and advertise their products. The technology of image synthesis has many applications in the business world and scientific world as well as in the arts.

DANCE

In the past, the difficulty of preparing dance notation has meant that few choreographers have left behind a permanent record of their work. To produce a written dance manuscript takes many hours with graph paper and ruler. Even with such a score, another director may have difficulty recreating the same dance from the notation simply because it is hard to express movement, the interaction of dancers, or elaborate dance patterns in words or symbols. Furthermore, dance is a vision of a choreographer that takes shape during rehearsal. Although film can be used to record a dance as it is performed, a camera can only capture a small segment of movement on stage in detail (rather than each dancer simultaneously).

Supplement 11.5 Organization Promotes Museum Data Processing

Museum Computer Network, Inc., (MCN), a nonprofit organization, holds annual conferences and sponsors publications relating to museum computer networks. In addition, it offers members complete documentation on Griphos, a batch processing data management system. This system facilitates the indexing and controlling of museum inventories. Subscribers can also reference materials related to museum catalogues and computer applications in the MCN library. The library includes working papers and unpublished reports on museum data processing projects around the world.

Although computer graphics systems for dance notation are in the experimental stage, the concept underlying such systems is that the input is notation defining movements or patterns. The computer translates the data into a moving figure performing the dance on a computer screen. Once this technique is refined, it may be widely used by artists to:

- Choreograph new dance routines.
- Experiment with movement and sequences of movement in order to modify dance routines.
- Guide dancers in rehearsal so they can master the sequence of dance steps they are to perform.
- Record the finalized choreography of a dance and store that choreography for later recall.

Another use of computers in the world of dance is simply to manage the business of a dance company. Dance companies must pay performers and backstage workers. Props have to be built and stored, tickets sold, advertising planned, rehearsals scheduled, contracts written, theaters rented, funds raised, and new productions planned. Because management information systems are appropriate for all these activities, computers are in the front office of most dance companies today.

OTHER APPLICATIONS

There are numerous other applications for computers in the fine arts and humanities. For example, theaters use computers in ticketing, lighting, and set design. Museums keep inventory lists and schedule maintenance of their collections by computer. Both theater and museum directors have a budget and staff to manage, for which business programs are appropriate.

Many cities use a computer system as a clearing house of information on cultural activities. In Paris a computer keeps track of as many as 12,000 different arts events available in the city on any given day, from exhibits at major museums to concerts of classical and popular music. Visitors can access this data base at the Maison d'Information Culturelle. They might ask where Mozart is being performed that evening. In a matter of seconds, the time, place, program, conductor, and price of ticket will appear on screen.

Another application of computers is for **research** in the humanities, particularly in the social sciences and in disciplines utilizing quantitative data. Researchers in the humanities must store and manipulate data and utilize statistical tools just as researchers in scientific fields do. Archaeologists, for instance, use computers for pattern analysis, bracket dating, bore diameter date formulas, and excavation registers. Every artifact and its associated find-spot must be documented and keyed to numerical coordinates on site drawings. Patterns of post holes, pits, and foundations must be analyzed. The computer can generate descriptive statistics and measurements of central tendency and dispersion in the interpretation of site record data. Computers can also be used in restoring monuments of the past, such as the Buddhist temple Borobudur.

Much historical research is an analysis of information about economic, social, and political

Supplement 11.6 Computers Help Restore Borobudur

Borobudur is one of the greatest Buddhist monuments. It was built in the eighth century in central Java, Indonesia. The architecture is a huge, truncated pyramid built to surround a steep hill. The temple itself consists of five terraces, each representing one step leading to peace and tranquility. Bell-shaped domes (stupas) encase stone-sculptured Buddhas on each terrace. The terraces are also decorated with intricately carved blocks of stone illustrating episodes in Buddha's life.

In 1006 the temple was deserted following an earthquake and volcanic eruption. Over the years, neglect of the temple and erosion of the hill within led to Borobudur's decay. By 1960 the monument was in danger of collapse, its 1,300,252 stones in total disarray. Alarmed that civilization might lose this treasure of the past, UNESCO began Borobudur's reconstruction.

The restoration project was a gigantic jigsaw puzzle. Ten thousand stones had fallen from the main structure. Another 30,000 had to be dismantled for repair. Fifty-eight headless Buddha torsos and fifty-four unmatched heads were among the ruins.

A computer was used to catalog all stones and to keep track of the location of stones during the course of the project (for example, which stones were being treated where they were stored, and so forth). The computer also matched each Buddha to its stupa and helped determine where each fallen stone should be placed.

It took ten years of effort and an expenditure of $25 million to save Borobudur. Computers are contributing to similar restoration of projects in many parts of the world, especially in Egypt.

behavior. Historians cull records of numbers of people; casualties from war, famine, and disease; voting patterns; and so forth. By manipulating quantitative information of this nature, they learn about conditions in the past. Political scientists, economists, and sociologists study quantitative history as well, utilizing computers because of their speed and their ability to manipulate and analyze data. The ability of computers to store huge data bases is also an advantage.

SUMMING UP

Computer applications exist in all areas of the humanities. Computers can be a medium for the expression of ideas or a tool for that expression. A computer can also be programmed with guidelines that enable it to create original works in the arts. In addition, people with personal computers as well as professionals with access to minis and mainframes can benefit from the computer's ability to store, manipulate, and analyze data in the humanities.

Information technology has given artists new ways to express themselves creatively. At the same time, artists are being challenged by computers to study the creative process itself. As technology plays a growing role in the fine arts, the traditional concept of "art" will have to be redefined.

REVIEW QUESTIONS

1. How can computers contribute to artistic expression?
2. What advantages do word processors have over conventional typewriters?
3. How can CAI benefit students of:
   a. literature?
   b. music?
   c. art?
   d. dance?
4. What role can computers play in research in the humanities?
5. Can computers create original works of art? Explain.
6. How is electronic sound generated? What is the difference between analog and digital sound synthesis?
7. What do the following terms mean?
   a. delayed playback
   b. amplitude envelope
   c. timbre
   d. light pen
8. Describe how electronic music can benefit:
   a. the professional musician
   b. the amateur musician
9. Describe graphic hardware for:
   a. input of drawings or pictures
   b. output of drawings or pictures
10. Describe the use of computer graphics in commercial and non-commercial art.
11. How does computer technology facilitate film making?
12. How will computer-generated special effects change the way films are made in the future?
13. What are the advantages of computer animation over hand-drawn animation? The disadvantages?
14. How can computers contribute to the field of dance?
15. What are the reasons image processing has developed more slowly than data and word processing?
16. Give examples of data bases in the humanities that might be useful to the general public.
17. How do computers affect artists, even those without access to computer hardware and software?
18. How does real-time contribute to the arts?

DISCUSSION QUESTIONS

1. Compare the graphics capabilities of computers with the graphic capabilities of humans. Will the human artist be replaced by a machine?
2. How do computers help to bridge the gap between science and the arts?
3. What are the economic implications of computer use in the fine arts? The social implications?
4. Are computer graphics "art"?
5. Do you believe that computers will contribute to the evolution of new art forms? Explain.
6. Will computers change the content of what we teach in the humanities?
7. How can computers be used in branches of the humanities not discussed in this chapter, such as:
   a. religion?
   b. linguistics?
   c. sociology?
   d. other?
8. Is poetry the expression of a deeply felt emotion or the manipulation of sensory images? Can a computer be a poet?
9. Who benefits most from computer technology applied to the fine arts: the average individual or the gifted?
10. What do you believe should be the focus of future computer applications in the arts?

11. Do you agree with the quotation at the beginning of this chapter?

12. How does computer art and computer music compare with that produced by humans? Which do you prefer and why? Do you think a computer is capable of producing art superior to that produced by humans?

13. In January 1983 the computer was named "Man of the Year" by *Time*. Do you think the computer will ever be named "Artist of the Year," "Poet of the Year," or "Musician of the Year"? Explain.

EXERCISES

1. Critique some work of art created by a computer. Compare it with similar art produced by a human artist.

2. If you know how to program, write a program to:
   a. generate art by a formula with a changing parameter
   b. generate art using superimposed characters and printing them
   c. compose music

3. Evaluate a film or an animated advertisement that used computer technology.

Selected Annotated Bibliography

Bailey, Richard W., ed. *Computing in the Humanities: Papers from the Fifth International Conference on Computers in the Humanities*. New York: Elsevier North-Holland, 1982. Included are twenty papers written by mathematicians, statisticians, literary scholars, linguists, archaeologists, and musicians on topics of interest to both computer scientists and humanists.

Bonifer, Michael. *The Art of Tron*. New York: Simon and Schuster, 1982. This book describes the filming of *Tron*. It traces computer use in the production, including problems translating the story into screen effects. Many optical processes are discussed on a scene-by-scene, concept-by-concept basis. The book will please both film and computer buffs.

Casazza, Ornella and Paolo Franchi. "Art for the Ages," *Perspectives in Computing*, vol. 5, no. 1 (Spring 1985), pp. 4–13. Experiments in digital image processing point the way toward the application of computer technology in analyzing, restoring, and preserving works of art. This magazine is an IBM publication.

Cone, Lawrence L. "Skycam: An Aerial Robotic Camera System," *Byte*, vol. 10, no. 10 (October 1985), pp. 122–32. A microcomputer provides the control for Skycam, a mobile, remote-controlled camera system designed to bring three-dimensional mobility to motion picture and television camera operation.

"Creating Computer Art: A Special Report," *Popular Computing*, vol. 4, no. 1 (November 1984), pp. 73–90. This section includes articles on state-of-the-art hardware and software for original works of art. Tips are also given to amateurs on creating graphics on PCs.

Creative Computing, vol. 6, no. 6 (June 1980). This issue includes fourteen articles on computer graphics and seven on computer music. Some are "how to" articles, some are analytical, and others list program code.

Deken, Joseph. *Computer Images: State of the Art*. New York: Stewart, Tabot and Cleang, 1983. This book provides background information on image processing. The book includes a portfolio with sample computer graphics in medicine, advertising, movies, and flight simulation.

DeWitt, William H. *Art and Graphics on the Apple II/IIE*. New York: John Wiley & Sons, 1984. The author assumes the reader of this book knows BASIC. He attempts to convince programmers and artists that the field of computer graphics extends artistic imagination.

Dorf, Richard C. *Computers and Man*. San Francisco: Boyd and Fraser, 1977, pp. 311–40. A good discussion on computers and the arts. Many illustrations are included.

Fox, David and **Waite, Mitchell.** *Computer Animation Primer.* New York: McGraw-Hill, 1984. This book describes animation techniques, and shows how many sophisticated mainframe graphics effects can be created on a home computer. Sample programs illustrate the concepts discussed. A working knowledge of BASIC is needed to follow the text.

Glassner, Andrew S. *Computer Graphics User Guide.* Indianapolis: Howard W. Sams, 1984. This is a state-of-the-art primer on graphics concepts and techniques. The author explains that the "book does not cover the mathematics necessary to write computer programs, but provides a solid explanation of everything that those mathematics do."

Hofstadter, Douglas R. *Godel, Escher, Bach: An Eternal Golden Braid.* New York: Vintage Books, 1980. This 1980 Pulitzer Prize winner covers everything from computers to mathematics, from poetry to Zen Buddhism.

Kenealy, Patrick. "Product File: Graphics Workstation," *Mini-Micro Systems,* vol. 16, no. 7 (July 1983), pp. 165–83. The hardware and software for graphic workstation (both for graphic processing and graphic display) are described. A ten-page product table provides details on workstations from twenty-nine vendors.

Kerlow, Isaac Victor. "The Computer as an Artistic Tool," *Byte,* vol. 9, no. 10 (September 1984), pp. 189–206. The evolution of computer art, the creative process, conceptualization and design of a computer image, shading, color, texture, and the originality of computer art are the topics discussed.

Myers, Edith. "Cray Conquers H'wood," *Datamation,* vol. 30, no. 10 (July 1, 1984), pp. 24–27. The use of Cray X-MP-generated scenes for twenty-five minutes of film in the movie *The Last Starfighter* is described.

Peterson, Dale. *Genesis II: Creation and Recreation with Computers.* Reston, VA: Reston Publishing, 1983. The role of computers in the visual arts, music, literature, and games is traced in this book.

Prueitt, Melvin. *Art and the Computer.* New York: McGraw-Hill, 1984. The first part of this book treats conceptual foundations of computer art and methodologies for creating it; the second is an annotated collection of computer art.

Rabson, Carolyn and Gustave. "Hum a Few Bars," *Perspectives in Computing,* vol. 5, no. 1 (Spring 1985), pp. 24–33. The National Tune Index is helping to bring order to the chaotic state of documentation for music. This index provides a comprehensive, multifaceted tool for research in eighteenth-century American and British secular music. This magazine is an IBM publication.

Tucker, Jonathan B. "Making Music with Micros," *High Technology,* vol. 4, no. 7 (July 1984), pp. 53–63. Subjects covered in this informative article include sound synthesis, real-time systems, waveforms, recording and transcribing, and digital interface.

Watt, Dan. "Musical Microworlds," *Popular Computing,* vol. 3, no. 10 (August 1984), pp. 91–94. An excellent nontechnical discussion of computer music.

The Use of Computers in Government, the Military, and Politics

The greater the power at our disposal, the greater the number of insoluble problems we can solve.

JACQUES STERN

CHAPTER TWELVE

Key Words

campaigns	electronic voting	nine-digit zip code
Census Bureau	file swapping	political conventions
computer matches	fly-by-wire	Postal Service
computer security	individual rights	privacy
data integration	information misuse and abuse	radar
data integrity	Internal Revenue Service (IRS)	Social Security Administration (SSA)
Department of Defense	law enforcement	smart weapons
digital information and control systems	military communications	White House
	National Crime Information Center (NCIC)	

In the 1950s, the U.S. government was a leader in tabulating equipment and early computing systems. The first commercial computer, UNIVAC I, was placed in operation at the Census Bureau. The military, recognizing the potential of information technology for defense purposes, has supported computer research and development since the advent of computers and has also been a major purchaser of innovative computer systems.

But by the 1960s, civilian departments of the government lagged behind the private sector in the implementation of emerging technologies. This lag is not apparent, however, if one counts the number of computers in government today. The Federal Government still remains the single largest user of data processing systems in the world. It has over 18,000 large and medium-sized computers. In addition, hundreds of thousands of small computers and word processors are on the desks of civil servants. (Table 12.1 summarizes the growth of computer systems in government.)

However, computing capacity cannot be judged by numbers alone. A large portion of government computers are obsolete. Loss of government leadership in computing can be attributed to many factors. Lack of qualified and experienced data processing personnel has contributed to inefficient and ineffective management of government computing resources. Computer system procurement procedures in government are time-consuming, delaying timely replacement of outmoded equipment. Problems such as undocumented software, incompatibility of data, and failure to plan for system integration have hampered operations. Indeed, all of the problems associated with computer systems in business and industry seem to be compounded by government bureaucracy.

With mounting pressure to provide better public service at less cost, Washington is beginning to overhaul obsolete systems. The government is also applying computer technology to the solution of problems in domains not computerized in the past. Supplement 12.1 lists just a few examples of use of high technology in government today. Government computers are used to control air-traffic, to evaluate air and water pollution, to monitor NORAD's (North American Air Defense Command) ballistic early warning system, to handle deportation cases, to compute statistics on unemployment, to plan construction of Corps of Engineers dams, to allocate resources for maintenance of interstate highways, to process inspection data of customs officials—the list is endless.

This chapter will focus on the benefits of information technology at the White House, Census Bureau, and Internal Revenue Service. The use of

Supplement 12.1 Some Uses of High Technology in Government

- The National Weather Service collects information on temperature, air pressure, wind direction, and other climatic conditions from 100,000 stations, including stations located on weather balloons, satellites, airplanes, and ships at sea. This information is processed by computer for the preparation of daily weather maps and monthly and seasonal forecasts. A supercomputer installed in 1983 has doubled the forecasting accuracy.
- High-speed equipment has been installed at fifty-eight regional offices of the Veterans Administration. A full rundown of benefits for which a veteran is entitled can now be obtained in minutes. Computers process educational, hospital, and insurance claims of veterans as well.
- The Library of Congress is using a retrieval language called Scorpio to access legislative, bibliographic, and directory data bases. Files include a Congressional Record abstract file and a bill digest file. The library is also reproducing some of its rare documents onto digital-optical disks for storage and retrieval. Users will be able to view fragile collections, such as Civil War photos or valuable Audubon prints, on devices that resemble home videodisk players. The quality of detail and color on disks is higher than on conventional microfilm.
- Congressional committees are using online interactive budget formulation systems. These systems assist in authorization, appropriations, and budget resolution processes. Members can access historical funding information, current funding requests and decisions, and committee recommendations.
- Computer-controlled color plotters are used in map production by the Defense Mapping Agency. The system is interactive, allowing operators to edit digitized cartographic data.
- Janus, an advanced combat simulator, is being used to train officers for high-ranking command positions at the U.S. Army War College. When a battle zone is selected, the computer supplies detailed topographical maps of the area. During the war games, the computer keeps track of factors such as flight time of artillery shells or how fast a fireball will spread based on humidity, temperature, and wind speed. Janus operates in the real-time mode, processing two million programming instructions per second.
- The Treasury Department requires only a few employees to handle about 750 million checks issued annually. Check-issue and payment information on magnetic tapes are fed into computers to automatically reconcile check-issue and payment data. Reconciliation is usually completed within a few weeks after receipt of cashed checks. (In 1956, 600 clerks issued and reconciled the checks manually. Although only 300 million checks a year were issued at that time, the reconciliation process took months to accomplish.)
- The Department of Agriculture digitizes data from satellite photos in order to estimate acreage under cultivation around the world and thus make harvest predictions. A better crop assessment capability helps decision makers plan domestic agricultural policy.
- A Correspondence Management System stores Senators' statements on current issues. Staff members can access these statements and insert quotes in form letters when answering constituent mail. Congressmen can make inquiries regarding the current status of bills and resolutions using a system named LEGIS. SOPAD provides a summary of debates taking place in the House and Senate.

Computerized weather monitoring by the National Hurricane Center in Miami has dramatically reduced the number of deaths caused by powerful storms such as Hurricane Elena. (NASA)

Supplement 12.2 The Growth of the Information Technology Budget from 1982 to 1984 (Dollars in Thousands)

	1982 actual	1984 estimate
National Security and International Affairs (OSD, Army, Navy, Air Force, Marine Corps, SSS, EIBUS, USIA, AID, USITC, USTR, State)	4,448,434	6,106,633
Economics and Government (Commerce, Justice, Treasury, Transportation, GSA, OPM, HUD, IEMA, CAB, ICC, NTSB, USRA, SBA, PCC, IHLBB, SEC, OA, FTC, NCUA, FCC, FMC)	1,601,764	2,310,733
Human Resources, Veterans, and Labor (HHS, Education, Labor, VA, CPSC, RRB, ACTION, NLRB, FMCS, EEOC, OS & HRC, NEA, NEH, NAT MED BD)	1,176,601	1,454,246
Natural Resources, Energy & Science (Agriculture, Interior, Energy, Corps of Engineers, EPA, NASA, TVA, NSF, CFTC, NRC, Smithsonian)	1,856,965	2,323,305
Total	9,083,764	12,194,917

Table 12.1 Growth of computer inventory in the federal government

Fiscal year	Number of computer systems	Number of CPUs*	Percent owned	Percent leased
1950		2		
1951		3		
1952		5		
1953		7		
1954		10		
1955		45		
1956		90		
1957		160		
1958		250		
1959		403		
1960	Same As	531	19	81
1961	Number	730	15	85
1962	Of CPUs	1030	17	83
1963		1326	21	79
1964		1862	40	60
1965		2412	50	50
1966		3007	53	47
1967		3692	58	42
1968		4232	58	42
1969		4666	60	40
1970		5277	64	36
1971	5230	5934	73	27
1972	5803	6731	78	22
1973	6014	7149	81	19
1974	6450	7830	84	16
1975	6981	8649	87	13
1976	7527	9648	89	11
1977	8528	11124	91	9
1978	9299	12190	91	9
1979	10551	14333	92	8
1980	11055	15142	91	9
1981	12522	17503	91	9
1982	13058	18474	91	9

*Prior to 1971 each CPU (Central Processing Unit) was considered a computer system. In 1971 a "system concept" was introduced which recognized that a computer system may have more than one CPU.

Source: "A Five Year Plan: Meeting the Data Processing and Telecommunications Needs of the Federal Government." Washington, U.S. Government Printing Office, April 1983, Figure III-A-1.

Supplement 12.3 The Distribution: Federal Information Technology: Who Will Spend the Money in Fiscal Year 1984

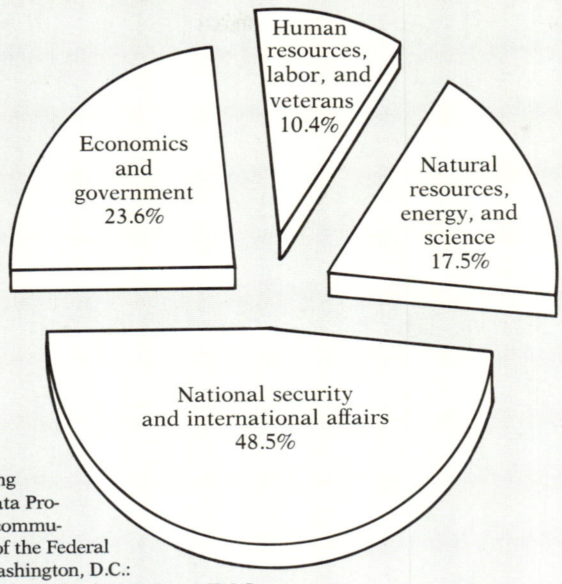

*Source: "A Five Year Plan: Meeting the Automatic Data Processing and Telecommunications Needs of the Federal Government." Washington, D.C.: Government Printing Office, 1983, Figure II-C-5.

computers for law enforcement, mail delivery, defense, and Social Security will also be discussed. These governmental applications have been chosen for discussion because of their impact on the daily lives of citizens, the magnitude of their computer operations, or the fact that they raise social concerns that must be resolved in this age of computers. The chapter closes with a look at computers in campaigns and elections.

THE WHITE HOUSE

The **White House** is more than just the President and his aides. It consists of twelve divisions, constituting a total work force of about 350 persons. Surprisingly, the White House has been one of the last bastions in Washington to enter the computer age. Although the Secret Service uses computers to check on visitors entering White House grounds and to perform office tasks, the overall use of computers at the White House has been quite limited until very recently. As late as 1981, the entire White House staff shared only thirty computer terminals. Even the massive federal budget was compiled largely by hand. While an IBM mainframe held a gold mine of figures, only system managers accessed the computer. A comprehensive computerized management tracking system considered during the Carter Administration never got off the ground.

In 1982, the Executive Office of the President began an office automation project. It started with installation of 177 IBM Displaywriters for clerical staff. At first these were stand-alone word processors. They were soon enhanced, however, to provide access to data bases, graphics, and electronic mail.

The next phase of automation consisted of the installation of management workstations for top-level presidential aides. This system, called the Executive Office of the President Network (EOP NET), enables staff to access personnel and financial data stored in White House mainframe computers for activities such as analysis of the federal budget. The network also provides an electronic mail link between the White House and twenty-two federal agencies for sending messages, reports, and budget information. (The eighteen-inch interior granite walls of the old Executive Office Building, with no conduits for running cables, was a major architectural problem in establishing this network.)

Other tasks of White House computers include scheduling Cabinet meetings, keeping track of official White House positions on political issues, and placing a digital version of the President's signature on presidential correspondence. Staff members have access to an electronic library of wire service stories and to the online network Nexis. (Data base services, of which Nexis is one, are discussed in Chapter 14.) Presidential assistants can use an IBM IRMA communications board to download data from the IBM mainframe to their desktop personal computers. Staff computers are leased, not purchased, so that they can be easily exchanged for new technology in the future.

THE CENSUS BUREAU

Census taking and data processing have been linked ever since the 1880s when Herman Hollerith was hired by the **Census Bureau** as a special agent. He designed a census machine that could read punched cards, a device used in the 1890 census count.

The Bureau became computerized in 1951 when a UNIVAC I was installed. UNIVAC remained in service until 1963 when it was replaced with more advanced processing hardware. Table 12.2 summarizes the historical evolution of census processing.

The volume of data handled by Census Bureau computers requires special equipment to speed data entry (see Figure 12.1). For the 1980 census, FOSDIC (Film Optical Sensing Device for Input to Computers) was designed to capture census responses in machine-readable form. GBF/DIME (which stands for geographic base files/dual independent map encoding) is a totally integrated system of computer programs, reference files, and standard clerical and operational procedures that contributed to a number of geographic processing functions.

Table 12.2 At the Census Bureau

Time	Method used	Unit of work*	Compile census
Before 1890	 Pen and ink	1	7–9 years
1890	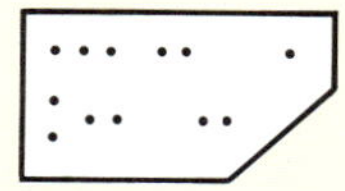 Manual punchcard	5	3–4 years
1950	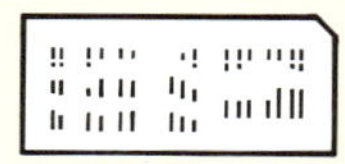 Electric punchcard	40	2–3 years
1951	 First computer	80	2 years
1980	 Modern computer	20,000	less than 1 year

*Work units of the "normalized" units used by the Census Bureau.
Source: Government document in public domain.

Nevertheless, many operations of the Census Bureau are still highly labor-intensive. A major acquisitions program is underway to replace existing computing capacity with more advanced information technology. An estimated $95.3 million will be spent through the fiscal year 1988 for computer hardware and software. New systems will include:

- *A geographic support system.* Information on maps will be translated into computer-readable (digital) form,

Figure 12.1 Part of the Census Bureau's computer system. Because this system handles such massive amounts of data, the issue is now whether to design a new system that anticipates future needs, or to continue to adapt the existing setup to growing pressures. (Burroughs Corporation)

and then merged with other geographic data for integrated geographic information files.

- *A decennial data capture system.* FOSDIC will be replaced by a new system to control the inventory of incoming census forms and capture respondent data.
- *An integrated bureau system.* This includes mainframe replacement, computer-assisted telephone interviewing, terminals, telecommunications, and general processing support.

In 1984 the Grace Commission (the formal name of this committe is the President's Private Sector Survey on Cost Control) criticized this plan as too large in scope. Large projects run a high risk of cost and time overruns and frequently do not accomplish desired objectives, according to the commission's members. They recommended that technology needs be segmented into smaller, more manageable projects and that only troublesome elements of the Census Bureau's operations be replaced.

The issue before the Census Bureau is one all major users of computers must resolve when planning to overhaul operations: when is a totally new, integrated computer system advisable as opposed to patchwork redevelopment of a system?

THE INTERNAL REVENUE SERVICE

In 1983 the 86,000 employees of the **Internal Revenue Service (IRS)** processed 171 million tax returns and collected $627 billion in revenue. Although equipped with forty major computers and hundreds of smaller systems, the agency still relies on paper and the human hand. Tax returns and over 500 million documents received annually are stored in hard copy. (These documents contain data from employers, banks, and stockbrokers on salaries, interest, and dividends.) Reams of paper now crowd the agency's 3.4 million cubic feet of warehouse space. Storage and manual retrieval of documents costs the IRS $35 million a year. Agency computers are used primarily for basic bookkeeping, to keep track of returns filed, and tax payments or refunds. Fewer than 10 percent of IRS examiners have access to a computer.

Recently, however, the IRS has stepped up efforts to automate. High priority is being given to the use of optical character recognition (OCR) equipment to process forms. OCR forms are replacing keypunch cards for use by employers when making federal tax deposits to authorized banks. The 1984 Form 1040EZ, the so-called short form for individual returns, is read by OCR equipment. Form 1099, used by banks to report interest payments, is scheduled for conversion to OCR next. In the future, some forms may be eliminated altogether. The agency is considering letting individuals file tax returns electronically over the telephone from personal computers.

Laser disk storage is also being planned. The IRS hopes to give tax examiners the ability to call a tax return for audit to a terminal screen without having to retrieve any paper documents. The agency is replacing its outdated mainframes with new equipment and rewriting its 2400 programs from assembly language to COBOL. (The current batch processing and online systems have been in place since 1962.)

The automation of collections is under development as well. The computer ranks delinquent accounts in order of priority. The most flagrant cases are brought to the screen when agents turn on their terminals. The computer is used to dial the phone number of the offender and to log promises to pay. If payment is not received within a given time period, the computer informs the agent so that follow-up can take place.

One of the problems with this system is that the IRS's master data base is kept separate from local files of collection agents. This means that individual agents may have to move from one terminal to another to get access to all of the information they need. Critics say that this lack of **data integration** is indicative of the shortsightedness of IRS planning. Agency officials explain that they settled for a two-computer system because they wanted to automate collections quickly.

Some aspects of IRS operations are controversial. Every year a sample of tens of thousands of Americans are selected for audit in order to give the IRS control data with which to compare the tax returns of others. The IRS also buys population-profile information from research firms to determine typical incomes for given neighborhoods. If an individual submits a low return from a high-income neighborhood, the return will be flagged for possible audit.

Even more controversial is the IRS's purchase of mailing lists from commercial marketing companies. These companies estimate the income of population segments from data about median income, family size, and other household statistics published by the Census Bureau for census tracts. The records of Motor Vehicle Departments are then matched with these income estimates. If an individual owns a 1970 Pinto, the income estimate is lowered. If a 1984 Cadillac, it is raised. By purchasing such information and matching it with taxpayer returns, the IRS can identify nonfilers or possible underfilers.

Many persons are concerned that **computer matches** of this type violate **individual rights**. Traditional tax evasion investigations are triggered by some evidence of wrongdoing. This is true because the limited resources of law enforcement make it impracticable to conduct dragnet investigations. But even more important, our constitutional system bars the government from investigating persons it does not suspect of committing a crime. It is against the Fourth Amendment to conduct unreasonable searches and seizures, so-called "fishing expeditions" in the hopes that some evidence of wrongdoing will turn up. Yet matching is nothing more than a fishing expedition, according to critics. Although no evidence of tax fraud exists, matching triggers intense scrutiny of the tax records of citizens.

It is also argued that presumption of innocence is at odds with computer matching. The burden is shifted to citizens to prove that they have indeed filed accurate tax returns, that they are free of guilt. Furthermore, citizens are denied due process of law insofar as individuals are not given notice that their names are being subjected to a match, and not given an opportunity to contest the results of the match. They are targeted for audit just because they belong to a category of persons who "might be" involved in tax fraud.

Most Americans agree that everyone should pay their fair share of taxes. It is the responsibility of the IRS to collect these taxes. The computer is a powerful tool helping the agency to fulfill its mandate. However, this power raises many social and ethical issues. Perhaps we need to redefine the privacy rights of citizens and the limitations of government in this modern age. Concerns of this nature will be discussed in greater detail in Part III, which focuses on the social impact of computers.

LAW ENFORCEMENT

Responsibility for **law enforcement** in this country does not rest with a single governmental body. We have local police departments, county sheriffs, state police, and 113 organizational entities at the federal level with law enforcement or investigative missions. Included are agencies such as the FBI,

Supplement 12.4 Electronic Ball and Chain

New Mexico's county jails are overcrowded. One proposed solution was given a ninety-day trial in 1983. Volunteer misdemeanor offenders were permitted to serve their sentences at home while wearing electronic bracelets to monitor their movements. Each bracelet emitted a digital code that was transmitted to a device connected to the wearer's phone. If the wearer wandered more than 300 feet from the phone, the telephone automatically signaled a monitoring computer. Tampering with the bracelet also sent a signal to the computer.

Those who participated in the experiment were work-release prisoners and probationers. Each time they left home for work or returned, the computer was alerted. Prison authorities could impose a curfew and make sure that it was followed without having a probation officer personally check on each individual.

Critics of the project say it violated personal privacy. Although a prisoner's privacy rights are more limited than those of other citizens, work-release probationers in the past have been trusted to leave jail during the day. Under the project, they were under twenty-four-hour, second-to-second surveillance. Many people also objected to the idea of electronic monitoring systems. What if the concept were extended to other areas? Might one go to court for a traffic offense and end up wearing a bracelet?

Many applications of computer technology have social implications. Electronic bracelets are just one example.

Immigration and Naturalization Service, Coast Guard, Secret Service, Drug Enforcement Administration, and Customs. Data processing supports the activities of all of these organizations. Examples of how computers contribute to law enforcement at both the local and national level follow.

In Local Communities

Most computer applications by the police at the local level are routine. Files containing information on vehicle accidents, parking tickets, traffic citations, and fine collections are common. Files of arrest data, crime statistics, stolen property, court dockets, and police workload are also usual. Word processing assists in the preparation of police reports. Accounting functions assist in payroll processing.

Nonroutine applications are those that contribute to law enforcement decision making and strategic planning. Examples include:

- Computer-aided dispatch
- Digital communications to mobile units, such as police cars
- Automatic vehicle location
- Direct data file access
- Voice data entry systems
- 911 emergency routing, automatic number identification, and location display
- Rapid, comprehensive management reporting

Some of these features are part of the police dispatching system used in Aurora, Colorado. Traditionally, two-way radio communications between dispatchers at headquarters and police officers in the field are used. Aurora's dispatching system consists of a central processing unit, a repeater site, and sixty-nine mobile dispatch terminals in police cars. When a call comes into the station, a clerk inputs the information into the computer and also gives it to the dispatcher. Two screens are at the dispatcher's console. One shows the location of all patrol cars on duty, the other the call data. The computer informs the dispatcher which available patrol car is nearest the complaint. The dispatcher alerts the patrol car with a loud beep. The officers in the car access the call data on their terminal and acknowledge that they

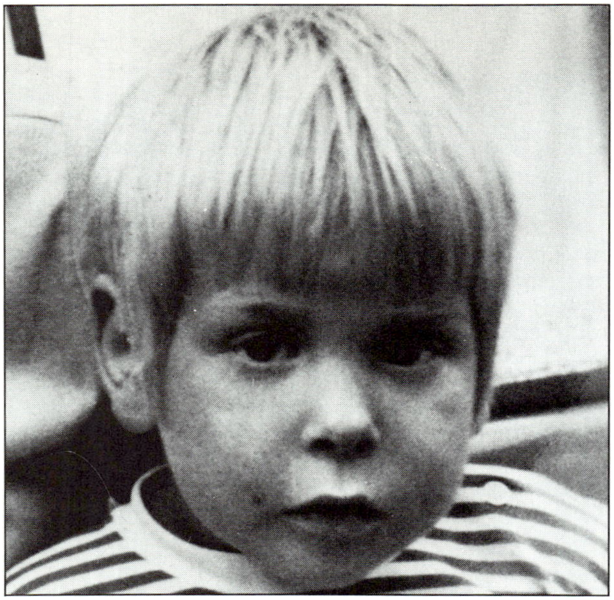

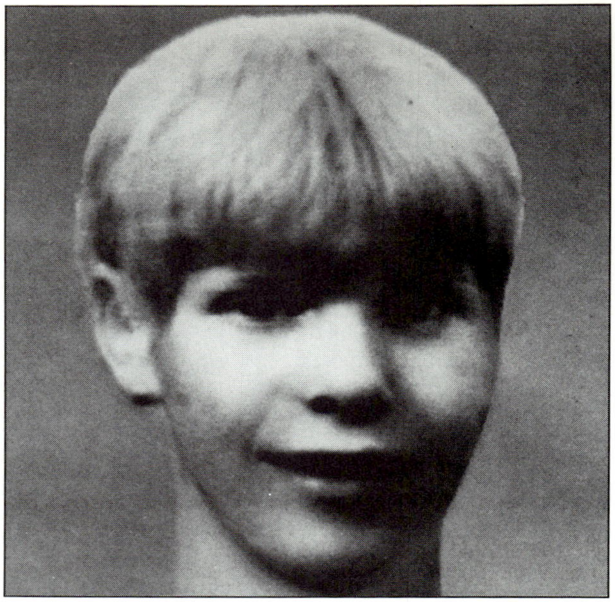

Figure 12.2 A photograph of a young boy. Based on this photograph (left), a computer was programmed to simulate a photograph (right) of the same child eight years into the future. In the case of missing children, this capability could prove useful in tracing their development over the years.

are responding by pressing an "in route" key. Meanwhile, the computer searches files stored in memory for information on names and addresses of persons involved in the complaint. Is there a history of violence at the address? Does one of the parties have a criminal record? Information that will help the officers plan their course of action is flashed to the patrol car terminal.

The National Crime Information Center

At the national level, the FBI has been a pioneer in digital detective work. Prior to 1967 its police files were on index cards. But in that year it established the **National Crime Information Center (NCIC)** and began to computerize files on missing persons, warrants, stolen property, securities, criminal histories, and registered property (for example, cars, boats, guns.) Today the NCIC has an annual budget of $6 million and houses fifteen million records, including eight million individual dossiers. Two IBM mainframes manage the records. Approximately 64,000 federal, state, and local police agencies, government prosecutors, and judges are authorized to access NCIC files. They can do so through more than 17,000 terminals linked to the center's data bases. Each day, the NCIC handles more than 260,000 information requests. (See Figure 12.2.)

Here is an example of how NCIC can contribute to law enforcement in local communities. Suppose a police officer is chasing a speeding car with an out-of-state license plate. The number can be radioed to the dispatcher who will run a check with the NCIC to determine whether the car has been stolen. By the time the vehicle is stopped, the police know whether more than a simple speeding ticket is in order. A name check with NCIC when the ticket is being issued will reveal whether the driver is a known criminal on the run. In essence, the NCIC provides officers with a computerized list of wanted persons and stolen property. This service is also available to federal law enforcement agents. Timely information of this nature, which alerts officers to situations that may be dangerous, can help save lives.

Supplement 12.5 The Computer and the Night Stalker

Computers might revolutionize criminal detection, if not crime itself. "There are a lot of people walking the streets out there who think they're home free," Orange County Police Lieutenant Richard Olson has noted, as reported in *Time*. He was musing on the fate of such criminals once California's automated fingerprint identification system, Cal-ID, is in place.

California's computerized fingerprint-matching system proved itself dramatically months before it was even scheduled to begin operation. The suppliers of the system were still loading California's massive volume of primary fingerprint data, digitized and translated into numerical data, into the computer when they were asked to make a trial run in an attempt to solve a very nasty problem.

For months the serial killer known as the Night Stalker had been terrifying California citizens and frustrating law enforcement agencies. By the time police had lifted a clean fingerprint from the steering wheel of a car thought to have been stolen by the Night Stalker, fourteen people had died at his hands. California State Attorney General asked Cal-ID's suppliers to stop what they were doing and search for a match.

Without a computer, fingerprint matching is tedious, time-consuming work. Further, fingerprints left at crime scenes are often next to useless. Los Angeles Police Commander Bill Rathburn was even quoted in *Time* as admitting that most dusting for prints is done strictly as PR, "to show people that we're doing something to pursue the criminal." Los Angeles police estimated that with one expert assigned to the case, comparing the suspected Stalker print to the prints in the city's paper records could have taken up to sixty-seven years.

Early computerized fingerprint-identification systems had their own problems in reliability and thoroughness, since they often ignored prints that were smudged or otherwise imperfect. Cal-ID, however, combined high-speed, custom-made chips with a new technique for analyzing prints and for comparing data with smudged prints that old systems would have overlooked as imperfect. The result, as Los Angeles officials soon discovered, was the blend of reliability and speed that criminal detection required.

Three minutes after the steering-wheel print went into Cal-ID, the computer delivered a list of ten possible matches headed by a first choice whose probability rating was four times as high as that of the next contender. Two days later, the suspect who topped the list, confirmed as chief suspect by the evidence at hand, was apprehended and at this writing is awaiting trial for the Night Stalker murders.

Musing on the huge roster of unsolved crimes in Los Angeles and on the fate of those who believe themselves to have gotten away with murder—as well as robbery, rape, and assorted other crimes—Lieutenant Olson said, "Once we get these computer systems working together, they're going to be in for a surprise."

The Dangers Inherent in Computerized Files

The incredible power of computers today coupled with the existence of so many law enforcement files containing personal data threatens individual **privacy** and creates a danger of **information misuse** and **abuse**. The fact that many of the files are secret, such as those in the Central Intelligence Agency and National Security Administration, adds to the problem.

For example, many police files lack **data integrity**: that is, the data is neither complete nor accurate. In a recent report, the Office of Technology Assessment (OTA), which sampled two groups of NCIC arrest records, found the 27 percent of the sampled files were incomplete and 20 percent were inaccurate. According to OTA, state-run computer-based criminal history systems are even more inaccurate than NCIC records. Many local files do not contain disposition data (that is, information about the decision rendered in a criminal case). Arrest records following a dismissal of charges are not expunged. Computer audits and checks for unsubstantiated entries are not run.

File swapping between agencies is another problem. Mistakes in local police records become incorporated in national data bases. An individual who has managed to correct a police file at home may be harassed in another state on the basis of the very same misinformation.

Many people believe that the growing collection of personal dossiers by the police threatens individual privacy. (Chapter 15 discusses personal dossiers and privacy at length.) Law enforcement agencies maintain that they need their record systems to maintain law and order. This is a volatile issue not easily resolved. We can expect growing public debate about the use of computers in law enforcement in the years ahead.

THE POSTAL SERVICE

The **Postal Service** no longer has a monopoly on the delivery of mail. Competitors in the form of package delivery companies and electronic mail networks have been edging in on the Postal Service's market. Since low postal rates are dependent on mass volume, a loss of customers could raise the cost of conventional mail delivery per item and require Postal Service users to pay more for their stamps. Higher costs might lower demand still further and set off a new cycle of postal rate increases.

The Postal Service hopes to meet the challenge of competitors by raising productivity through automation. A processing system is planned that will use optical character readers (OCR) to locate and read zip codes on letters. Then each letter will be printed with a bar code (a series of vertical bars and half bars) to represent the zip code in the address. Sorting will be performed by high-speed bar code reading equipment. This will eliminate the need for manual letter handling so that the Postal Service can reduce the number of its employees.

Another feature of planned automation is an expanded **nine-digit zip code**. The present five-digit code directs mail to the appropriate station or branch, but clerks must still memorize the routes of individual letter carriers. The four new digits will sort for local sectors (for example, several blocks, a large building), and segments (for example, one side of a city block, one floor in a large building, a cluster of mail boxes). It is expected that expanded zip codes combined with OCR readers and new bar code sorting machines will speed deliveries, reduce errors, and lower costs.

Another example of the application of information technology to the U.S. Post Office is a routing program called IVESS (Interactive Vehicle Scheduling System). The Postal Service has approximately 4,000 four-year contracts with private mail carriers. When contracts come up for renewal, IVESS helps redesign routes based on a data file of delivery stops, truck capacities and speeds, and related information. The program also makes a cost analysis of the economic advantages of route alternatives.

Despite the implementation of automated sorting and other computerized services, it is uncertain whether the U.S. Post Office will remain economically viable. If home shopping through personal computers becomes commonplace, for example, third-class advertising through the mail will drop in volume. (Home shopping is discussed in Chapter 18.) Another category of third-class mail, newspapers and journals, may diminish if electronic news begins to replace the printed page. (Electronic news is described in Chapter 14.) Once the electronic transfer of funds (EFT) for bill payment becomes the norm, first-class mail will likewise diminish in volume. (EFT is the subject of Chapter 18.)

In addition, many corporations are reducing their use of conventional mail by installing local networks for message delivery between in-house departments. Businesses may also adopt electronic mail for communications with vendors and clients if electronic mail proves more economical than the Postal Service in the future. Post Office automation costs are already being passed on to users. One company in Connecticut, considered "small" in terms of its data processing activity, has calculated that a nine digit zip codes will require:

- Changing 6 entry functions
- Expanding 40 disk files
- Altering 145 programs
- Recompiling 81 control procedures
- Writing 40 conversion programs

The very existence of conventional mail delivery is challenged by information technology.

Supplement 12.6 Killer Robots

PROWLER (Programmable Robot Observer With Logical Enemy Response), a robot that resembles a miniature tank, is designed as a mobile sentry. Its mission: to patrol an area such as a military airfield or pipeline and to identify intruders. Another possible application would be to patrol prison corridors at night. The advantage of PROWLER over human sentries is that a twenty-four-hour guard can be provided at less cost. In addition, the robot never falls asleep and will always obey orders.

In 1984 a prototype of the PROWLER was completed. The robot is equipped with microcomputers, artificial intelligence software, and distance-ranging sensors. It can also carry weaponry, including M60 machine guns and a grenade launcher. Future purchasers will specify what weapons they want and whether the robot needs human permission to open fire.

There are no plans in the U.S. to arm the PROWLER with lethal weapons. Instead, the robot will warn intruders to stay put, and then broadcast a warning to human guards. Critics of the PROWLER note that not all purchasers will exercise such restraint. How will the Western world react if the East Germans begin patrolling the Iron Curtain with a PROWLER that is armed with weapons?

The problem with smart weapons is that military technology has many potential civilian applications. There is no way to restrict technology, such as killer robots, to the battlefield.

But by incorporating that technology and developing new services and strategies, the Postal Service may survive.

MILITARY SYSTEMS

Computers were first used by the military in World War II. They calculated ballistic tables and determined the optimal mix of ships in convoys to minimize the danger of submarine attack.

The **Department of Defense** has been in the forefront of computer technology ever since. It has sponsored the development of computer systems and funded research in information technology. Over half of the government's complement of computers belongs to the military. The insatiable demand of the military services for smaller and faster computers, more reliable components, and larger storage capabilities has given impetus to the miniaturization of electronics. Experts claim that the development of microminiature circuitry has been the most significant military development of the past twenty years.

Digital Information and Control Systems

Digital information and control systems have resulted in the redesign of military equipment. Let us examine how airplanes have changed as an example.

Airplane cockpits are no longer a skein of wires, each instrument receiving information from sensors on a separate data path. Digital systems hook a large number of devices into a single data channel, called a data bus. A bus controller acts like a traffic policeman, operating according to programmed instructions or directions from the pilot. Information from one instrument can be automatically fed to another. For instance, data from the altimeter can be routed to the oxygen system or autopilot. The data will be continuously updated as well. Whole packages of information can be relayed, even to weapons hanging beneath the wings.

In ordinary aircraft, there is a mechanical or electrical linkage between pilot, rudder, elevators, ailerons, and engine. New technology enables pilots to **fly-by-wire**; that is, the pilot moves controls to tell the flight-control computer what action to take and the computer issues the necessary orders through the data bus system. A computer can react much faster to information supplied by sensors than a human and can continually adjust any number of complex controls. Some planes are equipped with parallel data buses and as many as four flight-control computers to keep the craft flying in case one system is damaged or fails. (The space shuttle has such a backup system.) Some planes have mechanical backup systems.

The X-29A, a fighter, is an example of a plane highly dependent on computers. It has three computers on board that make about forty adjustments per second to onboard controls. The pilot can also interact with the computers. Should all three computers fail, the plane will self-destruct within two-tenths of a second.

A second area where microelectronics has had a profound effect is on **radar**. Signal processing circuits today give lifelike images and provide much more information about range, bearing, and height of a target than could be provided in the past. Pulse-doppler radar in aircraft can pick out moving targets from the earth or sea below, and radar can peer into spinning turbines to identify jet engines. At present, processors handle approximately 750,000 operations a second; seven million a second are projected for the early 1990s. It is expected that advanced computers will soon be able to draw a three-dimensional picture of a target and check the profile against memory to see what the profile represents. Such radar will help solve an intractable problem of modern warfare: identification of friend or foe.

Microelectronic and digital systems facilitate **military communications** as well. In battle a commander needs to know the location of units on the move. We now have position-locating systems that provide this information automatically. The commander sets up a master station at a known location for transmission and receipt of data-code messages to and from field units. Each message contains the precise time of transmission based on atomic clocks, and the time difference from transmission to receipt is converted into distance to determine troop positions. The accuracy and rapid delivery of this information enables commanders to respond to changing field conditions and to execute complex troop maneuvers.

Still another contribution of modern electronics is **smart weapons**. Automatic gun loaders and seeker-guidance technology applied to tanks, torpedos, and missiles are examples. Today a missile computer can be supplied with the information formerly given pilots and can be programmed to make decisions during a mission. For example, in 1984 a Tomahawk missile hit its test target 400 miles from its launch site. It was guided in flight by an internal computer that held in memory a detailed map of the target area. Another advantage of computer-directed missiles is that they can fly faster and turn more quickly than manned aircraft and can fly into danger without risking a pilot's life.

Problems for the Pentagon

The Department of Defense has been criticized in the past for implementing technology so complex that the common recruit can neither operate nor maintain it. It has been charged that new "gadgets" have resulted in less military capability at higher cost.

To meet these objections, more emphasis is being placed on ease of use in the development of high-tech military systems. Reliability of such systems has improved and maintenance is far easier.

Yet mistakes are still made when it comes to deciding which systems to fund for development. One reason for these mistakes is that the gap between the decision makers and the technically qualified in the Pentagon is widening. Politics also plays a role in military appropriations. Furthermore, so many new technologies exist that the range of options is bewildering. Many of these technologies blur the traditional distinction between ground and air systems, fueling interservice rivalries. Deep-strike weapons, with various combinations of warheads, launchers, sensors, and guidance techniques, cause limitless jurisdictional arguments.

Another problem for the Pentagon is that heavy reliance on computers makes the defense of this country dependent on tight **computer security**. The destruction of hardware is not the only danger. An enemy might plant an embedded instruction in software causing missiles to retarget to friendly capitals or cause shipboard computers to garble communications in battle. A "Trojan horse" of this nature is difficult to detect even by the most skilled experts.

Supplement 12.7 Sample Problems with Computerization at the Social Security Administration

- It was estimated that it would take 6,000 to 9,000 work years to eliminate the minimum benefit level for three million people, a proposal of the President's fiscal year 1982 budget. Such a change would have required modification of virtually every program in the system.
- It took 20,000 man-hours to update programs to make 1982 cost of living increases in Social Security checks and another 2,500 hours of computer runtime to make the changes. (The same job could have been done in a relatively few days using a modern computer system, according to officials.)
- Social Security was recently three years behind its annual recomputation of benefits. The SSA acknowledges that billions of dollars in incorrect payments may result.
- Manual processing may be required to implement changes proposed by the President's budget since there is insufficient systems capability to get the required work done in time to achieve expected savings.

The 8,000 large computers used by the Department of Defense are scheduled for replacement with more advanced systems that include sophisticated, built-in security systems. But replacement will take at least five years. Until then, elaborate measures have been taken to limit access to military computers. Although secrets may be protected, restraints to prevent misuse may interfere with authorized computer access. This, in turn, may limit the usefulness of large military computer systems in the interim period.

SOCIAL SECURITY ADMINISTRATION

The Social Security Act of 1935, part of President Roosevelt's New Deal, provided for old age, survivors, and disability insurance; public assistance; and health and welfare services. Initially social security covered only workers in commercial and industrial occupations. However, successive legislative changes have expanded the program. The **Social Security Administration (SSA)**, that part of the Department of Health and Human Services responsible for administering social security programs, has grown accordingly.

Today SSA employs more than 80,000 people. It pays monthly benefits to over thirty-six million people. Each year the SSA processes more than 380 million annual wage reports from employers, 120 million health bills, 7.5 million new-claims applications, and 10 million requests for Social Security cards. Over 50 million beneficiaries received program benefits in the fiscal year 1982.

Computers were installed by the Social Security Administration in the 1950s to help automate record processing. At the time, those computers were "state of the art"—the best available. By the 1980s, however, data processing at SSA was in danger of total breakdown. Just mailing out the thirty-six million benefit checks each month represented a "daily miracle," according to the Social Security Commissioner. How did this situation arise?

As social insurance programs enlarged over time, a heavy administrative burden was placed on the SSA's data processing system. To speed implementation of new tasks, the SSA did not take time to redesign existing systems from the ground up. It never developed a long-range plan to guide systematic growth of its data processing capacity. An extremely complex patchwork system evolved as a result, encompassing a range of programming expertise and techniques developed from the 1950s through the 1970s.

Although the SSA has undergone four major transitions of computer equipment since the 1950s, software conversion has been merely a translation of existing programs to make them run on the newer equipment. An added complication is the lack of written documentation and the high turnover of personnel. So many undocumented program changes have taken place that no one knows how the system functions. Record storage at SSA is another huge problem. The agency still uses magnetic tapes instead of advanced mass storage technology. It takes 2,000 employees just to move the 14,000 reels of data needed for daily operations from storage facilities to the computers. Some of the consequences of the inefficiency and near-collapse of Social Security's computer operations are listed in Supplement 12.7.

In March 1982 the Social Security Administration announced a five-year modernization plan that has won support from both Congress and the Office of Management and Budget. In order to minimize the risk of service disruption, the plan proposes a step-by-step approach to modernization rather than building a new system from scratch. Software will be streamlined and hardware upgraded in increments. The five-year modernization effort will cost an estimated $479 million.

POLITICAL CAMPAIGNS

In addition to helping run the government, computers have helped politicians run in government elections since the 1960s. In the sixties, politicians began hiring computer firms to prepare campaign letters and solicit supporters for funds. The Republican National Committee bought its first computer in 1975. These early computers were mainframes and only candidates with large campaign funds could afford to use them.

By the 1980s, however, personal computers with low price tags were available. Virtually all candidates, even those running in state and local elections, could afford to add computers to their campaigns. (There are an estimated 500,000 elected public offices in this country. More than 750,000 candidates compete in each election cycle.) A microcomputer system appropriate for polling, direct mail, and voter targeting ranges from several thousand dollars to $10,000. Since many candidates run for office more than once, this cost can be spread over several campaigns.

Here are examples of ways computers can contribute to **campaigns**:

- *Financial management.* To prepare financial projections. To perform cash flow analysis and other accounting functions, including campaign budgeting. To use spreadsheets when drawing up financial reports.
- *Research.* To store data bases of possible convention delegates and their positions on issues. To analyze demographic data of political subdivisions. To sort voting statistics for analysis, such as percentages of women voters in a given district. To allocate campaign resources according to the most promising areas for a candidate. To store text of what every opponent has said about every issue. To store lists of people met and issues talked about.
- *Polling.* To generate lists of random telephone numbers, design samples, record poll answers, analyze results. Daily tracking of opinion helps determine trends and is used in planning campaign strategies.
- *Scheduling.* To schedule activities of candidates and staff. To print daily summaries of events for different classes of users (for example, the media might get one format, the candidate another).
- *Fund raising.* To solicit contributions. To tailor fund-raising appeals to the population segment represented in a particular mailing list. To store a catalog of donors. To automate "thank you" form letter mailing.
- *Word processing.* To write speeches. To prepare personalized campaign mailings (form letters with variable text). To prepare reports to meet state and federal election law requirements.

Software can be written for an endless variety of campaign chores. But candidates need not have programmers on their staffs. A number of microcomputer packages are on the market that serve basic campaign needs. Popular packages in 1984 included Campaign Manager, Politech L, and The Campaigner; these packages ranged in price from $500 to $1000. A system called Solon that included hardware and software and that was selling for $16,500 was also on the market.

The personal computer has revolutionized campaigns, particularly campaigns at the state and local level in which candidates establish and run their own support organizations. A critical element in campaigns is information management. Yet the short time period of a campaign does not allow for leisurely development of systems or procedures. Generalized software packages for personal computers, such as data base managers,

Supplement 12.8 Data Base of Congressional Voting Records

Since politicians use computers to keep track of voters in their districts, it is only tit-for-tat that voters use computers to keep track of the voting records of their representatives in Congress. Legi-Slate is such an online data base. It was originally designed to help lobbyists, corporations, and government entities keep track of congressional activity. But since its inception, many voter organizations have begun using the data base to decide how to distribute their campaign contributions.

Users can request a listing of which members of Congress supported specific pieces of legislation. The lists can be geographic, in relationship to party leadership votes, or ordered in any number of ranking schemes. The system saves interested parties hours of searching through the *Congressional Record* for vote counts.

spreadsheets, and word processing, provide candidates with efficient tools to manage information—tools that greatly facilitate running a campaign.

CONVENTIONS

The national **political conventions** in 1984 depended on an assemblage of computer gear unprecedented in political history. Estimates of the combined value of electronic aids at the Democratic Convention, for example, ranged from $1 to $1.25 million. Five communications-oriented facilities were installed:

- A credentials and data security network
- An electronic mail system
- A vote tabulation network
- A phone message distribution system
- A videotex service dispensing information about both the convention and points of local interest

Similar communication systems were part of the 1984 Republican Convention at Dallas.

In addition, both parties used computers for office chores in preparation for their conventions. Computers assisted in preparation of delegate lists, credentials, updated rules, schedules, and procedures. Word processors revised platform planks while graphics computers helped produce signs, floor plans, and presentation materials.

What is more, the news media covering the convention used computers as extensively as the political parties did, if not more so. Almost half of convention attendees were journalists who had portable and lap-size computers with modems enabling them to send stories to their home offices. TV anchormen covering the convention had access to the data bases of their networks, which provided them with details about delegates, such as their ethnic backgrounds, occupations, and political leanings. They could extract information about voting patterns through programs on mainframes, and keep a running tabulation on platform votes and the nomination process.

Automation at the 1984 conventions was a subject of much media coverage. By the 1988 conventions, use of electronics in politics may be so commonplace that little mention of it will be made in the press.

ELECTIONS

Elections are run by state and local election officials. There is no uniform method of preparing voter registration lists, no single procedure for casting ballots and tabulating results. While some communities have computerized ballot counting, many people still mark ballots with pencils or pull mechanical voting machine levers.

Electronic voting systems that allow voters to use computer technology to cast ballots from their homes are technologically feasible today but not likely to be implemented in the near future. One reason for this is concern about possible election fraud and much uncertainty regarding the social implications of electronic voting. More people might vote, but would greater voter participation necessarily lead to better government? Would electronic voting lead to more frequent elections? Would elected officials be hesitant to provide decisive leadership, choosing instead to follow the mood of a public not well informed on complex issues?

In all likelihood, electronic voting will be limited to opinion polls for some time to come. Most Americans would be hesitant to change election procedures before the consequences of changes were well understood.

SUMMING UP

Federal agencies recognized the value of computers back in the 1960s and were early leaders in the use of information technology. Businesspeople toured government facilities to learn what computers could do. Yet within a few short years, leadership in the field of computing shifted to the private sector. Washington was saddled with obsolete hardware, and the efficiency of government operations was steadily declining.

Many factors have contributed to this situation. The basic problem appears to be that government bureaucracy simply cannot cope with the dynamic nature of the computer industry. When making purchases, for example, it is the practice of the federal government to accept low bids. Since computer manufacturers discount their older hardware to make way for new models, a low price usually signifies obsolete technology. Furthermore, it takes government two to three years to process the paperwork for purchases. Protracted procurements mean that hardware is outdated before it is even installed.

In addition, government purchasing officers buy all types of equipment. Private industry has learned that specialists are needed to keep abreast of computer technology and to understand the needs of users. The salary structure of government also works against the use of appropriate expertise. The civil service is unable to compete with industry for the experienced professionals needed to write software and run computer operations.

One hopeful sign in Washington is the growing awareness that information systems need to be overhauled and that long-range automation plans should begin now. Although agencies need not incorporate the latest technology to fulfill their missions, up-to-date technology would contribute to better government.

Some federal agencies, of course, do utilize computers effectively even now. The National Aeronautics and Space Administration, the National Institutes of Health, and the House of Representatives are generally rated highly for their implementation of information technology. The Department of Defense supports computer research and development, and it implements advanced systems for weapons and strategic planning. By requiring defense computers to have COBOL compilers and new military systems to be programmed in Ada, the department is promoting widespread use of these languages. This is an example of how government can provide leadership in computing.

The same advantages of using computers apply to government as to other sectors of the economy. Computers are a fast, accurate, reliable, low-cost tool for large-volume information processing. They store large amounts of information and make it possible to process that information in ways that would be impractical, if not impossible, by other means. Computers can contribute to effective and efficient government, which ultimately benefits all citizens.

Today, low-cost microcomputers have the power that only large systems used to have. Perhaps government will be improved once personal computers are found on every bureaucrat's desk. Microcomputers have already had a noticeable effect on politics. They have proven to be a useful tool in fund raising and organizing campaigns. Candidates are no longer as dependent on power brokers and party backing in their quest for elected office as they were in the past.

The subject of computers in government is a large one that is difficult to compress into a single chapter. Each government department we have discussed was chosen because of the particular characteristics of its use of computers. The Census

Supplement 12.9 Computer Management of Disaster Relief

Disaster relief is essential after a community is devastated by hurricane, tornado, or flood. Immediately following the calamity, emergency medical treatment is the priority. Next, displaced families must be provided with food, shelter, and transportation. Within a few days, relief agencies must begin processing thousands of applications for financial assistance and home repairs.

Employees of the Federal Emergency Management Agency and state officials who participate in disaster relief must account for all government resources provided to victims. In the past, tracking and reporting of these resources was done manually. Records were kept on index cards and paper-and-pencil registers. Under the press of crushing work loads, accurate cost accounting and status reporting was next to impossible.

A new management information system called Carma has been developed to help federal and state workers administer disaster relief. Using Carma, workers can:

- Input basic application identification data.
- Record each family's special needs.
- Verify identification and eligibility data from separate sources.
- Assign cases to appropriate resource agencies.
- Track progress.
- Report daily progress online.

The developers of Carma (Planning Research Corporation and Culpepper Associates) hope that data gathered from Carma applications will be useful for disaster modeling. This modeling should help officials plan disaster relief so that more rapid assistance is available to victims when disasters actually occur.

Bureau was chosen because of its historical role in computer use and because it handles a large mass of input data that is processed in the batch mode. The IRS is like the Census Bureau in two respects: it uses batch processing and it handles personal records of citizens. The use of computers in such departments raises issues of privacy and fair use of data. The military and law enforcement agencies have been described as examples of departments that utilize online, real-time processing. The Social Security Administration was included in the chapter because its outmoded, outdated systems represent problems common in the government's use of computers. Finally, the White House and Post Office were selected because while most readers are familiar with these governmental entities, they may not be aware of how computers have affected or will soon affect their internal operations.

REVIEW QUESTIONS

1. Why do governmental agencies need computers? Are batch or online systems most common? Give examples of departments using these modes. Do computers contribute to governmental efficiency and effectiveness?
2. Why is the federal government no longer a leader in the use of information technology?
3. Describe computer applications at the:
   a. White House
   b. IRS
   c. post office
4. How will updating computer systems at the Census Bureau reduce costs in the 1990 census?
5. What is the purpose of computer matching at the IRS? Does matching violate individual rights?
6. What is the purpose of a nine-digit zip code?
7. Are computers effective in fighting crime? Describe computer systems used in law enforcement at both the local and national levels.
8. How can police data files threaten the average law-abiding citizen? Is data integrity an issue?

9. How has microminiature computer technology contributed to the defense of this country?

10. Is computer security more important at the Department of Defense than in other governmental departments? Explain.

11. What has led to current data processing problems at the Social Security Administration? How could the problems have been avoided? How can they be corrected?

12. Describe how a personal computer can aid a candidate running for office?

13. How can electronic gear at a political convention contribute to the nomination of a presidential candidate? Is the democratic process enhanced by electronics?

14. Discuss advantages and disadvantages of electronic voting.

DISCUSSION QUESTIONS

1. If you were in charge of modernizing computer systems in government, what steps would you take? List your priorities. Is more electronic gadgetry the answer? Would you favor mainframes and supercomputers or place emphasis on microcomputers?

2. What would make government bureaucracy more responsive to the dynamics of the computer industry?

3. Should all government agencies share one large computer system, including data bases? How would bureaucrats, politicians, and taxpayers benefit? What would be the dangers?

4. Do you agree with the view that security of government computer systems is more crucial than security in the private sector? Explain.

5. Comment on the statement: Computers in government are a great threat to personal privacy and individual rights.

6. Why are business organizations turning to electronic mail? Do you think that this will lead to a demise of the U.S. Postal Service?

7. Do you think that decisions on computer processing in government are more political than technological or economic? How should data processing decisions be made?

8. Could the federal government run without computers?

9. What changes do you foresee in the Post Office in coming years? Will services expand or decline?

10. Has computer technology improved the U.S. defense posture?

11. Who is responsible for the fact that processing in many government agencies is close to breakdown because of obsolete, overburdened computer systems? Discuss the Social Security Administration as one example.

12. Do you believe that computer technology will contribute to the decentralization of politics? To the ability of independents (that is, candidates without a party tie) to win office?

13. Describe changes in our democratic process that you foresee should electronic voting from homes be implemented.

14. How can the cost versus benefits of computer systems in government be assessed?

EXERCISES

1. Prepare a list of computer uses in local government that you think are desirable. Then interview an official to determine how computers are being used in your city's government. Investigate the reasons for any discrepancies between the two lists.

2. Research some recent computer applications (within the last two years) for:
   a. federal government administration
   b. defense
   c. city government
   d. transportation

3. Read a case study of computer crime in government. Identify why it occurred, how the crime was detected, what measures were taken to prevent further crimes of the same nature, and what sanctions were imposed on the offender. Now suppose that this crime had occurred in the private sector. Would the detection, correction, and sanctions have been the same? If so, why? If not, why not?

4. Consider a computer application in government that has a counterpart in business. How do the two systems differ? Why do they differ?

Selected Annotated Bibliography

Bruno, Charles. "The Electronic Cops," *Datamation*, vol. 30, no. 9 (June 15, 1984), pp. 115–24. Describes how computers have made law enforcement easier but also raises isues of data abuse and misuse.

Coniff, Richard. "Government By Computer," *Science Digest*, vol. 90, no. 12 (December 1982), pp. 55–56. The benefits and dangers of computer use in government are discussed.

Cook, Royer. "Predicting Arson," *Byte*, vol. 10, no. 10 (October 1985), pp. 239–45. Computer-based arson-prediction systems permit city officials and firefighters to store and analyze the large data sets necessary to pinpoint buildings where arson is most likely to strike.

Connolly, James. "IRS Still Depends on Paper in Computer Age," *Computerworld*, vol 18, no. 5 (January 30, 1984), p. 23. The new equipment being purchased by the IRS is described.

Government Computer News. This is a monthly journal with a newspaper format that was started in 1982. Each issue is about 100 pages long. An excellent reference on computers in government.

Gray, Martha. *Federal ADP Equipment: A Compilation of Statistics, 1981*. Washington, D.C.: Government Printing Office, 1982. An excellent set of tables on the numbers and types of equipment used in governmental agencies.

"How Uncle Sam Misuses Computers," *Business Week*, issue 2745 (June 28, 1982), pp. 88–90. This article describes the bureaucratic problems of government that contribute to obsolete information technology, in spite of the huge expenditures spent on government computers.

Meacham, Jim. "The New Masters," *The Economist*, vol. 291, no. 3 (May 21, 1983), pp. 5–32 Meacham surveys new weapons and equipment being used in the realm of conventional warfare and assesses their impact on military tactics.

Porter, Martin. "The PC Runs For President," *Personal Computing*, vol. 8, no. 3 (March 6, 1984), pp. 195–196 This is a case study of Senator John Glenn's use of a PC in the Democratic primaries in 1984.

President's Private Sector Survey on Cost Control: Report on Automated Data Processing/Office Automation. Washington, D.C.: Government Printing Office, 1983. This report is more commonly known as the Grace Commission report. Data processing problems in government, evaluations of proposed modernization plans, and recommendations for government automation are included in the report.

Smith, Rodney. "Getting Out the Vote," *Popular Computing*, vol. 4, no. 1 (November 1984), pp. 111–15. How use of computers for candidates running on low-budget campaigns can make a crucial difference. A review of political software and prices is included.

Smith, Rodney. "The New Political Machine," *Computerworld*, vol. 18, no. 29 (July 16, 1984), pp. ID19–25. Smith traces the history of computers in politics and describes how software packages can benefit candidates seeking election.

Walker, Paul. "Smart Weapons in Naval Warfare," *Scientific American*, vol. 248, no. 5 (May 1983), pp. 53–61. Precision-guided weapons, such as those used in the Falkland Islands war, challenge the Navy's plan to add expensive surface ships to the U.S. fleet.

"Washington Catches Up to the Computer Age," *U.S. News and World Report*, vol. 96, no. 13 (April 2, 1984), pp. 61 ff. A brief survey of computer use at a number of government departments is included in this article.

Watt, Peggy. "Democrats Computerize Politics," *InfoWorld,* vol. 6, no. 23 (July 23, 1984), pp. 23–25. The nature of nominating conventions has been changed by information technology, according to Watt. Electronic systems used in San Francisco at the 1984 Democratic Convention are described.

Watt, Peggy. "Micros in the White House." *Infoworld,* vol. 6, no. 35 (August 27, 1984), pp. 20–23. Office automation for White House staff is described.

The Eclipse of Slide Rules: Computers for Engineering, Science, and Research

Every great advance in science has issued from a new audacity of imagination.

JOHN DEWEY

CHAPTER THIRTEEN

Key Words

computational power	**microcomputer**	**parallel processing**
cost	**microminiaturization**	**pipelining**
instrumentation	**microprocessor**	**simulation**
online real-time computing (ORLT)	**minicomputer**	**speed**
mainframe	**multiprocessing**	**supercomputer**
	non-von machine	**vector processing**
	optical processing	

To illustrate the impact of information technology on engineering and the sciences, let's look at a problem in celestial mechanics as an example. When first generation electronic computers were being designed after World War II, W. J. Eckert, Dirk Brouwer, and G. M. Clemence realized that computers could be used to calculate ephemerides with unprecedented accuracy. (Ephemerides are tables giving the coordinates for celestial bodies at specified times within a specified period.) The project of this group of scientists was to calculate new ephemerides for the outer planets Jupiter through Pluto.

Eckert and his colleagues used the IBM Selective Sequence Electronic Calculator (SSEC) for their now classic calculation. This machine, which became operational in 1948, was the only machine then capable of the project. They used the SSEC to calculate heliocentric coordinates to nine decimal places for the planets at forty-day intervals for the years 1653 to 2060. The SSEC took approximately 120 hours to make the necessary computations and to punch cards. A human working forty hours a week with a mechanical desk calculator would have required eighty years to produce the tables, according to Eckert's estimate.

If we compare the SSEC with modern day computers, we can see how problem-solving capabilities have improved. A Radio Shack TRS-80 Model I microcomputer used to reproduce the ephemerides of Eckert's team took only ten hours and twenty-five minutes. A present-day supercomputer could probably solve the problem in two seconds or less.

This example shows that computers can be used to perform scientific tasks that are not feasible if they are done by manual processing or by the electromechanical devices of the past. It also points out that personal computers are quite capable of doing serious scientific work and illustrates the speed of supercomputers. With modern information processing technology, we may be able to solve some of the mysteries of the universe that have eluded us for so long.

This chapter opens by explaining what types of computers are appropriate for engineering, science, and research. Next, the contribution of computers to the work done in these fields is described. Sections are devoted to instrumentation and online control, the computational power of computers, and simulation. The chapter concludes by discussing supercomputers, since most of these machines are today used for scientific research.

WHAT SIZE COMPUTER IS APPROPRIATE?

Microprocessors, microcomputers, minis, mainframes, and supercomputers—all are used by engineers and scientists in their work.

For example, one finds **microprocessors** in instruments that monitor experiments and control equipment. The computational power of **micro-**

Supplement 13.1 Sample Computer Configuration for Scientific Research: A Single Lab at the Lawrence Livermore Facility

- *Large computers*
  1 Cray-1
  3 Cray-1S
  3 CDC 7600
  2 DEC PDP/10
- *Storage*
  3.4867×10^{12} bits (3.4867 trillion bits)* (Includes 40,000 reels of active tapes and 16,000 reels of archival tapes)
- *Network*
  Lawrence Livermore National Laboratory Network
  Activity: 2.9×10^{9} bits/hour
- *Peripherals*
  2 electrostatic page printers with 18,000 lines/minute
  4 microfilm recorders
- *Main Research Projects*
  Nuclear weapons research (80 percent of computational resources)
  Magnetic fusion energy
  Laser fusion
  Laser isotope separation
  Nonnuclear energy technologies
  Biomedical and environmental research

*One trillion bits of data is the equivalent of 12.5 billion English words or the number of words found in approximately 100,000 average-sized books.

computers and their ability to store and analyze data benefit engineers and scientists as well. Although microcomputers have limited capabilities compared to larger computers, they match, and even surpass, many giant machines of the last decade in their processing power. The fact that microcomputers cannot handle vast quantities of data is less of a limitation than one might think because many mathematical and scientific problems are characterized by comparatively little input and output. Thus when calculations must be performed on a relatively small quantity of data, a microcomputer can be a useful tool. Microcomputers can also be used as terminals on which to prepare data for input into a mainframe or to edit output for clearer presentation.

Minicomputers and **mainframes** are general-purpose machines capable of handling a range of problems. They are the mainstay of most large organizations that have centralized data processing needs. (As we saw in Chapter 2, the increase in computing power of minis has blurred the distinction between minis and mainframes. Many experts believe that minis are no longer a separate class of machines.)

The versatility of mainframes allows them to perform administrative functions (for example, recordkeeping, accounting) as well as data processing for applied science and basic research. They operate at speeds measured in nanoseconds, have large storage capacities, and can support hundreds, or even thousands, of online terminals.

Mainframes contribute to a wide variety of engineering and scientific endeavors. For example, they help biologists study the effects of pollutants on plants and animals. They assist physicists in research into the nature of the constituent particles of matter and the forces between them. Civil engineers use mainframes when designing dams, buildings, and tunnels; mechanical engineers use them to design automobiles and power plants. (Computer-aided design and other engineering applications in manufacturing are discussed in Chapter 8.)

The distinctive characteristic of **supercomputers** is their ability to quickly process gigantic quantities of numerical data. That is why they are commonly called "number crunchers." Disciplines where the problem-solving capabilities of supercomputers are required include aerodynamics, seismology, weather prediction, and nuclear weapons development.

SCIENTIFIC USES OF COMPUTERS

The contribution of computers to engineering, science, and research can be classified according to the work they do. Microprocessors are commonly embedded in scientific instruments. Data from the instruments may then be analyzed online by other machines. In addition, computers are valuable in science because they can perform complex computations or simulate the environment. Let's take a brief look now at each of these categories of work.

Instrumentation and Online Real-Time Computing

Computers contribute to **instrumentation** in a variety of ways. Computer-controlled telescopes, for example, detect and track satellites beyond radar range. Instruments also monitor trends in the tilt of the crater floor at Mount St. Helens, sending data to a large computer every ten minutes for analysis. One immediate benefit is that eruptions can be predicted by up to thirty minutes, giving scientists working at the site time to evacuate.

Computers also monitor spacecraft instrumentation from launch to landing. In 1984, just four seconds before liftoff, a computer detected a possible malfunction in a four-inch fuel valve of Discovery and stopped engine firing in mid-sequence to abort the mission.

Other examples of the marriage of computers and instrumentation are the medical imaging techniques discussed in Chapter 10. Working in conjunction with various kinds of sensors, computers are able to digitize images of the body (and of bodily processes) from perspectives never before possible.

In each of these examples, **online real-time computing (OLRT)** is the processing mode; that is, instantaneous processing takes place on data collected by the instrument sensors. There is no waiting for batch processing and no delay because the CPU has been dedicated to work of higher priority. Online real-time computing is needed to control a variety of engineering and scientific activities. Sometimes a person initiates the control action. More often, however, online control is provided by a computer that initiates action (under program control) when the process being monitored exceeds (or falls below) specified tolerance limits. The decision to abort the Discovery mission was made on this basis. The complexity of the instrumentation and the need to make split-second decisions are reasons why computers control launching of the space shuttle.

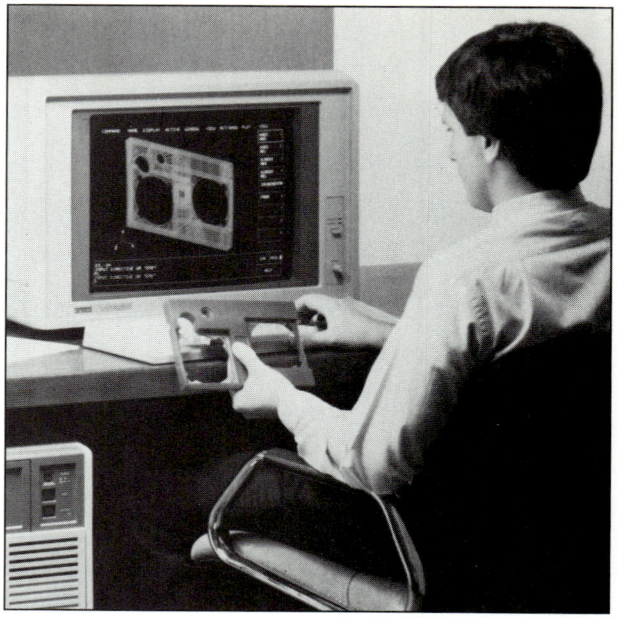

Figure 13.1 Going back the electronic drawing board. This designer is seeking a solution to a problem in a manufactured finished product. (Digital Equipment Corporation)

Massive and Complex Computation

Many problems in engineering and science require the solution to complex equations. Sometimes the ability to process massive amounts of data is a necessity. Computers have both capabilities. The **computational power** of computers assists physicists in generating random numbers for experimental input. It helps chemists in decoding the molecular structure of complex proteins And it helps geologists in predicting rock mass behavior under stress. Because of their computational power, computers are able to digitize film images from experiments with nuclear weapons or turn tables of crude data into pie charts or three-dimensional graphs. (See Figure 13.1.)

The authors recently participated in a planning model to determine ninety-seven optimum activity levels subject to 122 equality and inequality constraints using input data representing a set of 11,836 coefficients, some of which were six digits long. Clearly a computer was needed to solve a problem of this complexity. It is in relation to problems of this nature that the scientific community benefits from the computational power of a computer and the computer's ability to manage and manipulate data.

Figure 13.2 Using a computer to design a machine. Computer graphics permit an inventor to realize an idea without having to build physical models, making experimentation less expensive in the corporate setting. (McDonnell Douglas Corporation)

Figure 13.3 A digitizer and the image it produces. The operator enters the data by running the digitizer over the surface of the object. The resulting 3-D wire-frame image can be rotated, scaled, and otherwise manipulated on the screen. (Micro Control Systems, Inc.)

Simulation

Engineers and scientists commonly build models and then test these models under changing conditions. The model may be a scaled-down version of a real object, such as an airplane model that will be tested in a wind tunnel under varied conditions of wind velocity. Or it may be a set of mathematical expressions that represent a process or a complex system. In both cases, a computer can be programmed to answer "What if?" questions; that is, a computer can be programmed to calculate how changes in the environment of the model or changes in the design of the model affect the model's performance. This is called **simulation**. (See Figures 13.2 and 13.3.)

With simulation, scientists can study complex physical processes, such as plasma behavior. Computer-simulated crash testing can substitute for the real thing in aircraft design. Guidance in how to run chemical refineries can be provided by plant simulation. The oil industry simulates drilling strategies for different geological formations in its search for ways to boost recovery of oil deposits.

SCIENCE IN TRANSITION: THE ADVENT OF SUPERCOMPUTERS

Science is undergoing a structural transition as a result of the use of computers and particularly of supercomputers. To experimental and theoretical science, a new methodology has been added: information science. According to Neal Lane of Rice University,

> The current transition affects every discipline of science and engineering and every university engaged in scientific research. We expect that the new opportunities for scientific inquiry and industrial applications of science made possible by large-scale computation support will feed back into total scientific activity—in theory, experiment and computation.[1]

[1]"Supercomputers: Who'll Be the Fastest with the Fastest," *Physics Today* (May 1984), p. 61.

Supplement 13.2 Seismic Exploration

When mountains are created by geological processes or earth plates drift, layers of sedimentary rock may buckle, creating upfolds called "anticlines." In the search for oil and gas, geologists look for anticlines of porous rock where fossil fuels can become trapped.

Seismic exploration is a common method of locating and measuring potential traps. This exploration technique makes use of sound waves reflected from subsurface rock layers following a mechanical excitation (a chirp signal or pressure pulse from an explosive charge). The waves are detected and recorded by seismic reflection crews. The data is then analyzed by computer. Seismic exploration is an activity that generates more digital data for computer processing than any other human activity—an estimated 10^{15} to 10^{16} data bits annually. For such massive data processing, the use of supercomputers is appropriate.

For large-scale computation, supercomputers are needed. Most supercomputers to date have been located in government agencies with defense missions, such as the National Security Agency, or in federal laboratories like Lawrence Livermore. (The world's biggest user of supercomputers is the nuclear weapons laboratory at Los Alamos; it has ten). However, the use of supercomputers in industry is on the increase. Commercial sectors targeted for supercomputer sales are aerospace, oil and gas exploration, and automobile manufacture. Chemical, semiconductor, and biomedical concerns are also expected to be in the forefront of industrial supercomputer use.

Why is the extension of supercomputer use to industry significant? One reason is that supercomputers mean jobs and revenue to the computer industry, an industry of importance to the American economy. Supercomputer technology has contributed to the production of more powerful, lower level computers as well, which has enhanced American leadership in computing and been of benefit to computer users. Furthermore, fields that depend on supercomputers to process massive amounts of information, such as aerodynamic design, have been transformed and new technologies have been stimulated by the use of supercomputers. The argument goes that the country with the best supercomputers will in fact lead all others in scholarship, industry, and government. (Consider the national security implications, for example, if the U.S., which depends on supercomputers to develop weapons and plot defense strategies, falls behind in the supercomputer race.) The importance of supercomputers explains the shock waves caused by the Japanese plan to introduce a fifth generation computer in the 1990s, a computer expected to surpass present-day supercomputers in performance. (Chapter 19 discusses the Japanese challenge at length.)

THE PROBLEMS LIMITING SUPERCOMPUTER USE

Cost is one deterrent to supercomputer sales. The price tag of between \$5 and \$15 million (compared to \$3 million for a top of the line mainframe) is beyond the budgets of many potential users. Altogether, fewer than 100 supercomputers had been purchased by the early 1980s. Growth of the supercomputer market will depend, in part, on innovations that will lower the price of the machines.

The high price of supercomputers has been particularly detrimental to university communities. Although the potential contribution of supercomputers to research is recognized on college campuses, the money has not been available to purchase (or access) the machines. (Access fees at U.S. universities are typically between \$2000 and \$3000 per hour. In contrast, Japanese fees are as low as \$60 per hour as a result of government subsidies.) University research requiring the processing capability of a supercomputer has been limited as a result. Another consequence is that students have not gained experience using supercomputers or acquired the concepts needed to work in a supercomputer environment upon grad-

Supplement 13.3 Microchip Improvements

A program to develop very high-speed integrated circuits (VHSIC, pronounced "vissic") was launched by the Defense Department in 1980. Already VHSIC chips have improved by being reduced from a minimum-feature size of 5 microns on commercially available microcircuits to 1.25 microns. (A micron is about 40 millionths of an inch.) A second research phase is now underway. The goal is a minimum-feature size of 0.5 microns by 1989, a 100-fold improvement over devices of the 1970s. (To illustrate the miniaturization of 0.5 microns, imagine a U.S. map showing every house on every street in every city. This map could be printed on a single newspaper page if it were possible to print in 0.5 micron-wide lines.)

To reach their VHSIC goals, the Pentagon in 1980 selected nine contractors (from a dozen competitors) to perform nine-month program definition studies. By 1981, the field had been narrowed to six firms working on Phase One objectives. In October 1984, these three teams were awarded contracts for Phase Two: Honeywell, IBM, and TRW/Motorola. Each contractor has a different approach to the solution of the problem. The Pentagon believes that this parallel effort should help ensure VHSIC success.

graduation. This lack of a trained pool of users has hampered both sales and further development of supercomputers. Both government and industry have had difficulty hiring engineers and scientists with the training needed to conduct research using supercomputers.

Fortunately, this picture is changing. Colorado State and Purdue have purchased Cyber 205's and the University of Minnesota has acquired a Cray-1. In 1984 the National Science Foundation announced that it would establish supercomputer centers at Princeton, Cornell, the University of California at San Diego, and the University of Illinois—universities immediately dubbed "supercomputer U's." These machines will be the core of a network connecting some thirty other schools. In addition, no fewer than fifty teams at American universities are building supercomputers of their own. Innovative technology to reduce the price of supercomputer models is also being implemented.

A second factor limiting the supercomputer market is processing **speed**. Supercomputers are still too slow to solve some engineering and scientific problems. For example, to detect small operational faults in a nuclear power plant and to correct these faults before they become dangerous would require an increase in speed by a factor of 100. In the aircraft industry, design is still done part by part (that is, nose, tail, wings and so on) because supercomputers cannot simulate airflow around an entire airplane. Present day supercomputers would have to increase in speed 1000 times to do that.

One way to increase speed is **microminiaturization**—that is, by reducing the distance electronic signals have to travel through computer circuitry. The problem designers face with microminiaturization is how to dissipate the intense heat generated by current passing through dense circuitry of contemporary design. The solution used by Cray-1 was to circulate freon gas through cooling channels in the machine. Cray-2, which has a central processing unit only twenty-six inches high and thirty-eight inches long compared to the nine-foot length of the Cray-1, immerses the computer in a bath of fluorocarbon. This temperature control allows Cray-2 to function at speeds of more than one billion operations per second.

CMOS circuits (complementary metal-oxide semiconductors) that produce little heat are under development. So are gallium arsenide chips to replace silicon chips. (Electrons move more easily in gallium arsenide than in silicon.) Switches cooled to −273°C, called Josephson junctions, a cooling that will enable them to operate in a few trillionths of a second, are being researched by two Japanese companies. (Both General Electric and IBM formerly were engaged in similar research but have discontinued Josephson junction projects.) Biomolecular devices are also being considered.

All of these new technologies may contribute to greater supercomputer speeds in the future. Many experts believe, however, that we are reaching the

Supplement 13.4 Supercomputer Specs: Cray-2

	CRAY-2	CRAY-1
Number of CPUs	4, each more powerful than a CRAY-1	1 CPU
Internal memory (64-bit words)	256 million 64-bit words	1 million
Input/output processors	Virtually unlimited	Maximum of 4
Concurrent memory ports	4	4
Cycle time	4.1 nanoseconds	12.5 nanoseconds
Size (excluding peripherals)	16 square feet	100 square feet
Software support	Too new for third-party software; FORTRAN compiler; Pascal; C; subroutine library; considerable utilities; multitasking library	Third-party software; 77 FORTRAN; assembly language, scientific subroutine library and many utilities
Operating system	An interactive system based on UNIX called CX-OS	COS
Cost	$17.6 million	$10–15 million

Compared with CRAY-1, the next step in the evolution of supercomputers, CRAY-2, cuts processing time by more than half, from 12.5 to 4.1 nanoseconds. This advance is very significant in the business, military, government, and scientific realms in which these computing giants are needed and used. Further, the CRAY's huge memory capacity and its exceptional scalar and vector processing capabilities allow the CRAY-2 to solve problems in just minutes that previously had been simply too complex to address.

Using its state-of-the-art graphics capabilities, CRAY-2 renders its analyses into superbly detailed, informative, and often beautiful images. These pictures can be either CAD quality of the highest degree of detail or photograph-quality images statistically generated by particle systems. In the movie industry and other arenas involving video graphics, the capacity to cast millions of bits of information into visual form becomes a means of creating exquisitely detailed animated-film images.

The high cost of supercomputers such as the CRAY-2 still limits access to them, but the capability of the CRAY-2 to solve complex, multiphase problems in minutes makes it a very important supercomputer for the aerospace, petroleum, and automotive industries, and in science and engineering.

Supplement 13.5 Chip Processing Speed

A very high-speed integrated circuit (VHSIC) chip can perform multiplications of complex numbers at the rate of 100 million operations per second. To get an idea of this speed, imagine that every man, woman, and child in this country at once could multiply two complex numbers and get the answer within two seconds. A single VHSIC chip, measuring only 0.32 by 0.32 inches, could make the same number of calculations in the same time period.

The incredible speed of these chips in computing power is matched by an impressive gain in power over the current industry standard, since many more of the tiny components can be squeezed into smaller spaces than is true for less high-speed chips. Not long ago, packing thousands of transistors onto tiny squares of silicon was considered a monumental achievement, but superchips will soon hold tens of millions of transistors.

Another equally important advantage of the superchip is its tremendous precision. Up to now, computer technology has been too slow to represent radio waves. But the new superchips can represent lightning-quick phenomena precisely, in digital form.

An example are the pictures radioed back to Earth from distant planetary probes. With superchips, these images can now be processed digitally nearly as they arrive, in real-time, to remove static and interference, revealing dazzlingly clear images of planetary landscapes.

Supercomputers have drawn much attention as the cutting edge of the current revolution, but the superchip, soon to enter its second phase of development during which its speed will increase and its size diminish even further, is quietly pushing back limits on the full range of computer technology.

physical limits of speed for electronic computer hardware. The answer to increased performance may be to redesign the way computers solve problems. Since the 1940s, computer systems have been based on step-by-step, single-file sequential processing—a mode called the von Neumann approach. However, **non-von machines** that will process data in parallel are now being developed. They break problems into parts that can be worked on simultaneously. **Vector processing** is one step in this direction. Instead of processing single elements, the computer processes a one-dimensional array (a series of related items) consisting of many elements. Another non-von approach is called **pipelining**, whereby concurrent processing of data sets takes place with more than one operation performed at the same time.

Multiprocessing (two or more processing units under integrated control) and **parallel processing** (concurrent or simultaneous execution of two or more processes) are also architectures of promise. These architectures are of special interest to researchers in artificial intelligence who hope to develop systems to match human intelligence since the brain seems to work by means of parallel processing. With the dramatic drop in the cost of CPUs, the linkage of hundreds or thousands of processors working together is economically feasible. The difficulty is designing ways to divide problems in segments for multiprocessing and parallel processing and to coordinate many processors. Some machines with these architectures are already on the market. NASA's Goddard Space Flight Center uses a limited application computer built by Goodyear Aerospace called the Massively Parallel Processor with over 16,000 subprocessors. Bolt Beranek and Newman has marketed the Butterfly multiprocessors since 1984 with more than 100 subunits, and Intel has announced a 128-processor machine, the iPSC. But these machines cannot yet compete with supercomputers like those from Cray and Control Data.

Another way to increase speed may be through **optical processing**: that is, the replacement of electronics by laser light beams. Chapter 20 discusses technology under development for fifth generation computers that should also contribute to increased processing speed.

It may be some time before new technologies such as these are fully developed and implemented. Nevertheless, demand for supercomputers is on the rise. It is estimated that the supercomputer market will grow, up from forty machines shipped in 1984 to 200 annually in 1990.

Supplement 13.6 Scalar vs. Vector Processing

Von Neumann computers perform single-file sequential processing, called scalar processing. Let's examine how the computer solves the following problem using the von Neumann approach.

Calculate $C = c_1 + c_2 + c_3$

where: $a_1 + b_1 = c_1$

$a_2 + b_2 = c_2$

$a_3 + b_3 = c_3$

First, the computer adds a_1 and b_1 to get c_1. The answer is stored. Next it adds a_2 and b_2 to get c_2 and stores the answer. Then it adds a_3 and b_3 to get c_3. Finally, it calculates the sum of c_1, c_2, and c_3. Four operations are necessary to compute C.

In vector processing, all of the a's, b's and c's will be considered "vectors," and all vectors processed in one operation as follows:

In this example, the vectors are small, with only three elements each; moreover, there are only two vectors. But the technique can be used for computations in which the vectors are very large and in which there are many vectors. In such cases, the difference between vector and scalar processing can result in a significant increase in problem-solving speed.

$$\begin{vmatrix} a_1 \\ a_2 \\ a_3 \end{vmatrix} + \begin{vmatrix} b_1 \\ b_2 \\ b_3 \end{vmatrix} - \begin{vmatrix} c_1 \\ c_2 \\ c_3 \end{vmatrix} \quad \text{where } c = \begin{vmatrix} c_1 \\ c_2 \\ c_3 \end{vmatrix}$$

SUMMING UP

All types of processors contribute to engineering, science, and research—from microprocessors to supercomputers. Each serves a different function. Microprocessors are generally associated with instrumentation. The computational power of low-cost microcomputers is sufficient for many scientific problems with limited amounts of input and output. The graphics capabilities of microcomputers are also useful, as is their ability to prepare data for input into a larger computer system. Minis and mainframes are the workhorses of the scientific community. Their versatility, speed, computing power, low cost (in comparison to supercomputers), and ability to support large numbers of users (including users at remote locations connected through a telecommunications network) make them invaluable. Supercomputers are required in disciplines where massive amounts of data and complex calculations must be processed.

Workers in applied science and research benefit from the ability of computers to monitor and control instrumentation. They benefit from online computing capabilities, the computational power of the machines, and their ability to simulate the real world. Computers are no longer just tools for measurement and analysis. They have become the means for making new discoveries that may play an important role in shaping society in the future.

Until recently, supercomputers in this country were used primarily for weapons development, nuclear energy research, and weather prediction by government agencies and labs. This is changing. The demand for supercomputers is growing in commercial sectors and on college campuses. Firms that produce supercomputers are currently working to resolve two problems that limit supercomputer markets: cost and speed. Implementation of new production technologies and architectures should improve machines, help spur the sales, and increase the presence of supercomputers in and outside of scientific fields.

REVIEW QUESTIONS

1. How do computers benefit engineers, scientists, and researchers?
2. What types of computers are appropriate for scientific work? Discuss the benefits of each class.
3. Why do many scientific labs rely on mainframes? Why not purchase supercomputers since they are more powerful than mainframes?

4. Cite examples of engineering or scientific projects that use computers for:
   a. instrumentation
   b. online computing
   c. computational power
   d. simulation
   Explain how computers benefit the projects.
5. What are the advantages and disadvantages of using computer simulation?
6. Explain why many experts believe that science today is being restructured as a result of changed methodology.
7. Explain the change taking place in supercomputer use. Why is this change significant?
8. What factors hinder expanded use of supercomputers?
9. What new technologies are being researched and developed to increase the speed of computers?
10. What is a non-von machine?
11. Would the workstation for an engineer or scientist differ from that of an office worker? How?
12. Why do we need faster supercomputers?

DISCUSSION QUESTIONS

1. How does scientific processing differ from nonscientific processing? Give examples to illustrate this difference.
2. Are there special computing resources needed for simulation? What are they?
3. What computing facilities are appropriate for
   a. a professor of science?
   b. an engineer employed by a large firm?
   c. a researcher in a defense establishment?
   d. a researcher at the National Institutes of Health?
4. What are the economic, social, and political implications of computer use by:
   a. scientists?
   b. engineers?
   c. researchers?
5. Do you think that American leadership in the production of supercomputers is important? Explain your position.
6. Do you believe that the U.S. government should provide subsidies for supercomputer research?
7. Should the government provide a network of computing facilities for the use of scientists, researchers, and engineers? If so, what facilities should be available? How should these facilities be funded?
8. Why are the current crop of university graduates often called "the VAX generation"?
9. Give examples of commercial applications of supercomputers.
10. How have computers revolutionized the way engineers design and test products?
11. Does your university need a supercomputer? Why?
12. What is the relevance of supercomputers to national defense?

EXERCISES

1. Give examples of computer use in:
   a. chemistry
   b. graphics
   c. medical research
   d. structural analysis
   e. astronomy
   f. geophysics
   g. aerospace
   h. weather forecasting
   i. oil reservoir modeling
   j. automobile engineering
   k. particle physics
   l. defense
2. Visit a computer facility dedicated to engineering, science, or research. List the com-

puter resources at the facility and describe how they are used.

3. Interview a politician at the state or national level regarding the role government should play in the supercomputer race. Get specifics on policy and legislation the politician favors (or opposes).

4. Interview a student on your campus who is engaged in a scientific, engineering, or research project that uses computers. What problems does the student have getting computer time? Are adequate computing facilities available for the project? How could student access to computing resources be improved?

5. Interview a scientist or engineer (may be a faculty member) doing research using a computer workstation. What are the desirable features of the workstation?

Selected Annotated Bibliography

Alexander, Tom. "Computing with Light at Lightning Speeds," *Fortune*, vol. 10, no. 2 (July 23, 1984), pp. 82–88. Alexander predicts that soon light waves will replace electronics in computers and will help reduce the cost of processing. He also believes this emerging technology will crunch numbers faster than today's supercomputers.

Bak, Per. "Doing Physics with Microcomputers," *Physics Today*, vol. 26, no. 12 (December 1983), pp. 25–29. Bak argues that microcomputers (including personal computers at home) can do large-scale computations in physics with reduction in costs and increase in convenience to the researcher over mainframe use.

Chamberland, Dennis. "Amateur Astronomy and the Home Computer," *Astronomy*, vol. 11, no. 8 (August 1983), pp. 75–77. This article describes the use of microcomputers for computation and also for station keeping (maintaining logs, word processing, and output displays.) In addition, the author discusses how a microcomputer DBMS gives users problem-solving capabilities involving a large data base without requiring a mini or mainframe.

Davis, Dwight B. "Super Computers: A Strategic Imperative," *High Technology*, vol. 4, no. 5 (May 1984), pp. 44–53. Supercomputer features, including multiprocessing and pipelining, are discussed. The importance of supercomputers to government and universities is also examined.

Enke, C. G. "Computers in Scientific Instrumentations," *Science*, vol. 215, no. 4534 (February 1982), pp. 785–91. The ease of operation and degree of functional adaptability of computer interfaces for instruments are examined.

Freedman, David H. "Supercomputers Get Ready to Muscle into the Mainframe's Territory," *Infosystems*, vol. 31, no. 9 (September 1984), pp. 72–76. Supercomputers for data base manipulation as well as for numerical computation are being developed. The article discusses the commercial market for such machines and problems in their development.

Fullenwider, Ronald R. and Lefever, James P. "Computer Graphics and the Practice of Architecture." *IEEE Computer Graphic Applications*, vol. 1, no. 4 (October 1981), pp. 18–26. Excellent photographs and a well-written commentary explain how computers are used in the firm Albert C. Martin and Associates.

Houston, Tom R. "Why Models Go Wrong," *Byte*, vol. 10, no. 10 (October 1985), pp. 151–64. This article describes what a model is, how computers contribute to modeling, and some of the incorrect ways to develop or use models.

Hudson, C. A. "Computer Evolution," *Science*, vol. 215, no. 4534 (February 1982), pp. 818–25. CAD, CAM, and the emergence of other engineering systems are described.

Johnsen, Gregory. "Gallium Arsenide Chips Emerge from the Lab." *High Technology*, vol. 4, no. 7 (July 1984), pp. 44–51. The state of the art of gallium arsenide chips is examined. So are current applications and potential of the chips.

Johnson, Jan. "CRAY and CDC Meet the Japanese," *Datamation*, vol. 30, no. 4 (April 1, 1984), pp. 32–42. American and Japanese supercomputers are compared. The article also discusses design strategies in the two countries and evaluates prospects of domination at the "super" end of the market.

Karplus, Walter J. "The Spectrum of Mathematical Models," *Perspectives in Computing*, vol. 3, no. 2 (May 1983), pp. 4–13. A good discussion of mathematical modeling problems encountered in various scientific disciplines. Includes many good diagrams on different models.

Mulvey, John M. "Computer Modeling for State Use: Implications for Professional Responsibility," *IEEE Technology and Society Magazine*, vol. 2, no. 2 (June 1983), pp. 3–8. Computer modeling in state and federal agencies is discussed.

Metcalf, Michael. "The Role of Computing in High-Energy Physics," *Perspectives in Computing*, vol. 3, no. 4 (December 1983), pp. 20–31. Applications of computers in high-energy physics range from aiding in the design of accelerators and controlling their operation to online signal analysis, data analysis, and network communication.

Perspectives in Computing, Armonk, N.Y.: IBM Corp. This is a journal addressed to academia in scientific, engineering, and research work. Started in 1980 by IBM and issued quarterly, the journal includes many excellent and detailed articles on computer use, with colored illustrations when appropriate. Each issue includes a matrix identifying disciplines (y-axis) and articles (x-axis) of all issues.

Preiss, K. "Future CAD Systems," *Computer-Aided Design*, vol. 15, no. 5 (July 1983), pp. 223–27. A look into the future of a very important subject to all engineers and production personnel.

Stahr, Lisa B. "Working with Statistical Analysis," *Personal Computing*, vol. 8, no. 10 (October 1984), pp. 73–83. Packaged software for statistical analysis that is widely used by scientists and statisticians was once found only for mainframes and minis. Today such packages are also available for microcomputers and can produce graphics in color.

Sulentic, Jack W. "The Magic of Image Processing," *Sky and Telescope*, vol. 67, no. 5 (May 1984), pp. 407–11. An excellent article on computer enhancement techniques for image processing of stars and planets by computer. A diagram of the equipment is provided, as are excellent photographs of output.

Watts, J. W. and Peaceman, D. W. "The Simulation of Petroleum Reservoirs," *Perspectives in Computing*, vol. 5, no. 1 (Spring 1985), pp. 14–23. Mathematical modeling helps petroleum engineers estimate how much oil and gas can be produced from a subsurface reservoir under a variety of operating conditions.

Microcomputers on the March: Use at Home and at Work

The universe is full of magical things patiently waiting for our wits to grow sharper.

EDEN PHILLPOTTS

CHAPTER FOURTEEN

Key Words

back-end processor	in-house videotex systems	remote data base
bulletin board	mainframe terminal emulation	selection
CAI package	micro	small businesses
electronic news	microcomputer	teletex
front-end processor	modem	training
game packages	networks	videotex
home computer	personal computer (PC)	Viewtron
home management	Prestel	word processing
	professionals	
	protocol	

Microcomputers are small but complete microprocessor-based computer systems. They include a CPU, memory, input and output devices, interfaces, and a power supply. Microcomputers come in a wide variety of models, ranging from desktop size to portables that fit in a briefcase. In 1982, the market was dominated by 8-bit machines typically limited to 64K RAM and costing from $3000 to $5000. By the late 1980s, it is estimated that 32-bit, 256 and 512K microcomputers will be the norm, although price will remain roughly the same as at the start of the decade. Advances in technology are reducing the cost of microcomputer components at the same time that computing power is increasing.

Microcomputers are sold for home and business use. This chapter will describe common applications in both environments. The chapter will also look into the future to describe potential applications once a national communications infrastructure is available to link microcomputers with distant mainframes and data bases.

HOW MICROCOMPUTERS ARE USED AT HOME

In the late 1970s, low-priced microcomputers designed for family games and home management were put on the market. These machines were called **personal computers (PCs)** or **home computers** to distinguish them from microcomputer models customized for business applications. At first, buyers of home computers were primarily computer hobbyists and people with a computing background. They were challenged both by the potential of personal computers and their limitations. Their prior computer experience enabled them to make the systems run in spite of program bugs and poor documentation.

Soon, however, manufacturers began selling personal computers for home use to persons with no computing background. This group of customers requires systems that are easy to install, operate, update, and maintain. And since they lack programming skills, these users need off-the-shelf program packages. The computer industry has put a great deal of effort into the development of user-friendly systems for home use with the expectation that personal computers will someday be as commonplace as the family TV.

Sales of personal computers have been dampened, however, by the fact that many owners of PCs have broadcast their dissatisfaction with their pur-

Supplement 14.1 Comparison of Four Well-known Microcomputers as of 1985

	HP 110	Apple IIe	TRS-80	IBM PC XT
Manufacturer	Hewlett Packard	Apple Computer Inc.	Tandy Corp.	IBM
Purchase price	$2995	$1295	$219 without monitor	$4275
Memory size in bytes (min-max)	272K	64–128K	16–64K	256–640K
Address space	16-bit	8-bit	8-bit	16-bit
Operating system	MS-DOS	Apple Dos/ ProDos	Tandy or OS-9	PC-DOS, CP/M UCSD-Pascal
Input/output ports	2	10	2	1
Input/output channel speed* (bits/sec.)	5K	19.2K	300K	9600K

*Rate at which data can be transmited from and to peripherals.

chases. Often disappointment can be traced to the unrealistic expectations that the computer industry itself has fostered in the public. Certainly PC advertising implies that no intellectual labor is required to master a personal computer. Ads also give the impression that persons can effortlessly control their environment by installing a PC.

It is true that the steps involved in turning on a PC and loading it for game playing are simple. But use of a home computer as a word processor or as a tool of home management requires **training**. Users must wade through self-instruction manuals, attend personal computer classes, or seek help from the vendor who sold them their machine.

A recent training innovation has been the development of computer-based tutorials that are integrated with the software itself. A "help" code will bring a menu to the screen asking what type of help is needed. Perhaps the user of a word processing package doesn't know how to change margins, for example. When "Margins" is selected in the help menu, a window will open up on the screen explaining how margins are set. This training concept should make it easier to use home computers and improve customer satisfaction in the process.

At the present time, personal computers used in the home serve five major functions: they are used for playing games, for word processing, for home management, for CAI, and for communicating with data base services.

Games

Hundreds of **game packages** are on the market. Many are video adventures. For example, one can bring survivors to safety from a city under attack, search for gold and diamond treasure, rule an island surrounded by rebels and pirates, stage a helicopter rescue of delegates to a UN conference, or maneuver through a maze while avoiding monsters.

Strategy games, such as chess, checkers, and Go, are also popular. One version of chess has nine skill levels. Players can begin with opening moves (choosing either black or white), or they can set up board positions mid-game and continue to play from there.

Other games simulate an environment. A player can be an air traffic controller and direct both landings and takeoffs, or a tycoon trying to save a failing automobile empire.

The computer industry favors games, which have been a good source of revenue and have brought computers into the home. Children who play video games do not feel threatened by computer technology as so many of their parents do. In all likelihood, computer literacy will not be a problem when today's game players grow up.

Word Processing

Until quite recently, few families bought personal computers because they wanted **word processing**; instead, they would buy word processing packages after they purchased a PC for playing games. In the last few years, however, that pattern is changing as the all-around value of word processing is gaining in recognition. In the home, a word processing package can be used for correspondence, school term papers, Christmas card address lists, recipe storage, and club minutes and handouts, to name just a few applications. The family typewriter collects dust since it is far easier to produce mistake-free copy on a microcomputer. Another advantage of word processing is that a written document can be stored in computer memory for later retrieval. (For a full discussion of the advantages of word processing, refer to Chapter 7.)

Home Management

Personal computers can serve **home management** needs of users. The most popular type of program in this category is the financial package: that is, a package that will help with budgeting, bookkeeping, income tax preparation, and investment portfolio analysis. When family expenditures are input on a PC instead of being entered into a ledger book, the computer can keep track of information such as yearly income, credit card expenses, loan amortization, percent of total income spent on specific budget items, and checking and savings account balances. (See Figure 14.1.)

A number of diet and nutrition programs are available for families as well. One program suggests recipes for leftovers. Another calculates metabolic rates and caloric needs based on sex, height, age, and weight. PCs can also serve as an appointment calendar or a log for phone messages.

Figure 14.1 A home computer system. This user is organizing the household finances. (Atari)

Microcomputers can be be designed and programmed to respond to sensor signals for the control of home lighting, security, and heating and cooling systems. Indeed, computer control of this sort may become standard in homes of the future. More on this subject appears in Chapter 20.

Computer-Aided Instruction (CAI)

Although parents and grandparents often purchase CAI programs, learning programs are low on the wish list of most children. As a category, games are much more popular than **CAI packages** for home use.

The market for CAI is growing, however. Sales of CAI packages for adults, in particular, are increasing. In many technical subjects, information becomes obsolete after a few years. Professionals in such fields must constantly upgrade and update their knowledge. The home computer can provide self-paced instruction as an alternative to traditional classroom learning.

The problem with CAI for many adults is that it requires a great deal of self-discipline. Without the routine of classes, the need to study for scheduled exams, and teacher-student contact, it is often difficult to keep up one's motivation. For many adults, however, the convenience of learning at home outweighs the disadvantages of CAI.

Access to Remote Data Bases

Another popular way to use a PC is to access information of public interest from a **remote data base**. Data base services work by storing information in a host computer and financing the collection and storage of this information through an access fee charged to customers.

In order to access a data base, users must establish a telecommunications link between their microcomputers and the data base. In a typical setup, the user's microcomputer connects to the host computer of the data base service through a **modem**. The modem converts analog signals coming through a telephone line to digital signals that can be read by the user's home terminal and vice versa. Although telephone lines and modems are currently the most widely used telecommunications link, cable television, optical fibers, or satellite may also be used as the transmission mode. (Chapter 3 discusses modems and the telecommunications process in greater detail.)

The modem itself is commonly bought by users. It can also be built into microcomputer equipment at the time of manufacture. Data services charge customers a user's fee for access to information in their data bases. This may be a monthly fixed rate or it may be based on actual connect time to the host computer of the data service.

There are hundreds of database services to which PC users can subscribe. Among the more common are CompuServe, Dow Jones News/Retrieval Service, Newsnet, Dialog, and The Source. CompuServe has over 200 information categories that range from wine and food to electronics and communications. CompuServe subscribers can also send electronic messages to one another through the service's network. Messages can also be left on electronic **bulletin boards**, which are essentially files devoted to specified topics. Subscribers can add information or comments to the bulletin board file for others to read.

Newsnet allows users to pick key words relating to topics of interest; the service's computer will then find articles related to that topic. Dow Jones appeals to persons interested in financial news. Its more than 150,000 subscribers can access a data base containing stories of general interest reported by the media for that day, or they can read the *Academic American Encyclopedia*, the *Wall Street Journal*, or *Barrons*. A software service enables subscribers to chart performance of stocks and update and evaluate portfolios using the News/Retrieval Service. See Supplement 14.2 for a description of other public data bases.

Teletex and **videotex** are terms used to describe data services that include graphics-based data communications. The difference between the two is that teletex is a one-way service whereas videotex is interactive, allowing users to both send and receive information. For example, after viewing stock market prices, the videotex user might place a buy order. Figure 14.2 helps illustrate this difference. In addition, there are hybrid systems that consist of a one-way broadcast signal to a teletex receiver with return communication through the telephone.

Prestel was one of the first videotex services available to the public. It was initiated in 1979 in Great Britain. The system today provides over 180,000 pages of information on shopping, entertainment, exhibitions, gardening, travel, and news. Prestel is accessed from a family television, not a personal computer. This means that information access is not combined with general-purpose computing.

The system works as follows. Users have a numeric keyboard that connects to their TV, a device that resembles a TV remote control unit and calculator combined. They select the information they want from menus (index pages) that appear on the screen. First a general menu is displayed. This leads to more specific menus as users indicate their choices by pressing keys on the keyboard. (Figure 14.3 shows a sample of the tree structure used in programming the sequence of menus.)

In 1983, a similar service called **Viewtron** was introduced in south Florida. The terminal used by Viewtron consists of two parts: a small control unit that plugs into a phone jack and the family TV, and a wireless keypad. The price of the terminal in 1984

Supplement 14.2 Public Online Data Bases

An online data base is generally understood to be a collection of records held in computer storage from which users can retrieve information rapidly and immediately upon request from a terminal linked to the database computer by telecommunications. The records are commonly the machine-readable version of an abstracting or indexing journal, but they may be fact and numeric data bases as well. Accessed information may be displayed on the user's terminal screen or the information can be printed and mailed to the user.

In January 1984 there were over 1,700 public data bases available to users for a fee. And this number is growing. In the last six months of 1983 alone, more than 133 new data bases were added to the list.

The following is a brief description of sample online public data bases. They have been chosen to illustrate the range of topics and specialities available. The number of bibliographic records available online is impressive: over forty million unique references in the early 1980s, with an annual update rate of over six million more. This represents a resource pool far larger than most libraries can match.

- *Agistar.* Farm news, weather reports, market analysis from *Farm Future* and commodity prices. Updated every ten minutes.
- *Artbibliographies modern.* Art theory, ceramics, drawing, folk art, furniture, glass, interior design, painting, photography, prints, sculptures, textiles, town and country planning, and water color painting. Updated every six months.
- *ASI (American Statistics Index).* All statistical publications originating from the Federal government from 1973, updated monthly.
- *Balance of payments.* Contains over 60,000 quarterly and annual tabulations compiled by the International Monetary Fund for its 115 members.
- *BOOKSINFO (Books Information).* English language books in print in the U.S.A. from 1960, updated monthly.
- *CLAIMS/CLASS (Class codes, Assignee, Index, Method Search/Classification).* Index to the U.S. Patent Classification Scheme, from 1950, updated annually.
- *Dow Jones News/Retrieval.* Business, economics and management news and articles from *Dow Jones News Service, Barron's, New York Times,* and the *Wall Street Journal.* Contains a ninety-day file, updated daily.
- *Federal Index.* United States federal activities and public policy. Abstracts from *Congressional Record, Federal Register, Weekly Compilation of Federal Documents, Washington Post, Code of Federal Regulations, United States Code.* From 1976, updated weekly.
- *Magazine Index.* Cover-to-cover indexing of over 370 magazines from 1976, updated monthly.
- *MEDLINE.* Medicine and a wide range of related sub-fields as represented by the *Index Medicus* categorized list of medical subject headings. From 1977, updated monthly.
- *NASA (National Aeronautics and Space Administration).* Printed version, *Scientific and Technical Aerospace Reports* and *International Aerospace Abstracts,* from 1962, updated weekly.
- *Newsearch.* Daily index to articles, performance reviews, product listings, and news in nearly 400 American newspapers, magazines, and periodicals. Contains current month data, updated daily.
- *Sport.* Bibliographical information on international sport, physical education, recreation, and sport medicine. Includes over 80,000 citations from 1975, updated quarterly.
- *TOXLINE (Toxicology Information Online).* Includes information on drug chemistry, environmental pollutants, pesticides, pharmacology, teratology, from 1974, updated monthly.

Among the more common information service suppliers for online data bases are:

BRS (Bibliographic Retrieval Services)
Dow Jones
IRS (Information Retrieval Service)
Lockheed DIALOG (Lockheed Information Systems)
NLM (National Library of Medicine)
NYT (New York Times Information Service)
SDC ORBIT (System Development Corporation)

was $900: the monthly subscription rate, $12. In addition, telephone line charges of approximately one dollar per hour of access time were billed customers by Southern Bell. Viewtron plans to extend services to thirty-five metropolitan areas once it is established in Florida.

Other teletex and videotex services exist in the United States, but like Viewtron, they are still largely experimental. Further development of these services is currently hindered by a kind of double-bind: in order for such services to be economical, they must have a mass market; but before a mass market can be established, teletex and videotex must become economical. One way to help break this cycle is to develop standards for encoding graphic information. At the present time, six different videotex **protocols**—that is, the procedures or conventions used between communicating devices, such as terminals and computers

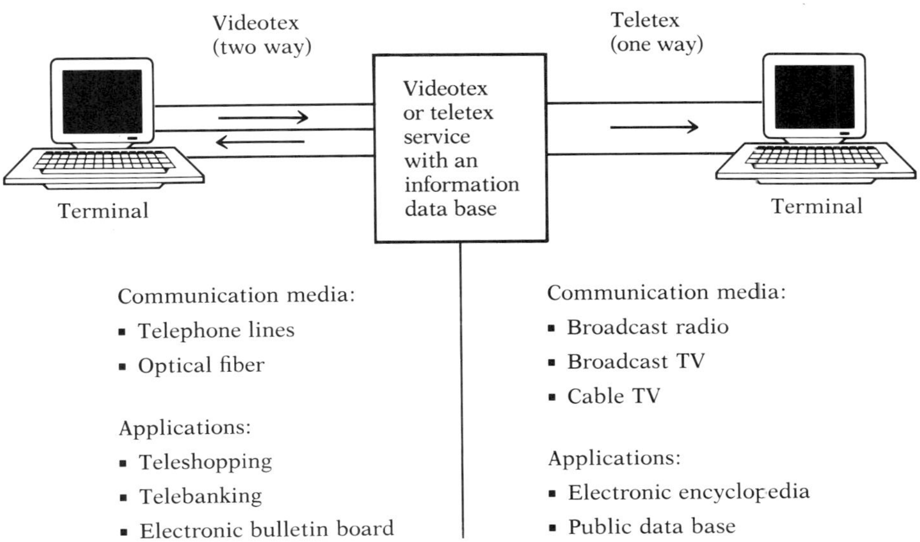

Figure 14.2 Comparison of Videotex and Teletex.

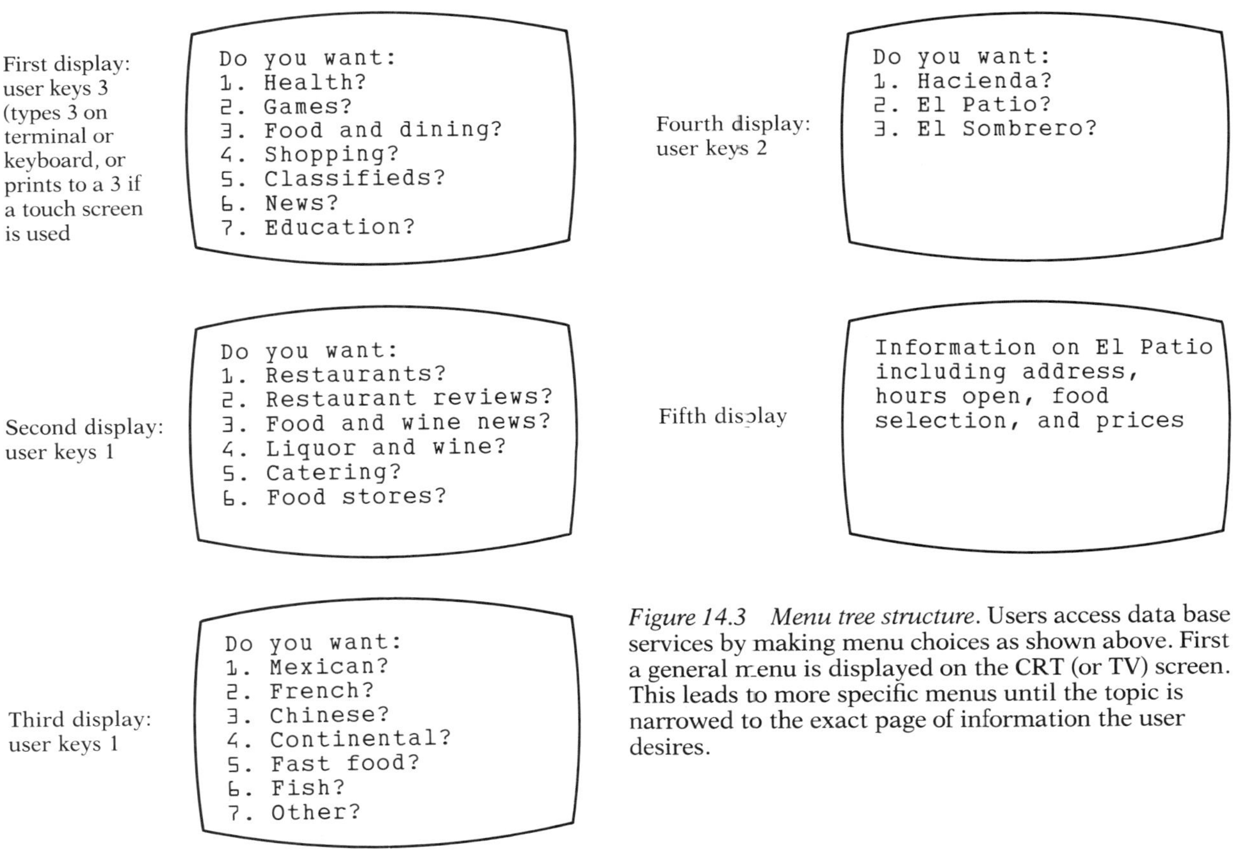

Figure 14.3 Menu tree structure. Users access data base services by making menu choices as shown above. First a general menu is displayed on the CRT (or TV) screen. This leads to more specific menus until the topic is narrowed to the exact page of information the user desires.

—are in use worldwide. This means that users cannot benefit from economies of scale and that they are limited in the services they can receive from a given equipment configuration.

PCs should not be viewed as competitors of videotex. On the contrary, growth in the PC market should broaden the base of potential videotex customers since PCs can be adapted to become videotex terminals. Data services like Dow Jones and CompuServe may provide information in the form of graphics and interactive services in the future, thus becoming true videotex systems.

In 1984, IBM, CBS, and Sears announced a joint venture in the videotex business. The system will send data to CRT screens, not TVs. Such a venture should promote IBM PCs and provide a market in which Sears can electronically merchandise its catalog and financial services. CBS will contribute its own experience with advertisers, news, textbook publishing, and educational software operations. This is an example of a videotex service that is being designed exclusively for the personal computer market.

HOW MICROCOMPUTERS ARE USED ON THE JOB

Since personal computers were introduced, they have increased in computing power and memory, making them useful machines for work. Today the terms "microcomputer" and "personal computer" have become interchangeable. Indeed, in terms of sales, far more machines called PCs by their manufacturers are purchased by organizations than by families for games and household management. (Note that the term **micro**, the shortened form of "microcomputer," is also used in computer literature to refer to a "microprocessor." The dual meaning of the term can be confusing.)

PCs for Professional and Small Operations

Authors are turning to the word processing capabilities of personal computers for writing articles and books. Salespeople use PCs to update financial

- *Accounting functions:* general ledger, accounts receivable/payable, FICA reports, W-2 forms, aging report, balance sheets, funds flow worksheets, cash requirements report, daily voucher report, transaction history.
- *Budget planner:* cash-flow projection based on changes in accounts receivable, inventory levels.
- *Property analysis system:* make appreciation and inflation estimates; generate ten-year schedules showing equity buildup, estimated appreciation, tax benefits, cash flow, return on investment.
- *Orders:* reports of open and back orders; order correction, on-hold orders, active orders, order confirmations, invoices; sales orders, salesmen commission, house profit tracked.
- *Payroll:* calculate hourly and monthly salaries; print checks including year-to-date deductions on stubs; master employee list; monthly recap of deductions, payroll subtotals, withholding, state and federal reports; overtime reports, absentee reports.
- *Taxes:* depreciation, amortization, multiple schedule C's and F's; support federal income tax schedules; "What if?" tax planner.
- *Inventory:* sales, returns, orders, receipts, cancelled orders; inventory scrap, loss, physical count; price list, status report, valuation; low stock, slow-moving; profitability by item, product group analysis, current inventory analysis.

Figure 14.4 Sample PC business programs.

records and prepare summary reports. In fact, a growing list of **professionals**—including, for example, consultants, insurance agents, accountants, and computer programmers—are discovering that work on a PC terminal at home is more productive than a long commute, jangling phones, and constant interruptions that are part of work in a corporate office. (Chapter 17 discusses the topic of telecommuting in detail.)

The computing power of a PC is appropriate for many **small businesses** as well. (In 1984, a microcomputer with random access memory of 256K, 10MB hard disk storage, a monitor and printer, plus general business software could be purchased for $6,000 to $11,000. For a small business with fewer than ten employees and monthly sales averaging about $20,000, such a system is quite adequate. (See Figure 14.4 for a list of some of the financial functions that can be performed on a PC.)

Supplement 14.3 Information Processing Industry Market Trends

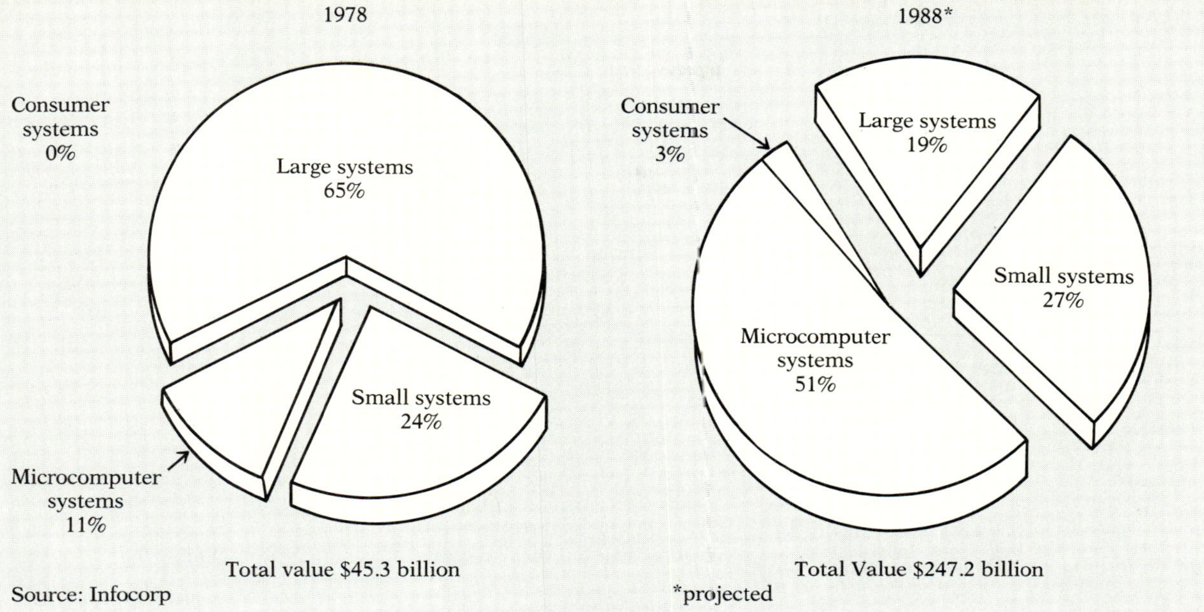

PC programs have also been designed for special purposes and particular groups. For example, one can purchase software packages for:

- *Billing and timekeeping.* Time and services are input, and the computer prepares bills according to a predetermined rate schedule. Designed for attorneys, consultants, and other professionals.
- *Church management.* Keeps lists of congregation members (names, addresses, and so on), prepares church directory, forecasts financial needs, tracks contributions, prepares contribution summary, and prepares tax records of church donations for members.
- *Construction management.* Provides job costing, budgeting, and financial statements.
- *School management.* Schedules classes; prints report cards, honor rolls, transcripts, class rosters, mailing labels, student data sheets; keeps records of textbooks, supplies, equipment; processes financial data.
- *Apartment house management.* Keeps records on every apartment and tenant, status of apartment, general journal of expenses and rents; generates monthly profit/loss statements, rent rolls, form letters, leases, renewals, nonpayment notices, terminations.
- *Harbor management.* Keeps master file of slips, moorings, and rental units; tracks rent due; prints statements; keeps accounts receivable records.
- *Employment agency consulting.* Keeps job description file and candidate data base to match needs of clients with candidate experience, salary, and education.
- *Architectural consulting and business management.* Draws maps and building perspectives; evaluates and structures rental projects (to calculate, for example, profits at full occupancy, operating expenses); analyzes beams, design, walls structure, heating and cooling load, lighting, and acoustics. Also used for project cost accounting, word processing, site analysis (for example, building size and parking relationships), and land evaluation.

The Use of PCs in Two Sample Occupations

To get a better feel for the usefulness of microcomputers on the job, let's take a closer look at how PCs are used in two particular kinds of work: farming and law practice.

Table 14.1 Sample agricultural networks

Name of service	Source of database software	Mode of service	Nature of service offered	Geographic range of service
Agnet	University of Nebraska	Online real-time interactive	200 applications (e.g. Beef Grower [cost of weight gain], Crop Budget [determine cost of production of various crops], Buyland [estimating economic value of land])	40 states and some foreign countries
CMN (*C*omputerized *M*anagement *N*etwork)	Virginia Polytech Institute	Online real-time, accessible at all times	70 application programs for farmers, bankers, extension specialists	44 states and Canada 500 users
FACTS	Purdue University	Online Interactive	Specialized on crop and livestock	
Comnet	University of Michigan	Online Interactive	Applications for extension agents and individual farmers	20 states
Agistar	Agri Data Resources, Inc. (private sector) Used by Commodity News Service	Update every 10 minutes on cattle, farm futures, grain, etc.	Information for farmers and ranchers to help planting and harvesting Analysis and advice using market data and commodity prices	Nationwide access

Farmers can use a PC to keep health and breeding records of stock. They can use the computational power of a microcomputer to establish a least-cost feeding program or least-cost pesticide and fertilizer mix. As in most businesses, farmers have a need for inventory lists, machine maintenance schedules, and financial records, all of which can be processed on a PC.

A telecommunications link to remote data bases is of particular value to farmers. The latest weather forecast is essential in deciding when to harvest, just as the latest commodity prices are valuable in deciding when to sell. In addition, most farmers and ranchers rely on universities and agribusiness firms for assistance in farm management and planning. Agricultural **networks** use electronics to bring information to the farm. (See Table 14.1 for a partial listing of agricultural data base services.) Agnet, one such service, has more than 200 management and information programs in its library. Any standard terminal that operates at either 300 or 1200 baud can access this service. Agnet also handles messages. Should grasshoppers become a problem, farmers in affected areas can be notified of infestation levels and spraying schedules through electronic bulletin boards and mailboxes.

Lawyers constitute another group which has been using microcomputers to cut costs and increase efficiency. A very powerful PC with letter-quality word processing capability could be purchased for between \$2100 and \$7000 in 1984. The PC can be used for routine correspondence and the preparation of long documents that require extensive editing, like negotiated contracts. The ability of a word processor to store paragraphs for wills, trust agreements, property settlements, and leases, means that lawyers do not have to prepare these repetitive documents from scratch for each new client.

Lawyers also purchase financial packages to run on their PCs: general ledger, payroll, timekeeping and billing, and programs to handle trust accounts. Database management programs are popular as well. They facilitate administrative tasks such as file management and information retrieval. A DBMS package enables the staff in a

Figure 14.5 An instant tailgate office. The portable computer extends a firm's computing capabilities to the job-site, airplanes, taxicabs—anywhere. (Data General Corporation)

law office to key information like client and case data just once, and then sort, select, and use that information in reports without having to rekey it.

With a communications link, attorneys can access legal information through online data bases like Westlaw and Lexis, the ABA/net, and Dialog. Dialog's data base, for example, includes a "Legal Resources Index" that contains more than 660 legal periodicals, newspapers, and magazines published since January 1980. Electronic bulletin boards enable a lawyer to ask for information from other lawyers with experience in specific fields. Specialized software packages for PCs are available for estate tax planning, for real estate closings, or preparation of immigration and naturalization forms, to name just a few.

Law and farming are just two of the many occupations in which speed, accuracy, storage capacity, processing capabilitiy, and communications facilities of microcomputers help cut costs, improve information access, and upgrade performance. (See Figure 14.5.)

Microcomputers in Large Organizations

The use of microcomputers is not limited to small organizations and businesses. Personal computers are challenging the high-budget areas of mainframe computers in corporate settings, governmental agencies, and large organizations as well.

Let's take a look at the advantages and disadvantages of microcomputers when they are used in large organizations. We will also briefly review the applications in these settings for which microcomputers are most appropriate. Finally, we will describe a technology that makes it possible to get the best of both worlds by combining the advantages of using microcomputers with those of mainframe computing.

Advantages The primary advantages of personal computers in the setting of a large organization have to do with cost to management and convenience for workers. A microcomputer on a worker's desk costs little more than a terminal for a large computer. Five users can be supplied with PCs plus printers for less than $25,000. To provide the same computing capacity on a large, heavily loaded computer might require supplemental hardware costing as much as $500,000. In the context of sums of this sort, a single application can often justify the purchase of a PC.

Furthermore, runtime on a mainframe is more costly than runtime on a PC, which is limited to the cost of electricity. Mistakes or runaway jobs that can wreak havoc with mainframe schedules, causing many users to suffer, affect only one user on a personal computer.

A third advantage of microcomputers is that users have complete control over their hardware, software, and data. They can run jobs at their own convenience and do not have to ask anyone's permission for computer access. They are not dependent on computer center schedules, are not required to justify projects to computer center personnel, and not forced to wait until a request for service rises to the top of a priority list. In certain domains microcomputer software packages are excellent. In recent years, software developers have greatly refined word processing systems, small data base systems, mail merge systems, spreadsheets, and interactive languages like BASIC.

Supplement 14.4 How One Restaurant Chain Uses a Microcomputer Network

A microcomputer/electronic cash register network has been installed at Studebaker's restaurant chain. Waitresses and bartenders use the electronic cash registers located behind the bar and in the lounge to keep running subtotals of client tabs. The microcomputer uses the data to process reports on gross, net, and total sales, average sales by department, and type of payment (cash, credit card, and house charge). The network can also track sales by individual staff members or register stations. In addition, managers can access information such as hourly sales or sales per brand of drink on a continuous and immediate basis.

The information provided by Studebaker's microcomputer network is used to make adjustments in restaurant service. The floor plan may be altered or waitress assignments changed during peak hours. A link to the home office mainframe lets executives know how well each branch is doing. The home office also centralizes accounting functions for the chain, including payroll, inventory by location, general ledger, and accounts payable and receivable.

Finally, microcomputers are convenient to buy and install. No lengthy appropriation process is necessary when purchasing a microcomputer. Both hardware and software are generally available through local vendors for immediate delivery. The equipment can be plugged in wherever there is an electric outlet. No special wiring or air conditioning is required. And perhaps most important of all, the user does not need extensive training to operate a microcomputer. Employees with prior experience using computers have no difficulty mastering a PC.

Disadvantages Despite all the advantages of personal computers, however, microcomputers will never replace mainframes because of their limitations. PCs are poor at moving large amounts of data. They cannot sort hundreds of thousands of records, an essential function in much business processing. They also lack the processing speed and memory capacity to handle complex problems.

Another more general disadvantage of using a microcomputer is that software packages are seldom exactly what a user wants. Yet making modifications to existing software, or writing a new program, is difficult and time consuming. Highly paid executives with microcomputers on their desks may wind up spending much of their time being data entry clerks, programmers, and machine operators. Some PC users get attacks of "analysis paralysis." They become so engrossed in the process of getting information out of a computer that they forget exactly what information they needed in the first place.

Another problem is that because microtechnology is advancing rapidly, PC hardware and software quickly become dated. Users find that new software won't run on old hardware or old software on new hardware.

Finally, microcomputers are difficult to control in a large organization. Maintenance is a problem when a mix of models and manufacturers are purchased. Data processing personnel are often at a loss to help users. How can they be expected to have expertise with dozens of different microcomputer brands? Security is an issue when no central authority monitors access to secrets and use of confidential data. Disks that should be locked in a safe may be carelessly stowed in a desk drawer. And PCs themselves can be easily stolen.

Application Areas Given these advantages and limitations, for what activities is a microcomputer appropriate in a large organization? The answer is that microcomputers are in fact appropriate for many isolated applications and for segments of larger processes. They are appropriate, for example, for handling financial calculations required to make decisions in tax planning, mergers and acquisitions, or investments. They are also appropriate for sorting and cross-referencing notes in product development, marketing, and sales, and for processing personal files of employees that contain data not useful to others in the organization. Project managers find microcomputers useful in scheduling work assignments and keeping track of

Supplement 14.5 Sample Network Configuration for Microcomputers and Mainframes

A broadband local area network (LAN) can connect microcomputers and terminals with varying equipment configurations in different departments in an organization. A broadband LAN allows the integration of data, voice, and video on the network.

This building has on its roof facilities for microwave and satellite communications. Buildings such as these are considered teleports.

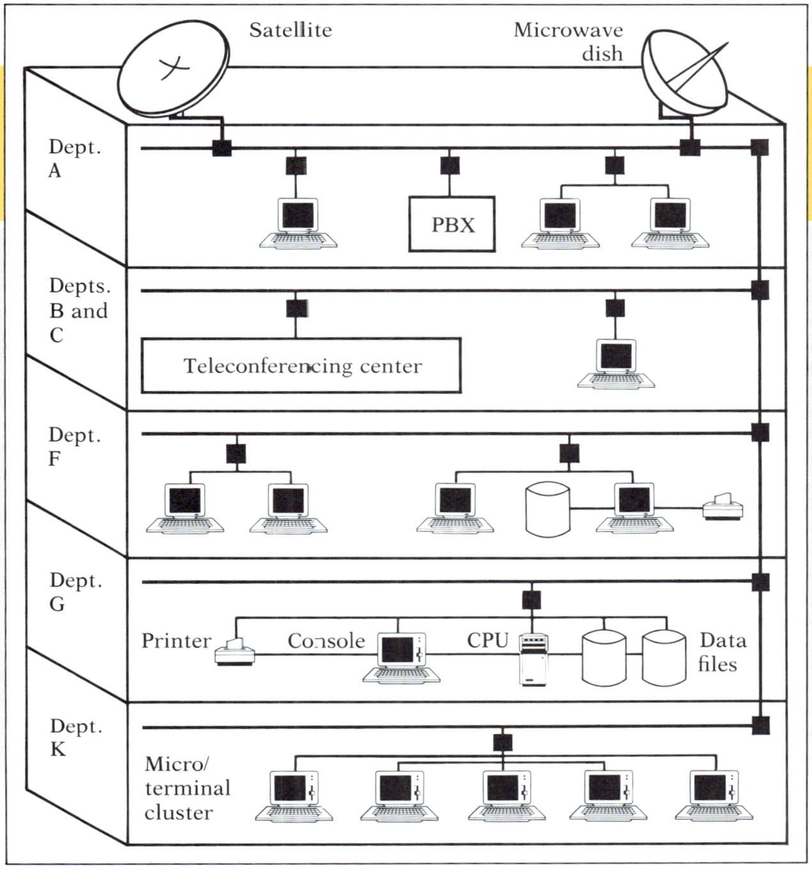

development costs; secretaries, in handling correspondence and preparing reports; foremen, in tracking tools and work-in-progress. In addition, microcomputers can serve as terminals for electronic mail; they can perform the function of electronic filing; and they can assist in personal administrative functions like message and calendar management.

Teletex and videotex, the graphics-based data base services described earlier in this chapter, also assist employees in their jobs. Two companies that have implemented **in-house videotex systems** are IBM and DEC. DEC's service is used primarily to access catalogs of printed material, including hardware manuals, sales promotion literature, and business forms. A user of DEC's system can punch in an order of selected catalog items which the central computer will in turn print as a shipping order.

Business use of videotex is particularly well suited to situations in which access to information will lead to a transaction, such as a phone call, letter, or purchase. The information displayed by a videotex system might be name lists, addresses, stock quotes, items for sale, or classified ads. Videotex might also be used to access facts, numbers, survey and financial information, or market projections. This information could serve as background or be used directly in decision making.

Access to a public data base is also possible from PCs within an organization. A service such as Dialog or The Source provides information of general interest, such as newspaper articles and reports—information that may be useful on the job.

Organizations with an inventory of old application systems that need to be updated often redesign them for microcomputers. Since many old systems were originally written for machines with much less processing capability than PCs currently have, transferring the work to a microcomputer is

Supplement 14.6 Mainframe Terminal Emulation

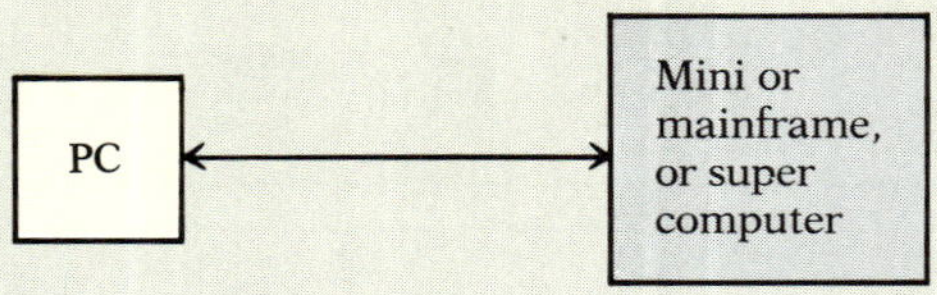

PC as "dumb" terminal accessing a larger computer for its processing or memory capacity

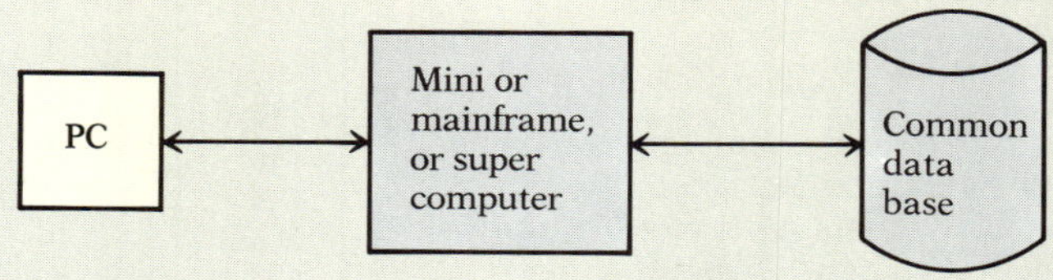

PC accessing a common data base through a larger computer

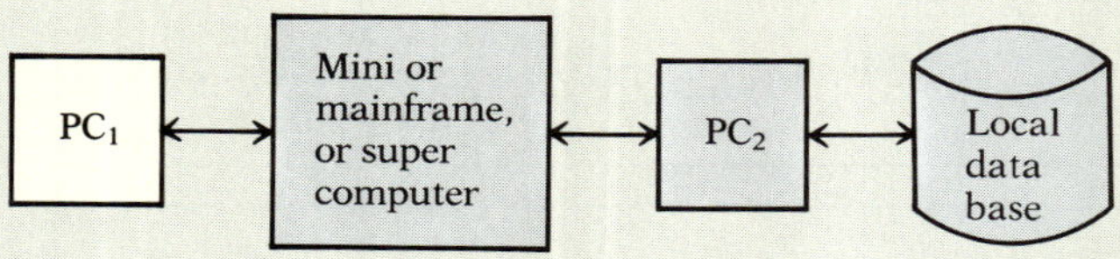

PC_1 accessing another PC (PC_2) for its local data base through a larger computer (wired to PC_2)

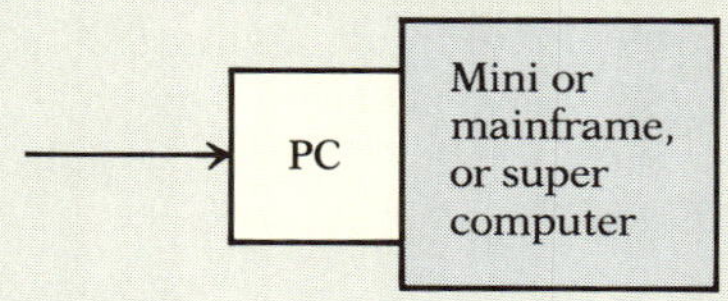

PC as a front-end processor to mini or mainframe

often feasible. Of course, data processing managers must plan the migration carefully. They must ensure that the data and programs are indeed the right size to be processed on a microcomputer. Users of the application must also be willing and able to take responsibility for operating the redeveloped system.

Terminal Emulation One factor that may contribute to the increased use of microcomputers in large organizations in years to come is the development of technology to link microcomputers with mainframes. This technology, called **mainframe terminal emulation**, allows microcomputers to act as input devices for mainframe transaction processing and as devices for display or storage of processed results. For example, since more processing capacity is needed than available on a PC to process financial planning packages or certain end-user oriented file management systems, such as NOMAD, FOCUS, and RAMIS, microcomputers can serve as "dumb terminals" (terminals with only simple input and output capabilities) to initiate mainframe processing of these packages.

Terminal emulation also allows microcomputer users to access data stored in common data bases; the PC can then process applications using that data. In addition, when a PC user is linked to the company's mainframe, he or she can access "turnkey systems" (complete systems and fully operational computer systems) developed in-house expressly for the use of employees in disparate departments.

In the near future it is expected that microcomputers will become active **front-end** and **back-end processors** for large-scale mainframe applications. For example, a microcomputer might replace a data entry terminal at a branch office, becoming a front-end processor. As a back-end processor, the microcomputer might be used to edit reports and distribute them electronically. When not needed for either front-end or back-end functions, the microcomputer might serve local needs; for example, for word processing or spreadsheet functions.

In the mid 1980s, many technical problems with terminal emulation are still unresolved. Too often user expectations exceed the state of the art. But the connection of microcomputers to mainframes is a priority of most data processing managers in large organizations. Both hardware and software personnel are working to solve these problems. The technology of terminal emulation will undoubtedly make advances in the near future.

PC APPLICATIONS IN THE FUTURE

As personal computers become common fixtures in homes and telecommunication networks are developed and refined, living patterns may change. For example, the morning newspaper may no longer appear in print. Instead, people may turn on a PC to learn what is happening in the world. From a menu of headlines, you will be able to select articles that have been delivered electronically from the data base of a news agency for display on a CRT screen. The home screen may provide access to news from foreign data bases transmitted by satellite as well. The real-time nature of **electronic news** means that reports on events can be transmitted as soon as they are keyed into the computer at the news center by a reporter. News from the past can also be accessed. One might retrieve all articles on a specified topic over a given time period, for example.

Electronic magazines and journals are also forecast for the future. In addition, books may be stored in a computer's data base for access from a PC. Imagine being able to ask a computer to prepare a bibliography on a given topic and then choosing a book from the list and selecting pages for viewing from its index. Entire libraries may be stored in computer memory in the future, with books accessed simultaneously by hundreds of readers. Users of electronic libraries might read the book on a CRT screen or obtain a hard copy by using a printer attached to their home computer.

Reservations for airlines through a home computer may be commonplace in the future. This service has in fact already begun on a trial basis. Instead of going through a travel agent, individuals can use their own terminals to access an online real-time reservation system. By typing a few instructions, it is possible to call up flight information to the screen—information on schedules, plane capacity, number of seats in first class, meals served, plane connections, cost, and so forth. Once the user has decided on the particular flight and date for travel, this information can be entered on the terminal along with name, phone number, number of seats, and other data requested by the system in the form of prompts that appear on the screen. It is even possible to specify special services needed, such as a salt-free diet or wheelchair assistance in boarding. Once all reservation data is input, the reservation service's computer confirms the reservation, charges the fare to the user's credit card, prints the ticket, and has it delivered by mail. A similar reservation service is feasible for trains, hotels, and rental cars.

Electronic mail may replace conventional mail service as described in Chapter 7. In France, the nationalized telephone company has calculated that the cost of printing and distributing phone books, coupled with the salary of 4,500 operators to provide directory assistance, is greater than the cost of providing each phone household with a liquid crystal or plasma display home computer. Telephone users in test cities are being given such a terminal to retrieve directory information. The terminal also has an electronic mail capability. If the system proves successful, it will be extended throughout France. It is possible that U.S. phone companies might offer similar services in the future.

Electronic banking and home shopping may also become widespread once personal computers are in every home. These applications are discussed in detail in Part III of this book.

HOW TO SELECT A MICROCOMPUTER

A large number of microcomputers are on the market. Choosing an appropriate model can be an agonizing decision. Whether you are buying a microcomputer for use at home or in the office, there are a number of factors that you should consider as you make your **selection**. These factors include:

- *Cost*. How much can you spend? Although many personal computers can be bought for less than $1000, these usually attach to a TV, exclude printers, and are oriented to entertainment, CAI, or home management.

Memory and storage may be too limited to be satisfactory for professional work. A more expensive, more sophisticated computer (that is, 16-, 32-, or 64-bit machines) ranging from $1000 to $10,000 may be required if the machine will be used for full-time work, whether in a home-office or in an organization.

- *Application.* Why is a microcomputer needed? If you know in advance how the microcomputer will be used, be sure software for that application is available before selecting hardware. Many buyers fail to realize that software packages are often written for specific equipment and are not portable from one microcomputer to another. It is thus important to keep in mind that software must be compatible with the microcomputer's operating system. MSX is the operating system used by Japanese manufacturers while American microcomputers generally use Unix, CP/M, or MS-DOS.

- *Features.* What is important to you, the buyer? A color video display? Large print on the CRT? A compact unit with a built-in disk drive? A keyboard that resembles a typewriter? A mouse or joystick? Buyers will not know what they really want unless they discuss features with other PC owners and try out different models. Visit sales outlets and computer shows and study your options before making a choice.

- *Peripherals.* What kind of storage devices and printers will best suit your needs? Cassette tapes are low-cost secondary storage but slow to access information. Floppy disks require a disk drive, often a separate piece of equipment. Hard disks have more storage capacity than floppies but cost more as well. When selecting a printer, evaluate speed, quality, noise level, and cost. Although you may not want telecommunications initially, consider the ease with which this capability can be added in the future. Look for expandability in the system you choose.

- *Availability of software.* Are software packages available? Unless you are a computer hobbyist or computer professional, do not plan to write all your own software. Choose a system with off-the-shelf packages.

- *Documentation.* Are instruction manuals easy to follow? It is a good idea to spend several hours in the store trying out models to see if you can follow their manuals before making a purchase. Unfortunately, many systems lack adequate documentation. Poorly written instructions often cause user dissatisfaction.

- *Guarantee and maintenance.* What will you do if the system breaks down? Although computers are reliable machines, they do need service from time to time. Check on the terms of the warranty and find out who is qualified to fix the microcomputer you are planning to purchase. Be sure to ask about the cost of service calls.

- *Terms.* What rent, lease, or purchase options are available on competitive models? Can special financing terms be arranged? Shop around. Some dealers offer discounts. Others may have sales that can save you money.

- *Reputation.* What is the reputation of the manufacturer of the machine you intend to buy and the reputation of the vendor selling it? No one wants to buy equipment from a company that is floundering or from a dealer who is insensitive to user problems once a sale is made. Many computer vendors have information centers in their stores and sponsor classes for their customers to help them take full advantage of their purchases.

Additional selection factors are listed in Figure 14.6.

Because many people who wish to buy microcomputers have no computing background, they don't feel qualified to evaluate technical features. They are intimidated by computer jargon and salesmen, and simply don't understand the meaning of terms like "byte," "DBMS," and "RAM." Computer literacy *is* important in selecting a microcomputer. Persons who buy a PC without first acquiring a background knowledge in computing may be talked into buying a machine totally inappropriate to their needs. The steps that should be followed in making a selection are listed in Figure 14.7.

Although a comprehensive market analysis would be wise before selecting a microcomputer, the size of the market makes such an analysis difficult. Table 14.2 gives some information about a few PCs in various price ranges that were on the market in 1984. In the mid-1980s, over 150 manufacturers were selling personal computers. (It is predicted, however, that only fifty microcomputer manufacturers will survive into the 1990s.)

- *Hardware*
  Bit size (8-bit, 16-bit, etc.)
  Internal memory
    ROM, PROM, or EPROM capacity
    RAM capacity
  External storage
    Media (cassette, tape, diskettes, hard disks)
    Number
    Capacity
  Peripherals (printers, other input/output devices)
  Speed
  Keyboard (shape, size, character set, layout, detachable)
  Screen (width, size, readability, tiltability, resolution)
  Color capability
  Graphics capabilities
  Pointer (cursor, mouse)
  Network access capability and interfaces
  External device interfaces
  User friendliness
  Computer size

- *Software*
  Operating system
  Choice of packaged software available
  Level of language access
  DBMS capability
  Windowing capabilities

- *Vendor*
  Reliability
  Reputation
  Services offered
  Financing possibilities
  Maintenance contract conditions

- *Other*
  Cost
  Documentation
  Type of equipment (general purpose, professional personal computer, etc.)
  Portability
  Serviceability (easy access to service, spare parts available
  Human factor considerations (ease of use, comfort)
  Training

Figure 14.6 Microcomputer selection criteria.

1. State computer processing needs.
2. Search for hardware (CPU and peripherals) and software (operating system and application packages) that meet these needs.
3. Take into consideration future needs, compatibility of equipment, ease of use, and delivery dates.
4. Select a vendor.
5. Negotiate financing, maintenance, and service contract.
6. Install equipment.
7. Learn how to use the equipment by utilizing documentation provided and/or attending classes.

Figure 14.7 Steps in acquiring a microcomputer.

SUMMING UP

This is the decade of the microcomputer. In 1984, microcomputers were the largest single segment of the information processing industry, roughly 37 percent of the total, representing $113 billion in sales worldwide. Growing microcomputer sales can be attributed to the continual drop in the price of PCs and their increased computing capability.

Microcomputers today are low in cost, user-friendly, and easy to install, update, and maintain. Software packages exist to meet the information processing needs of people with no programming skills. Many of these packages are menu-driven, with both editing and information retrieval designed for casual users. It's no wonder, therefore, that microcomputers have had a major impact on information processing at home and at work. The advantages and disadvantages of micros are summarized in Figure 14.8.

Families make use of PCs today for games, word processing, computer-aided instruction, home management, and access to external data

Table 14.2 PC market in different price ranges*

	Units sold		Dominant model	
Price range	**#**	**Percent of total**	**Model**	**Percent share**
$0–$499	4290	35.3	Commodore Vic-20	37.1
$500–$999	2850	22.9	Commodore C-64	67.7
$1000–$2999	2240	18.0	Apple IIe IIc	38.8
$3000–$5999	2270	18.2	IBM PC	32.5
$6000–$11,999	800	6.4	IBM PC XT	42.5
	12,450	100.8**		

*1984 prices
**The .8 here reflects the effects of "rounding."

Advantages

- Easy to use and access
- Full control of operations and applications
- Fewer environmental constraints
- Low cost:
  - Start up
  - Run time
- Independence from central computing system
- Computing power available when needed and not shared with others
- No contribution to overhead for shared computing resources (that is, operating and maintenance costs, room, security for a large computer system.)

Limitations

- No backup or access to other computers in periods of overload when in stand-alone mode
- Limits on:
  - Size of program used
  - Amount of data that can be sorted
  - Language of program
  - Software packages available
  - Speed of processor
  - Processing power of 16-bit (and smaller) machine
- Less established vendors than vendors of minis and mainframes
- Some programs less portable than programs for large computers
- Need communications link to have:
  - Large software systems, such as some DBMSs
  - Access to shared data bases

Figure 14.8 Advantages and limitations of microcomputers.

bases. Although teletex and videotex are still largely experimental in the U.S., their expansion should make electronic mail, electronic shopping, telenews, telereservations, and telebanking common by the end of this century.

In England and France, the fact that the post office, telephone system, and TV are nationalized has fostered innovative applications for home PCs—for example, the videotex service Prestel in England. The development of videotex services has been much slower here in the United States. One reason is that the telecommunications network for such services must be funded by private enterprise, not government. Uncertainty about rulings of the FCC which controls communications in this country, the failure of legislation to keep pace with rapid technological advances, and the slowness of U.S. judicial processes in resolving disputes are also factors that have slowed the development of a national telecommunications infrastructure. Cost is an additional factor. But a communications network would cost less than the $70 billion spent in a recent ten-year period for national highways.

Microcomputers play a role at work as well as at home. According to many industry observers, there will be a PC on the desk of every white collar worker by the year 2000. At present most microcomputers in organizations are stand-alone machines used to access and manipulate the personal files of employees. For large and complex problems, workers must turn to mainframes. In the future, microcomputers that are linked to nationwide networks may be the norm. Furthermore, once technical bugs with terminal emulation are solved, microcomputer users will have a choice. They will be able to operate their PCs in a stand-alone mode, or use them as terminals to access the data and the processing capability of mainframes.

REVIEW QUESTIONS

1. Why does the computer industry favor the sale of PC games?
2. What changes have occurred in microcomputers over the past ten years?
3. How can word processing be of value in the home?
4. Describe three home management applications for personal computers.
5. What is the difference between a remote data base service like CompuServe and videotex? What purposes do each serve?
6. Will videotex through a family TV cut into the market of PCs for home use? Explain your answer.
7. How can personal computers assist someone running a small business?
8. What are electronic bulletin boards? Give examples how they can be used.
9. Would a microcomputer on the desk of a manager in a large organization be useful? How?
10. How can mainframe terminal emulation serve a PC user?
11. What are the advantages and disadvantages of microcomputer use in a large organization?
12. Discuss problems with hardware, software, and maintenance when PCs are used in:
    a. small businesses.
    b. large organizations.
13. Can videotex serve people in their jobs? What is the difference between in-house videotex and remote videotex? How might each contribute to the work of an engineer?
14. Describe ways in which family lifestyle might be affected once PCs are as commonplace as TVs in the home.
15. Why is it a good idea to consider the availability of software packages before choosing a microcomputer model?
16. How can documentation affect customer satisfaction with a PC purchase?
17. Describe three applications for a PC:
    a. of an educational value.
    b. for recreation.
    c. for controlling a home environment.
    d. for a small business operated out of a home.
    e. for a large business.

18. Discuss the differences (if any) between:
    a. microprocessors
    b. microcomputers
    c. home computers
    d. personal computers
    e. desk computers
    f. portable computers

DISCUSSION QUESTIONS

1. How do you view growth in the market for personal computers? With alarm or with anticipation? Why?
2. If you were to own a PC, how would you use it?
3. What trends do you foresee for personal computer use in the United States in the near future?
4. You are responsible for choosing one personal computer for educational purposes, one for business use, and one for family pleasure. Will the selection of these PCs differ in:
    a. make?
    b. storage?
    c. speed?
    d. peripherals?
    e. software?
5. Discuss the advantages and disadvantages of microcomputers used in large organizations.
6. How do you think a national telecommunications infrastructure should be financed? Who should be responsible for its development?
7. The PC will have a sociological, psychological, and economic impact on individuals and on society. Comment on this statement.
8. The microcomputer has brought electronics into a new era. It is altering the structure of our society. Comment.

EXERCISES

1. Interview someone who owns a personal computer. Discuss how the PC is used. What are the advantages and limitations of the computer?
2. Visit an organization using a remote online data base accessed by a microcomputer. Describe how the data base service is used.
3. Imagine that you are given the responsibility of selecting a microcomputer for use in one of your classes. Describe your needs and select a computer. What will it cost? What criteria did you use in selecting the:
    a. vendor?
    b. model?
    c. peripherals?
    d. features?

Selected Annotated Bibliography

Barlow, Mike. "The Smart House Comes of Age," *Personal Computing*, vol. 6, no. 10 (October 1982), pp. 112–20. Use of micros in the home is described.

Blundell, Gregory S. "Bringing In Personal Business Computers," *Small Business World*, vol. 10, no. 9 (September 1982), pp. 24–31. The author stresses that managers should learn to use microcomputers now while they are still in the stand-alone phase. This will prepare them for microcomputer networking, a mode of computing that is sure to become widespread and one with great business potential.

Brown, Gary D. and Sefton, Donald H. "The Micro vs. the Applications Logjam," *Datamation*, vol. 30, no. 1 (January 1984), pp. 96–104. Small computers can help eliminate the three-year backlog of development and maintenance work of typical data processing departments. The article describes what microcomputers can and can't do.

Byte, vol. 7, no. 12 (December 1982). This is a special issue on computer games for PCs and arcades. An interesting article on game design techniques written by an Atari employee is included.

———, vol. 8, no. 7 (July 1983). This issue is devoted to videotex. Applications (including home banking and shopping) and issues (like privacy) are discussed.

Deken, Joseph. *The Electronic Cottage.* New York: Bantam Books, 1981. A description of how the computer revolution will change the home.

Emmett, Arielle. "Electronic Bulletin Boards," *Personal Computing,* vol. 7, no. 6 (June 1983), pp. 64–69. Computer bulletin boards provide new forums for the exchange of information and ideas. Emmett suggests steps for setting one up yourself.

Gabel, David. "How A Computer Can Control Your Home," *Personal Computing,* vol. 7, no. 3 (March 1983), pp. 49–55. The author starts with the premise that we have the technology right now to build "smart houses" and then proceeds to tell how to do it.

Gillard, Collen and Smith, Jim. "Computer Crime: A Growing Threat," *Byte,* vol. 8, no. 10 (October 1983), pp. 398–424. The proliferation of personal computers adds to problems of security in information processing.

Hedberg, Augustin. "Choosing the Best Computer For You," *Money,* vol. 2, no. 11 (November 1982), pp. 68–112. This is a microcomputer purchase guide for persons lacking a technical background. Discusses applications, peripherals, interfaces, and software. Specifications for thirty-eight different products are included.

Grabb, Donald Evan. "An Annotated Bibliography of Recent Books—Technical Topics for the IBM PC Family," *Byte,* vol. 10, no. 11 (Fall 1985), pp. 11–35. The forty-one books reviewed fall into seven categories: hardware, Intel PC microprocessors and assembly languages, high-level languages, graphics, data communications, miscellaneous, and references. The annotations cover content, intended audience, writing style, and estimate the value of the book to the reader.

High Technology, vol. 5, no. 11 (November 1985). This issue includes several articles on micros at work. Topics include a business outlook for micros, a technology overview, and applications for manufacturers, technicians, professionals, educators, and consumers.

Isshiki, Koichiro R. *Small Business Computers: A Guide to Evaluation and Selection.* Englewood Cliffs, N.J.: Prentice-Hall, 1982. This is a text on small computers: configuration, selection, acquisition, installation, benefits, and pitfalls.

Latamore, G. Berton. "The Business Connection," *Popular Computing,* vol. 4, no. 5 (March 1985), pp. 75–80. Describes how online data services provide fast, accurate information to PC users.

Lodhal, Thomas M. "Micro-Power For Managers," *Management Technology.* vol. 1, no. 8 (August 1983), pp. 28–35. Architecture, network potential, portability, and price of small computers are discussed.

PC World, ed. *Get More Out Of Your PC.* San Francisco: PC World Communications, 1983. This is a special issue of collected articles on spreadsheets, word processing, database management, communications, and other applications.

Rubin, Charles. "Farming Smarter with a Computer," *Personal Computing,* vol. 7, no. 6 (June 1983), pp. 96–101. Rubin shows how farmers can use spreadhseets and other programs in managing small and large farms. Trends in farm management are also discussed.

Stahr, Lisa B. "Working With Statistical Analysis," *Personal Computing,* vol. 8, no. 10 (October 1984), pp. 73–83. Until recently, packages for statistical analysis were available only on mainframes and used by scientists and mathematically oriented users. Now such packages are available to all users on microcomputers. Furthermore, output is not limited to tables but can be an attractive graph in color.

Today: The Videotex Computer Magazine. Videotex even has a monthly journal started in 1982. The magazine includes contributed articles, tutorials, and an "industry watch" section.

Wilkins, Robert P. "How Lawyers Can Use Microcomputers," *Byte,* vol. 9, no. 5 (May 1984), pp. 160–67. The author discusses how attorneys can benefit from word processing, number crunching, information management, communications, electronic spreadsheets, and specialized software packages for microcomputers.

Young, T. R. "The Lonely Micro," *Datamation,* vol. 30, no. 4 (April 1984), pp. 100–14. The focus of this article is on training users to take full advantage of their microcomputers.

The Social Implications of Computers

The change brought about in the workplace and at home by computer technology has social repercussions. The computer era requires new skills, new attitudes, and new patterns of living. Although jobs have been created in information services, other jobs have been lost to robots and automation. Power within organizations and the world community at large is being restructured because of modern methods of collecting, processing, and distributing information. Machines are even challenging the way people view themselves. Once machines have vision, natural language understanding, and intelligent capabilities, will the value of human life be undermined?

Part Three addresses the social impact of this age of information. Chapter 15 deals with the threat of data banks to the privacy of individuals. Chapter 16 discusses artificial intelligence. The impact of computers on employment is the subject of Chapter 17, electronic monetary systems are covered in Chapter 18, and examples of information technology as an agent of change are given in Chapter 19. The book closes with a look at the future. Chapter 20 describes ongoing research in fifth generation computing and makes some predictions about what it will be like to live in a telematic society.

PART THREE

Privacy: The Threat of Data Banks

Advanced technology has created new opportunities for America as a nation, but it has also created the possibility for new abuses of the individual American citizen. Adequate safeguards must always stand watch so that man remains master and never the victim of the computer.

RICHARD NIXON,
ADDRESS TO THE NATION,
FEBRUARY 23, 1974

CHAPTER FIFTEEN

Key Words

accuracy
code of fair information practices
data bank
Fair Credit Reporting Act of 1971
fair use
Federal Privacy Act of 1974
gatekeeping
linkage
matching
one-time expenditures
operational costs
personal dossier
Privacy Protection Study Commission
right to privacy
routine use exception
videotex records

Green eye-shades, high stools, ledgers, and pens: these were the tools of clerks who manually processed records in the past. As society modernized, the number and complexity of records increased. In response to this growing workload, recordkeeping has become automated. Today, the use of computers in government, service organizations, and industry for the processing of records is widespread. Without being explicitly aware of the fact, this country has made an irrevocable commitment to computerization. There is no turning back.

Individuals interact with a multitude of computerized record systems in their daily lives. Most transactions, such as filing an insurance claim or cashing a paycheck, result in the collection of personal data that is stored in a computer data bank. The growth of data banks has led to a collision between the need of both private and public institutions for information about their clients on the one hand and the right to privacy of individuals on the other.

The issue of privacy is the subject of this chapter. First the rise of vast data banks will be examined. Public concern over the accumulation of personal information in these data banks and issues such as accuracy, fair use, and computer matching will be examined. The provisions of the 1974 Privacy Act restricting the use of personal data by government agencies will be described. The chapter closes with a look at both potential privacy abuse arising from recent technology and at the cost of privacy measures.

COMPUTER DATA BANKS

Data of a personal nature is collected by every organization that has dealings with the public. Name, address, and telephone number are data elements that are collected for most files. In addition:

- Credit information and purchases appear in charge account files.
- Family history, health record, and disabilities appear in medical files.
- Age, height, weight, color of eyes, social security number, and traffic citations appear in Department of Motor Vehicle records.
- Income, deductions, sick leave, dependents, education, employment record, and references appear in work personnel records.
- Number of vehicles, types, insurance coverage, and past accidents appear in insurance records.
- Religious affiliation and contributions appear in church records.

The list could go on and on. The average person's name appears in thirty-nine local, state, or federal files and forty private sector files. Just about every salient fact about every individual is in a computer file somewhere.

Although recordkeeping has always been a part of organized society, isolated bits of personal

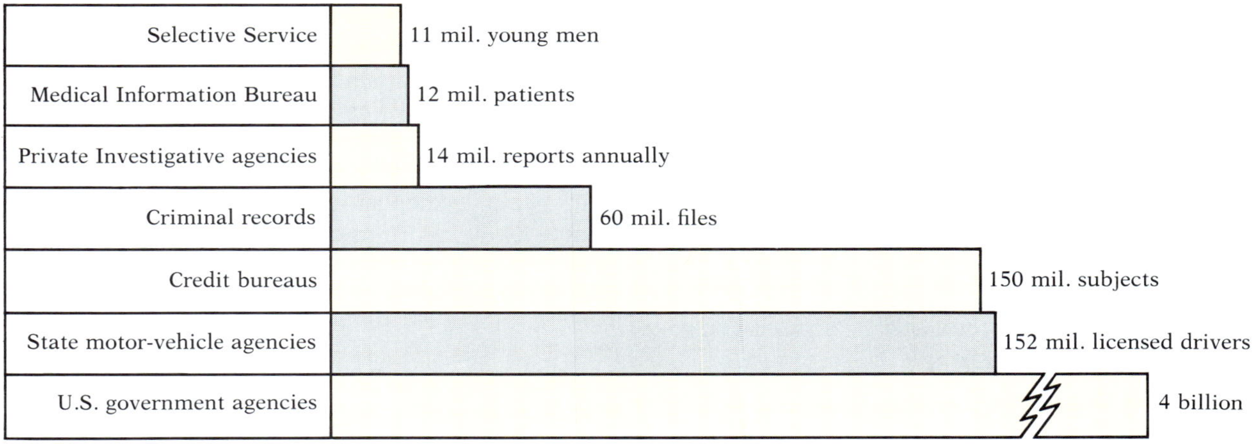

Figure 15.1 *Who has personal data on file?*

*Source: *U.S. News & World Report*, April 30, 1984, pp. 46–47.

information do not threaten privacy. With computers, however, pools of data can be collected—pools that constitute comprehensive **personal dossiers**. We have the technology to store the intimate details of an individual's life. How many times has Mr. Jones been married? Has his appendix been removed? What was his bar bill last year? How does Mr. Jones spend his off-work hours? A study of a data pool makes it possible to draw a profile of Mr. Jones' behavior. Few Americans want such a profile in the public domain. They believe they have a **right to privacy**, including the right to control the collection, the dissemination, and use of information about their personal lives.

This explains opposition to the proposal in the 1960s for a Federal Data Center with records on each American. The public was outraged at the prospect of government being in possession and control of detailed information on the lives of citizens. They did not want an Orwellian society with Big Brother (that is, the government) collecting files on citizens.

Linkage of data bases through high-speed communication networks poses the same threat to individual privacy as a single, all-inclusive **data bank,** since scattered personal data can then be readily accessed and combined. What is needed are common data elements to link files. When Congress considered mandating universal use of Social Security numbers as personal identifiers in the early 1970s, those opposed argued that a universal identifier would facilitate file integration, undermining privacy.

To study the problem, a special advisory group of the Department of Health, Education, and Welfare (HEW) was formed. Its 1973 report entitled "Records, Computers, and the Rights of Citizens" is credited with providing the intellectual foundation for much of the privacy legislation in the 1970s, including the placement of restrictions on Social Security number use. The report proposed **a code of fair information practices**. The HEW code states that privacy is a matter of mutual concern between recordkeeper and subject. It affirms that the custodian of data is responsible for timeliness, accuracy, and security of data. It also states that personal information should not be used for a purpose other than that for which it is gathered.

THE PROBLEM OF ACCURACY

Accuracy of stored data is a principal component of the HEW fairness code. Unfortunately, one of the weak areas in computer systems is auditing mechanisms for accuracy. It simply isn't practical and would be far too costly to check the validity of all information stored in data banks. Figure 15.1 shows a sample of the number of personal records in computer files, all of which are subject to error.

As described in Chapter 6, mistakes are often made at the time of data collection, data preparation, and data input. In the 1960s, the Army collected files on potential "subversives" using the code 134.295 to indicate that a person was a non-Communist while 135.295 indicated Communist Party membership or advocacy of communism. The arbitrary manner in which data was collected on the political activities of citizens, the assignment of codes without the knowledge of the individuals involved, the lack of challenge procedures, the fact that a single digit separated the codes—all of these factors contributed to the likelihood of error. This is a good example of why so many Americans fear computer data banks.

Required proof of data accuracy at the time of collection is common only when data is crucial to an organization's operation. For example, a birth certificate must accompany an application for a passport. But the certificate is not required when applying for a bank loan since loan approval does not depend on the applicant's exact age. Yet a birth date mistake in bank records takes on importance if that mistake is passed on to another organization where the information is vital.

Most data bank administrators claim that they have no obligation to determine the accuracy of information they receive from others. This is the position of TRW Information Service, a company which sells thirty-five million credit reports each year to 24,000 subscribers throughout the country. Each month TRW receives computer tapes from thousands of companies containing the status of their customer accounts. TRW computers then lift, organize, and store information from the tapes so that it can be supplied to clients making credit checks. This service could not be provided if TRW were forced to check the accuracy of the information on each tape.

Inaccuracy of data files is not a trivial problem. Each year some 350,000 people register formal complaints about mistakes in TRW's reports. Some 100,000 of these complaints annually result in changes to information stored in TRW computers. How many incorrect entries are not noticed? How many mistakes are not corrected?

In the United States, the federal government has an estimated four billion records. Millions of personal records exist in credit agencies, commercial banks, medical institutions, police departments, schools, charge account files, and places of work. Consider the potential for harm should only 1 percent of these records be in error. Errors may:

- *Result in inconvenience and frustration.* Most readers have experienced computer billing errors.
- *Prevent people from obtaining goods and services to which they are entitled.* Unwarranted cutoffs of benefits due to errors in Social Security Administration files are not uncommon, for example.
- *Ruin reputations and disrupt lives.* For example, in 1976 Michael DuCross was arrested as AWOL from the Marine Corps and held five months in the Camp Pendleton brig before the government discovered an error in its computerized files. DuCross had never been AWOL and had been legally discharged from the Marines in 1969.

One way to reduce errors is to allow individuals the right to inspect personal records and challenge mistakes that they find. The problem is that mistakes may be circulated before they are identified. An individual has no way of knowing which organizations have copied an error and stored the error in their files.

Consider the plight of Lucky Kellener, a Los Angeles lawyer who occasionally paid his brother's rent. When the brother was evicted, Kellener's name mistakenly appeared in papers filed by the landlord in court. Based on information drawn from court records, Kellener was subsequently listed as an undesirable tenant in the computer of U.D. Registry, Inc. (a company that provides landlords with information on prospective tenants.) Three years later when Kellener tried to rent a larger apartment for himself, he was repeatedly turned away with lame excuses, such as "Someone was here before you." Finally, one landlord unintentionally let out the secret: the existence of a computer blacklisting service with his name on the list.

Kellener's experience illustrates why civil lib-

Supplement 15.1 Computer Check Leads to False Arrest

William Jones was stopped by a Los Angeles County sheriff for a minor traffic violation in 1979. The sheriff radioed information from Jones' driver's license to the computerized warrant system used by the county. When the system indicated several outstanding warrants under the name of William Jones, Jones was taken to the police station and booked. In spite of repeated protests that he was *not* the man in the warrants, Jones spent two weeks in jail before being cleared by the courts. He lost his job during the interim, had to drop out of junior college, and was called to active duty in the National Guard because he missed weekend training while in jail.

A class-action suit on behalf of Jones and four others who had also been falsely arrested was filed in 1980 against the City of Los Angeles by The Center for Law in the Public Interest. The suit charged that the Automated Wants and Warrants Systems used by the city violated constitutional and civil rights of the plaintiffs.

In 1984, Los Angeles Superior Court approved a settlement of the case—a settlement requiring the city to adopt policy and procedural changes in making arrests. From that point on, police were required to use stricter criteria when matching a suspect to a computerized warrant. The percentage of weighted descriptions that must match to make a "hit" has been increased from 62 percent to 72 percent. (These descriptions include license number, hair color, address, and so forth.) In addition, all available manual records must be searched before jailing a person who claims to have been falsely arrested.

It was not the intention of the suit to shut down the computer warrant system altogether, but merely to force the city to impose safeguards in its use. All parties to the settlement believe that the revisions should reduce the chance of false arrest in the future.

ertarians are concerned with the growth of computerized data banks, the unmonitored exchange of data, and the existence of errors in stored data. It also raises the question of fair use of personal information, the topic of the next section.

FAIR USE OF DATA

To most Americans, privacy includes the right to control the use of personal data. We view secret files as a threat to individual freedom. We want limits placed on data collection to prevent institutions from gathering personal information that has no relevance to their legitimate needs. We also want to restrict access to personal data that has been collected.

There is a market value to personal information. Merchants can determine where to direct their advertising from such information. They can draw up lists of persons who like the outdoors and to whom camping equipment might appeal or lists of Cadillac owners who might be attracted to diamond jewelry. Does the sale of a mailing list for advertising purposes violate privacy? A **fair use** restriction gives individuals the right to participate in this decision. Fair use means consent must be obtained before personal data in a data bank is shared with others. After all, data pools are attractive targets for all types of groups. Consider the value of information regarding who goes camping weekends or who likes diamond jewelry, to a thief.

Fair use restrictions also address the "gatekeeping" issue. **Gatekeeping** is controlled access to services, privileges, benefits, or opportunities. An example of gatekeeping is the point-scoring method used by many credit agencies to determine whether an individual is a good credit risk, based on age, salary, duration of employment, and so forth. In this case, gatekeeping serves a legitimate business interest. But gatekeeping can also be used to discriminate. There is an ill-defined area of gatekeeping practices that go against the American grain.

Computer processing facilitates gatekeeping just as it does the unrestricted exchange of personal data. As stated by the U.S. Privacy Protection Study Commission,

> The ability to search through hundreds of thousands, or even millions, of records to identify individuals with particular characteristics of interest is at once the most important gain and the most im-

Supplement 15.2 Smart Cards

Most Americans carry credit cards in their wallets. On the back of each card is a magnetic stripe containing up to 1,700 bits of information (approximately 45 words), such as name, address, credit number, and so forth. Today we have the technology to produce a "smart card" of the same size containing 2 megabytes of information (approximately 400 typewritten pages). Some smart cards are computer systems, containing a chip-sized microcomputer, memory, and external communications to access devices. Manufacturers are also producing smart keys, smart bracelets, and smart medallions to be worn on a neck chain with the same features.

The U.S. Army uses the technology of smart cards for a data tag worn by each soldier. The tags contain the soldier's 201 personnel file (about 34,000 bytes of information) plus medical and financial records. (When a soldier goes into combat, the tag is purged of all data except name, rank, and serial number in case of enemy capture.)

For civilians, smart cards have many potential applications. They might be used to store an individual's medical history. Such a card would be very useful to doctors in case of emergency. The cards might serve as an employee ID and to store employment data, such as security clearances to enable individuals to enter restricted areas. The cards might represent electronic money, authorizing purchases up to a given total; with each purchase, the transaction would be recorded on the card and the allowable total debited.

Smart cards raise questions of privacy. Recruits in the army are given no choice about wearing a data tag. But would you choose to carry in your pocket a smart card containing personal medical data or a record of your financial transactions?

A microcomputer card. The card's active portion and contact points measure less than two centimeters in diameter, yet it goes a long way toward permanently eliminating the need for paper records in financial transaction. (Groupe Bull)

Supplement 15.3 Sample Credit File

UPDATED CREDIT PROFILE

IDENTIFICATION NO.

Page	Date	Time	Port	Identification No.
1	12-14-85	11:12:37	AC33	18-010858/48

Subscriber Name/Company Name / Status Comments	Date Reported	Date Opened	Client Code / Type	Acct. Code	Amount	Balance	Balance Date / Amount Past Due	Payment Profile
WARDS			8422520	0			787228371	
CURR ACCT	3-85	10-79	CHG	28	-$100	$0	9-17-85	000-00-0000
PLUS SYSTEM SERVICES			3250029	1			59717625211a5281	
CURR ACCT	9-85	12-77	CRC	REV	$200	$0	10-31-85	00000000000
ROCKY MOUNTAIN BANKCARD			5150032	1			4713002868791	
CUR WAS 30	12-85	2-82	CRC	REV	$1700	$12	10-31-85	00000000000
FNB OF RIVERSIDE			9524263	3			198965996	
CURR ACCT	10-85	4-83	UNK	24	$5800	$927	11-19-85	
FNB OF ALBANY			4201024	1			4332420525993180 4	
CURR ACCT	9-85	11-80	CRC	REV	$1900	$0	9-15-85	000000000-0
SEARS			8718447	0			62302603941	
CURR ACCT	3-85	7-82	CHG	REV	$200	$0	8-30-85	00000000000
END								

portant source of potential harm stemming from the automation of large-scale personal data record-keeping systems.[1]

Fair use restrictions are an attempt to minimize this potential for harm.

PRIVACY LEGISLATION

The first major legislation to deal with the problem of data banks and privacy was the **Fair Credit Reporting Act of 1971**. According to this act, individuals have the right to access to their own credit files and correct credit errors.

The next important piece of legislation was the **Federal Privacy Act of 1974**, which set guidelines for the collection, maintenance, use, and dissemination of personal information by federal agencies. This act defines the following rights of citizens:

1. *Right of notification.* Each agency that maintains a system of records is required to publish in the *Federal Register* at least annually a notice of the existence and character of the records. This must include name and location of the information system, categories of records maintained, uses of the records, and policies regarding access and disposal. When records are disseminated to other agencies under compulsory legal processes, reasonable effort must be made to notify the individuals involved.
2. *Right to accuracy and relevance.* Agencies are charged with collecting and maintaining information that is current and accurate. They may only keep records that are relevant and necessary to accomplish their mandates.
3. *Right to confidentiality.* Agencies must establish administrative, technical, and physical safeguards to protect the security and confidentiality of records.
4. *Right to access.* Knowing the existence of recorded data is not sufficient if access to that data is restricted or the data unintelligible (coded or recorded on magnetic tape, for example). The act recognizes an individual's right to access one's own record and review and copy it.
5. *Right to challenge.* Amendment of records may be requested when an individual believes personal data is not accurate, relevant, timely, or complete.
6. *Right for correction.* The act states that procedures should be established for record amendment.
7. *Right of control.* No records may be made available for another purpose without an individual's consent. (Exceptions are listed; for example, records for law enforcement or use by the Census Bureau.) Only the information necessary to accomplish the purpose of the agency may be collected.
8. *Right to redress.* Individuals may bring civil action in district courts against agencies that fail to comply with provisions of the act and be rewarded damages. Officers and employees of agencies are also liable to criminal penalties for willful disclosure of information to any person not entitled to it.

The Privacy Act also created the **Privacy Protection Study Commission** to determine whether additional standards were needed to protect personal data in the records of government and private organizations. During eighteen months of study and testimony, the commission examined matters such as the confidentiality of tax and bank records and the use and misuse of mailing lists. The final report of the Commission, delivered to Congress and the President in 1977, counseled against federal legislation to extend the Privacy Act to the private sector. But the Commission recommended that the philosophy and principles of the act should be adopted by others. An important contribution of the Commision was that it switched the focus in the privacy debate away from ways to curb harm caused by privacy abuse and toward the positive concept of fairness in recordkeeping.

[1]U.S. Privacy Protection Study Commission, Final Sixteen Report, 1977.

Supplement 15.4 The Fair Credit Reporting Act

The Fair Credit Reporting Act of 1971 gives individuals the right to access their credit files, to correct errors, and to present their side of any disputed issue. Though credit bureaus may charge a fee for record access (usually $5 to $8), access must be granted free of charge to individuals who have been denied credit.

Inaccurate information called to a credit bureau's attention must be investigated and corrected within two weeks. Should an individual so request, the bureau must send a revised credit report following error correction to anyone who received the erroneous credit history within the past six months. In case of disagreements regarding record accuracy, an individual has the right to file a statement of up to 100 words for inclusion in the record stating his or her case.

This act helps to ensure that financial data is accurate. However, an individual's privacy is not protected by the act since a subject's consent is not required before financial data of a personal nature is released to clients of the credit bureau.

Supplement 15.5 Privacy Threatened by Stolen Password

Access to files of TRW Information Services, the largest credit-reporting agency in the U.S., is by a password (a number code). In 1984, TRW officials acknowledged that a stolen TRW password had been posted on electronic bulletin boards. As a result, the credit histories of more than ninety million Americans were vulnerable to unauthorized access. (It has not been announced whether anyone actually took advantage of the code.) As soon as TRW learned of the security breach, the code was changed.

Increased TRW privacy safeguards might make it more more difficult and expensive to make legitimate credit checks for customers. However, following the password incident, TRW announced that it plans to tighten system security. Company officials are undoubtedly evaluating privacy vs. cost and convenience tradeoffs.

Since 1974 many state and local laws modeled on the HEW privacy code have also been passed. For example, in many states privacy standards have been legislated for universities and public schools, state agencies, criminal justice communities, health-care providers, and insurance companies. A large number of private organizations and firms have adopted privacy policies on their own initiative. IBM, for example, has endorsed four principles of privacy, as show in Figure 15.2.

PRIVACY IN GOVERNMENT

What is the government's record on privacy? Poor, according to the House Committee on Government Operations. This committee has accused the Office of Management and Budget of ineffective enforcement of the Privacy Act. Articles in the popular press and testimony at Congressional hearings also point to an unsatisfactory record.

Many problems arise from the language of the Privacy Act. When first introduced on Capitol Hill, the act permitted *no* exchange of personal data among federal agencies without the consent of the individual involved, unless the exchange was a "law enforcement" disclosure relevant to the investigation of a specific violation of law. However, in committee the act was amended to permit "routine use" exchanges. In Senate and House debate the **routine use exception** was defined as data exchanges necessary for "housekeeping" by federal agencies.

Four principles of privacy

For some time now, there has been a growing effort in this country to preserve the individual's right to privacy in the face of expanding requirements for information by business, government and other organizations.

In searching for appropriate guidelines, private and governmental groups have explored many avenues and considered many aspects of the privacy question.

As a company with a vital interest in information and information handling, IBM endorses in their basic purpose four principles of privacy which have emerged from various studies, and which appear to be the cornerstones of sound public policy on this sensitive issue.

1. Individuals should have access to information about themselves in record-keeping systems. And there should be some procedure for individuals to find out how this information is being used.
2. There should be some way for an individual to correct or amend an inaccurate record.
3. An individual should be able to prevent information from being improperly disclosed or used for other than authorized purposes without his or her consent, unless required by law.
4. The custodian of data files containing sensitive information should take reasonable precautions to be sure that the data are reliable and not misused.

Translating such broad principles into specific and uniform guidelines will, of course, not be easy. They must by thoughtfully interpreted in terms of the widely varying purposes of information systems generally.

In particular, the proper balance must be found between limiting access to information for the protection of privacy on the one hand, and allowing freedom of information to fulfill the needs of society on the other.

But solutions must be found. And they will call for the patient understanding and best efforts of everyone concerned. In this search, IBM pledges its full and whole-hearted cooperation.

IBM

Figure 15.2 IBM's policy on privacy. Courtesy of International Business Machines Corp.

Following passage of the act, the Office of Management and Budget (OMB) repeated this definition in the guidelines it gave federal agencies to assist them in complying with the act. These guidelines stated that routine uses are those "that are appropriate and necessary for the efficient conduct of government and in the best interest of both the individual and the public," such as agency "housekeeping measures." To make certain that this was not an unlimited category, it was added that, "a 'routine use' must be not only compatible with, but related to the purpose for which the record is maintained."[2] Critics of the government believe that the common practice of computer matching violates the Privacy Act as interpreted in these OMB guidelines.

Matching began in 1977 when HEW sought payrolls of federal employees from the Civil Service Commission and the Department of Defense to be matched against welfare files to detect welfare fraud. Both agencies were reluctant to make disclosures because of the strictures of the 1974 Privacy Act. Nevertheless, they did so lest it appear that they were sheltering welfare cheaters. They accepted the routine use exception as justification for the match.

Computer matching at the federal level has been regulated since 1979. At that time the OMB issued guidelines to be followed by federal agencies when planning computer matches of personal record systems. The guidelines state that:

- A notice must be published in the *Federal Register* justifying how disclosure of information for matching is compatible with the purpose for which the information has been collected.
- Interagency agreements on data use must be written.
- Controls on the disposition and return of records must also be established.
- Notices must be sent to the OMB and Congress concerning the creation of new systems of records as a result of any computer match.

[2]*Federal Register*, 28953 (July 9, 1975).

In 1982 OMB guidelines were again revised by the Reagan Administration to help agencies relate the procedural requirements of the 1974 Privacy Act to the operational requirements of computerized matching.

The OMB guidelines do provide some restrictions on matching programs. Government critics charge, however, that the restrictions are easily circumvented. For example, a notice in 1980 in the *Federal Register* by the Veteran's Administration justified information disclosure for matching purposes as follows:

> An integral part of the reason that these records are maintained is to protect the legitimate interests of the government and, therefore, such a disclosure is compatible with the purposes for maintaining these records.[3]

According to this reasoning, any disclosure by a government agency of personal data for matching is justified. After all, all federal records are purportedly maintained for the "legitimate interests of government."

MATCHING: FAIR USE OR ABUSE?

Since the 1970s, computer matching by federal and state officials has become commonplace. Some sixty different federal programs that depend on the income level of an individual to determine eligibility use matching programs in an effort to prevent fraud. Eligibility for Head Start, weatherization grants, disaster loans, and welfare are examples. Matching of Selective Service lists with driver's license records helps locate males aged eighteen to twenty-four who have not registered for the draft. Matching provides the government with addresses of student-loan defaulters on the federal payroll. Matching also identifies "runaway parents" entitled to tax refunds (funds that can be diverted to court-ordered child support). The IRS uses matching to identify persons living in high-income neighborhoods who have paid less tax than their estimated income according to commercial mailing lists.

Although matching could be done by manual processing prior to computers, it was time-consuming and costly and, as a result, infrequent. The speed of computer processing and the ability of computers to store large amounts of data facilitate the efficiency and effectiveness of matching. That is why the question of whether matching constitutes fair use of personal data is a contemporary issue.

Persons who favor matching believe it is an important tool in the fight against corruption and fraud. Those opposed argue that matching violates the rights of individuals. They cite the Fourth amendment, which guarantees constitutional protection against unreasonable searches and seizures, the principle of presumption of innocence, and due process of law as incompatible with computer matching. (Chapter 12 explains this line of reasoning with regard to matching by the Internal Revenue Service.) They also point out the dangers of decision making on the basis of matching since few data bases are "clean and accurate," and few matches take into consideration extenuating circumstances.

Matching is not limited to government. The technique is employed by businesses, private organizations, and individuals who own and operate computers. The question being raised today is whether restrictions should be placed on matching. If so, what restrictions and how can they be enforced?

The privacy issue has not been solved by the 1974 Privacy Act. According to Alan F. Westin, a well-known commentator on privacy, Americans see privacy as one of the central quality-of-life issues of our time, an issue that has not been solved and that is not fading away. Rather, it is going to become more intense, "as [the issue of] privacy serves as the handle with which a still considerably alienated public seeks to define and install greater measures of individual or social control over an organizational system whose powers have been vastly increased by computer uses in the last 20 years."[4]

[3]Quoted in Jake Kirchner, "Privacy: A History of Computer Matching in Federal Government," *Computerworld*, vol. 15, no. 12 (December 14, 1981), p. 15.

[4]Alan F. Westin, "The Impact of Computers on Privacy," *Datamation* 25, no. 24 (December 1979), pp. 193.

Supplement 15.6 Profiles

Investigators construct profiles of persons who commit crimes based on their experience. Most commonly, profiles are "red flag" lists of characteristics. Profiling helps law enforcement agents identify suspects of a crime or persons who *might* commit a given crime.

For example, a male who purchases a one-way airline ticket at the last minute and pays for it in cash fits the profile of a highjacker or drug courier. Although the individual has done nothing wrong, he may be stopped and questioned by airport security. In Florida, if the same doctor-lawyer combination is involved in a number of insurance claims for bodily injury, they may be investigated to make sure they are not part of a fake accident ring. One computer firm identifies workers in its employ under the age of thirty-five who have higher than average absenteeism, requests for time off, lateness, sick leave, accidents, and Worker's Compensation claims—all characteristics of drug users. An employee who fits this profile may be asked to undergo a blood or urine test to determine whether the person is a drug addict.

Do profiles constitute an invasion of privacy? Should we use electronics to facilitate profile matching of computerized information? Few persons object to the use of profiles when searching for persons who have committed a given crime. However, when the goal is deterrence or prevention of crime—the identification of potential offenders—objections are often raised that the civil liberties of citizens are being violated. The problem is one of striking a balance between individual rights and a community's interest.

PRIVACY AND VIDEOTEX

The recent growth of videotex services may further erode personal privacy. Companies that sell videotex services compile, as a matter of course, records of services accessed from each household— records that document home banking, home shopping, reservations, stock market purchases, telemail, and so forth. The advantage of these records over similar records kept by banks, stores, travel agents, and other institutions is that they are all in one location. In effect, the records constitute dossiers on subscriber behavior.

Who owns **videotex records**? Without a law or service contract to the contrary, the company that collects the records owns them, according to a 1976 U.S. Supreme Court ruling. That means that videotex vendors can sell dossiers to retailers, pollsters, direct mailers, credit investigators, or other groups that have a commercial interest in personal data.

A second problem with videotex is that users are not protected from eavesdropping. Federal law governs "wire communications" but defines the term as transmission provided by common carriers such as the telephone company. This probably exempts the cable services that carry videotex from restrictions on eavesdropping. While the law prohibits "aural interception," furthermore, no mention is made of data and text transmission. Electronic mail, for example, does not transpire in an aural mode.

Many cable firms have adopted codes of behavior regarding the privacy of subscribers and are urging the videotex industry to pass industry-wide privacy standards. In addition, several states have already passed laws to protect the privacy of videotex users. Legislation to that effect is also being considered by Congress. The law always lags behind advances in technology. (The drafters of the law against wiretapping, for example, obviously did not anticipate videotex.) To ensure that privacy is not abused in this age of computers, we must continually be alert to the privacy implications of new technology.

THE COSTS OF PRIVACY

There are two types of expenditures involved when organizations adopt privacy policies: **one-time expenditures** to initiate privacy measures and recurring **operational costs**.

The first category includes the cost of analyzing privacy needs and designing privacy procedures. Special equipment may have to be purchased: for example, badge readers to keep unauthorized per-

Supplement 15.7 Privacy in the Back of a Cab

Electronic signboards are being installed in New York cabs. They are set in the glass partition between cabbie and passenger and deliver ten-second computer-controlled commercials called Taxigrams. In 1984, individual advertisers paid $10.29 a month for each cab which displayed its message during each four-minute advertising cycle.

Just think of the potential of this advertising mode. In the future, the computer may be programmed to adjust its message sequence according to passenger profile codes punched by the driver. For example, a teenager might be bombarded with messages of coming rock concerts and advertising for stores specializing in current fashions. The three-piece suit client might be told about expensive places to dine.

Does advertising to a trapped audience constitute an invasion of privacy? In this age of electronics, our privacy may be assaulted from unexpected quarters.

Supplement 15.8 Privacy and Electronic Mail

One usually thinks of the privacy issue in association with record-keeping systems. However, electronic mail is as vulnerable to privacy invasion as data banks. Electronic mail may contain personal information in the message. In addition, personal information can be obtained by studying who is the sender and who the addressee of the message. The latter can establish a relationship between groups of people. Should such knowledge be available to interested parties, such as law enforcement agencies, without a warrant and without the consent of message senders and recipients?

Privacy issues that must be addressed in relation to electronic mail include:

- Who owns information transmitted by electronic mail systems? The sender? The owner of the hardware? The transmission carrier?
- Does unauthorized access to electronic messages violate the law? Does such access constitute search-and-seizure without due process of law for those whose messages are intercepted?
- Are records of who sends and who receives messages in the public domain?
- Should users of electronic mail have the same protection as telephone users? What laws protect them? What federal law protects privacy when electronic mail crosses state lines?
- What is the legal liability of the carrier of electronic mail if messages are delivered to the wrong party?

sons from access to files containing personal data. Special software may have to be written: for example, a program to check user acess codes.

The main component of operational costs is salaries, primarily for clerks handling notification, access, challenge, correction, and erasure procedures. The cost of monitoring privacy procedures and resolving disputes should also be added to this category, as should fees paid for legal advice. Other operational costs include computer time for running programs related to privacy, rental or maintenance of security equipment, and supplies.

How much do privacy policies cost? Implementation of the 1974 Privacy Act has been estimated at $36 million for development, with annual operations an estimated $37 million five years later. A major problem in making such an estimate is that measures to ensure privacy also serve other organizational interests. For example, many of the measures that protect personal data also reduce the danger of lost records and work to guard government secrets and to circumvent sabotage of facilities. How can cost figures for privacy and security be separated?

Operational costs usually peak after passage of privacy legislation, when many people exercise new rights of access and challenge, and then stabilize at a lower level. When the 1971 Fair Credit Reporting Act was passed, one credit agency reported that the number of access requests to personal records rose by a factor of 2,000. One can only guess whether a similar increase would occur were the 1974 Privacy Act extended to the private sector.

SUMMING UP

Paperwork plagues organizations, and paperwork costs are rising. Information technology is a powerful paperwork cost-cutting tool. The recordkeeping ability of computers aids decision making and improves the efficiency and effectiveness of government and private organizations in their delivery of goods and services.

But this recordkeeping ability of computers also threatens individual privacy. The speed of computer processing, the collection of vast data banks, instantaneous retrieval capabilities, and telecommunications facilitate access to personal data. The 1974 Privacy Act restricts the use of personal data by U.S. federal agencies. But the provisions of the act have not been as strictly interpreted as many groups, who are concerned over the erosion of individual rights, would like. For example, matching is a common government practice. Many persons believe that matching undermines fair use protections in the Privacy Act. Perhaps special legislation on matching to protect individuals from privacy abuse is needed.

The 1974 Privacy Act does not extend to the private sector. Although many states have passed legislation incorporating similar features, most Americans believe that their privacy is not adequately protected. They know that advances in technology have given millions of individuals access to information data bases. They know that the possession of personal data banks and communications technology can lead to social control, the nightmare of George Orwell's *1984*.

Privacy issues are today being widely discussed. Where should the line between efficiency and privacy be drawn? Or to put it another way, how much privacy should be sacrificed in the interests of efficiency?

In 1982, Justice Louis D. Brandeis was confronted with a wiretapping case: at issue, privacy invasion made possible by new technology. In his dissenting opinion Justice Brandeis wrote,

> Experience should teach us to be most on our guard to protect liberty when the government's purposes are beneficent. Men born to freedom are naturally alert to repel invasion of their liberty by evil-minded rulers. The greatest dangers to liberty lurk in insidious encroachments by men of zeal, well-meaning but without understanding.[5]

[5] *Olmsted v. U.S.*, 2777 U.S. 438 (1928). (Dissenting Opinion.)

It would be wise to keep this counsel in mind as we implement computer technology and seek a balance between the privacy rights of individuals and the interests of government and business.

REVIEW QUESTIONS

1. Why has privacy become an issue in this age of computers? Is the issue different from privacy concerns prior to the advent of computers? Why is privacy important?
2. What threat does the existence of a computerized personal dossier pose to personal privacy? Describe some of the common privacy abuses of computerized information systems.
3. What was the purpose of the proposed Federal Data Center? Why was its existence opposed? Do you favor such a center? Explain your reasons.
4. How do high-speed telecommunications between remote data banks threaten personal privacy?
5. What was the contribution of the 1973 HEW Report?
6. Discuss the problem of accuracy in data banks. Cite examples of harm from data inaccuracies. Have you had personal experience with errors in computerized files? Describe your problem.
7. Discuss the concept of fair use of personal data. How does the gatekeeping issue relate to fair use? Give examples.
8. What privacy protection is legislated by the 1974 Federal Privacy Act?
9. Discuss the routine use exception of the 1974 Federal Privacy Act. Do you believe that matching is justified by this exception? Support your position.

10. Discuss the arguments for and against matching.
11. Why is videotex vulnerable to privacy abuse? How can such abuse be prevented?
12. What does it cost for an organization to initiate privacy measures? Why is it difficult to determine exact costs?

DISCUSSION QUESTIONS

1. In your judgment, is the Privacy Act of 1974 adequate? Should it be extended to state governments, universities, businesses, and other organizations?
2. If you were the head of an organization not bound by a privacy code, would you institute privacy measures? What measures? What obligation do you believe private organizations have regarding the privacy of client records?
3. Would your answer to Question 2 differ if you were the head of:
   a. a university?
   b. a hospital?
   c. a small business?
   d. an art gallery?
   e. a multinational corporation?
4. Do you support the idea of a universal personal identifier for all citizens of the U.S.? What are the advantages and disadvantages of being assigned a personal identifier at birth?
5. How can the conflict between the need for data privacy and the need for data access be resolved? What tradeoffs can be made?
6. Are laws in the U.S. adequate for detecting, discouraging, and punishing privacy violations? What new laws would you recommend? Should these be local, state, or federal laws?
7. Is the cost of privacy measures worth it? How can an organization decide whether security precautions to ensure privacy are worth the cost?
8. Are you concerned about violations of your privacy in a computerized society as:
   a. a student in an educational institution?
   b. a patient in a hospital?
   c. a depositor in a bank?
   d. a buyer of stocks and bonds through a large securities firm?
   e. a citizen of a state?
   f. a citizen of the U.S.?
   g. a church-goer?
9. Do you believe that the medical history of you and your family should be available to medical researchers? Are you concerned that your medical history, if made accessible, might be used for unauthorized purposes? What guarantees would you want to ensure privacy? Can such guarantees be trusted?
10. Do you believe that compiling census data is an invasion of the privacy of citizens? Is the gain to society from census reports worth the invasion of citizen privacy?
11. What dangers do home computers pose to personal privacy? How can privacy invasion using home computers be prevented?
12. Do you think our society collects too much data? Is all of the data necessary for the efficient functioning of government and private institutions?
13. Who should decide what information is sensitive and should not be collected because it violates our privacy?
14. Should the verification of the accuracy of data files be mandatory? What are the advantages and disadvantages of such a requirement?
15. Do the FBI and police at the state and local levels benefit from National Crime Information Center files (see Chapter 12)? Do these files threaten the privacy of individuals? How can the needs of law enforcement for information on individuals be balanced against the privacy rights of individuals?

EXERCISES

1. If your library has access to an online data base, observe and record how bibliographical data on research references can be retrieved. What are the advantages and cost elements of such an online data bank? Does such a data bank threaten your privacy?

2. List online data bases with which you have transactions, such as airline reservations, car rental reservations, and so forth. Make a list of the data elements collected by these data bases. Does the information they collect violate your privacy? How can your privacy be protected?

3. Find out what personal data is collected in your community by:
   a. sports coach
   b. hospital
   c. doctor
   d. church
   e. university
   f. bank

   Is all of the data necessary in order for each of the above to perform their duties? What information should *not* be collected?

Selected Annotated Bibliography

Burnham, David. "Tales of a Computer State," *Nation*, vol. 235, no. 17 (April 20, 1983), p. 1 ff. This article details many examples of privacy abuse resulting from data base errors.

Bushkin, Arthur L. and Schaen, Samuel I. *The Privacy Act of 1974: A Reference Manual for Companies*, McLean, Va.: System Development Corporation, 1978. The subtitle is an apt description of the book. It discusses the coverage of the act, basic compliance requirements, technical considerations for implementation, and the establishment of appropriate safeguards.

Galloway, Joseph L. "How Your Privacy Is Being Stripped Away," *U.S. News and World Report*. vol. 96, no. 4 (April 30, 1984), pp. 46–48. The growth of data banks and dangers of matching are discussed.

Gordon, Hedy. "The Interface of Living Systems and Computers: The Legal Issues of Privacy," *Computer/Law Journal*, vol. 3, no. 3 (Fall 1980), pp. 877–90. There is little legal precedent concerning computers and the invasion of privacy. Legal policy that should be implemented is suggested.

Gottlieb, C. C. and Borodin, A. *Social Issues in Computing*. New York: Academic Press, 1973. This is a good discussion of data banks, dossiers and their threat to privacy. Unfortunately, the discussion of these issues is spread throughout the book, with the result that readers must use the index to locate relevant sections. The search is worth the trouble, however.

Hoffman, Lance J. et al. *Computers and Privacy in the Next Decade*. New York: Academic Press, 1980. This book is a set of readings and commentary written by well-known experts in the field (including W. H. Ware, Paul Armer, Rein Turn, Abbe Mowshowitz). The discussion is balanced and very provocative. Included are articles on privacy, the personal computer, electronic funds transfer, transborder flow, and non-uniform privacy laws. Problems and issues arising from the need to preserve individual autonomy and to protect public order in future decades are also addressed.

Kirchner, Jake. "Privacy: A History of Computer Matching in Federal Government," *Computerworld*, vol. 15, no. 12 (December 14, 1981), pp. 1–16. A good discussion of Project MATCH.

Nash, Deanna C. and Bollier, David A. "Protecting Privacy in the Age of Hometech," *Technology Review*, vol. 83, no. 8 (August/September 1981), pp. 67–75. Interactive home media are at risk for four types of exposure: intrusion, interception, misuse of information, and aggregation of individual or household information. Safeguards are discussed.

Neustadt, Richard M. "Privacy and Videotex Systems," *Byte*, vol. 8, no. 7 (July 1983), pp. 96–103. Two-way services bring with them the potential for abuses, according to the author. They generate files of subscriber behavior and can be easily intercepted.

Smith, Robert Ellis. "Privacy: Still Threatened," *Datamation*, vol. 28, no. 10 (September 1982), pp. 296–306. Smith has impressive credentials: publisher of *Privacy Journal* and author of *Privacy: How to Protect What's Left of It*. In this article the author differentiates between privacy and security issues, discusses fair information practices, and introduces the new challenges to privacy posed by home computers and videotex.

A Challenge to Humans: Artificial Intelligence

Machines can and do transcend some of the limitations of their designers, and . . . in doing so they may be both effective and dangerous.

NORBERT WEINER

CHAPTER SIXTEEN

Key Words

artificial intelligence (AI)	**knowledge base**	**Samuel checker program**
expert systems	**knowledge information processing systems (KIPS)**	**speech understanding**
heuristics	**language translation**	**Turing test**
intelligence	**language understanding**	**ultra-intelligent machines (UIM)**
	pattern recognition	

Computers already process numeric data and text far faster than humans, without error or fatigue. They are also able to retrieve far larger amounts of data and to do so with better recall than the human mind. Work is in progress to develop hardware and software for tasks previously considered the unique prerogative of humans—that is, for tasks that require reasoning, learning, and self-improvement. Will computers eventually be able to do everything that humans can do and be more proficient as well?

Researchers are seeking an answer to this question. Professionals in psychology, linguistics, mathematics, engineering, and computer science are working together to construct computer systems to automate human tasks. Many terms have been used to describe this field of study but artificial intelligence is the catchword that is most commonly used. The term "artificial intelligence" refers to the capability of a device to perform functions that are normally associated with human intelligence.

The purpose of this chapter is to provide readers with background on artificial intelligence by discussing its historical evolution and its goals and objectives. Although artificial intelligence holds much promise for the future, few fields are as controversial. This chapter will also examine the nature of this controversy.

THE EVOLUTION OF ARTIFICIAL INTELLIGENCE

In 1956, a summer institute was organized at Dartmouth College to exchange ideas about ways of making machines behave intelligently. All of the scientists attending the conference believed that thinking could indeed take place outside of the human brain. All agreed that the digital computer would be the best nonhuman instrument for this purpose. Many of the conference participants were already engaged in projects to enhance the problem-solving capabilities of computers. Some were programming computers to play games and prove theorems, activities that require reasoning. Others were interested in problems of **pattern recognition** (recognition of forms, shapes, or configurations by automatic means) and language (translation and understanding by machines of human language). At Dartmouth, participants reported on the progress of their work and discussed directions for future research.

Many expressions were used at Dartmouth to describe complex information processing and machine learning, including the term "artificial intelligence." This term has gained widespread popularity in spite of the objection of many scientists that there is nothing artificial about machine intelligence. The Dartmouth conference is usually credited with naming and formally launching artificial intelligence as a new field of endeavor.

DEFINING INTELLIGENCE

Artificial intelligence (AI) is the capability of a machine to perform operations associated with human intelligence. But what is **intelligence**?

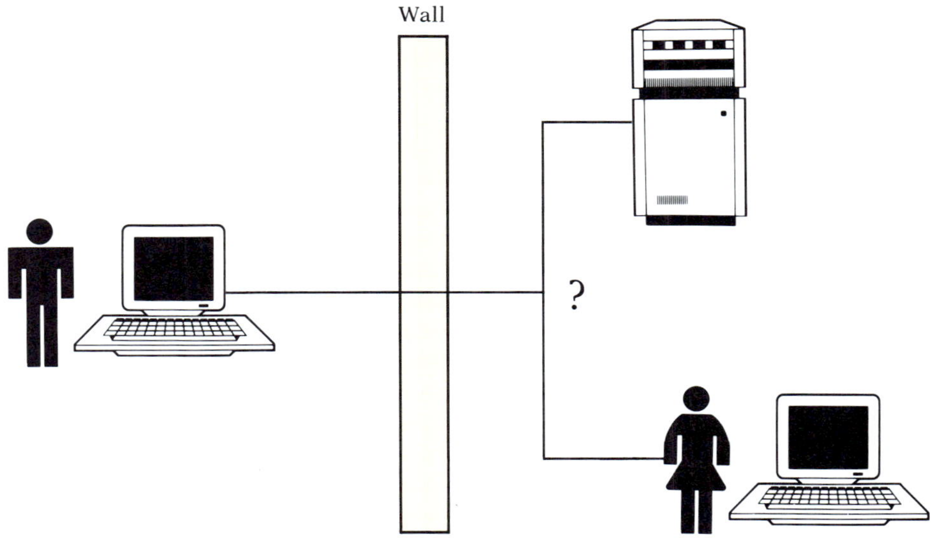

Figure 16.1 The Turing Test. In the Turing test a human communicates with an unseen respondent through a terminal, not knowing if the respondent is a person or a machine. If the tester mistakes computer answers for human answers, the computer successfully passes the Turing test.

Webster's dictionary describes intelligence as the ability to learn or understand from experience. The faculty of reasoning, the ability to perceive relationships, and the power of thought are also given as attributes. Other lexicographers add creativity and originality as essential components of intelligence.

These definitions only add to the problem of defining intelligence since they make the list of terms that need to be defined even longer. What constitutes "learning"? What is "thinking"? What is "creativity"? Can learning, thinking, and creativity be measured?

It is argued that computers have demonstrated intelligence by proving geometry theorems (including Pythagoras' theorem) and finding solutions to problems in logic and calculus. Computers have been programmed to rediscover laws from physics such as Archimedes' law of displacement and Ohm's law for electric circuits. As early as the 1960s, computers composed music, produced graphic art, and designed an electric motor. Certainly we would attribute intelligence to humans performing the same activities.

CAN MACHINES THINK?

"Can machines think?" is the type of question philosophers like to debate. Since humans think, perhaps one way of deciding whether a machine can think is to see whether a machine can be mistaken for a human. Alan Turing, a British mathematician challenged by the problem of developing a criterion of thinking, suggested such a test. He proposed a "conversation" over a teleprinter circuit between a human and an unseen respondent. If the average human could not correctly decide whether the respondent was a person or machine, it would have to be admitted that the respondent was thinking (see Figure 16.1).

If one accepts the validity of the Turing test, a chess match in 1978 might be used to support the thesis that machines can think. In this match, a computer program, Chess 4.7, was challenged by David Levy. Levy commented after the game that the computer responded like a human.

The responses of a computer in a **Turing test** depend on programming and the data base stored in computer memory. Unless programmed to calculate averages, a computer cannot figure the average of 2 and 6 although this is a simple problem. Unless updated with recent Wall Street quotations, it cannot give the current price of AT&T stock. Of course, the computer can be programmed to give evasive answers, such as "I'm not interested in the stock market." And it might fool an interrogator when asked questions such as "What is the color of your hair?" by being programmed to brag about its charms. The nature of the test prevents the interrogator from demanding a demonstration that such charms exist.

Many anecdotes can be cited of computers fooling people for short periods of time into believing they are human respondents, not machines. But no computer has yet been built that can imitate humans indefinitely. Failure of the Turing test does not mean that computers do *not* think (nor does passing the Turing test prove that they *do*) since it can be argued that the test itself is not a valid test of thinking.

CAN MACHINES LEARN?

If learning is an attribute of intelligence, perhaps machine intelligence can be demonstrated by showing that a computer can learn.

In the 1950s, Arthur Samuel programmed a computer to play checkers to test his hypothesis that machines can indeed learn. His checker program identified and stored winning game strategies (and losing strategies), and copied winning moves in subsequent play (while avoiding losing moves). As a result, the program Samuel wrote soon played a better game than Samuel himself. In time, the computer even beat state checker champions. The **Samuel checker program** demonstrated that self-improvement could be programmed, that computers could learn from experience. It was a major contribution to early AI research.

When Samuel first began writing his checker program, he considered programming a decision tree. All possible paths from each decision point (each checker) would be delineated. The computer would be given the task of searching the various paths leading to the end of the game and then selecting a path that would lead to a win.

This technique is illustrated in Figure 16.2 for tic-tac-toe, a simpler game than checkers. Only a partial tree is illustrated, showing some of the options that follow a single initial move. A more complex tree could be prepared showing all game moves. If the complex tree were input, the computer could be programmed to search all paths in the tree in order to identify a winning strategy after each move by an opponent.

Given the speed of computers, a tic-tac-toe decision-tree search doesn't take long. (This strategy is used to search data structures for many simple business problems.) However, a decision tree for a game of strategy is much more complex. Samuel calculated the need to search 10^{21} moves for a game of checkers. In chess, an exhaustive search of only three moves for each player from a given decision point involves a search of 1.8 billion possibilities. A computer can make such a search, but it would be time-consuming and costly.

Samuel decided a more promising approach for his game of checkers would be to employ **heuristic** rules of thumb to identify winning strategies. (In heuristic problem solving, solutions are discovered by evaluating progress made toward the end result, a guided trial-and-error approach.) Heuristic principles in the checker program would shorten the decision tree search by pruning the tree. Using heuristics, a computer might be programmed to mark the center square in tic-tac-toe as a first move, disregarding all other possibilities. In chess, the knight might be kept from the edges of the board since half the possible movement of the piece is lost there. Samuel's problem was to devise a set of rules for choosing promising paths to search, rules that would lead to a checkers win and eliminate dead-end searches. (Rules of thumb can contribute to game losses if they are ill-conceived.)

One way to eliminate unpromising alternatives is to formulate a strategy and investigate only those paths consistent with that strategy. A fire chief who analyzes past fires by type, time, and place, and trains firefighters to recognize and meet similar emergencies, has a strategy for training that eliminates preparation for unlikely conflagrations. In the event of the unexpected, however, the plan for training may prove incomplete. Samuel realized in writing his checkers program that both his heuristics and planned game strategy were possibly inadequate.

A third element was, therefore, added to his program, that of pattern recognition. Successful

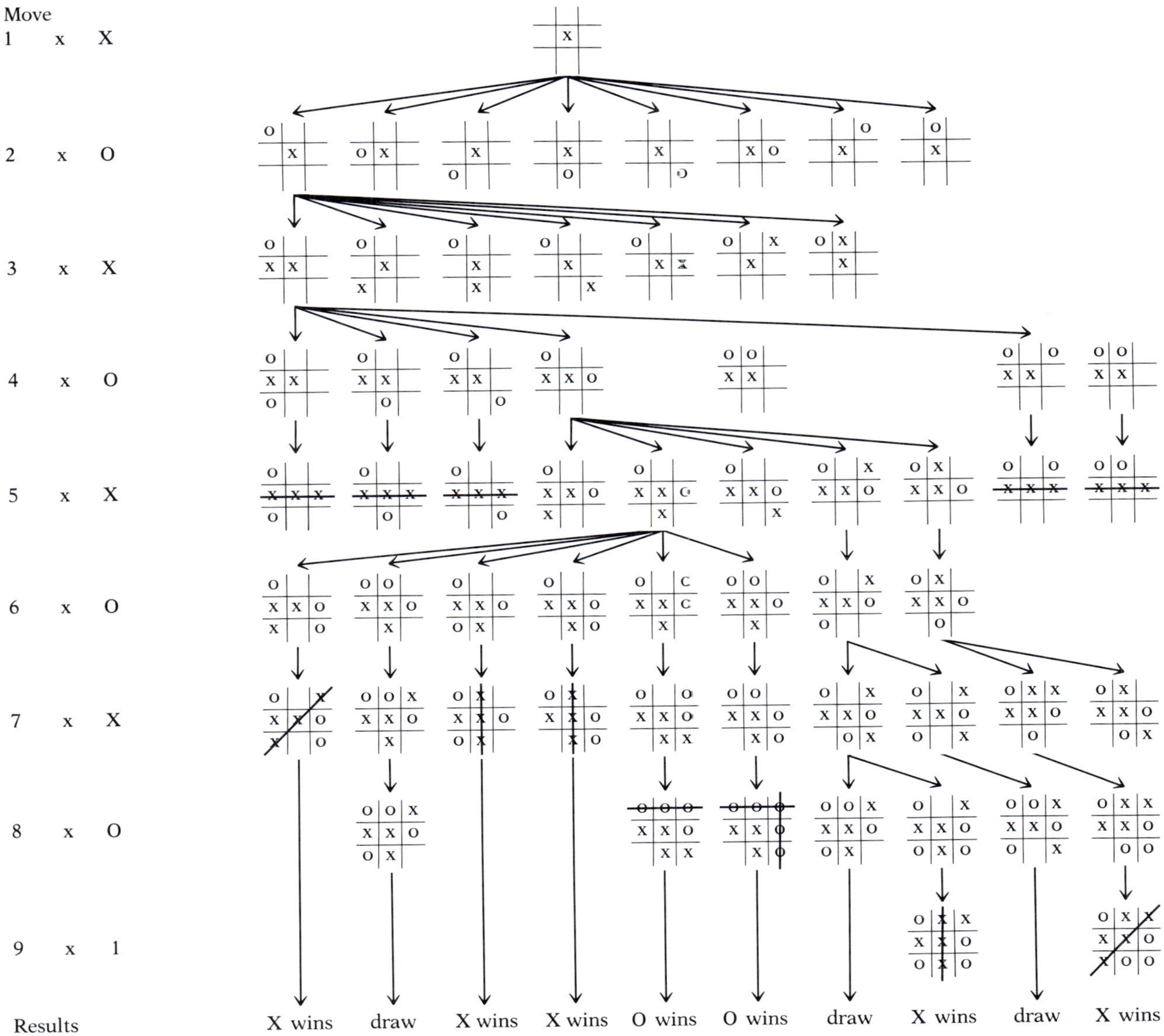

Figure 16.2 Partial decision tree for tic-tac-toe. This diagram is a partial decision tree for tic-tac-toe tracing one branch of the tree leading to a win for X, should the first move of X be the center square. Row 1 shows the initial move of X. Row 2 shows the possible responses of 0. To simplify the diagram, Row 3 takes one of these responses and lists all possible counter moves for X, while Row 4 pursues options for 0 for some of the possible X choices in Row 3. Rows 5, 6, 7, and 8 show possible winning game strategies for X after the move in Row 4.

Supplement 16.1 Facts vs. Heuristics

Fact: Plants need water.
Heuristic: Water house plants when the soil feels dry to the finger.

Fact: Zinfandel is a full-bodied, dry, red wine.
Heuristic: Red wines are usually best with beef.

Fact: Rice increases in bulk when cooked in water.
Heuristic: Allow 1 cup of uncooked rice for 4 servings.

Fact: The height of a person depends on bone growth.
Heuristic: Double the height of a child at age 2½ to determine the child's adult height.

Although heuristics guide our thinking, they are not always true. Unlike facts, a heuristic often has to be changed to fit the variables in a given environment.

game players often make standard moves to common board positions or develop their own set of responses to familiar game patterns. Samuel programmed the computer to identify and store winning game patterns, including winning game patterns used by opponents. These patterns were then used in game playing by the computer.

Samuel's programming of decision trees, heuristics, and pattern recognition rules resulted in a checker program that learned, a program that could modify itself as result of experience. Although never a world-class checker master, the program improved its performance with each game.

Since Samuel's pioneering learning program, many others have contributed to the subject of machine learning. Researchers have approached the problem from two different angles. On the one hand, studies of the physiology of the human mind have resulted in attempts to construct computers that match the manner by which the brain appears to process information. This explains the interest of AI researchers in parallel processing, described in Chapter 13. Other researchers are searching for electronic solutions to problem solving that do not necessarily follow the methods used by the brain. The emphasis is rather on designing hardware and software that will match the *results* of human thought.

LANGUAGE UNDERSTANDING

Programming a computer to understand ordinary natural language is one of the most difficult challenges in computer science. It is believed that many future commercial applications of computers will require interchange between humans and machines in English or other natural languages. This is why both industry and government (the U.S. Defense Department in particular) are interested in language research. The problem challenges persons in the field of artificial intelligence since **language understanding** seems to be close to the essence of human thought.

Language research has taken many directions. One is **language translation**. Indeed, the Japanese have declared that a major goal for their fifth generation computers, projected for the 1990s, is Japanese-English translation. One translation approach has been storing dictionaries and rules of grammar and syntax in computer memory so that word-by-word translation can take place. Early results in this direction proved far from satisfactory. For example, "The spirit is willing but the flesh is weak," translated by this method into Russian, then back into English, resulted in "The vodka is strong but the meat is rotten." The ambiguities in the meanings of words that are intrinsic in natural languages and other semantic problems are major stumbling blocks in any translation effort.

Joseph Weizenbaum has produced a family of

Supplement 16.2 ELIZA Put to the Test

Upon arrival at work early one Saturday morning, a vice president of Bolt, Bernak and Newman, Inc. found the following message attached to a PDP-1 computer teletype terminal: "Type all messages into this teletype and end them with a period."

Assuming that the teletype was linked to the home of a colleague, Dr. Daniel Bobrow, the officer initiated the following conversation.

VP:	Do you think I can use the computer this morning?
Response:	Why do you ask?
VP:	I might be able to make some additional sales.
Response:	Why aren't you sure?
VP:	My prospective customers have never seen a demonstration of the system.
Response:	Does this mean very much to you?
VP:	Of course it does.
Response:	You seem very positive about that.
VP:	This is ridiculous.
Response:	What do you mean by ridiculous?
VP:	Is there any reason why I can't use the computer now?
Response:	Tell me about your prospective customers.
VP:	Please dial me up on 491-1850

When the VP got no response or phone call (note the missing period), he was decidedly irritated. Thinking someone was playing games with him, the VP phoned Dr. Bobrow for a explanation, waking him from a sound sleep. Dr. Bobrow burst into laughter when the VP related the conversation. The teletype, Bobrow explained, was linked to a computer. The VP had been communicating with ELIZA.

*Source: *Newsletter of the Special Interest Group on Artificial Intelligence of the Association of Computing Machinery*, December 1969, and Z. W. Pylyshyn, *Perspectives on the Computer Revolution*, Englewood Cliffs, N.J.: Prentice-Hall, Inc., 1970, pp. 347–48.

programs called DOCTOR that make it possible for patients to converse quite naturally with a computer through a terminal. For example, his program ELIZA provides responses similar to those given by some psychotherapists by rephrasing human statements or giving standard replies, as in this exchange:

> ELIZA's opening statement (appears on CRT screen): Do you have any problems?
> Human (types response on terminal keyboard): Yes, I am unhappy.
> ELIZA: Why are you unhappy?
> Human: My friend is mean to me.
> ELIZA: Tell me about your friend.

ELIZA's stock of stored sentences and programmed rephrasing has fooled many persons into believing they were conversing with a doctor, not a computer. But Weizenbaum cautions against the simple and superficial level of language understanding of his DOCTOR programs and denounces the use of such programs in clinical situations.

In order for a computer to truly understand a natural language, the machine must know the meaning of words in context. It must understand metaphors, appreciate the unstated goals and beliefs of the speaker, be able to perceive inferences, and recognize the underlying motivations of characters in a given context. In addition, the computer must be able to handle inconsistent information and judge the plausibility of sentences. For example, understanding of the sentence, "John ate up the compliments," depends on recognition that the object of the verb is, strictly speaking, inappropriate for its action and that the statement therefore constitutes a kind of metaphor. Understanding the sentence "Mary jumped ten feet when she heard the news," requires the ability to recognize exaggeration.

In 1977 Terry Winograd of MIT demonstrated that a computer could "understand," to a limited extent, both verbal language and geometrical manipulations. His work was one of the early breakthroughs in language understanding. Winograd programmed a computer to carry on protracted conversations, recognize and use colloquial sentence fragments, correctly interpret pronouns, and

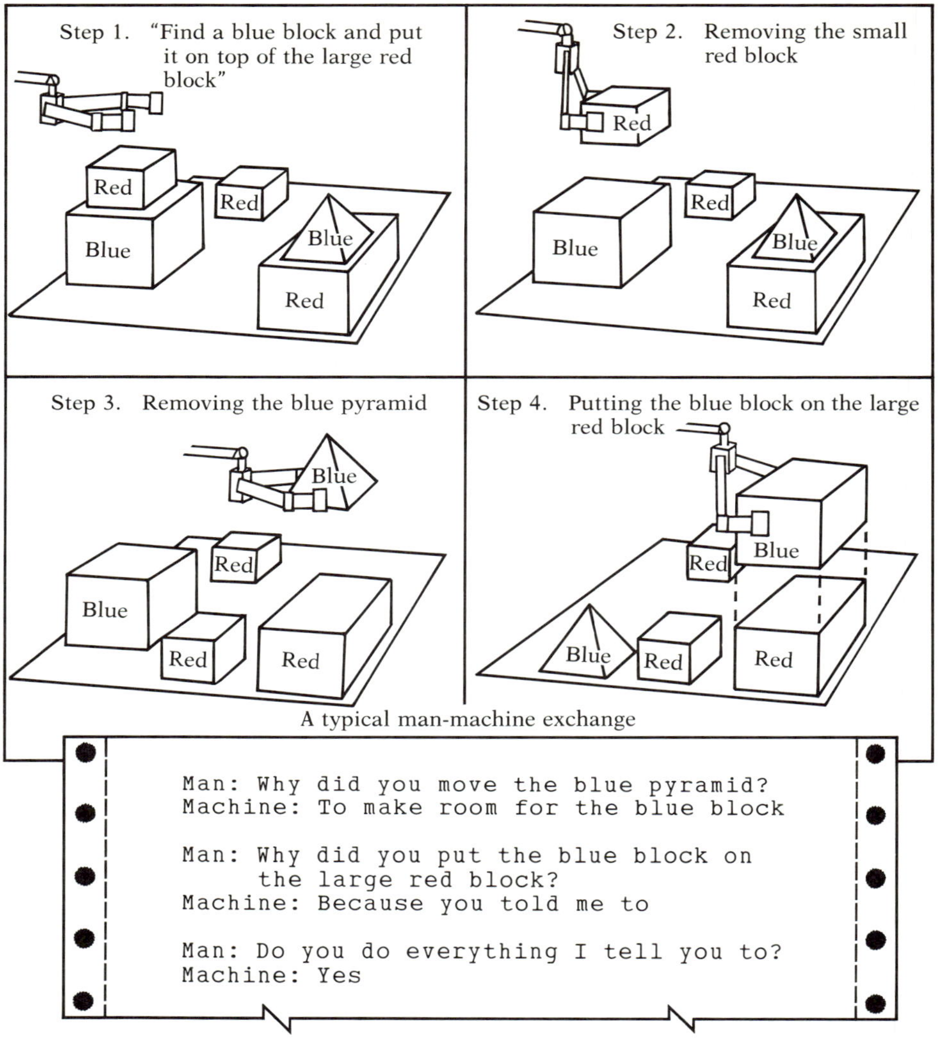

Figure 16.3 Winograd's program for block manipulation. This figure illustrates the level of language understanding of Winograd's program. Note that several actions are required by the robot arm to carry out the command in Step 1.

Source: Tom Logsdon, *Computers & Social Controversy*. Potomac, Maryland: Computer Science Press, 1980, p. 247.

derive meaningful interpretations from many ambiguous constructions. Although the environment had constraints placed on it (see Figure 16.3), the achievement was significant.

Many researchers regard language understanding as a problem of modeling common sense. The best programs to date can deal with language in narrow, limited domains but have not been able to extend understanding to a broad range of experience. (See Supplement 16.3 for an example.) More knowledge of human cognition may be needed before computer systems can be designed to simulate common sense. Even with this knowledge, there is no certainty that common sense can be programmed. Some scientists doubt whether machines will ever be able to perform tasks that require a common sense understanding of the environment in which they operate.

Supplement 16.3 INTELLECT, a Natural Language Program

INTELLECT, developed by Artificial Intelligence Corporation (AIC) of Waltham, Massachusetts, is a program that allows a manager to get information from a computer without having to ask a computer expert for help. People who work with computers every day quickly master the rules for using a computer. That is, they learn the codes they need, how to program commands, how to work through menus, and so forth. Managers who are occasional computer users, however, seldom know how to get information they want from a computer. INTELLECT, a product of extensive artificial intelligence research, is programmed for them.

INTELLECT takes an English-language request typed in by the user and translates this request into a form that the computer can process, taking into account the peculiarities of the data base being queried. This may sound easy but it isn't. The computer must have knowledge about the user's intention and background in order to make this translation. For example, if a manager types, "What is the average earnings of the salesmen in New York?" the program must be able to determine from the data base that New York has two meanings, city and state. It must then respond by asking the manager which he means.

Each time INTELLECT is sold for a commercial application, a dictionary of appropriate vocabulary is developed by AIC and added to the program. This may even include corporate slang. Ford uses INTELLECT to handle questions about which cars have met which environmental rules. Du Pont uses it to handle questions about sales and production of polymers and resins. INTELLECT is successful because it operates in a limited domain. It cannot understand natural language outside of that domain.

Supplement 16.4 Speech Recognition System

IBM has developed an experimental speech recognition system using voice input to create office documents. Five thousand words, consisting of business correspondence vocabulary, are stored in computer memory in "base form" pronunciation models constructed from a 200-element alphabet of sound "labels."

Spoken words are compared by the system with the label models of its base forms. (The way an individual pronounces different sound labels is obtained during a 20-minute training session. Only these individuals are permitted to use the system.) The system also calculates the probability that words will occur in certain contexts based on its analysis of twenty-five million words of office correspondence. (The system statistically predicts the likelihood of the next word given the previous two identified. If the third word is unlikely, the previous words will be reevaluated and possibly changed.)

These techniques enable the system to correctly identify the spoken words in its vocabulary 95 percent of the time.

Research is also being conducted in the related field of **speech understanding** (a combination of speech recognition and language understanding). The potential in all environments for computers with language and speech understanding is mind-boggling. Imagine a homemaker able to give instructions to a stove by talking instead of setting time and temperature controls, a foreman able to direct the movements of robots by speech, or a general able to target a cruise missile by voice.

EXPERT SYSTEMS

Researchers in artificial intelligence are also working in the field of **expert systems**. Expert systems are programmed to ask users to supply information on a problem. The computer then processes the information and reaches conclusions normally requiring human expertise.

An example is MYCIN, developed at Stanford University, which recommends drugs and treatment for patients with bacterial infections. MYCIN asks questions regarding patient symptoms and general health, and requests information on medical history and test results. The dialogue below is an example of the type of information exchange that takes place. A computer terminal is used to display questions and key answers.

MYCIN: From what site was Culture 1 taken?
Answer: Blood
MYCIN: When?
Answer: 1985
MYCIN: When in 1985?
Answer: December 1985
MYCIN: What is the weight of the patient?
Answer: 125 pounds

The diagnosis of MYCIN is based on a set of decision rules (over 300 in an early version) regarding bacterial infections. That is, the computer diagnoses the problem from the information entered into the system by following the logic of programmed rules. An example of such a rule is as follows:

IF the infection type is primary bacteremia and the site of culture is one of the sterile sites, and the suspected point is the gastrointestinal tract,

THEN there is evidence that the organism is bacteriodes.

The computer data base contains information on drugs and treatment for each diagnosis the system makes. This information is drawn from computer memory and displayed on the terminal screen once the user-supplied information is processed and a diagnosis is reached.

One problem with computer diagnosis is that a correct diagnosis requires carefully defined decision rules. Expert systems such as MYCIN cannot be programmed by the average computer analyst. The programming of facts and rules requires the knowledge of a specialist in the field in which the system claims expertise. This field must be narrowly defined so that possibilities are limited and the amount of data to be programmed is manageable. The specialist must be dedicated to, or at least not antagonistic to, the concept of expert systems and be willing to work with a person skilled in programming.

Another limitation of computer diagnosis is that an accurate, updated data base is essential. Furthermore, a human expert is necessary to ensure that the treatment recommended by the computer is appropriate. These limitations explain why expert systems for diagnosis are restricted to narrow medical domains and are not commonly used in clinical practice. There is still much to be learned by AI researchers before the expertise of humans in medicine and other subject areas can be matched by machine. MYCIN is described in this chapter because it illustrates how expert systems work and because it has served as a model for other expert systems, since it was one of the first expert systems to be developed.

MYCIN has many features of interest. For example, it uses decision rules of diagnosis to identify whether or not necessary symptoms exist by working *backward* from the rules to deduce the symptoms (this process is called "backward chaining"). MYCIN also uses probabilities and certainty factors for each branch of the question-answer tree to calculate the degree of confidence the system has in its diagnosis. In addition, MYCIN can answer questions regarding how a diagnosis has been reached. For example, it might cite Rule 251 in its data base as the key to its diagnosis, and state that rule upon request.

Dialogue between MYCIN and a physician may remind the doctor of important diagnostic decision rules or symptoms associated with a particular illness. Such a dialogue also has another useful purpose: it can help locate faults in the program, such as the absence of a crucial decision rule or the need to add recently marketed medications to the data base. One of MYCIN's strengths lies in the fact that many users contribute program modifications and help update the data base.

Another example of an expert system in the medical field is MECS-AI, a system developed by a team at Tokyo University for problems of the thyroid. The program incorporates 200 decision rules for the diagnosis of twenty thyroid diseases. The reasoning for each diagnosis is explained (with

Supplement 16.5 Sample of Expert Systems Currently in Use or Under Development

System	Knowledge domain	Function performed
AQ11	Medicine	Diagnosis of plant diseases
CASNET	Medicine	Medical consulting, infectious diseases
CONGEN	Chemistry	Determining chemical structure of an unknown compound
DENDRAL	Chemistry	Hypothesizing molecular structure from mass spectrograms
DIPMETER ADVISER	Oil industry	Oil exploration
EL	Electrical industry	Analyzing electrical circuits
GUIDON	Medicine	Computer-aided instruction
HASP (SU/X)	Machine acoustics	Problem solving
INTERNIST/CADUCEUS	Medicine	Consultant in internal medicine
HASP/SIAP	Defense	Passive sonar surveillance system
MACSYMA	Math	Mathematical formula manipulation
MECHO	Machine industry	Problem solving and planning
MOLGEN	Biology	Planning DNA elements and genetic engineering
MYCIN	Medicine	Infectious disease treatment consultant
PECOS	Programming	Problem solving
PROSPECTOR	Mining industry	Mineral exploration
PUFF	Medicine	Diagnosis of lung diseases
R1	Computer industry	Computer configurations (VAX-11/780 systems)
SACON	Engineering	Diagnosis
SECHS	Chemistry	Search
SOPHIE	Electronics	Computer-aided instruction
SYNCEM	Chemistry	Search
VM	Medicine	Measurement and interpretation
XCON	Computers	Diagnosis of computer malfunctions

special explanations given for look-alike symptoms). Case histories are cited to back up conclusions. The system also accepts patient progress reports and will update its diagnosis.

Supplement 16.5 is a list of sample expert systems that have been implemented in medicine and other fields. Systems are under development in most of the hard sciences and applications have been proposed in many professions and occupations, such as law, agriculture, and even plumbing. Such systems have many educational uses. For example, medical students have found MYCIN helpful when studying infectious diseases. Expert systems can serve as a training device. Written classroom materials derived from expert systems are often superior to materials developed from conventional sources.

Other uses for expert systems include:

- *Advice to experts on unfamiliar issues.* For example, a lawyer who seldom engages in tax planning might consult the expert system TAXADVISOR.
- *Preliminary screening for experts to save them time.* For example, computerized tax files might be reviewed by an expert system when tax laws are changed to identify clients whose portfolios should be reviewed.
- *Solutions to common problems for nonexperts and diagnosis of conditions that make consultation with a human expert imperative.*
- *Temporary consultant when human expert is not available.*

Supplement 16.6 Developing AUDITOR, an Expert System

AUDITOR is an expert system that assists auditors in assessing a company's allowance for bad debts. To formulate the knowledge base for this system, its developer, Christopher Dungan, asked expert auditors to list factors or clues they use in examining the allowance for bad debts. Then the auditors were asked to give relative weights to each factor. Finally, the auditors were asked about the existence and nature of relationships between factors.

This information was next assembled in approximately fifty rules using the programming language AL/X developed at the University of Edinburgh. In the testing phase, AUDITOR was used in real and hypothetical cases. The opinions of expert auditors were solicited in order to refine the rules.

Finally the system was validated in two ways.

1. Auditors who helped develop the system tested it against ten cases taken from audit working papers.
2. Two other auditors, one using the program, the other using traditional auditing procedures, evaluated eleven cases and compared results.

There was more than 90 percent agreement between the expert system AUDITOR and the human auditors in both validation procedures. The validations supported the belief that the rules were accurate and that the system merited the label "expert system."

GOALS OF AI

Why are AI researchers focusing on machine equivalents of human processes? Because advances in language and speech understanding, relevance extraction, deduction, vision, discovery techniques, and other topics listed in Figure 16.4 are required to reach the ultimate goal of AI. This goal is to move beyond traditional computer applications that operate on only two levels, data and programs, to **knowledge information processing systems (KIPS)** that will combine (1) the problem-solving ability of computers, and (2) the algorithm power of decision models, (3) with the know-how of experts and (4) a self-modification capability.

Should KIPS prove feasible, they will incorporate both machine learning and a knowledge base. Unlike present data bases which store explicit information, a **knowledge base** will consist of facts stored in computer memory plus IF-THEN rules that allow information to be created from these basic facts. Let us take an example of family relationships to explain this difference. In the structured data base common today, all relationships must be entered.

Example: Tom is Billy's parent.
Tom is Steve's brother.
Steve is Billy's uncle.

In a knowledge base, inference rules allow relationships to be derived from input. From the data

Mary is Billy's parent.
Mary is Jane's sister.

the information that Jane is Billy's aunt could be derived by programming the following IF-THEN rule.

IF (PARENT X Y) and (SISTER X Z), THEN (AUNT Z Y).

The bulk of information in a knowledge base is inferred in this manner. When new facts are added to the base during use, new relationships between the facts will be derived—relationships that the user does not have to input. Indeed, the user may be totally unaware of the existence of these relationships.

A knowledge base is another feature the Japanese plan to incorporate in their fifth generation computers announced for the 1990s.

COMPARING HUMAN AND COMPUTER CAPABILITIES

Humans have some capabilities that machines may never be able to duplicate. As Lewis Garret put it,

Perception	Pattern recognition (vision, voice, images, language) Relevance extraction Language understanding
Remembering	Information retrieval Question-answering
Thinking	Deduction Heuristics Inferences
Learning	Induction Discovery Generalization
Motivation by goals	Goal seeking Optimization (of goals) Satisfying (of goals)

Figure 16.4 Topics of AI research.

Man is inventive and flexible. He perceives, abstracts, and associates quite well, drawing on broad experience to make decisions and check reasonableness. However, he is forgetful of detail, inaccurate, and subject to boredom and fatigue.[1]

Computer systems are in general faster than humans, and both accurate and consistent in recalling and processing information. However, they currently lack the flexibility of humans. They also lack the ability to function independently since they must be programmed and operated by humans. Other differences between the human brain and computers are listed in Table 16.1.

[1]Lewis E. Garret, "Primer on Artificial Intelligence," *The Best of Creative Computing*, vol. 2, Morristown, N.J.: Creative Computing Press, 1977.

Table 16.1 Comparison between human brain and computers

Area of comparison	Computer 1960	Computer 1980	Computer 2000	Human
Memory density (bits/cm^3)	10^3	10^5	10^9	10^{16}
Computing power (switches/second)	10^{12}	10^{13}	10^{15}	10^{12}
Speed (cycles per second)	10^6	10^8	10^{10}	10^2
Total density (circuits/cm^2)	10	10^2	10^5	10^7
Accuracy	Superior, especially in numeric computation			
Visual domain				Superior
Auditory domain				Superior
Fatigue	No loss of efficiency of effectiveness because of fatigue			Tires easily
Breakdown	Breaks down completely if few connectors are destroyed			Has some of the same capabilities
Problem-solving strengths	Defined and well-structured problems			Ill-defined, ill-structured problems as well as defined well-structured problems
Ability to adapt to changed conditions	Limited			High
Life	5–30 years			75 years
Ability to correlate and analyze masses of data	Good			Poor

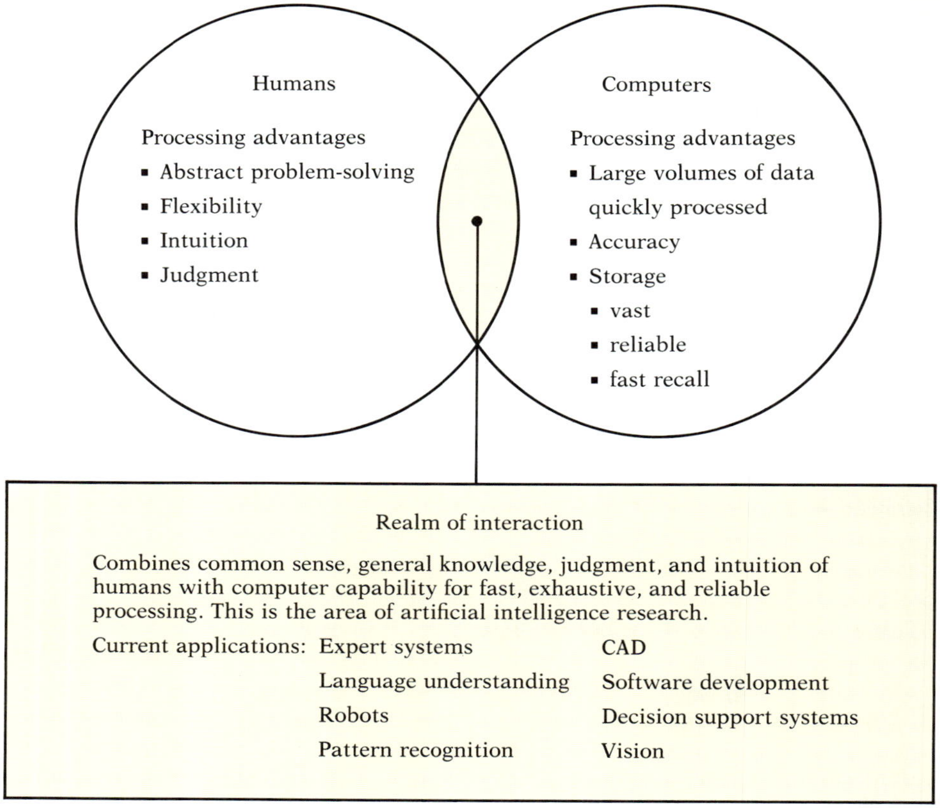

Figure 16.5 Areas of comparative advantage.

Society will benefit most if the complementary strengths of humans and computers are utilized. Figure 16.5 shows areas where men and machines have comparative advantages and illustrates that there is a realm of interaction where humans and computers together can be more effective than either alone. We need man's aesthetic and emotional sensitivity to temper machine rationality. In any case, as Lord Bowden, a distinguished British scientist, argues, it would be futile to try to duplicate humans with computers in a world already overpopulated by intelligent beings that are produced quite easily, relatively cheaply, and in an enjoyable way.

Some people prophesy a future in which the capacity of computers to learn will be used to design improvements in computer hardware and software—improvements that add to the capabilities of the machines. These new capabilities combined with learning may, in turn, trigger new design improvements, a cycle that may be repeated until **ultra-intelligent machines (UIMs)** have been developed.

Marvin Minsky, an MIT scientist, cautions that machine intelligence may cause problems as well as solve them.

> It is unreasonable to think that machines will become *nearly* as intelligent as we are and then stop, or to suppose that we will always be able to compete with them in wit or wisdom. Whether or not we could retain some sort of control of the machines, assuming that we would want to, the nature of our activities and aspirations would be changed utterly by the presence on earth of intellectually superior beings.[2]

[2]Richard C. Dorf, *Computers and Man*, 2nd ed., San Francisco: Boyd & Fraser Publishing Company, 1977, p. 405.

Supplement 16.7 Vision for Robots

Until recently, it has been difficult for robots to remove parts from a bin when assembling circuit boards or microcomputers on an assembly line because robots typically cannot see three dimensionally. Systems that have been developed for three-dimensional vision take up to an hour to "see" an image, much too long for practical use in manufacturing.

Two scientists, Berthold Horn and Katsushi Ikeuchi, working at MIT's Artificial Intelligence Laboratory have developed a new vision system that can "see" an image in one minute. Their system uses a video camera, a computer programmed in LISP (a language used in AI projects), and a modified version of the Fisher-Price Company's "Rack-and-Stack" toy. They call this system "photometric stereo vision." It works by rasterizing (breaking into electronic segments) the image of a part. This image is then stored in computer memory. When the robot must withdraw that part from a parts bin, three lights from different directions are flashed on the bin creating a stereo effect. This enables the computer brain of the robot to recognize the part no matter what position it is in.

This vision system may be used in electronics and computer manufacturing. Another possible application is rudimentary inspection of finished assemblies.

Whether machines will be developed in the future that surpass humans in intelligence remains to be seen. Clearly computers today have more intelligence than in the past and strides are being made to increase machine capabilities.

AI CONTROVERSY

Will our society be able to assimilate intelligent machines? Should we call a halt to further research in AI? What are the social, psychological, ethical, and human implications of developing machines with problem-solving capabilities that surpass human capabilities in many domains? Although researchers in artificial intelligence have been discussing these questions among themselves for some time, the public has only recently begun to address these issues. Is it possible that people will begin to feel subservient to machines and no longer value human life? Some psychologists fear that intelligent machines will so threaten man's self-image that pathological behavior may result. Culture shock may be many magnitudes greater than described by Alvin Toffler in *Future Shock*.

Joseph Weizenbaum, an eminent computer scientist whose program ELIZA was discussed earlier, recommends that we identify and specify worthy national goals for AI instead of pursuing AI research blindly without knowledge or concern for the consequences. He argues that there are certain tasks which computers *ought* not be made to do, independent of whether computers *can* be made to do them.

Weizenbaum's critics counter that researchers can never assess the prospective benefits of a contemplated invention. Indeed, a given line of research may prove both beneficial and harmful to society. Consider the development of radar and advances in aircraft which are useful in both peace and war.

Without doubt, computers will change the way we work and alter social patterns in the future. It is not surprising that the field of artificial intelligence has become controversial since the direction of AI research may well decide the nature of these changes.

SUMMING UP

Although the number of commercial artificial intelligence applications is currently limited, the field of AI has generated much excitement. Research in the representation of knowledge and in machine learning has progressed. Language and speech understanding are being pursued. It is hoped that individuals will soon be able to converse with computers in a natural language, such as English, without having to learn a formalized computer language, such as BASIC or Pascal. Expert systems are also being developed that incorporate the knowledge of specialists to aid humans in making decisions about difficult problems. At this point, however, expert systems have only been developed in a few domains.

It is conceivable, but by no means certain, that research in artificial intelligence will lead to the creation of ultra-intelligent machines (UIMs) that surpass the capabilities of the human intellect. Clearly, many people already feel threatened by computers with limited artificial intelligence and question whether such machines will enhance the quality of human life. They are afraid that machine efficiency will be given priority over human concerns in the future and that decision making will no longer depend on trust, faith, compassion, and other values that humans cherish. Indeed, many people believe that mechanization is incompatible with humanism.

Others look forward to advances in artificial intelligence. They foresee a future in which humans direct the use of intelligent machines for the benefit of all mankind.

REVIEW QUESTIONS

1. What is artificial intelligence? What problems of definition arise in this discipline?
2. What is the Turing test? What assumptions are made in the test? Does application of the test to computers prove that computers can think?
3. What was the purpose of the Samuel checker program? Did it succeed in meeting its purpose?
4. What are heuristics? Give examples of the application of heuristics in a field of your choice.
5. What is pattern recognition? Compare pattern recognition in Samuel's checker program to a security device that opens a safe on the basis of handprints.
6. What two approaches to machine learning are used by AI researchers?
7. What makes language understanding by computer so difficult? Why does the subject interest persons in AI?
8. What is an expert system? How are expert systems developed? How do they work?
9. What is the meaning of KIPS? Compare KIPS with computer information systems currently in use. How will KIPS be an improvement?
10. Compare the human brain with a computer.
11. Discuss the controversy that surrounds AI. What point of view does Joseph Weizenbaum represent?

DISCUSSION QUESTIONS

1. Do you agree with the statement, "Artificial intelligence is the most promising subdiscipline in computer science?" Explain your answer.
2. Discuss obstacles to the success of AI. How can these obstacles be overcome?
3. In AI research what should be the role of:
   a. government?
   b. industry?
   c. academia?
4. What disciplines outside of computer science can and should contribute to AI research? What types of contributions can they make?
5. Do you agree that computers can think and demonstrate intelligence? Explain your reasoning.
6. Do you believe UIMs are feasible? How might society be altered by the introduction of UIMs? What dangers do you foresee? What steps should be taken now to prepare society for such machines?
7. How will intelligent computers affect:
   a. business?
   b. government?
   c. defense?
   d. homemakers?
   e. industry?

8. Why is it taking so long to develop products that incorporate pattern recognition and computer language understanding? What are the obstacles to commercial applications of AI?

9. Do you believe that research in AI is desirable and should be supported? Or do you believe such research should be stopped? Why? Who should do the supporting or the stopping?

10. Give examples of expert systems that might be developed in your field of interest given the present state of AI technology. Do you think that expert systems will put people out of work? Threaten you in your chosen profession? If so, what can you do about it?

11. In what areas have AI applications been successful? What prerequisites are necessary for successful application of artificial intelligence?

12. Do you share the view that computers are already smart . . . and getting smarter at a frightening rate?

EXERCISES

1. Review a film that you have seen in which a computer demonstrated intelligent behavior.

2. Visit an organization using robots that can be categorized as intelligent robots (or read about such robot use). What did the robots do? How was their intelligence exhibited?

3. Read a fictional account about an intelligent computer. How was this intelligence demonstrated? Do you think that advances in computer science might make this fiction fact in the future?

4. Find articles describing applications of AI research. What applications are under development?

5. Interview a user of an expert system. Describe the advantages and limitations of the system from the user's viewpoint.

6. Make a list of intelligent features you think computers should incorporate.

7. Give an example of a dialogue you might have with an intelligent computer for:
   a. data entry.
   b. debugging a program.
   c. searching for data in a data base.
   d. use of a computer system or component.

8. Construct a set of heuristic rules that can be used to play a board strategy game such as Chinese checkers or chess.

9. A knowledge base contains the following information and inference rule:
   Person: John. Person: Mary.
   Relationship: John is the husband of Mary.
   Inference rule: IF X is the husband of Y THEN Y is the wife of X.
   Could you use the above knowledge base to answer these questions?
   a. Who is the husband of Mary?
   b. Is John the husband of Mary?
   c. Are John and Mary married?

Selected Annotated Bibliography

BYTE, vol. 10, no. 4 (April 1985). This is a special issue devoted to the subject of artificial intelligence. Included are articles on vision systems, the brain as a computer model, parallel networks, and expert systems.

Coffey, Margaret L. "Intelligent Terminals: The Best of Both Worlds," *Datamation*, vol. 28, no. 4 (April 1982), pp. 104–10. This article discusses the availability of intelligent terminals for secretarial jobs in offices, and use in factories and laboratories for monitoring and control.

Dertouzos, M. L., and Moses, Joel, eds. *The Computer Age: A Twenty-Year View*. Cambridge, Mass.: The MIT Press, 1979. This is an excellent collection of articles on the controversy over AI, with pieces by such AI notables as Daniel Bell, Joe Weizenbaum, Herbert Simon, and Marvin Minsky.

Evans, Christopher. *The Mighty Micro*. London: Victor Gollancz Ltd., 1979. This book has good chapters on the nature of intelligence, the evolution of intelligent machines, and UIMs. The author focuses on the contributions to artificial intelligence of the British scientific community.

Fersko-Weiss, Henry. "Natural Language," *Personal Computing*, vol. 9, no. 11 (November 1985), pp. 93–96. With natural-language systems, users direct their computer in commonplace English, not cryptic commands. The author describes how such systems work.

————. "Expert Systems," *Personal Computing*, vol. 9, no. 11 (November 1985), pp. 97–105. Personal computers are beginning to diagnose problems, to make reasonable judgements, to decide optimum courses of action, and to give advice. Fersco-Weiss describes sample expert systems and how they work.

Kent, Ernest W. *The Brains of Men and Machines*. Peterborough, N.H.: Byte Publications, 1981. The author has done a good job discussing the functions and operations of a brain in lay terms. He suggests that the structure of the brain is not applicable to machine design.

Logsdon, Tom. *Computers and Social Controversy*. Potomac, Maryland: Computer Science Press, 1980. Chapter 9, entitled "Era of Intelligent Machines," is an example of the standard treatment on the subject of AI found in many texts. A bibliography, exercises, and proposed student projects are provided.

McCorduck, Pamela. *Machines Who Think*. San Francisco: W. H. Freeman and Company, 1979. The content of this book is as provocative as the title. The author brings the background of a reporter and feelings of a novelist to the subject. Development of AI is seen through the eyes of participants in AI history. The book is rich in anecdotes and well written.

Michaelsen, Robert and Michie, Donald. "Expert Systems In Business," *Datamation*, vol. 29, no. 11 (November 1983), pp. 240–46. AUDITOR, TICOM, TAXADVISOR are three of the expert systems discussed. The authors discuss how expert systems are applicable to business environments.

Pournelle, Jerry. "Artificial Experts," *Popular Computing*, vol. 4, no. 1 (November 1984), pp. 59–62. Discusses some of the dangers of relying on programs that aren't truly expert. The example cited is psychological diagnosis.

Rich, Elaine. "The Gradual Expansion of Artificial Intelligence," *Computer*, vol. 17, no. 5 (May 1984), pp. 4–12. Describes Macsyma, the Programmer's Apprentice, and the LISP tutor as examples of automated help facilities to illustrate the useful role that AI systems can play.

Schank, Roger. "The Current State of AI: One Man's Opinion," *The AI Magazine*, vol. 4, no. 4 (Winter-Spring 1983), pp. 3–8. Schank claims that AI is in a state of disruption. He suggests that there are two primary views of the purpose of AI: study of the mind with a new tool and creation of a new technology. He discusses both what would constitute major advances in AI and also the unsolved problems that are important to AI. He sees AI as not a discipline in its own right but as a contributor to many other disciplines.

Stefik, Mark, and Aikins, Jan, et al. "The Organization of Expert Systems," *Artificial Intelligence*, vol. 18, no. 2 (March 1982), pp. 135–173. Excellent coverage on the organization of expert systems. The article does not require prior knowledge of AI jargon.

Waltz, David L. "Artificial Intelligence," *Scientific American*, vol. 247, no. 3 (September 1982), pp. 118–32. A survey of AI from the programmer's viewpoint. The article includes excellent diagrams of different models, such as Winograd's block world, a tree structure in chess, and the plan and program logic of SHRDLU. A discussion of cultural dependency and learning is also included.

Webber, Bonnie Lynn, and Nilsson, Nils j., eds. *Readings in Artificial Intelligence*. Palo Alto, CA: Tioga Publishing, 1981. Articles written by respected researchers in the field of AI are included. Recommended are pages 2–22, 289–333, and 410–28.

Winston, Patrick Henry. *Artificial Intelligence*, 2nd ed. Menlo Park, Calif.: Addison-Wesley, 1984. The first chapter of this book discusses the types of AI problems computers can solve and will be of interest to students in computer literacy courses. Subsequent chapters are more appropriate for advanced computer science students.

"Why Can't A Computer Be More Like A Man?" *The Economist*, vol. 282, no. 7219 (January 9, 1982), pp. 77–81. This article discusses the difficulty of programming the general knowledge of humans despite the fact that researchers are developing and refining AI techniques.

Jobs in Jeopardy? The Impact of Computers on Employment

If it keeps up, man will atrophy all his limbs but the push-button finger.

FRANK LLOYD WRIGHT

CHAPTER SEVENTEEN

Key Words

administrators	fixed cost	telecommuting
breakeven point	leisure	total cost
compensation	machine processing	training programs
computer processing	managers	unemployment
factory work force	manual processing	variable cost
	office automation	
	professionals	

Mankind has always sought ways to make work easier. Primitive man shaped hand tools and crude weapons for the hunt. Simple machines, like the wheel, lever, and inclined plane, came next. Complex mechanisms fueled by the energy of coal, gas, and oil followed. And then came automation, the substitution of machines for manpower. Today we have computers able to do many tasks more efficiently than the human brain.

Each new invention has led to changes in the work force. Although new jobs have been created, other jobs have become obsolete, causing loss of employment and hardship for many families. Limited dislocation of labor has generally been accepted by the public because of the compensating benefits of improved working conditions and standards of living. Computer technology, however, may rend the social fabric far more than mechanization in the past. Indeed, critics of computerization charge that we may be creating an economy in which potentially unlimited output can be achieved by systems of machines requiring little cooperation from human beings. Is massive unemployment in the offing?

This chapter will examine the nature of work in the United States and the problems of displacement and unemployment. First, the economic reasons for the widespread use of information processing today will be explained. Then we will examine the changes in the structure of the jobs of office workers, blue collar workers, professionals, and managers brought about by information processing. We will also explore some of the ways of mitigating the adverse effects of displacement and unemployment as a result of automation. The chapter closes with a look at two possible trends of the future, telecommuting and increased leisure, both of which can be attributed to advances in information technology.

THE ECONOMICS OF AUTOMATION

Today employers have a choice. They can (1) process information manually using paper and pen; (2) utilize electromechanical devices such as typewriters, adding machines, and sorters; or (3) profit from advances in electronics by making use of computers.

Manual processing is suitable when the volume of data to be processed is small. This is because **fixed costs** (for example, a desk) plus **variable costs** (for example, supplies and the wages of clerks) for small-volume processing are lower than fixed plus variable costs for other processing modes.

As the volume of data to be processed grows, however, manual processing loses its competitive advantage. The reason for this is the cost of wages and fringe benefits. In data processing as in other segments of our economy, labor performed by hand is an expensive commodity. For large-volume manual processing, labor is the major portion of

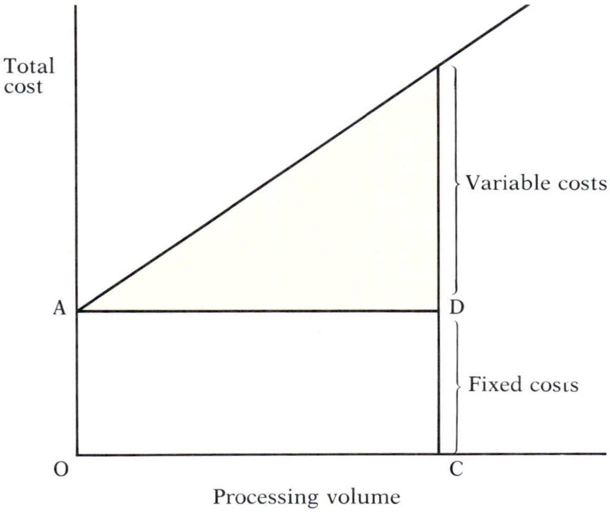

Figure 17.1 Manual processing cost components. Fixed costs (OA) remain the same regardless of volume. Note that variable costs become a large portion of total cost as volume grows. Therefore, employers focus their attention on ways of reducing labor for large volumes of data processing. (The shaded area shows how variable costs increase with volume.)

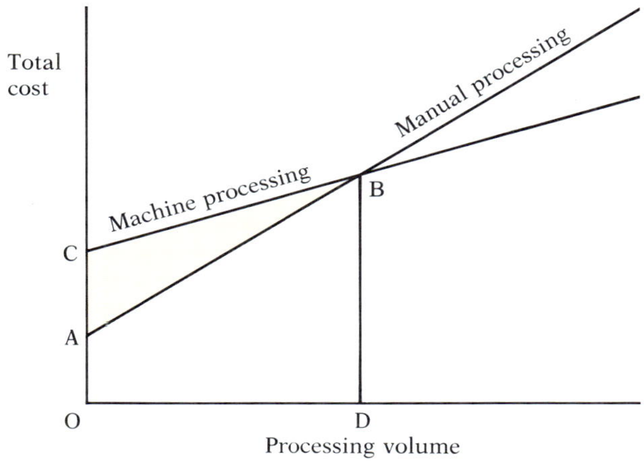

Figure 17.2 Manual processing compared to machine processing. OA represents fixed cost for manual processing: OC, fixed cost for machine processing. Beyond the breakeven point B, representing processing volume OD, machine processing is warranted. The shaded area shows savings that would accrue if manual instead of machine processing were employed for volume OD. Beyond OD, savings result from machine processing.

total cost, which is the sum of fixed and variable costs. (See Figure 17.1 for a diagram showing the relationship between fixed, variable, and total cost.) Every time employees receive a pay raise or more fringe benefits, variable costs increase and the total cost slope becomes steeper (assuming there is no change in productivity).

When data is processed by machines such as adding machines, cash registers, calculators, and sorters, the cost per unit of work is reduced since labor is no longer a major cost ingredient. But the initial investment in equipment (fixed cost) is greater than fixed costs for manual processing.

Figure 17.2 compares manual and **machine processing** for a given task. Note that manual processing has a total cost advantage for low-volume processing. But with an increase in volume, a **breakeven point** is reached. In this context, the breakeven point is the point where total manual processing cost equals total machine processing cost. For greater volume, machine processing is more economical (that is, for volume greater than OD in the figure).

Machines vary in price according to the task they perform. The amount of labor and level of skill, which, in turn, affects the wages of employees, also vary from one activity to another. These factors affect total processing cost. Nevertheless, the basic economic principle illustrated in Figure 17.2 holds true: large volumes of data can be processed more economically by machine than by hand.

Let's add a total cost line for **computer processing** to Figure 17.2. This is shown as EL in Figure 17.3. At the present time, the price of most computers is more than the price of electromechanical devices, so that the starting point on the x-axis representing computer fixed cost (OE) is high. (This may soon be untrue because computer hardware is rapidly dropping in price.) Since computers have lower operating expenses than electromechanical devices, the slope of the total cost line (EL) is flatter than the slope for electromechanical devices (CK). As a result, large-volume data processing (beyond OG) is most economical when data is processed by computer.

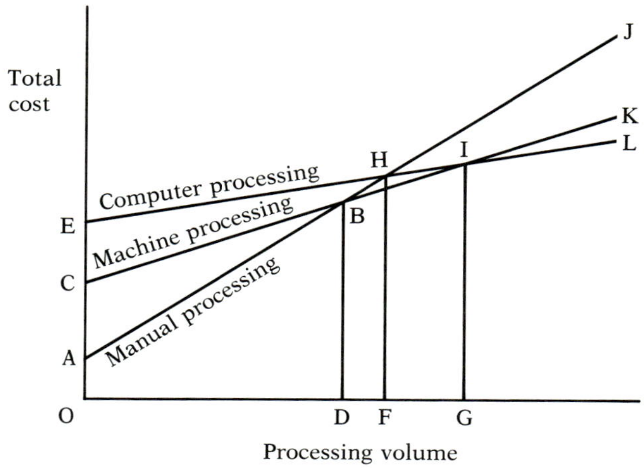

Figure 17.3 Comparison of manual, machine, and computer processing. This figure shows that the slope of the total cost line for computer processing is flatter than that of manual and machine processing. This is because computer variable costs are minimal. However, initial costs for computer processing are higher than for manual or machine processing. For processing volumes less than OD, manual processing is least costly. For volumes ranging from OD to OG, machine processing is most economical. Volume of processing must exceed OG before computer processing is economically justified. (H and I represent breakeven points.)

In the information-rich environment of today, employers need to keep costs down while processing vast amounts of data in order to remain competitive. Computers are increasingly being perceived as the answer to this need. The installation of computers, in turn, means that work procedures are changing, job descriptions are being rewritten, lines of responsibility are being altered, decision making is being transformed, and new work skills are coming into demand. Everyone agrees that computers are making radical changes in the way work is done. But whether there will be a net job gain (more new jobs created than jobs lost) as a result of computerization is the subject of much debate.

AUTOMATION AND JOBS

There is a wide range of opinion regarding the effects of automation on employment. This is apparent in both scholarly publications and the popular press. One author will predict that office automation will enable American business to create twenty million new jobs before the end of the century. Another will assert that there are 20 million office workers in this country whose jobs will be put to risk one way or another by office automation. Some experts believe automation will make American industry more competitive in world markets, creating new jobs as trade expands. Others believe high technology will eliminate more jobs than it creates.

The concern that machines might cause **unemployment** has existed since the beginning of the industrial revolution. An historical view (see Figure 17.4) shows that workers displaced by mechanization have been able to move to jobs in other sectors of the economy. In 1820, 85 percent of the work force was engaged in agriculture; in 1870, this figure was 53 percent, and in 1984, it was about 3 percent. If the amount of work to be done were static, these numbers would have resulted in massive unemployment. But new jobs have been created to absorb farmers moving to cities as well as craftsmen whose hand labor has been replaced by factory machines. In the past, mechanization resulted in higher output and an expansion of employment. The debate today is whether computerization will have the same results.

Although we have experienced some rise in unemployment levels since the computer revolution began in the 1950s, many factors have contributed to this rise. These factors include inflation, the oil crisis, an alteration of the demographic composition of our population, business cycle fluctuations, and changes in the morale of labor and corporate management. The U.S. has not, however, experienced the kind of large-scale domestic unemployment that was forecast thirty years ago when computers entered the commercial marketplace.

Indeed, the overall number of jobs has grown. Employment statistics since 1951 show a gain of 50 percent in civil occupations, from sixty to ninety million employed. Some of the new jobs are directly related to computer technology. Of the 2,130,000 new jobs in manufacturing, for example, 31 percent have been in the field of electronics. The production of computers and computer-related

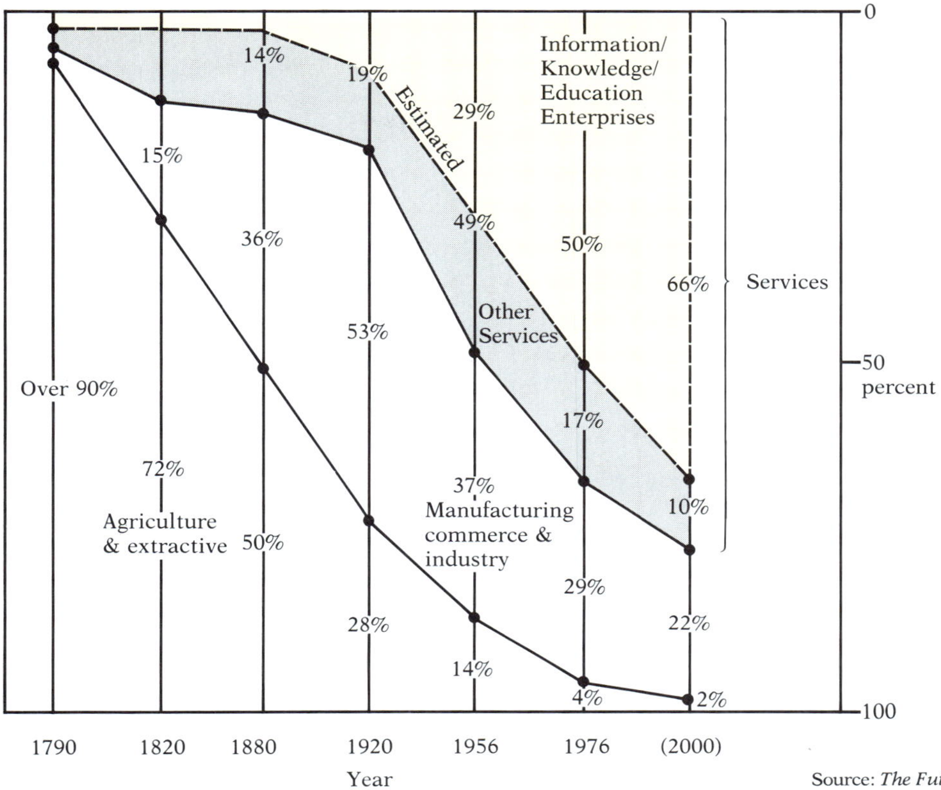

Figure 17.4 Workforce distribution. The composition of the workforce has altered drastically since 1790. The postindustrial age is dominated by information/knowledge/education activities.

Source: *The Futurist*, vol. 15, no. 2 (April 1981), p. 24.

Supplement 17.1 Automating the Clothing Industry

The clothing industry has traditionally been labor-intensive. But automation is coming to the basic stages of clothing production: design, pattern making, fabric cutting, and stitching.

Computer-aided design is relatively easy with rigid materials, such as steel. To design clothing, the computer must be able to depict the drape and fall of soft material on the body, a much more complex problem. However, computers with this capability are expected to reach the market soon: prototypes have already been developed.

Computerized pattern-drawing and cutting systems are available that can add features (such as pockets) to standard patterns, make size adjustments, and calculate how to cut the cloth with minimal fabric waste. The pattern is then stored on magnetic tape, fed into a numerical control machine, the fabric is cut automatically.

Garment assembly and sewing is usually done by an assembly line of workers at sewing machines. Delivery of pieces to be assembled has been automated by a pulley system that carries the pieces to sewing workstations. Singer has developed a microprocessor-controlled sewing machine with an arm that can grasp fabric and move it through the machine. A human operator first guides a sample through the sewing motions: the machine repeats the operator's movement for the fabric pieces that follow. But thus far, only simple sewing operations can be automated. Most of the sewing must still be done by people.

Supplement 17.2 Online Job Search Services

More than a million jobs are available at any one time in the United States. To find an applicant to fill a technical, professional, or managerial position may take six to eight weeks, and the search costs the employer an average of $6,000. This includes the cost of running advertisements or paying a recruiter's fee, and the cost of screening resumés and interviewing prospective employees. When a top executive is being sought, a "head hunter" (an executive-search recruiter) is commonly paid a commission to find the right applicant for the job.

A number of computerized job-search services have been established in this country to assist job seekers and employers. Resumés of applicants and information on jobs can be accessed online. An example of an executive-search service of this nature is Career Network. This network service is provided by a number of recruiting firms that share resumés and nation-wide job listings. (The network might be compared to multiple listings in real estate.)

Career Network is available on The Source, a public data base service. In 1984, firms using the Career Network paid an annual fee of $2,800 to The Source, but no royalties or commissions. Job seekers paid only a connect fee to The Source to look through open positions. Applicant profiles were listed online for six weeks at a cost of $28.

Other electronic job data bases operate in a similar manner. Examples are CareerSystem, Inc., CARI (on GE Computer Network) and Computer Job Bank (on CompuServe).

services has created an estimated three million jobs. In the telephone, telegraph, and typesetting industries, where unions have strongly resisted automation, studies show that the total number of jobs has risen despite computerization. As one commentator puts it, "In industrialized countries, the present evidence indicates that computing has not had the unsettling effect on employment forecast by many . . . the effects have been similar to those accompanying other technological innovations."[1]

The creation of new jobs should continue through the 1990s according to the Institute of Economic Analysis (IEA) of New York University. This conclusion is based on a dynamic input/output model of the U.S. economy that the Institute has developed. The model incorporates three technological scenarios, each scenario representing an alternative path the U.S. economy might follow between 1980 and 2000.

[1]Tom Logdson, *Computers & Social Controversy*. Potomac, Maryland: Computer Science Press, 1980, p. 276.

Supplement 17.3, drawn from the study, compares the number of persons seeking jobs with the number of jobs available. Historical figures are included as well as projections for 1990 and the year 2000. (Figures are from the U.S. Departments of Labor and Commerce, and the IEA model.) These figures lead the Institute to conclude that the labor-saving effects of computer-based automation will not result in significant unemployment in this century.

The optimism of the Institute regarding the employment picture in the next fifteen years is not shared by all labor experts. Many of the assumptions of the IEA model can be challenged. Even if the model proves accurate, the threat of massive unemployment is not discounted, merely delayed. But perhaps society will have time to change attitudes toward work and leisure, time to restructure jobs and reallocate manpower. If we are innovative, flexible, and receptive to change, we may be able to reap the benefits of computer technology without massive social disruption of the workplace.

THE IMPACT OF COMPUTERS ON JOBS

Without doubt, computers will reshape the labor force. Let's look at specific categories of jobs to see what the impact of information technology will be.

Supplement 17.3 Available Jobs and Demand for Employment According to IEA Model and Other Sources, 1963–2000

		1963	1967	1972	1977	1990	2000
Jobs available	Employment, IEA Model[a]	62.8	69.6	78.2	86.2	124.1	156.6
	Other sources[a,b]	62.8	70.9	78.1	87.4	111.0 to 123.9	- -
Supply of workers	Civilian labor force[c]	71.8	77.3	86.5	97.4	123.9 to 138.3	132.8 to 157.4

[a]Includes private sector employment plus employment in public education and health. Excludes public administration, armed forces, and household workers. Employment is for IEA scenario that assumes the fastest technological progress and most rapid adoption of available technology of the three scenarios IEA has developed.
[b]Entries for 1963 through 1977 are from the U.S. Department of Commerce.
[c]Entries for 1963 through 1977 are from the U.S. Department of Labor.

Source: Wassily Leontief and Faye Duchin, "The Impacts of Automation On Employment, 1963–2000." New York: Institute for Economic Analysis, September 1983, p. 15.

Office Automation

As described in Chapter 7, computers are automating office work. According to recent estimates, over ten million office employees in the United States already work with video terminals. Companies producing **office automation** equipment are experiencing a 40 percent growth rate, selling computer systems for data capture, storage, retrieval, processing, and distribution of information. An estimated 25 to 30 percent of office jobs will be fully automated by 1990 according to a study by Siemens, a German corporation.

The reason why automation has not reduced the need for clerical personnel to date is that office workload is expanding. With easier document production and retrieval, more documents are being produced and retrieved. Because of word processors, more letters are being written. More information is being analyzed now that we can capture and process data electronically. In short, office computers are not being used to save labor, but to improve accuracy, to facilitate better utilization of resources, and to do jobs that simply couldn't be done before.

Will this trend continue? The answer is yes, *if* the chief justification for office automation in the future is promoting growth. A growth model will mean that jobs will be restructured but not lost. Much of the drudgery of office work will be eliminated by automated machinery while new jobs at a slightly higher level will be created. On the other hand, if employers focus on cost-cutting rather than growth, automation will in fact result in the elimination of jobs. Office work will be turned into an assembly line operation, so that clerical employees who remain employed will be little more than extensions of machines. This will make it harder than in the past for clerical workers to advance to supervisory positions and higher skill levels.

Computers in the Factory

The computer revolution is another step in the substitution of machine labor for human labor. Although today's machines are controlled electronically, not mechanically or electromechanically, they are first cousins to machines introduced at the start of the industrial revolution.

But unlike machines of the past, which had limited applications and thus affected the labor force of only a single industry, computers threaten workers in all industrial sectors. Since computers can be programmed to do a variety of tasks, computer use is not restricted by the product being manufactured. Experts predict that 65 to 75 percent of the entire **factory work force** may be displaced by computers in coming years. With numerical control, process control, and CAD, jobs in manufacturing are being lost forever.

Robots are also displacing workers. By 1990, an estimated 70,000 to 200,000 robots will be in the workplace. These robots will be programmable and hence multipurpose. They will have vision and touch discrimination, and they will also be adaptable, incorporating artificial intelligence features that enable them to learn from experience. Objection to robots on the job may be self-defeating for labor. Without robots, U.S. industry may become noncompetitive, resulting in a flood of low-priced imports and the investment of American capital in factories abroad. Loss of jobs at home would be the by-product.

Recognizing that computers will displace workers, unions are no longer bargaining for job security (retention of workers in specific jobs) but for employment security (a guarantee that workers will be retrained, not fired, if their skills become obsolete). Employment security puts the responsibility for placing workers in new jobs on the employer. Labor leaders are well aware that factory workers can no longer depend on narrow vocational skills acquired at the start of their careers. Workers will have to participate in recurrent retraining throughout their entire work lives as jobs are automated and more and more computers (and robots) are placed in factories.

Computers for the Professional

Computers are tools that enhance the work of **professionals** while removing the tedium of many tasks. Information access is improved. Large amounts of data can be manipulated with speed and accuracy. The abilities of computers to answer "What if?" questions, to simulate environments, to illustrate concepts through graphics, and to make inferences and intelligent deductions are among those used by professionals to great advantage. Intelligent computer systems are an aid to the professional, not a job threat at the present time. Of all groups in the work force, the professional gains most and risks least by the computer revolution.

Administration by Computer

Much of the work of **administrators** and **managers** entails dealing with people and solving ill-structured problems. Often these problems involve nonquantifiable data variables that cannot be programmed. For example, both administrators and managers hire new employees, plan the utilization of human resources, mediate disputes, motivate staff, and dismiss unsatisfactory workers. These tasks require knowledge of personalities within an organization and insight into human interaction. Personnel management is a realm that may never be computerized.

There are, however, a large number of decisions to be made at management levels that require information collection and analysis. An estimated 80 percent of managerial decisions can be programmed for solution by computer in areas such as accounting, finance, and manufacturing. There are also many problems that are best solved by a partnership of manager and computer.

> These are decisions where managerial judgment . . . will not be adequate, perhaps because of the size of the problem or the computational complexity and precision needed to solve it. On the other hand, the model or data alone are also inadequate because the solution involves judgment and subjective analysis. Under these conditions the manager *plus* the system can provide a more effective solution than either alone.[2]

Middle managers are more vulnerable to displacement by computer than persons at top echelons. But for the most part, they are less vulnerable to job displacement than office and blue collar workers. (See Figure 17.5 for an assessment of the impact of computers on all levels of employ-

[2]Peter G. W. Keene and Michael S. Scott Morton, *Decision Support Systems: An Organizational Perspective*. Reading, Mass.: Addison-Wesley Publishing Co., Inc., 1978, p. 86.

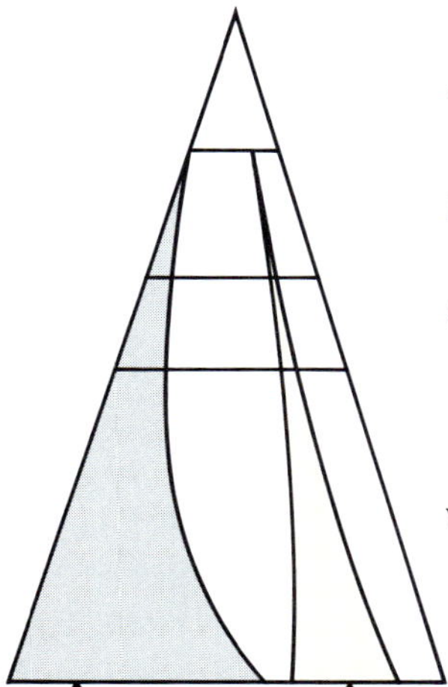

Figure 17.5 Unemployment and displacement caused by computer technology at different levels of an organization. Note: The actual number of persons who lose jobs or are displaced by computer technology will vary widely from one organization to another. This figure is an approximation of unemployment and displacement in a typical firm. Note also that this diagram is not drawn to scale.

ment.) It should be noted, however, that computers have changed administrative and managerial jobs. In particular, the manner in which quantitative decisions are reached has been altered. Administrators and managers today must be able to state problems for machine solution, and the ability to evaluate large amounts of processed data has become more important than hunch and intuition, the basis of much decision making in the past. This means that individuals who do not learn to utilize computers effectively for decision making may lose their jobs to persons with computer skills.

STRATEGIES TO RESHAPE THE WORK FORCE AND MITIGATE TECHNOLOGICAL DISPLACEMENT

Computer technology promises enormous potential benefits provided economic manpower and industrial relations policies are attuned to the problem of creating new, better paid, and more satisfying jobs, and also provided that economic policy measures are taken to create consumer demand so that the economy continues to grow. This section will discuss strategies that can be adopted by unions, management, and government to reshape the work force to meet the challenge of the computer age.

Retraining and Redistribution of Manpower

The planning and implementation of computer systems have a long lead time. This time can be used by organizations to retrain workers, restructure jobs, and transfer employees to other duties if the new system will take away jobs. One way to establish a climate receptive to change is to add worker representatives to the system development process from departments that will be affected by implementation of the new technology. This helps employees understand the need for computers and the benefits they will derive when gains are made in the organization's competitive posture. Such participation should also help to prevent the alienation that results when employees feel they lack both recognition for their skills and control over the content of their work. According to Arthur Francis and Paul Willman,

> At the plant and company level, if the impact of innovation involves deskilling, large scale labor shedding, and hence, heightened conflict, it will say more about the design and implementation decisions effected than about the "inevitable" consequences of microprocessors.[3]

The same observation could also be made regarding the impact of microcomputers, minis, and mainframes.

Many companies have formalized **training programs** to upgrade the skills of workers, so that they can switch to new jobs when displaced by automation. Employers usually finance in-house training. Both American steel and auto workers have agreed to have a certain amount of money per worker per hour withheld so that it can be pooled for retraining. Some organizations allow employees to attend outside classes on company time. Some provide individual counselling and job referral as well.

[3]Arthur Francis and Paul Willman. "Microprocessors: Impact and Response." *Personnel Review*, Spring 1980, 9:16.

Supplement 17.4 A Thirty-five Hour Work Week?

IG Metal, the metalworkers' union in West Germany, is the world's largest trade union. It is also in the forefront of the fight for a thirty-five-hour work week. The union claims that it will give workers a nicer life and will increase employment, stimulating the economy. Half of the cost of such a program will be returned to employers in the form of higher productivity, union representatives argue.

German employers claim that a thirty-five-hour week will add 16 to 20 percent to wage costs and ruin their recent improvement in international competitiveness.

A major problem is motivating employees to take advantage of educational opportunities. Another problem is designing retraining programs leading to jobs and programs that fit the aptitudes and educational backgrounds of employees in need of new employment. Many jobs created by computerization, such as computer-aided design, require higher education, not simple retraining. Unfortunately, there are fewer jobs for the undereducated and unskilled in an automated society since repetitive physical tasks are easily mechanized. Some unions try to protect workers in these categories with no-layoff union clauses, seniority protection, transfer rights, and extended layoff notice periods. These strategies may work if the industry is strong, but not if a firm must automate and retrench to remain competitive and survive.

Another solution to the threat of unemployment is early retirement and extended vacations in order to spread the work load among those in need of a job. A reduction in working hours is also a possibility. Understandably, these solutions are favored by workers only if they result in no loss of real net income.

Monetary Compensation

Some corporations give employees severance pay when they are put out of work by computers. Such **compensation** is usually a lump sum intended to be used for job training and relocation, but it is more commonly used for groceries and rent during the search for a new job. Many labor experts suggest that employees would be better served if redundancy payments were in the form of counseling, education, job referral, and moving expenses to new jobs. This type of package is being negotiated with employers by some unions.

Another form of compensation when workers are laid off is payment by industry to union pension funds to finance early retirement and annual wage guarantees. Remaining full-time workers are the principal beneficiaries of this type of payment, not those who lose their jobs. Coal miners under John L. Lewis adopted this strategy, preferring an industry with a few highly paid workers to one with many miners receiving marginal pay.

Possible Government Responses to Unemployment

There is general consensus that government is expected to provide the climate for a sound economy. The White House and Congress are held accountable when high unemployment exists. Most corporate managers and labor leaders agree that they cannot handle the problem of technological unemployment alone and recommend that policy be formulated at the national level to deal with human resources. For example, the government might shift priorities from welfare to job creation, or establish protectionist policies for new industries. Government has the power to increase public spending, to add to the money supply, to revise tax laws, to extend benefits to persons out of work, and to create civil service jobs, all of which have a bearing on employment.

TELECOMMUTING

Let us now turn to the impact of computer technology on where, not how, work is done.

Supplement 17.5 Second Thoughts About Working at Home

Although a home office frees one from a daily commute to work, some workers discover that traffic jams at rush hour are preferable to telecommuting. The following are sample negative reactions to working at home:

- My professional and home life have become too intertwined. I can never get away from my work.
- I've gained sixty pounds. My terminal is too close to the refrigerator.
- I feel isolated working at home. There is no incentive to work hard, no sense of personal accomplishment, no social contact, no feeling that I am part of a team.
- Everyone interrupts me—the dog, the kids, the mailman, the neighbors, even my spouse who knows better. I'm just too available.
- There have been no raises, no promotions since I've had a home office. I'm afraid I'm jeopardizing career advancement by being a teleworker.
- I'm getting claustrophobia (we simply lack the space) and my wife doesn't want me home during working hours.

A number of legal and economic considerations have given employers second thoughts about telecommuting as well. The safety of expensive equipment kept at home is an issue. Who is liable if thieves steal a video terminal from a home office? Privacy and security of data is also a concern.

Telecommuting, the substitution of telecommunications for transportation to a downtown office, is a new trend affecting the labor force. To eliminate lost time and lost productivity and the expense involved in a long commute, neighborhood centers and workstations at home are beginning to replace the central office.

Telecommuting is appropriate for jobs that can be done from remote terminals linked to a central mini or mainframe. The advent of microcomputers also makes telecommuting an option for workers with a personal computer, and data and programs of their own. Close to 60 percent of U.S. workers can be classified as information workers. Many of these employees could quite easily work out of their homes. In 1984, more than 200 employers had telecommuting programs of some kind under way, ranging from one or two people up to almost 100. Some commentators predict that there will be ten million teleworkers by 1990.

Telecommuting was first talked about during the Arab oil embargo in the mid 1970s. It was recognized that roughly 5 percent of U.S. oil use was for commuting and that a savings of 190,000 barrels of oil a day could be gained if 20 percent of commuters stayed at home. A few corporations did experiment with home workers at the time (for example, Control Data Corporation and Continental Bank of Illinois) but not until the 1980s did the idea come of age. By that time reports on the success of experimental alternative work site programs were in circulation, and the benefits of telecommuting were better understood. In addition, the personal computer was on the market, a factor contributing to the economic feasibility of home workstations.

The percentage of time an employee telecommutes varies from one organization to another. Some companies have no main office at all. All work is done at dispersed workstations joined in a network. Informal meetings take place in low-rent neighborhood centers or at the homes of employees. Sometimes a company will establish a small satellite office with or without an electronic link to the main office. This type of alternative work site is classified as telecommuting since the time and cost of commuting to a downtown office is avoided. Other organizations design work assignments so that employees who operate out of their homes spend one or two days each week at the main office. Many commentators on telecommuting believe that this latter arrangement will become the norm.

The Benefits of Telecommuting

One of the primary benefits of telecommuting is increased productivity. Workers claim that there are fewer distractions away from the central office. Gains in productivity of 20 to 40 percent are not uncommon among professionals. However, it should be recognized that many persons work best in a structured environment or when they interact socially with others. Not everyone has the work habits and planning skills to direct their own activities. Careful screening of candidates is necessary to ensure that productivity is not lost, instead of gained, by telecommuting.

In service-oriented organizations, telecommuting is a good way to extend hours of operations. For example, employees at home can take orders and answer customer queries. J.C. Penney uses telecommuting for some of its catalog-order telephone centers. Companies that have seasonal peak volumes, or certain hours of the day with heavy service demand can handle the load by telecommuting without tying up office space.

When organizations are recruiting new employees, telecommuting can help attract applicants. Many persons like the idea of flexible scheduling instead of the standard 8-to-5, Monday-to-Friday work week. Some people are most productive in the early hours of the morning or late at night. When working at home employees can choose which hours to work. Organizations trying to hire professionals where demand exceeds supply may find that the option of telecommuting gives them a recruitment edge.

Telecommuting is also attractive to persons with family responsibilities (a young child or aged parent) who may be unable to work at certain hours of the day or cannot take the time to commute. Persons with medical disabilities who are unable to leave home can also enter the work force through telecommuting.

Telecommuting can be an alternative to corporate transfers. Many employees today resist relocation. A common reason is that a spouse is employed and unwilling (or unable) to uproot. Whatever the objection, a valued employee who might resign rather than move can be retained when telecommuting is an alternative to a transfer. In addition, the employer avoids the cost of the relocation (commonly $30,000 or more) or the cost of hiring a replacement.

Finally, telecommuting is advantageous because it reduces office space requirements. Downtown locations cost an average of $4,000 to $10,000 per workstation. With telecommuting, such overhead expenditures are minimized. Furthermore, telecommuting means that space is not a constraint when changes in the workload are proposed. Organizations can expand rapidly without worrying where to put people, or retrench without being saddled with expenditures for unused space.

Implementation

Careful planning is required for telecommuting to be successful. The people selected must work well on their own. Their assignments must be jobs that can be done away from the main office. Data processing personnel, data entry clerks, systems engineers, and systems programmers are good prospects. Technical or documentation writers and data processing training specialists who must develop educational materials are also good candidates for telecommuting. (The latter might also hold classes at a remote site.)

Persons selected for telecommuting should be trained to cope with off-site employment while managers should be trained to supervise subordinates from a distance. Remote work does not mean all contact with co-workers is lost. On the contrary, training should include ways to remain in continued contact through electronic mail, phone, regularly scheduled meetings, memos, report routings, and so forth. There is some evidence that persons who opt for telecommuting look only at the short-term benefits (less commuting, reduced expenditures for gasoline, meals, clothing), not realizing the problems associated with working alone. A training period can help employers evaluate whether the right candidate for telecommuting has been chosen and help employees gain a realistic view of telecommuting as a work mode.

LEISURE

Computer technology has still another impact on labor: it increases **leisure**. The work week has been diminishing since the 1850s. The computer revolution is hastening this reduction of work hours. Increasingly, the changed nature of employment brought about in part by technology is leading to extended vacations, earlier retirements, and fewer hours on the job.

While free time is increasing over all, it is not being evenly distributed throughout society. Clerical workers, craftsmen, laborers, and factory workers see their leisure increasing. Farmers, managers, and professionals, on the other hand, work disproportionately long hours. Leisure time is also affected by social class, minority status, geographical location, religion, age, and sex.

Sociologists are concerned that the people least able to cope with leisure are the people most likely to have it. Will free time be spent sitting passively before the TV watching game shows? If increased leisure is to be the norm, we need more capital and planning for the development of leisure time activities. We need better sporting and recreational facilities. We should also redesign educational institutions to foster broader interests in young people and to include more part-time and nondegree programs for adults that will widen their horizons and help them prepare for a leisure society.

The same information technology that is responsible for creating much newfound leisure can contribute to the enjoyment of free time. Video games are already very popular. We may soon be able to view the Sistine Chapel or explore the Louvre in Paris using home computers. Computers may also be used to dispense an open network of educational services.

Attitudes toward leisure in the United States are mixed. Many persons enjoy work and cannot imagine what they would do without it. Most people would like more time to spend with their families, to read, to listen to music, or to engage in various sports. At the same time, they fear not working, being brought up on the Puritan work ethic, which extolls work and condemns nonwork as laziness. A change in attitude toward work and leisure may become necessary in this age of computers. Self-worth should not be tied to a job. We can only hope that free time leads to enriched lives instead of social disorder.

SUMMING UP

Computer processing is cost-effective for large-volume and structured processing. Since we live in an information-rich society, computers are replacing manual processing and electromechanical data processing devices in offices as employers seek ways to keep their costs down. Robots are also replacing workers in many factory jobs, particularly jobs that involve repetitive manual tasks or jobs in environments hostile to human life.

When computers first became commercially available in the 1950s, it was predicted that they would create massive unemployment and throw society into unprecedented economic and social disorder. To date, this has not occurred. The overall number of jobs in the country has grown, and unemployment figures, though high, can be attributed to a variety of factors including business cycle fluctuations, demographic changes, and the state of the world economy—in short, not solely to computerization. The unsettling effects of computers have been similar to those accompanying other technological innovations in the past.

Computers do, however, have a decided impact on the structure of employment in this country, particularly in manufacturing where robots, numerical control, process control, and computer-aided design have displaced workers. Office automation and the use of management decision-support systems are also changing the nature of work in the office. Telecommuting is a new trend changing where work is done.

Strategies that industries can follow to assist persons displaced by computers include retraining programs, manpower redistribution, and monetary compensation. Both government and unions can also take actions to help protect jobs, to create new jobs, and to cushion the impact of lost work.

Change in employment patterns as a result of computerization has contributed to the increase of leisure time in this country. We must develop leisure activities to combat boredom. We must change our attitudes toward work so that the experience of not working does not give individuals a feeling of worthlessness and alienation.

REVIEW QUESTIONS

1. What is the difference between automation and computerization? Can one isolate the effects of computerization from those of automation in the unemployment and displacement of workers?
2. Are fixed or variable costs the deciding factor when a decision is made regarding the appropriate mode of processing? Explain.
3. What are the comparative advantages of:
   a. manual processing?
   b. machine processing?
   c. computer processing?
   Why is computer processing favored by most large organizations today?
4. What is a breakeven point? How is it determined? What is its significance?
5. Has the computer caused unemployment? Have more jobs been lost than created in this age of information? Explain.
6. Why do some observers believe office work will increase, and others, that office work will decrease in the future?
7. What is the difference between job security and employment security?
8. Which sectors of the work force have been most, and least affected by computerization? Will only certain levels of employment, certain segments of the economy, or certain industries be affected?
9. Discuss ways a reduction in the number of jobs might be distributed among workers.
10. How can government play a role in creating jobs?
11. What is telecommuting? Who benefits from telecommuting?
12. Describe some of the problems employers face when implementing telecommuting.
13. How does a computer society affect leisure?
14. What structural changes will be necessary in our society when we have more leisure?

DISCUSSION QUESTIONS

1. Will the use of computers rend the social and economic fabric of the U.S.? How will computer use affect employment levels in other countries of the world?
2. Is unemployment demeaning? Explain your answer.
3. How would you define leisure? How will leisure be affected by computers?
4. Do you believe that computerization will lead to mass unemployment and widespread leisure?
5. What sectors of society in your community have the least leisure? Why? Do you foresee the uneven distribution of leisure in the future? Why?
6. Comment on the following statement: Leisure does not contribute directly to a nation's gross national product; therefore, leisure is unproductive.
7. Who should be responsible for safeguarding jobs? Government? Unions? Chambers of Commerce? Is full employment a worthy goal?
8. Do you foresee massive unemployment resulting from computerization in this century? What measures should be taken now to prevent high levels of unemployment?
9. Is unemployment a price that must be paid for the benefits of high technology?
10. Do you believe telecommuting is a trend of the future? Would you like to work at home? Why or why not?
11. What effect do you think telecommuting will have on:
    a. office complexes in downtown centers?
    b. shopping malls?
    c. pollution?
    d. employee-employer relationships?

12. What is the greatest threat to employment in the factory: NC (numerical control), PC (process control), CAD (computer-aided design), CAM (computer-aided manufacturing), or robots? Will this threat increase or decrease in the late 1980s and 1990s?

13. How will computers affect the work ethic in this country?

14. Should we have national leisure policies for:
    a. workers?
    b. the elderly?
    c. the unemployed?
    What policies would you recommend?

15. Do you perceive computers as a threat to your future with regard to employment possibilities? To the future of other members of your family?

EXERCISES

1. Interview a union leader or teacher of labor economics in your community. Describe their views for (or against):
    a. robots.
    b. computers in the office.
    c. computers in the factory.

2. Read about a recent union strike in which computer use was at issue. Discuss the position of both sides in the dispute. If you were the arbitrator in the case, what would your decision be? State your reasons.

3. Let us imagine that you employ 200 workers but must retrench to remain in business. What criteria would you use to decide which employees to let go?

4. You are the manager of a grocery store. It will cost $30,000 to acquire a computer. Operating costs will be $2/$1,000 of sales for the computer compared with $20/$1,000 of sales for manual processing, which has a $5,000 fixed cost. What sales volume would justify a computer?

Selected Annotated Bibliography

Ayers, Robert and **Millet, Steven M.** *Robotics, Applications and Social Implications.* Cambridge, Mass.: Ballinger Publishing, 1983. A good discussion of the impact of robots on employment (Chapter 5), productivity (Chapter 6), and policy (Chapter 7).

"Experiences With Tele-Commuting." *EDP Analyser*, vol. 20, no. 11 (November 1982), pp. 1–16. Telecommuting options are described as are the job characteristics most conducive to remote work. Concerns of employees who have been telecommuters are also raised.

Forester, Tom, ed. *The Electronics Revolution.* Oxford: Basil Blackwell Publishers, 1980. This book includes an excellent selection of articles on computers and their effect on employment. Topics include automation, the impact of microprocessors, the role of government, displacement, and how computer users view the impact of computers on employment. Pages 353–56 contain a guide to literature on the subject. The material reviewed is from both the U.S. and United Kingdom.

Gilchrist, Bruce. "Computers and Employment: The U.S. Experience," In Lavington, S. H., ed. *Information Processing 80*. Amsterdam: North Holland Publishing Company, 1980, pp. 919–24. Gilchrist approaches the subject at three levels: national, industrial, and personal. He also identifies steps society can take to ease the burdens put on some individuals by computerization.

Giuliano, Vincent E. "The Mechanization of Office Work," *Scientific American*, vol. 247, no. 3 (September 1982), pp. 148–64. A shift from paper work to electronics can improve productivity, service to customers, and job satisfaction, according to the author.

Gordon, Gil E. "The Office Away From the Office," *Computerworld*, vol. 18, no. 38 (September 17, 1984), pp. ID/1–8. Early telecommuting programs, advantages, appropriate home jobs, and prime employee candidates are the topics addressed.

Kirchner, Englebert. "At The Mercy of Machines," *Datamation*, vol. 28, no. 9 (September 1982), pp. 254–57. Kirchner discusses two opposing scenarios regarding office automation: job gains and job losses. The applicability of each scenario depends on whether employers are promoting growth or cutting costs.

Martin, James. *The Telematic Society*. Englewood Cliffs, N.J.: Prentice-Hall, Inc., 1980. In Chapter 19, pp. 170–76, the author predicts a three-and-a-half-day work week in the future, but not for all sectors of the economy. He believes that eventually increased leisure will change society as drastically as the industrial revolution did. Martin is provocative if not always persuasive. This book is the successor to Martin's *Wired Society*.

Norman, Colin. "The New Industrial Revolution," *The Futurist*, vol. 15, no. 1 (February 1981), pp. 31–40. Changes that microelectronics will bring to the workplace are described. The emphasis is on robots.

Olson, Margrethe H. "Remote Office Work: Changing Work Patterns in Space and Time," *Communications of the ACM*, vol. 26, no. 3 (March 1983), pp. 182–87. Behavior and organizational and social problems that occur with telecommuting are discussed. The author also contrasts satellite work centers, neighborhood work centers, flexible work arrangements, and work at home.

Renfro, William L. "Second Thoughts on Moving the Office Home." *The Futurist*, vol. 15, no. 3 (June 1982), pp. 43–48. This article discusses problems home workers face, such as loss of social contacts, career barriers, and sharing cramped quarters with family.

Simon, Nora and Minc, Alain. "Computerizing Society," *Society*, vol. 17, no. 3 (January-February 1980), pp. 25–30. The authors (who are from the Ministry of Finance in France) look at the computer industry and the social implications of computing on employment from the European viewpoint. The article is a well-written and refreshing discussion of the implications of computing.

Swartz, Gail Garfield and Neikirk, William. *The Work Revolution*. New York: Rawson Associates, 1984. The authors are pessimistic that more jobs will be created by automation than destroyed. They recommend work week reductions and a $40 billion program of public service jobs financed by increased taxation.

Electronics Supplant Cash

Money is merely information, and as such can reside in computer storage, with payments consisting of data transfers between one machine and another.

JAMES MARTIN

CHAPTER EIGHTEEN

Key Words

automated clearing house (ACH)
automated teller machine (ATM)
benefits of EFT
critical mass
electronic funds transfer (EFT)
Electronic Fund Transfer Act
embezzlement
float
home banking
home shopping
identifier
index
network
point-of-sale terminal (POS terminal)
privacy
reliability
security
teleshopping

Throughout history, people have looked for convenient methods of paying for goods and services. Cattle, salt, crops, and shells are examples of early forms of money. Commodities were later replaced by coins and paper money, a more portable form of exchange. Even more convenient than currency are checks and credit cards.

We have now developed banking and payment systems which use the speed and efficiency of computers to process transactions involving currency, checks, and credit cards. We can also transfer funds by computer from one account to another without the use of written checks. This process is called **electronic funds transfer (EFT)**. Eventually currency and checks may be eliminated altogether. If this happens, we will become a cashless, checkless society.

This chapter describes the terminals through which electronic transactions take place and various aspects of electronic funds transfer, including how it works and what are the benefits of dealing with money in this way. In addition, the chapter will explore the implications of a cashless society with regard to control, privacy, law, and lifestyle.

AUTOMATED TELLER MACHINES

An **automated teller machine (ATM)** is an unattended transaction terminal to handle customer deposits and withdrawals twenty-four hours a day. Some ATMs are located inside bank lobbies; some are found in shopping malls or other public locations. Users must insert a special card into the ATM to initiate a transaction. This card has the user's account number and credit limitation encoded in the magnetic stripe on its back. Most ATM systems have an additional security feature. They require users to enter a personal identification code (a password) before the ATM will begin to process a given transaction. An ATM will "swallow" a card used in several unsuccessful attempts to activate the system. This prevents someone with a stolen card from making trial and error attempts to break the password. (ATMs also swallow outdated or defective cards.)

Instructions for a deposit or withdrawal are displayed on a one-line ATM screen. By pressing appropriate keys, the customer can direct the ATM computer to carry out the transaction desired. ATMs are most commonly used to dispense cash.

Some ATMs are self-contained units. Others are connected in a network so that every transaction is cleared with a central computer. This prevents users from overdrawing their credit limitations by making withdrawals at a number of ATMs within a short period of time. (See Figure 18.1.)

POINT-OF-SALE TERMINALS

Most readers are familiar with **point-of-sale terminals (POS terminals)** found in retail establishments to record sales transactions. This information is processed by computer to produce accounting and inventory control reports for the store's management. Less common is the use of POS terminals to monitor charge accounts with credit limits within a given store. The sale of merchandise

Supplement 18.1 Magnetic Cards to Secure ATMs

Recently Swedish banks have adopted a new type of ATM identifier card to safeguard Sweden's network of automated teller machines. Existing magnetic stripe cards are being replaced because they can be altered, copied, or erased if exposed to magnetic force. The new cards have encoding on the back that is structured into wet magnetic tape material during the tape manufacturing process, a technology developed by Watermark Magnetics. This results in permanent encoding that cannot be altered. Existing ATM hardware can be converted to read the new cards for about $25. Bank officials believe that the new technology is a cost-effective solution to problems of card counterfeiting and magnetic data alteration.

recorded on the POS terminal debits (deducts from) the customer's credit limit by the amount of the sale.

POS terminals can also be used for check and credit card authorizations. In this case, the terminals are part of a telecommunications network linking them with banks and credit agencies. Some POS systems immediately debit the amount of purchase from the customer's bank account and deposit the money to the store's account. This electronic transfer of funds requires a telecommunications link from the store to the customer's bank, and a link between the banks where the customer and store have accounts.

Home computers may also be used as POS terminals, allowing users to select and order merchandise and pay for the goods with electronic transfer of funds. A later section in this chapter is devoted to home shopping.

ELECTRONIC TRANSFER OF FUNDS

In 1965, Thomas Watson, chairman of IBM at the time, made the following prediction:

> In our lifetime we may see electronic transactions virtually eliminate the need for cash. Giant computers in banks, with massive memories, will contain individual customer accounts. To draw down or add to his balance, the customer in a store, office, or filling station will do two things: insert an identification into the terminal located there [and] punch out the transaction figures on the terminal's keyboard. Instantaneously the amount he punches out will move out of his account and enter another.
>
> Consider this same process repeated thousands, hundreds of thousands, millions of times each day, billions upon billions of dollars changing hands without the use of one pen, one piece of paper, one check, or one green dollar bill. Finally, consider the extension of such a network of terminals and memories—an extension across city and state lines spanning our whole country.[1]

Although we have not eliminated money altogether, Watson's prediction about electronic funds transfer is becoming a reality. Billions of dollars are moved daily from one account to another using computers and telecommunications without any currency exchange or paper to record and process transactions. (The term "electronic transfer of funds" is misleading since no physical transfer takes place as the name implies. Many persons object to the name EFT for this reason.)

An example is the direct deposit of Social Security checks by the federal government, a program in effect since 1975. The Treasury Department uses EFT for recurring payments, such as transfer of funds for government employees' life insurance programs. In the private sector, many corporations deposit weekly paychecks by EFT and preauthorize account debits such as monthly interest payments. The use of EFT for telephone bill paying is common among banks and their corporate clients. In the early 1980s, Chase transferred

[1]Reprinted by permission of IBM.

Figure 18.1 Banking in the cashless society. Cash and checks could disappear from our everyday lives as the developing technology allows us to conduct our financial transactions with magnetic-stripe and microprocessor cards. (NCR Corporation)

between $5 and $7 billion a day using EFT at the request of corporate customers. Some banks, like Madison National, use EFT to provide discount brokerage services.

Here is an example of how EFT works. An organization that substitutes EFT for checks in accounts payable transactions will key accounts payable information on tape (that is, the names of payees, accounts, and banks to which deposits should be sent). The information will be sent electronically to the nearest **automated clearing house (ACH)**, a computerized version of the traditional check clearing house. The ACH then transfers funds into banks where vendors hold accounts.

Let's take a closer look at the components of an EFT system.

THE COMPONENTS OF AN EFT SYSTEM

EFT systems require electronic means for authorizing transactions, communications networks to link data files (which in this case are bank accounts), and information systems capable of pro-

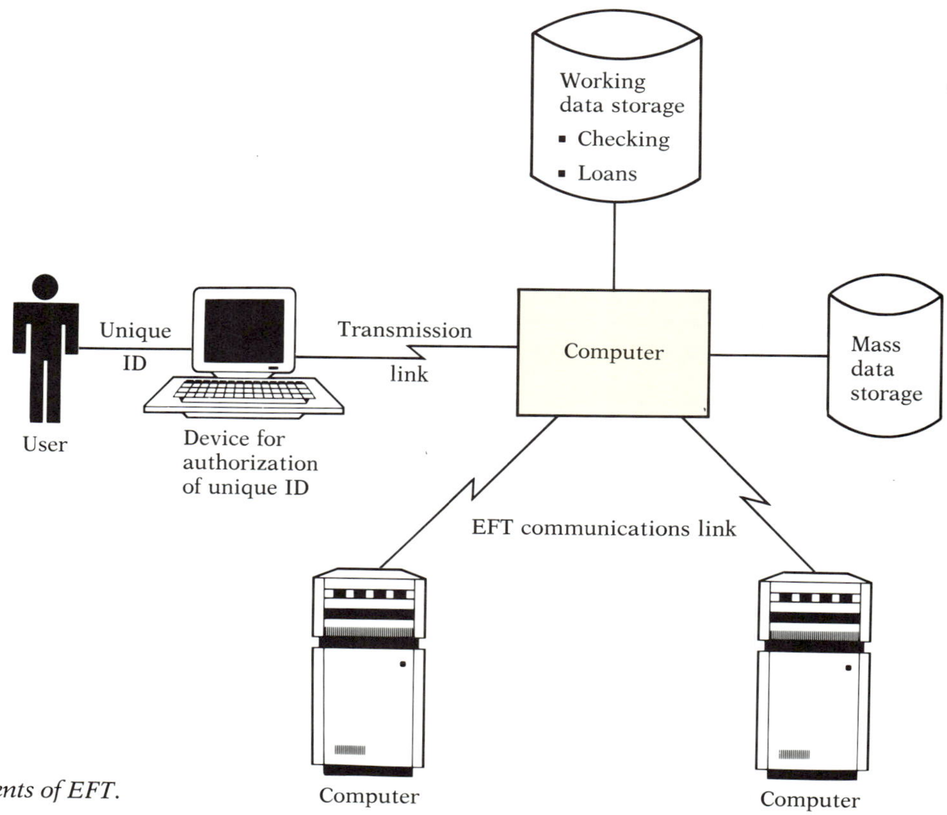

Figure 18.2 System components of EFT.

Supplement 18.2 Electronic Food Stamps

A pilot program is being initiated by the U.S. Department of Agriculture to replace paper coupons in the food stamp program with EFT. Grocery stores will be equipped with special POS terminals to automate food stamp transactions. An individual who qualifies for food stamps will be issued a photo identification card. The dollar value of the individual's benefits is placed in a special account.

When groceries are purchased, the checkout clerk will enter the card and a four-digit personal identifier code (supplied by the shopper) on the POS terminal. Through EFT, the amount of the food stamp transaction will be electronically debited from the account of the shopper. Unused benefits remain in the account until the next purchase. They cannot be converted into cash.

The system should prevent illegal trafficking in coupons for cash, coupon counterfeiting, and problems associated with theft and loss of coupons. Furthermore, unauthorized persons will be prevented from receiving benefits.

cessing desired transactions. Each of these essential components is discussed in this section. Figure 18.2 illustrates these basic components.

Electronic Transaction Authorization

If you have ever tried to buy groceries or new clothing by check, you know that some form of identification may be demanded. A driver's license will usually suffice. This is an **identifier** to link you, the check writer, to the funds in your checking account. This identifier helps the clerk decide that you are indeed authorized to withdraw funds from the checking account. The clerk matches the information on the identifier with information preprinted on your check.

Electronic funds transfer requires a machine-readable identifier so that unauthorized, fraudulent attempts to transfer funds will be recognized by the electronic system as such. A number of machine-identification technologies have been developed. Badges or cards that can be read by machine, such as those used in ATMs, are one alternative. Signature readers and equipment to distinguish between hand shapes, fingerprints, or voices are also possibilities. Such machines are practical applications of pattern recognition research. Note that some authorization systems require an identifier and a machine reader (for example, a card and card reader), while others require a pattern recognition device only (for example, a fingerprint reader).

Although many authorization systems are currently on the market, no system is as yet entirely problem-free. Cost is one difficulty. Signature and voice recognition devices are too expensive to be used widely, and they have the limitation that both signatures and voices may change over time. Many persons object to the use of fingerprints, perhaps because they have been used in the past to identify criminals. Indeed, the very concept of a unique identifier is under attack since it raises the specter of a police state. Most EFT systems use card identifiers at the present time. System computers check lists of lost, stolen, or cancelled cards before approving transactions. However, the user of an unreported stolen card might succeed in making a fraudulent EFT transaction.

Networks

EFT requires a computer **network** to link the person initiating the transfer, the account where funds are stored, and the recipient's account. (Networks are explained in Chapter 3.) Network communications should be easy to initiate, transmission time should be minimal, and the cost of transmission should be low. Network security is essential since the bits of data that pass through the network can represent enormous sums of money.

There are many parties with vested interests in the development of networks for EFT. These include:

Supplement 18.3 Smart Cards Replace Checkbooks

Smart cards, identical in size and shape to plastic credit cards, are being used in a pilot program in France for financial transactions. The cards have an embedded microchip that holds account information and balance in its memory.

At the beginning of each month, a certain amount of money is transferred to the card's account according to an agreement reached between the cardholder and the bank. The first time the card is inserted in a reader each month, the amount is automatically added to the previous balance recorded in the card's memory. When paying for goods, the card will record the date and value of the transaction and a new balance will be calculated by the microchip. The French smart card can handle about 200 transactions, the equivalent of eight paper checkbooks.

It is expected that service-oriented industries, in particular, will benefit from financial smart cards. There will be no need to maintain communications lines with central computers to verify the credit of customers. Reader terminals are currently located at hotels, car-rental depots, and airport ticket counters.

- Computer manufacturers.
- Manufacturers of communications equipment.
- Public and private carriers that provide communication services.
- Financial institutions and their clients.
- Government bodies that regulate banking.
- Government bodies that regulate communications.

Reconciling the diverse and often competing interests of these groups has slowed the development of a communications infrastructure in this country. In Europe communications are nationalized so that the development of EFT depends on government policy. In the United States, however, networks for EFT are developed by the private sector. This adds to problems of standardization and complicates both legal and regulatory issues.

Electronic Processing Capability

Once a requested EFT transaction is relayed to a customer's bank by telecommunications, the transaction is recorded and processed by computer without the use of paper media. (However, hard-copy statements reporting EFT transactions and account status are sent to bank clients each month.)

THE BENEFITS OF EFT

One of the **benefits of EFT** expected in the future is a reduction in the cost of making financial transactions. Over forty billion checks are processed annually in the United States. The cost of check stock, the cost of check writing, and the cost of check audits and controls are saved when organizations (or individuals) switch to EFT. As communications costs drop, network transactions should also be lower than stamps for mailing checks.

Each of the forty billion checks passes through an average 2.4 institutions during processing. Although banks report little difference between the cost of check processing and EFT processing at the present time, banks should realize savings when EFT volume increases. System components will reduce in price, and experience with EFT should improve cost efficiency. Already significant cost differentials exist between ATM and branch banking. An ATM machine costs approximately $40,000; a brick-and-mortar branch with limited drive-in facilities costs $300,000 or more. The cost of an ATM transaction is also lower than the cost of processing a paper check—approximately 42¢ for a local ATM transaction vs. more than $1.00, according to one source.

When electronic banking was first introduced, it was feared that people would object to dealing with ATMs. But shorter lines, convenient locations, and the ability to make financial transactions at any hour of day or night have in fact attracted users. Many people also like the privacy of ATM transactions. They feel more comfortable conducting business with a machine than interacting with a bank employee. One study has shown that minority groups prefer terminals because machines (unlike people) cannot discriminate.

Home Banking

Home banking is an offshoot of EFT. A wide range of financial services is available to individuals with home computers and a telecommunications link with a bank. These include:

- *Bill payment and account-to-account transfers.*
- *Financial management services.* For example, portfolio analysis, tax data collection, budget and cash-flow programs, and general investment information.
- *Administrative services.* For example, listings of bank hours and locations, loan rate and annuity tables.
- *Reporting services.* For example, periodic statements, balance and status inquiries, transaction histories, service charge summaries.

The service that customers seem to like best is statement display, the ability to review account activity since the last hard-copy statement.

Home banking does more than save people trips to the bank; it is like having a financial counselor in the home. In addition, bank services are convenient and accessible at any time of day or night, weekdays and weekends. Banks benefit because they can broaden their customer base by offering home banking services. They also are able to cut back office costs with EFT (that is, on costs associated with check processing). An officer of First Wisconsin National Bank predicts that 10 percent of all households will be using home banking by 1990.

Home banking must generate sufficient income to cover operating expenditures and start-up costs. A market must exist before home banking can be initiated. Banks are faced with the classic chicken-and-egg syndrome. The number of home banking services they offer determines the number of customers they attract: the number of customers determines how many services can be offered. Marketing success depends on finding the **critical mass**. In this context, the term critical mass refers to the optimum mix of banking services to encourage customer participation, at a price that makes the service economically viable for all persons involved (that is, profitable to the provider and cost-effective for the consumer).

The cost of home banking services in 1984 was in the $8 to $15 per month range. Many experts believe that home banking, to be viable, must be offered with other information services, such as videotex. Others believe that the ultimate providers of home banking will be third-party vendors. For example, Sears, in partnership with CBS and IBM, is planning ATMs and in-home banking in various forms for its customers.

Home Shopping

With EFT, **home shopping** (also called **teleshopping**) is feasible. The key to home shopping is that payment for selected purchases can be authorized from a home terminal.

Home shopping is a feature offered by many videotex home information systems being introduced across the country. Viewtron, described in Chapter 14, is an example of such a system.

Selection of goods may be through catalogs or newspaper advertisements called to the screen. Although the pleasure of window shopping and the ability to handle merchandise is lost, many systems allow viewers to rotate items displayed on the screen or view them in close-up. An advantage of home shopping is that the time spent searching for specific items can be reduced.

In the future it may become possible to key in descriptions of wanted items on a home terminal. Suppose a blue silk dressing gown with a bamboo design in size 6 is desired. Once these specifications are keyed in, the search for such a dressing gown will be done by computer. The names of stores stocking dressing gowns that meet the description will be flashed on the screen and the price of the dressing gowns listed. Customers will be able to view the merchandise on the screen, place an order, and authorize payment without ever leaving home.

If such home shopping systems take hold, they will change marketing patterns. Merchants will have to **index** their goods and provide these indexes to an information utility. Shopping centers will lose customers if buyers chose to make most purchases from their homes. Stores might become warehouses, transacting all business electronically. Fewer sales personnel and less display space would be needed. Shoplifting might cease to be a problem.

The concept of teleshopping can be extended to real estate transactions, to the selection of a plumber to unclog a pipe, to the purchase of airplane tickets, or to reservation systems for rental cars and motel rooms. Theoretically, one could bet on a horse race using EFT. It should be recognized, however, that while home shopping is technologically feasible and is implemented on a limited scale at present, it may not become commonplace very soon.

REGULATION OF EFT

In 1974 Congress created the National Commission on Electronic Fund Transfers. The commission was directed to recommend legislation providing for the development of public and private EFT systems. The commission held hearings for two years, providing a forum for industry, professional, and consumer groups to voice their views on EFT.

In 1978 the **Electronic Fund Transfer Act** became law. This was followed by Regulation E in 1980, issued by the Federal Reserve Board, which sets forth implementation provisions for the act. Regulation E affects the issuance of "access devices," initial disclosure of terms and conditions for EFT accounts, liability of consumers for unauthorized transfers, documentation of transfers, preauthorized debits and credits, and procedures for error resolution.

Many legal issues regarding EFT are not addressed in the 1978 act. For example, does an EFT terminal constitute a bank branch? (Federal courts have ruled that ATMs accepting deposits constitute a branch.) Under the McFadden Act passed in 1927, federal banks are unable to expand their services in jurisdictions where state banks are restricted. A national bank is, therefore, forbidden from establishing a branch in states that disallow branching. How will the McFadden Act be interpreted by the courts in disputes between state and national banks over EFT?

Obviously banking laws such as the McFadden Act need to be updated to deal with the complex legal issues raised by EFT. There is general agreement that new legislation is needed, but no agreement regarding what the new legislation should be.

Another problem currently confronting legislators is that small banks, unable to afford terminal equipment and unable to offer the range of computer services offered by larger banks, want protective legislation. They are afraid that EFTs will lead to concentration of deposits in fewer and fewer banks, creating bank monopolies. Alarmists see Citibank spreading westward and Bank of America eastward, swallowing smaller financial institutions in their paths. Although antitrust laws should prevent bank monopolies, resistance to EFT is partially based on this fear.

ISSUES INVOLVED IN IMPLEMENTING EFT

A variety of issues are slowing the spread of EFT. These issues include the financial implications of transactions that have no interval of delay and problems regarding security of data, lack of public confidence in computer transactions, cost, and the preference for cash. The remainder of this chapter will focus on these issues.

Float

When payments are made by check, there is usually a two-day to seven-day period between the time the check is written and the time the check is cashed. The amount of money in transit but not yet collected is called **float**. Float is, in effect, an interest-free, short-term loan to the check writer.

Instantaneous EFT payments eliminate float and the possibility of earning interest on these short-term loans. In fact, a company that pays bills by EFT but receives payment by conventional

Supplement 18.4 Bank of America Network

An international network of common data bases linking 100 locations is being built by Bank of America. Called International Banking System (IBS), the network will cost an estimated $500 million in the next seven years.

By 1988, Bank of America will have automated all of its foreign exchange and money trading, funds movement, correspondent banking services, and general ledger and accounting functions. For the bank's first data center in London (which covers Europe, the Middle East, and Africa), an estimated 150 separate data processing programs have been written (approximately five million lines of code). Most of the services available in London will be replicated at the other data centers. Data centers are planned for Hong Kong, Singapore, San Francisco, and other undisclosed locations.

Hardware at the London data center includes IBM 3081 and 3083 mainframes and an Amdahl V/8. To interface with the world, a message switching environment with DEC 11/70 minicomputers connected to the mainframes is featured. Communications systems used by IBS include everything from dedicated telephone lines to leased satellite transponders. Four systems handle operational database functions: Comet, for liability management; Astra, for credit and marketing; Aries, for payments; and Gemini, for accounting, including maintenance of customer accounts and of the bank's own general ledger.

Jay Cook, senior vice president of Bank of America's Global Systems Services, explained the reasons for building this world encompassing data network as follows:

> We are doing this partly to keep competitive and also to meet the demands of the marketplace. Multinational corporations want information. They want to be able to execute quickly, and once they execute they want to know what has been done. International banking has been a (communications) maze in the past . . . We hope to be able to sell this network and these services to other banks, rather than have them build something comparable.[2]

[2]Charlie Howe, "Wiring The World," *Datamation*, vol. 30, no. 16 (October 1984), p. 58.

checks stands to lose money. Loss of float is a principal reason why cash managers oppose EFT. On the other hand, if all expenditures and receipts were EFT transactions, the loss of float might be balanced by early receipts and other financial advantages. For example, real-time information on the status of funds helps firms manage their money to minimize idle funds.

Security and Privacy

As EFT networks expand and new electronic financial services are offered to the public, opportunities for embezzlement will increase. System designers must recognize system weaknesses, anticipate embezzlement attempts, and develop hardware and software to foil system intrusion. This is much easier said than done, in part because the technology that must be secured is constantly changing. (See Chapters 3 and 6 for discussions of security in communications and security of computer systems.) The number of potential embezzlers with computer expertise is also expanding.

Although most victims of computer crime do not want their identity publicized (they fear that their business might be hurt by loss of public confidence), there are EFT embezzlement cases on record. For example, a computer consultant to a bank transferred $10.2 million of the bank's money to his Swiss account by using his knowledge of codes and telecommunication security.

Not all electronic embezzlement requires computer expertise. Consider this example. A New York City customer, who had inserted his card in an ATM, was told by the next person in line (a con artist) that the machine was out of order. The customer then moved to an adjacent machine without clearing the first one. The con artist watched to see what code the customer used to initiate the transaction, and then returned to the first ATM, which was still open and active, entered the code, and withdrew $300 (the maximum allowed) from the customer's account.

Tight EFT **security** can contribute to individual **privacy** with regard to financial matters. But many persons fear that EFT will be one more

Supplement 18.5 $40,000 ATM Theft

Although neither police nor bank officials will give details, an apparent freak flaw in ATM security resulted in a theft of nearly $40,000 over one weekend in 1984 in Springfield, Massachusetts. An ATM software package, not the hardware itself, was allegedly to blame. According to reporters on the scene, a local man discovered an input code that enabled him to make repeated ATM cash transactions that did not register as withdrawals. With the help of two friends, he made as many as 250 withdrawals in one night.

Two of the men were detained when they tried to buy tickets to Hawaii because they fit the standard profile of hijackers—they had no luggage and attempted to purchase their tickets with cash. They were linked to the ATM embezzlement because cash was stuffed in their pockets, underwear, and shoes.

source of gathering personal data for data banks and personal profiles. Certainly, an analysis of bill payment through EFT could reveal an individual's spending patterns, travel movements, drinking habits, debts, health status, and so forth. The work of the IRS and law enforcement agencies would be easier if authorities were allowed to monitor EFT. For example, by tracing the terminal a suspect used for EFT transactions, the police would know where to focus search for the suspect.

Will government decide that the social advantages of EFT surveillance outweigh privacy rights? The concern of many citizens that EFT will contribute to the erosion of individual privacy may slow public acceptance of EFT.

Lack of Public Confidence

Many readers have had personal experience with computer errors, such as persistent dunning for a bill already paid. The credibility of computer transactions is in general somewhat tarnished. It is no wonder the public is concerned about the **reliability** of EFT and is therefore reluctant to eliminate the paper backup of checks. Indeed, most computer specialists would be uncomfortable with a cashless society given the current state of technology. A checkless, cashless society will not become a reality until the public gains confidence in EFT efficiency and accuracy.

Cost

Many banks offer free checking account services for customers who maintain a given balance. There is, therefore, little financial advantage to these customers in shifting to EFT since most banks charge for EFT services.

Preference for Cash

Many people like the feel of cash. It gives them a sense of achievement, triumph, power, even exhilaration. Retirees have expressed unhappiness with direct deposit of their Social Security checks. They want to handle their money, and they like the social contact they have with tellers and other bank customers when they deposit their own checks.

A cashless, checkless society might take away some of the joy of living, some of the satisfaction a worker feels when handed a weekly paycheck. Although EFT may prove to be the most efficient means of making financial transactions, it may not satisfy human needs. It is possible, however, that design features may make the "fun" of transacting business through a terminal outweigh the pleasure of handling cash.

SUMMING UP

Money need not be tangible. Data on financial transactions that is transmitted through telecommunication lines is a form of money and can be used to replace hard currency and checks.

One advantage of the electronic transfer of funds is that a large number of transactions can be processed quickly and efficiently. In addition, processing costs for many financial transactions are reduced. Furthermore, EFT is convenient and can

- *Checking*
  Reconciliation
  End-of-month statements
  NOW accounts
- *Savings*
  Passbook savings
  Statement accounts
  Money market certificates
  IRA
- *Installment loans*
  Simple interest
  Add-on
- *Mortgage loans*
- *Bill payer services*
- *Automatic teller machine services*
- *General ledger*
  Assets and liabilities
  Capital net worth
  Income and expenses
- *Administration*
  Payroll
  Budget
  Personnel
  Forecasting
  Accounts receivable
  Accounts payable

Figure 18.3 Sample of bank reports generated by computer.

extend many services, such as home banking and home shopping, to families.

Disadvantages include the high capital cost required to establish EFT networks and loss of float. There are legal issues and problems regarding security and privacy to be resolved. Resistance to EFT may occur because persons like to have cash literally "in-hand."

Requirements for an EFT system include (1) unique customer identification; (2) reliable, inexpensive, and accessible devices to read the identification and authorize the transaction; (3) networks to link customers and banks; and (4) hardware, software, and computer personnel to process and store transactions.

Technologically, a cashless, checkless society is feasible. But it may be some time before coins and paper money become extinct. At the present time, banks and large organizations are the major users of EFT. EFT services to individuals are expanding, but home banking is moving more slowly than anticipated. One reason may be that ATMs, POSs, and consolidation of back office automation in banks have priority and are using up technical resources.

Discussions regarding computers and money usually center around EFT, since EFT is a contemporary issue. It should be remembered, however, that even without EFT, computers are essential to the operation of banks. They are used to record and process check transactions. They also control and keep track of loans and other client services. (Figure 18.3 lists a sample of bank reports generated by computer.) Computers also generate reports required by federal regulatory agencies and calculate up to fifty-two ratios for the ratings of CAMEL (capital asset quality, management, earnings, and liquidity).

REVIEW QUESTIONS

1. What is an ATM? What are the advantages and limitations of ATM transactions?
2. What functions do POS terminals perform?
3. Do electronic transaction terminals reduce the amount of paperwork for banks? Explain.
4. What is the objective of EFT? Can this objective be obtained with current technology?
5. Give examples of EFT use today.
6. List and describe the components of an EFT system.
7. Can EFT systems be made as secure as checks and drafts? What increased security measures would you recommend?
8. What has slowed the expansion of EFT in this country?
9. Compare the advantages and disadvantages of EFT with check processing.
10. What is the meaning of critical mass? Has lack of critical mass slowed the development of home banking? Why?
11. How is indexing related to home shopping? How can indexing save a shopper time?

12. Describe EFT regulation.
13. How does the issue of float relate to EFT?
14. Discuss reasons EFT has been slow to gain public support in this country.

DISCUSSION QUESTIONS

1. What do you think will be the future of:
   a. checks?
   b. plastic credit cards?
   c. currency?
   d. financial documents, such as stock certificates?

   Justify your position and state the time frame for your predictions.
2. What would you recommend as an identifier when making electronic transfer of funds at the:
   a. consumer level?
   b. business level?
   c. national agency level?
3. Should the government implement a nationwide EFT network? Discuss the problems of state/federal regulation of communications and banking.
4. How would home shopping affect retail trade and economic activity? Would it strengthen our economy?
5. How would home shopping change the style and structure of advertising? Would it lead to the demise of newspapers because they would lose advertising revenue?
6. How would home shopping change marketing? Retail jobs? The business center of your town? The price of goods?
7. Would you be willing to pay for home banking? How much? Who would benefit most from home banking?
8. Will home banking increase the danger of bank errors? Will it affect the consumer adversely in any way? How?
9. What are the dangers of home banking to privacy?
10. Do you favor cash in your pocket? Will it make any difference to you if currency and bills are replaced by EFT? Will it affect your lifestyle?
11. Will it be easier to keep financial records in a cashless society?
12. It is suggested that banking and shopping provide us with social contact that will be lost in a cashless society. Will this be a social problem? For whom?
13. Is disruption of society inevitable during and following the transition to EFT? What stratas of society will be affected?

EXERCISES

1. Visit a local bank and interview one of the officers. List the officer's views on the advantages of EFT to:
   a. the bank
   b. the customer
   c. society
2. Interview a user of EFT in your town. Does the user think security and privacy of EFT are adequate? What changes would the user like initiated to improve EFT customer service?
3. Report on recent state and federal EFT legislation. What problems does the legislation address? Who opposed the legislation? Why? Do you think the legislation is adequate or is further legislation needed?

Selected Annotated Bibliography

Bartimo, Jim. "Should You Try Banking by Computer?" *Personal Computer*, vol. 9, no. 11 (November 1985), pp. 61–7. This article includes the banks' view of computer banking as well as tips for managing personal banking at home.

Bencin, Richard L. "Electronic Marketing in the 1990s," *Advanced Management Journal*, vol. 48, no. 2 (Autumn 1983), pp. 51–58. This article discusses a new approach to selling that would use electronic technology. Topics discussed include CRT-assisted telephone marketing calls, the creation of eligibility factors for a good product/buyer match, survey data of client needs, computer software for direct mail, and teleadvertising.

Bequai, August. *The Cashless Society: EFTS at the Crossroads*. New York: John Wiley, 1981. An overview of the social, political, and economic problems that will come with a cashless society. Subjects examined include the threat to privacy, the reduction in competition among banks, the increase in computer-related crimes, and whether EFTS facilities should be operated by a government monopoly.

Boatright, Earl. "Electronic Funds Transfer: Why the Benefits Outweigh the Costs," *ICP Interface*, vol. 18 (Summer 1983), pp. 14–16. This article argues that a requirements analysis, including an assessment of security controls, accuracy, productivity, future cost containments, and customer service, is needed before automation is begun. Wire transfer of funds, automated clearing house, and ATMs are the electronic banking services discussed.

Bukowski, Robert. "ATM System Concerns For Senior Bank," *Bank Administration*, vol. 59, no. 2BE (February 1983), pp. 28–32. ATM system configuration determines level of service and degree of risk. Batch and alternative online ATM configurations are compared.

Fistell, Linde. "POS Technology Expands Users' Options," *Canadian Datasystems*, vol. 13 (September 1981), pp. 27–32. Sample POS hardware, including compact holographic scanners and modular and portable systems, are described.

Guynes, Steve. "EFTS Impact on Computer Society," *Computers & Security*, vol. 2, no. 1 (January 1983), pp. 73–77. Threats to EFT security are discussed. The security methods reviewed include an audit log, a password system, encryption, and reliable identifiers.

Logsdon. Tom. *Computers and Social Controversy*. Potomac, Maryland: Computer Science Press, 1980. Chapter 12, "Computers and Our Monetary System," is recommended (pp. 307–32). It discusses consumer and governmental responses to EFT.

Svigals, Jerome. *Computerworld*, vol. 43, no. 18 (October 29, 1984,) pp. In Depth/1–6. Pressures on the banking industry, including deregulation, national deficit, and internal problems (for example, personnel costs), are discussed.

Warfe, George J. "Signature Dynamics—Tomorrow's ID," *Bank Administration*, vol. 57, no. 1 (January 1981), pp. 33–40. This article discusses the advantages of signature dynamics (the measurement and analysis of the speed and rhythm of pen tip motion as people sign their signatures) over PIN (personal ID) numbers and plastic cards for transaction security.

Society in Transition: Information Technology as an Agent of Change

It is the business of the future to be dangerous. . . . The major advances in civilization are processes that all but wreck the societies in which they occur.

ALFRED NORTH WHITEHEAD

CHAPTER NINETEEN

Key Words

age of information	joint research ventures	research and development (R&D)
antitrust litigation	laws	self-image
decentralization	maximum separation	Semiconductor Research Cooperative (SRC)
distributed data processing (DDP)	Microelectronics & Computer Technology Corporation (MCC)	transborder data flow
government policies	network style of management	technology transfer programs
information-rich environment	1956 IBM Consent Decree	unbundling
Japanese model	nodes	

1956 was the turning point. In that year, white-collar workers outnumbered blue-collar workers for the first time in American history. More persons were engaged in clerical, technical, and managerial positions than in the production of goods. Scholars recognized that society was being restructured and that the industrial era had come to an end. They thought the post-industrial economy would be based on services.

However, it soon became apparent that a majority of service workers were actually engaged in the creation, processing, and distribution of information. And with each advance in the electronic handling of information, the number of information occupations has grown. Today's economy is based on the mass-production of information in:

- Printing and publishing trades.
- Communications and telecommunications industries: for example, broadcasting, periodicals, libraries, and teleprocessing.
- Knowledge professions: for example, educators, engineers, bureaucrats, insurance people, lawyers, doctors, bankers, technicians, managers, stock brokers, research scientists, and journalists.
- Companies engaged in the manufacture or distribution of information processing equipment, supplies, and services.

We have entered a new age, the **age of information**.

The transformation of the United States into a society whose principal source of wealth and power is information is changing the way we work, the way we play, the way we make decisions, the way we communicate with one another, and the way we think about ourselves. (See Table 19.1 for a summary of differences between the industrial and the information age.) This transformation is altering the balance of power within organizations and in the world at large. There is virtually no aspect of society untouched by the computer revolution.

This chapter will discuss some of the legal, political, ethical, and social issues that must be addressed in an information society.

COMPUTERS AS A SOURCE OF POWER

Information technology can contribute both to the concentration of power and to its diffusion. For example, computers can be used for purposes of repression and social control: for instance, for surveillance of the ruled. Yet they can also involve people in the decision-making process: for instance, community action on issues is facilitated through networks.

When information technology is first introduced, it increases the power of persons who understand how to use that technology. Persons in positions of leadership have an enhanced ability to defend their interests. The grip of specialists is strengthened since they can gain greater mastery of their specialities by using computer resources.

Professional elites cannot, however, lock up computer resources. The knowledge that gives the

Table 19.1 Comparison of the industrial and information age

Characteristic	Industrial Age	Age of Information
Basic resource	Oil, coal, gas, electricity, and nuclear energy	Information
Strategic resource	Capital and labor	Knowledge
Technology	Production technology using machine tools	High tech, such as computer technology, telecommunications, genetics
Labor	Semi-skilled and skilled production workers	The knowledge worker
Workplace	Office Factory	Electronic office Automated factory

elite its power can be transferred to others by information technology. In many ways, computers are a democratizing force. One reason is that data, once computerized, is stripped of ambiguity, while data management programs help order and simplify complex data sets. As a result, the transfer of knowledge is facilitated. In addition, we are developing user-friendly systems to enable persons with no computing background or expertise to share data and use it in meaningful ways. Moreover, in recent years computers have come within the budget range of most organizations and many individuals. A large segment of the general public today has access to computing resources. There is evidence that bureaucratic structures in this country are giving way to horizontal links between persons at all levels of society as a result of telecommunications and computer networking, a further indication that knowledge (and power) are being diffused by information technology.

In the sections that follow, three examples of the impact of computers on organizational and national power structures are examined. The trend toward decentralization, transborder data flow, and the challenge posed by information technology to the Soviet bloc are discussed.

Decentralization

In corporations and large organizations, **distributed data processing (DDP)** is becoming a common processing mode. A number of separate computing facilities, called **nodes**, are established within the organization to replace (or supplement) mainframes or minis at a central location. Each node is under the operational control of local management, and each site may have unique equipment and data base configurations according to local processing needs. A telecommunications link with headquarters allows centralized control over policies. But day-to-day decision making is delegated to managers at each node.

This decentralization is possible because of technological developments in computing. Low-cost telecommunications make networks economically feasible. Low-cost microcomputers and minis, with processing capabilities exceeding many former large computers, can now be purchased for the distributed nodes.

The result is a new **network style of management** replacing the bureaucratic hierarchy that was formerly characteristic of most corporations. As stated by Intel's Vice Chairman Robert Noyce,

> What we've tried to do is to put people together in ways so that they make contributions to a wider range of decisions and do things that would be thwarted by a structured, line organization.[1]

The trend toward **decentralization** is apparent throughout society. The concentration of power in the old industrial north has been diminished as factory after factory has closed. Hundreds of thou-

[1]Quoted in John Naisbitt, *Megatrends*. New York: Warner, 1984, p. 222.

sands of jobs have been lost as we have shifted out of the industrial era. According to John Herbers of the *New York Times*,

> The urban landscape from the Northern tier of states from Massachusetts to Minnesota is marred by vacant factories, warehouses and great open spaces where such buildings stood, visual testimony to a great migration whose impact on the nation is becoming increasingly clear.[2]

This migration is a shift in population and economic strength to the West where many new, high-tech industries are located, and to the Sunbelt where petrochemicals, oil, and space age technology are concentrated. (Mild climate, open spaces, and a perceived higher quality of life are also factors contributing to the decision of many families to move.) John Naisbitt, author of *Megatrends*, states that the old economic, financial axis between New York and Chicago is being replaced by a new axis between Los Angeles and Houston.

In addition, many city dwellers are moving to small towns and rural communities as businesses decentralize and open new facilities away from city centers. (The 1980 census reports that the counties adjacent to metropolitan areas are the fastest growing counties.) Telecommuting also contributes to decentralization since teleworkers can live far away from corporate headquarters.

The geographic decentralization of our population has been accompanied by a like-movement of personal income, pension funds, and investment. Since the allocation of seats in the House of Representatives is based on population, political power is shifting as well. The election of President Reagan in 1980 put a Westerner in the White House, a Republican who encouraged the flow of political authority from Washington and toward the states and localities.

Decentralization is a great facilitator of social change. It gives individuals more opportunity to tackle problems locally and gives impetus to grassroots political activity. The computer is not the only force in modern America promoting decentralization, but it is a major one.

[2]*Ibid*, p. 233.

Transborder Data Flow and the Third World

Information technology has improved financial management of transnational corporations. Large amounts of data on markets and economic conditions can be sent to headquarters by telecommunications. This flow of data across national borders, called **transborder data flow**, and the use of computers to handle and analyze the data improves decision making in most areas. As a result, the competitiveness of multinationals on world markets is enhanced.

Transborder data flow is the subject of much concern to the poorer nations of the world. As stated by Louis Jorvet,

> Information is power, and economic information is economic power. Information has an economic value and the ability to store and process certain types of data may well give one country political and technological advantage over other countries. This, in turn, may lead to a loss of national sovereignty through supernational data flows.[3]

In the Third World, it is feared that transborder data flow will hinder the establishment of domestic information resources. The reason is that telecommunications makes it much less costly to utilize remote computing power than to develop local processing capability. Without computing resources of their own, Third World countries will be dependent on foreign computer centers, a dependence that is politically unacceptable to many nations. Development in other fields may also be blocked since information technology has spin-off effects and is a tool for development in all disciplines, such as medicine, agriculture, and government. Computers are already eroding the value of one of the principle assets of developing countries, their abundant supply of inexpensive labor. Once robots automate factories in the West, there will be less incentive for companies to invest in Third World economies.

[3]Quoted by John Eger, "Transborder Flow," *Datamation*, vol. 24, no. 12 (November 15, 1978), p. 50.

Supplement 19.1 Liability for Transborder Data Flow

The Organization for Economic Cooperation and Development (OECD) is a forum for discussions on transborder data flow by the developed nations. Privacy and data protection are two subjects addressed in the OECD Privacy Guidelines, an international voluntary agreement negotiated and adopted in 1980. Signatories have agreed to keep personal data in electronic record systems at a minimum standard.

Recent discussions at the OECD have focused on the following problems:

- Legal liability for system failure.
- Negligence or inaccurate messages or data.
- EFT.
- Copyright protection for data bases and software.
- Unauthorized access to computers in the context of international data transmission.

Since members of the OECD have different legal traditions, international agreement on these problems is difficult to achieve. One important outcome of discussion on these problems may be to alert OECD members of the need to update their domestic liability laws. Reform at the national level would help promote international data transmission and encourage international trade in information goods and services.

Leaders of the Third World see their countries falling farther and farther behind the developed world. They are asking for technological assistance. They believe that the rich nations have a moral obligation to assist poor nations and bear responsibility as former colonial powers for their plight. They claim that assistance will actually benefit the West since economic disaster in the Third World could lead to political radicalization and to lost markets.

Yet programs to bring computer technology to the Third World are not free of controversy. According to many experts, the premise that the developing nations can leapfrog into the information age is naive at best. They cite lack of technological resources, including data, hardware and software, and experienced personnel to program and operate systems, as major problems. Because educational facilities are limited, there is no pool of potential users trained in computer use. It takes time to learn how to implement computer systems and to use information technology effectively. Growth in computing, it is argued, must pass through Nolan's stages of growth. (See Chapter 8 for a discussion of Nolan's growth curves.)

Some critics claim that **technology transfer programs** impose Western values and definitions of progress on the Third World for less than altruistic reasons and that, in effect, we are simply looking for computer markets. There is also concern that the benefits of information technology will work to further entrench the privileged in the Third World rather than reaching persons most in need of help.

The Challenge to Russia

Statements made by senior party members and academicians in Russia indicate that the Soviets acknowledge the impact of electronics on labor and the importance of introducing electronic equipment into their economy. At the present time, the USSR has an industrial economy. It is estimated that Russia lags ten to twelve years behind the West in the field of information technology. The USSR has the capability of moving into the information age, but the question is whether its present centralized social structure could survive.

The problem that faces the Soviet bloc is that an information-based economy depends on an **information-rich environment**. Data must exist, and that data must be objectively tested against reality. The exchange of data and system-wide interaction must also be possible.

These conditions are not present in Russia because data is linked to ideology. Data frequently represents what the system wants or needs to know rather than representing behavior. In general, the communist party filters information and then decides whether or not to make it public. There is prior censorship of almost everything generated through official channels. Not even street maps or telephone directories are readily available to the public. Newspapers, journals, and books must adhere to the party line.

Widespread access to computing resources in Russia will undermine the ability of those in power to control the flow of information. To censor all information passing through computer networks would take increasing amounts of time and energy of the political elite. How will the Soviets cope with the movement toward local autonomy in operational matters that is fostered by computing?

The West is a marketplace of ideas. We are establishing bibliographic data bases with references to most of the world's professional knowledge. We are developing tools to facilitate the search for information and its rapid retrieval, including interactive languages and mass storage techniques. There are few restrictions on the creation, manipulation, or exchange of information.

If communism is to compete with the West, Russian specialists must have the same access to professional knowledge as their Western counterparts. An expanded electronics industry is necessary as is an educated, informed citizenry. For this to occur, Russian society will have to be restructured. Communist ideology will be challenged in the process.

CHANGE IN NATIONAL POLICY

In this country, altered directions of national policy also demonstrate that computers are an agent of social change. For example, a new relationship between the United States government and the microelectronics industry is under consideration. The reason is that America's position as a world leader in information technology has eroded since the 1970s. In a knowledge-based economy, **research and development (R&D)** can be an indicator of coming innovation. Both federal and corporate investment in R&D have declined in the U.S. at a time when other countries are intensifying their research through organized and planned national efforts. To stimulate research and development of generic information technology in the United States, a new alliance of government and industry may be needed.

Already the Japanese are challenging U.S. leadership in microelectronics and artificial intelligence. It is common in Japan for a multicompany consortium to be organized and subsidized by the Ministry of International Trade and Industry. This consortium picks a research objective (or market penetration objective), assembles top-flight scientists to develop relevant technology, and then passes this technology to member companies for the development of commercial products. This approach has been very successful, allowing the Japanese to capture many markets from U.S. firms (for example, the TV, automobile, and semiconductors markets).

In view of the importance of information technology to the U.S. economy, perhaps the **Japanese model** should be followed. Many experts believe that the government should recognize that R&D of generic information technology is too expensive and too complex for U.S. computer firms to tackle on their own. They propose the following five measures:

1. Government tax incentives for research and capital spending in the microelectronics industry.
2. Government grants to universities and laboratories to strengthen existing microelectronics research groups and to establish new ones. It is also suggested that a national microelectronics laboratory be established.
3. An expanded government role in regulation and standardization to increase the compatibility of electronic products.
4. Government financial support to university faculty and students working on microelectronics theory, technology, and policy.
5. Government support of electronics-related career training in secondary schools and colleges.

Whether these recommendations will be adopted or not remains to be seen. The fact that such **government policies** are under serious consideration is an indication of the changing relationship of government and industry in this age of information.

THE QUESTION OF MONOPOLY

Let us now look at the issue of monopoly in relation to information technology. The computer industry has been shaped by antitrust litigation. But the industry, in turn, has reshaped American attitudes toward big business and forced change in federal regulation of the industry. This interplay has had a profound effect on jobs and markets.

Antitrust Action Against IBM

Computer firms have been involved in litigation over the question of size and monopolistic practices since 1932 when the government filed its first antitrust suit related to computing, a suit charging IBM and Remington Rand with restraint of trade for monopolizing the market for punched cards. Since that time, IBM has been a party to many antitrust suits. The company's size and leadership in pricing have made it a natural target for charges that it violates antitrust principles.

Antitrust litigation has had a profound impact on IBM and on the entire structure of the computer industry. For example, when computers were first put on the market, IBM did not sell its hardware but leased it to customers. In 1952, an antitrust suit by the government charged IBM with restraint of trade for its restrictive leasing agreements and price discrimination. The suit led to an out-of-court settlement, called the **1956 IBM Consent Decree**, in which IBM agreed to offer customers the option of buying or leasing equipment. This enabled a number of small companies to enter the leasing market. They could now purchase IBM equipment and lease it themselves. They competed with IBM's leasing operation by depreciating equipment over a longer lifetime than IBM and by accepting a lower unit profit margin.

In another provision of the decree, IBM agreed to establish a separate service subsidiary and to release technical information on machine maintenance. Today the independent services segment of the computer industry consists of over a thousand companies, many of which have become substantial enterprises. Without the 1956 Consent Decree, these companies could not have entered the marketplace and survived competition with IBM.

Antitrust pressure is also cited as instrumental in IBM's 1969 **unbundling** decision to no longer price hardware offerings to include software and services. This decision gave impetus to firms specializing in software, education, and maintenance.

Although antitrust litigation has contributed to changes in computing, it has not prevented the continuing domination of IBM. In January 1969, the Department of Justice again filed an antitrust action against IBM, calling for divestiture, divorcement, and reorganization of the company. (The intent was to force IBM to split into two or three smaller companies.) It was charged that IBM's share of the general-purpose digital computer market (mainframes) was in excess of 70 percent, leaving competitors "patently vulnerable." IBM, in defense, asserted that the data processing industry consisted of more than 6,000 companies, the corporation's own share of the market being only 32 percent.

The case dragged through the 1970s at enormous cost to both IBM and the taxpayer. By 1978, 80,000 pages of transcript had been recorded, yet the suit was still far from settlement. Although many people were frustrated by the interminable delays, others were not surprised at the endless litigation, blaming the government's lack of aggressive prosecution of the case. Attorney General Griffin Bell suggested an alternative to action through the courts: namely, resolving major antitrust issues through the legislative process.

> The process would necessarily be more political, but the questions at hand in a sense are political. They involve the basic restructuring of American Industry and the shape of the American Economy.[4]

Bell's views may have contributed to the passage of recent legislation to lower antitrust barriers (as described later in this chapter), but probably had no direct bearing on the outcome of the suit against IBM.

[4]Quoted in Linda Flato, "Washington's Concern with Antitrust Stalemates," *Datamation vol. 25, no. 7 (July 1979), p. 89.*

In January 1982, after thirteen years of litigation, the 1969 antitrust suit against IBM was dismissed. IBM declared itself "totally vindicated." During the course of the suit, the corporation had become bigger than ever. Its annual revenues had tripled and its share of the market was undiminished. Many observers of the trial agreed that the suit had long outlived its relevance. By 1982, competition centered in markets for small computers, communications, computing services, and software, not mainframes.

It is still too early to state what the social implications of the settlement will be, but some experts predict that IBM, unshackled by legal and political restraints, will expand into new markets, moving relentlessly against competitors. Others suggest that IBM, because of its size, will restructure and split of its own accord, the very action that the government was trying to force.

The AT&T Settlement

Another landmark antitrust case was resolved in 1982 when a settlement was reached in a seven-year-old antitrust suit against AT&T. According to the settlement, AT&T was freed from restrictive federal regulation. The settlement now allows AT&T to compete in whatever business it chooses, including computing. Prior to the settlement, the principle of **maximum separation** was central to regulatory schemas governing AT&T and other firms in the communications industry. Under maximum separation, the generation of information was kept separate from its flow in order to prevent the concentration of power over information. This principle prevented the merging of communications and computing since no single firm could enter both markets.

The 1982 settlement allows AT&T to compete with firms such as IBM, ITT, RCA, and General Telephone and Electronics for markets in office automation, home banking, and even computer manufacture. Computer firms, IBM in particular, will undoubtedly challenge AT&T's dominance in the field of data communications in turn. In all likelihood, the merging of computing and communications will serve the interests of consumers. It should foster innovative computing applications, such as home shopping and electronic mail, and lower costs to the consumer.

This history of antitrust litigation shows that concern over monopoly has helped structure the computer industry, an industry responsible for our transition from an industrial society to an information-driven economy. Antitrust litigation has also raised issues that are the subject of much debate today. One such issue is, "How bad is bigness?" Customers benefit from economies of scale. In addition, to compete on world markets we need investment in research and development that only large firms can afford. Another issue raised by antitrust litigation is, "If a computer company is to be 'broken up,' on what basis should it be done? How should data processing be defined?" If disks and tapes are considered separate markets equal in size, then a firm that sells 80 percent of all disks but no tapes would have a monopoly. But if disks and tapes are considered together, the firm would have only 40 percent of the total. A third issue has to do with the usefulness of antitrust litigation. People are asking, in effect, if it is in the public interest to spend tens of millions of dollars in government antitrust suits. The dismissal of the suit against IBM and the AT&T settlement in 1982 may signal a change in Washington and in the country as a whole regarding the value of antitrust litigation.

Lowered Antitrust Barriers

In the past, American firms have been wary of entering into **joint research ventures** because of uncertainty regarding their legal status under antitrust laws. Antitrust guidelines say that no more the 25 percent of any market is allowed to collaborate in a given consortium.

Recent legislation passed by the House and Senate has relaxed antitrust barriers. Congress recognizes that research consortia are a way to improve U.S. productivity and competitiveness. Consortia are favored by the Reagan Administration since they are organized and financed by the private sector and do not require direct government intervention.

In 1982, the **Semiconductor Research Cooperative (SRC)** was founded, the first U.S. consortium in electronics and computing. Thirty-five companies are members. They pool funds to sponsor research on microelectronics at key universities around the country. While results of SRC-funded projects will appear in technical literature available to the public, members of the SRC will be the first to look at results and will, therefore, have a lead time in developing commercial applications of the research.

The **Microelectronics & Computer Technology Corporation (MCC)**, which started operation in 1983, focuses on bringing together a pool of highly trained scientists and engineers for in-house research. MCC has eighteen corporate sponsors and a budget of more than $70 million. Its objectives include developing new methods of packing integrated circuits, expert systems to assist in writing software, and computer-aided design of very large-scale integrated circuits. It also has a program called Advanced Computer Architecture that is comprised of four independent projects devoted to parallel processing, artificial intelligence, data base management, and human interface with computers.

MCC's proprietary data on new processes, techniques, and prototypes will be limited to those companies funding each particular program. Licensing of patented technologies will be limited to sponsor companies for up to three years. Thereafter, licenses will be available to the general public.

According to the Reagan administration, consortia like SRC and MCC should help improve America's competitive position in computing. The government also favors joint ventures in chemical, TV, and other industries to help revitalize the economy. Whether American firms will relinquish their traditional independence and self-reliance remains to be seen. Antitrust laws are no longer the barrier to cooperative efforts that they once were. On the other hand, many firms believe trade secrets give them a competitive edge. They may be reluctant to work with competitors in a consortium to develop new technologies.

LEGAL DILEMMAS

Another area in which the computer has had a decided impact is in the realm of law. A dilemma confronting computer users today is that the law has not kept pace with technological developments in computing. As a result, courts must apply antiquated legislation to modern technology. For example, antitrust is regulated by the Sherman Act of 1890 and Clayton Act of 1914, laws written long before the advent of computers. Moreover, more than forty sections of the United States Code can be cited to provide sanctions for computer-related criminal conduct although they make no explicit reference to computers. This means that the statutes must be interpreted by the courts when a case involves computer resources. Whether an action is legal or not in computing is often difficult for the public to assess.

Only a few **laws** specifically address computing issues. These include the Privacy Act of 1974, the Information Act of 1975, and the Electronic Fund Transfer Act of 1978. Because so few laws have been written to cover issues facing computer manufacturers and computer users, it is not always apparent what the legal ramifications of a policy or course of action will be. In addition, individuals involved in computing are often uncertain regarding their rights.

Let's look at the problem of protecting computing resources as an example. The Patent Act of 1952 gives inventors a legal monopoly over their inventions for a period of seventeen years. This act applies to computer hardware only. The legal status of software is not so clear-cut. In 1972 the Supreme Court struck down a patent application for software on the basis that programs are ideas expressed in mathematical algorithms. One may not patent an idea.

If not patentable, can programs be copyrighted? Are they the equivalent of literary or artistic creations? Are programs protected by trade secret laws? There has been considerable litigation regarding software questions, and many decisions have been rendered in state and federal courts. But the issue of software rights is still not fully resolved. Perhaps the answer is national legislation specifically defining proprietary rights for software.

Liability is another legal area in which there are many uncertainties. Who is responsible when computer programs fail? The system designer who has not adequately defined the job? The programmer who used faulty logic? The manager responsible for financing and approving the project? Does the Uniform Commercial Code, which imposes an implied warranty of fitness of goods, apply to computer programs?

Liability is also unclear when leaks of proprietary data occur in time-sharing systems or when hackers use unauthorized computer time. And who is liable when a robot causes injury to a human?

The legislative process is deliberate and slow. Although there is agreement on the need for new laws on computing issues, there is no agreement what these laws should be. One of the challenges of the 1980s will be to update the law so that the change in society fostered by computer technology can occur within a legal framework.

COMPUTERS AND SELF-IMAGE

Perhaps the most profound change being brought about by information technology is in the way people view themselves. The range of problems that computers can solve is increasing and computers are demonstrating their ability to think, be creative, and learn. Some philosophers and psychologists see human beings and computers as two different species of a more abstract genus called "information processing systems." This concept forces us to reflect on the nature of mind and the nature of life. What makes mankind unique?

The idea that people occupy a privileged position in the universe has been challenged before in history. Copernicus made us discard the view that the earth is the physical center of the universe. Darwin cast doubt on our role as the centerpiece of creation. Freud made us aware of the human being's instincts and drives, and defined the self as integrally involved with the unconscious. And now computers threaten our **self-image** by causing us to think of ourselves as parallel processing machines.

Will a flattened, mechanical view of human nature evolve in this age of computers? Or will we begin to see the human as a complex being, a mix of logic and emotion, with no machine counterpart? If we cede reason to the computer, will we increasingly focus on the soul and spirit of the "human machine"?

Some experts suggest that society will begin to value the emotional qualities of humans, qualities that have been suppressed in the past, as we seek to differentiate mankind from machine. More appreciation may be given the arts and more support given to artists who enrich our emotional lives. It may become acceptable to express our feelings rather than bottle them up inside. Sensitivity, rather than macho behavior, may become a cultural standard. Crying may become acceptable in adults.

Other experts fear that computers are increasing human alienation. Humans beings, they say, compare themselves to machines and see only their inferiority and obsolescence. Computer communications result in a loss of human connections since messages are sent from machine to machine, eliminating social contacts at the workplace. How can human dignity and feelings of self-worth survive in such a society? (See Figure 19.1.)

Sherry Turkle, author of *The Second Self: Computers and the Human Spirit*, suggests that we are living with a new and deeply felt tension as we try to resolve contradictory notions about our value as humans. We once defined ourselves with respect to our differences from animals. Today it's our differences from computers that concern us. She closes her book by saying,

> One thing is certain: the riddle of mind, long a topic for philosophers, has taken on new urgency. Under pressure from the computer, the question of mind in relation to machine is becoming a central cultural preoccupation. It is becoming for us what sex was to the Victorians—threat and obsession, taboo and fascination.[5]

SUMMING UP

There is virtually no aspect of society untouched by the computer revolution. We must adjust to decentralized decision making to accommodate the trend toward distributed data processing at work. We must adjust to decentralization of our popu-

[5]Sherry Turkel, *The Second Self*, New York: Simon and Schuster, 1984, p. 313.

Figure 19.1 One popular film's pessimistic view of the future. The world of **Bladerunner** is populated by robots like Pris and Batty who have been programmed to believe that they are human. (© 1982 The Ladd Company)

lation as people move from the older centers of industry in the North now that information, not manufacturing, is the basis of our economy.

We are also learning that information technology has political ramifications. The development of countries in the Third World may depend on access to computer technology and control over transborder data flow. Russia's competition with the West may depend in large part on the USSR becoming an information state, even though such a state would challenge the ideology of communism.

National policy in the United States is shifting as we face competition in information technology. The relationship of government to industry is being redefined. Antitrust barriers have been lowered to allow joint research ventures. The merging of computing and communications is now permissible. In addition, our legal structure is being changed to provide protection and avenues of redress for the computer industry and computer users.

Finally, the computer requires us to think about who we are. If our intellectual abilities can be matched and possibly surpassed by machines, do humans have a unique and special role in the universe? Are we merely chemistry and program? Computers have given these questions immediacy and urgency.

REVIEW QUESTIONS

1. What is the "age of information?" What are its characteristics? How does it differ from the industrial age?
2. Do computers contribute to centralization? How?
3. What is DDP? What effect does DDP have on decision making in an organization?
4. Describe how computers have contributed to decentralization of American society.
5. What is transborder data flow? How have computers contributed to this situation?
6. What is the relationship of transborder data flow to concentration of power?
7. What are the arguments for and against the transfer of technology to the Third World?

8. Will information technology bring social change to countries within the Soviet bloc? How?

9. Why are many people suggesting that a new relationship between government and the computer industry should be forged? Give examples of government policy that could affect research and development in microelectronics. How can national policy help the computer industry in the U.S.?

10. How has antitrust litigation shaped the computer industry in the U.S.? Why has IBM been a frequent party to antitrust suits? How have the suits affected IBM?

11. Why is the 1982 antitrust settlement of the government's action against AT&T of significance to the computer industry? What does maximum separation mean?

12. Do the Japanese represent a threat to American leadership in computing? Why?

13. What is the purpose of joint research ventures? Why have antitrust barriers been lowered? How can consortia serve American interests?

14. Describe some of the problems that arise when technology moves at a faster pace than state and national legislatures.

15. Has the law in the United States inhibited or protected the computer industry?

16. How do computers threaten mankind's self-image?

DISCUSSION QUESTIONS

1. Do the computer elite have more power than it should, or have computers contributed to decentralization and diffusion of power? Can both be true? What factors would contribute to shared computing power?

2. Do you agree that we live in an information society? What are the advantages of an information society over an industrial society? How will your life be different from the lives of your parents and grandparents as a result of the new importance of information?

3. Comment on the statement, "Information is power and power corrupts." Do you see this happening? Give examples.

4. What are the benefits or disadvantages of restricted transborder data flow to:
   a. multinational companies?
   b. underdeveloped or Third World countries?
   c. freedom of information?
   d. international trade?

5. Does the United States have a moral obligation to help developing countries in:
   a. computer use?
   b. computer production?
   c. training computer personnel?

   If so, who should provide the help?
   a. private business
   b. individuals
   c. government

6. Comment on the following statement: Computers threaten the very existence of communist countries?

7. Is U.S. leadership in computing threatened by the Japanese? Will we lose our leadership as we have in the automobile and TV industries?

8. Should the U.S. government intervene to help (or control) the computer industry? Is so, how? If not, why not?

9. Should the computer industry be regulated by government?

10. Should the government prosecute computer firms under antitrust laws to prevent them from becoming too big? How might antitrust litigation affect:
    a. innovation?
    b. consumer choice?
    c. consumer prices?

11. Comment on the following statement: The passage of statutes is too slow a process to be responsive to the fast-moving and dynamic computer industry.

12. How do you think software should be protected?
13. What does the computer industry need most: entrepreneurs, capital, government protection, researchers and scientists, more R&D investment, or growth in computer applications? Justify your position.
14. Should the computer industry in the United States be protected by quotas and tariffs from competition from abroad?
15. Should the transfer of computer technology to friends and foes in the world be controlled? If so, by whom and how?
16. Would it be in the best interest of the consumer to have an unrestricted computer industry?
17. Do you believe that competition between IBM and AT&T will serve the interests of the end user? What can be done to maximize the benefits of such confrontation and minimize the negative effects?
18. How does the computer affect your view of yourself? How can a computerized society enhance the way individuals view themselves? What would be the impact of a lowered self-image?

EXERCISES

1. Make a list of the most important social issues in the United States that have arisen because of computers. Rank them in order of importance from your point of view.
2. Identify two different groups of information workers and list the characteristics you think workers in each group should have. Then interview persons employed in each group. Compare their views on information workers with your own.
3. Read an article or book by Sherry Turkle or Joseph Weizenbaum. Summarize their views on the social implications of computers.

Selected Annotated Bibliography

Association for Computing Machinery Committee on Computers and Public Policy. "A Problem-List of Issues Concerning Computers and Public Policy," *Communications of ACM*, vol. 17, no. 9 (September 1974), pp. 495–503. Although this list is many years old, the sixteen social issues it voiced have not been solved. A short background and a series of provocative questions are provided for each issue.

Burton, Robert P. "Transnational Data Flows: International Status, Impact and Accommodation," *Data Management*, vol. 18, no. 6 (June 1980), pp. 27–34. This is a report on guidelines for the protection of privacy and transborder flow of personal data by the Organization of Economic Cooperation and Development, of which the United States is a member.

Cristo, Thomas K. "The Law and DP: A Clash of Egos," *Datamation*, vol. 28, no. 9 (September 1982), pp. 256–58. Cristo complains of the chasm between lawyers and EDP personnel. Computer people should realize that laws exist to redress legitimate grievances, while lawyers should realize that computers are not mysterious and mystical objects.

Dray, James and Mernosky, Joseph A. "Computers and a New World Order," *Technology Review*, vol. 86, no. 4 (May/June 1983), pp. 12–16. Problems in the transfer of computer technology to Third World countries are reviewed. The French effort, Centre Mondial Informatique et Resource Humaine, is described.

Fishman, Katherine Davis. *The Computer Establishment*. New York: McGraw-Hill, 1982. The history of computers has been written in this book in an anecdotal fashion, making the book easy for nontechnical people to read. A series of profiles of memorable personalities (for example, Seymour Cray and Thomas Watson) and a synopsis of memorable events in computing are included.

Forester, Tom, ed. *The Microelectronics Revolution.* Oxford, U.K.: Basil Blackwell, 1980. Part three of this book discusses the social impact of computers and the information society. A very powerful set of articles (and replies) are included by distinguished social commentators, including Herbert Simon, Joe Weizenbaum, Margaret Boden, Theodore Lowi, Bruno Lefevre, John Garrett and Geoff Wright, and Daniel Bell.

Malik, Rex. "Communism vs. the Computer," *Computerworld*, vol. 17, no. 28 (July 9, 1984), pp. ID/35–48. This article was adapted from a May 1984 essay in *Intermedia*, the journal of the International Institute of Communications in London. The topic discussed is whether the USSR can survive the information age.

Naisbitt, John. *Megatrends*. New York: Warner, 1984, 333 pp. Naisbitt outlines ten trends that represent major changes in America as we move from the industrial age to an era where information and services dominate the economy.

Noble, David F. "Is Progress What It Seems To Be?" *Datamation*, vol. 30, no. 19 (November 15, 1984), pp. 140–54. The author, a professor of the history of technology at MIT, explores the ramifications of technological progress. He charges engineers and scientists with being the servants of technology rather than the masters. Noble also discusses science as a social power, computers used for monitoring machines and humans, the displacement of workers, and the limitations of human control.

Sauvant, Karl P. "The Growing Dependence on Transborder Data Flows," *Computerworld*, vol. 17, no. 26 (June 25, 1984), pp. In Depth/19–24. Although transborder data flow serves international corporations, it can hinder less developed nations from developing their own information resources.

Sheridan, Thomas. "Computer Control and Human Alienation," *Technology Review*, vol. 83, no. 1 (October 1980), pp. 61–73. People who program computers find interaction with computers fulfilling. For many others, dealing with computers can be intimidating. Sheridan discusses the factors that make control by computers so alienating.

"The Great Debates: Technology and National Policy," *High Technology*, vol. 4, no. 10 (October 1984). The section contains a number of articles on the efforts in the U.S. and abroad to develop and maintain a competitive edge in the high technology. Especially recommended is "R&D Consortia: Can U.S. Industry Beat the Japanese at their Own Game" (pp. 46–52).

Turkle, Sherry. "Computers as Rorschach," *Transactions of Social Science and Modern Society*, vol. 17, no. 2 (January/February 1980), pp. 15–24. Turkle reminds the reader that Rorschach is perhaps the best known and most powerful of psychology's projective measures and that a computer's capacity as a projective device resembles that of Rorschach. The author looks at the computer as a metaphor and as a projective medium and suggests "that this subjective side of the computer presence is highly relevant to understanding issues concerning computation and public life."

———*The Second Self: Computers and the Human Spirit*. New York: Simon Schuster, 1984. Turkle is not as interested in what computers do, as in the "subjective computer"—the way the machine enters social life and psychological development. She is concerned with what humans will be like in the future.

Weizenbaum, Joseph. *Computer Power and Human Reason*. San Francisco: W. H. Freeman, 1976. This book, written by a computer scientist turned humanist, is a classic. Weizenbaum examines what computers can and cannot do and make recommendations about what computers should not do. The book has provoked controversy in computing as well as in the social sciences.

Tomorrow: A Telematic Society

Did we come here to laugh or cry?
Are we dying or being born?

CARLOS FUENTES

CHAPTER TWENTY

Key Words

concurrent programming	inference engine	parallel programming
context data	intelligent programming	practopia
electronic advertising	intelligent software	task decomposition
electronic encyclopedia	knowledge base	telematic
electronic home	knowledge-based management system	ultra large-scale integration (ULSI)
electronic news	learning	very large-scale integration (VLSI)
fifth generation	multiprocessor systems	vision systems
human-machine interface	networks	wired society

Many new technologies will shape tomorrow. Genetic engineering, holography, robotics, and space science are examples. But perhaps the greatest impact on the entire fabric of society will come from the integration of telecommunications and computing. The French have coined the term "telematique" to describe this integration, the English version being **telematic**. Our future will be a telematic society in which the computer serves as a computational machine and as a communications device. Telematics will transform not only the workplace, but also the daily lives of citizens.

This chapter will describe hardware and software under development for a new generation of computing systems, advances that will contribute to a telematic future. The social impact of telematics will also be discussed.

MAKING PREDICTIONS

The ability to look ahead is a rare gift. Too often, predictions fail to match the reality of the future. It is amusing to read that a committee of the British Parliament failed to recognize the merit of Thomas Edison's incandescent lamp. In 1878, the committee reported that Edison's ideas might be "good enough for our transatlantic friends but unworthy of the attention of practical or scientific men."

The following prediction made in 1922 was also far off the mark:

> It is highly unlikely that an airplane, or a fleet of them, would ever successfully sink a fleet of Navy vessels under battle conditions.

This prophecy was made by Franklin Roosevelt, who later served as president and commander of the American armed forces during World War II.

If it is so hard to envision the future, why devote a chapter to tomorrow? The reason is that we must try to anticipate the future so that we, as a society, have time to plan for change. We may need to revise our educational system to provide young people with the skills required in the workplace of tomorrow. We may have to restructure our government, revise the law, and alter our attitudes. Social change proceeds slowly. We must begin to lay the groundwork for the future today.

It is not as difficult to forecast technological innovation in computer science as it is in many other fields. The gestation period for new technology is generally five to twenty years, from the time of invention to commercial application. This means that professionals who study current research and development can make predictions about the performance of computer systems to be marketed in this century with some measure of certainty.

Supplement 20.1 Emerging Integrated Circuit Technology

1984–87
- Gallium arsenide crystals
- Mid-UV and deep-UV wavelength imaging
- Reactive ion etching
- Optical stepping
- E-beam wafer writing
- Ion implantation
- Planar plasma etching
- Ion milling
- Fully automated process segments

1987–1990
- Robotic interface with automatic equipment
- Software-controlled processing
- Holographic imaging
- X-ray storage ring energy for imaging
- Ion beam imaging
- Laser doping and imaging:
- Resist-less imaging (ion beam and laser)
- All-dry resist developing and etching
- Novel IC structures like 3-D superlattices

Source: Elliot, David J. "How Smart the Computer: Status and Future on Building Its Brain." *AFIPS Conference Proceedings*. Reston, Virginia: AFIPS Press, p. 141.

Whatever the consensus about the direction of advances in computer technology, there is diversity of opinion regarding its social impact. This chapter will present some opposing viewpoints. The predictions presented will serve a useful purpose if they stimulate discussion on the future since the first step in planning for tomorrow is to envision what the future may be.

FIFTH GENERATION COMPUTING

The first four generations of computers have all shared a single basic design: the Von Neuman processor that executes simple instructions in sequence. Improvements have come by making individual parts run faster and by increasing storage capacity. By the end of the 1980s, it is estimated that conventional systems should be able to execute 100 million sequential instructions per second and access gigabytes (billions of bytes) of memory.

The problem is that the ability to process instructions with speed does not guarantee that a problem can be solved quickly. For one thing, increased processing capability can lead to tons of output, obscuring the solutions to problems. System designers are now addressing the issue of information indexing and data management so that users in the future will not be overwhelmed by a glut of information.

Furthermore, computer scientists recognize that software must do more than fulfill the predetermined information needs of users. Programs must also help define information needs. They must help users recognize a problem, help them draw the problem's boundaries, help them access information relevant to the problem's solution, and then solve the problem.

In 1981, the Japanese announced an ambitious plan to develop a new generation of computers (the fifth). These computers will run at faster speeds and have increased processing capability, machine intelligence, and enhanced input/output capabilities. Since the Japanese announcement, similar projects have been proposed in the United States and Europe. All of the programs are concentrating research in the same basic areas: very large-scale integrated circuits, new computer architectures, knowledge-based problem-solving systems, improved human-machine interfaces, and networking.

Very Large-Scale Integrated Circuits

Very large-scale integration (VLSI) is a basic field of **fifth generation** research. (The term **ultra large-scale integration [ULSI]** is used by some fifth generation researchers.) Present design and fabrication techniques are not available to build the

Supplement 20.2 New-generation Technology in Office Automation

- *Users.* Secretaries, managers, administrators
- *Applications.* Integration, storage, and retrieval of all types of office information, improved access to information-management systems voice commands, voice output, natural language used for queries, data entry, and commands, integration of the telephone system with office computing systems; expert systems to assist office procedures and management decisions; teleconferences.
- *Components.* Powerful personal work stations with voice recognition and output, image digitization, and high-resolution graphics display, local area networks linked to the telephone network and wideband networks to central mainframe computing systems; powerful data-base management software; parallel data-base machines.

complex VLSI chips and wafers required for a new generation of machines. The first step, therefore, is to develop VLSI design tools to assist in the design of next generation chips and wafers, and to support the manufacture of experimental designs during the course of the research.

Computer Architectures

Unlike monolithic supercomputers of today, fifth generation computers will be compact, high-performance **multiprocessor systems**. They will be made up of small specialized units that operate in parallel, allowing the computer to perform many operations at once. Each unit will solve portions of the problem under the direction of a control unit that integrates the work of the specialized processors. The components of a fifth generation computer will vary according to the needs of the user. If a vision system is required, for example, a vision system will be added, just as we add components to a stereo system today.

A lot of research still needs to be done on multiprocessor architectures. The main goal is to develop a usable, highly functional system that will increase speed of processing as more components are added. This goal is dependent on **concurrent** or **parallel programming**—that is, programming system components so that they execute two or more processes simultaneously—which no one yet knows how to do well. In addition, there is still only a limited understanding of **task decomposition**, which is the process of deciding how one subdivides a complex problem into small segments for parallel processing. Multiprocessor experiments to date have shown that additional processors may decrease performance because of the "too many cooks" syndrome. In effect, the processors start tripping over each others' toes. The problem to be resolved is how to use a large number of processors effectively in a given application.

Disk storage is another area of system architecture under research. Two promising technologies should contribute to increased memory: optical storage and vertical magnetic recording.

Knowledge-Based Problem-Solving Systems

Fifth generation computers will use **intelligent software**—that is, software that incorporates AI features—to solve complex problems. The building blocks of such software will be:

- A **knowledge base**: a body of expert knowledge on a particular subject.
- **Context data**: information built up by the system about the situation in which the problem arises.
- An **inference engine**: a computer program that provides strategies to draw inferences and produce solutions to the problem under analysis.
- A **knowledge-based management system**: a system to automatically organize, control, update, and retrieve knowledge (both data and rules) stored in memory.

Supplement 20.3 New-generation Technology in Retailing and Service Industries

- *Users.* Consumers, retailers, advertisers, marketing department, purchasing department, sales personnel, service companies, lawyers, travel agents, advertising agencies, publishers.
- *Applications.* Computer-based catalogs for browsing and shopping; remote ordering and shopping from consumers' homes or office terminals; support for teleconferences between sales personnel and customers; accounting, billing, and invoicing systems; inventory management, automated Yellow Pages; data-base and expert systems for searching property and court records; trip and travel planning; tax and financial planning and analysis; stock-market and commodity-market information, diagnostic and trouble-shooting information on cars and major appliances.
- *Components.* Hardware and software to support multimedia information systems combining image, graphical, and textual data, work stations for access to multimedia information systems; natural-language and voice commands for browsing and searching through on-line catalogs by telephone or terminal; expert-help systems, wideband networks and protocols to permit communication between user terminals and remote information systems.

When these building blocks are combined, the result will be a computer able to select an appropriate line of reasoning to solve a complex problem. The computer will then search for data relevant to the problem and arrive at a solution.

Intelligent programming is another software objective of researchers. Intelligent programming implies that the user tells the computer what to do, not how to do it. The computer itself writes the "how to" instructions according to software that gives the machine instructions about writing programs. That is to say, the computer takes over the burden of programming.

The ultimate goal of intelligent programming will be to automatically convert problems into efficient computer program solutions. The user will merely present a problem to the computer, letting the machine determine the nature of the problem and how best to solve it. (Software will, of course, direct the machine in making this determination.) Then the computer will program itself for the solution.

Improved Human-Machine Interfaces

Natural language understanding is one goal of the effort to create improved **human-machine interfaces**. Once computers can understand English (or any other natural language like French or Japanese), users will not have to learn programming languages or follow rigid input formats to utilize computer processing power. Instead, users will be able to speak commands or key input in sentence structures of their mother tongue. Computers will produce speech output, so that interactive dialogues between user and computer will be possible in some subject domains.

Vision systems are also under development. They will enable computers to recognize patterns, to recognize specific locations from pictures, or to detect particular objects in view. Machines that can see and understand their environment are needed for robotic applications.

Finally, future output display systems will automatically determine how to present numbers, text, and graphic information according to the needs of the user.

Networks

Fundamental to fifth generation computing will be **networks** that enable computers at dispersed locations to share resources. Computers will be connected to local area networks (LANs), and local area networks will be interconnected in a nationwide network.

Large-scale integrated circuits and telecommunications technology have already solved some of the hardware problems related to networks. We currently have local area networks capable of carrying many megabytes of information. Satellites and fiber optic land lines interconnect clusters of local area networks.

Various software-related problems, however, still need to be resolved. For example, the development of software to interface between computers built by different manufacturers (computers that vary in architecture and protocols) still requires work. The next generation of computers will also require distributed operating systems that synchronize processing when several nodes work on aspects of a given problem in parallel. Distributed data bases must also be implemented so that computers in the network can obtain information from any network node.

RESEARCH APPLICATIONS

Imagine the processing power of a contemporary mainframe or supercomputer packaged as a personal computer sitting on your desk at home. In the future you may ask questions or discuss your problems with the computer. If you ask an ambiguous question, the computer will respond with questions of its own to clarify what you want to know, and then write a program to solve the problem. If the store of the computer's knowledge is insufficient to solve the problem, it will draw the information it needs via network communications from a remote data base. In other words, your PC will become a counselor, able to solve problems on an expert, professional level. This is one goal of fifth generation research.

Although no such computer exists, progress has been made in many areas of research essential to such a system and to fifth generation computing. Advances have been made in high-speed data storage and retrieval, expert systems, voice recognition for limited vocabularies, networks to access remote data bases, high-level programming languages, voice output, high-resolution graphics, and image input. Supplements 20.2 through 20.10 suggest application areas for advanced technologies that have already been demonstrated in research settings. One can expect implementation of these applications in the near future.

COMPETITORS IN THE FIFTH GENERATION RACE

Many observers believe that future world leadership in computing will belong to the nation that wins the race for a fifth generation computer. Let us now look at the leading competitors.

Japan

The Japanese have a well-funded, long-range national program to develop a fifth generation computer by the 1990s. Rather than basing their entire program on predictions of what the needs of the 1990s will be, the Japanese are trying to design information systems and develop computers that will make an ideal society in the 1990s possible. Under the auspices of the Ministry of International Trade and Industry, eight Japanese firms have formed a consortium called the Institute for New Generation Computer Technology to develop the new technology, with each firm contributing about forty researchers. The total budget for the ten-year project is an estimated $200 million.

Many experts believe the research required for a fifth generation computer will take more than ten years. In the past the Japanese have not demonstrated an ability to develop innovative software, a weakness that may hamper their ability to meet their research objectives for fifth generation computers. Some of the objectives may even prove to be entirely unobtainable.

On the other hand, the Japanese have demonstrated their technological competitiveness in other industries, and their previous hardware projects have been quite successful. Western computer manufacturers take the Japanese challenge very seriously indeed. They recognize that a successful project will place the Japanese in a position of dominance, giving them technical and industrial leadership in the world-wide information processing industry.

The United States

The United States has been funding research for the past twenty years in some of the key technologies of fifth generation systems: for example, in microelectronics and artificial intelligence. But the Japanese announcement of their fifth generation project has led to a more concerted research effort in this country.

Supplement 20.4 New-generation Technology in Industrial Automation

- *Users.* Manufacturers of goods; designers of manufactured products, product and plant engineers.
- *Applications.* Automated factories —computer-aided design (CAD), computer-aided manufacturing (CAM), and robotics, inventory management, product-cost estimating, control and routing of production runs, expert systems for design
- *Components.* High-speed parallel data-base storage and retrieval software to integrate all types of information related to design and manufacturing, high-level programming languages for robots, libraries of modular designs and robot-control routines, theorem proving and planning techniques for design verification and robot control, combined expert systems and simulation for CAD, parallel processors for CAD and CAM work stations supporting high-resolution graphics

Supplement 20.5 New-generation Technology in Education

- *Users.* Students at all levels including professionals and adults.
- *Applications.* Intelligent computer-aided instruction (CAI) systems that permit students to direct and control the presentation of course material; computer-based training for adults and professionals; computer-based assistants that explain how to use computing systems.
- *Components.* Software and specialized processors to support voice commands, voice output, and natural language interaction with intelligent CAI systems; specialized hardware for graphics and images, libraries and remote access to courses via digital networks; improved human-computer interfaces; cognitive modeling of the learner.

Some forty American universities and thirty major corporations are engaged in computer research directed at new generation computing. There is a growing recognition, however, that this piecemeal approach to research may not meet the Japanese challenge, in part because of the increasing cost of microelectronics research. American computer firms are beginning to form research consortia, as described in Chapter 19. Politicians are also exploring the possibility of a national technology policy that would foster joint-research projects like those in Japan.

The federal government has a vested interest in computer research. Fifth generation computing technology is important to national security in areas such as aircraft and weapons design, simulations, and cryptology. Advanced systems are needed in order to build up strategic strength in relation to the Soviet bloc. Future research in physics, chemistry, and math may also depend on such systems.

The U.S. wants to maintain world leadership in information technology. It would not like to be in a position of having to rely on a foreign supplier for the technology it needs. For these reasons, the federal government may step up its support of fifth generation research. In 1984, the Defense Advanced Research Projects Agency announced a new program that points in this direction. This program, called Strategic Computing and Survivability, will foster a new generation of intelligent supercomputers for military use. Its objective is the development of high-performance VLSI-based hardware and multiprocessor software for computers with the ability to see, reason, plan, and even supervise the actions of military systems.

Europe

In information technology, the Europeans are losing ground to the Americans and Japanese. The result is a negative balance of trade in information

Supplement 20.6 New-generation Technology in Health Care

- *Users.* Physicians, hospitals, patients, the handicapped, the disabled.
- *Applications.* Expert systems for diagnosis and prescription; data-base systems for medical records; monitoring and management of hospital patients; national data bases of information on available organs, health supplies and services, and disease statistics, automatic analysis of laboratory tests, on-line access to medical journals, textbooks, and laboratory and research results, intelligent search and retrieval entries in a medical data base, reading machines for the blind; computer-controlled wheelchairs; robot arms to aid the disabled in feeding and in manipulating objects; sensory prostheses
- *Components.* Specialized parallel processors and software for expert systems and data-base systems, natural-language processing and voice input and output; phone and remote-terminal access to data bases and expert systems; specialized hardware to acquire, analyze, and display information from laboratory tests.

Supplement 20.7 New-generation Technology in Arts, Culture, and Leisure

- *Users.* Public at large.
- *Applications.* Multimedia computer "books" that allow browsing through images, text, and sound data; digital recording and storage of and access to music, painting, and graphic arts via digital music and image systems; a computer-based artist's palette to assist musical and graphical composition; intelligent home robots and toys.
- *Components.* Large-scale storage systems; wideband digital communication to access cultural information and entertainment; high-resolution digital sound input/output; graphical and image input/output devices, such as electronic paintbrushes and solid-state cameras.

technology products. There is also a negative balance of patents, which shows that Europe is failing to develop a strong technological base within its industries. In the long run, the race for fifth generation technology may influence Europe's ability to survive as an economic entity.

In 1982, the European Strategic Programme on Research in Information Technology (ESPRIT) was formed by the common market countries to improve Europe's competitive posture in the computing field. Research in five areas will be supported by ESPRIT: advanced microelectronics, software technology, advanced information processing, office automation, and computer-integrated flexible manufacturing. ESPRIT has committed approximately 11.5 million ECU (economic community units, roughly equivalent to U.S. dollars) to support some three dozen projects.

WHERE WE ARE HEADED

Computers that incorporate fifth generation technology will provide access to the universe of knowledge. Online retrieval of information will instantly put users in touch with a substantial part of mankind's collective memory. Let's now consider ways in which our daily lives may change as a result.

Instant News

Today, reporters compose articles on computer consoles. Copy is edited on a video display screen and computers generate electronic signals to control the typesetting and printing of newspapers.

The newspaper of the future may be paperless, called to a computer screen by readers. From a menu, subjects of interest will be chosen (for example, foreign affairs, weather, consumer news). The reader will then scan headlines in order to select specific articles for screen display. **Electronic news** may consist of hundreds of pages of information drawn from news sources all over the world and translated into whatever language is preferred by the reader. Moreover, the news may be selected according to the personal profile of the reader that is stored in computer memory.

Supplement 20.8 New-generation Technology in Aerospace

- *Users.* Pilots, air traffic controllers, scientists and engineers studying and exploiting space and remotely sensed earth resources.
- *Applications.* Air-traffic control monitors, autonomous deep-space exploration, earth-resources monitoring, semiautomatic correction and analysis of weather data, autonomous manufacturing in space.
- *Components.* Networks of ground-based and satellite-based sensors with programs for automatic data reduction and storage in large-scale distributed data bases, robots capable of autonomous planning, expert systems for fault diagnosis and repair of autonomous spacecraft, learning programs to form and verify hypotheses; self-replicating machines for space manufacturing.

Supplement 20.9 New-generation Technology in the Military

- *Users.* Strategic planners, field and fleet commanders, intelligence analysts, weapons designers, maintenance and logistics staff.
- *Applications.* All aspects of planning and decision support; communication, command, and control, supply and support logistics; remote sensing and surveillance; cryptography, intelligent and autonomous weapons systems; expert consultants for maintenance and fault diagnosis in the field or at sea; autonomous vehicles for hazardous environments.
- *Components.* Management information systems with remote access and distributed data bases; large-scale parallel processors and storage systems; expert systems and knowledge-acquisition systems.

It should be noted that when electronic news is technologically feasible, a number of factors may constrain implementation, like cost, user acceptance, lack of demand, government regulations, or legal restrictions. A long lead time may also be needed to develop required hardware and software. Other potential computer applications described in this chapter may likewise never become commonplace.

Electronic bulletin boards, which are limited to narrower topics of interest than electronic news, will be another common news source in the future. (Electronic bulletin boards were described in Chapter 14.) The main difference between contemporary and future bulletin boards will be in the scope of the population pool that uses them: low-cost communications and a network infrastructure extending worldwide will enable persons with similar interests to share information wherever they may live.

Classified ads will also be available electronically. Such ads can be continuously updated (that is, new items can be added, sold items can be deleted). In addition, software will match potential buyers and sellers. Teleshopping, described in Chapter 18, is a further extension of **electronic advertising**. Moreover, when a network infrastructure is in place, buyers won't be restricted to local markets. Search programs will assist them in locating rare or specialized items from distant dealers.

Electronic mail, described in Chapter 7, will be an additional source of instant news. Today, electronic mail is used primarily in the business world, but in the future, electronic mail will serve families as well. Most households will undoubtedly own a terminal and transmission costs will be low. A message sent by electronic mail may become as commonplace as telephone call today.

Electronic Encyclopedias

The ancient Greeks had a dream of a comprehensive organization of knowledge. Computers may make this dream possible at last. Information technology gives us the tools to digitize and elec-

Supplement 20.10 New-generation Technology in Science and Engineering

- *Users.* Research scientists, design and field engineers.
- *Applications.* Expert systems for fault diagnosis; expert systems capturing and applying scientific expertise; intelligent human-machine interfaces to existing computing systems used for simulating physical processes; improved analytic tools such as symbolic algebra programs; computer-aided design; integrated data bases of scientific and engineering information, including technical papers, experimental data, and design specifications; information browsing systems and expert systems for retrieving information from scientific data bases under voice and natural-language control; expert systems for geological analysis and mineral prospecting.
- *Components.* Improved and more powerful data-base management systems including large storage systems, parallel data-base and expert-system processors; distributed data-base systems, networks for access to remote data bases; software and hardware for input and output of graphics, image, voice and textual data knowledge-engineering techniques to acquire and represent expertise.

tronically store written text, color illustrations, film clips, and sound recordings in computer memory. We may soon be capable of creating a comprehensive **electronic encyclopedia** containing most of the world's knowledge. Computers are already storing knowledge compendiums in certain fields. For example, the U.S. National Library of Medicine has an online information system called MEDLARS that keeps track of the thousands of medical journals published annually throughout the world.

Unlike hard-copy encyclopedias, electronic encyclopedias will store sound as well as images and text, and will be continually updated. (One of the disadvantages of hard-copy encyclopedias is that once printed, they cannot be changed until the next edition.) Furthermore, all information on a given subject can be quickly retrieved when information is stored in computer memory. (Scholars currently spend hours in libraries going through bound encyclopedias, card catalogs, and journal indexes trying to locate information on topics of interest.) (See Figure 20.1.)

The computerization of information will also redefine the role of libraries and librarians. Libraries will be archives of books of historical interest and small collections of general-interest hard-copy media. Librarians will be trained subject specialists who index and cross-reference information so that it can be stored in and retrieved from computer storage with ease. Librarians will also be technical consultants who help library users access information utilize information technology to best advantage.

The major controversy over encyclopedias in the past has been control over what information was printed and what information was left out. One early publisher instructed his printers to remove sections he didn't approve of. History is rewritten in the encyclopedias of many nations to fit the political ideology of the state.

Figure 20.1 A magnetic stripe reader. The device could be checking the validity of a card, debiting or crediting the holder's account, or loading information from a computer onto the card. (NCR Corporation)

Supplement 20.11 Oxford English Dictionary Goes Online

Oxford University Press has announced a plan to place its thirteen-volume dictionary in an electronic data base. A staff of 120 people has been assigned for data entry of the 20,000 printed pages of the dictionary, pages that contain some sixty million words. Once data entry is completed, it is possible that the dictionary will be available online, on magnetic tape, on laser/video disk, or possibly on a single integrated circuit, according to a spokesman from Oxford University Press.

The project will cost an estimated $10 million. The British government has awarded the company $420,000 for the project; IBM United Kingdom, an additional $1.4 million. The University of Waterloo in Ontario will survey potential uses and also help develop the software needed to take advantage of the electronic dictionary.

The problem of control is aggravated with global electronic encyclopedias. Who will select materials for inclusion? If an electronic encyclopedia is an integrated system for the storage and retrieval of all of the world's knowledge, who will control indexing and validation? Will politicians, librarians, an academy of scholars, world leaders, or commercial interests determine the contents of human knowledge? Since the way scholars and average citizens view the world is dependent on their knowledge base, the effort to store all information electronically may touch off major power struggles in the future.

Learning in the Future

From birth, children of the future will be exposed to information technology. They will quickly learn how to manipulate their environment through computers and how to obtain information on any subject they wish.

Consider, for example, computer toys made of a soft pliable material, designed for toddlers to handle. Very young children will learn that by touching the toys in certain ways, they can animate them or create music and color displays.

The educational uses of computers will also be revolutionized. When asked about monkeys, for example, the computer of the future may first ascertain the reason why the question has been asked in order to narrow the subject. Using artificial intelligence technology, the computer may then determine the level of understanding of the questioner so that the material can be automatically adjusted. Thus a child of five might be shown film clips of monkeys playing in the jungle, while a seventh grader who has to write a three-page paper might be guided in selecting a topic and then given information appropriate for a junior high school student. Certainly, information technology has the capacity to enhance children's **learning**. But will it?

Some educators say yes. With the electronic storage of knowledge, these educators argue, the importance of rote learning will diminish. Children will learn by discovery rather than by more traditional forms of exposition, they say. More emphasis will be placed on strategies for dealing with information —that is, on ways to get information, step-by-step problem solving, and the use of information in decision making—rather than on simply knowing information. According to this line of reasoning, in short, children of the future will be taught to think.

Other educators believe that learning requires the mastery of basic concepts so that events and natural phenomena can be understood. There is no substitute for scholarship, and scholarship is hard work, they argue. Computers are merely a distraction. They entertain children, making it appear that learning is taking place, but they actually foster mediocrity and illiteracy instead. Computers do motivate children, but not to study.

Still another view is that computers will have little impact on education. Computers may be used as nothing more than electronic workbooks adapted to fit the rather rigid structures that frequently characterize schools today. According to this vision of the future, it takes more than advances in technology to enhance learning; a change in the attitudes of parents and teachers towards education is needed as well. Many of today's key decision makers in society grew up before computers, and few of them have an understanding of computer-based technology. Changes in education may have to wait until today's children enter decision-making ranks.

The Electronic Home

Houses in the future will be more than structures for habitation. They may serve as companions, counselors, servants, and household managers as well.

To begin with, comfort and security will be monitored by home computers in the years ahead. Lights will turn on automatically when someone enters a room and off when the person leaves. Temperature will be controlled by computer: windows will be opened and shut, and the furnace or cooling systems activated as needed. Ground moisture will be monitored and sprinkler systems turned on when the soil is dry. The computer will keep track of persons in the house and signal an alarm for unidentified movement, automatically dialing the police for help.

Although many of the subsystems just described already exist, home computers in the future will, in all likelihood, be master controllers of all the electronic systems in the house. Furthermore, they will monitor aspects of home living that are not monitored today. For example, when a dishwasher begins to leak or drains become plugged, the problem will be identified by the computer before it becomes chronic. The computer will then give the householder fix-it advice. If the computer does not have sufficient information stored in memory, it will consult with the computer of a neighboring house or search a remote repair data base.

Stove heat will be shut off when food begins to burn. Food supplies will be monitored and shopping lists automatically prepared when food stocks are low. Menus will be suggested for well-balanced meals, incorporating a family's favorite recipes. The home computer will adjust the room environment according to who is in the room and what the occupant is doing. If the person is studying, white noise may be generated to block out street sounds. If the person is relaxing, the sound of soft wind or raindrops may be produced. Or if the room is being used for sleeping, the temperature of the room will be lowered.

Screens, loudspeakers, and printers of all types will be everywhere around the house. The computer will also project holographs (three-dimensional output), according to predictions. If you ask for Beethoven's first symphony, music will begin to play. If you ask for a view of the interior of Notre Dame Cathedral, a hard-copy photograph will be produced. If you decide to take a trip, the computer will check the weather, make your reservation, write your ticket, arrange payment through EFT, provide you with information on local customs, give you a screen preview of sights you will see, and organize a quick language course with videotapes so you can learn phrases you will need in your travels.

Robots will tend to household chores such as vacuuming, mowing the lawn, ironing clothes, and preparing meals. The computer may scan daily news in order to give you an oral synopsis of the day's events. Having built a profile of each person living in the house, it will know exactly what will interest you. It will be able to carry on lengthy conversations when you want to talk, adjusting to your mood. It will tell jokes to cheer you or gossip if you so choose. Imagine home computers able to adopt the personality of Marilyn Monroe or Michael Jackson if you want to be entertained, or the voice of your mother when you want comfort and advice on personal problems.

Networks of home computers should be able to coordinate the use of natural resources to eliminate waste in the future. For example, household computers might coordinate electricity use within a community to spread demand throughout the day.

In many ways, the house of the future will behave like a living creature. **Electronic homes** will stimulate, entertain, teach, serve, and protect the family.

Supplement 20.12 Supermarket for the Future

A robot issues a magnetic-tape parking lot ticket and opens the parking lot gate to shoppers at this supermarket. At the door of the store, a welcoming robot greets customers. Within the store itself, a minirobot moves among shoppers, announcing special sales and new products.

Shoppers push carts that are equipped with built-in calculators to help keep track of purchases. Prices are displayed on the shelves by light-emitting diode displays updated daily by the store's central computer. When a customer reaches for an item, sensors detect the customer's hand, triggering a recorded description of the item.

Meat is cut to the desires of each customer by a robot. The robot also weighs, wraps, and prices the order.

After shopping, customers roll their carts onto a monorail track that conveys their purchases to the checkout counter where POS terminals scan the items to calculate a total. Time, date, and item descriptions are recorded, and a receipt is printed. Information on the sale is utilized by inventory control software, which monitors stock and places orders when supplies fall low. The stockroom itself has no human workers. All unloading and stockroom shelving is done by robots.

When store shelves need to be replenished, the appropriate containers with the needed items are automatically selected. A conveyor belt transfers the containers to robot carts, which in turn deliver the goods to various store locations.

This store is not fantasy. A supermarket belonging to Seiyu, a Japanese supermarket chain, recently opened with these features. According to Seiyu president Seiji Tsutsumi, "Allowing machines to perform these jobs for which they are most appropriate results in improved store management systems, and, in general, gradually ushers in the age of new information media and mechatronics."[2]

[2]Besher, Alexander. "The First Computerized Market." *InfoWorld*, vol. 6, no. 39 (September 24, 1984), pp. 103–04.

A TELEMATIC SOCIETY

We are already in the first stages of a **wired society**. Automated offices and factories are reshaping the workplace. The role of computers in medicine, sports, the fine arts, government, science, and research is expanding (see Figure 20.2). We have electronic banking and shopping, telemail and telenews, and we are beginning to compile the knowledge of the world in data bases with remote access. Progress is being made in computer vision, high-level languages, speech understanding, knowledge data bases, parallel processing, inference engines, intelligent programming, and so forth. The question all of these advances pose, of course, is whether the quality of life will really be improved.

Optimists see freedom from drudgery, intelligent management of natural resources, and the elimination of war and poverty in our future. They predict a new Renaissance since more time will be available for cultural pursuits. Access to the world's knowledge will contribute to mankind's understanding of the universe, they say. Interactive communication tools will stimulate empathy with others and help bind human ties. The home will again become the focus of daily life, promoting family togetherness. National boundaries will lose their importance as a world community is born.

Figure 20.2 Computerized shoes and their accompanying software. Data such as time, distance, and calories used are entered automatically into the shoe while running. Later, data can be loaded into the computer for storage and analysis. (Puma USA, Inc.)

Supplement 20.13 Projections for the Future

1985 to 1990

- Fifty percent of all assembly and 30 percent of all manufacturing will be computer controlled.
- Fifty percent of the manufacturing workforce will be skilled, working in computer automated, computer-controlled plants.
- One-third of homes will have computers.
- Videotex will become more common for home shopping and home banking.
- Microprocessors will be common in autos.

1990 to 1995

- Twenty percent of information workers will be telecommuters.
- Expert systems will exist in many professional fields.
- Microprocessors will be used extensively in helping the sick and disabled.
- Some cities may have 50 percent of factories automated and integrated.
- Fifth generation systems with AI in I/O and processors will be marketed.
- Integrated management information systems with some AI features will be common.
- Paperless offices will become more common.
- Smart machines in the home will become more common.

1995–2000

- Eighty percent of homes will be equipped with microcomputer control systems (as common as TVs during the 1970s).
- There will be thirteen million telecommuters.
- Expert systems will exist in most professional fields.
- Intelligent management information systems will be common.
- There will be many wired cities.
- Smart cards will be commonplace.

Pessimists see illiterates glued to game shows on video screens in the world of tomorrow, waited on hand and foot by domestic robots. They see responsibility for managing cities, running factories, growing crops, and distributing goods and services delegated to intelligent computers. Surveillance systems with little regard for personal privacy will be the norm. Individuals, they say, will sever all ties with the human race in favor of computer companionship since computers will indulge every selfish wish. With self-selective media, people will filter out unwelcome news, preferring to live with virtual realities—that is, with imaginary constructions of the world—rather than with physical realities.

In *The Third Wave* Alvin Toffler sees a middle course for society, a **practopia** that is neither the best or worst of all possible worlds. He sees,

> A civilization no longer required to put its best energies into marketization. A civilization capable of directing great passion into art. A civilization facing unprecedented historical choices—about genetics and evolution, to choose a single example—and inventing new ethical or moral standards to deal with such complex issues. A civilization, finally, that is at least potentially democratic and humane, in better balance with the biosphere and no longer dangerously dependent on exploitative subsidies from the rest of the world.[1]

Clearly, technology itself will not decide our future. It is the way we use technology that will decide how we live, work, learn, and think. We must begin now to construct a society that can meet the revolutionary challenges of advanced technology. We have a destiny to create.

SUMMING UP

Research on fifth generation systems is underway. Very large-scale integrated circuits, advanced computer architectures, knowledge-based problem-solving systems, human-machine interfaces, and networks are the principal areas of work. Advanced systems will be used in all of the application areas discussed in this book. We will have automated offices, factories, and schools. Computers with

[1]Alvin Toffler. *The Third Wave*. New York: William Morrow, 1980, p. 375.

intelligence will contribute to decision making, health care, the humanities, government, science, and engineering. We can expect changes in leisure as well as changes in work. We can also expect a redefinition of community, family, and home.

Not all of the predictions made in this chapter will come to pass. Some of the goals of fifth generation computers may prove technologically infeasible. Some uses of computers may prove too costly to develop. Other factors that may slow or prevent implementation of the applications described in this chapter include limited resources, government regulatory schemas, high risk in realizing capital investments, product development priorities in other fields, lack of markets, government interference (for example, through unfavorable tax policies), legal restrictions, and lack of user acceptance.

REVIEW QUESTIONS

1. What is a telematic society? Is all this talk about a wired society pure conjecture or are we near implementation?
2. Why is it difficult to make predictions regarding the future of computing?
3. How will fifth generation computers differ from the preceding generations?
4. What do the Japanese expect to achieve from their fifth generation project? What are the short-term and long-term objectives and potential? How has their plan affected the United States?
5. Describe developments that can be expected in the coming decade in:
   a. computer architecture
   b. peripherals
   c. software
   d. applications
6. What are the advantages and disadvantages of intelligent programming?
7. What advances in networking are proposed for fifth generation systems?
8. Discuss applications that will be feasible in the near future as a result of on-going research in fifth generation systems.
9. Compare American, Japanese, and European strategies for the development of fifth generation technology.
10. How will instant news differ from printed newspapers?
11. Discuss the concept of electronic encyclopedias. What implementation problems exist? How will they affect the general public? Scholars?

DISCUSSION QUESTIONS

1. Do you believe that the Japanese fifth generation project will succeed? State your reasons. How will success change your life?
2. In the United States, what role should the following groups play in preparing for a wired society:
   a. federal government?
   b. business?
   c. churches?
   d. universities?
   e. clubs or special-interest groups?
3. Do you look to the future of computing with anticipation or dread? Explain. How will a wired society affect:
   a. quality of life?
   b. environment?
   c. economics?
   d. education?
   e. leisure?
4. Which application area do you think will show greatest growth in the next decade?
5. Discuss six negative effects of computers on society.
6. How do you think computers in the year 2000 will affect:
   a. privacy?
   b. the work week?
   c. housekeeping?
   d. education?
   e. recreation?
   f. transportation?

7. Do you believe that artificial intelligence will be part of future computer systems? Why?

8. Do you think fifth generation computers will be developed by 1990? Explain.

9. What priorities would you give to fifth generation research? Why? Are there some research objectives that you think should be abandoned because they are not in the interests of society? Which ones?

10. Some futurists speculate that living in a wired society will make people smarter. Do you agree?

11. Do you believe that a wired society will lead to more individualization or more conformity? Why?

12. What effect will a wired society have on nationalism?

13. How will a wired society change our concept of time and reality?

14. It was once believed that the invention of writing would cause people to lose their ability to remember. It is now said that human memory will be affected by fifth generation systems. Do you agree or disagree? Explain.

15. Will humans be more concerned with material things in a wired society than at present?

16. Many commentators fear that a knowledge elite will be created in a wired society? How would you define a "knowledge elite"? Do you think the rise of such a group would be a threat to society? A benefit?

17. Will humans be better educated in the future or will illiteracy prevail in the year 2000? Will society recognize the need for education?

18. What sort of status symbols will a wired society have?

19. One view of the future is that information in the future will be a commodity. It is feared that the "commoditization" of information may lead us into a new version of the dark ages because information will not be accessible to the masses for the reason that they will not be able to afford it. Comment.

20. It has been charged that the U.S. and its allies want to use the information technology to exploit the rest of the world. The term "information imperialism" is used in this context. Do you think charges are valid?

21. Describe a home you would like to build in the future.

22. Would you recommend a course in computer literacy for:
    a. farmers?
    b. friends?
    c. office workers?
    d. your parents?

    Why or why not?

EXERCISES

1. Research computer applications that have recently been put on the market that incorporate fifth generation technologies.

2. If you were given $15,000 to buy computer resources for your home, what would you buy and why?

3. Imagine that you are a school superintendent. What revisions would you make to the school curriculum for grades 1–12 to help students prepare for a computerized future? Explain your assumptions.

4. Interview an officer in a company or service organization in your community that is computerized. What problems does the officer have hiring employees with computer skills?

5. Design a home of the future.

Selected Annotated Bibliography

Datamation Staff Report. "Pushing the State of the Art," *Datamation*. vol. 311, no. 19 (October 1, 1985), pp. 68–84. This report is on computer research projects by the U.S., Esprit, France, Japan, the United Kingdom, Scandanavia, and the USSR.

Denken, Joseph. *The Electronic Cottage.* New York: Bantam Books, 1981. A preview of the computer revolution in the home.

Feigenbaum, Edward A. and McCorduck, Pamela. *The Fifth Generations: Artificial Intelligence and Japan's Computer Challenge to the World.* Reading, Mass.: Addison-Wesley, 1983. AI and Japanese competition with the U.S. are both emotional issues. The authors suggest that the U.S. should not bet on the Japanese or against them but should instead take advantage of whatever research they accomplish and apply it in the U.S.

Fredricks, G. and **Schaff, A., eds.** *Microelectronics and Society: For Better or for Worse.* Oxford, U.K.: Permagon Press, 1982. This is a report of the Club of Rome, which is famous for its *Limits to Growth* and known for its "prediction of mankind" issues. The report takes a world view of microelectronics, focusing especially on its impact on developing countries.

Jones, Thomas E. *Options for the Future.* New York: Praeger Publishers, 1980. Any discussion of the future must be based on assumptions that vary from one author to another. In this book, Jones reviews and critiques the views of Bell's "Post Industrial Society," Brzezinski's "Technocratic Age," a Delphi panelist's view of the "Abundant Age," Meadows's "Limits of Growth," and Kahn and Wiener's "Post Industrial Culture."

Lemly, Brad. "Other Voices, Other Futures," *PC Magazine*, vol. 4, no. 1 (January 8, 1985), pp. 133–36. Twelve commentators make predictions regarding the future role of computers.

Loye, David. "The Brain and the Future: First Ripples of the Wave," *The Futurist*, vol. 16, no. 3 (October 1982), pp. 21–24. This issue is subtitled "The Future from 1990." A good discussion on communications of the future and policy impact analysis is included.

Martin, James. *Telematic Society: A Challenge for Tomorrow.* Englewood Cliffs, N.J.: Prentice-Hall, 1981. Martin is a technologist and a specialist in telecommunications. This book, one of twenty-eight by the author, is a successor to *The Wired Society*. It discusses the impact of computers and telecommunications on medicine, news, shopping, factory, home, and cities.

McCorduck, Pamela. "Introduction to the Fifth Generation," *Communications of the ACM*, vol. 20, no. 9 (September 1983), pp. 629–30. Fifth generation project goals, phases of implementation, budget, and organization are discussed. The author is a journalist who writes for non-computer scientists as well as for the technical audience of *Communications.*

Teich, Albert H., ed. *Technology and Man's Future.* 3rd edition. New York: St. Martin's Press, 1981. The book contains an excellent set of articles on forecasting, assessing, controlling, and reshaping technology. Particularly noteworthy are the articles by Paul Goodman, "Can Technology Be Humane?" and Langdon Winner, "The Political Philosophy of Alternative Technology."

"The Race is Still Open," *The Economist*, vol. 290, no. 7368 (November 17, 1984), pp. 88–93. Britain's response to the challenge of Japan for fifth generation technology.

"The State of Computing," *Computer*, vol. 17, no. 11 (October 1984). This is a special IEEE centennial. Included are articles on the mini and microcomputer industries, computer education, supercomputing, microcomputing in the 1980s, computers in military and space sciences, expert systems, pattern recognition, computing in medicine, and speech processing. The articles should help readers assess both the state of technology now and directions we are heading.

Toffler, Alvin. *The Third Wave.* New York: William Morrow, 1980. Unlike *Future Shock* by this same author, which emphasized the personal and social cost of change, this book "emphasizes the equally important cost of not changing certain things rapidly enough." Among topics discussed by Toffler are the electronic cottage, families of the future, and the corporate identity crisis.

"Trying to Predict the Future," *Personal Computing*, vol. 3, no. 13 (Mid-October 1984), pp. 30–44. This article, drawn from a special issue on educational computing, includes comments on computers and education by Terrel Bell, Seymour Papert, Joseph Weizenbaum, and other noted experts. Topics covered are computer literacy, the future of computers in the classroom, the changing nature of schools, computers for people no longer in school, questions of equity, and computers in future society.

Wheeler, Hesh. "Beyond Partnership," *Datamation*, vol. 30, no. 14 (September 1, 1984), pp. 149–52. Cooperative efforts for technology development, such as MCC (Microelectronics and Computer Technology Corp.) are discussed. The role of the Department of Commerce in developing cooperative guidelines and advising groups is also described.

Withington, Frederic G. "Winners and Losers in the Fifth Generation," *Datamation*, vol. 29, no. 12 (December 1983), pp. 193–209. Withington has made predictions in the past with a fair degree of accuracy. In this article he compares the U.S. with Japan and Europe in four areas of competition: large-scale integrated circuits, disk drives (mag and optical), supercomputers, and knowledge-based problem-solving machines.

Glossary

The definitions in this glossary have been written in simple terms in order to facilitate understanding. Readers who wish a complete technical glossary of computer terms should consult a computer dictionary such as the *American Standard Vocabulary of Information Processing* published by the American National Standards Institute. Computer dictionaries can be found in most libraries.

Abacus A calculating device, consisting of beads or balls that slide along wires on a frame; used as a counter or memory aid for solving arithmetic problems.

Access The manner in which data is stored in or retrieved from the memory of a computer system. See *direct access*, *random access*, *remote access*, and *serial access*.

Access controls Procedures to restrict the approach to computing resources, to identify users requesting computing services, and to limit processing to authorized users for authorized purposes only.

Access directory A list of all users authorized to access computing resources. The directory, generally stored in the computer memory, may specify limitations on specific resources to be accessed, type of access, security level, and permissible time of access.

Access time The amount of time that passes between a request for data and the availability of that data.

Accuracy Correctness, freedom from error.

Accumulator A storage location (register) within the computer that holds the results of arithmetic, logical, and input/output (I/O) operations.

Ada A high-level programming language originally developed by the Department of Defense for use in military systems.

Address A memory location used for storing information. An address can be in the computer (memory address) or on the storage media (disk address).

ALGOL An acronym for *ALGO*rithmic *L*anguage, a modular structured programming language used for scientific and mathematical operations.

Algorithm A step-by-step process used to solve a problem in a finite number of steps or procedures.

Alphabetic characters Characters limited to the English alphabet (A to Z).

Analog Pertaining to the use of physical measurements (for example, distance, rotation, voltage) to represent numerical variables in computer computation.

Analog computer (1) A computer that uses analog representations; (2) a computer that processes analog data. Contrast with *digital computer*.

Analog signal A continuous electrical signal representing a condition (such as temperature or the position of game control paddles). An analog signal can be any frequency or strength.

Analyst See *systems analyst*.

APL An acronym for *A Programming Language*, a powerful interactive language for scientific and mathematical computations.

Application program A program written for or by a user for a defined purpose (for example, accounts payable, word processing).

Application software Software programs that perform a specific user-oriented task, such as balancing a payroll. Application software can be either purchased as a package or custom designed by a programmer.

APT An acronym for *A*utomatically *P*rogrammed *T*ool, a language for programming numerical control machines.

Arithmetic and logic unit (ALU) The element in the central processing unit (CPU) that manipulates data for arithmetic, logical, and control functions.

Array An arrangement of quantities in rows and columns.

Artificial intelligence (AI) The ability of a computer to imitate certain human actions or skills, such as problem solving, decision making, perception, and learning.

ASCII An acronym for the *A*merican *S*tandard *C*ode for *I*nformation *I*nterchange. This code is widely used to represent numbers, letters, or characters in computer memory and to transmit them from one computer to another. ASCII assigns a unique binary number code to each character.

Assemble To translate a symbolic language program into a machine language program. This is accomplished by replacing the symbolic operation codes and addresses with the operation codes and addresses that the computer was designed to interpret.

Assembler A computer program that converts (or translates) assembly language programs into a form (machine language) that the computer can understand. The assembler translates mnemonic instruction codes into binary numbers, replaces names with their binary equivalents, and assigns memory locations to data and instructions.

Assembler program Instructions written in assembly language, where there is a one-to-one correspondence between the assembly language instructions and the instruction and data formats of the computer.

Assembly language A programming language in which the programmer can use mnemonic instruction codes, labels, and names to refer directly to their binary equivalents. The assembler is a low-level language since each assembly language instruction translates directly into a specific machine language instruction.

Attribute A characteristic.

Authoring language A language used by instructors to write programs for computer-aided instruction.

Authoring system A computer program used for the preparation of computer-aided instruction software.

Automated teller machine (ATM) Unattended terminal that provides banking services, such as the limited withdrawal of cash by customers from their accounts.

Automated factory A factory that uses computer hardware and software, numerical control, process control, computer-aided design, and robots.

Automation The use of self-operating equipment and electronic devices to replace humans in production, inspection of parts, control of work processes, or performance of routine or repetitious work.

Backup (1) A copy of a file that is stored for safekeeping. The copy is for use should the original be damaged or lost; (2) redundant equipment or procedures that can be used in place of a component or storage medium that fails.

Backward recycling Provision of additional information or drill in computer-aided instruction for students who have not mastered the concepts under study. Backward branching is the programming technique employed.

BASIC An acronym for *B*eginner's *A*ll-purpose *S*ymbolic *I*nstruction *C*ode, a relatively easy to use programming language that is available in many small computer systems.

Batch processing A traditional method of data processing in which transactions are collected and then processed as a single unit.

Baud A unit used to measure the speed of data transmission. One baud is equivalent to one bit per second. To determine the number of characters per second, divide the number of bits per second by 10.

Binary The basis for calculations in all computers. This two-digit number system consists of digits 0 and 1, which are represented in the computer as the presence or absence of small electrical pulses.

Biofeedback A technique that attempts to control involuntary body functions, such as the rate of a person's heartbeat. A machine is used to monitor the function and to provide a signal when changes occur.

Biomechanics The study of movement, force, and velocity relating to muscular activity.

Bit A contraction of *bi*nary digi*t*, the smallest unit of information that the computer recognizes. A bit is equivalent to the absence or presence of an electrical pulse (0 or 1). Bits are usually grouped in nibbles (4 bits), bytes (8 bits), or larger units.

Branch A set of instructions that are executed between two successive decision instructions.

Break even point In costing, the point of intersection between a cost curve and corresponding revenue curve.

Bubble memory A storage device that uses reversals of magnetic polarity in magnetic domains (bubbles) to represent the binary states 0 and 1. This storage device is able to store data after power is removed.

Buffer A storage area that is located in the central processing unit (CPU) or in a peripheral and that is used to temporarily hold data awaiting further processing.

Bug A mistake in a program or in an electrical circuit. Eliminating the mistakes is known as *debugging*.

Bulletin board A computer network service that provides for the posting of or access to information and messages. Only terminals connected to the network have access to the service.

Bus (1) A circuit used for transmitting data or power; often a circuit that acts as a common connection among a number of locations. (2) A path over which information is transferred from any of several sources to any of several locations.

Business data processing The use of computers to process data for business purposes (for example, recording and calculating payroll information).

Byte A group of bits (usually 8). A byte can be used to represent one character (number or letter) of information, all or part of binary numbers, and machine language instructions.

CAD/CAM Acronyms for *c*omputer-*a*ided *d*esign and *c*omputer-*a*ided *m*anufacturing. Collectively, an integrated system that uses computers to perform both design and manufacturing operations.

calculator Generally and historically, a device for carrying out logic and arithmetic computations.

Canned program A software package developed and made available (that is, sold by software houses or provided free by vendors) to multiple users who have similar needs and problems.

Cassette A reel of magnetic tape.

Cassette tape storage Storage of data on a serial device that records magnetically on a removable tape cassette.

Cathode ray tube (CRT) An electronic vacuum tube, such as a television picture tube, that can be used to display graphic images, text, or numerical data on visual display terminals.

Central processing unit (CPU) The part of the computer that interprets machine language processing instructions and then controls the execution of the instructions.

Centralized data Data that is stored and maintained at a single site and shared by users.

Centralization: The concentration of decision making in an organizational structure.

Channel (1) A path for electrical data transmission between two or more stations; (2) a hardware device that connects the central processing unit (CPU) and main storage with the input/output control units; (3) synonymous with "circuit," "line," "link," "path," "facility."

Character Any letter, number, symbol, or punctuation mark.

Check A process for ensuring the accuracy of data.

Check digit A digit that is added to a digit string that is used for the purpose of checking the accuracy of input data. The check digit is calculated by a formula that draws upon the values of digits in the string.

Checking program A specific type of diagnostic (error-discovering) program that examines programs or data for mistakes.

Chip A thin wafer which holds the integrated circuits of electronic components.

Circuit A means of communication between two or more points. For example, a telephone linkage is normally a two-wire or four-wire circuit.

Circuit board A board with chips mounted on it, connected by imprinted circuits. Circuit boards can usually be easily removed or added to computers.

COBOL An acronym for *CO*mmon *B*usiness-*O*riented *L*anguage. A high-level programming language designed for business data processing on large computers.

Collage The addition of texture to a graphic image on a computer screen.

Command An order to the computer in the form of (1) words and numbers typed on a keyboard, (2) words spoken into a microphone, (3) positions of a game paddle or joystick, and so on.

Common data base Pooled data integrated for common use as a shared resource.

Communications The successful and unaltered transmission of intelligence from the point of origin to the point of reception.

Communications line Any medium, such as a wire or telephone circuit, that connects a remote station with a computer.

Communications link The physical means by which one location is connected to another for the purpose of transmitting and receiving data.

Communications program Software that controls and supports the communications between the computers and terminals in a data communications network.

Compatibility (1) The ability of an instruction, program, or component to be used on more than one computer; (2) the ability of computers to work with other computers that are not necessarily similar in design or capabilities.

Compile To translate into machine language a computer program written in another programming language. This can be done by converting the overall logic structure of the program, by generating more than one machine instruction for each symbolic statement, or by combining both methods.

Compiler A translation program that converts high-level instructions into a set of binary instructions (object code) for execution. Each high-level language requires a compiler or an interpreter. A compiler translates the complete program, which is then executed. Every change in the program requires a complete recompilation. Contrast with *interpreter*.

Computer A system designed for the manipulation of information, incorporating a central processing unit (CPU), memory, input/output (I/O) facilities, power supply, and cabinet.

Computer application The use of a computer to solve a specific problem or to accomplish a particular task.

Computer graphics The use of computer capability to create, transform, and display symbolic and pictorial representations.

Computer-independent language A programming language that requires translation or compilation to any one of a variety of computer languages.

Computer literacy A basic understanding of computers. There is still no agreement about the exact meaning of this term. Some people argue that knowledge about computer applications and social implications constitutes literacy. Others insist that the term requires an understanding of the technology of computers. Still others consider the ability to program (and often to program in a specific language) a prerequisite to literacy.

Computer network A computer system consisting of two or more interconnected computing units.

Computer program A series of instructions that a computer can interpret and execute to achieve a desired result.

Computer system Information processing equipment that operates as a unit. A computer system consists of a central processing unit (CPU) with main storage, input/output channels, control units, direct access storage devices, and input/output devices connected to the system.

Computer-aided drafting and design (CADD) The use of a computer to assist in the creation, modification, and representation of a design.

Computer-aided design (CAD) The use of a computer to assist in the creation or modification of a design.

Computer-aided manufacturing The use of computer technology in the operation and control of a manufacturing process.

Computer-assisted instruction (CAI) The direct use of a computer for the facilitation and certification of learning; that is, using the computer to make learning easier and more likely to occur (facilitation), as well as using the computer to create a record verifying that learning has occurred (certification).

Computer-integrated manufacturing (CIM) The coordination by a computer of all functions and operations in a computerized factory.

Computerized axial tomography The use of a computer to analyze a series of cross-sectional scans to construct a three-dimensional image.

Computer-managed instruction (CMI) Use of a computer to oversee instruction and to direct students to learning resources.

Concentrator A device that provides communications capability between many low-speed channels. Usually different speeds, codes, and protocols can be accommodated on the low-speed side. The concentrator may have the ability to be polled by a computer, and may in turn poll terminals.

Concordance An alphabetical index of all major words in a text showing the contextual occurrences of each word.

Concurrent programming The programming of system components to operate simultaneously.

Conditional instruction An instruction that is executed only when a specified condition or set of conditions is satisfied.

Configuration The group of devices that make up a computer or data processing system.

Console The part of a computer that the operator or maintenance engineer uses to communicate with the computer.

Control A management function that involves observing and measuring organizational performance and environmental activities and making changes when expectations and standards are not met.

Control program A program that is designed to schedule and supervise the performance of data processing work by a computing system.

Control unit (1) The part of the central processing unit (CPU) that directs the sequence of operations, interprets coded instructions, and sends the proper signals instructing other computer circuits to carry out the instructions; (2) a device that controls the reading, writing, or display of data at one or more input/output devices.

Controller A device used to manage a peripheral device such as a CRT, printer, or disk drive.

Convention General agreement or acceptance of certain practices.

Conversational Pertaining to a program or a system that allows a user to carry on a dialogue with the computer, usually by means of a terminal. In a "conversational mode," the computer responds to input quickly, permitting the user to maintain a train of thought. See *interactive*.

Conversion (1) The process of changing from one method of data processing to another or from one data processing system to another; (2) the process of changing the form of representation in data processing (for example, to change from decimal representation to binary representation).

Copy-protected format The storage of programs on a medium that prevents the program from being copied with standard equipment.

CP/M The name of a common operating system.

CRT display device A display device on which images are produced on a cathode-ray tube (CRT).

Cursor An electronically generated symbol that appears on the display screen to tell the operator where the next character will appear.

Custom software Tailor-made computer programs prepared for a specific purpose. Contrast with *packaged software*, in which the programs are written for general purposes.

Cycle (1) A period of time during which a set of events is completed; (2) the repetition of a set of operations in the same sequence. The operations may be subject to variations on each repetition.

Daisy wheel A printing wheel composed of spokes with characters at the end of each spoke.

Data Facts, numbers, letters and symbols that become usable information when processed.

Data acquisition The means by which data is selected and accumulated to be processed into a meaningful and useful form.

Data bank A comprehensive collection of libraries of data. A library consists of files, which contain records, which are in turn comprised of individual data elements.

Data base A collection of interrelated data files or libraries organized for ease of access, update, and retrieval.

Data base administrator (DBA) Person to whom authority has been delegated to coordinate, monitor, and control the data base and related resources, including the data element dictionary and data directory system.

Data base management system (DBMS) A generalized set of computer programs that control the creation, maintenance, and utilization of the data bases and data files of an organization.

Data capture A method whereby recorded information is read by an optical reading device and sent to a computer for processing.

Data collection The accumulation of data in a form usable by a computer.

Data element A fact or observation collected and recorded as data.

Data hierarchy The organization of characters, data elements, records, and files that make up a data base.

Data input Data used by programs to produce output.

Data, machine-readable Data that is acceptable as input to a particular machine.

Data management A major function of operating systems that involves organizing, cataloging, locating, storing, retrieving, and maintaining data.

Data network Telecommunications network designed specifically for data transmission.

Data organization The way data is arranged within a data set (for example, sequential organization or partitional organization).

Data processing (DP) The manipulation of data by following a sequence of instructions to achieve a desired result.

Data processing system A network of machine components capable of accepting information, processing it according to a plan, and producing the desired results.

Data security Protection of computerized information by various means, including cryptography, locks, identification cards and badges, restricted access to the computer, passwords, physical and electronic backup copies of the data, and so on.

Data transmission The sending of data from one part of a system to another part.

Debug To find and eliminate mistakes or problems in computer software or hardware.

Decision support systems (DSS) Computerized applications used by management for decision making. These applications often use mathematical and statistical models (such as linear programming, CPM, or PERT) in operations research and management science.

Dedicated A term applied to a computer or piece of hardware that is used exclusively to perform a single task.

Demodulation The conversion of data represented as an analog signal for transmission over communication lines into a digital signal that can be processed by data processing equipment. The reverse of *modulation*.

Device In computers, a piece of hardware that performs a specific function. Input devices (for example, keyboards) are used to get data into the central processing unit. Output devices (for example, a printer or display monitor) are used to remove data from a computer in some usable form. Input/output devices (for example, terminals or disk drives) are able to perform both input and output functions.

Digit A single character, 0 through 9, A through Z, or a special symbol such as $, %, ¢, #, or +.

Digital Pertaining to the use of a discrete medium to represent data. A discrete medium is anything that is counted to determine its value, such as sticks, markers, bits, and so on.

Digital computer A computer that operates on digital data by performing arithmetic and logical operations on the data. Contrast with *analog computer*.

Digital-to-analog converter Device that transforms a digital computer's electrical pulses into a continuous analog signal in order to relay information or power to a nondigital device outside of the computer.

Direct access (1) A storage method in which data is stored randomly on a volume rather than immediately following the previous entry. The data is then retrieved by reference to its location rather than by reference to previously stored data. (2) Pertaining to the process of storing and retrieving data without regard for previously stored data. Synonymous with *random access*. Contrast with *serial access*.

Disk A circular plate with magnetic material on both sides. This plate rotates so that data can be stored and retrieved by one or more "heads" that transfer the information to and from the computer. The computer-readable information may be placed on a floppy or a rigid (hard) disk, and may have information on one or both sides. Also known as "diskette" or "disc." See also *floppy disk*.

Disk drive Unit into which sofware is loaded.

Disk pack A removable direct-access storage volume containing a number of magnetic disks on which data can be stored. Disk packs are mounted on a disk storage device.

Disk storage The storage of data on direct-access devices that record the data magnetically on rotating disks.

Display A representation of data using a visual medium.

Display unit A terminal device that presents data visually, usually by means of a cathode ray tube.

Distributed data processing (DDP) The arrangement of computers within an organization in which the organization's computer complex has many separate computing facilities all working in a cooperative manner, rather than the conventional single computer at a single location. Frequently an organization's central files are stored at the central computing facility, with the geographically dispersed smaller computers calling on the central files when they need them.

Document A record that contains information written for human use. This record can be provided in a written or printed form (such as in a user manual) or it can be displayed on a computer terminal.

Documentation (1) The preparation of the information recorded in documents; (2) in data processing, the collection of documents that pertain to an information system.

Dot matrix A pattern of closely positioned dots that form a letter, number, or other symbol.

Dot matrix printer A printer that forms characters by printing tiny dots to print letters or numbers.

Downtime The period of time during which a computer is not operating.

Dumb terminal Terminal with no independent processing (or storage) capability.

Dynometer An instrument used in athletics to measure muscle strength.

Electromechanical data processing The use of electromechanical devices, such as typewriters and calculators, to process data information.

Electromechanical device A processing device that uses both electrical and mechanical principles, such as a keypunch, collator, or tabulator.

Electronic encyclopedia Information that commonly appears in a printed encyclopedia and that can be accessed electronically through a device such as a computer terminal.

Electronic funds transfer (EFT) An electronic payment transaction system using computers and telecommunications instead of traditional cash or checks.

Electronic home The use of electronic devices in the home for applications such as environmental control, security, recreation, shopping, mail, and home banking.

Electronic mail The transmission of mail using electronic devices and telecommunications as a substitute for the physical mail delivery traditionally performed by the post office.

Electronic mailbox An address in a computer system where messages sent by electronic mail can be stored for access by an authorized recipient.

Electronic news Information that is commonly printed in a newspaper and that can be accesed electronically through a device such as a computer terminal.

Electronic office An office that uses computers to process many secretarial and administrative tasks.

Electronic voting The use of computer systems to record and count the number of votes cast in an election.

Electrostatic printer A printer that supplies an electrical charge through dot-matrix pins onto special paper to shape the desired characters.

Electrothermal printer A dot matrix printer that presses heated pins in the shape of the desired character against heat-sensitive paper.

Emulate To cause a computer to accept the same data and execute the same programs with the same results as another computer system.

Encrypt To scramble or convert into code.

EPROM An acronym for *e*rasable *p*rogrammable *r*ead *o*nly *m*emory; ROM chips that can be programmed to contain software applications and then erased and reprogrammed with new instructions.

Ergonomics The science of human engineering, which combines the study of human body mechanics and physical limitations with industrial psychology.

Execution cycle The sequence of steps performed in carrying out a computer instruction.

Executive routine A control program that coordinates the execution of other programs.

Expert system A system that performs at or near the level of human experts.

External memory See *external storage.*

External storage (1) A storage device other than main storage. For example, storage on magnetic tape or direct-access devices. Synonymous with *external memory*, *auxiliary storage*, and *secondary storage*. (2) A storage area that supplements another storage area. Contrast with *main storage*.

Factory-wide management information system (FMIS) The linkage of functional information subsystems within a factory to produce information designed to aid plant managers in the performance of their duties.

Feedback The return of part of the output of a machine, process, or system to the computer as input for another phase, especially for self-correcting or control purposes.

Field A subdivision of a record that contains a particular category of data; for example, a date, an amount, or a name.

Fifth-generation computer Associated with intelligent supercomputers planned by the Japanese for the 1990s.

File A logical collection of data, designated by name and considered as a unit by a user. A file consists of related records. For example, a payroll file (one record for each employee, showing rate of pay, deductions, and so on) or an inventory file (one record for each inventory item, showing the cost, selling price, number in stock, and so on).

Final output Processed data produced in a usable form.

Firmware Programs that reside in hardware; for example, software stored on a chip.

Float A sum of money representing outstanding checks.

Floppy disk A flexible disk encased in a protective jacket; used for storing data. See *disk.*

Flowchart A graphical representation of a procedure or computer program.

Font A full assortment of characters in a particular size and style (for example, large print for preparing transparencies, italicized print for emphasis, and so on).

Format A specific arrangement of data.

FORTRAN An acronym for *FOR*mula *TRAN*slating system. A language primarily used to express arithmetic formulas in computer programs.

Fourth generation language Refers to a class of very high-level languages often in an interactive mode. Many data base management systems incorporate a fourth generation language as a query language.

Gatekeeping Controlled access to services, privileges, benefits, or opportunities.

General-purpose computer A computer that is designed to perform a wide variety of functions.

Generation (of computers) Applies to the evolution of computers. Computers using vacuum tubes were called first generation computers. Second generation refers to computers using transistors; third generation, to the use of integrated circuits; and fourth generation, to large-scale integration of circuits.

Graphics Presenting information pictorially rather than alphanumerically.

Graphics plotter A device that can provide multicolored hard-copy representation of complex graphic patterns.

Graphics tablet An input device used to digitize a picture or drawing for computer processing.

Hacker (1) A person who enjoys learning or knowing about computer systems; (2) one who is good at programming and programs enthusiastically; (3) a person who uses deceptive or illegal means to gain unauthorized access to computer systems.

Handshaking An electronic process in which communicating units query one another to ensure that each is ready for transmission and that information will not be lost.

Hard copy Information generated by a computer and normally printed on paper.

Hard disk A rigid version of a floppy disk, made of aluminum and used for storing large amounts of data. See *disk*.

Hardware The electronic circuits, memory and input/output components of a computer system. Components made of steel or metal that one can see and touch. Contrast with software.

Head Device inside a disk drive that is used to read, write, and erase information on a disk.

Heuristic Pertaining to exploratory methods of problem solving which pursue solutions by continually evaluating progress toward the final result. Contrast with algorithm.

Hierarchy of data The organization of data into successive levels. For example, in a logical arrangement, a data base consists of files, which consist of records, and so on. In a physical arrangement, words consist of bytes, which consist of bits.

High-level language A programming language in which the statements represent procedures rather than single machine instructions. FORTRAN, COBOL, and BASIC are three common high-level languages. A high-level language requires a compiler or interpreter.

Home computer Usually refers to a microcomputer located in a residence for family use.

Host computer The main central processing unit in a network of distributed terminals or smaller computers.

Human factors Physiological, psychological, and training factors to be considered in the design of hardware and software, and the development of procedures. These considerations are necessary to ensure that humans can interface with machines efficiently and effectively.

Hybrid computer A computer that processes data through the use of both analog and digital representation of data.

Impact printer A printer that operates by causing print elements to strike paper.

Image mixing The addition of texture and color to an image on a computer screen to provide a three-dimensional effect.

Implement To put into effect.

Index (1) An ordered list of the contents of a file or document, and the corresponding reference notations used to identify or locate those contents; (2) to prepare such a list; (3) a table used to locate the records of a sequential data set.

Inference engine Name given to the control structure of an artificial intelligence problem solver in which the control is separate from the knowledge.

Information processing See *data processing*.

Information retrieval system A computing system application designed to recover specific information from input data.

Information system A system that utilizes manual, electromechanical, and electronic data processing systems, as well as personnel and operating procedures, to collect and process data and then disseminate output.

In-house Pertaining to a system used only within a particular company or organization, where the computing is independent of any external service.

Input (1) Data or programs entered into a computer system; (2) the act of entering data into a computer; (3) data used by programs and subroutines to produce output.

Input device Any machine that allows entry of commands or information into the computer. An input device could be a keyboard, tape drive, disk drive, microphone, light pen, digitizer, or electronic sensor.

Input manual Documentation that describes the format and procedures for data entry.

Input/output (I/O) That part or procedure of a computer system that handles communications with external devices.

Instruction A coded message that specifies what action a computer must take. The terms *command* and *order* are often used as synonyms.

Instruction cycle The fetching and decoding of a computer instruction so that the central processing unit (CPU) knows what action to take.

Instruction set The set of instructions that a computing system is designed to be capable of performing.

Integrate To make into a whole by unifying the parts.

Integrated circuit (IC) A module of components manufactured as a single, solid unit. Integrated circuits can be contrasted with discrete components (such as transistors, diodes, capacitors, and resistors) that are manufactured individually and then assembled into circuits. Integrated circuits are used as logic and storage circuitry.

Intelligence The capacity to acquire and apply knowledge, and to use thought and reason in problem solving.

Intelligent software Programs that incorporate features of artificial intelligence.

Intelligent terminal A terminal that is programmable and can therefore process its messages; for example, checking validity of input. Contrast with *dumb terminal*.

Interactive Commonly used to describe a software program that provides give and take between the operator and the machine. The program may ask a question to elicit a response from the operator or present a series of choices from which the operator can select. See *conversational*.

Interface The juncture at which two computer components (hardware and/or software) meet and interact with each other. Also applies to human-machine interaction.

Intermediate output Output that is stored for future use as input.

Internal memory Storage that is directly controlled by the central processing unit (CPU). See *main memory*.

Internal storage Storage within the computer proper.

Interpreter A translation program used to execute statements expressed in a high-level language. An interpreter translates each such statement and executes it immediately. Instructions can be freely added or modified in the user program, and execution may be resumed without delay. Contrast with *compiler*.

Job A series of tasks executed by the computer to perform a specific function. Included are the programs, linkages, files, and instructions to the operating system required for execution of the tasks.

Joystick An input device normally consisting of a vertical stick that can be tilted in any direction to indicate direction of movement.

K Computer shorthand for the quantity 1024 (usually approximated as 1,000) which is 2^{10}. The term is usually used to measure computer storage.

Key A field of data in a record that is used for accessing the record.

Key data element Data element used to link files.

Key terminal A terminal with keyboard for data entry.

Key word A significant or informative word in a title, abstract, or text that is used to describe the document.

Keyboard The panel of keys that is connected to a computer and used to enter data. It looks similar to the keys of a typewriter.

Keypunch A device with keyboard used to punch holes in a card to represent data.

Knowledge base Artificial intelligence data bases that are collections of facts, inferences, and procedures corresponding to the types of information needed to solve problems.

Knowledge engineering An artificial intelligence approach focusing on the use of knowledge.

Knowledge system An intelligent computer program that uses knowledge and inference procedures to solve difficult problems.

Knowledge-information processing system A system that combines the problem-solving ability of a computer and the algorithm power of decision models with the know-how of experts and a self-modification capability. Such systems do not currently exist. They are a goal of researchers in artificial intelligence.

Language See *programming language*.

Large-scale integration (LSI) The combining of about 1000 to 10,000 circuits on a single chip. Typical examples of LSI circuits are memory chips, microprocessors, calculator chips, and watch chips.

Laser printer A printer that forms an electrostatic image on paper by reflecting laser beams off a rotating disk containing characters.

Light pen An input device for a CRT. It records the emission of light at the point of contact with the screen.

Link The physical communication path between two nodes or switching centers.

Linkage Term used in programming for a coded instruction that connects two separately coded routines.

LISP An acronym for *LIS*t *P*rocessing language, the basic artificial intelligence programming language.

Load Process of transferring information from a peripheral storage device to the computer's main memory.

Local area network (LAN) A telecommunications network used to connect computers with other computers, peripherals, and workstations that are in fairly close proximity.

Log To record or document important events.

Logging Recording data in the time sequence that events occur.

Logical data element Data element that is independent of the physical data media on which it is recorded. Logical data elements are grouped by use and meaning

Logical file A collection of one or more logical records.

Logical organization An arrangement of data into an orderly, structured, functional whole from the point of view of the end user. Contrast with *physical organization*.

Logical record A record that is defined by the information it contains rather than by its physical environment. Portions of the same logical record may be located in different physical records.

Low-level language A language that is easily understood by the computer. In a low-level language, programs are hard to write (by programmers) but can be quickly executed by machine. Examples are machine or assembly language.

Machine A device, such as a computer, that performs or helps in performing a human task.

Machine-dependent Pertaining to the procedures or programs created for a specific computer system. Contrast with *machine-independent.*

Machine instruction An instruction in a source language that is equivalent to a specified sequence of machine instructions.

Machine language Set of coded instructions that can be directly executed by a computer's central processing unit (CPU).

Machine-independent Pertaining to procedures or programs created without regard for the computer system that will be used to process them.

Machine-readable Pertaining to data in a form that can be read by a peripheral or read directly by a computer.

Magnetic disk A flat circular storage medium with a magnetic surface. Data can be stored on this plate by the selective magnetization of portions of the flat surface. This form of storage permits random access to the data.

Magnetic drum A drum capable of storing data, used as a bulk memory device.

Magnetic ink An ink that contains particles of a magnetic substance. These particles can be detected by magnetic sensors.

Magnetic ink character recognition (MICR) The machine recognition of characters printed with magnetic ink. Contrast with *optical character recognition.*

Magnetic tape A tape that stores data on a magnetic surface. Data is stored by selective polarization of portions of the surface.

Main memory The internal memory of the computer contained in its circuitry, as opposed to peripheral or external memory (tapes, disks, and so on).

Main storage (1) The area in the computer where data is stored; contrast with auxiliary or *external storage.* (2) All program-addressable storage from which instructions may be executed and from which data can be loaded directly into registers.

Mainframe A large general-purpose computer with fast processing time. Appropriate for corporations, research organizations, universities, and governmental agencies.

Maintenance Any activity intended to correct or prevent faults in computer hardware or software, including tests, measurements, replacements, adjustments, and repairs.

Malfunction The effect of a fault or of the unexpected functioning of hardware.

Manual data processing Processing done by hand (without the aid of a computer).

Mark-sense device A device that reads a document for specific marks in particular locations written with an electrographic pencil and converts the marks into machine-readable form.

Mass storage (online) The storage of a large amount of data that is readily accessible to the central processing unit (CPU) of a computer.

Master file A file that is relatively permanent. (Some data in the file never changes while other detailed data will change as a result of updating.)

Match To compare the identity of two or more items of data. This process is used in updating a master file from a detailed transaction file.

Material requirements planning (MRP) A computer program that plans and controls the flow of materials required for specified levels of production.

Medium The physical device on which data is recorded (for example, paper tape, cards, magnetic tape).

Memory The section of the computer where instructions and data are stored. Each item in memory has a unique address that the central processing unit (CPU) can use to retrieve information.

Menu A list of alternative actions displayed on the terminal screen for selection by the user.

Micro (1) One-millionth; (2) an abbreviation used for the words microprocessor and microcomputer. This term causes confusion in computer circles because of its multiple meanings.

Microcomputer A small but complete microprocessor-based computer system, including CPU, memory, input/output (I/O) interfaces or devices, and power supply.

Microfiche A sheet of microfilm on which it is possible to record a number of pages of microcopy.

Microfilm A roll of film on which documents are photographed in a reduced size.

Microminiaturization A production process that puts a large number of functions and logic on an integrated circuit.

Microprocessor A small electronic central processing unit (CPU) that can interpret instructions and make calculations.

Minicomputer A general term describing a class of small mainframe-type digital computers.

Mode The method of performing a particular operation (for example, the "binary mode" or the "interpretive mode").

Model A computer reproduction or simulation of a real or imaginary person, process, place, or thing. Models can be simple or complex; artistic, educational or entertaining; a mathematical representation or part of a game.

Modem The shortened form of *MO*dulator-*DEM*odulator; a device that transforms a computer's electrical pulses into audible tones for transmission over the phone line to another computer. A modem also receives incoming tones and transforms them into electrical signals that can be processed and stored by the computer.

Modify (1) To alter a part of an instruction or routine; (2) to change data that has been stored.

Modulation The conversion of a digital signal generated by a computer into an analog signal for transmission through a telecommunications channel such as a telephone wire. The reverse of *demodulation*.

Monitor (1) A microcomputer program that directs operations of the hardware; (2) a video display terminal.

Mouse A pointing device used to identify a location on a CRT screen for making additions or changes to data. The pointer is controlled by a person who moves the mouse in two dimensions on a flat surface, such as a table top.

MS-DOS A common operating system.

MSX An acronym for *M*icro*S*oft E*X*tended Basic, software for microcomputers developed by Microsoft Inc. as a standard for Japanese microcomputers sold in the U.S.

Multimedia center A room for information processing and retrieval using a variety of media (for example, screens, printers, plotters, microfilm readers, teleconferencing terminals, color-animated graphics, and so forth).

Multiplexer A hardware device that allows the handling of multiple signals over a single channel.

Multiprocessing system A computer system that employs two or more interconnected processing units. This allows it to execute programs simultaneously.

Multiprogramming The permitting of more than one program to timeshare machine components.

Nanosecond A billionth (1/1,000,000,000) of a second.

Natural language A spoken, human language such as English, Spanish, Arabic, or Chinese. Compare to *programming language*.

Natural language processing Processing of natural language by a computer to facilitate communication between humans and the computer, or for other purposes such as language translation.

Network An interconnection of computer systems, terminals, and communications facilities.

Node (1) An end point of any branch of a network, or a junction common to two or more branches of a network; (2) any station, terminal, terminal installation, communications computer, or communications computer installation in a computer network.

Numeric Expressed by a number or numbers. Synonymous with "numerical."

Numerical control (NC) The use of numeric data to provide the instructions for operating a machine.

Object program Software translated into machine language by an assembler or compiler. Same as "object code." Contrast with *source program*.

Offline Used to describe equipment that is neither connected to, or under the control of, the central processing unit (CPU). Contrast with *online*.

Offline input device A peripheral for data entry that is not under the direct control of the central processing unit (CPU).

Online Used to describe equipment that is directly connected to the central processing unit (CPU) and in operational-ready condition. Contrast with *offline.*

Online processing Processing of input data in random order, without preliminary sorting or batching. Contrast with *batch processing*.

Online real time A computer system that receives input data, processes it, and returns results within sufficient time to control the operating environment.

Online system In teleprocessing, a system that permits the entry of data from the point of origin into the computer or one that transmits data directly to the place where it is used.

Operand (1) That which is operated upon. (2) Information entered with a command name to define the data on which a command processor operates and to control the execution of the command processor.

Operating system A collection of programs for operating the computer. Operating systems perform housekeeping tasks, such as input/output between the computer and peripherals, and accept and interpret information from the keyboard.

Operation (1) A computer activity specified by a single instruction; (2) a program step executed by a computer.

Optical character recognition (OCR) The machine identification of printed characters through use of light-sensitive devices. Contrast with *magnetic ink character recognition*.

Optical reader A device that interprets handwritten or machine-printed symbols, and then stores the information on a storage medium or transmits the information to a computing system.

Optical scanner A light-sensitive device used to scan printed or written data and then generate an analog or digital signal to represent the data scanned.

Output (1) Any processed information coming out of a computer via any medium (print, CRT, and so on); (2) the act of transferring information to these media.

Output device A machine that transfers programs or information from the computer to some other medium. Examples of output devices include tape, disk, and bubble memory drives; computer printers, typewriters, and plotters; the computer's video display screen; robots; and sound synthesis devices that enable the computer to talk and/or play music.

Packaged software A program designed to be marketed for general use that may need to be adapted to a particular installation.

Pascal A programming language first developed to teach programming concepts. Its use has extended to business and scientific applications.

Password A secret identification code keyed by the user and checked by the system before the user can gain access to the system. Each user or group of users has a unique password.

Pattern recognition The automatic identification of shapes, forms, or configurations (such as fingerprints or signatures).

Peripheral Computer equipment that supports the central processing unit (CPU) to provide the system with outside communication.

Peripheral-bound A system that backlogs because of the slowness of peripheral equipment.

Personal computer (PC) Commonly refers to a microcomputer.

Physical file A set of physical records.

Physical organization The arrangement of physical records of data. Contrast with *logical organization*.

Physical record A record from the standpoint of the manner or form in which it is stored, retrieved, and moved; that is, one that is defined in terms of physical qualities. A physical record may contain all or part of one or more logical records.

Picosecond One-trillionth (1/1,000,000,000,000) of a second.

PL1 An acronym for *P*rogramming *L*anguage, version *1*. A high-level language developed by IBM. PL1 is an all-purpose procedure-oriented language for both scientific and business applications.

Plot To draw or diagram by connecting the point-by-point coordinate values.

Plotter A mechanical device for drawing lines under computer control.

Point-of-sale (POS) terminal A peripheral commonly used in retail stores to perform data handling functions such as recording and monitoring sales transactions.

Policy A course of action or guiding principles.

Portability Software properties that permit use of the sofware in another computer environment.

Practopia Describing a computerized society that is neither the best nor worst of possible worlds.

Primary storage Internal storage within a computer.

Primitive data Synonymous with raw data.

Printer A computer output device that produces computer output on paper.

Priority A rank assigned to a data processing task that determines the order in which it will receive system resources.

Privacy The right of an individual to control the collection and disclosure of data about personal affairs.

Process control (PC) The use of computers to monitor a continuous production process (for example, monitoring the generation of electricity).

Procedure The course of action taken for the solution of a problem.

Processor A hardware device capable of performing operations upon data.

Program A sequence of instructions directing a computer to perform a particular function; a statement of an algorithm in a programming language.

Program error Any mistakes or problems in a computer program that prevent the computer from performing the proper computations.

Programmer Person who writes computer programs.

Programming language A set of symbols and rules that can be used to specify an algorithm in a computer-executable form.

PROLOG An acronym for *PRO*gramming in *LOG*ic, a language that lends itself to inference making. Used extensively in artificial intelligence.

PROM An acronym for *p*rogrammable *r*ead *o*nly *m*emory; an internal computer memory that can be programmed only once.

Prompt A message that is provided by the computer system to help the user.

Protocol The rules governing how two pieces of equipment communicate with one another.

Query language A high-level language that allows users quick access to a data base. The language, usually English-like, allows users to bypass the process of defining, creating, implementing, and testing of transactions.

Random access An access method whereby each record of a file or location in memory can be accessed directly by its address. Contrast with *sequential access*.

Random-access memory (RAM) (1) Provides quick access to any storage location point because it allows for searches that scan vertically and horizontally, instead of sequentially. Computer internal memories and disk memories are RAM devices. (2) That non-permanent part of main memory that can be both read from and written on, in contrast to ROM, which is read-only memory.

Read To accept data (from a disk, card, and so on) for storage and/or processing.

Read-only Pertaining to a type of access that allows data to be read but not modified.

Read-only memory (ROM) Permanent memory, stored on a chip, that is used to perform routine functions such as instructing the computer during power-up. ROM can also be used to store a language.

Read-write head A small electromagnet used for reading, recording, or erasing polarized spots on a magnetic surface.

Real time Pertaining to the processing of data in synchronization with the actual occurrence of events.

Real time processing Processing data rapidly enough to provide results useful in directly controlling a physical process or guiding a human user.

Record A collection of data items that is stored on a disk or other medium and that may be recalled as a unit. Records may be fixed or variable in length. One or more records usually make up a data file.

Remote processing A method of using a computer system from a location that is distant from the central processing unit (CPU).

Ring network Computer systems linked in a circular pattern. Access from one system to another can be clockwise or counter-clockwise.

Robot A machine, composed of sensing devices, links, and joints, that performs specific manual tasks. The machine is governed by a microprocessor or microprocessors.

Run The execution of a program by a computer.

Search A systematic examination of available information in a given field of interest.

Secondary storage See *external storage*.

Security Measures taken to prevent access to or manipulation of data, documentation, equipment, or programs without authorization.

Semiconductor A substance that does not conduct well at low temperatures. However, when heat, light, or voltage is applied, the conductivity improves.

Sensor Any device that monitors the external environment for a computer. Types of sensors include photoelectric sensors that are sensitive to light; image sensor cameras that can record visual images and transform them into digital signals; pressure sensors that are sensitive to any kind of pressure; sensors that record infrared information; and ultrasonic transducers that produce a high-frequency sound wave that bounces off objects and lets the computer calculate the distance between itself and those objects.

Separation of responsibility An organizational principle that divides computer operations into separate functions. This division reduces the likelihood of security violations by restricting the scope of tasks assigned to each employee.

Sequence (1) The order in which items are arranged according to a specified set of rules; (2) in sorting, a group of records whose control fields are in ascending or descending order, according to the collating sequence.

Sequential access A storage method (such as on a magnetic tape) in which data can only be reached or retrieved by passing through all intermediate locations between the current one and the desired one. Contrast with *random access*.

Sequential processing An access method for storing or retrieving data blocks in a continuous sequence, using either a sequential-access or a direct-access device.

Service program A program that provides general support for the operation of a computer system. Also known as a "utility program."

Shell document Text stored in a computer which can be copied, and then modified with word processing, for a variety of purposes (for example, form letters or contracts that are individualized by filling in names and addresses at the time of printing).

Simulation A computerized reproduction, image, or replica of a situation or set of conditions.

Smart product A manufactured item with an embedded microprocessor.

Smart terminal See *intelligent terminal*.

Soft output Computer output that is nonpermanent in nature, such as a display on a CRT screen. Some devices have the capability of converting a soft output to a hard copy through a printer or a plotter.

Software A general term for computer programs involved in the operation of the computer.

Source program A program that must be translated into machine language before use.

Special-purpose computer A computer that is designed to perform a restricted class of tasks.

Spreadsheet Packaged software used largely, but not exclusively, for planning. A spreadsheet quickly computes the cells in a matrix, given input values that change.

Stand-alone system A computer system that does not require a connection to another computer.

Standard An accepted authority or established measure for operation, behavior, or performance.

Star network The arrangement of linked computer systems in a pattern that resembles spokes of a wheel. Each node is connected to a central computer system, and, through this center, to other nodes.

Storage The general term for any device that is capable of holding data that can later be retrieved.

Supercomputer The fastest type of mainframe computer, appropirate for processing many large numbers. (This work is often called "number-crunching").

Symbol A representation of something by reason of association or convention.

Synthesizer Equipment that uses solid-state circuitry to duplicate the sounds of musical instruments.

System Usually refers to a group of related hardware and/or software designed to meet a specific need.

Systems analyst An individual who analyses and designs information systems, and performs many related functions in the development and maintenance of a system.

Tape An inexpensive medium for storing data that can only be accessed sequentially.

Tape drive A device that moves tape past a read/write head when data is being stored on the tape or retrieved.

Tape unit A storage device that consists of a tape drive, reading and writing heads, and associated controls.

Telecommunications (1) Pertaining to the process of communicating over long distances through the transmission of signals (for example, telegraph, radio, or television); (2) the conversion, control, and transmission of data between a computer system and remote devices.

Telecommuting The use of computers and telecommunications by an employee who works at home instead of commuting to an office.

Teleconferencing Two-way communication between two or more groups (or three or more persons) remote from one another, using electronic means.

Telemail See *electronic mail.*

Telematic The American equivalent of the French word "telematique" meaning the combination of computers and telecommunications to produce results greater than could be achieved by either alone.

Teleprocessing The processing of data that is received from or sent to remote locations by way of telecommunications lines.

Teleshopping The use of computers and telecommunications from the home for the selection of purchases.

Teletex A one-way information service.

Terminal A keyboard plus a CRT and/or printer that can be connected to a computer.

Time sharing A method of sharing the resources of the computer among several users. The computing speed of time-sharing systems makes it appear that the computer is running different jobs simultaneously.

Timeliness The availability of output when needed by the user.

Transborder data flow The transfer and transmission of data across national borders.

Transaction file A data file containing relatively temporary or current data to be processed along with a master file.

Transistor A semiconductor device for controlling the flow of current. Developed by Bell Laboratories, then part of AT&T.

Translator (1) A device that converts information from one system of representation into equivalent information in another system of representation; (2) a routine for changing information from one representation to another.

Translation program A program that changes information from a high-level language to machine language.

Transmission The sending of data from one location to another, leaving the source data unchanged.

Unbundling The discontinuation of the practice of grouping services, programs, and training with hardware sales by a computer hardware manufacturer.

UNIX An operating system developed by AT&T.

Update To modify information.

User-friendly Descriptive of both hardware and software that are designed to assist the user by being scaled to human dimensions, self-instructing, error-proof, and so on.

Vacuum tube An electron tube that has an internal vacuum; the dominant electronic element found in first generation computers.

Validation Process of checking compliance of data with preset standards and verifying data correctness.

Vendor A supplier or company that sells computers, peripherals, or computer services.

Very large-scale integration (VLSI) In practice, the compression of more than 10,000 transistors on a single chip.

Videotex An interactive two-way information system using a TV screen or computer terminal screen as a display device.

Voice recognition equipment An input device that will enter data spoken by a human.

Wafer Many silicon chips linked together to increase efficiency and lower cost of production.

Wand A portable scanning device often used in stores and factories to read data for computer processing.

Winchester disk Another term for a hard disk, an information storage device with a very large capacity.

Window Partial area on a CRT screen for display of documentation or program results. Windows enable terminal users to view several displays simultaneously.

Wired society The dependence of society on computers and telecommunications for activities formerly performed manually or by mechanical and electrical means.

Word A unit of data or the set of characters that occupies one storage location. In most minicomputers, a word is equal to two bytes.

Word processor A text editor system for electronically writing, formatting and storing letters, reports, and books prior to printing.

Word processing (WP) The creation, modification, and production of documents, letters, and manuscripts using electronic text-editing software and equipment.

Workstation A location containing computer resources (hardware and software) needed by employees in an organization to perform specific work tasks.

Write (1) To copy information usually from internal storage to external storage; (2) to transfer information to an output medium.

Xerographic printer A printer that forms a negative image on an electronically charged plate, then electrically transfers the image to a photoconductive surface where ink is applied. The positive image is formed on electrically charged paper that passes over the surface and attracts the ink.

Index

Photographs courtesy of: American Robot™; Adidas; Apple Computer, Inc.; Artronics, Inc.; AT&T Bell Laboratories; AutoCAD™/Autodesk Inc.; Boeing Commercial Airplane Company; Broderbund Software, Inc.; Burroughs Corp.; Peter Byron/U.S. News & World Report; Casio Microcard Corp.; Cauzin Systems Inc.; Cermetek Microelectronics; Mark Chester; Cogito Systems; The Computer Museum—Boston, MA; Contour Medical Systems, Inc.; Ian Currington/Floating Point Systems; Dallas Semiconductor; Data General Corporation; Datasouth Computer Corporation; Del Mar Group, Inc.; Digital Equipment Corporation; Dilip Menta/Contact; Ericsson; Evans Sutherland; Floating Point Systems, Inc.; Ford Motor Company; Fujitsu Limited; General Electric; Genigraphics Corporation; Gould Electronics, Inc.; Groupe Bull; Hattori Corporation of America; Hewlett-Packard Company; Honeywell, Inc.; Houston Instrument; International Business Machines Archives; Inforite Corporation; Intel Corporation; Intermec®; International Business Machines Corporation; Interstate Electronics Corporation; Kurzweil Computer Products, Inc.; Lasar Video, Inc.; Maison de Marie-Claire/Bouchet/Gribas/Karsala; McDonnell Douglas Corporation; Megatek Corporation; Micro-Card Technologies/Health Management Systems; MicroComputers Accessories, Inc.; Micro Control Systems, Inc.; Motorola, Inc.; NASA; NCR Corporation; Oberon International; Plus Development Corporation; Polaroid Corporation; Puma USA, Inc.; Radio Shack, a Division of Tandy Corporation; Research Libraries Group, Inc.; Robot Defense Systems, Inc.; Sperry Corporation; St. Benedict's Farm; San Francisco Ballet; Sanders Associates Inc.; Sperry Univac, a Division of Sperry Corporation; Telos Software; Telentry Systems; Texas Instruments Inc.; Viewtron Corporation of America; Virginia Wesleyan College; Western Union Corporation; Brian Wolff; Xerox Corporation